DUKE OF YORK

Father of America's Slave Society

BY EDWARD DOTEN

THE DUKE OF YORK:
FATHER
OF AMERICA'S SLAVE SOCIETY

This book is for nonprofit educational purposes for the general public and for school curricula teachers are able to distribute to students.

There are certain conditions set forth below for using and copying the book.

The book is copyrighted. You are free to share the book, and portions of the book, with others, and to copy it. The book is subject to the conditions that you cannot modify any material in the book and you must always give full credit to me, Edward Doten, as author, and to *www.DukeYork.org* as the source of the first edition.

If you wish to quote the book, you may do so subject to the same conditions of giving me, Edward Doten, and *www.DukeYork.org* full credit.

I make no claim for material cited to or derived from other copyrighted publications or for material in the public domain, except as to the collection and organization of such material. Except as indicated, I have obtained documents and information quoted herein from identified or public sources. This book provides background information and opinion. Since I am not a professional academic historian regarding slavery, I rely entirely upon the sources quoted or cited.

The first edition of this book is available to be downloaded without charge at *www.DukeYork.org.*

* * *

Images are from *slaveryimages.org.*

* * *

Cover Design by Dr. Carlton Calhoun
www.HireCarltonCalhoun.com

Library of Congress Control Number: 2022921436
ISBN: 978-1-947741-74-4

TWO IMPORTANT WARNINGS

First, if you are sensitive or squeamish, then you may prefer not to read this book. The book describes *phenomenally gruesome violence.* I was *disturbed on many occasions* by my research and by the information I believe necessary to convey in order to provide an accurate description of slavery. *This is not your typically carefully-censored and whitewashed high school discussion of slavery.*

Second, the language of the time was rough and crude, and often would be considered to be deeply offensive today. I have chosen to quote directly from books and other materials by or about Frederick Douglass, Harriet Tubman, Sojourner Truth, Solomon Northup, Harriet Jacobs, William Wells Brown, David Walker, and others, who themselves are quoting, or were, slaveholders or others who disrespected African-Americans. The books, and the quotations, use dialect. To be true to the historical value of the material, *I deliberately have not deleted words they used, even if those words may offend.* Again, if you disagree with that approach, or if you are sensitive or squeamish, then you may prefer not to read this book. I do not condone racism or racial discrimination or prejudice of any kind.

In memory and recognition of America's Slavery Heroes—Harriet Tubman, Frederick Douglass, Sojourner Truth, Harriet Jacobs, Solomon Northup, William Wells Brown, Jermain Loguen, Frances Ellen Watkins Harper, Lt. Juan Bautista (Prince) Witten and the Florida Army of Black Warriors, Nat Turner, David Walker, and many other brave African-Americans, both slave and "free"—far too numerous to name—who fought bravely and valiantly against their bondage and discrimination to attain great heights and success, and in addition, in memory of the abolitionists, both "free" African-Americans—especially William Still, the Father of the Underground Railroad—and whites, who provided invaluable assistance to slaves, often in violation of federal and state laws and at great risk of harm to themselves

§ § §

It is time for America to recognize, and to teach our children that, through their exemplary courage, words and actions, these African-American heroes contributed mightily to American history and culture and should be held up to America's youth as role models

§ § §

Their contributions to America were so significant that many of America's Slavery Heroes deserve to be recognized in America's history on a par with the Founding Fathers (including George Washington and Thomas Jefferson) and Abraham Lincoln,
each of whom also contributed significantly to America

TABLE OF CONTENTS

CHAPTER ONE:
MEET
AMERICA'S SLAVE SOCIETY

"Slavery and race are not at the periphery of the American experience[.]
They're at the very core of what America is."
Author James Swanson[1]

"Were I about to tell you the evils of Slavery …
I should wish to take you, one at a time, and whisper it to you.
Slavery has never been represented; Slavery never can be represented."
William Wells Brown[2]

§ § §

What did your schools teach you about slavery?

Did they teach that slavery was "something that happened 150 years ago?"[3]

"SOMETHING"

"[S]omething that happened 150 years ago"
Mitch McConnell, Majority Leader, U.S. Senate

For those who believe that slavery occurred long ago, consider this:

Slavery in America was only two life spans ago. A person born in 1940 would have been 82 years old in 2022. A person born in 1858 during slavery and before the Civil War was 82 in 1940.

Although slavery occurred not so long ago, in some sectors of American society, including some school systems, there is a deliberate effort to de-emphasize—to sanitize—it. My schools in the 1950s mentioned slavery only briefly and then moved quickly on to other subjects.

I was not taught that America's slave society was one of the worst crimes against humanity in World history, a genuine Reign of Terror.

I was not taught that slavery for millions of people lay at the core of America's society, culture, political life, and government for hundreds of years, the majority of America's history

I was not taught that "[B]y 1770, slave raids had depopulated whole regions of coastal West Africa."[4]

---

1 Author James Swanson, quoted in Ruane, "It was the nation's largest auction of enslaved people. Now, a search for descendants of the 'weeping time'" at C1 (Wash. Post, Oct. 13, 2019) at *gratefulamericanfoundation.com/weeping-time/*, accessed Nov. 3, 2020.

2 William Wells Brown, *"In A Lecture delivered before the Female Anti-Slavery Society of Salem"* in E. Greenspan, ed., WILLIAM WELLS BROWN: A READER at 108 (Univ. of Georgia Press, Athens, 2008).

3 Mitch McConnell quoted in Rosenberg, "Mitch McConnell's ancestors owned slaves, according to a new report. He opposes reparations" (Wash. Post. July 8, 2019) at *www.washingtonpost.com/politics/2019/07/09/mitch-mcconnells-ancestors-owned-slaves-according-new-report-he-opposes-reparations/*, accessed Sept. 19, 2020.

4 Harper, "Slavery in the North," at *slavenorth.com/emancipation.htm*, accessed Sept. 20, 2020.

I was not taught that, at the time of the Civil War, America was one of the last few countries in the New World practicing slavery.

I was not taught that—

> "During the half century after the legal end of slave importation, *the slave population of the United States surpassed not only that of any other country in the New World,* but, after abolition of slavery in the British colonies in the 1830s, *that of all of them combined.*"[5]

I was not taught that "by 1860, approximately two thirds of all New World slaves lived in the American South."[6] That compares to Brazil, Cuba, and Puerto Rico, the only other then-remaining New World slave societies.

Have you paused to imagine the process by which an African, a human being, was converted into a thing, a chattel one hundred percent submissive and obedient to his or her master's wishes? Think about what was required to do that to someone who had lived freely in Africa with friends, family, and community?[7]

§ § §

In America, many people "learned" that slavery was cured—washed away—by the Civil War, amendments to the Constitution, and Civil Rights Laws in the 1960s. People say, "But I had nothing to do with slavery." On an individual level, that likely is true. This book is a means, however, to learn about African-Americans and their predicament and why many are angry today.

Despite the overriding significance of slavery to America for a period extending for most of America's history, many wish to sweep slavery under the rug. Especially in the South, many schools taught that the Civil War was about "states' rights," but in reality, that misnomer was simply a code for the "right" to practice slavery and to extend it into new territories.

The lingering effects of the comprehensive slave society are not so easily erased.

This brings me to a key perspective.

America's harsh and intense political divide regarding racial issues is a direct consequence of the falsities taught by, and omissions committed by, America's schools decades ago. Many middle-aged and older Americans—like me—were "taught" by such school districts and teachers.[8]

As a consequence, I knew truly little about the extensive abuses of slavery, and virtually nothing about the astoundingly ghastly slave trade, until I began my research.

The same is true of millions of other middle-aged and older Americans, and many younger ones, as well.

Meanwhile, many, even if not all, African-Americans know what happened 150 years ago. It happened to their grandparents and great grandparents. The information is passed from generation to generation in family conversations.

---

5 P. Kolchin, **AMERICAN SLAVERY 1619-1877** at 94 (Hill and Wang, 2003) ("Kolchin"). Emphasis added.

6 Mintz, "Historical Context: American Slavery in Comparative Perspective" at *www.gilderlehrman.org/history-resources/teaching-resource/historical-context-american-slavery-comparative-perspective,* accessed Oct. 6, 2020.

7 See "Chapter Five: *The Duke's Slave Trading Legacy—Africans in Transition: From People to Things.*"

8 See *"Chapter Six: The Duke of York's Creation on a Rampage—Sanitizing History is Fraudulent Education."*

The resulting radically different educations lead to an inability to understand each other.

Through my retirement research, I learned that, for more than 200 years, America and the American colonies were home to a vicious slave society.

In the South, and for most of those 200 years, in the North, slavery was a key source of labor. Even after most Northern states abolished slavery, they continued to profit from it through lucrative business relationships with Southern planters and through active participation in the slave trade and in the markets for cotton, sugar, and other slave-produced commodities. All Americans benefited from a broad range of essential and other slave-produced products—clothing and other cotton goods, sugar, rice, tobacco, and indigo—at lower prices than if paid labor had produced the products.

Slavery was at the core of the American society, culture, and economy. It pervaded virtually all significant aspects of American political life. Pursuant to the Constitution, the slave society had an exaggerated political strength that enabled it to dominate much of America's political structure, including at the state level and, at the federal level, in Congress, the Presidency, and the Supreme Court.

I quickly learned that slavery actually was a crucial factor central to America's political, social, cultural and economic development equivalent or comparable in significance to:

- The settlement of both the Northern colonies and the Southern colonies
- The Revolutionary War
- The Westward expansion
- The Civil War
- The industrial revolution

I was surprised to learn that the form of slavery practiced in America had originated, and had been promoted aggressively in the American colonies, as an official English government policy for the government's profit. That official government policy was not a capitalist conspiracy.

THE TRAIL OF TEARS

"The Slave Trail of Tears is the great missing migration—a thousand-mile-long river of people, all of them black, reaching from Virginia to Louisiana. …

"This forced resettlement was 20 times larger than Andrew Jackson's 'Indian removal' campaigns of the 1830s, which gave rise to the original Trail of Tears as it drove tribes of Native Americans out of Georgia, Mississippi and Alabama. It was bigger than the immigration of Jews into the United States during the 19th century, when some 500,000 arrived from Russia and Eastern Europe. It was bigger than the wagon-train migration to the West, beloved of American lore. This movement lasted longer and grabbed up more people than any other migration in North America before 1900.

"The drama of a million individuals going so far from their homes changed the country. It gave the Deep South a character it retains to this day; and it changed the slaves themselves, traumatizing uncountable families.

"But until recently, the Slave Trail was buried in memory. …"

Ball, "Retracing Slavery's Trail of Tears" (Smithsonian Magazine, Nov. 2015) at *www.smithsonianmag.com/history/slavery-trail-of-tears-180956968/*, accessed Nov. 3, 2020.

I was astonished to learn that, beginning in the 1660s, the form of slavery practiced in American colonies, and then the American states, in many respects was more inhumane than the forms of slavery practiced at the time by the Dutch, Spanish, French and West Africans and even in the colonies before 1660.

Then, I learned even more disturbing information.

I began to learn that, in New York, slaves were punished for rebelling by burning them at the stake only three decades before the Declaration of Independence (and in South Carolina, as late as 1828, half a century after the Declaration).

I continued my research.

I was aghast to learn that slaves in America were broken on the wheel, and literally were roasted for hours over slow-burning fires, with the explicit intention of increasing their torture as a warning to other slaves to remain submissive. They were gibbetted, i.e., placed in cages and suspended in the air for all to watch them die or to view their bodies.

"Branding a Negro Woman", *Slavery Images: A Visual Record of the African Slave Trade and Slave Life in the Early African Diaspora,* accessed November 14, 2020, *http://slaveryimages.org/s/slaveryimages/item/1976*

Even after the Revolution, they were wrapped in straw and burned. They were beheaded; mutilated by slicing ears, noses, hands, feet, and hamstrings, and by knocking out teeth, so they could be identified if they were captured after running away. They were branded like cattle. At times, the slave society even posted the heads of executed slaves along public roads as a terrorist warning to other slaves not to resist their fate.

HARRIET JACOBS

"Only by experience can any one realize how deep, and dark, and foul is that pit of abominations."

H. Jacobs, Incidents in the Life of a Slave Girl at 6 (1861), available from the Library of Congress at *www.hathitrust.org/digital_library*

This is America. How could so many of such shameful acts have been committed in America, not only in the 1700s, but some of them even into the mid-1800s? That was long after the Declaration of Independence declared "We hold these truths to be self-evident, that *all* men are created equal, that they are endowed by their Creator with certain unalienable rights, that among these are life, liberty, and the pursuit of happiness."

My schools did not teach me that America, which stood in the 1900s so boldly as a beacon of freedom against the dictatorships of communism and fascism, was itself only a few decades earlier, for millions of people, a brutal, all-consuming dictatorship.

My schools did not teach me that, for many others who disagreed morally with the slave society, America spread a blanket of repression and fear. Abolitionists and others who objected to slavery, or who only questioned it, were relatively safe so long as they kept quiet. If, however, they became too vocal against the pervasive repression or if they assisted fugitive slaves, they too could suffer greatly. They could be prosecuted under the Fugitive Slave Law, and could be attacked physically, and murdered, by mobs even in non-slave states.

Especially in slave states, America's constitutional guarantees in its Bill of Rights of freedom of speech, freedom of the press, and freedom of religion were held hostage to the slave society. The Bill of Rights did not apply to the states. The slave society could not endure any view that did not re-affirm slavery.[9]

Of course, America has progressed far since the time of slavery. So, what is the point of concealing this momentous feature of America's history? Why promote a fraudulent version of history? Why encourage a false patriotism?

As I continued my research, I learned even more astonishing information. I learned that, in sharp contrast with America when Florida was a still Spanish colony—not part of America until 1821—there were legally-established towns of truly free blacks. Many of the free blacks were escaped slaves from America. Florida welcomed them with open arms and grants of freedom, making them fully-functioning citizens.

I also learned that, at the time of the Civil War, not only Canada welcomed fugitive slaves in the North, but Mexico in the South automatically granted fugitives freedom once they crossed the Rio Grande from Texas and Louisiana.

WHAT IS A "SLAVE SOCIETY"
VS. "A SOCIETY WITH SLAVES?"

"What distinguished societies with slaves was the fact that slaves were marginal to the central productive processes; slavery was just one form of labor among many. ... In societies with slaves, no one presumed the master-slave relationship to be the social exemplar.

"In slave societies, by contrast, slavery stood at the center of economic production, and the master-slave relationship provided the model for all social relations: husband and wife, parent and child, employer and employee, teacher and student. From the most intimate connections between men and women to the most public ones between ruler and ruled, all relationships mimicked those of slavery."

I. Berlin, Many Thousands Gone: The First Two Centuries of Slavery in North America at 8 (Harvard Univ. Press, 1998)

What a divergence from life in America!

Yet, there is more still. I learned that as late as three-quarters of a century following the Declaration of Independence, routinely, even in the nation's capital, slave traders marched slaves on foot under the lash in chained gangs, known as "coffles," for hundreds of miles and even a thousand miles.

Can you imagine undertaking such a walk? In chains?

When I first read that information, I was confused. I did not understand how that could be true. How could people possibly have been treated in that manner in America? Yet, it was true.

Why didn't my schools teach me about slave coffles?

9 See *"Chapter Six: The Duke of York's Creation on a Rampage—The Slave Society's War on Abolitionists."*

I think both you and I know the answer.

All of those horrible, unthinkable events occurred in America. Yet, there was much, much more.

Those events were "something that happened 150 years ago!"

That "something" also "happened" in America, with full governmental support, 200 years ago, and 300 years ago, and more than 350 years ago.

That "something" was what America actually was!

FORMER TEXAS SLAVE

"Don't let them tell you nothing about slavery ... You don't know nothing about being a slave until you been one."

R. Campbell, An Empire for Slavery—The Peculiar Institution in Texas, 1821-1865 at 261 (Louisiana State University Press, 1989)

THE BIRTH IN THE 1660s OF AMERICA'S REIGN OF TERROR

Major events in American slavery occurred approximately a century apart. They can be considered distinct Phases:

- Phase 1: The beginning in the 1660s with the English government's incentivization, promotion, and legalization of a brutal form of slavery through the leadership of the Duke of York and other governmental actors.
- Phase 2: The middle in the 1770s and 1780s with the Revolution, the creation of the American nation free of the English government, the issuance of the Declaration of Independence and, only a little later, ratification of the Constitution.
- Phase 3: The end in the 1860s with the Civil War and the ratification of the 13th, 14th, and 15th Amendments to the Constitution, followed by a decade of Reconstruction, and then by Jim Crow segregation and oppression.
- In a sense, there also was a Phase 4: Another century later, it is notable that America enacted the Civil Rights Laws in the 1960s to effectuate at last the intent of the 13th, 14th, and 15th Amendments.
- There also is now a Phase 5: Despite all that has already occurred, African-Americans still have not achieved equality in key areas. Important remnants of slavery persist, especially with regard to deficient educations,[10] which in turn is responsible for many serious racial inequities.

In Phase 1, America's slave society was born through the fatherhood of the Dule of York and the motherhood of the American colonies:

- American slavery's Reign of Terror had its beginnings in New York, Maryland, Carolina, and Virginia in the 1660s
- Except in New England (which enslaved Native American warriors in wars and traded them to the Caribbean for Africans), the forms of indentured servitude and slavery practiced by the Dutch, Spanish, and French in what is now America often were less inhumane than the slavery that the English devised and that became true American slavery; the same is true of the forms of servitude practiced before 1660 in the Maryland and Virginia colonies and West Africa

FORMER TEXAS SLAVE

"A White Lady was here the other night
wanted to know about slavery time
and when I started to tell her she said
she didn't want to hear that stuff.
I told her the half hadn't been told
if she didn't want to hear that,
it wasn't nothing to tell."

R. Campbell, An Empire for Slavery—The Peculiar Institution in Texas, 1821-1865 at 115 (Louisiana State University Press, 1989)

---

10 See "*Chapter Seven: Moving Forward??—Remnants of Slavery: Intolerable Discrimination in Education.*"

- ▶ The true form of American slavery, incentivized, promoted, and legalized initially by the English, was an especially inhumane hereditary form of slavery that, within a brief time, became focused specifically on Africans
- ▶ The true form of American slavery was devised as official English government policy for the profit of the English government in the form of tax revenues on slave-produced commodities and in the form of slave-trading revenues for the government's monopolistic Royal African Company
- ▶ To promote what became the true form of American slavery, the English provided specific property tax, tariff, and land grant incentives to encourage American settlers to buy slaves and put them to work

There is one specific individual who, with his brother, King Charles II, and their colleagues, was especially instrumental in devising and promoting the English form of slavery in America.

That individual is the Duke of York, James Stuart, who later became King James II.

True American slavery did not begin in Virginia in 1619 with captives taken by the English from a Portuguese ship. That episode was not the beginning of the true form of American slavery.

Those individuals, while certainly not volunteers, were treated in key respects more as indentured servants than "slaves"[11] in the sense in which slavery became practiced in America after 1660.[12]

The character of slavery in the American colonies changed once the Duke of York and King Charles II came to power in the 1660s with the Restoration of the English monarchy.

Moreover, almost another century before 1619, the Spanish brought genuine slaves (although again not in the sense of true American slavery) into Spanish Florida[13] and South Carolina (where the first American slave revolt occurred in 1526).[14] That also was a less inhumane form of slavery[15] than was practiced in America as promoted by the Duke of York.

Illustrating both the presence of slaves in what became America long before 1619, and less inhumane characteristics of the Spanish form of slavery, after a trip during the late 1520s from Florida to Texas by boat, and following an initial capture by Native Americans in Texas, a Spanish slave named Esteban ("one of the greatest explorers in the history of North America"[16]), led a small group of Spanish explorers on foot to Baja

---

11 Brewer, "Slavery, Sovereignty, and 'Inheritable Blood': Reconsidering John Locke and the Origins of American Slavery" at 1048 (American Historical Review Vol. 122, Issue 4, Oct. 2017) ("Brewer");
I. Berlin, MANY THOUSANDS GONE: THE FIRST TWO CENTURIES OF SLAVERY IN NORTH AMERICA at 30-31 (Harvard Univ. Press 1998) ("Berlin").

12 Berlin, at 30-32, 34-37.

13 L. Rivers, SLAVERY IN FLORIDA—TERRITORIAL DAYS TO EMANCIPATION at 2 (Univ. Press of Florida, 2000) ("Rivers"); K. Deagan and D. MacMahon, FORT MOSE: COLONIAL AMERICA'S BLACK FORTRESS OF FREEDOM at 7, 12, 16 (Univ. Press of Florida and Florida Museum of Natural History, 1995) ("Deagan and MacMahon").

14 Deagan and MacMahon, at 13, 16.

15 Rivers, at 2; Deagan and MacMahon, at 7; J. Landers, BLACK SOCIETY IN SPANISH FLORIDA at 2-3 (Univ. of Ill. Press, 1999) ("Landers").

16 R. Goodwin, CROSSING THE CONTINENT 1527-1540 at 7 (HarperCollins Publishers, 2008) ("Goodwin").

California. At Baja, in the mid-1530s, they met other Spanish explorers who had enslaved Native Americans in what is now America's Southwest and Northern Mexico. Esteban's expedition wended its way across the continent 300 years before Lewis and Clark's expedition.

HARRIET TUBMAN

"Slavery ... is the next thing to hell."

K. Larson, Bound for the Promised Land—Harriet Tubman, Portrait of an American Hero at 54 (Ballantine Books, 2003). Footnote omitted.

After shepherding the expedition across the continent, in recognition of his abilities Esteban was appointed "as the de facto military commander of the first Spanish expedition deep into territory that is now Arizona and New Mexico in search of the mythical lands of Cibola and the Seven Cities of Gold."[17]

What an adventure! How exciting to contemplate!

The Duke of York and his colleagues and successors never would have granted slaves such responsibility, freedom, or access to military armaments. In the Duke's America, that flexibility was not possible.

17 Goodwin, at 6-7, 11.

WHY THE DUKE OF YORK IS THE FATHER OF AMERICA'S SLAVE SOCIETY

> "To understand the origins of slavery, we need to pay more attention to how various laws and policies enabled it across the empire, to who was behind those policies, to who profited the most from those policies via customs on imported staple crops, and to how those policies were initially rationalized. Slavery was created in legal pieces—pieces written, approved, and rationalized in hierarchical political contexts by Charles II and his brother James II. It took force to implement and get access and control enslaved labor and collect taxes; the power of empire was critical to each part of slavery's development."
>
> **Dr. Holly Brewer[18]**

Meet the Father of America's Slave Society—the Duke of York.

The Duke of York was, in modern terms, one of the greatest criminals in American—and World—history. The Duke was a true international terrorist.[19]

In the mid-1660s, James Stuart was the Duke of York. He was the younger brother of King Charles II. In 1660, King Charles II assumed the throne in the Restoration of the monarchy in Britain following the Interregnum. During the Interregnum, Oliver Cromwell had assumed power following the beheading of King Charles I, King Charles II's and the Duke of York's father. After King Charles II died in 1685, James, the Duke, became King James II. He was deposed in 1688 in the Glorious Revolution leading to the accession to the throne of Queen Mary II, James' daughter, and her husband, King William III.

The Duke of York's status in the 1660s as a primary leader of English forces in the New World and elsewhere arose from his roles as the King's brother and representative, as the Admiral of the English Navy, and as the chief executive and largest shareholder of a slave-trading governmental monopoly, the Royal Adventurers.[20] The Royal Adventurers, however, fell on difficult financial times, and was reorganized as the Royal African Company. Again, the Duke served as the chief executive and largest shareholder ("a controlling interest"[21]).

100,000 AFRICANS

"During the years from 1673 to 1689, ... the Royal African Company exported slaves from Africa at an annual rate of 6,120, making a total of 104,040."

J. Rawley and S. Behrendt, THE TRANSATLANTIC SLAVE TRADE at 135 (Univ. of Nebraska Press, 2005)

The Duke was not the only person responsible for slavery in America, but he filled a particularly pivotal role. The English were not the only nation to practice slavery, but they practiced it principally in their American and Caribbean colonies, as opposed to England itself. Moreover, their form of slavery was different—even less sensitive to slaves' humanity—than other forms of slavery.

18 Brewer, at Abstract. Footnotes omitted.

19 For additional information regarding the Duke of York's significance to American slavery, see *"Chapter Three: The Duke of York Promotes Slavery."*

20 James Stewart" at *www.commonwealthbooksllc.homestead.com/jamesm—Duke-of-York.html*, accessed Sept. 28, 2020.

21 L. Harris, IN THE SHADOW OF SLAVERY—AFRICAN-AMERICANS IN NEW YORK CITY, 1626-1863 at 26 (Univ. of Chicago Press 2003) ("Harris").

The Duke had extensive power. He used his appointment by King Charles as Admiral of the English Navy to direct English military policy both in Africa and in New York.

Further, as CEO of the Royal African Company, the Duke had a monopoly on the English slave trade with the colonies.

True American slavery had to be created. Despite a few contemporaneous exceptions, and slavery centuries earlier, the English did not practice slavery extensively within England. Dr. Edgar McManus states that "[C]hattel bondage had disappeared in Northern Europe prior to the colonial era."[22] Hilary Beckles cites historian David Eltis as "tell[ing] us that, while just over 10% of England's population had been classified as slaves in 1086, slavery was not a feature of later 14th century English society."[23]

Dr. McManus adds that "the [English] settlers brought over no legal precedents for dealing with slaves."[24]

There are a few English judicial decisions relating to slaves, but without serious discussion of the validity of slavery within England itself. The English did not provide for slavery in the common law.[25] Thus, English precedents for slavery did not provide a body of slave law. Yet, in the American colonies, the English did not adopt other already-existing less inhumane forms of slavery. In England's American and Caribbean colonies, slavery was, in an authentic sense, designed and promoted by the English, *sui generis,* with the Duke of York as a central pro-active official executing the governmental policy in the American colonies.

John Codman Hurd explains the peculiarity that England itself did not have slavery, although its colonies did. He adds that prior English practices did not disqualify anyone as a citizen based upon race or color; once slave status was removed, the person became a British subject:[26]

> Before our Revolution, all free persons within the dominions of the king of Great Britain, whatever their color or complexion, were native-born British subjects—those born out of his allegiance were aliens. *Slavery did not exist in England,* but *it did in the British colonies.* Slaves were not, in legal parlance, persons, but property. The moment the incapacity, the disqualification of slavery, was removed, they became persons, and were then either British subjects or not British subjects, according as they were or were not born within the allegiance of the British king. ...

In America, however, as promoted by the Duke of York, slavery was based upon race. Later, this was taken to its ultimate extreme by the Supreme Court,[27] which decided that not only slaves—but no African-Americans, even if "free"—were recognized in America as "citizens."

---

22 E. McManus, BLACK BONDAGE IN THE NORTH at 57 (Syracuse University Press 1973) ("McManus, Black Bondage in the North").

23 Beckles, at 12.

24 McManus, Black Bondage in the North, at 57.

25 J. Hurd, THE LAW OF FREEDOM AND BONDAGE IN THE UNITED STATES, Vol. II, at 88 carryover footnote (Little, Brown & Co., 1862), available from the Library of Congress at *www.hathitrust.org/digital_library* ("Hurd"). Emphasis added.

26 Hurd, Vol. II, at 88 footnote. Emphasis added.

27 *Dred Scott v. Sandford,* 60 U.S. 393, 15 L. Ed. 691 (1857).

The Duke, his brother, King Charles II, and their colleagues fashioned and promoted their especially brutal form of English slavery in New York and other English colonies to the South.

Prior to that occurrence, the Dutch had practiced slavery in New Netherland, including New Amsterdam (which became New York City under the Duke). Dr. Hilary Beckles explains the Dutch slavery:[28]

> Dutch legal provision for the control and regulation of slaves resembled that of [the] French more closely than it did that of any other European state. The Dutch West India Company, for example, was simultaneously determined to discipline its slaves, benefiting from their labour as alienable property, while at the same time insisting that slave owners had an obligation to provide for the social, educational and religious guidance and instruction of their slaves.

The Dutch granted many of their slaves "half freedom" to live their own lives, with occasional obligations.[29] Dr. Edgar McManus describes the Dutch system of slavery as being "as mild as the realities of chattel slavery probably allowed" with "none of the mutual hatred in New Netherland of the sort that brutalized slave relations in other colonies."[30] Dr. Ira Berlin cites Dutch slaves living on their own, establishing families, working on their own, baptizing their children, suing and being sued in court, and drilling in the militia.[31]

Dr. Alan Singer states: "In Dutch New Netherland permanent, racially based, hereditary slavery was not a clearly established institution. However, this changed once the British took control."[32]

The Spanish and French practiced forms of slavery in colonies that became Florida, Louisiana and Texas, and other states formed in whole or in part from them. Again, however, those forms of slavery often gave slaves at least a degree of recognition of their humanity.

Dr. Hilary Beckles states:[33]

> [W]hile the [Spanish] *Siete Partidas* and the [French] *Code Noir* attempted to balance repression with protection, English law reflected no such concern.
>
> Instead, English law on slavery reflected only the need for constant vigilance on the part of the white population against the black ...

The French *Code Noir* granted slaves many legal protections not adopted by the English, such as a right to marry legally with masters' permission, a right against separation of families, punishment for masters and

---

28 Beckles, "Slave Voyages—The Transatlantic Trade in Enslaved Africans" at 68 (United Nations Educational, Scientific and Cultural Organization) ("Beckles").

29 McManus, Black Bondage in the North, at 57-58; Harper, "Slavery in the North," at *slavenorth.com/newyork.htm.* Citation omitted.
See also "William Penn and James, Duke of York" at *pennsylvaniahistory.wordpress.com/2012/08//11/William-penn-and-james-duke-of-york,* accessed Sept. 28, 2020.

30 E. McManus, A HISTORY OF NEGRO SLAVERY IN NEW YORK at 11 (Syracuse University Press 1996) ("McManus, Slavery in New York").

31 Berlin, at 52.

32 A. Singer, NEW YORK AND SLAVERY—TIME TO TEACH THE TRUTH at 53-54 (Excelsior Editions, State Univ. of New York, Albany, 2008) ("Singer").
See also "William Penn and James, Duke of York" at *pennsylvaniahistory.wordpress.com/2012/08//11/William-penn-and-james-duke-of-york,* accessed Sept. 28, 2020.

33 Beckles, at 66.

overseers engaging in excesses against slaves, a right to medical care, and a guarantee of full rights of citizenship upon achieving freedom.[34] The existence of the legal protections does not mean that slaveholders always honored them, but the English did not provide their slaves the same legal benefits.

ENGLISH INDUCEMENTS TO SETTLERS TO PURCHASE SLAVES

- Land grants for each slave purchased in Virginia, New Jersey, and Carolina
- Property tax incentives for slaves directly from Africa
- Favorable tariffs for slaves directly from Africa

In the 1520s, the Spanish entered Florida and the territory that became Mexico, almost a century before the English entered Virginia and considerably more than a century before the Duke defeated the Dutch in New York.

Like the Dutch and French, the Spanish treated their slaves with more humanity than the English, again with protections not adopted by the English. "Slaves could buy their freedom, maintain family cohesiveness, and sue their masters for mistreatment. Governors and rulers often freed slaves as a reward for service to the Crown."[35] Free blacks in Spanish Florida had full rights of citizenship. The Spanish allowed free blacks to form their own towns,[36] and as noted earlier, created an army of free black warriors upon whom the Spanish colony depended for defense.[37] Later, Mexico also offered freedom to fugitives, allowing them to work or join the military.[38]

The Duke of York never would have permitted such conditions.

His official military position as Admiral was a crucial factor in the substantial growth of the slave trade. Dr. Brewer states: "Charles II gave his brother a commission at the beginning of the war with the Dutch in 1664 that allowed him to attack wherever he liked; James chose the Dutch-occupied forts off the coast of Africa."[39] She adds: "As a consequence of [a treaty with the Portuguese] and Charles II's earlier acquisition of the forts on the African coast, England transported more than half of the slaves sent to all of the New World by [the middle of the Eighteenth Century]."[40]

34 "Le Code Noir" at *thelouvertureproject.org/index.php?title=Le_Code_Noir,* accessed Sept. 19, 2020. See also Rodrigue, "Slavery in French Colonial Louisiana" at *64parishes.org/entry/slavery-in-french-colonial-louisiana.*

35 Deagan and MacMahon, at 7.

36 See, e.g., Deagan and MacMahon, at 7.

37 Rivers, at 4; Landers, at 3. See generally, e.g., Cusick.

38 A. Baumgartner, SOUTH TO FREEDOM: RUNAWAY SLAVES TO MEXICO AND THE ROAD TO THE CIVIL WAR at 1-2, 3 (New York: Basic Books, 2020) ("Baumgartner"). See also Grant "South to the Promised Land," at 78, 85, 88 (Smithsonian July-August 2022) ("Grant").

39 Brewer, at 1048, n. 22.

40 Brewer, at 1073.

"English Castle at Anamabou", Slavery Images: *A Visual Record of the African Slave Trade and Slave Life in the Early African Diaspora,* accessed November 15, 2020, *http://slaveryimages.org/s/slaveryimages/item/2087*

Slaveryimages.org states: "In 1698, the Royal African Company described the facilities at Anomabo, which included 'twelve great guns ... a large tank or cistern ... and a Negroe-house for one hundred and fifty Negroes. This fort ... opens a trade ... for gold, corn, palm-oyl and oyster-shells; also a very great trade for slaves.' See Royal Africa Company, A Particular of the Royal African Company's Forts and Castles in Africa (London, ca. 1698)."

Further, King Charles II was in clear ultimate control in Virginia and other colonies. In addition, the Duke, and representatives functioning with him, such as William Berkeley and George Carteret, were royalists who discharged King Charles' slavery policies in the American colonies. Illustrating the Duke's influence in Southern colonies, among other things, the Duke's Royal African Company "maintained a factor or business agent at Jamestown to over see the sale of slaves."[41]

Dr. Holly Brewer describes how King Charles used the government's land policy to promote the growth of large plantations founded on slave labor, with "promised 'headrights' of thirty to fifty acres of land in Virginia to anyone who bought a servant, whether white or black." Dr. Brewer begins by outlining the monarchy's power:[42]

> Legal concepts of dominion or lordship justified both monarchy and proprietary power. Charles I and later Charles II granted proprietors not only the land but also the right to govern the inhabitants of colonies such as Barbados, Carolina, and New York. Despite notable exceptions in New England and Pennsylvania, in most cases Stuart kings chose men who shared such principles—whether as royal governors, appointed officials, or great proprietors.

41 "The Angolan Connection and Slavery in Virginia" at *www.historyisfun.org/learn/learning-center/the-angolan-connection-and-slavery-in-virginia/*, accessed Oct. 13, 2020.

42 Brewer, at 1045. Footnotes omitted.

She then describes how the English land policy operated in practice:[43]

> In practice, *the legal concept of dominion took the form of headrights, which encouraged lordship, large estates, and bound labor.* Barbados's first proprietor, the Earl of Carlisle, gave men ten acres of land for each servant they owned. By royal proclamation, Charles I and Charles II *promised "headrights" of fifty acres of land in Virginia to anyone who bought a servant, whether white or black.* Charles II instructed Governor Thomas Culpeper that "every person that shall transport or carry servants thither shall, for every servant soe carried and transported, have set out to him, upon the Landing and Imployment of such servant, Fifty acres of land, To have and to hold to him the said Master, his heirs and assigns for ever."

The offer was attractive to large numbers of settlers, who then acquired many slaves and extensive land:[44]

> Between 1635 and 1699, Virginians claimed four million acres for importing 82,000 white and black "servants." In August 1664, Charles II likewise agreed to "granting away the first million acres alloweing thirty acres per head to [masters who import] men women and Children white or blacke, for the latter further the Plantation as much and Doe as much produce the goods that shall pay Custome and fill shipps." Note here the claim that "blacke" laborers were even better than white at producing crops to be taxed in England. The king even permitted respectable Englishmen who "have good Estates, & doe ingage to bring on more people" to claim the headrights that would accord with their plans to import that many people.

A 1909 book discussing slavery in Virginia, states that "[I]t was not until 1661 that the institution of slavery was recognized in Virginia by statute law."[45]

Dr. Brewer explains how the English government's policy led to the creation of large slave plantations:[46]

> A prosperous man who planned to import "an hundred hands" could claim thirty acres for every person he planned to buy, and therefore the king would reward him with a contiguous estate of three thousand acres. Masters thus assembled large plantations with bound labor under royal aegis.

Of course, slave performed much, or all, the hard labor in the creation of those plantations They cleared rock and boulders and cut and uprooted countless tress to prepare fields for planting.

Dr. Brewer adds: "By encouraging mass production of staple crops that were heavily taxed, royal headright policy dramatically increased crown revenue."[47]

Thomas R.R. Cobb, a slaveholder and an influential proslavery advocate and legal scholar in the late antebellum period, reinforces the description of the English government's, and especially the Duke of York's, land-for-slaves policy. Mr. Cobb points specifically to the Duke's likely role in the promotion of slavery in New Jersey through the policy:[48]

---

43 Brewer, at 1045-46. Footnotes omitted.

44 Brewer, at 1046. Footnotes omitted.

45 B. Munford, VIRGINIA'S ATTITUDE TOWARD SLAVERY AND SECESSION at 16 (Longmans, Green, and Co., 1909; reprinted by Negro Universities Press, 1969).

46 Brewer, at 1046.

47 Brewer, at 1046.

48 T. Cobb, AN INQUIRY INTO THE LAW OF NEGRO SLAVERY IN THE UNITED STATES OF AMERICA Vol I, at cxlix. (T. & J. W. Johnson & Co., 1858) ("Cobb"), available from the Library of Congress at *www.hathitrust.org/digital_library.* Footnotes omitted.

> New Jersey, it is known, was dismembered from New York when New Netherlands was conquered by England in 1664. In the next year, a bounty of seventy-five acres of land was offered by the proprietaries for the importation of each able-bodied slave. This was doubtless done in part to gain favor with the Duke of York, then President of the African Company.

Douglas Harper largely confirms Mr. Cobb's description of the New Jersey policy ("offered 60 acres of land, per slave, to any man who imported slaves in 1664").[49]

The English government also utilized its land policy in Carolina, evidencing the Duke's influence through the Royal African Company. In 1663, proprietors, who were members of the Royal African Company, offered land to settlers who brought slaves into the Colony ("20 acres of land for every black male slave and 10 acres for every black female slave brought to the colony within the first year").[50] That was contemporaneous with the Duke's work in devising slavery in New York and elsewhere in America.

Note the interesting confluence of the dates given for active pursuit of the land-for-slaves policy—1664 in each of Virginia and New Jersey and 1663 in Carolina. That was not a coincidence. It was shortly after the Restoration of the Monarchy in England in 1660 and the rise to power of King Charles II and the Duke of York.

Thus, at numerous points during the early colonial era, when slavery was in the process of creation in American colonies, we see the heavy hand of English royalty in search of tax revenues after 1660.

Dr. Brewer states:[51]

> only with the restoration of hereditary monarchy in 1660 did colonies pass laws enshrining hereditary slavery: Barbados in 1661, Virginia in 1662, Jamaica and Maryland in 1664. These laws were a response to Charles II's explicit requests to his governors in 1661 to support the RAC [Royal African Company] and to codify their laws. William Berkeley of Virginia, like other governors, had to obtain the approval of Charles II and his Council of Foreign Plantations for all laws.

Those new laws had grave impacts upon slaves' lives. Importantly, in Virginia before 1660, the laws relating to servants were much different. Dr. Brewer states that, in earlier Virginia: "African servants, like English, had jury trials, could witness (if they could swear an oath), could be manumitted, and could own land and servants themselves when freed."[52] Dr. Ira Berlin describes the early Virginia servants who famously entered Virginia in 1619 as achieving freedom after serving terms of years; they also had families, and acquired land.[53]

Dr. Berlin cites the following rights afforded at least certain "slaves" in the Chesapeake region (Virginia and Maryland) before 1660:[54]

- "[F]arm independently"
- "[M]arry"

---

49 Harper, "Slavery in the North," at *slavenorth.com/newjersey.htm*, accessed Sept. 19, 2020.

50 "Slavery in South Carolina" at *www.womenhistoryblog.com/2008/07/slavery-in-south-carolina.html*, accessed Sept. 19, 2020.

51 Brewer, at 1050.

52 Brewer, at 1048.

53 Berlin, at 30-32.

54 Berlin, at 30-32, 34-35.

- "[B]aptize children"
- "[G]ain[] their freedom"
- "[N]o law yet enshrined African slavery in either Maryland or Virginia"
- "[R]arely worked more than five and a half days a week during the summer," with "a general reduction of labor" in winter
- "Custom ... required masters and mistresses to provide their servants sufficient food, clothing, and shelter, and limited the owners' rights to discipline subordinates"
- Citing to a seventeenth-century Chesapeake guide, "the planter customarily permitted 'his Servant a parcell of clear ground to plant some Tobacco in for himself, which he may husband at those idle moments he hath allowed him'"
- "[S]ome servants and slaves also gained access to provision grounds where they raised not only corn and vegetables to subsist themselves and their families, but also tobacco, which they sold in conjunction with their owner's crop, and occasionally in competition with it"
- "They also kept hogs and cattle, which they—like their owner—pastured in the region's open-range forests and swamps"
- "Slaves also traded directly with planter-merchants, assigned their debt to others, and rented land to add to their own fortunes"
- "[T]here was no part of the economic life of the Chesapeake in which they did not participate"
- "[I]n short, into the middle years of the seventeenth century and perhaps later, slaves enjoyed the benefits extended to white servants in the mixed labor force"

In Maryland, like Virginia, harsher laws began to appear in the 1660s and thereafter.[55] Thus, under the English, there was a coordination, beginning in the mid-1660s in the legalization and active promotion of slavery in New York, on a contemporary basis with Virginia's and Maryland's enactment of harsher slave laws.

The following summary illustrates the Duke of York's pervasive power regarding slavery in America:

- The Duke was instrumental in the enactment of New York laws in 1665 and later years—as part of enactments known as the "Duke's Laws"[56]—"recogniz[ing] the existence of slavery as a legal institution"[57]
- The "Duke's Laws" legalized the English form of slavery, which was more harsh than contemporary forms of slavery and servitude[58]

---

55 A GUIDE TO THE HISTORY OF SLAVERY IN MARYLAND at 27-31 (MD State Archives and Univ. of MD 2007) ("Slavery in Maryland").

56 THE COLONIAL LAWS OF NEW YORK FROM THE YEAR 1664 TO THE REVOLUTION, Vol. I, at xii, 6 et seq. (1894), available from the Library of Congress at www.hathitrust.org/digital_library ("Colonial Laws").

57 See, *e.g.*, McManus, Slavery in New York, at 24; McManus, Black Bondage in the North, at 60. Footnote omitted.

58 See, *e.g.*, McManus, Black Bondage in the North, at 56-61; Harris, at 27-28; Singer, at 53-54.
See also Deagan and MacMahon, at 7; "Florida History Built on Slavery" at *usslave.blogspot.com/2013/06/florida-history-built-on-slavery.html* (quoting Dr. Jane Landers), accessed Sept. 19, 2020; Rivers at 2, 3, 4; Rodrigue, "Slavery in French Colonial Louisiana" at *64parishes.org/entry/slavery-in-french-colonial-louisiana*, accessed Sept. 19, 2020; "Le Code Noir" at *thelouvertureproject.org/index.php?title=Le_Code_Noir*, accessed Sept. 19, 2020.

- The Duke was the Admiral of the English Navy
- The Duke was also the chief executive and largest shareholder of the Royal African Company
- In 1664, the Duke defeated the Dutch at New Amsterdam, after which the City and the Colony were named New York in his honor[59]
- As Admiral, in battling the Dutch for control of the slave trade, the Duke gained Dutch forts in Africa, facilitating the English trade through his Royal African Company[60]
- The Royal African Company had a governmentally-decreed monopoly on the slave trade in the American colonies[61]
- Benefiting from the former Dutch forts and from its slave trading monopoly, the Royal African Company, led by the Duke, brought more than 100,000 Africans from Africa to the New World[62]
- The Duke branded many, if not all, of the slaves he brought to the New World with his initials, "DY"[63]
- Unlike the Dutch, French and Spanish, the "Duke's Laws" introduced true chattel slavery into New York, recognizing the status of slaves as things, brutes, chattels, property to be used as masters desired[64]
- The Duke and his colleagues, and their successors, enacted laws, and accepted practices, granting slaveholders and other whites broad powers to punish slaves, even for minor offenses[65]
- The Duke and his colleagues enacted laws establishing the hereditary character of American slavery, with the result that children born to slave women were themselves automatically slaves for life[66]
- The Duke and his colleagues enacted laws establishing the racial character of slavery, focusing American slavery upon Africans, moving away from Native American slavery,[67] and "presum[ing]""all Negroes ... to be slaves"[68]
- The Duke and his colleagues opened the port of New York to slave trading and auctions, used the port to promote slavery on an active basis, and turned the port into the early center for the slave trade in America[69]

---

59 Thomas, at 13; "Colony of New York: A Brief History" at *www.celebrateboston.com/history/new-york.htm*, accessed Sept. 19, 2020; Harris, at 26; "New York State Name Origin" at *statesymbolsusa.org/symbol-official-item/new-york/state-name-origin-state-quarter/origin-new-york*, accessed Sept. 19, 2020.

60 Brewer, at 1047-48 n. 22, 1073.

61 Singer, at 53; Slavery in Maryland at 4; Cobb Vol I, at cxliii-cxliv.

62 Brewer, at 1047. Footnote omitted.
See also "James Stewart" at www.commonwealthbooksllc.homestead.com/james—Duke-of-York.html, accessed Sept. 28, 2020.

63 Beckles, at 86.
See also "William Penn and James, Duke of York" at pennsylvaniahistory.wordpress.com/2012/08//11/William-penn-and-james-duke-of-york, accessed Sept. 28, 2020.

64 McManus, Slavery in New York, at 80, 81; E. McManus, Black Bondage in the North, at 62.

65 See, e.g., McManus, Slavery in New York, at 80, 81-82; Singer at 54.

66 See, e.g., McManus, Black Bondage in the North, at 60-61; Harris at 28.

67 See, e.g., McManus, Black Bondage in the North, at 60-; Harris at 28; Singer at 53.

68 McManus, Black Bondage in the North, at 60-61.

69 See, e.g., Harris, at 26-27, 28; Singer, at 57; McManus, Slavery in New York, at 24.

- The Dukes' (and King Charles IIs') promotion of slavery's legalization and expansion was for economic purposes—increasing shipping and production of manufactured goods, crops, and other slave-produced commodities that the Crown could tax in order to increase the English government's wealth and from which the Royal African Company received, through its active trading, substantial increased slave trading revenues[70]
- The Duke opposed representative government and, as governor of New York, opposed creation of a legislative assembly, caused dissolution of an assembly, and declined to approve a "Charter of Liberties" that an assembly had submitted to the Duke for his final approval, as was required for all New York laws at the time[71]
- After 1685, the Duke was also King James II of England, until deposed in 1688, during which time, he continued execution of the governmental slave policies[72]

New York City, County and State unjustifiably are named in honor of this criminal and international terrorist—the Father of America's Slave Society.

The Duke of York was not an imperfect American patriot born into an already-existing slave society, as in the case of George Washington, Thomas Jefferson, and Abraham Lincoln. Rather, as an opponent of representative government and a Charter of Liberties, the Duke was, and remains, an "enemy" of all Americans, both whites and African-Americans. The Duke, with King Charles II, was one of the key instigators of slavery in America, and is the only slave trader—in modern terms, a criminal and international terrorist—honored in the names of a major American city, county and state.

While Americans bestow great honors upon the Duke, the English disliked him so much they deposed him!

---

70 Brewer, at 1045-48.
See "Chapter Three: The Duke of York Promotes Slavery—Why Charles II and the Duke of York Promoted Slavery: Follow the Money."

71 Colonial Laws Vol. I, at xiii-xvii
See "Chapter Three: The Duke of York Promotes Slavery—The "Duke's Laws" and His Opposition to Representative Government."

72 Brewer, at 1054-55; Colonial Laws Vol. I, at xvii. Footnote omitted.

TIME LINE: THE MONARCHY CREATES A MONSTER

The following Time Line, which is excerpted from Appendix I, identifies key events in the early days of slavery and indentured servitude in the American colonies.

The Time Line reflects then-contemporary systems of slavery in other cultures (Dutch, Spanish and French) and the form of indentured servitude existing in Virginia prior to the Restoration of the English Monarchy and the Duke's rise to power in the American colonies.

Thus, the Time Line indicates how the absolutist Stuart Kings after the Restoration—King Charles II and King James II (the Duke of York)—rejected available precedents. They could have created a system of slavery that was less inhumane than the one they imposed in the American colonies.

They did not.

The Time Line also indicates the important slave trading role of Queen Anne, the Duke's (and King James II's) second daughter.

THE TERRORIST SLAVE SOCIETY

Year	Event(s)
1526	Spanish bring slaves to Florida; Spanish slaves have certain rights as human beings that the English later denied
1526	First slave revolt in what is now America at Spanish colony of Vasquez de Allyon (now in South Carolina); revolt stymies Spanish settlement
1528-36	Illustrating greater rights of Spanish slaves, Spanish slave, Esteban, leads Spanish expedition across North America, joining Spanish explorers in Baja California 300 years before Lewis & Clark; later is appointed as de facto military commander in search of the Seven Lost Cities of Gold
1619	The English take captives from a Portuguese ship and trade them for food at Point Comfort, Virginia; the captives receive treatment with important rights as human beings that the English later denied
1620	Pilgrims land at Plymouth with indentured servants, including my twelfth generation great grandfather, Edward Doten
1626	Dutch West India Company imports 11 Africans as slaves in New Netherland; slaves in New Netherland have certain rights as human beings that the English later denied
1641	Massachusetts enacts statute legalizing ownership of slaves taken captive in wars or purchased from others, which is incorporated into the Articles of the New England Confederation
1652	Rhode Island adopts similar statute
ca. 1655	Illustrating the rights of the early Virginia captives, Anthony Johnson, an early captive who became a free black slave holder and land owner through land grants, wins a dispute in court against a white property owner over ownership of a slave claimed by Mr. Johnson
1660	Restoration of the Monarchy in England; King Charles II takes the throne, then appoints his brother, James Stuart, Duke of York, as Admiral of the Navy
1660	The English government forms the Royal Adventurers, a slave trading monopoly; after reorganization, the government names the company the Royal African Company; during the Duke's control, the Royal African Company ships more than 100,000 slaves to the New World, branding many, if not all, of them with the Duke's initials, "DY"
1661	King Charles II appeals to colonial governors to enact laws supporting slavery and the Royal African Company
1661-75	England, in alliance with Portugal, fights for and ultimately gains control of Dutch forts on West African coast; the forts and associated African trading relationships, prisons, and other facilities are vital to the English slave trade
1662	King Charles II marries Catherine de Braganza, a Portuguese princess, whose dowry includes claims of West African forts controlled by the Dutch

1662	Virginia begins enacting restrictive laws formalizing brutal slavery at direction of English monarchy
1663	Slaves and indentured servants plot rebellion in Gloucester, Virginia; plot is disclosed; four plotters hanged
1663	Royal African Company officials offer land to Carolina settlers purchasing slaves (20 acres per male slave, 10 acres per female slave)
1664	English aggressively promote land-for-slaves policy, rewarding slave purchasers; the more slaves, the more land awarded (in Virginia, 50 acres per slave; in New Jersey, 60-75 acres per slave)
1664	Maryland begins enacting restrictive laws formalizing brutal slavery at direction of English monarchy
1664	Duke of York defeats Dutch in New Amsterdam and receives Charter from King Charles II granting the Duke control of the colony; New York is named "in honor" of the Duke
1664-88	James Stuart, as Duke of York and later as King James II, opposes representative government in New York and vetoes a Charter of Liberties petitioned by the people
1665	New York, under Duke of York, begins enacting restrictive laws, known as the "Duke's Laws", enshrining brutal slavery
1685	Duke of York takes English throne as King James II following death of King Charles II; continues slave policies and denial of representative government
1685	French King Louis XIV promulgates the *Code Noir,* granting slaves certain rights as human beings denied by the English
1686	Spanish government begins offering escaped slaves sanctuary in Florida, with rights as free citizens; over time, American slaves escape to Florida in large numbers
1688	King James II is deposed; William and Mary assume the English throne
1702	Queen Anne, second daughter of the Duke of York (King James II), assumes English throne
1702 *et seq*.	English enact additional laws placing even more restrictions on slaves; still more restrictive enactments occur over many years
1708	Slaves revolt on Long Island, killing a white family; the government hangs two male slaves and burns a slave woman at the stake
1712-13	Queen Anne obtains the *Assiento*, a slave trading monopoly contract with the Spanish, pursuant to which the English supply hundreds of thousands of slaves to the New World over several decades
1712	Slave rebellion in New York; slaves kill seven whites and set fires; dozens of slaves arrested; several slaves commit suicide to avoid capture; more than 20 slaves executed; slaves burned at the stake and broken on the wheel
1738	Spanish Florida establishes Fort Mose, a free black town

What is terrorism?

How would you view a government or a cult, domestic or foreign, that, with full official, societal and religious support:

- Directly attacks civilians with military forces
- Relies for its chief source of labor upon trafficking in, purchasing, and trading hundreds of thousands of captured human beings based upon their race
- Enslaves millions of human beings in a brutal smothering servitude
- Repeatedly rapes and impregnates slave women who have no power to resist, and then enslaves their children for life
- Beats slaves in their daily lives and lavishly whips disobedient slaves
- Coerces slaves to perform back-breaking labor for long hours day after day
- Routinely chains gangs of slaves, including children, to make forced long-distance marches
- Deprives slaves of basic necessities for routine comforts of life
- Destroys slaves' families, tearing young children literally from their parents' arms, and separating spouses from each other never to be seen again
- Gains political power based upon the size of the slave population; the more slaves, the more power[73]
- Uses the most barbaric punishments imaginable against escaping and rebellious slaves

> **"TERRORISM"**
>
> "the systematic use of terror especially as a means of coercion"
>
> "Terrorism" at www.merriam-webster.com/dictionary/terrorism, accessed Nov. 5, 2020

Is it not fair to characterize such actions as "terrorism"?

Those are the horrors to which a substantial proportion of America's, and the American colonies,' population—ultimately millions of people—was subjected for more than 200 years.

That was slavery in America.

America's slave society was sadistic. There simply is no way to soften the description in an honest manner.

That is "something that happened 150 years ago."

It represented a genuine Reign of Terror.

The Reign of Terror was a way of life in America for hundreds of years, for the majority of America's history, even today.

America's slavery had two vastly different worlds—

---

73 See *"Chapter Four: America's Slavery Contradictions—The Constitution Contemplated and Protected Slavery."*

- The world of white citizens: Filled with freedom and opportunity
- The vastly different world of slaves: A living hell *for life* without hope

Actually, there was a third world for supposedly "free" African-Americans. That world had theoretical "freedom," but without basic rights, such as, among others, the right to travel freely, including the right even to cross the border into a supposedly "free" state; the right to receive an education; the right to receive service at businesses offering public accommodations, such as hotels, restaurants, theaters, and transportation; the right to be employed for work on the basis of merit; the right to enter a skilled profession or to begin a business without prohibitive resistance from competing whites; the right to live where one wanted upon paying the price; the right to vote; and the right to serve on juries.

EXCEPTIONAL INHUMANITY OF AMERICAN SLAVERY, EVEN IN ITS TIME

In what became the English colonies, the initial form of labor often originated as a less harsh form of servitude than the slavery ultimately adopted. The early forms of servitude were often indentured servitude or sometimes slavery. That slavery, however, while still brutal, was less inhumane than under the system promoted by the Duke of York and the English government.

Colonies in which less inhumane servitude was practiced before their adoption of the English form of slavery include the following:[74]

- The colony that had been New Amsterdam, including New York and parts of New Jersey
- Virginia
- Maryland
- Carolina Colony, which became North Carolina and South Carolina
- Georgia

In a paper prepared for the United Nations Educational, Scientific and Cultural Organization, Dr. Hilary Beckles states:[75]

> The English form of slavery contrasts, at least in legal terms, with the forms of slavery legalized by the Dutch, French and Spanish, which included "the right to family life, leisure time, religious instruction, or access to law to protest against cruel treatment."

Kathleen Deagan and Darcie MacMahon state in their book published by University Press of Florida and Florida Museum of Natural History, that:[76]

> The Spanish slave code provided certain rights for slaves. Slaves could buy their freedom, maintain family cohesiveness, and sue their masters for mistreatment. Governors and rulers often freed slaves as a reward for service to the Crown. After 1492, this slave code was brought to the Americas by the Spaniards, and underlaid many of the differences between the lives of some Spanish-African slaves and the lives of many slaves in the English colonies.

In the Smithsonian, Richard Grant reinforces Deagan's and MacMahon's portrayal:[77]

> Even though slavery existed in New Spain, American runaways were usually granted asylum by the Spanish authorities, because the American form of slavery was regarded as far more brutal and dehumanizing. In New Spain, for example, slaves were subjects of the Spanish crown, not property, and it was illegal to separate husbands and wives or to impose excessive punishments.

74 Georgia began as a colony in 1732.

75 Beckles, at 52, 66-67, 86

76 Deagan and MacMahon, at 7

77 Grant at 78, 84. See also Baumgartner at 23-24.

Dr. Leslie Harris describes the less inhumane treatment of Dutch slaves in New Netherland before the Duke of York's emergence:[78]

> In New Netherland, African slaves could testify in court and bring suit against whites; had the same trial rights as whites; could own property, except real estate or other slaves; and could work for wages.

Dr. Harris adds that "Dutch Reformed [Church] ministers performed marriages for a significant number of enslaved and free blacks, "and "[a]s the slaves married and had children," the Dutch West India Company "allowed them to form separate households" She continues that "In addition to permitting slaves in New Netherland to own material goods and earn wages, the Dutch West India Company and the Dutch government allowed them to petition the government and to use the courts to settle disputes." She cites two specific instances in which slaves were able to bring suit in court successfully against whites, in one instance for wages due and in the other for damage to a slave's cow.[79] The Dutch permitted slaves to be taught to read and write. In addition, the Dutch West India Company offered a number of slaves 'half freedom,' permitting the slaves to pursue their lives, subject to obligations to provide service "in times of need" and to pay an annual tribute.

Unlike slaves under the English system who could not own property, the Dutch West India Company eventually gave some slaves land, so they could engage in agriculture. Dr. Harris further observes that:[80]

> In 1663, just before the British took over the colony, the Dutch granted unconditional emancipation to half-free blacks in the colony, who numbered about seventy-five. Their children were probably included in the number.

The French *Code Noir,* while allowing brutality against slaves, also stated:[81]

> **Article XXVII**. Slaves who are infirm due to age, sickness or other reason, whether the sickness is curable or not, shall be nourished and cared for by their masters. In the case that they be abandoned, said slaves shall be awarded to the hospital, to which their master shall be required to pay six sols per day for the care and feeding of each slave. ...
>
> **Article XLIII**. We enjoin our officers to criminally prosecute the masters, or their foremen, who have killed a slave under their auspices or control, and to punish the master according to the circumstances of the atrocity...
>
> **Article XLVII**. Husband, wife and prepubescent children, if they are all under the same master, may not be taken and sold separately. We declare the seizing and sales that shall be done as such to be void. For slaves who have been separated, we desire that the seller shall risk their loss, and that the slaves he kept shall be awarded to the buyer, without him having to pay any supplement. ...
>
> **Article LV.** Masters twenty years of age may free their slaves by any act toward the living or due to death, without their having to give just cause for their actions, nor do they require parental advice as long as they are minors of 25 years of age.
>
> **Article LVIII**. We declare their freedom is granted in our islands if their place of birth was in our islands. We declare also that freed slaves shall not require our letters of naturalization to enjoy the advantages of our natural subjects in our kingdom, lands or country of obedience, even when they are born in foreign countries.

---

78 Harris, at 16.

79 Harris, at 17, 20-21.

80 Harris, at 23, 26.

81 Le Code Noir" at thelouvertureproject.org/index.php?title=Le_Code_Noir, accessed Sept. 19, 2020.

> **Article LIX.** We grant to freed slaves the same rights, privileges and immunities that are enjoyed by freeborn persons. We desire that they are deserving of this acquired freedom, and that this freedom gives them, as much for their person as for their property, the same happiness that natural liberty has on our other subjects.

In addition to those examples, Dr. Beckles states that slavery in West Africa was far different from the English form of slavery promoted by the Duke of York:[82]

> [R]ecent research into African history has suggested that the term "slave" would only have been appropriate for newly acquired captives, who had not yet undergone the elaborate process of adoption and assimilation. The concept of a "slave", then, is a complex one in West-African history, having very different meanings to that denoted by the chattel slaves of the later transatlantic slave trade.
>
> Aside from these problems of definition, slavery as an institution in Africa was also widely used as a means by which outsiders could become assimilated into the local kinship system. It could also act as a mechanism by which certain persons were kept in a subordinate position for labour purposes for a defined period of time, and as a social marker that indicated an absence of kin and a state of non-belonging. However, the emphasis in all such cases was upon the possibility of exiting from the state of slavery through gradual integration into family, household and kin structures. Indeed, in most cases, such African "slaves" were persons having specified rights and obligations, including the right to family, cultural identity and, ultimately, to freedom, and these rights were part of general customary understanding. Above all, enslavement was not confined to members of a single ethnicity or culture.

Dr. Harris agrees. She describes how slaves' expectations based upon African slavery could have been far different from the English form of slavery imposed in the American colonies, leading to the 1712 slave revolt in New York:[83]

> New Yorkers identified the majority of the rebels as Koromantine and Pawpaw Africans, part of the large group of Africans who arrived in New York City between 1710 and 1720. Koromantine and Pawpaw Africans trained their men in their communities in the conduct of guerilla warfare. These Africans' knowledge of slavery in Africa entailed more rights and privileges than accorded to slaves in British North America. In the Akan-Asante society from which these slaves came, slaves or their children could eventually be absorbed into the community as equals. Masters rewarded faithful slaves with the opportunity to inherit land and to work for themselves. Not every slave experienced such privileges, but the possibility of such rewards eased the condition of slavery there.[84]

In summary, America's slavery, as promoted by the Duke of York and his colleagues and successors, was considerably different and more inhumane than slavery as often legalized or practiced in other cultures contemporary with, or immediately preceding, the origination of slavery in the territory that became America.

Although those precedents were available to the Duke, and to his colleagues and successors, he and they chose to implement in America a punishing form chattel slavery and, over time, to focus that form of slavery on one specific racial group—Africans.

---

82 Beckles, at 23-24.

83 Harris, at 38.

84 See "*Chapter Six: The Duke of York's Creation on a Rampage—Who Were the Slaves?*"

AMERICA CHOSE DESPOTIC REPRESSION OVER HUMANITY

"the great sin and shame of America"[85]

Frederick Douglass

§ § §

Of course, slaves did not like slavery. Once slave traders brought hundreds of thousands of Africans to America, and that number increased into the millions, white citizens discovered that they had a tiger by the tail—an exceptionally large African-American population, full of anger and hostility, uneducated and unskilled, generally without means to make an independent living.

Dr. Peter Kolchin quotes Thomas Jefferson as stating in 1820:[86]

> We have the wolf by the ears, and we can neither hold him, nor safely let him go. Justice is in one scale, and self-preservation in the other.

Dr. Hilary Beckles states:[87]

> The management of ... slave societies was no easy matter: the Africans did not wish to be enslaved, and they vigorously opposed their condition. As a result, such slave societies were maintained less by consensus and more by force and cruelty, depending for their stability on a combination of militia control, urban constables and garrisoned soldiers. ...
>
> In all the colonies, slavery laws laid the foundations for elaborate systems of repression. ...

All of those slaves were dangerous to the very existence of white citizens and to the property of white citizens. Slaves would, and did, kill masters and their families. Slaves would, and did, commit arson and otherwise damage or destroy property. Slaves would, and did, steal food and other necessities of life. After all, their labor was stolen day after day by their masters, and indirectly by society at large in support of the masters. If simply released, wrathful slaves could wreak far more havoc and become a burden on society.

Moreover, slavery led to wealth. Lonnie Bunch, Secretary of the Smithsonian Institution, adds: "In the years before the Civil War, the amount of money invested in slaves was more than the amount of money invested in railroads, banks, and businesses combined. This was the economic engine of Europe and the United States."[88]

Greed and perceived economic necessity claimed the day. It was not sufficient for Americans to live reasonably comfortable lives, based on the fruit of their own efforts, on all that land expropriated from the Native Americans. America could not become truly wealthy without slave labor—labor stolen from other human beings. Wage workers and voluntary indentured servants alone could not, or would not, do the job.

So, guess what? They decided to compel Africans to do the work that whites disliked. Oh, and they didn't pay the Africans either.

---

85 F. Douglass, MY BONDAGE AND MY FREEDOM at 442 (1855), available from the Library of Congress at *www.hathitrust.org/digital_library* ("Douglass, My Bondage and My Freedom").

86 Kolchin, at 89.

87 Beckles, at 62.

88 "The Slave Ship" at *cbsnews.com/news/the-slave-ship-60-minutes/*, accessed Oct. 6, 2020.

This is reflected in diverse sources. One is in Pennsylvania steel mills, where white ironmasters asked for restrictions on slave importation to be eased because there was an insufficiency of white workers "for the hard conditions that prevailed in the bloomeries and mills repelled free workers."[89]

A second source is a slave master and proslavery legal scholar, Thomas R.R. Cobb. Mr. Cobb provides the following views of why slavery was legalized in Georgia in the 1700s (which was governed at the time by trustees). Mr. Cobb emphasizes, among other things, that white workers "were utterly unable to do service" and describes the advocacy of religious figures in favor of slavery:[90]

> The trustees provided laborers in indented white servants, in their judgment better adapted to the wants of the colonists. Experience soon proved the fallacy of their reasoning. The contests between them and the colonists were unceasing and stubborn on this point. The best and wisest of the latter joined in the universal demand for slave labor. ... *[T]he white servants imported, for more than half the year (from March till October), were utterly unable to do service,* and to so deplorable a state did the colony arrive, that at last *the pastor of these hardy Germans (Mr. Bolzius), beseeched the trustees "not to regard any more our or our friends' petitions against negroes."*

Since the slaves were hostile, however, they had to be beaten into submission.[91] That made them even more angry, hostile and dangerous. Whites knew this, and profoundly feared the slaves. Remember that, in a number of states, the slave population outnumbered, or was close to equaling, the white population. In some rural areas, the slaves greatly outnumbered the white population. This occurred not only in the Deep South. For example, "At the end of the 18th century, Maryland was the third largest slave state and, 58% of Prince George's [County] population was enslaved."[92]

CONTRASTING AFRICANS' LIVES IN EUROPE IN MID-1800s

"Soon after the arrival of his daughters, Mr. [William Wells] Brown [in exile due to the Fugitive Slave Law] placed them in one of the best seminaries in France, where they encountered no difficulty on account of their complexion. The entire absence of prejudice against color in Europe is one of the clearest proofs that the hatred here [in America] to the colored person is solely owing to the overpowering influence of slavery. Mr. Brown's daughters, after remaining in France one year, were removed to the Home and Colonial School in London, the finest female educational college in Great Britain. Here, as well as in the French school, the girls saw nothing to indicate that the slightest feeling of ill-will existed on the part of the students towards them, because of their color."

J. Brown, Biography of an American Bondman by His Daughter at 74 (R.F. Wallcut, 1856), available from the Library of Congress at *www.hathitrust.org/digital_library*

By choosing to move forward under those conditions, colonial America also found it necessary to become still more repressive. Slaves responded by adopting passivity and docility as a façade presented for the benefit of white people, but not reflective of inner emotions. For large numbers of slaves, the internal hatred was magnified. Even seemingly passive and docile slaves harbored hostility. There simply is not a way to beat a helpless person brutally without fostering rage, hostility, and hatred in return.

89 Beckles, at 42-43.

90 Cobb, Vol I, at cli. Footnotes omitted. Emphasis added.

91 See "Chapter Five: The Duke's Slave Trading Legacy—Africans in Transition: From People to Things."

92 Bordewich, Review of W. Thomas, WHEN SLAVES HAD THEIR DAY IN COURT (Yale Univ. Press, 2020) at C7 (Wall St. J., Nov. 14, 2020) at www.wsj.com/articles/a-question-of-freedom-review-slavery-on-trial-11605282554, accessed Nov. 14, 2020.

So, from fear and guilt, white America—terrified of rebellion and of African-Americans in general and needing to destroy resistance to submission—practiced the brutal English approach to slavery. America increasingly tightened the shackles on the slaves, and adopted ever-more punitive laws.

As stated by Dr. Beckles, "slave revolt and conflict over slavery were permanent features" of slave societies:[93]

> [F]or three and a half centuries, a dominant political feature of all colonial societies in the Americas was the fear of rebellion by African slaves, and the development of complex systems of defence against possible insurrection, as well as the creation of socio-cultural institutions that effectively excluded blacks attests to the seriousness with which anti-slavery activities were viewed. Maintaining the slave-status of blacks in such societies, against a background of the threat of mass rebellion, was a priority of most colonial administrations, and this was all the more important since no colonial slave society was politically stable, and slave revolt and conflict over slavery were permanent features of them.

Such slavery was ubiquitous in America.

Both before and after the Declaration of Independence, slavery deeply penetrated everything in America—politics, social life, religion, and the economy, both North and South.[94]

---

93 Beckles at 174-75.

94 See "Chapter Six: The Duke of York's Creation on a Rampage—Slavery Was a National Institution: North and South.

RATIONALIZING SLAVERY: "FOR THEIR OWN GOOD"

"poor pagans whom Christians have thought to consider cattle"[95]

New York Weekly Post-Boy

"Our ancestors were transformed from human personalities into private property."[96]

A. Philip Randolph

§ § §

For the preponderance of America's existence from the founding of the colonies, more than 200 years of America's history, slavery defined and built America and pervaded all important aspects of American life.

To put it into perspective, even today, that period remains the majority of America's history. America has chosen to ignore or at least substantially to diminish the vital importance of slavery's historical role.

There have been only 16 decades since slavery ended in 1865, and only seven decades since the Supreme Court's decision in *Brown v. Board of Education*[97] declaring that segregated schools were unconstitutional. Still today, extreme discrimination in education continues unabated.[98]

Whatever the specific lifestyle of slaves, however, Christians pretended that this slavery was for the African-Americans' good. After all, in Africa, they had no chance of going to a Christian Heaven. The perception was that, in Africa, the slaves had been inferior beings living in huts and following what American whites regarded as weird cultural practices and pagan religions. Now, as slaves in America, they had a chance of salvation and civilization, although they still were viewed as dirty, unreliable, undesirable, and inferior.

Others argued that slavery was a "positive good," with superior living conditions over workers in the North. One example is George Fitzhugh, a vocal proponent in favor of slavery.

Mr. Fitzhugh characterized slavery, contrasting it with Northern capitalism, as "a beautiful example of communism," as follows:[99]

> We find in the days of Sir Matthew Hale, a very singular pamphlet attributed to him. It was an attempt to prove that two healthy laborers, marrying and having in the usual time four children, could not at ordinary labor, and with ordinary wages, support their family. The nursing, washing, cooking and making clothes, would fully occupy the wife. The husband, with the chances of sickness and uncertainty of employment, would have to support four. Such is the usual and normal condition of free laborers. With six children, the oldest say twelve years of age, their condition would be worse. Or should the husband die, the family that remained would be still worse off. There are large numbers of

95 McManus, Black Bondage in the North, at 151, quoting *the New York Weekly Post-Boy,* March 24, 1760, edition.

96 Quoted at Gates, "Slavery by the Numbers," at *www.theroot.com/slavery-by-the-numbers-1790874492,* accessed Sept. 19, 2020.
See *"Chapter Five: The Duke's Slave Trading Legacy—Africans in Transition: From People to Things."*

97 *Brown v. Board of Education,* 347 U.S. 483 (1954).

98 See *"Chapter Seven: Moving Forward??—Remnants of Slavery: Intolerable Discrimination in Education."*

99 G. Fitzhugh, SOCIOLOGY FOR THE SOUTH at 28-29 (1854), available at the Academic Affairs Library, Univ. of North Carolina at Chapel Hill, docsouth.unc.edu. Emphasis added.

> aged and infirm male and female laborers; so that as a class, it is obvious, we think, that under ordinary circumstances, in old countries, they are incapable of procuring a decent and comfortable support. The wages of the poor diminish as their wants and families increase, for the care and labor of attending to the family leaves them fewer hours for profitable work. With negro slaves, their wages invariably increase with their wants. The master increases the provision for the family as the family increases in number and helplessness. *It is a beautiful example of communism, where each one receives not according to his labor, but according to his wants.*[100]

John C. Calhoun, a famous orator, is known in part for his speech in 1837 defending slavery as a "positive good," seeking to place abolitionists on the defensive. John Calhoun was Vice President from 1825 to 1832, and thereafter served as a U.S. Senator. He delivered his "positive good speech" on the Senate floor, presenting his view of the positive attributes of slavery and forecasting a split in the Union.

The following is an excerpt from Senator Calhoun's speech:[101]

> *We of the South will not, cannot, surrender our institutions.* To maintain the existing relations between the two races, inhabiting that section of the Union, is indispensable to the peace and happiness of both. It cannot be subverted without drenching the country or the other of the races. … But let me not be understood as admitting, even by implication, that the existing relations between the two races in the slaveholding States is an evil:—far otherwise; I hold it to be a good, as it has thus far proved itself to be to both, and will continue to prove so if not disturbed by the fell spirit of abolition. I appeal to facts. *Never before has the black race of Central Africa, from the dawn of history to the present day, attained a condition so civilized and so improved, not only physically, but morally and intellectually.*
>
> In the meantime, the white or European race, has not degenerated. It has kept pace with its brethren in other sections of the Union where slavery does not exist. It is odious to make comparison; but I appeal to all sides whether the South is not equal in virtue, intelligence, patriotism, courage, disinterestedness, and all the high qualities which adorn our nature.
>
> But I take higher ground. I hold that in the present state of civilization, where two races of different origin, and distinguished by color, and other physical differences, as well as intellectual, are brought together, *the relation now existing in the slaveholding States between the two, is, instead of an evil, a good—a positive good.* I feel myself called upon to speak freely upon the subject where the honor and interests of those I represent are involved. I hold then, that *there never has yet existed a wealthy and civilized society in which one portion of the community did not, in point of fact, live on the labor of the other.* Broad and general as is this assertion, it is fully borne out by history.

Fortunately, we have an extensive record from the slaves themselves regarding the actual characteristics of slavery they experienced. This includes the words of America's Slavery Heroes written in the form of narratives by or about Frederick Douglass, Sojourner Truth, Harriett Tubman, Harriett Jacobs, Solomon Northup, William Wells Brown, and others.

---

100 See *"Chapter Six: The Duke of York's Creation on a Rampage—The Story of Bomefre: Death of a Lonely Loyal Servant."*

101 "Slavery a Positive Good" at *teacherpress.ocps.net/stephenhansen/files/2016/07/Calhoun-Slavery_a_Positive_Good_.pdf,* accessed Sept. 19, 2020. Emphasis added.

A BOILING POT: THE DEPRAVED SLAVE SOCIETY

"The main cause of slave revolts was slavery."[102]

Dr. Marcus Rediker

§ § §

America's slave society was a tight lid on a boiling pot. At times, the lid blew off.

Slaves were not simply "property." In reality, they were people, human beings.

So, sometimes, slaves fought back. That made whites even more fearful. The most famous such incident is known as "Nat Turner's rebellion" in 1831 in which slaves killed approximately 55 to 60 people. There were other notable slave revolts in New York, South Carolina, Louisiana, North Carolina, and Virginia, among other places.[103]

CONVERTING DOLLARS

For those who wish to convert dollars from the time of slavery into current money, $1,000 in 1850 would be equivalent to $33,322.82 today.

So, a multiple of 33 is fair.

"Value of $1,000 from 1850 to 2020" at www.officialdata.org/us/inflation/1850?amount=1000, accessed Sept. 19, 2020

In TWELVE YEARS A SLAVE, Solomon Northup estimates his slave value as $1,000, or $33,000 today.

More often, slaves resisted by dragging their heels, feigning illness, running away, sabotaging their work, and stealing or damaging their masters' property. Some escaped through suicide.

Such a society was unhealthy and depraved. After the American Revolution, reacting to the ideals of the Declaration of Independence, abolitionists began to increase in numbers. Many Americans experienced moral qualms about what their society had done. The movement began slowly.

Over the succeeding eight decades, however, stirred by the urgent voices and writings of America's Slavery Heroes and others, abolitionism matured into a powerful social force. The words of the Declaration, as well as passionate speeches by people like Frederick Douglass, Sojourner Truth, Frances Ellen Watkins Harper, and William Wells Brown, haunted, and also inspired, them. The writings of Douglass, Brown, William Lloyd Garrison, Theodore Weld, and other escaped slaves and abolitionists motivated them. Nat Turner's and other slave rebellions disturbed them. John Brown's raid on the federal armory at Harper's Ferry and his moving words at his trial made it inevitable.

Even then, the stubbornness of the slave society, determined to preserve its way of life, still made the incredibly bloody Civil War necessary. Emphasizing its all-encompassing malice, the slave society was willing for its own citizens to experience, and to inflict, hundreds of thousands of deaths, and a million and a half

102 M. Rediker, THE SLAVE SHIP: A HUMAN HISTORY at 299 (Penguin Books, 2007) ("Rediker").

103 See generally, T. Gray, THE CONFESSIONS OF NAT TURNER (T.R. Gray, 1831), available from the Library of Congress at *www.hathitrust.org/digital_library* ("Gray").
See *"Appendix I: American Slavery Time Line,"* which identifies some of the notable slave revolts.

casualties, in attempting to preserve its "ownership" of other human beings and to export slavery into new territories.

Yet, there were the ever-present fears of what could happen if all those hostile, uneducated people simply were released while unable to provide for themselves without land or marketable professional skills. Further, much of the population, including even abolitionists, were racist at heart, considering African-Americans to be inferior and undesirable. The same was true of the majority of whites in the South who did not own slaves.[104]

As one potential solution, many Americans considered plans to send the African-Americans somewhere else. Thomas Jefferson flirted with the concept of recolonization by sending African-Americans back to Africa. Dr. Patrick Rael states that "Prominent Americans lent their names, credibility, and fortunes to the [American Colonization Society], including Henry Clay, Andrew Jackson, Francis Scott Key, James Monroe, Daniel Webster, and Bushrod Washington." Supreme Court Justice John Jay was among the members.[105]

Dr. Rael adds that a group known as Colonizationists Across the Hudson—[106]

> warned that free blacks constituted a degraded class that "would provoke a civil and servile war" unless something were done to control them. They suggested the physical removal of black people, so that "the enormous mass of revolting wretchedness and deadly pollution" would be removed from the nation's shores.

The American Colonization Society was instrumental in creating the African nation of Liberia to receive freed slaves, although a substantial proportion died from disease, the climate, and wars with local tribes.[107]

Abraham Lincoln, who was willing to preserve the Union early in the Civil War at the cost of continuing slavery, proposed paying masters for their slaves, and sending the freed slaves down to South or Central America. Washington, DC, actually did pay masters for their slaves, offered freed slaves money to leave the country, and even paid some to do so.[108]

Most former slaves and "free" African-Americans resolutely resisted colonization, however, choosing to remain where they had been born and lived all their lives.

Not only freed slaves were skeptical of the proposed compromise, but slaveholders doggedly opposed it. They were wedded to their way of life and social organization, built upon slavery. They claimed to believe that slaves were treated well and, given Southern "paternalism," were quite happy.

The slaves told a different story.

So did the pervasive white fear of the slaves.

---

104 Kolchin, at 179, 180, 181.

105 Rael, "Chapter 4: The Long Death of Slavery," in Berlin and Harris at 137 ("Rael"). Footnote omitted.

106 Rael, at 137. Footnote omitted.

107 "The American Colonization Society" at *www.whitehousehistory.org/the-american-colonization-society,* accessed Sept. 19, 2020; "How a Movement to Send Freed Slaves to Africa Created Liberia" at *www.history.com/news/slavery-american-colonization-society-liberia,* accessed Sept. 19, 2020.

108 "DC Emancipation Day" at *emancipation.dc.gov/page/ending-slavery-district-columbia,* accessed Sept. 19, 2020.

AN "ACTUAL REIGN OF TERROR"

"There exists at this moment, throughout the Southern States, *an actual Reign of Terror.*"[109]

William Lloyd Garrison, quoting the New York Tribune

"[C]rimes which would disgrace a nation of savages. There is not a nation on the earth guilty of practices more shocking and bloody, than are the people of these United States, at this very hour.

"Go where you may, search where you will, roam through all the monarchies and despotisms of the old world, travel through South America, search out every abuse, and when you have found the last, lay out your facts by the side of every-day practices of this nation, and you will say with me, that, for revolting barbarity and shameless hypocrisy, America reigns without a rival."[110]

Frederick Douglass

"Slavery is a crime … against God, and all the members of the human family … ."[111]

Frederick Douglass

"Liberty and life were stolen and sold[.]"

"Human beings delivered, sorted, weighed, branded with marks of commercial enterprises and loaded as cargo on a voyage without return[.] *One of the largest migrations in history was also one of the greatest crimes of history.*"[112]

George W. Bush, U.S. President

---

109 W. Garrison, THE NEW "REIGN OF TERROR" IN THE SLAVEHOLDING STATES, FOR 1859-60 at iii (American Anti-Slavery Society, 1860). Emphasis added.

110 Douglass, "What to the Slave Is the Fourth of July?" (July 5, 1852) at "Text of Douglass's Speech" at *www.owleyes.org/text/what-to-the-slave-is-the-fourth-of-july/read/text-of-douglasss-speech#root-162*, accessed Nov. 5, 2020.

111 F. Douglass, My Bondage and My Freedom, at 379.

112 "Slavery one of the greatest crimes of history: Bush" at *www.smh.com.au/world/slavery-one-of-the-greatest-crimes-of-history-bush-20030709-gdh2ew.html*, accessed Sept. 19, 2020. Emphasis added.

REIGN OF TERROR

"A period of brutal suppression
or intimidation by those in power"

"Reign of Terror," American Heritage® Dictionary of the English Language, Fifth Edition (Houghton Mifflin Harcourt Publishing Company 2016), quoted at *www.thefreedictionary.com/The+Reign+Of+Terror,* accessed Sept. 19, 2020

In the mid-1800s, simply granting freedom to slaves was not the only potential choice to be made. That was too easy. Ending slavery meant war, and that meant hundreds of thousands of deaths and 1½ million casualties in a population only ten percent of today's population.

Slavery was substantively an unadulterated "Reign of Terror."

This is the slavery that America sanitizes.

The following are certain characteristics of the English form of slavery as practiced in America for more than two centuries:

- America practiced slavery against an eighth of its population, in specific states 50% or more by the time of the Civil War
- By the time of the Civil War, slaveowners owned approximately four million human beings in America;[113] the number of slaves in America was the proportionate equivalent, based on the current U.S. population, of 40 million slaves—approximately the population of the State of California or twice the population of the State of New York
- A significant percentage of slaves were children
- Not only slaveowners, but America, as a matter of *national* governmental policy through the Fugitive Slave Laws of 1793 and 1850, regarded millions of human beings as chattels—property to be bought, sold, leased, mortgaged, bred, worked as oxen and horses in the fields, brutalized routinely and tortured, until at times they died from excessive labor, disease, abuse or neglect

SLAVERY WAS A CRIME AGAINST HUMANITY

"slavery is now recognized as a great crime."

A Guide to the History of Slavery in Maryland, at 1 (MD State Archives and Univ. of MD 2007)

"The transatlantic slave trade is now generally accepted to have been a crime against humanity, even in those countries on both sides of the Atlantic that actively participated in it."

Beckles, *Slave Voyages—The Transatlantic Trade in Enslaved Africans* at 10 (United Nations Educational, Scientific and Cultural Organization)

"one of the greatest crimes against humanity in history."

Lonnie Bunch, Secretary, Smithsonian Institution quoted in "What happened when Trump visited the African American History Museum" (Aug. 31, 2019), at *www.chron.com/national/article/What-happened-when-Trump-visited-the-African-14404817.php,* accessed Sept. 19, 2020

113 "Black and slave population of the United States from 1790 to 1880" at *www.statista.com/statistics/1010169/black-and-slave-population-us-1790-1880/#:~:text=By 1860%2C the final census taken before the,free African Americans in all of the US.,* accessed Sept. 19, 2020.

- That national law obligated all governmental officials and citizens—even in so-called "free" states, which actually themselves had been slave states only shortly before—to assist in capturing escaped slaves, with judges rewarded for sending fugitive slaves back to their masters
- "[A]bout one million slaves ... [were] moved west between 1790 and 1860" in the "internal slave trade," routinely by means of slave coffles, to cotton plantations, mostly from the Upper South, with "a devastating impact" for slave families[114]
- Countless churches and ministers, even if not all, provided religious justification for slavery, emphasizing among other things, biblical passages to the effect that slavery was righteous, that slaves should obey their masters, and that slaves should be punished if they did not

All of those "somethings" "happened" openly, with widespread official political, religious, and social support, including by acts of Congress, enactments of state legislatures, acts of Presidents, and decisions of the courts, including the Supreme Court.

CONVERTING POPULATION

According to U.S. Census data, the population of the United States in 1860 was over 31,000,000, and in 2019, the U.S. population was approximately 330 million.

So, a general multiple of 10 is fair.

"1860 United States Census, Introduction" at viii at *www2.census.gov/library/publications/decennial/1860/population/1860a-02.pdf; "World Population review" at worldpopulationreview.com/states/,* accessed Sept. 20, 2020

That means four million slaves in 1860 was the proportional equivalent of 40 million slaves in America today.

The 1½ million Civil War casualties was the proportional equivalent of 15 million casualties today.

Out of an estimated 12.5 million Africans who had been transported forcibly toward the New World, including but not limited to America, an estimated 10.7 million survived the transportation phase, known as the "Middle Passage."[115] Thus, an estimated 1.8 million died from disease, brutality, murder, or suicide in the actual shipping process.[116]

Using the multiplier of ten to make a comparison to America's current population, it was the proportionate equivalent today of 125 million slaves shipped to the New World as a whole and 18 million Middle Passage slave deaths.

Yet, there are "conservative" estimates of a far greater number of total deaths associated with the slave trade.

In addition to the 1.8 million estimated African deaths in the course of the Middle Passage itself, Dr. Marcus Rediker estimates that another 1.8 million Africans died during capture, marching to the African Coast, and storage awaiting transfer to the slave ships, and an additional 1.5 million Africans, now "slaves," died shortly after they arrived in the New World. His "conservative"

114 Kolchin, at 96; Slavery in Maryland, at 11.

115 Gates, "Slavery by the Numbers" published at www.theroot.com/slavery-by-the-numbers-1790874492, accessed Sept. 20, 2020. This source agrees that by 1860, there were 3.9 million slaves in America out of a total African-American population of 4.4 million.
See also "Trans-Atlantic Slave Trade Database" at slavevoyages.org, accessed Sept. 20, 2020.

116 See "Chapter Five: The Duke's Slave Trading Legacy—The Triangular Trade and the Middle Passage: Key Role in Genocide."

estimate of total deaths associated with the slave trade (including from disease and abuse shortly after arriving in the New World) is at least five million deaths for a "yield" of nine million surviving slaves out of an initial 14 million captives.[117]

Those numbers alone would mean that, proportionately to current population, a comparative 50 million Africans died. That is equivalent to the combined current populations of California, Nevada, and Arizona, and approximately 15 percent of America's current population.

There are other estimates in the tens of millions of deaths during the capture and shipping phases alone, omitting deaths after New World arrival.[118]

That Reign of Terror was a genocide and a holocaust.[119] America's history includes knowing, purposeful participation in one of the worst genocides in World history. It is fraudulent "patriotism" to attempt to brush this off as merely "something that happened 150 years ago."

Placing in perspective the number of victims of America's Reign of Terror, to compare against the 1.8 million slave deaths in Middle Passage shipping alone, the following genocides have occurred since 1900:[120]

- "The Herero and Namaqua Genocide"—an estimated 65,000 to 110,000 deaths in Namibia by German Colonialists in 1904
- "The Armenian Genocide" (disputed by the Turks), during the First World War—an estimated 1.5 million Armenian expulsions and deaths during a war with Turkey
- "The Cambodian Genocide," 1975-1979— Pol Pot led the Khmer Rouge movement that resulted in an estimated two million deaths
- "The Rwandan Genocide," 1994—"over 800,000 mainly Tutsi Rwandans" at the hands of a Hutu dominated government
- "The Srebrenica Massacre, or Genocide," 1992-95—an estimated 8,000 Bosnian Muslim men and boys by Bosnian Serbs in what has been called the "Srebrenica Massacre"
- "The Darfur Genocide," ca. 2003—"more than 2.7 million people were forced to flee their homes" in Sudan in fighting between Janjaweed fighters and black Africans

The Nazi Holocaust led to millions of deaths, with varying estimates of the total. Commentators often use six million.

All of the foregoing genocides were terrible crimes against humanity, and each was a Reign of Terror in its own right. Together, they create a context within which to evaluate the slave trade and America's slave society.

---

117 Rediker, at 5.

118 See *"Chapter Five: The Duke's Slave Trading Legacy —The Triangular Trade and the Middle Passage: Key Role in Genocide."*

119 See *"Chapter Five: The Duke's Slave Trading Legacy—Genocide and Holocaust."*

120 What Is Genocide" at *www.theholocaustexplained.org/what-was-the-holocaust/what-was-genocide/the-cambodian-genocide/,* accessed Sept. 20, 2020.

RECOGNIZE AND HONOR AMERICA'S SLAVERY HEROES

Despite the hardships, heroic slaves, former slaves, and "free" blacks overcame incredible adversity and triumphed in awakening America's principled citizens to an obligation to end slavery.

In this dismal environment, from the depths of despair, there were triumphs of the human spirit. There were people I call "America's Slavery Heroes," including especially those who escaped slavery by overcoming great odds and courageously confronting great personal risks. Those African-American Heroes opposed and, with active dedicated support from "free" African-Americans and sympathetic whites, who themselves took great risks, ultimately defeated the very institution of slavery that King Charles II, the Duke of York, and their colleagues and successors created and promoted. Those Heroes, with their abolitionist allies, reversed America's deal with the Devil—devotion to the Hellish torment the Duke of York and America's colonial governments had created and America's state and national governments had enforced.

> **BLACK CODES**
>
> "The Black Codes were a series of statutes and laws enacted in 1865 and 1866 by the legislatures of the Southern states of Mississippi, Alabama, Georgia, Louisiana, Virginia, Florida, Tennessee, and North Carolina following the end of the Civil War at the beginning of the Reconstruction Era. The Black Codes were created to restrict the freedom of ex-slaves in the South."
>
> "Black Codes" at *www.american-historama.org/1866-1881-reconstruction-era/black-codes.htm#:~:text=The%20Black%20Codes%20were%20laws%20that%20were%20introduced,of%20ex-slaves%20was%20restricted%20in%20numerous%20ways%20including%3A*, accessed Sept. 20, 2020

Nevertheless, once slavery was in place, ending it was no easy task. Even when colonists sought to restrict the slave trade, the English government resisted.

Further, simply releasing hundreds of thousands, and eventually millions, of helpless, uneducated and unskilled people on the street, was a perceived "problem" that whites feared and with which many wrestled. When it was finally accomplished through the 13th Amendment, the results were not attractive, as various forms of "substitute slavery"—statutory and other forms of "apprenticeship" and "indentured servitude"—took form pursuant to Black Codes and otherwise for many decades. Significant remnants of slavery continue today, especially regarding educational inequities.

The slaves and former slaves I am calling "America's Slavery Heroes" are Heroes for all Americans. America's youth—both African-Americans and others—should know about and gain inspiration from their heroism. The following are brief synopses regarding a few of them:

► ***Harriet Tubman (Born ca. 1820; died 1913)***

Harriet Tubman was an unbelievably heroic individual. Ms. Tubman was only five feet tall, but extremely strong and determined. She had been severely injured when younger, having been struck in the head by an iron weight thrown by a white at another slave. The injury caused seizure episodes throughout her life. After escaping from her slave master on Maryland's Eastern Shore of the Chesapeake Bay, with help from William Still—the Father of the Underground Railroad—Ms. Tubman courageously returned an estimated 13 times to rescue an approximate 70 to 80 family members, friends, and other slaves. She provided escape directions to countless others. Ms. Tubman was proud to say that as a conductor on the Underground Railroad, she never lost a passenger. During the Civil War, she served in significant roles, including as a nurse, spy, cook, and military leader. She led a Union Army force in South Carolina that freed hundreds of slaves. After the end of slavery, Ms. Tubman assisted older African-Americans and operated a nursing home in Upper New York State.[121]

"Frederick Douglass, American abolitionist, ca. 1865", Slavery Images: A Visual Record of the African Slave Trade and Slave Life in the Early African Diaspora, accessed November 15, 2020, http://slaveryimages.org/s/slaveryimages/item/1531

▶ ***Frederick Douglass (Born ca. 1818; died 1895)***

Frederick Douglass was the best known abolitionist and anti-slavery speaker and an effective political leader. He is recognized, with Harriett Tubman, as one of the most prominent African-American abolitionists. He was one of the earliest advocates of women's rights.

Douglass' effective and highly-popular oratory came at a time when oratory was a leading form of entertainment. His emergence as an especially articulate orator and his Narrative, published in 1845, were significant developments in the battle against slavery. He later added political activism, supporting the Liberty Party and later Abraham Lincoln.

Like Harriet Tubman, Mr. Douglass escaped from Maryland. A fugitive slave himself, he was passionate and extremely articulate. After the enactment of the Fugitive Slave Law of 1850, he went into exile in England, where he continued his speaking. After English friends purchased his freedom, Mr. Douglass returned to America, publishing prolifically and successfully on slavery issues.[122]

▶ ***William Still (Born 1821; died 1902)***

William Still, a "free" black, often known as the Father of the Underground Railroad, was the operating head of the Philadelphia Anti-Slavery Society. He was a key individual assisting fugitive slaves in escaping to freedom.

Mr. Still maintained confidential records of the fugitives who passed through his office, which he published in a comprehensive volume after slavery ended.[123] The records Mr. Still kept and eventually published after the end of the Civil War describe in detail almost 1,000 Underground Railroad "passengers." Among other things, Still was instrumental in assisting fugitives who came to Philadelphia under the guidance of Harriet Tubman.

---

121 See generally Larson; S. Bradford, SCENES IN THE LIFE OF HARRIET TUBMAN (1869), available from the Library of Congress at www.hathitrust.org/digital_library ("Bradford").

122 See generally F. Douglass, THE NARRATIVE OF THE LIFE OF FREDERICK DOUGLASS (1845), available from the Library of Congress at *www.hathitrust.org/digital_library* ("Douglass, Narrative"); Douglass, My Bondage and My Freedom.

123 W. Still, THE UNDERGROUND RAILROAD: A RECORD at (Philadelphia: Porter & Coates, 1872), available from the Library of Congress at *www.hathitrust.org/digital_library* ("Still, 1872 Edition").

In one remarkable encounter, as Still interviewed one escaped slave from the South, he realized that the slave was Still's own brother who was searching for his mother. It was a joyous reunion.

After the Civil War, Still fought diligently against discrimination. Over time, he also became successful in business.

► ***Sojourner Truth (Born ca. 1797; died 1883)***

Sojourner Truth "walked away" from her slave master's premises in Upper New York State early one morning. Ms. Truth brought a successful suit against her master for selling her son to a Southerner, the first such case brought by a former slave. The sale had violated New York law prohibiting sales of slaves out of the State. She was successful; the defendant was compelled to achieve the return of her son.

A strong religious figure, Ms. Truth became a prominent and popular outspoken lecturer against slavery and in favor of women's rights.[124]

► ***William Wells Brown (Born ca. 1814; died 1884)***

William Wells Brown was a slave in Missouri. Among other experiences, his master leased him to a slave trader who would collect gangs of slaves and ship them from Missouri to the South, including Natchez, Mississippi, and New Orleans, by riverboat. Eventually, Mr. Brown was acquired by others who took him on a riverboat to Cincinnati. He then escaped in the middle of January into Ohio, a "free" state. As a fugitive slave, however, he remained at risk of capture, so he traveled at night, hiding during the day.

With his eye on the North Star, Brown headed toward Cleveland. While exhausted, freezing cold, and ill, he encountered a Quaker couple who nursed him to health. The man was named "Wells Brown." William had no last name (and had been whipped several times for trying to use his own name, William, as a slave). He gladly accepted the offer of "Wells Brown" to use that name in combination with "William."

While working on boats on Lake Erie after he reached Cleveland, Mr. Brown saved almost four dozen slaves, assisting them in reaching Canada, hidden on the boats.

Mr. Brown became a prominent and effective abolitionist speaker and a prolific author of narratives, memoirs, novels, a play, a travelogue, a song book, and other publications. Brown was the first published black playwright and published other "firsts." Among other books, Brown authored historical books regarding blacks, including **THE NEGRO IN THE AMERICAN REBELLION: HIS HEROISM AND HIS FIDELITY**, an historical work about black soldiers during the Revolution. In the first chapter of that book, Brown describes repeated instances of heroism and bravery of blacks in the cause of the American Revolution. He portrays Crispus Attucks, "the first to fall," and discusses the deep respect shown by the colonists to Attucks and other victims of the Boston Massacre at a public funeral and through annual recognition for years thereafter.[125]

---

124 See generally Dictated by S. Truth, written and edited by O. Gilbert, SOJOURNER TRUTH'S NARRATIVE AND BOOK OF LIFE (1875), available from the Library of Congress at *www.hathitrust.org/digital_library* ("Truth's Narrative and Book of Life").

125 W. Brown, THE NEGRO IN THE AMERICAN REBELLION: HIS HEROISM AND HIS FIDELITY at 4 (Lee & Shepard, 1867), available from the Library of Congress at www.hathitrust.org/digital_library.

In 1853, Brown wrote a novel titled **CLOTEL**, or, **THE PRESIDENT'S DAUGHTER: A NARRATIVE OF SLAVE LIFE IN THE UNITED STATES,** the first novel written by an African-American. He first published the book in London, where he resided at the time. The novel describes, as fiction, lives of two mulatto daughters born to Thomas Jefferson and one of his slaves.[126]

As a fugitive, Mr. Brown was forced into exile in England after enactment of the Fugitive Slave Law of 1850. He was joined by his two daughters, and lived in France and England, where his daughters attended schools. He continued speaking actively in Europe about the evils of slavery. At an international exhibition in London, he and others conducted a demonstration at the American exhibit, publicizing the use of slave labor to produce goods on exhibit. Once English friends purchased his freedom, he returned to America. He traveled thousands of miles in Northern states from New England to Missouri as an abolitionist orator.[127]

Back in America, Mr. Brown eventually became Dr. Brown, a medical doctor. He practiced medicine for the rest of his life.

▶ ***Frances Ellen Watkins Harper (Born 1825; died 1911)***

Born "free," Frances Ellen Watkins Harper was educated in her uncle's black academy in Baltimore. A poet and accomplished author, she devoted her life in opposition to slavery as a forceful and articulate abolitionist speaker. She also fought for womens' rights. Although little known today, Ms. Harper was quite well-known in mid-Nineteenth Century America. She particularly emphasized the rights of black women.[128]

While Sojourner Truth often sought accommodation with white women, Ms. Harper did not hesitate to issue direct challenges to them, such as "You white women speak here of rights. I, as a colored woman, speak of wrongs."[129]

Ms. Harper disagreed with certain leaders of the womens movement, such as Elizabeth Cady Stanton, who opposed the 15th Amendment, referring to black men in insulting terms. Harper fought for the Amendment.

---

126 W. Brown, CLOTEL, or, THE PRESIDENT'S DAUGHTER: A NARRATIVE OF SLAVE LIFE IN THE UNITED STATES, WITH A SKETCH OF THE AUTHOR'S LIFE (London, Partridge & Oakey, 1853), Academic Affairs Library, Univ. of North Carolina at Chapel Hill, available at docsouth.unc.edu.

127 See generally W. Brown, NARRATIVE OF WILLIAM W. BROWN, A FUGITIVE SLAVE, WRITTEN BY HIMSELF (Anti-Slavery Office, 2nd ed. 1848), available from the Library of Congress at *www.hathitrust.org/digital_library*; J. Brown, BIOGRAPHY OF AN AMERICAN BONDMAN BY HIS DAUGHTER (R.F. Wallcut, 1856), available from the Library of Congress at *www.hathitrust.org/digital_library* ("J. Brown").
See *"Chapter Six; The Duke of York's Creation on a Rampage—A Bill of Sale."*

128 See generally F. Foster, ed., A BRIGHTER COMING DAY: A FRANCES ELLEN HARPER READER Introduction (New York: The Feminist Press at the City University of New York, 1990) ("Foster"); "Frances Ellen Watkins Harper" at www.*africanamericanpoetry.org/frances-e-w-harper*, accessed March 1, 2022.

129 "Inspiring Speeches by Frances Watkins Harper, 19th-Century Reformer & Author" at *www.literaryladiesguide.com/author-quotes/inspiring-speeches-by-frances-watkins-harper*, accessed March 1, 2022; "Shall Not Be Denied" at *www.loc.gov/exhibitions/women-fight-for-the-vote/about-this-exhibition/new-tactics-for-a-new-generation-1890-1915/western-states-pave-the-way/i-speak-of-wrongs-frances-ellen-watkins-harper/*, accessed March 1, 2022.

▶ ***Harriet Jacobs (Born ca. 1815; died 1897)***

Harriet Jacobs repeatedly declined her slave master's persistent sexual advances, enticements, and threats. In order to avoid him, Ms. Jacobs hid by living in a tiny attic space for seven years in the home of her "free" grandmother until she could escape to the North to be with her children. She wrote her memoirs about her ordeal and the unique brutality of slavery for slave women.[130]

▶ ***Jermain Loguen (Born 1813; died 1872)***

After escaping from slavery in Tennessee, Jermain Loguen[131] made his way through Canada to Syracuse, where he established himself as a noted and eloquent abolitionist speaker and fierce opponent of slavery. He became an ordained minister in the African Methodist Episcopal Zion Church, preaching at multiple locations in Upper New York State.

He remained a fugitive slave for his entire life until the ratification of the 13th Amendment. Despite offers by others to purchase his freedom, Mr. Loguen refused. He openly dared the slave society to come to Syracuse to capture him and return him to slavery.

Despite his status as a fugitive himself, Mr. Loguen aggressively provided assistance and sustenance to large numbers of fugitives from slavery. His contributions as a "stationmaster" operating a "depot" for the Underground Railroad were so valuable that he was known as the "King of the Underground Railroad."

He "built an addition to his home for the specific use of fugitives."[132] "[H]is basement was fitted with bunks and other equipment for fugitive slaves."[133] He "regularly put his home address in the newspapers inviting any fugitive from slavery to drop in at any time."[134] "In 1859 [he] openly announced in the papers that twenty fugitives would be at his home during a donation visit, so people could get to know those whom they were helping."[135]

Loguen assisted a number he estimated at 1,500 refugees for the nine years after enactment of the Fugitive Slave Law of 1850.[136] In calendar year 1856 alone, he reported assisting 186 fugitives.[137] In 1854, he "reported 200 passengers."[138]

---

130 See generally H. Jacobs, INCIDENTS IN THE LIFE OF A SLAVE GIRL (1861), available from the Library of Congress at *www.hathitrust.org/digital_library* ("Jacobs").

131 J. Loguen, THE REV. J. W. LOGUEN, AS A SLAVE AND AS A FREEMAN, A NARRATIVE OF REAL LIFE (Syracuse: J.G.K. Truair & Co., 1859), Academic Affairs Library, Univ. of North Carolina at Chapel Hill, available at *docsouth.unc.edu* ("Loguen Narrative").

132 C. Hunter, TO SET THE CAPTIVES FREE: REVEREND JERMAIN WESLEY LOGUEN AND THE STRUGGLE FOR FREEDOM IN CENTRAL NEW YORK, 1835-1872 at 138 (Hyrax Publishing, 2013) ("Hunter").

133 "Jermain Wesley Loguen (1813-1872)" at *www.blackpast.org/african-american-history/loguen-jermain-wesley-1813-1872/*, accessed March 14, 2022.

134 Hunter at 13. Footnote omitted.

135 Hunter at 145.

136 Hunter at 155.

137 Hunter at 144.

138 Hunter at 155. Footnote omitted.

In a dramatic event in Syracuse known nationally as the "Jerry Rescue," when federal Marshalls had arrested a fugitive named Jerry, Mr. Loguen famously led a massive crowd breaking into the jail where Jerry was held, freeing him.[139] Abolitionists then transported Jerry to Canada. It was a striking demonstration of abolitionist barriers confronting the slave society, even after the enactment of the Fugitive Slave Law of 1850.

► *Solomon Northup (Born ca. 1807; died post-1857)*

Solomon Northup was a "free" African-American living with his family in Upper New York State. As a skilled fiddler, he traveled to Washington to work in a circus. In Washington, he was drugged and kidnapped, a widespread problem for "free" African-Americans. He was sold to slave traders in Washington, and shipped to the New Orleans slave auction, where he was purchased. Having been savagely beaten for telling people he was "free," Mr. Northup simply bided his time. After twelve years, he was able to identify a white man who would mail a letter for him back to New York about his location. His family and friends then gained his freedom. Illustrating the diabolical effects of the prohibitions against testimony by even supposedly "free" African-Americans, when he sued his slave trader in Washington, DC, as an African-American he was not permitted to provide testimony, so that the operative evidence in the case was the slave trader's denials.[140]

► *Lieutenant Juan Bautista (Prince) Witten (Born ca. 1758; died 1835) and Florida's Army of Black Warriors*

Lieutenant Witten was a slave who escaped to Spanish Florida with his family where they were granted their freedom. Trained by a skilled guerilla warrior from the Haitian revolution, Lt. Witten was a highly-respected officer in the Spanish Florida army of black warriors. The black army, numbering into hundreds, and perhaps 1,000, saved St. Augustine when it was under siege by slaveholder forces and U.S. Army troops in the secretive Patriot War of 1812. The secret War was conducted with the knowledge of President James Madison and Secretary of State James Monroe while the War of 1812 was in full sway. Lt. Witten and his guerilla army ambushed and defeated the slaveholders and U.S. Army troops in a decisive battle.[141]

NAT TURNER

"I heard a loud noise in the heavens, and the Spirit instantly appeared to me and said the Serpent was loosened, and Christ had laid down the yoke he had borne for the sins of men, and that I should take it on and fight against the Serpent, for the time was fast approaching when the first should be last and the last should be first."

T. Gray, The Confessions of Nat Turner (T.R. Gray, 1831), available from the Library of Congress at *www.hathitrust.org/digital_library*

► *Nat Turner (Born 1800; died 1831)*

In 1831, Nat Turner, devoutly religious, instigated the most famous of slave revolts. In Southampton County, Virginia, Mr. Turner led a large group of slaves in attacks against slaveholder families living on

139 See "Chapter Six: The Duke of York's Creation on a Rampage—The Jerry Rescue."

140 See generally S. Northup, TWELVE YEARS A SLAVE (1853), available from the Library of Congress at *www.hathitrust.org/digital_library* ("Northup").

141 See generally Rivers; Landers.

rural plantations, killing 55 to 60 whites before the Army defeated them. The uprising fueled substantial white fears, and even panic, across the South. Fearful whites assaulted and murdered large numbers of blacks. The slave society reacted by enacting even more repressive restrictions upon slaves.[142]

- ***David Walker (Born 1796; died 1830)***

David Walker was not a slave himself, but was the son of a slave. An early version of Malcolm X and Colin Kaepernick, Mr. Walker was the author of a small, strongly outspoken book entitled **"APPEAL TO THE COLORED PEOPLE OF THE WORLD."**[143] The **APPEAL,** which was terrifying to the slave society, led to sizable bounties offered for Mr. Walker, dead or alive. He criticized not only whites, but also slaves for their passivity, encouraging them to be ready for an uprising when the time was right. Mr. Walker, who operated clothing stores on the Boston waterfront, sewed copies of the **APPEAL** into the lining of clothing worn by sailors going South. Seaports in the South prevented black sailors from disembarking for fear they might bring copies on shore. African-Americans who could read, would read it to slaves.[144] PBS states that: "Copies of the Appeal were discovered in Savannah, Georgia, within weeks of its publication."[145]

There are numerous other African-Americans from the time of slavery who also deserve special honor.

America's Slavery Heroes, some virtually unknown in white, and even black, America today, deserve far more credit and recognition than they receive. They were a driving force when America reformed the Constitution by ratifying the 13th, 14th, and 15th Amendments and thereby became a much different nation. They contributed every bit as much to America as did the Founding Fathers and Abraham Lincoln, and should be recognized in proportion to that contribution.

They deserve to be recognized with a National Slave Memorial on the National Mall in Washington.

---

142 See generally Gray, THE CONFESSIONS OF NAT TURNER (T.R. Gray, 1831), available from the Library of.

143 See generally D. Walker, APPEAL TO THE COLORED PEOPLE OF THE WORLD, BUT IN PARTICULAR, AND VERY EXPRESSLY, TO THOSE OF THE UNITED STATES OF AMERICA, WRITTEN IN BOSTON, STATE OF MASSACHUSETTS (1829), Academic Affairs Library, Univ. of North Carolina at Chapel Hill, available at docsouth.unc.edu ("Walker").

144 "David Walker's Appeal to the Colored Citizens of the World" at *www.davidwalkermemorial.org/appeal,* accessed Sept. 20, 2020.

145 "David Walker's Appeal" at www.pbs.org/wgbh/aia/part4/4h2931.html, accessed Sept. 24, 2020

CHAPTER TWO: AMERICA'S SLAVE SOCIETY WAS A TERROR SOCIETY

THE SLAVE SOCIETY'S MESSAGES OF TERROR

"Slavery makes it necessary for the slaveholder to commit all conceivable outrages upon the miserable slave. It is impossible to hold the slaves in bondage without this."[146]

Frederick Douglass

"Born in violence, slavery survived by the lash. … [E]very stage of master-slave relations depended either directly or indirectly upon physical coercion."[147]

Dr. Peter Kolchin

"The labor of the slave is constant toil, wrung out by fear."[148]

William Leftwich, Son of a Slaveholder

"While the slave masters took to their sitting rooms, book-lined libraries, and private clubs to affirm their gentility, they drove their slaves relentlessly, often to the limits of exertion. Those who faltered faced severe discipline. In the process, millions died.

"Such a regime had to rest upon force. Violence was an inherent part of slave society … . [V]iolence was not only common in slave societies, it was also systematic and relentless; the planters' hegemony required that slaves stand in awe of their owners. Although they preferred obedience to be given rather than taken, planters understood that without a monopoly of firepower and a willingness to employ terror, plantation slavery would not long survive. The lash gained a place in slave societies …[149]

Dr. Ira Berlin

§ § §

Until the 13th Amendment was ratified in 1865, America—as a dominant element of its economy, culture and political structure—was a slave society. Although Northern non-slave states abolished slavery, and although slavery in the North often gave slaves certain flexibility that slaves in the South did not have,[150] the Northern states continued to provide substantial active support to Southern slavery in the form of critical business services—commodities trade, finance, insurance, shipping, and a variety of other capacities. Additionally, the federal government provided essential support to slaveholders through the Fugitive Slave Law of 1793, the

146 "(1845) Frederick Douglass, 'My Slave Experience in Maryland'" at *www.blackpast.org/african-american-history/1845-frederick-douglass-my-slave-experience-maryland/*, accessed Sept. 20, 2020. Emphasis added.

147 Kolchin, at 57.

148 T. Weld, AMERICAN SLAVERY AS IT IS: TESTIMONY OF A THOUSAND WITNESSES at 49 (American Anti-Slavery Society 1839), available from the Library of Congress at *www.hathitrust.org/digital_library* ("Weld").

149 Berlin, at 98. Footnote omitted.

150 Berlin, at 56-57.

Fugitive Slave Law of 1850, and the Supreme Court's decision in the Dred Scott case[151] denying even "free" African-Americans access to the federal courts on the basis that they were not "citizens" protected by the Constitution.[152]

America's slavery was extremely violent. For most slaves, the violence and threat of violence occurred on a consistent, daily basis.

Without fear, violence and terror, the slaves would not have been motivated to work exhaustively without pay or to live in the squalid conditions to which they were subjected. If the slaves did not labor unceasingly, slaveholders, as well as others dependent upon slavery, would not profit.

Slaveholders deliberately sought out and applied against slaves the most brutal instruments of terror that could be conceived. They consciously applied those instruments of terror to their purpose in a manner designed and intended to inflict upon slaves as much fear, and agony as was possible.

For emphasis, I repeat:

For the more than two centuries of American slavery, for the majority of America's history, America as a nation, and before that, the American colonies, intentionally inflicted consistent pervasive terror upon a population that grew into millions of helpless civilians derived from a distant foreign continent who had caused America no harm.

POWER OF THE SLAVE MASTER

"The power of the master must be absolute to render the submission of the slave perfect. In the actual condition of things it must be so. There is no remedy."

Supreme Court of North Carolina, 1829, quoted by Philadelphia Judge George Stroud in G. Stroud, A sketch of the laws relating to slavery in the several states of the United States of America at 10, footnote (H. Longstreth, 1856), available from the Library of Congress at *www.hathitrust.org/digital_library*

Americans inflicted that terror, in a systematic and deliberate manner, in order to bring into sharp focus for each individual slave, and for all slaves as a group, the following well-defined messages of terror:

Slaves Are Things, Animals[153]

- You are a slave for life; you have no chance for freedom, no protection and no recourse
- We own you; you are our property
- You are a thing to us, a chattel, the inferior equivalent of farm animals, cattle, horses, or swine, not human beings

151 *Dred Scott v. Sanford*, 60 U.S. 393 (1857).

152 See *"Chapter Six: The Duke of York's Creation on a Rampage—Slavery Was a National Institution: North and South."*

153 See *"Chapter Five: The Duke's Slave Trading Legacy—Africans in Transition: From People to Things."*

Slaves Society's Power

- We can treat you as we wish in our sole discretion
- Especially in agricultural settings, we can and will force you to labor from the break of day well into the night, without rest and on only one very quickly-consumed meal during the day, whipping you if you slow down, stretch your back, attempt to catch your breath, or attempt to tend to your children
- If you resist, we can and will punish you using inhuman methods, including killing you painfully, without consequences to us
- We can inflict pain upon you, even without cause, simply to demonstrate our absolute control over you or for our own amusement, without consequences to us
- If you resist our punishment, we can whip you mercilessly, even if it kills you, without fear of legal consequences
- We can, in our sole discretion, damage your internal organs with whips, rods, and paddles; mutilate you as punishment or for identification in case you run away; and brand you
- You will not be permitted to be insolent to any white people
- We require you to have written "passes" in order to leave your masters' premises; any white person can challenge you to demand to see your pass, and further, can inflict brutal punishment on you if you do not have one and can kill you if you resist
- We can, in our sole discretion, compel you to wear heavy iron collars, chains, weights, and head cages, with or without gags to prevent you from eating if you escape
- We can collect you forcibly into chained gangs (known as "coffles") of hundreds of slaves to march long distances

SLOW FIRE

"Tom, a slave convicted of murdering Adrian Beekman and Henry Brasier, was sentenced to be 'burned with a slow fire that he may continue in torment for eight or ten hours.'"

E. McManus, Black Bondage in the North at 129-30 (Syracuse Univ. Press 1973). Footnotes omitted.

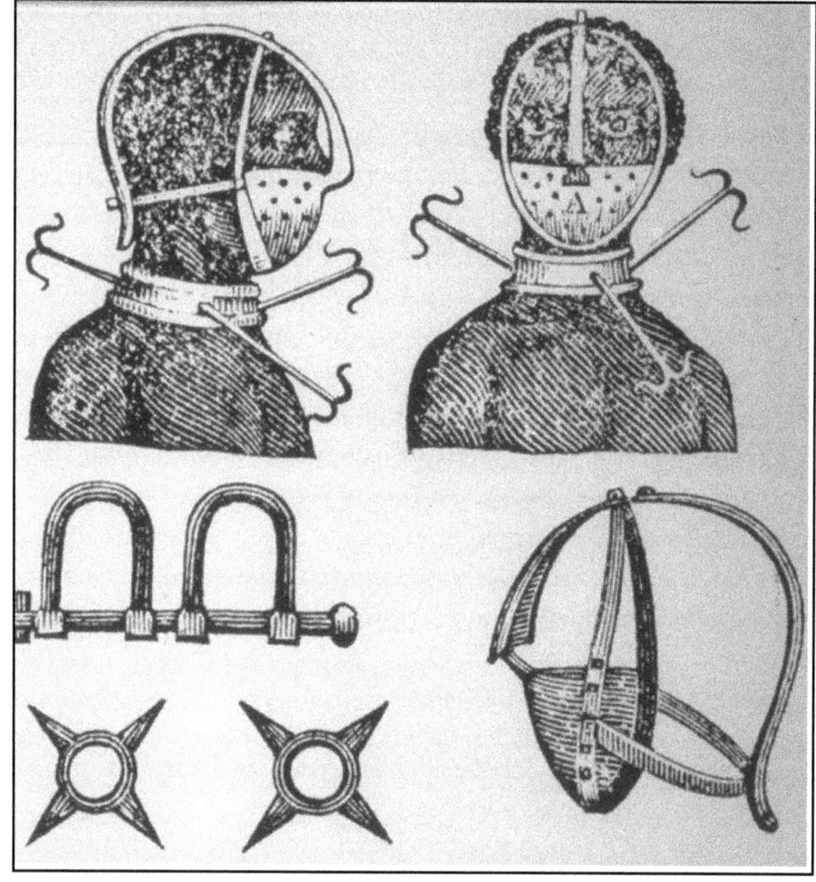

"Iron Mask, Neck Collar, Leg Shackles, and Spurs, 18th cent.," *Slavery Images: A Visual Record of the African Slave Trade and Slave Life in the Early African Diaspora,* accessed November 15, 2020, *http://slaveryimages.org/s/slaveryimages/item/1298*

THE BRUTAL WHIPPING OF MATT.

"Whipping a Slave, Virginia, 19th cent.," *Slavery Images: A Visual Record of the African Slave Trade and Slave Life in the Early African Diaspora,* accessed November 15, 2020, *http://slaveryimages.org/s/slaveryimages/item/1237*

"Paddling a Slave, U.S. South, 1845," *Slavery Images: A Visual Record of the African Slave Trade and Slave Life in the Early African Diaspora,* accessed November 15, 2020, *http://slaveryimages.org/s/slaveryimages/item/1255*

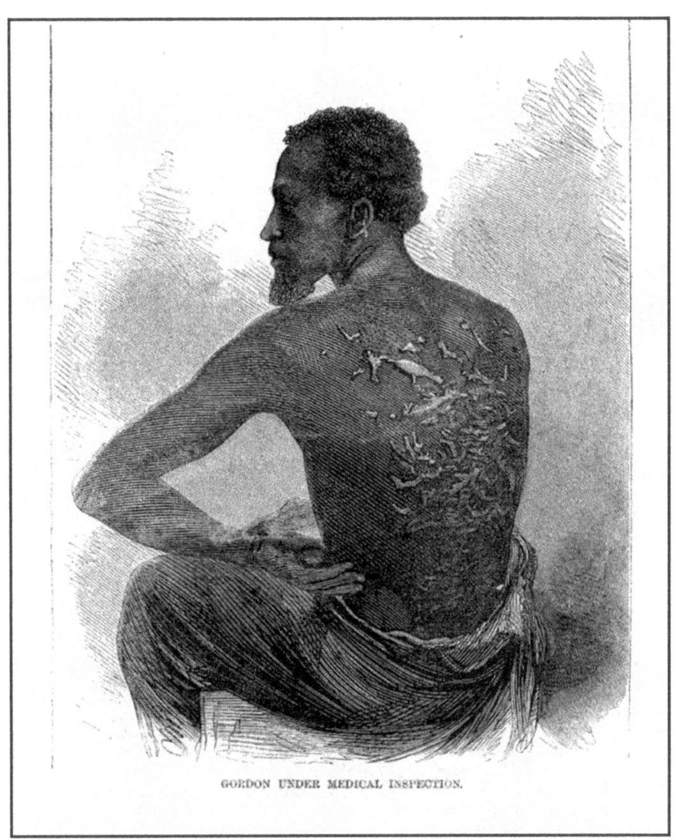

GORDON UNDER MEDICAL INSPECTION.

"Gordon Under Medical Inspection," *Slavery Images: A Visual Record of the African Slave Trade and Slave Life in the Early African Diaspora,* accessed November 15, 2020, *http://slaveryimages.org/s/slaveryimages/item/1236*

Denial of Common Comforts and Conveniences of Life

- We will deny you education about even basic reading and writing
- We are not obligated to provide you, and at our option based solely upon our economic considerations and sense of humanity, we can deny you, adequate food, clothing, and housing
- We can, in our sole discretion, deny you food and starve you
- We can, in our sole discretion, deny you decent clothing, regardless of the weather or season
- We can compel you to live in housing conditions suitable only for farm animals, and sometimes worse
- We can restrict your ability to gather with your friends for relaxation, celebration, religious services, funerals, or instruction of any kind
- If you are sick or aged, we can neglect your medical care in our discretion, based solely upon our own economic considerations
- We can, at our option, conduct medical experiments upon you with or without your consent

> **GIBBETING**
>
> "Gibbeting was the practice of locking criminals in human-shaped cages and hanging them up for display in public areas as a warning to others. The gibbet itself refers the wooden structure from which the cage was hung. In most cases, criminals were executed prior to being gibbeted. However, criminals were occasionally gibbeted alive and left to die of exposure and starvation."
>
> "A Look Back at the Disturbing Practice of Gibbeting" at *allthatsinteresting.com/gibbet*, accessed Oct. 27, 2020

Sexual Dominance

- You must submit to our sexual advances for our own pleasure, without consequences to us
- We will own your children as slaves for life—even if they also are our own children
- If you are a female, we can require you to have babies that we can sell to slave traders

> **"HAPPY," "CHEERFUL" SLAVES**
>
> **Virginia Seventh Grade Textbook:**
>
> "Life among the Negroes of Virginia in slavery times was generally happy. The Negroes went about in a cheerful manner making a living themselves and for those for whom they worked. They were not so unhappy as some Northerners thought they were."
>
> Dean, "'Who Controls the Past Controls the Future:" The
>
> Virginia History Textbook Controversy at 332 (Virginia Magazine of History and Biography, vol 17, no. 4, 2009)

Family Prevention and Destruction

- You will not be permitted to have a marriage license or family relationships recognized by law
- You will not be permitted to marry in a church
- We can separate you, in our sole discretion, from your informal spouses whom you love dearly and can take your children, even tiny babies, away from you

Denial of Legal Rights

- You will not be able to enter into contracts
- You will not be able to own property

- You will not be permitted to conduct business transactions unless we choose to permit it
- You will not be able to earn income unless we choose to permit it
- You will not be able to bring legal actions in court
- You will not be able to testify in court against white people
- You cannot provide testimony or other evidence in court, or to legislative bodies, regarding the treatment you or other slaves receive, even if it involves torture or murder

No Freedom

- You will not have a right to purchase your freedom
- Pursuant to a Supreme Court ruling, you are not, and cannot be, an American citizen with access to federal courts for protection; even if you are ever "freed," you will not be a citizen

Infliction of Terror

- If you attempt to run away, as an example to terrorize other slaves, we can kill you if you resist capture, and at least will inflict unbelievable pain on you that you will experience literally for weeks, and even months, afterward and the scars of which you will bear for life
- If we imagine that you have committed, or intend to commit, crimes of violence, we can lynch you without trial
- If you attempt, or if we imagine that you plan, rebellion, as an example to terrorize other slaves, we can, and often will, kill you, using the most agonizing methods we can devise, in the presence of hundreds, even thousands, of people who will not do anything about it, except to hear your screams and to watch you die prolonged and excruciating deaths

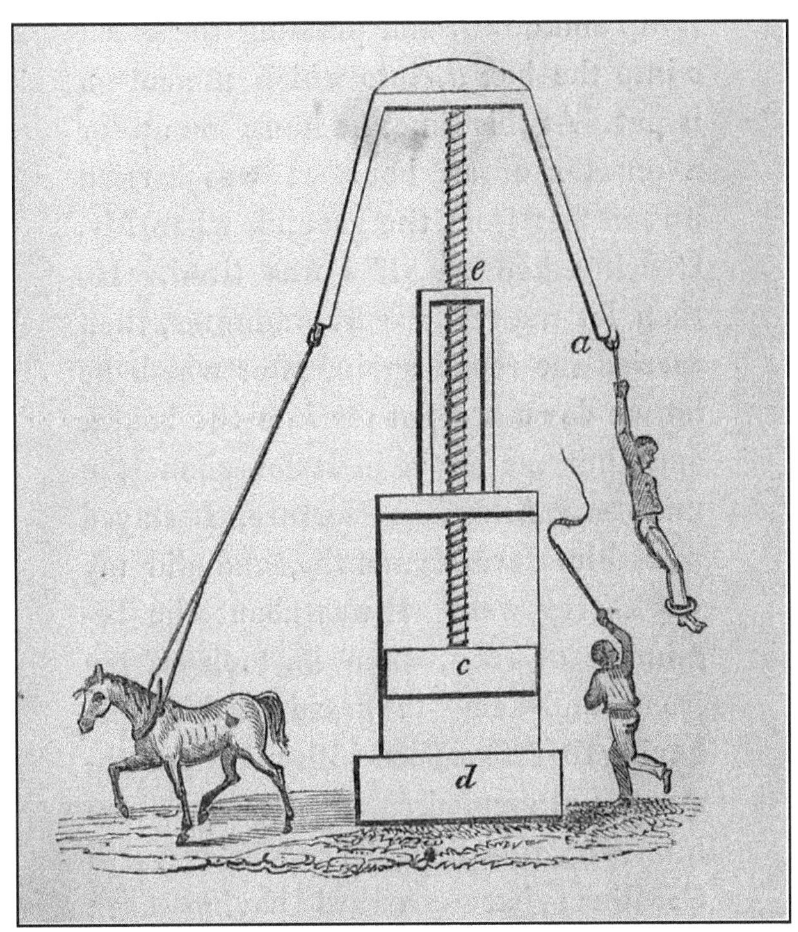

"Cotton Machine Used for Punishing Runaways, South Carolina, 1830s", *Slavery Images: A Visual Record of the African Slave Trade and Slave Life in the Early African Diaspora,* accessed November 15, 2020, *http://slaveryimages.org/s/slaveryimages/item/1206*

Governmental Protection for Slavery

- The federal, state, and local governments will enforce our property rights in you, even in states that prohibit slavery within their own borders

- Should you escape, officials and citizens in all states are prohibited from helping you, and are obligated to assist in your capture and to return you to slavery; judges are paid to do so
- The government will not protect you—in fact, the government is against you and will protect our property rights in you and our right to treat you as we wish
- The Declaration of Independence and its lofty ideals will not protect you
- The Constitution will not protect you, and in fact, it protects the slave society

Instruments of Terror

The instruments of terror applied against you, as examples intended and designed to terrorize other slaves and their children, include the following, among others:

- Guns for hunting you, if you run away, or for overpowering you if you are rebellious
- Whips made of hard, dried cowhide strips with knots deliberately fashioned to cut and tear your flesh as we administer literally hundreds of lashes to your naked, bleeding back while your bound arms are raised above your head and tied to a post or tree
- Vicious bloodhounds specially trained to hunt, attack, and wound you deeply
- Heavy paddles with holes drilled to increase your pain
- Stocks, to which your ears may be nailed, and in which we may hold you in immovable positions for many hours and even days
- Blocks covered with spikes and sharp pegs upon which you must stand for hours or days
- Gallows for hanging you publicly (and of course, trees for lynching you publicly or privately)
- Stakes for burning you alive publicly—at times over slow fires intended to impose the most lengthy and brutal pain and suffering imaginable
- Gibbets in which you can be starved to death while on public exhibit
- Wheels for breaking your bones and bodies until you die
- Spears for impaling you

MENDACIOUS NEGROES

"One of the consequences of the want of liberty in the slave is his disqualification to be a witness in cases affecting the rights of freemen. …

"In the United States the rule is enforced, without exception, in all cases where the evidence is offered for or against free white persons. In most of the States this exclusion is by express statutes. In others, by custom and the decision of the Courts. In all the slaveholding States, and in Ohio, Indiana, Illinois, and Iowa, by express statute, the rule has been extended to include free persons of color, or emancipated slaves.

"That this universal exclusion of a negro from testifying may, in many supposable cases, operate harshly and to the defeat of justice, especially in reference to the cruel treatment of slaves, is an undeniable fact; and yet it is equally true, that the indiscriminate admission and giving credit to negro testimony would not only, in many cases, defeat justice, but would be productive of innumerable evils in the relation of master and slave. …

"That the negro, as a general rule, is mendacious, is a fact too well established to require the production of proof, either from history, travels, or craniology."

T. Cobb, An inquiry into the law of Negro slavery in the United States of America, Vol I, at 226, 230, 232-33 (T. & J. W. Johnson & Co., 1858), available from the Library of Congress at *www.hathitrust.org/digital_library*

"Hanging a Slave, South Carolina, 1850s", *Slavery Images: A Visual Record of the African Slave Trade and Slave Life in the Early African Diaspora,* accessed November 15, 2020, *http://slaveryimages.org/s/slaveryimages/item/1231*

Ultimate Terror Message

To magnify the message of terror, we can, and at times will, place on spikes, along public roads, the heads of slaves executed for rebellion, with the intention that the heads be seen by other slaves, and by slave children, to bring home *as powerfully as possible* to those helpless human beings, the following messages:

You must obey us in all matters—
regardless of what we demand of you

You must submit completely to us

This is the best life you ever will have

You have no hope

CHAPTER THREE: THE DUKE OF YORK PROMOTES SLAVERY

NEW YORK HONORS THE DUKE

When England seized New Netherland in 1664, King Charles II renamed both the province and its capital New York in honor of the new proprietor, his younger brother James Stuart, Duke of York and heir apparent to the crown.

Thomas Archdeacon[154]

§ § §

Much changed when New Amsterdam became a British colony in 1664, including the name of the colony. *New York is named after the Duke of York*, the brother of the King, who was the head of the Royal African Company responsible for British involvement in the trans-Atlantic slave trade.

Dr. Alan Singer[155]

§ § §

The Duke of York is the Father of America's Slave Society.[156]

The Dutch had controlled New Amsterdam as the key city in New Netherland.

Once the English gained sway, the names of New Amsterdam and New Netherland were changed to "New York" in the Duke's honor.

Not only were the Duke's actions inconsistent with the standards of his own time, but the Duke's personal actions were contemptable by today's standards—he was a slave trader as the head of the Royal African Company who brought more than 100,000 Africans to the New World. Not only that, the Duke branded many, if not all, of his slaves with his initials.

Yet, America chooses to honor this rogue. It is abundantly clear that New York City and State are named in honor of the Duke of York (as opposed to the current Duke of York). To be specific, New York is not named after the City of York, England.[157]

The following are multiple resources for you to think about, since it is a crucial consideration in recognizing how America chooses to "honor" the Duke.

---

154 T. Archdeacon, NEW YORK CITY, 1664-1710: CONQUEST AND CHANGE at 32 (Cornell Univ. Press, 1976) ("Archdeacon").

155 "New York History Blog, Historical Views and News from The Empire State—Reckoning with Our Legacy of Slavery" (Oct. 21, 2019), Comment by Alan J. Singer, at *www.newyorkalmanack.com/2019/10/reckoning-with-our-legacy-of-slavery/*, accessed Sept. 22, 2010. Emphasis added.

156 See *"Chapter One: Meet America's Slave Society—Why the Duke of York Is the Father of America's Slave Society."*

157 In contrast, see "City of York—The First Capital of the United States" at *www.yorkcity.org/about/history/*, accessed Sept. 22, 2020,which refers to the City of York, Pennsylvania, as follows: "The City of York, Pennsylvania—named for York, England …"

For example, in **THE SLAVE TRADE—THE STORY OF THE ATLANTIC SLAVE TRADE: 1440-1870,** Hugh Thomas refers to:[158]

> the role of James, Duke of York (*after whom New York is, so inappropriately, named*), as president of the Royal African Company …"

In her book, **IN THE SHADOW OF SLAVERY—AFRICAN-AMERICANS IN NEW YORK CITY, 1626-1863**, Dr. Leslie Harris states:[159]

> [I]n 1664, the British took over the colony of New Netherland, resolving the century-long struggle between the Dutch and British over ownership of the territory. The British government *awarded the colony to the Duke of York, who renamed both New Netherland and New Amsterdam New York.*

An online article titled "Colony of New York—A Brief History" states:[160]

> New York, originally called New Netherlands, was so n*amed in honor of the Duke of York and Albany,* England, to whom the territory was granted on its conquest from its first settlers, the Dutch.

Yet again, StateSymbolsUSA.org states:[161]

> *New York was named after the English Duke of York and Albany* (and the brother of England's King Charles II) in 1664 when the region called New Amsterdam was taken from the Dutch. The state was a colony of Great Britain until it became independent on July 4, 1776.

Likewise, netstate.com states that New York State is named "to honor" the Duke:[162]

> THE STATE NAME: *New York was named by the British to honor the Duke of York and Albany*, the brother of England's King Charles II, when New Amsterdam was taken from the Dutch in 1664, New York became the name of the state and the city.

Thomas Archdeacon states that when the Duke conquered New Amsterdam, and the province was renamed in his honor, "The king then promised his brother James jurisdiction over the territory 'from the west side of the Connecticut River to the East Side of De La Ware Bay.'"[163] This was renewed after the English regained control following a brief period of Dutch had hegemony.[164] He continues: "In contrast with the Dutch West India Company, which had used slavery to implement colonial policy, James Stuart and the Royal African Company used New York to foster slavery. By the end of the seventeenth century, trading in human lives had

---

158 Thomas, at 13. Emphasis added.

159 Harris, at 26. Emphasis added.

160 "Colony of New York: A Brief History" at *www.celebrateboston.com/history/new-york.htm*, accessed Sept. 23, 2020. Emphasis added.
See also "William Penn and James, Duke of York" at *pennsylvaniahistory.wordpress.com/2012/08//11/William-penn-and-james-duke-of-york*, accessed Sept. 28, 2020.

161 New York State Name Origin" at *statesymbolsusa.org/symbol-official-item/new-york/state-name-origin-state-quarter/origin-new-york*, accessed Sept. 22, 2020. Emphasis added.

162 "The State of New York" at *www.netstate.com/states/intro/ny_intro.htm*, accessed Sept. 22, 2020. Emphasis added.

163 Archdeacon, at 37.

164 Archdeacon, at 100.

become a staple of the province's economy."[165] Indeed, "Blacks composed as much as 20 percent of New York's population in 1703."[166]

In summary, New York City, the County of New York, and New York State are named "in honor" of an international criminal and terrorist.

Incidentally, the Duke's full title was the Duke of York and Albany. The City of Albany—the capitol of New York State—also is named "in honor" of the Duke ("Albany was named after the Duke of York's Scottish title, 'Duke of Albany' in 1664 when the English took control of the area").[167]

---

165 Archdeacon, at 43.

166 Archdeacon, at 46.

167 "Amazing Albany Facts" at *www.albany.org/media/amazing-facts/*, accessed Sept. 22, 2020.

DUKE OF YORK AS KEY GOVERNMENTAL SLAVE TRADER: ROYAL AFRICAN COMPANY

"We hereby for us, our heirs and successors grant unto the same Royal African Company of England … that it shall and may be lawful to … set to sea such as many ships, pinnaces and barks as shall be thought fitting … for the buying, selling, bartering and exchanging of, for or with any gold, silver, Negroes, Slaves, goods, wares and manufactures …

"Witness the King at Westminster the seven and twentieth day of September [1672)

"BY THE KING"

Charter of the Royal African Company[168]

§ § §

"In order to counter Dutch control over the supply of African slaves to the English colonies, the government of King Charles II participated in forming a slavetrading company in 1663 called the Royal Adventurers, which traded in Africa. This company was financed by some of the leading aristocrats at Court, including the Duke of Buckingham and the Duke of Albermarle. *The King's brother, the Duke of York, was also elected president of the company.* In this way, *the monarch and government of England formally engaged in the development of the transatlantic slave trade,* since, though the company also traded in ivory and gold, *slaves were its single most lucrative commodity.* …

"[The Royal African Company, after reorganization,] *soon became the largest single company involved in the slave trade,* having a remit to supply the English colonies with slaves at [a] competitive unit price… .

"The 30 years following the establishment of the Royal African Company saw *a substantial upsurge in the size of the transatlantic trade. …"*

Dr. Hilary Beckles[169]

Pursuant to a charter from King Charles II, the Royal African Company actively traded slaves with the colonies. The monopoly lasted until after the end of the Duke's reign as King James II in 1688.[170]

During the period beginning in the 1660s, slavery became much more widespread throughout the American colonies.

As described by proslavery advocate, Thomas R.R. Cobb, the Royal African Company was highly active in the slave trade:[171]

---

168 H. Thomas, THE SLAVE TRADE—THE STORY OF THE ATLANTIC SLAVE TRADE: 1440-1870 at 196 (Simon & Schuster, 1997) ("Thomas").

169 Beckles, at 52. Emphasis added.

170 See "*Appendix II: King Charles II's 1664 Charter Granting to the Duke of York Authority Over New York.*"

171 Cobb, Vol I, at cxliii-cxliv.

During the reign of Charles II (1662), a third company with exclusive privileges was chartered. The Duke of York, the King's brother, was at the head of this company. …

In 1672, the fourth and last exclusive company was chartered, under the name of the Royal African Company, including among its stockholders, the King, his brother, the Duke of York, and others of distinguished rank. This Company continued its existence until the Revolution in 1688, when Parliament abolished all exclusive charters. They continued their operations, however, seizing the ships of private traders. …

BRITISH ORGANIZED THE SLAVE TRADE

"The British entry into the slave trade made it an established business and gave it organization. They established spheres of influence that controlled where different nations could trade."

J. Clarke, "African Resistance and Colonial Domination: The Africans in America" in Y. Ben-Jochannan and J. Clarke, New Dimensions in African History at 31 (Brawtley Press, 1991)

K.G. Davies confirms that that "the new company was to deal chiefly in negroes."[172]

Mr. Cobb continues by describing the Duke's strong influence evidenced in New York, where "[t]he slave code differed but little from that of Virginia," after the Duke defeated the Dutch in New Amsterdam. In New Jersey, which was created from the New Netherland/New York Colony, colonists sought to gain the Duke's favor by encouraging slavery through the English government's land-for-slaves policy (60 to 75 acres per slave).[173]

John Codman Hurd confirms the strong early power and influence of the Duke over the English government's activities:[174]

The Duke of York's patent or charter of the provinces acquired from Holland, empowered him and his assigns to govern the inhabitants by such ordinances as he and his assigns should establish … .

Mr. Hurd states further that the Duke had "full and absolute power and authority:"[175]

The patent to the Duke, dated March 16, 1664, for the lands lying between the Connecticut and Delaware rivers, granted to him, "his heirs, deputies, agents, commissioners, and assigns," *"full and absolute power and authority,* &c." …

History.com states that "According to the Navigation Act of 1660, only English-owned ships could enter colonial ports."[176] Another website at Pennsylvaniahistory.wordpress.com agrees, citing Dr. Alan Singer: "When the Duke took over New York one of the first actions of the new authority was to grant the colony port privileges and the right to use warehouses to ships engaged in the slave trade."[177]

172 K. Davies, THE ROYAL AFRICAN COMPANY at 60 (Atheneum, 1970) ("Davies").

173 Cobb, Vol I, at cxlix; Harper, *"Slavery in the North" at slavenorth.com/newjersey.htm*, accessed Sept. 22, 2020.

174 Hurd, Vol. I, at 124.

175 Hurd, Vol. I, at 278 footnote. Emphasis added.

176 What was the Royal African Company?" at *www.history.com/news/what-was-the-royal-african-company,* accessed Sept. 28, 2020.

177 "William Penn and James, Duke of York" at *pennsylvaniahistory.wordpress.com/2012/08//11/William-penn-and-james-duke-of-york,* accessed Sept. 28, 2020.

Thomas Archdeacon states that the Duke of York "dispatched Edmund Andros to be governor-general of his province," adding that the Andros government "took action to reduce Dutch influence and to bring the province fully into England's economic orbit by forbidding vessels from the Netherlands to bring goods to New York." In addition, "Governor Andros put into effect in the province the Duke's laws … ."[178]

Mr. Hurd adds that, even when colonies resisted further slave importation, the English Government overrode the colonists' wishes:

> To this power may be referred the frequent rejection of colonial laws restricting the introduction of African slaves.

Mr. Hurd explains the English government's enthusiasm for slavery by citing an English statute in 1697 referring to the profitability of the slave trade for the English government by stating:[179]

> the trade to Africa is highly beneficial and advantageous to this kingdom, and to the plantations and colonies thereunto belonging … .

History.com states that "By the end of the 17th century, England led the world in slave trading, and would continue to do so throughout the 18th century."[180]

This English government policy was continued for many decades. Mr. Hurd cites an English statute 50 years later titled "An Act for extending and improving the trade to Africa" reiterating the benefit to the government.[181]

The Duke of York actively promoted slavery in part through his "full and absolute power and authority" over the enactment of laws known as "the Duke's Laws." Mr. Hurd describes this, as follows:[182]

> The first local legislation under the English government was that published under the authority of the Duke of York, as proprietor, and known in the history of the colony as "the Duke's Laws."

EARLY BRITISH SLAVE TRADING

"The exact proportions of the slave trade can be estimated only approximately. From 1680 to 1688 we know that the English African Company alone sent 249 ships to Africa, shipped there 60,783 Negro slaves, and after losing 14,387 on the middle passage, delivered 46,396 in America."

W.E.B. Du Bois, The Negro at 155 (Henry Holt & Co., Thornton Butterworth Ltd., 1915), available from the Library of Congress at *www.hathitrust.org/digital_library*

The early writings of Messrs. Cobb and Hurd find significant support in publications by modern historians in addition to Dr. Beckles, quoted at the beginning of this section.

178 Archdeacon, at 100-01.

179 Hurd, Vol. I, at 174.
See also "*— Why Charles II and the Duke of York Promoted Slavery: Follow the Money*" below.

180 "What was the Royal African Company?" at *www.history.com/news/what-was-the-royal-african-company*, accessed Sept. 28, 2020.

181 Hurd, Vol. I, at 175.

182 Hurd, Vol. I, at 278. Footnote omitted.

The impact of the Royal African Company had reached far South of New York and New Jersey into the Carolina Colony. The website, History of American Women, states that:[183]

> Slavery was encouraged from the outset of the Carolina Colony. The four proprietors of the colony were members of the Royal African Company, a slave trading company. In 1663, the proprietors encouraged settlers to acquire slaves with the promise that they would be given 20 acres of land for every black male slave and 10 acres for every black female slave brought to the colony within the first year. This encouragement worked; by 1683, the black population was equal to the white population.

Dr. Holly Brewer describes the immense magnitude of the Royal African Company's slave trading ("more than 100,000 souls from Africa to the New World").[184]

The precise date on which the Company's slave-trading ended is not entirely clear. Douglas Harper states[185] that "the Royal African Company's monopoly on African coastal slave trade was revoked by Parliament in 1696." The Royal African Company's tight hold on the slave trade before the Company's revocation following the end of King James II's reign is cited in **A GUIDE TO THE HISTORY OF SLAVERY IN MARYLAND,**[186] with a reference to "The end of the Royal African Company's slave trade monopoly in 1698 …."

Thus, the Duke of York, through his power over the enactment of slave laws in New York, through his official position as Admiral of the English Navy, and through his monopolistic Royal African Company, was a key player—indeed, *the* key player, with his Brother, King Charles—in the expansion of the harsh and inhumane English form of slavery in the American colonies and in the promotion of African slavery as a supply of labor without which the colonies would not thrive.

Reflecting the brutality of the slavery the Duke promoted, he was himself a particularly pitiless individual—he branded many, if not all, of the slaves the Royal African Company purchased in Africa, and shipped and sold in the New World with his initials, "DY."[187]

183 "Slavery in South Carolina" at *www.womenhistoryblog.com/2008/07/slavery-in-south-carolina.html,* accessed Sept. 22, 2020.

184 Brewer, at 1047.

185 Harper, "Slavery in the North," at slavenorth.com/profits.htm, accessed Sept. 22, 2020.

186 Slavery in Maryland, at 4.

187 Beckles, at 86.

DUKE OF YORK'S DISTINCTIVE ROLE IN PROMOTING AMERICAN SLAVERY

> "The Duke of York's patent or charter of the provinces acquired from Holland, empowered him and his assigns to govern the inhabitants by such ordinances as he and his assigns should establish . . . ."
>
> **John Codman Hurd**[188]

> "From the first, the British exhibited a deep commitment to African slavery. Like James II, Duke of York—the proprietor of New York—many of those who invested in the colony were also stockholders in the Royal African Company, which enjoyed the exclusive privilege of supplying slaves to Britain's New World colonies. Not surprisingly, the number of slaves grew steadily . . . ."
>
> **Dr. Ira Berlin and Dr. Leslie Harris**[189]

§ § §

Slavery in the American colonies was a product of a monarchy accustomed to peasantry in England and indentured servitude in the colonies. The absolutist Stuarts who ruled England after the Restoration ruled from the top down, and the Duke of York—James Stuart—applied that ideology unceasingly.[190] The Stuarts did this because it was good for their "business," which was collecting taxes for a dominant government and revenues for the government's slave trading company.

Accordingly, as Dr. David Eltis states:[191]

> At some point in the 1660s, ... the annual number of Africans arriving the in the English Americas began to exceed the number of Europeans, a pattern that quickly came to hold for the Americas as a whole until the slave trade was suppressed in the decades after 1807.

As Frederick Douglass stated in 1855, "England is often charged with having established slavery in the United States . . . .[192]

Virginia, which previously had practiced slavery resembling indentured servitude, did not legalize slavery through statutory enactment until 1662,[193] and Maryland, which also had relied heavily on slaves approximating indentured servants, enacted its slave laws beginning in 1664.[194]

THE GOVERNMENT "COMPELLED" SLAVERY

"Though the condition of slavery in the colonies may not have been created by the imperial legislature, yet it may be said with truth, that the colonies were compelled to receive African slaves by the home government."

J. Hurd, The Law of Freedom and Bondage in the United States, Vol. I at 208 n. 2 (Little, Brown & Co., 1862), available from the Library of Congress at *www.hathitrust.org/digital_library*

---

188 Hurd, Vol. I at 124.

189 I. Berlin and L. Harris, SLAVERY IN NEW YORK at 10 (The New Press, 2005) ("Berlin and Harris").

190 Brewer, at 1047.

191 D. Eltis, THE RISE OF AFRICAN SLAVERY IN THE AMERICAS at 195 (Cambridge Univ. Press, 2000) ("Eltis"). See "*—Why Charles II and the Duke of York Promoted Slavery: Follow the Money*" below.

192 Douglass, My Bondage and My Freedom at 376-77.

193 Brewer, at 1048.

194 Brewer, at 1048; Slavery in Maryland, at 3, 4.

While this was the "English form of slavery," it does not mean that similar laws were in effect in England.

Instead, as John Codman Hurd describes, in England "there was no principle on which a domiciled negro could be thus held in involuntary servitude."[195] He states further that "The weight of judicial decision had been that negroes were not chattels in England[.]"[196]

Before the English came to New York, the Dutch had created a class of African landowners, giving them land as a means of gaining their assistance in resisting Native Americans. The Dutch trusted the Africans to serve in militias. Although the Dutch regarded the Africans as inferior, and required them to pay an annual tribute and to perform occasional public service, the Africans "married in Dutch churches, sued in Dutch courts, celebrated Dutch festivals, and took Dutch names."[197]

"Broomstick Wedding, Virginia (?), 1840s", *Slavery Images: A Visual Record of the African Slave Trade and Slave Life in the Early African Diaspora,* accessed November 15, 2020, *http://slaveryimages.org/s/slaveryimages/item/637*

That changed quickly once the English took over New York. They began enacting laws legalizing slavery. Dr. Ira Berlin and Dr. Leslie Harris state that "From the first, the British exhibited a deep commitment to African slavery. ... Not surprisingly, the number of slaves grew steadily..."[198]

The English government moved deliberately step by step to effectuate its improvised form of slavery. To begin, after King Charles II and the Duke came to power, Dr. Edgar McManus states: "[T]he laws promulgated by the Duke of York ... recognized slavery as a legal institution."[199]

This was accomplished by limiting the looser forms of servitude applied by the Dutch to servitudes involving a contractual relationship—"those who willingly sell themselves into bondage."[200] Thus, under the English, a servant without a formal contract with a definable term of years was legally a slave for life. Dr. Leslie Harris

195 Hurd, at Vol. I, at 378

196 Hurd, at Vol. I, at 379.

197 Berlin and Harris, at 8.

198 Berlin and Harris, at 8.

199 McManus, Black Bondage in the North, at 60.

200 McManus, Black Bondage in the North, at 11-12. See also McManus, Slavery in New York, at 24.

states, however, that "just before" the English "took over the colony," the Dutch had freed unconditionally all of their "half-free" servants, "probably" including their children.[201]

Dr. Harris, Dr. Ira Berlin and Christopher Moore outline a variety of rights and privileges Dutch slaves had experienced, but that were denied by the English, such as marriage and family life, earning income, participation in religious services and baptism, serving in the militia, and access to the courts. The Dutch even granted some slaves and their wives freeholder status.[202]

Dr. McManus states further that, in New York, "Under the proprietary rule of the Duke of York," the English policy toward slavery became clear as soon as sovereignty passed from the Dutch, "enter[ing] an era of unprecedented expansion," with officials "instructed to promote the importation of slaves by every possible means:"[203]

> With the establishment of English control in 1664, slavery entered *an era of unprecedented expansion. Under the proprietary rule of the Duke of York* colonial policy was shaped to a large extent by the Royal African Company. ... *[T]he ... Royal African Company used the colony to implement slavery.* From the start of the English occupation the creation of *a commercially profitable slave system* became a joint project of both government and private interests. *The Duke's representatives in New York—governors, councilors, and customs officials—were instructed to promote the importation of slaves by every possible means.*

McManus adds that the English used New York's port facilities "to promote the use of slave labor:"[204]

> The Laws of 1665 recognized the existence of slavery as a legal institution. Port privileges and warehouse priorities were given to ships carrying African slaves, and *measures were adopted to promote the use of slave labor.*

Dr. Leslie Harris points to the British promotion of slavery seeking "to make the New York colony a major market for slaves:"[205]

> With British rule, slavery in New York gained a new stringency, and free blacks, too, were affected by the new rulers' desire to control slaves. British colonists' concern with regulating slavery resulted from Britain's increasing involvement in the African slave trade. *The Duke of York held a controlling interest in the Royal African Company, which sought to make the New York colony a major market for slaves.*

Dr. Jill Lepore describes the in specific terms:[206]

> It was cheaper for New York slave traders to import directly from Africa; buyers in New York paid customs duties of only forty shillings "For every Negro and other Slave, of 4 years old, and upwards, imported directly from *Africa,*" compared to four pounds (or eighty shillings) for those "From all other places."

---

201 Harris, at 26

202 Berlin and Harris, at 8-9; C. Moore *"Chapter 1, A World of Possibilities: Slavery and Freedom in Dutch New Amsterdam,"* in Berlin and Harris, at 38-39 *et seq* ("Moore").

203 McManus, Slavery in New York, at 23. Emphasis added. Footnotes omitted.

204 McManus, Slavery in New York, at 24. Emphasis added. Footnotes omitted.

205 Harris, at 26-27. Footnotes omitted. Emphasis added.

206 J. Lepore, "Chapter 2: The Tightening Vise: Slavery and Freedom in British New York" in I. Berlin and L. Harris, ed., SLAVERY IN NEW YORK at 61 (The New Press, 2005) ("Lepore").

Dr. Harris also notes special property tax incentives to settlers purchasing slaves imported directly from Africa.[207]

Dr. McManus points out that, since the English limited indentured servitude to those who entered into it willingly, the English laws brought about notable change, stating: "This ended the informal apprentice and indenture system of the Dutch whereby white servants could be bound for indefinite terms."[208]

Dr. Harris describes the spread of a "parallel" pattern of the innovative New York slave laws ("the colony's first laws regulating slavery") to "Virginia and other southern colonies, signifying the entrenchment of slavery throughout mainland North America."[209]

Dr. McManus continues that prohibition in 1679 of Native American slavery "completed the policy of restricting slavery to bondsmen of African origin," and "These measures greatly stimulated the importation of African slaves."[210]

Dr. Harris describes how the English focused their slave laws on Africans ("Negroes only shall be slaves"):[211]

> [I]n 1706, the British ... passed a law stating that *"Negroes only shall be slaves."* The 1706 law also formally discounted religion in determining enslavement. The provincial assembly's law stated that "baptism shall not alter the condition of servitude of the Negro slave." This legally sundered the already tenuous connection between Christianity and freedom for African slaves. And in the same law, the British insured the hereditary nature of slavery by having children inherit their mothers' condition of slavery or freedom.

The English also legislated the hereditary form of slavery—the status of the offspring of a slave and a free person was determined by the status of the mother. As stated by William Goodell, "Slaves being held as Property, like other domestic animals, their Offspring are held as Property, in perpetuity, in the same manner."[212] Thus, like all children of slave women, even the child of a white master and a slave woman was a slave to the father-master.

Negroes, "as a class," "were presumed to be slaves," and were required to carry the burden of proof that they were free, while white people had no such burden of proof.[213] Freedom was difficult to prove, however, since presumed slaves (and their potential African witnesses) could not testify in court against whites.[214] As stated by William Goodell, "Slavery is upheld by suppressing the testimony of its victims."[215]

W.E.B. Du Bois also recognizes the key role of the Duke's Royal African Company, and the changes wrought by the English slavery system, stating that, after its reorganization, "the 'Royal African Company' ... carried on

207 Harris, at 26-27. Footnotes omitted. Emphasis added.

208 McManus, Slavery in New York, at 24.

209 Harris, at 27.

210 McManus, Slavery in New York, at 24. Footnotes omitted.
See also McManus, Black Bondage in the North at 12.

211 Harris, at 28.

212 W. Goodell, THE AMERICAN SLAVE CODE IN THEORY AND PRACTICE at 248 (American and Foreign Anti-Slavery Society, 1853) ("Goodell").

213 McManus, Slavery in New York, at 61.

214 See, *e.g.*, McManus, Slavery in New York, at 80.

215 Goodell, Part II, Ch. III, at 300.

a growing [slave] trade for a quarter of a century," adding that the English became "the world's greatest slave-trader" pursuant to "the governor's instructions:"[216]

> The final terms of peace [between England and Netherlands] ... surrendered New Netherlands to England, and opened the way for England to become *henceforth the world's greatest slave-trader.* ... It was left to the English, with their strong policy in its favor, to develop this trade. ... *[T]he trade continued to be encouraged in the governor's instructions.*

Dr. Holly Brewer describes the legal enactments of the English ("pieces written, approved, and rationalized in hierarchical political contexts by Charles II and his brother James II") as key to the origination of slavery in the colonies, including not only New York, but also Virginia and elsewhere.[217]

Dr. Singer adds that "in 1665, a law recognized the status of slavery in the Colony," and cites "a series of measures" at the local level "formaliz[ing] the slave system," such as "recogniz[ing] the right of slaveholders to use physical violence, short of lethal force, to punish" slaves, "prohibit[ing] more than four Africans and Native Americans from meeting together and Africans and Native Americans from possessing guns," and imposing a curfew "on enslaved men and women over the age of fourteen."

As time passed, slave laws became increasingly oppressive. According to Dr. Singer, in 1702 "New York's first comprehensive slave code was adopted which equated slave status with being African." He describes the 1702 law as forbidding trade with slaves, reiterating the limits on assembly, and "confirm[ing] the right of 'any Master or Mistress of slaves to punish their slaves for their Crimes and offenses.'"[218] Dr. McManus opines that "[t]he system of course rested on naked force... ."[219]

GOVERNMENTAL TAX INCENTIVES

"Colonial officials encouraged the company's trade in New York by removing the property tax on slaves and imposing tariffs on imported slaves that favored African imports"

L. Harris, In the Shadow of Slavery—African-Americans in New York City, 1626-1863 at 26-27 (Univ. of Chicago Press 2003)

Dr. Harris describes how the restrictions on slaves, and even "free" African-Americans, increased following a slave revolt in New York in 1712. New York City enacted a prohibition on any slave over the age of 14 being on the "streets after sunset without a lantern by which he or she could be clearly seen." Punishment for a violation was 39 lashes. Moreover, due to white fears of even "free" African-Americans, "Slaves freed after 1712 could not own real estate. The laws penalized both free blacks and whites who entertained slaves or sold them alcohol, but fined blacks at twice the rate of whites." New York City became "an increasingly hostile place for free blacks."[220]

216 W.E.B. Du Bois, THE SUPPRESSION OF THE AFRICAN SLAVE TRADE TO THE UNITED STATES OF AMERICA 1638-1870 at 17-18 (Longmans, Green & Co., 1896), available from the Library of Congress at *www.hathitrust.org/digital_library.* Emphasis added.

217 Brewer, at Abstract. Emphasis added.

218 Singer, at 53-54.

219 McManus, Slavery in New York, at 80.

220 Harris, at 39.
See also Lepore, at 80-81.

It is noteworthy that Virginia's and Maryland's slavery laws, coinciding with enactments in New York, also paralleled those of New York in content.[221] This should not be a surprise, since Virginia and Maryland authorities, like the Duke in New York, also answered ultimately to King Charles II.

221 See "Virtual Jamestown: Laws on Slavery" at *www.virtualjamestown.org/laws1.html,* accessed Nov. 10, 2020; Slavery in Maryland, at 27-31.

WHY CHARLES II AND THE DUKE OF YORK PROMOTED SLAVERY: FOLLOW THE MONEY

King Charles II and his younger brother, the Duke of York, had significant governmental economic incentives—tax receipts and slave-trading revenues—for encouraging, indeed actively promoting and even incentivizing, the cruel English slavery.

As noted in the preceding section, the Duke and his colleagues used tax incentives—lower property taxes and reduced import tariffs on slaves they brought directly from Africa[222] —to promote the sale of slaves imported via the Royal African Company.[223] As a highly-significant additional incentive, they dangled the attractive land offer to settlers.

Confirming Dr. Brewer's analysis of the Crown's practices to reward coerced labor, Dr. Peter Kolchin cites a Virginia plantation owner, John Carter, who received 4,000 acres of land as a headright for importing 80 indentured servants in 1665 to work for him.[224]

Dr. Brewer explains the government's motives behind the land grant policy, observing that "[t]obacco customs paid the national debt and paid for James II's custom collectors, navy, and standing army:"[225]

By encouraging mass production of staple crops that were heavily taxed, *royal headright policy dramatically increased crown revenue.* Even in 1636, Virginia tobacco generated £42,000 in net crown revenue for Charles I. After 1660, Parliament granted Charles II higher taxes on tobacco and sugar imported into England, and rates increased again in 1685 at James II's request. By 1687, gross crown receipts from tobacco taxes were £725,648 out of net crown income of just over £2,000,000. Tobacco customs paid the national debt and paid for James II's custom collectors, navy, and standing army of 40,000 men.

Dr. Brewer observes that as of approximately 1687, "Tobacco and sugar taxes together made up at most a third of total crown revenue."[226]

She identifies the Duke of York's Royal African Company as a central player in the execution of the government's policy:[227]

> After the Restoration, principles of hereditary status, especially hereditary servitude, complemented crown revenue. Hereditary servitude thus became an organizing principle behind the king's empire. *Charles II's first step was to establish the Company of Royal Adventurers Trading into Africa, later the Royal African Company (RAC), under the leadership of his brother James, Duke of York,* and with most of the royal family as members. Promising his governors to supply the colonies with "conditional [English] servants and blacks," *Charles II coordinated colonial policy with the African trade by promoting RAC factors, or salesmen, to powerful colonial posts,* such as Thomas Modyford to the governorship of Jamaica in 1664.

222 Harris, at 26-27, 28. Footnotes omitted. Emphasis added.

223 Harris, at 26-27. Footnotes omitted. Emphasis added.

224 Kolchin, at 9.

225 Brewer, at 1046-47. Emphasis added.

226 Brewer, at 1047 n. 20.

227 Brewer, at 1047. Emphasis added.

K.G. Davies states that James made a handsome profit from his investment in the Company:[228]

> James II … held fully paid-up stock of £3,000; he received in dividends £3,480 and sold for about £5,730. Thus his total profit was £6,210 spread over seventeen years, the equivalent of an annual return of twelve percent.

Having devised a plan for the demand side of the slave-trade, English acquisition of former Dutch forts on the African Coast—through the Duke of York's military leadership as Admiral—was another key by providing for the supply side of the slave trade in Africa. According to Dr. Brewer, that " provided a base of operations for the RAC trade in Africans." It also led to the "creat[ion] of alliances with African princes, who sold their enemies to the English," denied landing rights to European slave-trading competitors, and furnished facilities, such as prisons to hold slaves pending shipment to the New World:[229]

> One motive for Charles II's marriage in 1662 to Catherine de Braganza, princess of Portugal, was her dowry, which included the legal right to Portugal's castles on the African coast that the Dutch "illegally" occupied, according to a secret part of Charles II's marriage treaty. Between 1661 and 1675, *Charles and James allied with the Portuguese to fight Dutch control of over a dozen castles off the African coast. Once conquered, such castles provided a base of operations for the RAC trade in Africans. As admiral of the fleet as well as director of the Royal African Company, James, Duke of York—with an open license from his brother to attack where he wished—directed the war toward Africa.* The new castles *created alliances with African princes, who sold their enemies to the English as servants*, prevented other European ships from landing, provided prisons for human cargo, and served as sites of exchange.

Dr. Brewer adds that "with the restoration of hereditary monarchy in 1660 … colonies pass[ed] laws enshrining hereditary slavery." The English government strongly reinforced the land-for-slaves policy through enactment of slave laws in "response to Charles II's explicit requests to his governors" following the 1660 restoration of the monarchy:[230]

> Likewise, only with the restoration of hereditary monarchy in 1660 did colonies pass laws enshrining hereditary slavery: Barbados in 1661, Virginia in 1662, Jamaica and Maryland in 1664. *These laws were a response to Charles II's explicit requests to his governors in 1661 to support the RAC and to codify their laws.* William Berkeley of Virginia, like other governors, *had to obtain the approval of Charles II and his Council of Foreign Plantations for all laws.*

ENGLISH GOVERNMENT INCENTIVES TO SETTLERS TO ACQUIRE SLAVES

Incentives:
- Reduced property taxes
- Reduced customs duties for slaves imported directly from Africa
- Landgrants—the more slaves owned, the more land granted

Goals:
- Tax receipts on increased commodity production by slaves
- Slave-trading revenues for monopolistic Royal African Company

Brewer describes how the new post-1660 laws were harsher than the prior laws and practices. Before 1660, African servants had important rights and privileges, although the legal environment was in flux with "a gradual process of policymaking:"[231]

228 Davies, at 74.

229 Brewer, at 1047. Emphasis added.

230 Brewer, at 1048. Emphasis added.

231 Brewer, at 1048-49. Emphasis added.

> *Before 1660, colonial laws treated "servants"—as both whites and blacks were usually called—similarly, if badly.* English subjects became servants when they "indented" themselves to a ship captain to pay the costs of passage. Their indentures, or contracts, allowed them to be bought and sold. Others were kidnapped and sold without contracts, as were most Africans sold to English colonists by privateers who raided Portuguese and Spanish settlements. *African servants, like English, had jury trials, could witness (if they could swear an oath), could be manumitted, and could own land and servants themselves when freed.* But in some colonies, courts began to treat Africans as more permanent, and even hereditary, servants, with arguments that those who were not Christian and not subjects had fewer rights, with little legal certainty. Slavery was not an abstraction, but a *gradual process of policymaking* that stripped particular people of the rights of subjects and fostered a hierarchical social order.

The 1660 rise of the English monarchy is critical, however, to identifying the beginning of American slavery:[232]

> *Only after the 1660s did elements of slavery emerge,* and only after 1705 did full slavery emerge in Virginia, if one measures slavery by the legal structure that made it both a powerful and a viable institution.

A cornerstone of the new legal regime was the creation of hereditary slavery—children born to slave mothers were automatically slaves for life, and were owned by the mothers' owners:[233]

> *Virginia's post-1660 laws about bond slavery followed royal ideals that emphasized heredity.* The 1662 law creating a holiday celebrating Charles II's restoration "to the throne of his royall ancestors" was followed by the law making bond slavery hereditary: *"All children borne in this country shall be held bond or free only according to the condition of the mother."*

In summary, King Charles II, the Duke of York and their colleagues and successors promoted a vast change in laws and practices governing slavery in the American colonies beginning with the restoration of the English monarchy in 1660.

The motives supporting the English government's proslavery policies were based on profit—increased tax revenues on slave-produced commodities and slave-trading revenues for the government's Royal African Company.

232 Brewer at 1049.

233 Brewer, at 1049. Emphasis added.

THE "DUKE'S LAWS" AND HIS OPPOSITION TO REPRESENTATIVE GOVERNMENT

The Duke of York was able to promote brutal slave laws because he dominated the legislative process in New York. How he used his power against all of the people of New York demonstrates that power.

The rigid control that the Duke of York maintained on the legislative process demonstrates starkly his ability to create in New York the English form of slavery based on the over-whelming dominance of the masters and complete submission of the slaves. He did this contemporaneously with English government colleagues who engaged in similar practices in New Jersey to please him, and with his colleagues in Virginia, Maryland, and Carolina who enacted parallel laws.

There is a significant distinction between the actions of the Duke of York and America's Founding Fathers who created the Declaration of Independence. As English royalty and a Stuart, the Duke adamantly refused to accept representative government and a "Charter of Liberties" approved by an "assembly," which the Duke rejected.

America's Founding Fathers provided at least for whites—although not for slaves or "free" African-Americans (who generally could not vote and ultimately were not considered to be citizens)—a representative government, with checks and balances, and a Bill of Rights applicable to the federal government setting forth important foundations for liberty.

In contrast, Dr. Holly Brewer states that the Stuarts—King Charles II and the Duke of York—"suppress[ed] representative government," with the Duke preventing a legislature:[234]

> The Stuarts [including the Duke] not only legitimated the formal enslavement of Africans, they ... *suppress[ed] representative government* and appoint[ed] local oligarchs to rule. In 1674, when James became governor of New York, he *allowed no legislature.*

She adds that "James II [the Duke] ... advocated ... absolute obedience for everyone:"[235]

> *James II had advocated principles that enshrined hereditary hierarchy and absolute obedience for everyone.* James II's efforts to strip his subjects of rights grew from his absolutism, which made all subjects into slaves; such slavery was part of a continuum that ended in slavery in the Americas.

JAMES STUART AS ABSOLUTIST

"Life was a matter of simple polar opposites: good and bad, right and wrong, obedience and disobedience. Kings should command, subjects were duty bound to obey. A king was to be guided by his conscience and his counsellors. It was not up to subjects to tell him what to do."

J. Miller, The Stuarts at 184-86 (Hambledon Continuum, 2006)

A five-volume compilation of New York's colonial laws, published by the New York State Printer in 1894, demonstrates the strong opposition of the Duke of York not only to representative government, but also to a bill of rights ("Charter of Liberties") sought by the general public of white citizens. Volume I of the compilation begins with an Historical Note written by Robert C. Cumming in 1894 discussing at length the

234 Brewer, at 1051. Emphasis added.

235 Brewer, at 1054-55. Emphasis added.

processes of adoption of early New York laws. Mr. Cumming was the Chief Clerk of the New York Statutory Revision Commission, and therefore worked under the Commission's oversight.

The following excerpts from Mr. Cumming's Historical Note in 1894 demonstrate the Duke of York's resistance to the demands of the people for a representative Assembly and a "Charter of Liberties." First, King Charles II granted the Duke control of New Netherland, which became "New York" in the Duke's honor, with full law-making authority, subject only to the King's ultimate authority:"[236]

> Upon the assumption that the sovereignty to the New Netherlands was vested in the crown of England, Charles II, on the 12th of March, 1664, *granted to his brother, the Duke of York, the territory embracing Long Island and New York.* ... By the terms of the charter the Duke of York, his heirs, deputies, agents, commissioners and assigns, were *empowered "to correct, punish, pardon, govern and rule all such the subjects* of us, our heirs and successors, as shall from time to time adventure themselves into any the part or places aforesaid ... *according to such laws, orders, ordinances, directions and instructions as by our said dearest brother or his assigns shall be established* ... so always as the said statutes, ordinances and proceedings be not contrary to but as near as conveniently may be agreeable to the laws, statutes and government of this our realm of England." The charter *further empowered the Duke of York to appoint governors and other officers,* and generally to establish a local government within the territory embraced in the terms of the charter.

Having achieved full control in New York, the Duke then appointed Richard Nicolls as New York's Governor. He also provided for the government of the Province and for enactment of laws known as "the Duke's Laws," which were "transmitted to England for confirmation:"[237]

> **COURT OF ASSIZE**
>
> "Assize, in law, a session, or sitting, of a court of justice. It originally signified the method of trial by jury. During the Middle Ages the term was applied to certain court sessions held in the counties of England ... ."
>
> "Assize" at *www.britannica.com/topic/assize,* accessed Oct. 27, 2020

> During the year 1664 *Richard Nicolls was appointed governor of New York by a commission from the Duke of York,* the original, of which seems to have been lost, but which undoubtedly conferred upon him in substantially the same terms, the powers of local government within the province, which by the terms of the charter were conferred on the Duke of York, his deputies and assigns. ...
>
> Annually the justices and the high sheriff were to meet with the governor and his council in the court of Assizes at New York, which afterwards became the general court of the province.
>
> Two days after the surrender of New York, Governor Nicolls in a letter to Captain Young promised that "Deputys shall in convenient time and place, be summoned to propose and give their advice in all matters tending to ye peace and benefitt of Long Island." And shortly afterwards, a circular was addressed to the inhabitants of Long Island requesting them to send two delegates from each town to a convention to be held at Hempstead on the last day of February, 1665. In accordance with this call, delegates from each town met at Hempstead on March 1, 1665. T*he most important action of the meeting was to prepare, or more properly to confirm, a body of laws, which afterwards came to be known as*

236 COLONIAL LAWS, Vol. I, Historical Note by Robert C. Cumming at xi. Citations omitted. Emphasis added. See "*Appendix II: King Charles II's 1664 Charter Granting to the Duke of York Authority Over New York.*"

237 Colonial Laws, Vol I, at xi to xii. Citations omitted. Emphasis added.

> *the "Duke's Laws."* ... A number of additions and amendments were made by the court of Assizes, and afterwards the Code was transmitted to England for confirmation. ...

According to Mr. Cumming, "The 'Duke's Laws' ... continued in effect throughout the province, except as modified by later enactments of the assizes, the governor and council, or the governor, council and assembly, probably, until 1691;—certainly as late as 1687 ... ."[238]

The form of government approved by the Duke consisted of the Governor and the Court of Assizes advising the Governor, acting subject to the Duke's oversight, with no elected Assembly. The Court of Assizes "was little more than the mouthpiece of the Duke or the Governor." The Court of Assize "insolently rejected" a petition by the people for an Assembly:[239]

> The meeting at Hempstead *can hardly be called a legislative assembly.* After the promulgation of the Duke's Laws, the Court of Assizes, in a limited sense, acted as a legislative body. However, *it was little more than the mouthpiece of the Duke or the Governor in the promulgation of edicts, which it had no share in framing. The people were dissatisfied and petitioned for the assembly* which had been promised by Nicolls. The petition was *insolently rejected* by the Assizes: "It doth not appeare that Col. Nicolls made any such promise & ye Governors instructions directing him to make no alterations in ye lawes of ye Governmt settled before his arrivall, they cannot expect his Honor can comply wth them therein ... .

Having rejected the petition for an Assembly, the Court of Assize bluntly informed the people that they should just obey ("obedience and submission") the laws enacted pursuant to "his R. Hss. Commission:[240]

> "for their desire to know what is required of them, *There is nothing required of them but obedience and submission to ye Lawes of ye governmt* as appeares by his R. Hss. Commission wch hath often beene read unto them."

In 1667, Francis Lovelace was appointed to succeed Mr. Nicolls as Governor.[241]

After New York was temporarily retaken by the Dutch in July 1673 for a brief period, and then subsequently relinquished in a treaty in February 1674, the Duke re-instated the prior English laws and ordered that the prior laws be once again recognized, except as he "confirmed" any changes:[242]

> *A new charter was granted to the Duke of York* on the 29th of June, 1674, in *substantially the same terms as the former charter,* embracing the same territory. ...
>
> By commission, dated July 1, 1674, Edmund Andros was appointed governor of the province, and was empowered by his commission "to performe and execute all and every ye powers wch. are by ye said letters patents graunted unto Mee to be excuted by Me my Deputy Agent or Assignes." ...
>
> T*he Duke of York,* on July 1, 1674, among other matters *instructed the new governor* as follows:
>
> > "As to ye formes of justice, *I thinke it best for you to put in execution such laws, rules and ordrs as you find have been established by Coll. Nicolis and Col. Lovelace, and not to vary from them but upon emergent necessities,* and ye advice of your Councill and the gravest & experienced persons

238 Colonial Laws, at xii. Citations omitted. Emphasis added.

239 Colonial Laws, at xii. Citations omitted. Emphasis added.

240 Colonial Laws, at xiii.

241 Colonial Laws, at xiii.

242 Colonial Laws, at xiii-xiv. Citations omitted. Emphasis added.

> there; and *if any such alteration be made, that it be only temporary for a yeare, and if it be not confirmed by me within that time, then to be utterly voyd at ye end of that yeare and of noe force at all, as if such alteracon or new law never had been prmitted."* ...

Thus, the Governor re-confirmed the effectiveness of the Duke's laws:[243]

> On August 6, 1674, *the Duke of York instructed the new governor to put in execution the "Duke's Laws,"* except those requiring amendment or alteration ...; and on November 9, 1674, shortly after his arrival at New York, *Governor Andros by proclamation* conforming to the instructions *declared "that the same Book of Laws formerly establisht and in force under his royal highnesse government is now again confirmed by his Royal Highnesse* the which are to be observed and practiced together with the manner and time of holding Courts therein menconed as heretofore." ...

Thereby, the Duke maintained tight control over the enactment of laws in New York through the body of laws known as "the Duke's Laws." "Thus the province continued to be governed by the Duke's Laws, with such amendments as the governor and council, with the approbation of the Duke of York, saw fit to adopt."[244]

The Duke flatly rejected "the demand of the people for a representative assembly." The Duke stated: "touching Generall Assemblyes wch ye people there seems desirous of in imitacon of their neighbour Colonies, I thinke you have done well to discourage any mocon of yt kind:"[245]

> *During the years prior to the second occupation by the Dutch, the people of the colony were restless and discontented, demanding by petition and otherwise, some form of representative assembly.* As free born Englishmen the principle of no taxation without representation, had been inculcated in their minds, and already the mode of government of the colony by the edict and decree of royal officers, was sowing the seeds of the Revolution. T*hat the demand of the people for a representative assembly had reached the ears of the Duke of York, is evident from a letter written to Governor Andros on April 6, 1675, in which the Duke said:*

DUKE REJECTS ASSEMBLY OF THE PEOPLE

"First yn, touching Generall Assemblyes wch ye people there seems desirous of in imitacon of their neighbour Colonies, I thinke you have done well to discourage any mocon of yt kind, both as being not at all comprehended in yr Instructions nor indeed consistent wth ye forme of government already established ... ."

Duke of York

> "First yn, *touching Generall Assemblyes* wch ye people there seems desirous of in imitacon of their neighbour Colonies, *I thinke you have done well to discourage any mocon of yt kind, both as being not at all comprehended in yr Instructions nor indeed consistent wth ye forme of government already established,* not necessary for ye ease or redresse of any greivance yt may happen, since yt may be a easily obtained, by any peticon or othr addresse to you at the Generall Assizes (wch is once a yeare) where the same persons (as justices) are usually present, who in all probability would be theire Representatives if another constitucon were allowed." ...

243 Colonial Laws, at xiv.

244 Colonial Laws, at xiv. Citations omitted. Emphasis added.

245 Colonial Laws, at xiv-xv. Citations omitted. Emphasis added.

Mr. Cumming's Historical Note continues that the Duke "suspect[ed] [such Assemblies] would be of dangerous consequences," criticized "the aptness of such bodyes to assume to themselves many priviledges wch prove destructive to, or very oft disturbe the peace of ye governmt," and added "[n]either doe I see any use of them:"[246]

And later, on the 28th of January, 1676, *the Duke wrote to Governor Andros* as follows:

> *"I have formerly writt to you touching Assemblyes* in those countreys and have since observed what severall of your lattest letters hint about that matter. But unless you had offered what qualificacons are usuall and proper to such Assemblyes *I cannot but suspect they would be of dangerous consequence, nothing being more knowne than the aptness of such bodyes to assume to themselves many prlviledges wch prove destructive to, or very oft disturbe the peace of ye governmt wherein they are allowed. Neither doe I see any use of them* wch is not as well provided for, whilst you and your councell governe according to ye laws established (thereby preserving every man's property inviolate) and whilst all things that need redresse may be sure of finding it, either at ye Quarter Sessions or by other legall and ordinary wayes, or lastly by appeale to myselfe. But howsoever if you continue of ye same opinion, I shall be ready to consider of any proposalls you shall send to yt purpose." ...

> Whether Andros continued of the "same opinion" does not appear, but at any rate, n*o form of representative assembly was established* under his administration.

> A new Governor, Thomas Dongan, was appointed in 1682, with instructions to finally establish an Assembly of freeholders:[247]

ASSEMBLIES ARE TROUBLESOME

"nothing being more knowne than the aptness of such bodyes to assume to themselves many prlviledges wch prove destructive to, or very oft disturbe the peace of ye governmt wherein they are allowed. Neither doe I see any use of them wch is not as well provided for ... ."

Duke of York

> Col. Thomas Dongan was commissioned governor of New York, September 30, 1682. With his commission he received instructions directing him "to issue of Writts or warrts of Sumons to ye sev'all Sheriffes or other proper offlcrs in every part of yor said government *wherein you shall expresse that I have thought fitt that there shall be a genll Assembly of all the Freeholders, by the prsons who they shall choose to reprsent ym* in ordr to consultting wth yourselfe and the said council what laws are fitt and necessary to be made and established for the good weale and governmt of the said Colcny and its Dependencyes." ...

> Governor Dongan arrived in New York in August, 1683, and at a meeting of the Council held at Fort James on the 13th of September following, *it was determined to summon an assembly in accordance with the instructions to the Governor,* to be held at the city of New York on October 17, 1683. Writs or orders were issued directing the inhabitants to choose their representatives "in the Generall Assembly to be held at New York October ye 17th, 1683." Each riding on Long Island was entitled to two representatives; Staten Island, one; Esopus, two; Albany and Renslaerswyck, two; Schenectady, one; Pemaquid, one; The Islands about New York, one; and New York, four.

An Assembly met in October 1683, with laws it passed to be subject to "the assent of the governor and council," and thereafter "[a]ll bills ... were to be transmitted to the Duke of York for confirmation or rejection:"[248]

---

246 Colonial Laws, at xv. Citations omitted. Emphasis added.

247 Colonial Laws, at xv-xvi. Citations omitted. Emphasis added.

248 Colonial Laws, at xvi. Citations omitted. Emphasis added.

> On the 17th of October, 1683, the representatives thus elected met in General Assembly, and constituted the first representative legislative body in the colony of New York. By the terms of his instructions Governor Dougan was directed to let the Assembly know that it was to be entitled to free debate. *All bills were to receive the assent of the governor and council, and were to be transmitted to the Duke of York for confirmation or rejection.* Laws assented to by the governor were to be good and binding *until rejected by the Duke of York, from which time they were to be null and void.* The governor was given power to cause the General Assembly to be summoned and to adjourn and dissolve the same, as he saw fit. …

The Governor signed all the laws that the Assembly passed, with one extremely critical exception—"the charter of liberties:"[249]

> At this session fifteen Acts were passed which received the signature of the Governor. … *It does not appear that any were disapproved except the charter of liberties.* … After a session of nearly three weeks, the legislature adjourned, enacting
>
> > "That according to the usage, custome and practice of the Realme of England, a Sessions of a General Assembly be held in this province once in three years att least."
>
> The second meeting of the legislature commenced in October, 1684, at which thirty-one acts were passed, which received the assent of the Governor. …

It can be seen, then, as described by Mr. Cumming in his Historical Note, that the Duke of York "vetoed" the "first act of the Assembly of 1683 … to pass 'the charter of Libertyes and privileges,'" which "did not meet with favor from the Duke of York:"[250]

> *The first act of the Assembly of 1683 was to pass "the charter of Libertyes and priviledges* granted by his Royall Highnesse to the inhabitants of New Yorke, and its dependansyes," *whereby the representatives attempted to confirm by legislation, the liberties and privileges, which they conceived were granted to them by the Duke of York in his commission to Governor Dongan.* … This assumption of the representatives, although receiving the assent of the governor, *did not meet with favor from the Duke of York, and was vetoed* March 3, 1684.

Mr. Cumming opined in his 1894 Historical Note that the Duke only had granted an Assembly "with great reluctance" and that the Assembly's "passing the Charter of Liberties and privileges only tended to increase his prejudice against representative bodies:"[251]

> It was *with great reluctance, that the Duke of York ever granted to the colony of New York a legislative Assembly,* and it is probable that the action of the assembly in *passing the Charter of Liberties and privileges only tended to increase his prejudice against representative bodies.*

After King Charles II died, the Governor allowed election of a new Assembly, but that Assembly was dissolved "in view of a new commission and instruction received by the governor:"[252]

> Before another meeting *news of the King's death was received,* and it was deemed expedient to dissolve the present assembly, which was done by proclamation, dated August 13, 1685, … and *writs were issued by the governor directing the elections of representatives to a General Assembly* to be held in October, 1685.

---

249 Colonial Laws, at xvi. Citations omitted. Emphasis added.

250 Colonial Laws, at xvi-xvii. Citations omitted. Emphasis added.

251 Colonial Laws, at xvii. Citations omitted. Emphasis added.

252 Colonial Laws, at xvi. Citations omitted. Emphasis added.

> This Assembly passed six acts which received the assent of the governor ..., and then adjourned to September, 1686. It was further prorogued until March, 1687, and *finally, in view of a new commission and instruction received by the governor, reposing the power of legislation in the governor and council, the Assembly was dissolved on January 20, 1687.*

In 1686, the Duke of York, now King James II, authorized New York's Governor to make laws without mention of any role for an Assembly. He gave specific direction to declare the Charter of Liberties to "bee forthwith repealed & disallowed" and further subject[ed] all laws to the King's "approval or disapproval:"[253]

NO CHARTER OF LIBERTIES

"Declare Our Will & pleasure that ye said Bill or charter of Franchises bee forthwith repealed & disallowed."

Duke of York

> At any rate, in June, 1686, the former Duke of York, now James II, King of England, issued a new commission, with *instructions to Governor Dongan, whereby he empowered him, with the advice and consent of the Councll,* or major part of them, *"to make constitute, and ordain Laws, Statutes, and Ordinances for the publick peace, welfare & good Government of our said Province and of the people and inhabitants thereof."* ... In the instructions accompanying the commission, *the governor was directed "to Declare Our Will & pleasure that ye said Bill or charter of Franchises bee forthwith repealed & disallowed." (This was the charter of Liberties and privileges, which had already been vetoed.)* The instructions further provided that all other Laws, Statutes & Ordinances already made, continue in force until new laws were enacted; *that copies of new laws be transmitted to the King within three months for approval or disapproval; that laws disapproved were to be void from thenceforth;* and that in enacting laws *the style of enacting the same be by the Governor and Council.* ...
>
> The governor and council met December 9, 1686. His Excellys Instructions being read and considered it is "Ordered, that all the branches of the revenue & all other laws that have been passed since the yeare 1683 *except such as his Matie has repealed* remaine & continue as they now are till further consideracon." ...

In July 1688, a new Governor, Sir Edmund Andros, was appointed, but laws remained subject to the King's approval:[254]

> A change in the government of the Colony had been determined on in England. The entire country from the St. Croix to the Delaware was consolidated under one government, and Sir Edmund Andros was appointed governor. ... So far as the making of laws was concerned, the powers conferred on Andros were substantially the same as those possessed by Governor Dongan.

Finally, after King James II 's removal from the English throne in 1688, New York was permitted to have an Assembly once William and Mary gained power through the Glorious Revolution. That policy continued thereafter:[255]

> *Thus things continued until the accession of William of Orange to the English throne ...*
>
> In the meantime Henry Sloughter was appointed governor of New York by commission, dated January 4, 1690. ...

253 Colonial Laws, at xvii-xviii. Citations omitted. Emphasis added.

254 Colonial Laws, at xviii. Citations omitted. Emphasis added.

255 Colonial Laws, at xviii-xix. Citations omitted. Emphasis added.

> *The commission of Governor Sloughter authorized the calling of a Legislative assembly,* and on March 20, the day after his arrival in New York, *writs for the election of representatives to the new Assembly were Issued.* Pursuant to this call the new Assembly met April 9, 1691, and from that date until the Revolution, the representatives of the people in General Assembly participated in the making of laws for the government of the Colony.

Thus, as the foregoing history demonstrates, the Duke of York maintained his stern domination over the New York legislative process. That enabled him to create the English form of slavery in the Colony. The Duke, an absolutist, did all he could to prevent representative government and the adoption of a Charter of Liberties in New York, even for white settlers. Only after his reign as King James II ended with the rise of William and Mary did the white citizens of New York receive the benefit of a stable representative Assembly.

The dominance of New York laws by the Duke of York, later King James II, places direct responsibility upon him for the content of New York's slave laws enacted during his governance from 1664 until the English deposed King James. King James' successors, William and Mary, James' oldest daughter, followed by Queen Anne, also his daughter, did nothing to ease the misery of the slaves initiated by James. Queen Anne and her successors continued the English government's pursuit of and heavy reliance upon the slave trade and black slavery.

THE DUKE'S DAUGHTER, QUEEN ANNE, CONTINUED HIS SLAVERY PROMOTION

"The last and most notable *asiento* was that granted to the British South Sea Company, in 1713, by a provision in the Treaty of Utrecht. This contract entitled the company to send 4,800 slaves to Spanish America annually for 30 years and to send one ship *(navío de permiso)* each year to engage in general trade."

Britannica.com[256]

§ § §

The Duke of York's (King James II's) royal successors continued his slavery practices. Especially King James' second daughter, Queen Anne, continued his promotion of slavery, with lasting consequences. With King Charles II, James II, and Queen Anne, slavery was a Stuart family business. Since they were reigning monarchs, slavery was a governmental undertaking.

Queen Anne served immediately after William and Mary, beginning in 1702 until 1714. In 1713, Queen Anne procured for Britain the *Asiento*—a long-term contract—with Spain pursuant to which Britain supplied Spain's colonies with hundreds of thousands of slaves for decades. The following excerpts demonstrate Queen Anne's significant role in slavery, through the Royal African Company:

> In 1713, in the Treaty of Utrecht, Britain won the *asiento,* the right to be the sole supplier of slaves to Spain's colonies in South America for 30 years. The British government sold the contract to the newly formed South Sea Company (SSC). The Royal African Company was the SSC's main supplier of slaves. Queen Anne was allocated 22.5 percent of the SSC stock.[257]
>
> § § §
>
> In 1713 an agreement between Spain and Britain granted the British a monopoly on the slave trade with the Spanish colonies. Under the *Asiento de negros,* Britain was entitled to supply those colonies with 4,800 African slaves per year for 30 years. The contract for this supply was assigned to the South Sea Company, of which Anne held some 22.5 percent of the stock.[258]
>
> § § §
>
> Anne was the second daughter of James, Duke of York (later James II), and Anne Hyde. ...
>
> Queen Anne continued the tradition of royal support for the British slave trade. In 1712 she announced that she had secured an exclusive contract for the British nation to provide enslaved Africans for the Spanish West Indies for thirty years. The Government sold the contract to the newly founded South Sea Company for £7.5 million. Queen Anne also secured over 20% of the stock for herself.[259]

Under Queen Anne and the *Asiento,* Britain's slave trade expanded dramatically.

---

256 "Asiento de negros" at *www.britannica.com/topic/asiento-de-negros,* accessed Oct. 14, 2020.

257 "The Business of Enslavement" at *www.bbc.co.uk/history/british/abolition/slavery_business_gallery_06.shtml.*

258 "Anne: Queen of Great Britain and Ireland" at *www.britannica.com/biography/Anne-queen-of-Great-Britain-and-Ireland*, accessed Oct. 14, 2020; Thomas, at 231.

259 "Queen Anne" at *www.npg.org.uk/learning/digitalhistpry/abolition-of-slavery/queen-anne*, accessed Oct. 14, 2020.

Lord Hugh Thomas states that, before Queen Anne's reign, under the leadership of her father, James Stuart, "By the end of the seventeenth century, as much as three-fifths of the income of the [Royal African Company] derived from the sale of slaves. Between its foundation and 1689, the company indeed exported just under 90,000 slaves … ."[260]

This governmental business expanded under Queen Anne, even before the *Asiento.* According to Lord Thomas, "By 1710, [the British] were selling well over ten thousand slaves a year to the Indies, the Spanish empire included; the French sold fewer than thirteen thousand in the twelve years 1702-13.[261]

Once Queen Anne obtained the *Asiento,* Britain's slave trade expanded yet further. Lord Thomas stated that "In the 1730s, British ships carried perhaps 170,000 slaves in all—for the first time, probably more in ten years than the Portuguese carried to Brazil."[262]

Just as America honors the Duke of York in the names of New York State, New York City, New York County, and the City of Albany, the State of Maryland honors Queen Anne in the names of the City of Annapolis,[263] Maryland's Capitol, and Queen Anne County.[264]

---

260 Thomas, at 203.

261 Thomas, at 231

262 Thomas, at 246

263 "History of Annapolis" at *www.annapolis.gov/588/History-of-Annapolis#:~:text=The Many Names of Annapolis The capital of,of Lord Baltimore%2C who owned the proprietary colony.,* accessed Oct. 15, 2020.

264 "Queen Anne's County, Maryland" at *www.ereferencedesk.com/resources/counties/maryland/queen-annes.html,* accessed Oct. 15, 2020.

CHAPTER FOUR: AMERICA'S SLAVERY CONTRADICTIONS

AMERICA'S BECOMES A NATION IN 1776, AND CHOOSES TO PERPETUATE THE REIGN OF TERROR

Once the English were out of the picture, America had an opportunity to re-evaluate slavery. When America became a nation, it was free to choose the character of nation it was to be.

With national independence, America chose Phase 2 of America's Reign of Terror.

There were distinctive pressures to bring an end to slavery, and as I discuss below, certain Founding Fathers wanted to do just that.

Other Founding Fathers had considerable qualms about slavery, and recognized it as an immoral institution. Some expected, or at least hoped, that slavery would die out over time. Yet, they could not bring themselves to incur the wrath of the slave society and of their political allies and social friends to end it. Perhaps they lacked the power to do so in the face of the slave society's strength. Many regarded African-Americans as inferior.

Unlike the Duke of York, the Founding Fathers did not create slavery. They had lived with it all their lives. It had always been an accepted part of their existence. In addition, most of the Founding Fathers possessed substantial wealth in the form of the human bodies of the slaves. In the 1770s, slavery existed everywhere—North and South. The abolitionist movement was not particularly strong at the time, although it certainly did exist.

This Chapter discusses the Founding Fathers lack of political will, and perhaps the absence of power, to do what they knew was right.

FOUR KEY EVENTS

Although it is possible to identify important occurrences associated with American slavery, four events stand out:

- The Duke of York's defeat of the Dutch at New Amsterdam (beginning Phase 1 of the Reign of Terror)
- The signing of the Declaration of Independence (beginning Phase 2)
- The invention of the cotton gin, which made implausible any hope for slavery's end
- The ratification of the 13th Amendment to the Constitution (beginning Phase 3)

Other noteworthy events during slavery include the following:

- Nat Turner's rebellion, which struck terror throughout the South and enhanced even more the deep white fear of their slaves
- The enactment of the Fugitive Slave Law of 1850, which not only gave slaveowners the right to pursue their fugitive slaves into supposedly "free" states, but required officials, and even common citizens, in those states to assist in the capture of the fugitives, forbidding citizens from assisting the fugitives; one result was enhancement of the abolitionist movement
- John Brown's Raid on the federal armory at Harper's Ferry, the sheer occurrence of which caused such devasting fear in the slave society that it made the Civil War inevitable
- Election of Abraham Lincoln less than a year after John Brown's execution, which although Lincoln was not an abolitionist, made clear to the slave society that it would not be able to dominate the federal government as had occurred prior to that time
- The Civil War within only 18 months after John Brown's raid at Harper's Ferry, which was shockingly devastating to the nation, with 1.5 million casualties, including 620,000 or more deaths; proportionately, today that would equate with 15 million casualties, or approximately 75% of the current population of New York State
- The Emancipation Proclamation, as much an economic document targeting the South's wealth as a freedom document. The Proclamation purported to free the slaves of slaveholders in the Confederacy. It was enforceable only in territory held by Union troops. The Proclamation did not, however, free slaves in slave states remaining in the Union (Kentucky, Missouri, Maryland, West Virginia, and Delaware, with a few slaves remaining in New Jersey). The District of Columbia freed its slaves in 1862, shortly before the Proclamation was issued. Maryland freed its slaves in 1864, prior to the 13th Amendment. West Virginia freed its slaves in 1865 at the time the State voted to ratify the Amendment. The remaining Union slave states did not free their slaves until final ratification of the 13th Amendment in 1865.

> **CASUALTIES OF WAR**
>
> There were an estimated 1.5 million casualties reported during the Civil War.
>
> A "casualty" is a military person lost through death, wounds, injury, sickness, internment, capture, or through being missing in action.
>
> "Civil War Casualties" at *www.battlefields.org/learn/articles/civil-war-casualties,* accessed Sept. 29, 2020

English Defeat of the Dutch (1664)

As discussed earlier, the Duke of York's defeat of the Dutch at New Amsterdam in 1664 resulted in his ability, together with King Charles II, and their colleagues, to promote the English form of slavery in the American colonies on a widespread basis. Until then, indentured servitude, or slavery similar to indentured servitude, had been practiced in Maryland, Virginia and elsewhere, and slavery had been practiced to a limited extent in the American colonies, especially in New England, as well as in Dutch New Amsterdam and in the Spanish colonies in Florida and Northern Mexico (which later became the Republic of Texas).

To reiterate, the Duke—James Stuart, who later became King James II—and his brother, King Charles II, brought into play, with the English form of slavery, a new more severe form of brutality.[265]

As Dr. Holly Brewer describes,[266] immediately after the restoration of the English monarchy in 1660, it was the Duke and his brother, King Charles II, who promoted slavery aggressively for the English monarchy's financial purposes.

As incentives to settlers to purchase slaves, Dr. Leslie Harris and Dr. Holly Brewer describe[267] how the English provided incentives for settlers' purchases of slaves imported directly from Africa. They also caused the enactment of strict slave laws.

The result was the rapid spread of the English form of slavery, based upon brutal laws promoted by the Duke of York and King Charles, throughout the American colonies from New York down to the Carolinas. As other territories and states emerged, they too copied those laws.

It should never be overlooked, however, that the Duke of York's efforts began in a receptive New York that itself benefitted greatly from slavery and practiced some of the most inhumane practices imaginable. This was not in Alabama, Mississippi, Louisiana, Georgia or Carolina or any other state in the Deep South that Northerners love to blame for slavery. To the contrary, the North's own role was significant.[268]

Declaration of Independence and Constitution (1776/1788)

The Declaration of Independence was a significant highly-influential and inspirational document. The Declaration did not itself speak against slavery explicitly, although an early draft had "attack[ed]" slavery.[269] Nevertheless, the Declaration's ideals motivated opposition to slavery over the following decades leading to the Civil War. Frederick Douglass and other African-Americans relentlessly refused to allow whites to overlook their hypocrisy in the light of the Declaration.

True, the signers of the Declaration were themselves imperfect, especially as measured by today's standards. They knew they were hypocritical, but struggled with the process for freeing slaves, concern over the potential for loss of significant "property value," substantial fear of African-Americans, concern about freeing so many uneducated and generally unskilled people without visible means of support, and their belief that blacks were inherently inferior to whites.

---

265 See generally Singer; McManus, Slavery in New York; McManus, Black Bondage in the North; Harris.

266 Brewer, at 1045-47, 1051.

267 Harris, at 26-27, 28; Brewer at 1046. Footnotes omitted. Emphasis added.

268 See *"Chapter Six: The Duke of York's Creation on a Rampage——Slavery Was a National Institution: North and South."*

269 "(1776) The Deleted Passage of the Declaration of Independence" at *www.blackpast.org/african-american-history/declaration-independence-and-debate-over-slavery/*, accessed June 13, 2022.

Nevertheless, the Declaration of Independence set a tone inspiring abolitionists and encouraging states to enact abolition laws.

Over time, especially with the persistent admonishment of eloquent slaves, former slaves, and "free" blacks, such as Frederick Douglass, Sojourner Truth, Frances Ellen Watkins Harper, Harriet Jacobs, Jermain Loguen, William Wells Brown, and David Walker, increasing numbers of white Americans were haunted by the bold statement that:

> We hold these truths to be self-evident, that all men are created equal, that they are endowed by their Creator with certain unalienable Rights, that among these are Life, Liberty and the pursuit of Happiness.

CONSTITUTION'S PROVISIONS
PROTECTING OR RECOGNIZING SLAVERY

- Return of fugitive slaves to their owners
- Continued importation of slaves by means of the international slave trade for 20 years
- Three-Fifths Compromise regarding representation in Congress (which also apportioned electoral votes for President), giving the slave society exaggerated influence in the new nation
- Insurrection clause contemplated use of military force to suppress slave rebellions

In contrast, the Constitution did not incorporate the Declaration's ideals. To the contrary, the Constitution was written from the perspective of inequality—it protected slavery. That was true especially in the Constitution's provision facilitating recapture of fugitive slaves, which fostered the Fugitive Slave Laws of 1793 and 1850. The Constitution contained provisions contemplating the validity of slavery. The Declaration of Independence did not.

The Constitution gave birth ultimately to the Supreme Court's infamous decision in the Dred Scott case that African-Americans were not "citizens," even if "free."[270]

To repair its damage, the Constitution was required to be amended radically. That occurred with the ratification of the 13th, 14th, and 15th Amendments. The 14th Amendment overturned the Dred Scott decision by declaring that "All persons born or naturalized in the United States, and subject to the jurisdiction thereof, are citizens of the United States and of the State wherein they reside." Those post-Civil War Amendments effectively incorporated into the Constitution for the first time the central freedom and equality principles of the Declaration of Independence.

Invention of Cotton Gin (1793)

The invention of the cotton gin was instrumental in the spread of the Duke of York's form of slavery in America. It destroyed any realistic hope for a rapid end to slavery.

Coincident with the invention of the cotton gin and shortly thereafter, "widespread soil depletion and frequent economic crises plagued the Chesapeake."[271] In Virginia and Maryland in particular, although not solely, tobacco became less profitable as a crop.

270 *Dred Scott v. Sanford,* 60 U.S. 393 (1857).

271 R. Halpern and E. Dal Lago, ed., SLAVERY AND EMANCIPATION at 123 (Blackwell Publishers, Ltd., 2002) ("Halpern and Dal Lago").

Under those conditions, cotton became King. As explained by Dr. Andrew Torget,[272] prior to the cotton gin's innovation cotton cloth had been considered by textile mills in Britain as more desirable than wool for many purposes. He adds that cotton clothing and other cotton products, however, could not be manufactured in substantial quantities. The British mills had difficulty obtaining a sufficient supply of cotton in order to engage in large-scale textile product manufacturing. Cotton was difficult to produce in quantity due to the tight integration of the seeds with fibers in the cotton bolls.

"The First Cotton-Gin", *Slavery Images: A Visual Record of the African Slave Trade and Slave Life in the Early African Diaspora,* accessed November 16, 2020, *http://slaveryimages.org/s/slaveryimages/item/1119*

As Dr. Torget describes, the cotton gin, invented in 1793 by Eli Whitney, made it possible to remove the seeds from cotton bolls mechanically much more easily, quickly and economically than it had been to remove the seeds laboriously by hand.[273] With the cotton gin, cotton could be produced efficiently for Britain's textile mills. Once again, the North also is deeply implicated, as New York merchants competed with British merchants for cotton bales in New Orleans.[274] Therefore, attention focuses appropriately upon textile mills in New England and elsewhere in the North, as well as in Britain, which benefited from slavery.

Dr. Torget states that:[275]

> a revolution in cotton had begun in Europe during the early 1800s when the burgeoning British textile industry developed an insatiable hunger for cotton as a cheaper more comfortable, more durable alternative to wool. The crop became, almost overnight one of the most valuable commodities in the Atlantic world, unleashing an economic storm that soon swept across the Atlantic ocean and began reshaping the North American continent.

He adds that "nearly half" of Britain's export economy in the 1840s was in the form of "manufactured cotton products," and "most of Great Britain's raw cotton supply—82 percent—came from the southern United States."[276]

272 A. Torget, SEEDS OF EMPIRE—COTTON, SLAVERY, AND THE TRANSFORMATION OF THE TEXAS BORDERLANDS, 1800-1850 at 3-4, 7-10 (Univ. of North Carolina Press, 2015) ("Torget").

273 Torget, at 35.

274 Torget, at 88-89, 125-26.

275 Torget, at 23.

276 Torget, at 212.

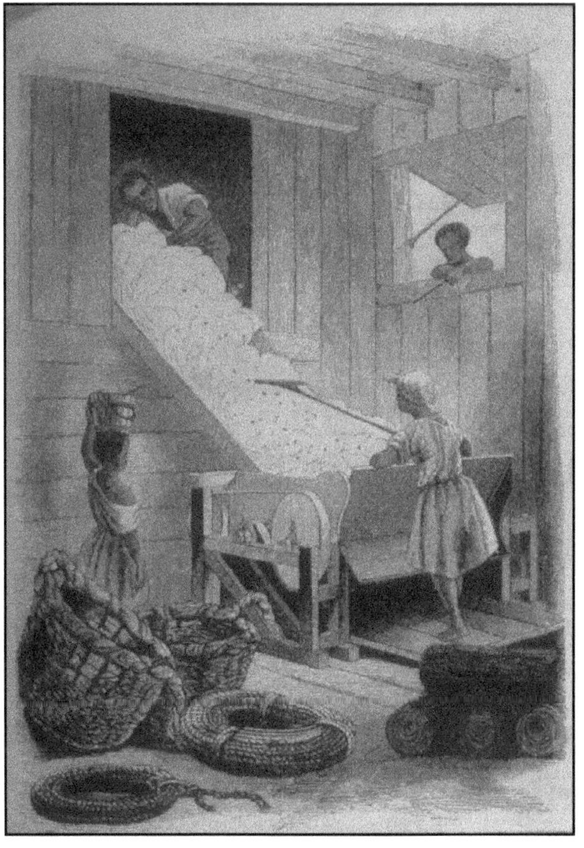

"Ginning Cotton, U.S. South, 1850s", *Slavery Images: A Visual Record of the African Slave Trade and Slave Life in the Early African Diaspora,* accessed November 16, 2020, *http://slaveryimages.org/s/slaveryimages/item/1170*

The cotton gin revolutionized American slavery, and impacted slaves tremendously and destructively. It led to a forced migration far greater than the migrations forced on Native Americans ("20 times large").[277]

Dr. Rick Halpern and Dr. Enrico Dal Lago describe the causes of the migration:[278]

> A production boom pushed hundreds of farmers and impoverished planters to settle the "Old Southwest," leaving depleted areas together with their slaves and, in the process of migration, causing the dissolution of thousands of slave families. Other upper South masters sold their slaves to the labor hungry planters of the cotton "black belt," fueling an internal slave trade which flourished until the Civil War.

Dr. Torget continues that "[o]ne of the largest migrations in United States history ensued, as hundreds of thousands of Americans poured into the Gulf Coast region that would become the Cotton South ... ." This was because "alluvial soils and a long growing season promised ideal conditions for cultivating" cotton.[279]

Fertile land in the South was especially suitable for growing cotton, especially along river beds, such as the Mississippi River.[280] Largely due to the ability to grow cotton in quantity, the populations of Alabama, Mississippi and Louisiana grew rapidly,[281] so that they became states within about 20 years. Given Mexico's ambivalence and hostility toward the institution, that was followed a decade and a half later by the Texas revolution and the creation of that North American nation founded on slavery.[282]

Yet, the process of growing cotton itself was labor intensive. The farmers and planters needed laborers. Who could be more desirable to cost-conscious planters than laborers who were denied pay? Thus, there also was an explosion of the slave population in the South.

277 Edward Ball, "Retracing Slavery's Trail of Tears" (Smithsonian Magazine, Nov. 2015) at www.smithsonianmag.com/history/slavery-trail-of-tears-180956968/, accessed Oct. 12, 2020 ("Edward Ball").

278 Halpern and Dal Lago, at 123-24.

279 Torget, at 4, 23.

280 Torget, at 43.

281 Torget, at 258.

282 See generally, R. Campbell, AN EMPIRE FOR SLAVERY—THE PECULIAR INSTITUTION IN TEXAS, 1821-1865 (Louisiana State University Press, 1989) ("Campbell"); and Torget.

Dr. Torget describes "voracious new markets for slaves along the Gulf Coast." Since the international slave trade had been prohibited, planters turned to the internal slave trade to fill their need.[283]

Those developments coincided with the decline in tobacco prices, so that tobacco planters shifted to less labor-intensive crops, such as cereals and corn.[284] Slaves became less valuable to the former tobacco planters. As Dr. Peter Kolchin describes,[285] there was a shipment of over a million slaves between 1790 and 1860 from the Upper South—especially Maryland and Virginia—to the slave auction in New Orleans where the Southern and Southwestern planters would purchase the slaves at higher prices.

Dr. Henry Gates states that "[o]f the 3.2 million slaves working in the 15 slave states in 1850, 1.8 million worked in cotton."[286]

The movement of slaves is associated with the development in the 1830s and 1840s of the shameful slave market in an area of Washington, DC, which became Alexandria, Virginia. The slave traders in Alexandria would purchase slaves at lower prices from Upper South planters, and would send the slaves for sale in New Orleans.[287]

"Slave Coffle, Washington, D.C., ca. 1819", *Slavery Images: A Visual Record of the African Slave Trade and Slave Life in the Early African Diaspora,* accessed June 7, 2022, http://slaveryimages.org/s/slaveryimages/item/197

In Kentucky, Louisville developed its own slave market, with slave traders moving slaves South from Kentucky using boats on the Ohio and Mississippi Rivers.

Slaves could be transported on ships, as was Solomon Northup, of TWELVE YEARS A SLAVE fame, a "free" African-American who was kidnapped in Washington, DC, or they could be placed in callous, merciless, and sickening slave coffles. Slave traders drove slaves literally on foot, like cattle, 1,000 miles from Alexandria, Virginia—effectively, Washington, DC, the Capital of "The Land of the Free"—to the New Orleans slave auction, or alternatively, to Louisville, Kentucky, to be shipped South on riverboats.

Slave traders force-marched women, men, aged and injured slaves, and children in chains through numerous states and countless local communities, witnessed by thousands upon thousands of silent whites, as well as other slaves and "free" African-Americans, in sun, rain, wind, and cold, dressed in rags, with or without shoes.[288]

283 Torget, at 43.

284 Slavery in Maryland, at 12.

285 Kolchin, at 96.

286 Gates, "Slavery by the Numbers" at *www.theroot.com/slavery-by-the-numbers-1790874492,* accessed Sept. 29, 2020.

287 Sweig, "Alexandria to New Orleans: The Human Tragedy of the Interstate Slave Trade, Part II" (The Connection Newspapers, Oct. 8, 2014) ("Sweig") at *m.connectionnewspapers.com/news/2014/oct/08/alexandria-new-orleans-human-tragedy-interstate-sl/,* accessed Sept. 29, 2020.

288 See "Chapter Five: The Duke's Slave Trading Legacy—The Internal Slave Trade: Coffles and Auctions."
See also "Chapter Six: The Duke of York's Creation on a Rampage—The Story of Eliza: Children Torn from a Mother's Arms."

Another aspect of the migration was the kidnapping and enslavement of "free" African-Americans, as occurred to Solomon Northup. Kidnap victims frequently were children.[289]

This is another in the litany of the "something that happened 150 years ago."

13th Amendment's Ratification (1865)

The 13th Amendment provides:

> Neither slavery nor involuntary servitude, except as a punishment for crime whereof the party shall have been duly convicted, shall exist within the United States, or any place subject to their jurisdiction.

Since the Constitution contemplated slavery as a valid system of labor, it was necessary to ratify the 13th Amendment to bring an enforceable, complete end to slavery.

The Emancipation Proclamation did not accomplish that. The Proclamation purported only to free slaves in Confederate states, not in Union states.

The Civil War did not free the Union slaves either. The War's end in favor of the Union, however, created an atmosphere that made the 13th Amendment possible.

The Civil War did result in earlier freedom for slaves, but only in Confederate territories controlled by Union armies. Union generals sought to enforce the Emancipation Proclamation where they could and when slaves escaped to the relative security of Union lines.

Yet, of course, the end was an arduous, bloody, drawn out scenario. Even today, important vestiges of slavery remain, most importantly with respect to deep persistent educational inequality.[290]

---

289 G. Stroud, A SKETCH OF THE LAWS RELATING TO SLAVERY IN THE SEVERAL STATES OF THE UNITED STATES OF AMERICA at 50 footnote (H. Longstreth, 1856), available from the Library of Congress at *www.hathitrust.org/digital_library* ("Stroud").

290 See *"Chapter Seven: Moving Forward??—Remnants of Slavery: Intolerable Discrimination in Education."*

THE REVOLUTION WAS ABOUT FREEDOM, BUT NOT FOR SLAVES

America's Founding Fathers undertook the American Revolution to achieve freedom for themselves and their families.

While the Revolution was not about freedom for slaves, I have not seen convincing evidence that the American Revolution was for the purpose of the preservation of slavery.

To the contrary, as stated by Dr. Rick Halpern and Dr. Enrico Dal Lago:[291]

> After the Revolution, most white intellectuals were convinced that slavery was morally wrong and would eventually die out, especially if assisted by gradual measures designed to facilitate emancipation without provoking a sudden change in society.

They note also the rise of capitalism, according to which:[292]

> labor should be free, and labor relations were best based on the mutual agreement of consenting parties. Slavery violated all the basic tenets of classical capitalism, based as it was on coerced labor and violence. Partly for these reasons, slavery started to be seen as an economically inefficient system.

Slaves, former slaves, and "free" African-Americans fought on the American Side.

For example, Crispus Attucks, a former slave or an escaped slave, depending on interpretation, was the first casualty of the American Revolution.

William Wells Brown, an escaped slave himself, tells the story of Mr. Attucks' early role in the Revolution:[293]

> Both in the Federal Convention to frame the Constitution, and in the State Conventions to ratify the same, it was admitted that the blacks had fought bravely against the British, and in favor of the American Republic; for the fact that a black man (Crispus Attucks) was the first to give his life at the commencement of the Revolution was still fresh in their minds. Eighteen years previous to the breaking out of the war, Attucks was held as a slave by Mr. William Brown of Framingham, Mass., and from whom he escaped about that time, taking up his residence in Boston. The Boston Massacre, March 5, 1770, may be regarded as the first act in the great drama of the American Revolution. "From that moment," said Daniel Webster, "we may date the severance of the British Empire." The presence of the British soldiers in King Street excited the patriotic indignation of the people. The whole community was stirred, and sage counsellors were deliberating and writing and talking about the public grievances. But it was not for "the wise and prudent" to be the first to act against the encroachments of arbitrary power. "A motley rabble of saucy boys, negroes and mulattoes, Irish Teagues, and outlandish Jack tars" (as John Adams described them in his plea in defence of the soldiers) could not restrain their emotion, or stop to inquire if what they *must do* was according to the letter of any law. Led by Crispus Attucks, the mulatto slave, and shouting, "The way to get rid of these soldiers is to attack the main guard; strike at the root; this is the nest," with more valor than discretion, they rushed to King Street, and were fired upon by Capt. Preston's Company. Crispus Attucks was the first to fall: he and Samuel Gray and Jonas Caldwell were killed on the spot. Samuel Maverick and Patrick Carr were mortally wounded.

---

291 Halpern and Dal Lago, at 88

292 Halpern and Dal Lago, at 87

293 W. Brown, THE NEGRO IN THE AMERICAN REBELLION: HIS HEROISM AND HIS FIDELITY at 3-5 (Lee & Shepard, 1867). Emphasis in original.

> The excitement which followed was intense. The bells of the town were rung. An impromptu town meeting was held, and an immense assembly was gathered.
>
> Three days after, on the 8th, a public funeral of the martyrs took place. The shops in Boston were closed; and all the bells of Boston and the neighboring towns were rung. It is said that a greater number of persons assembled on this occasion than were ever before gathered on this continent for a similar purpose. The body of Crispus Attucks, the mulatto slave, had been placed in Faneuil Hall, with that of Caldwell, both being strangers in the city. Maverick was buried from his Mother's house, in Union Street; and Gray from his brother's, in Royal Exchange Lane. The four hearses formed a junction in King Street; and there the procession marched in columns six deep, with a long file of coaches belonging to the most distinguished citizens, to the Middle Burying-ground, where the four victims were deposited in one grave, over which a stone was placed with this inscription:—
>
> "Long as in Freedom's cause the wise contend,
> Dear to your country shall your fame extend;
> While to the world the lettered stone shall tell
> Where Caldwell, Attucks, Gray, and Maverick fell."
>
> The anniversary of this event was publicly commemorated in Boston, by an oration and other exercises, every year until after our national independence was achieved, when the Fourth of July was substituted for the Fifth of March as the more proper day for a general celebration. Not only was the event commemorated, but the martyrs who then gave up their lives were remembered and honored.
>
> For half a century after the close of the war, the name of Crispus Attucks was honorably mentioned by the most noted men of the country who were not blinded by foolish prejudice.

Another African-American, Prince Hall, the "Father of Black Masonry," "was one of a few blacks who fought at the battle of Bunker Hill."[294]

Certainly, more slaves fought on the British side. The British offered slaves freedom in return for joining the British forces. Yet, that did not lead slaveholders to instigate the Revolution, already in progress. There were slaves who accepted the offer, although "no mass uprising of slaves occurred."[295]

Graham Hodges and Alan Brown state that 42% of the 642 runaway slave advertisements included in their compilation occurred during the period from 1775 to 1783. The book states that "In the American South, tens of thousands of fugitives, followed armies, formed their own battalions, and practiced a guerrilla war against the slavocracy," and cite "3,000 former slaves and free blacks who left New York with the British."[296]

Lord Dunmore, Governor of Virginia, offered freedom to slaves of rebels, if those slaves defected to the British. During the Revolutionary War, "some five thousand Chesapeake slaves" defected to the British lines in response to Lord Dunmore's offer of freedom. Some of them joined a British "Ethiopian Regiment." The

294 "Prince Hall Freemasonry" at *freemasoninformation.com/what-is-freemasonry/family-of-freemasonry/prince-hall-freemasonry/*, accessed Sept. 29, 2020.

295 Kolchin, at 70-72.

296 G. Hodges and A. Brown ed., "PRETENDS TO BE FREE"—RUNAWAY SLAVE ADVERTISEMENTS FROM COLONIAL AND REVOLUTIONARY NEW YORK AND NEW JERSEY at xxxiii-xxxiv (Fordham Univ. Press 2019) ("Hodges and Brown").

"Peter Salem at the Battle of Bunker Hill, Boston, 1775", *Slavery Images: A Visual Record of the African Slave Trade and Slave Life in the Early African Diaspora,* accessed November 15, 2020,

American Revolutionary forces did not make the same offer of freedom for voluntary service without the consent of the slaves' masters.[297]

With such offers (another was made by British General Henry Clinton), many slaves left their servitudes during the Revolution. Following the War, the British transported approximately 3,000 slaves to Nova Scotia over American objections.[298]

The context in which the Virginia Governor issued the Dunmore Proclamation is revealing. In particular, the Dunmore Proclamation itself evidences Lord Dunmore's action from the ship to which he had been forced to retreat ("GIVEN under my Hand on board the ship WILLIAM, off NORPOLE, the 7th Day of NOVEMBER, in the SIXTEENTH Year of His MAJESTY'S Reign.")

297 Slavery in Maryland, at 7-8.
See also Russell and Hodges, "Chapter 3: Liberty and Constraint: The Limits of Revolution" in Berlin and Harris at 96 ("Russell and Hodges").

298 Russell and Hodges, at 96-97, 104-06.

According to the Gilder Lehrman Institute:[299]

> In April 1775, John Murray, the Earl of Dunmore and Virginia's royal governor, threatened to free slaves and reduce the capital, Williamsburg, to ashes if the colonists rebelled against British authority. In the months that followed, Dunmore's position became increasingly desperate. His troop strength fell to just 300 men and, on June 8, fearful of being attacked, he abandoned the Governor's Palace in Williamsburg for the safety of a British ship.

In other words, armed insurrection was already in progress, Lord Dunmore having been driven out of Virginia, prior to the issuance of the Dunmore Proclamation.

The Dunmore Proclamation took the following steps:[300]

- Declared "Martial Law"
- "[R]equire[d] every Person capable of bearing Arms, to [resort] to HIS MAJESTY'S STANDARD, or be looked upon as Traitors to His MAJESTY'S Crown and Government," subject to penalties including "forfeiture of Life, confiscation of Lands, &c. &c."
- "[D]eclare[d] all indentured Servants, Negroes, or others, *(appertaining to Rebels,)* free that are able and willing to bear Arms, they joining His MAJESTY'S Troops as soon as may be"[301]
- Directed "His MAJESTY'S Leige Subjects, to retain their [Qui?rents], or any other Taxes due or that may become due, in their own Custody, till such Time as Peace may be again restored"

Note that the Proclamation did not offer freedom to slaves owned by planters remaining loyal to the English government.

I have not seen substantial evidence that Lord Dunmore's Proclamation caused slaveholders to revolt. He issued the Proclamation after hostilities already were in progress. Instead of revolting, slaveholders could have retained their slaves by remaining loyal to England.

I also have not seen substantial evidence that events in England relating to slavery caused slaveholders to revolt. One such potential development was a judicial decision by Lord Mansfield in the Court of King's Bench in England, holding in *Somerset v. Stewart*[302] that the English common law did not provide for slavery. The decision, in 1772, denied claims by a purported slaveowner temporarily on a visit to England to sell and export to Jamaica a slave then in England. The slave had escaped, and been recaptured. Slavery did not exist legally in England. While slaveholders in British colonies were concerned about the decision, by the time of the decision, the Boston Massacre and additional unrest among colonialists in America had already occurred. In addition, Lord Mansfield's narrow decision did not speak to slavery in the colonies.

Could individual slaveholders have favored the Revolution as a means to preserve slavery? Theoretically, that is conceivable. Yet, I have not seen evidence of it and certainly not of mass slaveholder support of the Revolution for that reason.

---

299 "Lord Dunmore's Proclamation, 1775" at *www.gilderlehrman.org/history-resources/spotlight-primary-source/lord-dunmores-proclamation-1775*, accessed Oct. 7, 2020.

300 "Proclamation of Earl of Dunmore" at *www.pbs.org/wgbh/aia/part2/2h42t.html*, accessed Sept. 29, 2020.

301 Emphasis added.

302 Somerset v Stewart (1772) 98 ER 499.

NORTHWEST ORDINANCE

The Northwest Ordinance, which was adopted initially under America's Articles of Confederation, preceded the Constitution. The Ordinance strongly reflected America's contradictions regarding slavery—both a desire to inhibit slavery's spread and yet a desire to protect the financial interests of slaveholders.

America gained control over the Northwest Territory from Great Britain in the 1783 Treaty of Paris after the end of the Revolution.[303] The Territory lay South of Canada and the Great Lakes, West of the Appalachian Mountains, North of the Ohio River, and East of the upper Mississippi River. It encompassed the present states of Ohio, Indiana, Illinois, Michigan and Wisconsin.[304]

After various states ceased their claims on Western land dating to colonial times, the Northwest Ordinance was enacted in 1787 by the Congress of the American Confederation.[305]

The Ordinance resolved the slavery issue for the Territory. It was not long, however, until 1803, when America made the Louisiana Purchase from France, presenting a new extensive territory for argument about expansion of slavery. The admission of Texas to the Union in 1845 and the settlement of the Mexican-American War in 1848 added still more territory for bitter debates, and in Kansas, a war, between slavery and abolitionist forces.

Among other things, the Northwest Ordinance contemplated, and provided a process for, admission of new states in the Northwest Territory when their populations reached 60,000.[306] New states were to be equal in status to the older pre-existing states.[307] Pending admission of new states, the Territory was to be administered by the federal government and a Governor, Secretary, and three judges appointed by the federal government. A legislature was to be elected once a territorial population reached at least 5,000 free male land owners.[308] The Ordinance "established important precedents" for admission of additional future states."[309]

---

303 "Northwest Territory" at *www.encyclopedia.com/places/united-states-and-canada/miscellaneous-us-geography/northwest-territory,* accessed Sept. 30, 2020.

304 Northwest Ordinance of 1787: Before the Constitution, an Early Federal Law Impacted Slavery" at *www.thoughtco.com/northwest-ordinance-of-1787-4177006,* accessed Sept. 30, 2020; "The Northwest Ordinance of 1787" at *history.house.gov/Historical-Highlights/1700s/Northwest-Ordinance-1787/,* accessed Sept. 30, 2020.

305 "The Northwest Ordinance of 1787 and Its Effects" at *www.americanhistoryusa.com/northwest-ordinance-1787-effects,* accessed Sept. 30, 2020; "Northwest Ordinance of 1787: Before the Constitution, an Early Federal Law Impacted Slavery" at *www.thoughtco.com/northwest-ordinance-of-1787-4177006,* accessed Sept. 30, 2020; "The Northwest Ordinance of 1787" at *history.house.gov/Historical-Highlights/1700s/Northwest-Ordinance-1787/,* accessed Sept. 30, 2020.

306 "Text of the Northwest Ordinance" at *www.varsitytutors.com/earlyamerica/text-northwest-ordinance#:~:text=Text of The Northwest Ordinance. Be it ordained,in the opinion of Congress%2C make it expedient.,* accessed Sept. 30, 2020.

307 "Northwest Ordinances" at *www.britannica.com/event/Northwest-Ordinances,* accessed Sept. 30, 2020.

308 "Text of the Northwest Ordinance" at *www.varsitytutors.com/earlyamerica/text-northwest-ordinance#:~:text=Text of The Northwest Ordinance. Be it ordained,in the opinion of Congress%2C make it expedient.,* accessed Sept. 30, 2020; "Northwest Ordinance of 1787: Before the Constitution, an Early Federal Law Impacted Slavery" at *www.thoughtco.com/northwest-ordinance-of-1787-4177006,* accessed Sept. 30, 2020.

309 "Northwest Ordinance of 1787: Before the Constitution, an Early Federal Law Impacted Slavery" at *www.thoughtco.com/northwest-ordinance-of-1787-4177006* accessed Sept. 30, 2020.

Generally, the Ordinance provided for a bill of rights, voting rights for free men (requiring more than minimal land ownership), surveying and division of land into gridded townships and small lots, and public land sales and distribution, with fee simple ownership in perpetuity.[310]

The Northwest Ordinance contained two significant provisions relating to slavery. One prohibited slavery in the states formed from the Northwest Territory, thereby limiting the spread of slavery. Thomas Jefferson was a vocal advocate for the provision.[311]

The prohibition of slavery in the Northwest Ordinance stated, as follows:[312]

> There shall be neither slavery nor involuntary servitude in the said territory, otherwise than in the punishment of crimes whereof the party shall have been duly convicted … .

That language, pursuant to which the federal government regulated slavery, later was followed closely in the 13th Amendment, which stated:

> Neither slavery nor involuntary servitude, except as a punishment for crime whereof the party shall have been duly convicted, shall exist within the United States, or any place subject to their jurisdiction.

The slaveholding states agreed to the Ordinance's prohibition of slavery in the territory in order to prevent competition with respect to growing tobacco, a labor-intensive crop thought to require slave labor. Due to the then-existing majority of slave states, even with the new free states, there would have been a political balance of free and slave states.[313]

In addition, however, the Ordinance provided vital protection for slavery and the property interests of slaveholders by incorporating a fugitive slave clause. In that sense, the Northwest Ordinance served as a significant proslavery precedent, foreshadowing both the Constitution's provision recognizing and protecting the property interests of slaveholders and the later Fugitive Slave Laws.

The language of the Ordinance preserving the property interests of slaveholders by allowing them to recapture and reclaim their escaped slaves in the Territory, stated, as follows:[314]

> Provided, always, That any person escaping into the same, from whom labor or service is lawfully claimed in any one of the original States, such fugitive may be lawfully reclaimed and conveyed to the person claiming his or her labor or service as aforesaid.

---

310 "The Northwest Ordinance of 1787 and Its Effects" at *www.americanhistoryusa.com/northwest-ordinance-1787-effects,* accessed Sept. 30, 2020; "Northwest Ordinance of 1787: Before the Constitution, an Early Federal Law Impacted Slavery" at *www.thoughtco.com/northwest-ordinance-of-1787-4177006,* accessed Sept. 30, 2020; "Northwest Ordinances" at *www.britannica.com/event/Northwest-Ordinances,* accessed Sept. 30, 2020; "Text of the Northwest Ordinance" at *www.varsitytutors.com/earlyamerica/text-northwest-ordinance#:~:text=Text of The Northwest Ordinance. Be it ordained,in the opinion of Congress%2C make it expedient.,* accessed Sept. 30, 2020.

311 "Northwest Ordinance" at *www.tjheritage.org/blog/2017/8/4/northwest-ordinance-1#,* accessed Sept. 30, 2020.

312 "Text of the Northwest Ordinance" at *www.varsitytutors.com/earlyamerica/text-northwest-ordinance#:~:text=Text of The Northwest Ordinance. Be it ordained,in the opinion of Congress%2C make it expedient.,* accessed Sept. 30, 2020.

313 "The Northwest Ordinance of 1787 and Its Effects" at *www.americanhistoryusa.com/northwest-ordinance-1787-effects,* accessed Sept. 30, 2020.

314 "Text of the Northwest Ordinance" at *www.varsitytutors.com/earlyamerica/text-northwest-ordinance#:~:text=Text of The Northwest Ordinance. Be it ordained,in the opinion of Congress%2C make it expedient.,* accessed Sept. 30, 2020.

That language placed the federal government squarely on record as defending existing slavery only a decade after the Declaration of Independence. The language was echoed, but strengthened, in the Constitution, as follows:

> No Person held to Service or Labour in one State, under the Laws thereof, escaping into another, shall, in Consequence of any Law or Regulation therein, be discharged from such Service or Labour, But shall be delivered up on Claim of the Party to whom such Service or Labour may be due.

The language of the Northwest Ordinance and the Constitution thereby formed a foundation for the Fugitive Slave Law of 1793 and the extremely oppressive Fugitive Slave Law of 1850.

After the Constitution was ratified, the Northwest Ordinance was reaffirmed in 1789 by the first Congress.[315]

In February 1860, Abraham Lincoln, who opposed the extension of slavery to America's new territories, cited the Northwest Ordinance as demonstrating the Founding Fathers' support for a federal government role in regulating slavery. Mr. Lincoln also noted the unanimous action of the first Congress following the ratification of the Constitution and President George Washington's signing of the legislation.[316]

America's contradictions regarding slavery continued until the Civil War, with an abolitionist movement that grew in strength and a slave society determined to protect, and persist in, its way of life at any cost.

---

315 "Northwest Ordinance" at *quaqua.org/northwest.htm#:~:text=Northwest Ordinance The Northwest Ordinancewas enacted in 1787%2C,Michigan%2C and other portions of the upper Midwest.*, accessed Sept. 30, 2020.

316 "Northwest Ordinance of 1787: Before the Constitution, an Early Federal Law Impacted Slavery" at *www.thoughtco.com/northwest-ordinance-of-1787-4177006*, accessed Sept. 30, 2020.

THE CONSTITUTION CONTEMPLATED AND PROTECTED SLAVERY

The Declaration of Independence was an idealistic document that served, over time, a substantial inspirational role for the abolitionist movement.

The United States Constitution was a functional document creating the details of America's representative form of government. The Constitution, as amended by its first ten Amendments—the Bill of Rights—is rightly regarded as a document designed to provide freedom to Americans and to protect Americans from the tyranny of despots, such as the Duke of York and later English monarchs.[317]

That was accomplished in part through a system of checks and balances to divide power so as to prevent excessive dominance by a single branch of government. The Bill of Rights was intended to guarantee critical freedoms.

In practice, however, the benefits of the Constitution, including the Bill of Rights, did not extend to African-Americans or to abolitionists advocating an end to slavery.

Dr. Hilary Beckles states that:[318]

> Jefferson's references to the right to life and liberty in the American Constitution were not meant to apply to Africans either in the public or in the private sphere. However, although such thinking did not find its way into Jefferson's vision for the enslaved Africans that made up a significant proportion of the new nation, the fear of insurrection on the part of the 700,000 black slaves in the mainland colonies, together with the discourse on human rights that was fuelling the American revolutionary war, combined to create political problems for the emerging nation, with both the issue of the slave trade and that of slavery demanding public discussion.

Additionally, the slave society simply ignored—without consequences—the Bill of Rights and freedoms it supposedly guaranteed. For decades, the government treated the Bill of Rights as inapplicable to the states. Thus, slave states routinely denied the right of free speech, the right of a free press, freedom of religion, the right to trial by jury, the right to due process, and the prohibition of cruel and unusual punishment.[319]

The Constitution protected the interests of slaveholders until the 13th Amendment prohibited slavery. The Constitution explicitly contemplated slavery in certain provisions.

Prior to the election of 1860, the Civil War, and the ratification of the post-Civil War constitutional amendments, slavery was a central defining force in America. This was facilitated considerably by key constitutional provisions giving slave states out-sized representation in Congress and in the presidential electoral college, and in turn, in the Supreme Court.

Interestingly, apart from the 13th Amendment prohibiting slavery, the Constitution never uses the words "slave" or "slavery." Further, when the Constitution otherwise refers to slaves, it uses the word "person," rather than the words "slave" or "property." Notice the subtle wordsmithing used.

---

317 See *"Chapter Three: The Duke of York Promotes Slavery—The 'Duke's Laws' and His Opposition to Representative Government."*

318 Beckles, at 182.

319 See *"Chapter Four: American Slavery in Practice—The Slave Society's War on Abolitionists."*

Until the election of 1860, the predominant view was that the Constitution was a proslavery document, in sharp contrast to the emphases in the Declaration of Independence upon freedom and equality of "all men." Not only Southern slaveholders held this view, but also key abolitionists associated with William Lloyd Garrison.

Another branch of abolitionism, associated with Gerrit Smith, Frederick Douglass (after he split with the Garrisonians), the Liberty Party (formed in 1839) and later the Free Soil Party and the Radical Abolitionists, and others situated especially in up-state New York argued that the Constitution could be viewed as an antislavery document. Despite specific provisions contemplating slavery, they believed the Constitution could provide a basis for freeing the slaves by antislavery public officials. Dr. James Oakes argues that there were, in effect, two Constitutions based upon these conflicting interpretations, although the document was the same. He outlines how President Lincoln used antislavery views of the Constitution in freeing the slaves not only through the Emancipation Proclamation, but also through military action protecting slaves escaping to Union lines.[320]

A NATION DIVIDED FROM THE BEGINNING

"The question of slavery was the great difficulty in the way of the formation of the Constitution. While the subordination and the political and social inequality of the African race was fully conceded by all, it was plainly apparent that slavery would soon disappear from what are now the non-slave-holding States of the original thirteen. The opposition to slavery was then, as now, general in those States and the Constitution was made with direct reference to that fact."

"Georgia Declaration of Causes for Secession" at *www.battlefields.org/learn/articles/declarations-causes#georgia,* accessed Sept. 30, 2020

One constitutional provision protected the property interests of slaveowners to their escaped slaves, and another provided for the continued importation for 20 years of slaves by means of the international slave trade ("viewed as deplorable even by many defenders of slavery"[321]). A third provision—the Three-Fifths Compromise—afforded slave states a greater degree of representation in Congress and in Presidential elections than the slave states would have had solely on the basis of their free white voting populations. In effect, the Three-Fifths Compromise gave the slave states 60 percent credit for their nonvoting slave populations. Another clause enabled federal military forces to battle slave insurrections.

The following are among the constitutional provisions recognizing slavery in America—

- Return of fugitive slaves to their owners (in effect until the adoption of the 13th Amendment)—

> No Person held to Service or Labour in one State, under the Laws thereof, escaping into another, shall, in Consequence of any Law or Regulation therein, be discharged from such Service or Labour, But shall be delivered up on Claim of the Party to whom such Service or Labour may be due.

Article IV, Section II, Clause 3

The Constitution thereby provided a foundation for the Fugitive Slave Laws of 1793 and 1850. Abolitionists argued in vain that the fugitives deserved due process under the Constitution. Under the 1850 Law, the

320 J. Oakes, THE CROOKED PATH TO ABOLITION: ABRAHAM LINCOLN AND THE ANTISLAVERY CONSTITUTION (New York: W.W. Norton and Company, 2021).

321 Kolchin, at 79.

federal government prohibited citizens in non-slave states from assisting fugitive slaves, and even required those citizens to assist in capturing fugitives.

- Continued importation of slaves by means of the international slave trade for 20 years—

> The Migration or Importation of such Persons as any of the States now existing shall think proper to admit, shall not be prohibited by the Congress prior to the Year one thousand eight hundred and eight, but a tax or duty may be imposed on such Importation, not exceeding ten dollars for each Person.
>
> **Article I, Section IX, Clause 1**

Dr. Donald Sweig explains the limits of this provision:[322]

> The Constitution, reflecting the needs and desires of Carolina and Georgia, prohibited interference with the importation of slaves by the federal congress until 1808, a period of 20 years. The need for such a prohibition is ample testimony of the inclination of many of the founding fathers to restrict the slave trade at the earliest possible date.
>
> Indeed, George Mason, of Fairfax County, opposed the ratification of the Constitution by Virginia because (among other issues) it allowed this "infamous traffic" to continue for another 20 years. The importation of blacks into the United States barely survived the 20-year protection provided by the Constitution. On March 2, 1807, Congress prohibited further importation of slaves after Jan. 1, 1808.

CONSTITUTIONAL PROVISIONS
PROTECTING SLAVERY

- Fugitive Slave Clause
- Three-Fifths Compromise
- Delay in Prohibition of International Slave Trade
- Insurrection Clause

Thomas R.R. Cobb, a proslavery advocate provides the following perspective regarding the delay in the ban upon the international slave trade until 1808:[323]

> Massachusetts, whose merchants were engaged in the slave-trade, joined with Georgia and South Carolina in demanding a few more years ere the final prohibition. The year 1808 was agreed upon.

Dr. Beckles takes a more conciliatory view, stating that "it was the Americans, once they had achieved their independence from Britain, who took the lead in the abolition of the transatlantic slave trade."[324]

Nevertheless, the 20-year protraction of the international slave trade led to a sharp increase in the importation of slaves ("more slaves entered the United States between 1787 and 1807 than during any other two decades in history"[325]).

322 Sweig, "Alexandria to New Orleans: The Human Tragedy of the Interstate Slave Trade, Part I" (The Connection Newspapers Online, Oct. 1, 2014) at *www.connectionnewspapers.com/news/2014/oct/01 /alexandria-new-orleans-human-tragedy-interstate-sl/*, accessed Sept. 30, 2020.

323 Cobb Vol I, at cliii. Footnotes omitted.

324 Cobb Vol I, at 183-84.

325 Kolchin, at 79

In the meantime, certain states, such as Virginia in 1778, enacted legislation prohibiting importation of slaves into the State.[326] Maryland did so in 1774.[327]

By silence, the Constitution also allowed the internal slave trade to persist unabated.[328]

► *Three-Fifths Compromise regarding representation in Congress (and therefore also apportioning electoral votes for President)—*

> Representatives and direct taxes shall be apportioned among the several Representatives and direct taxes shall be apportioned among the several states which may be included within this union, according to their respective numbers, which shall be determined by adding to the whole number of free persons, including those bound to service for a term of years, and excluding Indians not taxed, three-fifths of all other persons.
>
> **Article I, Section 2, clause 3**

The exaggerated political power that the slave society received through the Three-Fifths Compromise, in combination with the electoral college, enabled the slave society, by using its larger-than-life influence, to dominate America's politics not only at the state level, but also at the federal level. The slave society was able to elect an excessive number of representatives in Congress and received the benefit of an excessive number of state electors in Presidential elections. Further, through presidential judicial nominations and congressional judicial confirmations, the slave society also was able to dominate the Supreme Court. That led to proslavery judicial rulings.[329] Although slaves could not vote, the slave society received an outsized representation, based on 60 percent of the number of slaves in each state, lasting until after the Civil War. The more slaves owned in the slave states, the greater those states' political influence grew. Thus, on the backs of nonvoting slaves the slave society gained exaggerated power.

In Abraham Lincoln's speech in Peoria, Illinois, during the Lincoln-Douglass debates, Lincoln highlighted the Three-Fifths Compromise as unfair to Northern voters:[330]

> [T]here are constitutional relations between the slave and free States, which are degrading to the latter. We are under legal obligations to catch and return their runaway slaves to them—a sort of dirty, disagreeable job, which I believe, as a general rule the slave-holders will not perform for one another. Then again, in the control of the government—the management of the partnership affairs—they have greatly the advantage of us. By the constitution, each State has two Senators—each has a number of Representatives; in proportion to the number of its people—and each has a number of presidential electors, equal to the whole number of its Senators and Representatives together. But in ascertaining the number of the people, for this purpose, five slaves are counted as being equal to three whites. The slaves do not vote; they are only counted and so used, as to swell the influence of the white people's votes. The practical effect of this is more aptly shown by a comparison of the States of South Carolina and Maine. South Carolina has six representatives, and so has Maine; South Carolina has eight presidential

326 Kolchin, at 79.

327 Slavery in Maryland, at 6.

328 See *"Chapter Four: American Slavery in Practice— The Internal Slave Trade: Coffles and Auctions."*

329 See "*—George Washington, Thomas Jefferson, John Adams, and Other Founding Fathers—Supreme Court Justices*" below.

330 "Lincoln's Peoria Speech, October 16, 1854," at *www.nps.gov/liho/learn/historyculture/peoriaspeech.htm*, accessed Oct. 13, 2021.

> electors, and so has Maine. This is precise equality so far; and, of course they are equal in Senators, each having two. Thus in the control of the government, the two States are equals precisely. But how are they in the number of their white people? Maine has 581,813—while South Carolina has 274,567. Maine has twice as many as South Carolina, and 32,679 over. Thus each white man in South Carolina is more than the double of any man in Maine. This is all because South Carolina, besides her free people, has 384,984 slaves. The South Carolinian has precisely the same advantage over the white man in every other free State, as well as in Maine. He is more than the double of any one of us in this crowd. The same advantage, but not to the same extent, is held by all the citizens of the slave States, over those of the free; and it is an absolute truth, without an exception, that there is no voter in any slave State, but who has more legal power in the government, than any voter in any free State. There is no instance of exact equality; and the disadvantage is against us the whole chapter through. This principle, in the aggregate, gives the slave States, in the present Congress, twenty additional representatives… .

The Compromise was proposed by James Madison of Virginia specifically for the purpose of using nonvoting slaves to enhance the political power of the slave holding states:[331]

> Madison knew that the North would outnumber the South, despite there being more than half a million slaves in the South who were their economic vitality, but could not vote. His proposition for the Electoral College included the "three-fifths compromise," where black people could be counted as three-fifths of a person, instead of a whole. This clause garnered the state 12 out of 91 electoral votes, more than a quarter of what a president needed to win.

Thus, as occurs with the electoral college today, for decades America was effectively governed under the Constitution by unrepresentative governments. Only when the majority finally was sufficiently large and assertive, did America respond to the majority view. At that point, in its rage, the stubborn slave society created conditions for enormous destruction.

Illustrating the slave society's inflated power, the Three-Fifths Compromise and the electoral college could be, and was at times, decisive in the election of presidents. For example:[332]

> The effects of the 3/5 Compromise became evident at election time. In the election of 1800, Thomas Jefferson defeated John Adams by only 7 electoral votes. The election was clearly divided by the slavery issue. The north had predominantly gone with Adams, while the South sided with Jefferson. As the votes were counted, Northern politicians quickly realized that without the 3/5 Compromise, Jefferson would have [been] defeated. The fact that slaves had been counted as part of the South's representation had given Jefferson the victory. Later elections would have the same results. The election[s] of James Madison and Martin Van Buren would all be influenced by the 3/5 Compromise.

► *Insurrection clause*

> [The Congress shall have Power] [t]o provide for calling forth the Militia to execute the Laws of the Union, suppress Insurrections and repel Invasions
>
> **Article I, Section 8, Clause 15**

---

331 Kelkar, "Electoral College is 'vestige' of slavery, say some Constitutional scholars" (Nov. 6, 2016), at *www.pbs.org/newshour/politics/electoral-college-slavery-constitution,* accessed Sept. 30, 2020.

332 "Presidential Elections and the 3/5 Compromise" at *americanrevolutionblog.blogspot.com/2007/11/presidential-elections-and-35.html?m=1,* accessed Sept. 30, 2020.

The insurrection clause was used by the federal government to suppress slave rebellions, such as Nat Turner's rebellion in 1831 in Virginia and Charles Deslondes' rebellion in 1811 in Louisiana. The military also attacked fugitive slaves and truly free blacks in Spanish Florida. On the other hand, Lincoln found the clause useful in defeating the Confederacy.

Thus, the drafters of the Constitution were quite concerned about slavery issues, took slavery explicitly into account, and chose deliberately to protect it in the Constitution as an acknowledged American institution.

Despite all its short-comings, Frederick Douglass charitably expressed a forbearing antislavery view of the Constitution, stating in his famous speech, What to the Slave Is the Fourth of July?:

> Fellow-citizens! there is no matter in respect to which, the people of the North have allowed themselves to be so ruinously imposed upon, as that of the pro-slavery character of the Constitution. In that instrument I hold there is neither warrant, license, nor sanction of the hateful thing; but, interpreted as it ought to be interpreted, the Constitution is a GLORIOUS LIBERTY DOCUMENT. Read its preamble, consider its purposes. Is slavery among them? Is it at the gateway? or is it in the temple? It is neither.

GEORGE WASHINGTON, THOMAS JEFFERSON, AND OTHER FOUNDING FATHERS

Founding Fathers' Slavery Contradictions

My schools did not teach me that George Washington, Thomas Jefferson, Patrick Henry, James Madison and other of America's Founding Fathers were particularly large slaveowners. The sheer numbers of slaves they owned—often hundreds—were a revelation.

My schools taught only how those men were fervent about freedom, and how they risked their lives to fight for it. My schools did not teach how heroic slaves also risked their lives to fight for their own freedom and to escape slavery over the unwavering, and often violent, opposition of the slave society, the federal government, and state governments.

Presidents and Other Founding Fathers

Dr. Alan Singer states that Thomas Jefferson, George Washington and the four New Yorkers who signed the Declaration of Independence all owned slaves.[333]

Washington became a slaveholder at the age of eleven, when he inherited ten slaves from his father.[334] "Four of the country's first five presidents owned enslaved Africans … ."[335] Dr. Peter Kolchin states that, beginning with George Washington, eight of America's first 12 Presidents (for 49 of the first 61 years of America's history) were slaveowners.[336]

Other early Presidents who owned slaves were: James Madison (the fourth President, 100); James Monroe (the fifth President, 75 slaves); Andrew Jackson, the seventh President, 200 slaves).[337]

Others include:

- Martin Van Buren (eighth President, one slave)
- William Henry Harrison (ninth President, 11 slaves)
- John Tyler (tenth President, 70 slaves)
- James K. Polk (eleventh president, 25 slaves)
- Zachary Taylor (twelfth President, 150 slaves)

Underscoring the perseverance of slavery late into the eighteenth century, Andrew Johnson (seventeenth President), who became President when Abraham Lincoln was assassinated, had owned a reported eight

333 Singer, at 50.

334 "Jubilo! The Emancipation Century" at *jubiloemancipationcentury.wordpress.com/2013/02/18/list-of-slave-holding-presidents/*, accessed Oct. 1, 2020 ("Jubilo").

335 Singer, at 69.

336 Kolchin, at 3; "The Slaves Who Built Washington DC" at *zmblackhistorymonth2012.blogspot.com/2012/02/slaves-who-built-washington-dc.html*, accessed Oct. 1, 2020.

337 Reported number of slaves owned by U.S. presidents who served from 1789 to 1877 (throughout their lifetimes)" at *www.statista.com/statistics/1121963/slaves-owned-by-us-presidents/*, accessed Oct. 1, 2020.

slaves prior to his political life; President Ulysses S. Grant (eighteenth President), who became President in 1869 after the Civil War and after ratification of the 13th Amendment, had inherited a slave before he was President, but had freed the slave after two years.[338] James Buchanan (fifteenth President) is reported to have purchased two slaves, but to have converted their status to indentured servitude for terms of years.[339]

GIVE US LIBERTY

"Give us liberty or give us death!"

Harriet Tubman cited in K. Larson, Bound for the Promised Land—Harriet Tubman, Portrait of an American Hero at 181 (Ballantine Books, NY, 2003), quoting the Troy, NY, Daily News

Jefferson and Washington each owned hundreds of slaves, as visitors learn upon touring Mount Vernon and Monticello. Thomas Jefferson, America's third President, owned an estimated 600 slaves. George Washington, the first, owned more than 300 slaves (most actually owned by his wife, Martha, as dower slaves from an earlier marriage).[340]

Dr. Peter Kolchin also cites Patrick Henry ("Give me liberty or give me death") as "among the largest slave owners of [the] day."[341]

"WE HAVE THE WOLF BY THE EAR"

"I can say with conscious truth that there is not a man on earth who would sacrifice more than I would, to relieve us from this heavy reproach, in any practicable way. (sic) the cession of that kind of property, for it is so misnamed, is a bagatelle which would not cost me a second thought, if, in that way, a general emancipation and expatriation could be effected: and, gradually, and with due sacrifices, I think it might be. (sic) but, as it is, we have the wolf by the ear, and we can neither hold him, nor safely let him go. Justice is in one scale, and self-preservation in the other."

"Founders Online; Letter from Thomas Jefferson to John Holmes, 22, April 1820" at *founders.archives.gov/documents/Jefferson/03-15-02-0518,* accessed Aug. 15, 2020

Individual Founding Fathers expressed doubts regarding slavery, but actively practiced slavery and defended it during their lives.

An example is action taken by Thomas Jefferson hostile to escaped slaves in Spanish Florida. Spain had maintained a policy in its Florida colony welcoming escaped slaves as full and free citizens. The policy remained in effect until 1790, when Jefferson, as Secretary of State, negotiated its termination, calling it "essential" to good relations between Spain and America.[342]

Yet, Spanish Florida and its truly free black citizens remained important targets. President James Madison and Secretary of State, later President, James Monroe, "secretly sanctioned" the illegal and secret Patriot War of 1812 (which was *not* the War of 1812 occurring at the same time), in which U.S. Army troops supported slaveholders from Georgia, Florida, and Carolina, and

338 "Reported number of slaves owned by U.S. presidents who served from 1789 to 1877 (throughout their lifetimes)" at *www.statista.com/statistics/1121963/slaves-owned-by-us-presidents/,* accessed Oct. 1, 2020; Jubilo; "Slavery at Whitehaven" at *www.nps.gov/articles/slavery-at-white-haven.htm,* accessed Oct. 1, 2020.

339 Jubilo.

340 "Ten Facts About Martha Washington" at *www.mountvernon.org/george-washington/martha-washington/ten-facts-about-martha-washington/,* accessed Oct. 3, 2020.

341 Kolchin, at 70.

342 Landers, at 79.

their sympathizers, in attacking communities of free Africans, as well as Native Americans and the Spanish government, in Spanish Florida.[343]

While taking action inimical to slaves, Thomas Jefferson also expressed sympathy. In 1791, Jefferson engaged in an exchange of correspondence with Benjamin Banneker, a "free" African-American scientist and publisher of a widely-used almanac. In the correspondence, Mr. Jefferson expressed a desire at least to improve the slaves' conditions.[344]

Notably, John Adams, a key signatory of the Declaration of Independence and America's second President, did not own any slaves:[345]

> Did John Adams own slaves? No, and not only because of his family's moderate wealth. Adams was morally opposed to slavery and refused to employ slaves. His wife, Abigail Adams, went so far as to employ free blacks for labor as opposed to the two domestic slaves owned by her father.

As noted earlier, Mr. Adams opposed Thomas Jefferson in the presidential election in 1801. Mr. Adams lost by only seven electoral votes in an election in which slavery was an issue. The election was decided in Mr. Jefferson's favor by virtue of the Three-Fifths Compromise. Nonvoting slaves "counted as part of the South's representation had given Jefferson the victory."[346]

Similarly, John Quincy Adams, John Adams' son and the sixth President, did not own slaves and opposed slavery. He was, however, a member of a larger family through marriage with individuals who owned slaves. Both Adams also moved in social circles tolerant of slavery.[347]

Alexander Hamilton has a reputation for opposing slavery. One analysis states that Hamilton "abhorred slavery and at a few points in his life worked to help limit it. But any moral objections he held were tempered by his social and political ambitions. Throughout his life, like so many leaders of the time, he allowed or used slavery to advance his fortunes—both indirectly and through compromises he chose to make."[348] A more recent analysis based upon Hamilton's cash books and correspondence concludes that he owned a small number of domestic slaves, and assisted legal clients and family members in buying and selling slaves.[349]

---

343 Cusick, at 221.

344 "B. Banneker, letter dated Aug. 19, 1791, to Thomas Jefferson," available at *founders.archives.gov/documents/Jefferson/01-22-02-0049*, accessed Oct. 1, 2020; "Benjamin Banneker Biography" at *www.biography.com/scientist/benjamin-banneker*, accessed Oct. 1, 2020; "Thomas Jefferson, letter dated Aug. 30, 1791, to Benjamin Banneker" at *www.loc.gov/exhibits/jefferson/79.html*, accessed Oct. 1, 2020.

345 "John Adams and Slavery" at *www.johnadamsinfo.com/john-adams-and-slavery/89/*, accessed Oct. 1, 2020.

346 "Presidential Elections and the 3/5 Compromise" at *americanrevolutionblog.blogspot.com/2007/11/presidential-elections-and-35.html?m=1*, accessed Oct. 1, 2020.
See also "Electoral College is 'vestige' of slavery, say some Constitutional scholars" (Nov. 6, 2016), at *www.pbs.org/newshour/politics/electoral-college-slavery-constitution*, accessed Oct. 1, 2020.

347 Chervinsky and Hopkins, "The Enslaved Household of President John Quincy Adams" at *www.whitehousehistory.org/the-enslaved-household-of-john-quincy-adams*, accessed Oct. 1, 2020.

348 Klein, "Alexander Hamilton's Complicated Relationship to Slavery" at *www.history.com/news/alexander-hamilton-slavery-facts*, accessed Oct. 1, 2020.

349 Serfilippi, "'As Odious and Immoral a Thing': Alexander Hamilton's Hidden History as an Enslaver" (Schuyler Mansion State Historic Site, 2020) at *parks.ny.gov/documents/historic-sites/SchuylerMansionAlexanderHamiltonsHiddenHistoryasanEnslaver.pdf*, accessed Nov. 13, 2020.

In any event, Mr. Hamilton with John Jay, who was "one of the most prominent political figures of early America,"[350] "join[ed] together in establishing the New York Manumission Society," which advocated abolition, manumissions by slaveholders, founded the African Free School (which eventually had 800 students on seven campuses), and sponsored other programs easing the path for slaves and "free" African-Americans.[351]

Francis Scott Key, who wrote the Star Spangled Banner, presents contradictions representative of the time. On one hand, Mr. Key, a lawyer, represented successfully in judicial proceedings slaves seeking freedom as descendants of a white woman. Yet, he also owned slaves. In addition, as U.S. Attorney in Washington, DC, in 1836, years after he wrote the national anthem, Mr. Key prosecuted "a Northern bookseller, for 'seditiously' attempting to 'vilify' the national government simply by possessing abolitionist literature that he might distribute and that could encourage slaves to 'violence and rebellion.' Key hoped to show … 'that all abolitionist words were patently dangerous.'" Fortunately, the all-white jury disagreed.[352]

Contradictions

The slave-holding status of specific Founding Fathers, taken by itself, fails to describe their inconsistent opinions regarding slavery. Individual Founding Fathers had serious reservations about it, and were far advanced in their thinking in terms of their time when slavery was accepted not only throughout America, but widely throughout the New World.

For example, Benjamin Franklin owned slaves for a time, and "viewed [African-Americans] as inferior to white Europeans, as it was believed they could not be educated." After visiting a school for African-American children, however, he changed his mind. "In 1787 Franklin became the President of the Philadelphia Society for the Relief of Free Negroes Unlawfully Held in Bondage, often referred as the Abolition Society."[353]

Another Founding Father, George Mason of Virginia, exemplifies conflicts among the Founding Fathers. Although a Virginia delegate to the Constitutional Convention and regarded as author of specific provisions, Mr. Mason "was active in the convention for months before deciding that he could not sign same. He cited the lack of a bill of rights most prominently in his *Objections,* but also wanted an immediate end to the slave trade … ." At the same time, Mr. Mason "owned the second largest number of slaves in Northern Virginia."[354]

The Declaration of Independence and the Revolution did not end slavery, but demonstrated the inconsistencies slavery occasioned in the revolutionary context of a war for freedom. Dr. Edgar McManus states that:[355]

---

350 Rael, at 115.

351 Russell and Hodges, at 107, Rael, at 119, 121.

352 Bordewich, Review of W. Thomas, WHEN SLAVES HAD THEIR DAY IN COURT (Yale Univ. Press, 2020) at C7 (Wall St. J., Nov. 14, 2020) at *www.wsj.com/articles/a-question-of-freedom-review-slavery-on-trial-11605282554,* accessed Nov. 14, 2020.

353 "Slavery and the Abolition Society" at *www.benjamin-franklin-history.org/slavery-abolition-society,* accessed Oct. 1, 2020.

354 "George Mason and Slavery" at *gmufourthestate.com/2016/10/24/george-mason-and-slavery/,* accessed Oct. 1, 2020; Schwartz, "George Mason: Forgotten Founder, He Conceived the Bill of Rights" at *www.smithsonianmag.com/history/george-mason-forgotten-founder-he-conceived-the-bill-of-rights-64408583/,* accessed Oct. 1, 2020.

355 McManus, Slavery in New York, at 152.

> The Revolution intensified the opposition to slavery. ... So general was the ideological reaction that slavery was condemned by almost all the leaders of the Revolution. Washington, Jefferson, and Madison, slaveholders all, made statements supporting the principle of gradual abolition.

There also were counter-pressures. Aside from the loss of wealth that freedom for slaves would mean for influential slaveholders, America's leadership did not view freeing millions of slaves as a simple undertaking. There were concerns about how so many uneducated slaves could provide for themselves. White workers were concerned about the significant wage competition. Further, whites intensely feared African-Americans, and had concerns about theft, property damage, and personal safety based upon actual experience with behaviors by slaves often starving and deprived, especially when seeking to escape.[356]

So, we can view Thomas Jefferson, George Washington and other of America's founders certainly as less than perfect advocates of principles of freedom. Their sentiments for and against slavery were widely accepted at the time, but not universally. In his younger days, Mr. Jefferson opposed slavery on moral and practical grounds, and believed that slavery would gradually become extinct. As he observed America's growing slave society in his later years, Mr. Jefferson was less convinced of slavery's demise.[357]

The Slave Society's Persistence

So, slavery persisted in America. Apart from a growing number of Northern states that enacted abolition laws, slavery also expanded rapidly and substantially, especially after invention of the cotton gin.[358] Dr. Peter Kolchin states that "abolitionists were (at least during the 1830s and early 1840s) so lacking in influence that they posed little substantive threat to Southern interests."[359] He states that the result was that, by the time of the Civil War,

> far more slaves resided in the Southern states than in all the other remaining slave societies combined (Brazil, Cuba, Puerto Rico) and—together with Russian serfdom—Southern slavery had come to symbolize for much of the Western world a retrograde system resistant to change.

Dr. Kolchin describes the adamant resistance and power of the slave society:[360]

> Nowhere else did the defense of slavery turn into a veritable pro-slavery crusade, as it did in the United States; nowhere else did slave owners refuse to accept emancipation and go to war to preserve their interests.

Thus, powerful political and social issues delayed abolition. In instances when abolition finally did occur in Northern states, it often came in the form of prohibiting slavery for future children of slaves (and then only after they reached adulthood). It commonly did not mean freedom for existing slaves.

The Founding Fathers' lofty pronouncements in the Declaration of Independence about the rights to "Life, Liberty and the Pursuit of Happiness" set a tone for America that, over the next more than half century, provided encouragement to abolitionists. Those pronouncements, however, did not end, or even impede, slavery.

---

356 Kolchin, at 181.

357 Kolchin, at 77, 88.

358 Kolchin, at 4, 23.

359 Kolchin, at 190.

360 Kolchin, at 197.

Meanwhile, many abolitionists and others in the North retained and expressed their own, at times blatant, racist ideas regarding African-Americans. For example, Douglas Harper states that, when Oberlin College in Ohio took the lead in integrating in the 1830s by admitting a small number of African-Americans, viewed as a "radical" step at the time, the "chief proponent" of the integration plan "hastened to assure [students, faculty, and town residents] that he had no intention to let the place 'full up with filthy stupid negroes[.]'" Harper adds that: "The board of trustees tried to table the plan, but by now the abolitionists were aroused and would accept no retreat. In the end, in 1835, the trustees punted the decision to the faculty, which was assured of allowing black students to attend the school."[361]

Moreover, slavery in the South became a way of life. Resistance to its end was stronger than ever by the time of the Civil War.[362] It required the Civil War, with its one-and-a-half million casualties and hundreds of thousands of deaths, to end slavery. Even that did not complete the task, since even after the War, Union states continued to have slaves until the ratification of the 13th Amendment finally occurred.

Thomas Jefferson

Like other Founding Fathers, Thomas Jefferson was a man of contradictions. Dr. Peter Kolchin describes the evolution of Thomas Jefferson's views from a perspective that slavery was wrong and harmful to whites, as well as to slaves, to a resigned belief that it could not be extinguished early, mixed with concerns for providing for and protecting the slaves, and later greater resigned acceptance that slavery would continue.[363]

Dr. Kolchin states:[364]

> Jefferson never renounced his belief that slavery was wrong, but as he aged he abandoned his youthful conviction that it could be readily abolished.

Mr. Jefferson also expressed negative views regarding African-Americans. Dr. Alan Singer states that "In 1782, Thomas Jefferson argued that the 'real distinctions which nature has made' between the races would prevent Whites and Blacks from ever living together in a state of equality."[365]

Indeed, Mr. Jefferson did make such statements. They are expressed in his NOTES ON THE STATE OF VIRGINIA, which portrays Mr. Jefferson naively (especially in today's terms) struggling to understand African-Americans and the relationship between whites and African-Americans. His writings also reflect concerns about the welfare of slaves.

In addition, Mr. Jefferson described at length his generalized view of African-American characteristics that, in today's terms, are quite racist. Those are reflected in the text boxes at the end of this section.[366]

Yet, despite Mr. Jefferson's negative attitudes toward African-Americans, he and Sally Hemings, one of his slaves, had a lengthy intimate relationship after Mr. Jefferson's wife died. As a result, he had several African-American children. A tour of Monticello discloses that Ms. Hemings, with her and Mr. Jefferson's children (who legally were Mr. Jefferson's slaves), lived in dismal slave quarters, not in the nearby mansion.

---

361 Harper, "Slavery in the North," at *slavenorth.com/ohio.htm.*

362 Kolchin, at 185-86.

363 Kolchin, at 88-89.

364 Kolchin, at 88.

365 Singer, at 71. Citation omitted.

366 T. Jefferson, NOTES ON THE STATE OF VIRGINIA at 149-52 (J.W. Randolph, 1853), available from the Library of Congress at *www.hathitrust.org/digital_library* ("Jefferson"). Footnotes omitted.

Strangely, as a young woman, Ms. Hemings willingly agreed to be a slave to Mr. Jefferson on terms she negotiated:[367]

> Unlike countless enslaved women, Sally Hemings was able to negotiate with her owner. In Paris, where she was free, the 16-year-old agreed to return to enslavement at Monticello in exchange for "extraordinary privileges" for herself and freedom for her unborn children. Over the next 32 years Hemings raised four children—Beverly, Harriet, Madison, and Eston—and prepared them for their eventual emancipation. She did not negotiate for, or ever receive, legal freedom in Virginia.

Mr. Jefferson also favored colonization for freed slaves based on a belief that an irreconcilable racial divide could not result in friendly relations, given white prejudice and African-Americans' hostile feelings after their abuse in slavery. In that connection, he stated:[368]

> It will probably be asked, Why not retain and incorporate the blacks into the State, and thus save the expense of supplying, by importation of white settlers, the vacancies they will leave? Deep-rooted prejudices entertained by the whites; ten thousand recollections by the blacks of the injuries they have sustained; new provocations; the real distinctions which Nature has made; and many other circumstances, will divide us into parties, and produce convulsions, which will probably never end but in the extermination of the one or the other race.

Mr. Jefferson also expressed considerable concern regarding the condition of slaves and their treatment. In 1814, Mr. Jefferson stated in a letter to Edward Coles, in which Mr. Jefferson advocated a gradual emancipation approach similar to the approach used in New York and certain other states:[369]

> the love of justice & the love of country plead equally the cause of these people, and it is a mortal reproach to us that they should have pleaded it so long in vain, and should have produced not a single effort, nay I fear not much serious willingness to relieve them & ourselves from our present condition of moral and political reprobation.

According to Dr. Peter Kolchin, Thomas Jefferson did not free his slaves during his lifetime or "upon his death."[370] William Goodell states, however, that Mr. Jefferson freed five ("his own enslaved offspring"), out of his hundreds of slaves, subject to the approval of the Virginia legislature, as required by State law.[371]

---

367 "The Life of Sally Hemings" at *www.monticello.org/sallyhemings/*, accessed Oct. 2. 2020.

368 Jefferson, at 149.

369 "Letter dated Aug. 25, 1814, from Thomas Jefferson to Edward Coles" available at *www.encyclopediavirginia.org/Letter_from_Thomas_Jefferson_to_Edward_Coles_August_25_1814.*

370 Kolchin, at 89.

371 Goodell, at 276, 375. Emphasis in original.

THOMAS JEFFERSON ON AFRICAN-AMERICANS

"It will be right to make great allowances for the difference of condition, of education, of conversation, of the sphere in which they move. Many millions of them have been brought to, and born in America. Most of them, indeed, have been confined to tillage, to their own homes, and their own society; yet many have been so situated, that they might have availed themselves of the conversation of their masters; many have been brought up to the handicraft arts, and from that circumstance have always been associated with the whites. Some have been liberally educated, and all have lived in countries where the arts and sciences are cultivated to a considerable degree, and have had before their eyes samples of the best works from abroad. ... [N]ever yet could I find that a black had uttered a thought above the level of plain narration; never seen even an elementary trait of painting or sculpture. In music they are more generally gifted than the whites with accurate ears for tune and time, and they have been found capable of imagining a small catch. Whether they will be equal to the composition of a more extensive run of melody, or of complicated harmony, is yet to be proved. Misery is often the parent of the most affecting touches in poetry. Among the blacks is misery enough, God knows, but no poetry. Love is the peculiar oestrum of the poet. Their love is ardent, but it kindles the senses only, not the imagination."

T. Jefferson, Notes on the State of Virginia at 149-52 (J.W. Randolph, 1853), available from the Library of Congress at *www.hathitrust.org/digital_library*

MORE THOMAS JEFFERSON ON AFRICAN-AMERICANS

"They have less hair on the face and body. They secrete less by the kidneys, and more by the glands of the skin, which gives them a very strong and disagreeable odor. ... They are more ardent after their female; but love seems with them to be more an eager desire than a tender delicate mixture of sentiment and sensation. Their griefs are transient. ... ..."

T. Jefferson, Notes on the State of Virginia at 149-52 (J.W. Randolph, 1853), available from the Library of Congress at *www.hathitrust.org/digital_library*

George Washington

George Washington also was a large slaveholder, together with his wife, Martha. His actions reflect a commitment to slavery, as well as a degree of concern for the slaves.

Dr. Donald Sweig states:[372]

> It isn't easy for contemporary Americans to accept this fact about Washington, but there is no escaping it. Like nearly every prominent Virginian of the 18th century, he was a slave owner.
>
> By contemporary standards there can be no excusing slavery, but by the standards of his time and place Washington appears to have been relatively enlightened. There is ample evidence that Washington understood that his slaves were human beings who would make the most of their lives, whatever the external constraints imposed upon them, and that this included the formation and preservation of families.
>
> Many slave owners found it easier to regard their slaves more as chattel than as people. Not Washington.

"George Washington with Slave Laborers ", *Slavery Images: A Visual Record of the African Slave Trade and Slave Life in the Early African Diaspora,* accessed November 16, 2020, *http://slaveryimages.org/s/slaveryimages/item/1174*

Dr. Sweig observes that Washington's ownership of slaves added profoundly to his wealth, providing him with the time to pursue his career in the military and politics.[373] Dr. Erica Dunbar agrees: "Washington needed slave labor to maintain his wealth, his lifestyle and his reputation," although as he grew older, he contemplated "get[ting] quit of Negroes."[374]

Dr. Dunbar notes that Washington, as President, signed the Fugitive Slave Law of 1793, "which allowed fugitives to be seized in any state, tried and returned to their owners. Anyone who harbored or assisted a fugitive slave faced a $500 penalty and possible imprisonment."[375]

Illustrating Mr. Washington's commitment to slavery, Dr. Singer describes how, while residing in Philadelphia, Mr. Washington evaded "a Pennsylvania gradual abolition act by rotating enslaved Africans back

372 Sweig, "At Least George Washington Let His Slaves Have Families" (Wash. Post, Sept. 25, 1983) at *www.washingtonpost.com/archive/opinions/1983/09/25/at-least-george-washington-let-his-slaves-have-families/feca420d-c4ba-4563-9b88-5ba42f9b656b/*, accessed Oct. 2, 2020 ("Sweig, Washington").

373 Sweig, Washington.

374 Dunbar, "George Washington Slave Catcher" (NY Times, Feb. 16, 2015) at *www.nytimes.com/2015/02/16/opinion/george-washington-slave-catcher.html*, accessed Oct. 2, 2020 ("Dunbar").

375 Dunbar.

to his plantation in Virginia every six months."[376] Under Pennsylvania's gradual emancipation law, slaves who were in the State for six months would be free, so the Washingtons would remove their slaves from Pennsylvania before the six months had elapsed, thus "reset[ting] the clock."[377]

Contradictions emerge in Washington's relationships with his and Martha's slaves. For example, Mr. Washington had a slave chef named Hercules Posey. As a demanding chef, Mr. Posey ran the Washingtons' kitchen with a fabled "iron discipline," including over both enslaved African-Americans and white indentured servants and employees. He developed a strong reputation as a cook.[378]

WASHINGTON EXPRESSES OPPOSITION TO SLAVERY

"Before his death Washington said
'I can only say that there is not a man living who wishes more sincerely than I do to see a plan adopted for the abolition of it [slavery]; but there is only one proper and effectual mode by which it can be accomplished, and that is by Legislative authority; and this, as far as my suffrage [vote and support] will go, shall never be wanting [lacking].'"

"Jubilo! The Emancipation Century" at *jubiloemancipationcentury.wordpress.com/2013/02/18/list-of-slave-holding-presidents/,* accessed Oct. 2, 2020

Mr. Posey did not take advantage of opportunities for freedom in Virginia and even more so in Philadelphia. He was able to move about freely, always returning. Eventually, he left Mount Vernon on his own, but Washington later freed Mr. Posey in Washington's will.[379]

In contrast to Mr. Posey, while the Washingtons lived in Philadelphia, one of Martha's favorite slaves, a personal attendant named Ona Judge, at the age of 22, learned that Martha intended to give Ms. Judge to Martha's granddaughter ("who was known to have a fierce temper") as a wedding gift.[380] Thereupon, Ms. Judge escaped to New Hampshire. Ms. Judge simply walked away from the Washington's mansion during dinner, and took a ship North.[381]

Washington attempted for three years to bring Ms. Judge back.[382] He sent aides to New Hampshire to persuade Ms. Judge to return, but she refused unless the Washingtons would agree to free her in their wills. Despite the Fugitive Slave Law of 1793, which he had signed, Washington was reluctant to use force, which would offend Northern abolitionists.[383]

---

376 Singeer, at 4. Citation omitted.

377 Dunbar.

378 Ganeshram, "In 1795, George Washington gave thanks for liberty. The feasts chef had none." at R4 (Wash. Post, Nov. 22, 2020) at *www.washingtonpost.com/food/2020/11/19/washington-thanksgiving-hercules/,* accessed Nov. 27, 2020.

379 Ganeshram, "In 1795, George Washington gave thanks for liberty. The feasts chef had none." at R4 (Wash. Post, Nov. 22, 2020) at *www.washingtonpost.com/food/2020/11/19/washington-thanksgiving-hercules/,* accessed Nov. 27, 2020.

380 Dunbar.

381 "Martha Washington as a Slaveowner" at *www.mountvernon.org/george-washington/slavery/martha-washington-as-a-slaveowner/,* accessed Oct. 2, 2020.

382 Dunbar; "Ona Judge" at *www.mountvernon.org/library/digitalhistory/digital-encyclopedia/article/ona-judge/,* accessed Oct. 2, 2020 ("Mount Vernon Ona Judge").

383 Mount Vernon Ona Judge.

Mount Vernon's website states:[384]

> When Washington learned of Judge's request, he was furious. His response to her proposed deal reveals the tension between his stated antislavery principles and the reality of being a slave owner. He fumed to [an associate]: "To enter into such a compromise with her, as she suggested to you, is totally inadmissible ... for however well disposed I might be to a gradual abolition, or even to an entire emancipation of that description of People (if the latter was in itself practicable at this moment) it would neither be politic or just to reward unfaithfulness with a premature preference; and thereby discontent before hand the minds of all her fellow-servants who by their steady attachments are far more deserving than herself of favor."

UNGRATEFUL SLAVES

"The Blacks are so bad in their nature that they have not the least grat[i]tude for the kindness that may be shewed to them."

Martha Washington (1795) quoted at "Martha Washington as a Slaveowner" at *www.mountvernon.org/george-washington/slavery/martha-washington-as-a-slaveowner/,* accessed Oct. 2, 2020

After her escape, Ms. Judge lived her life in New Hampshire. She learned to read and write, gave newspaper interviews, married, and had a family. When Ms. Judge died at the age of 75 in 1848, she still had the status of a fugitive slave, since neither George nor Martha Washington had freed her.[385]

Washington took other actions in favor of slaveholders. As General, he objected when the British allowed slaves to escape to Canada after the War, claiming it violated the Revolutionary War peace treaty by failing to return "all confiscated property."[386]

Despite his actions to protect investments in slaves, Dr. Sweig describes George Washington as having been considerate of the family lives of the slaves he and Martha owned. Even so, however, Washington's slaves did not always have what one would regard today as a typical family life. Dr. Donald Sweig provides the following examples in the context of plantation properties Mr. Washington owned:[387]

> Mount Vernon slave families generally lived together, and those who did not were able to visit at night. Visits to and from spouses on other plantations also were common and perhaps frequent. Families were not indiscriminately separated .... Children under 13 usually lived with their mothers.

§ § §

> Washington's concern for maintaining the integrity of his slaves' families extended to the last year of his life. ... [H]e not only refused to sell any slaves but even to hire them out "because they could not be disposed of in families to my advantage, and to disperse the families I have an aversion."

George Washington provided in his will for his slaves to be freed following Martha's death. Martha Washington, however, did not follow George's act of freeing her own slaves in her will.[388]

384 Mount Vernon Ona Judge.

385 Mount Vernon Ona Judge.

386 Singer, at 50; Berlin and Harris, at 15.

387 Sweig, Washington.

388 Dunbar; Mount Vernon Ona Judge.

According to Mount Vernon's website:[389]

> Martha Washington … believed that slavery was part of the natural order, as many white people of the 18th century did.

Supreme Court Justices

America's first three Supreme Court Chief Justices owned slaves, but managed the issue very differently:

- John Jay, the first Chief Justice, who served until 1801[390]
- John Marshall, who served from 1801 until 1835[391]
- Roger Taney, who served from 1835 until 1864[392]

This is tremendously important in understanding the power of the slave society in early America. Until the Civil War, the Supreme Court's rulings dominated American law and America's legal management of slavery.

Chief Justice John Jay

Chief Justice John Jay was an active member of the New York Manumission Society, and actively opposed slavery.[393] He also came from a family of slaveholders, and owned slaves himself.

Chief Justice Jay argued, however, that he was more humane than other slaveholders:[394]

> Jay had an explanation for this seemingly contradictory practice: "I purchase slaves and manumit them at proper ages and when their faithful services shall have afforded a reasonable retribution."

JOHN JAY'S PERSPECTIVES

"Jay equated the cause of the rebellious colonist with that of the yearning-for-liberty slave. In 1777, he urged that New York's new state constitution provide for eventual abolition, and endorsed a resolution by the state constitutional convention calling for the end of slavery. 'Till America comes into this measure,' Jay wrote in private correspondence in 1780, 'her prayers to Heaven for liberty will be impious.' Such phrases echoed the thoughts of Thomas Jefferson, whose ruminations on the injustice of bondage caused him to 'tremble' when he reflected that 'God was just.' Unlike Jefferson, however, Jay suspected that blacks' natural capacities were 'probably' equal to whites', which to him made American hypocrisy all the more damning. 'To contend for our own liberty and to deny that blessing to others,' he wrote in 1785, 'involves an inconsistency not to be excused.'"

Rael, "Chapter 4: The Long Death of Slavery," in I. Berlin and L. Harris, ed., Slavery in New York at 115-16 (The New Press, 2005). Footnote omitted.

---

389 "Martha Washington as a Slaveowner" at *www.mountvernon.org/george-washington/slavery/martha-washington-as-a-slaveowner/*, accessed Oct. 2, 2020.

390 "The Papers of John Jay: Jay and Slavery" at www.columbia.edu/cu/libraries/inside/dev/jay/JaySlavery.html, accessed Oct. 9, 2020 ("Jay Papers").

391 Finkelman, "Master John Marshall and the Problem of Slavery" at lawreviewblog.uchicago.edu/2020/08/31/marshall-slavery-pt1/, accessed Oct. 9, 2020 ("Finkelman, Part 1").

392 "Roger Taney" at housedivided.dickinson.edu/sites/slavery/people/roger%ADtaney/#:~:text=0riginally%20from%20Maryland%2C%20Taney%20had%20been%20a%20slaveholder, accessed Oct. 9, 2020.

393 Jay Papers.

394 Jay Papers. See also Rael, at 117.

Chief Justice John Marshall

Chief Justice John Marshall, considered to be a "great" Chief Justice, served for three-and-a-half decades. His approach to slavery was quite different from that of Chief Justice Jay.

According to Dr. Paul Finkelman, Chief Justice Marshall owned over 250 slaves. He worked his slaves both in an urban household and on plantations that he and his sons owned. He gave slaves to his sons.

Justice Marshall also sold slaves at an auction to pay a son's debts, thereby likely destroying some slave families. He actively purchased slaves throughout his life. He did so even in instances ironically on the Fourth of July. One of those was as early as 1784, the first Fourth of July after the end of the Revolutionary War.[395]

Further, Justice Marshall never freed any of his slaves, not even upon his death, unlike George Washington. He made an offer of manumission to one favorite slave, together with $50, or alternatively $100 if the slave would emigrate to Liberia. The slave refused to leave his community for Liberia. The $50 offer was futile because the slave would have been required to obtain the approval of the Virginia legislature in order to remain in the State as a "free" African-American, and the $50 was not adequate to pay for a lawyer to seek the approval.[396]

Not only was Chief Justice Marshall a large slaveholder, but Dr. Finkelman analyzes Justice Marshall's legal opinions, finding that:[397]

> Chief Justice Marshall never wrote an opinion supporting black freedom. In some of these cases Marshall overturned lower court decisions, from slaveholding jurisdictions, emancipating the slave plaintiff. In cases involving the African slave trade Marshall was equally hostile to liberty, almost always siding with defendants, who had participated in the African slave trade in violation of U.S. law.

Moreover, "On the bench Marshall always supported slavery, even when statutes and precedent were on the side of freedom." [398]

In a related article, Dr. Finkelman expands on that analysis[399]:

> Marshall's analysis and jurisprudence in slave cases was often inconsistent from his rulings in other areas of the law. For example, in cases involving contracts or bankruptcy, he strongly advocated the application of natural law to reach outcomes that favored creditors. But when confronted with the African slave trade—which Congress had declared to be piracy—he concluded that natural law had no place in American jurisprudence.
>
> However, in freedom suits and in slave trade cases, the results of Marshall's jurisprudence were consistent. He always supported slaveowners when blacks claimed to be free. Similarly, he consistently failed to enforce the federal prohibitions on American participation in the African slave trade or, after 1808, the absolute prohibition on bringing new slaves into the United States.

---

395 Finkelman, Part 1.

396 Finkelman, Part 1.

397 Finkelman, Part 1. Emphasis in original.

398 Finkelman, Part 1.

399 Finkelman, "John Marshall's Proslavery Jurisprudence: Racism, Property, and the 'Great' Chief Justice" at *lawreviewblog.uchicago.edu/2020/08/31/marshall-slavery-pt2/*, accessed Oct. 9, 2020.

Dr. Finkelman also cites Justice Marshall's correspondence evidencing a[400]

hostility to free blacks and his fear of slave rebellions. He argued the entire nation "could be strengthened" by the "removal of our colored population." He believed the "danger" from free blacks "can scarcely be estimated."

Dr. Finkelman adds that Justice Marshall:[401]

petitioned the Virginia legislature for funds to support colonization, because of the "urgent expedience of getting rid in some way, of the free coloured population of the Union." Marshall declared that free blacks in Virginia were worthless, ignorant, and lazy and that in Richmond half the free blacks were "criminals."

Chief Justice Roger Taney

Chief Justice Roger Taney, who served immediately after Justice Marshall for another three decades also owned slaves early in life. Justice Taney was an ardent advocate of slavery.

While Justice Taney served, the Court issued several significant proslavery decisions, notably the *Dred Scott* decision (African-Americans, whether slave or "free," were not citizens and, therefore, not entitled under the Constitution to access the federal courts),[402] *Prigg v. Pennsylvania* (despite State law prohibiting capture of fugitive sales, a slaveowner had the right under the 1793 Fugitive Slave Law to enter into a free state to recapture a slave),[403] and *Jones v. Van Zandt* (a white abolitionist in Ohio was liable to a Kentucky slaveowner for assisting the owner's slave in escaping).[404]

His opinion in the *Dred Scott* decision,[405] in particular, stands as one of the most infamous Supreme Court decisions in American history.

Ironically, however, Taney "emancipated his own slaves in 1818," almost two decades before he became Chief Justice.[406]

"Dred Scott, ca. 1857", *Slavery Images: A Visual Record of the African Slave Trade and Slave Life in the Early African Diaspora,* accessed November 15, 2020, *http://slaveryimages.org/s/slaveryimages/*item/1508

400 Finkelman, Part 1.

401 Finkelman, Part 1.

402 Dred Scott v. Sandford, 60 U.S. 393, 15 L. Ed. 691 (1857).

403 Prigg v. Pennsylvania, 41 U.S. 539 (1842).

404 Jones v. Van Zandt, 46 U.S. 215 (1847).

405 Dred Scott v. Sandford, 60 U.S. 393, 15 L. Ed. 691 (1857).

406 "Roger Taney" at *housedivided.dickinson.edu/sites/slavery/people/roger%ADtaney/#:~:text=Originally%20from%20Maryland%2C%20Taney%20had%20been%20a%20slaveholder*, accessed Oct. 9, 2020.

AFRICAN-AMERICANS NOT "CITIZENS"

"A free negro of the African race, whose ancestors were brought to this country and sold as slaves, is not a 'citizen' within the meaning of the Constitution of the United States.

"When the Constitution was adopted, they were not regarded in any of the States as members of the community which constituted the State, and were not numbered among its 'people or citizens.' Consequently, the special rights and immunities guarantied to citizens do not apply to them. And not being 'citizens' within the meaning of the Constitution, they are not entitled to sue in that character in a court of the United States, and the Circuit Court has not jurisdiction in such a suit.

"The only two clauses in the Constitution which point to this race treat them as persons whom it was morally lawfully (sic) to deal in as articles of property and to hold as slaves."

United States Supreme Court, Syllabus for *Dred Scott v. Sanford*, 60 U.S. 393 (1857)

Summary

America's Founding Fathers were people. They acted within the context of their time, in which most, but not all, of America's leaders owned slaves. In important respects, they were extraordinary people. When they acted, as well as throughout their lives, slavery was favorably regarded and widely practiced and supported both in the North and South. At that time, the difficulties associated with emancipation were not figments of the imagination, but were considered to be serious concerns.

Frederick Douglass recognized the humanity of America's Founding Fathers, stating in his famous Fourth of July address:[407]

> Fellow Citizens, I am not wanting in respect for the fathers of this republic. The signers of the Declaration of Independence were brave men. They were great men too—great enough to give fame to a great age. It does not often happen to a nation to raise, at one time, such a number of truly great men. The point from which I am compelled to view them is not, certainly, the most favorable; and yet I cannot contemplate their great deeds with less than admiration. They were statesmen, patriots and heroes, and for the good they did, and the principles they contended for, I will unite with you to honor their memory.

The Duke of York, his brother King Charles II, and their colleagues, in contrast, were not American patriots. They acted contrary to common practices even among other cultures that practiced slavery at the time. They inaugurated a form of slavery that was particularly cruel. They laid the foundation for a form of American slavery that violated even those then-contemporary international standards.

407 Douglass, "What to the Slave Is the Fourth of July?" (July 5, 1852) at "Text of Douglass's Speech" at *www.owleyes.org/text/what-to-the-slave-is-the-fourth-of-july/read/text-of-douglasss-speech#root-162,* accessed Nov. 5, 2020.

ABRAHAM LINCOLN

Abraham Lincoln personified America's slavery contradictions. Unlike the Founding Fathers, however, President Lincoln was opposed unalterably to slavery.

In the simplistic, sanitized version of history my schools taught me, I "learned" that Abraham Lincoln was a single-minded abolitionist—the Great Emancipator. My schools did not teach about his cautiousness when confronted by difficult choices. My schools did not teach about his evolution in thinking about African-American equality, colonization, voting rights, and other issues. My schools did not teach about his policy ambivalence. My schools taught simply that President Lincoln opposed slavery—true—but not about his important efforts and compromises to resolve complex and difficult political and social issues in order to avoid an unimaginably disastrous calamity.

Instead, my schools taught simply that President Lincoln's Emancipation Proclamation freed the slaves. Of course, actually, it didn't, at least not in a legal sense, and certainly not in the Union states. My schools taught that Lincoln fought the Civil War to free the slaves. Again, he didn't—at least not at first—and later perhaps as much for strategic reasons of undermining the Southern economy, as well as to pursue humane choices.

His human complexity, making human choices in extremely difficult circumstances, does not mean, however, that President Lincoln was not a genuine American hero—he was.

Dr. Peter Kolchin states:[408]

> Lincoln's caution stemmed not from moral equivocation—he consistently reiterated his belief that slavery was wrong and ought to be abolished—but from potent practical considerations. ... The loyalty of Maryland, which harbored considerable pro-Confederate sentiment, was especially critical, for the state's secession would leave Washington, D.C., surrounded by enemy territory.

Dr. Kolchin adds that the War support of Northern Democrats was tenuous, reliable "so long as the war remained one to preserve the status quo; a war to overturn slavery, however, was an altogether different matter."[409]

Difficult Choices

President Lincoln worked in the context of a highly-charged and highly dangerous political milieu. Above all, he wanted to preserve the Union first, and then to deal with slavery after that. If the Union had not been preserved, the path to abolition of slavery would not have been available at all. The following are among the issues he confronted.

First, he faced legal considerations. For example, the Constitution limits the federal government's authority to intrude into state affairs. It was not at all clear that the federal government could simply declare slaves to be free.

Second, Southern politicians were heavily influential in Congress. To the extent legislation was needed, they were a crucial factor and hurdle.

Third, the Supreme Court was dominated by Justices friendly to slavery, so judicial action was unlikely.

---

408 Kolchin, at 202.

409 Kolchin, at 202.

Fourth, President Lincoln faced especially serious additional political difficulties. In order to win the War, and to free the slaves eventually, President Lincoln needed to engage in delicate balancing. Kentucky (which had declared neutrality), Missouri and, importantly, Maryland—all dedicated slave states—remained in the Union. If those states also had seceded, victory in the War would have been much more onerous for the Union, and probably impossible. Delaware, and to a much lesser degree, New Jersey, also were slave states.

In particular, if Maryland to the East had seceded, then Washington, DC, with Virginia to the West, would have been completely surrounded by hostile Confederate territory. The Union may have been compelled to abandon its Capitol. Underscoring Maryland's proslavery stance, in Baltimore, pro-Confederate sympathizers rioted in 1861, attacking Union soldiers from Massachusetts.[410]

Moreover, there were considerations of the welfare of the slaves themselves. Few of them had received education. Indeed, state laws forbade education of slaves, even regarding basic reading and writing skills. In some states, laws even prohibited education for "free" African-Americans. Rural slaves who worked as field hands, had no other skills. A major question was how, once those slaves were freed, they would be able to support themselves.

That issue tied directly to the issue of white fear. The whites had so badly mistreated slaves and other African-Americans that the whites were terrified of retribution. Angry slaves were ready to provide it. Whites feared crime—theft and violent crime—from freed slaves unable to make a living.

The loss of slaveholders' substantial "wealth" was an important consideration. Today, it may seem that the wealth of slaveowners should have been overlooked completely. Yet, at the time, large numbers of socially- and politically-influential planters and other slaveowners had made substantial investments in their slaveholdings. They were not ready voluntarily to let that affluence and source of income simply disappear to their own financial ruin.

As President, therefore, Lincoln was a leader with heavy responsibilities. If he could devise solutions that would avoid the War and preserve the Union, he wanted to do that.

As a President should do, Douglas Harper states that Lincoln's administration developed an affirmative proposal for ending slavery. The proposal provided for "gradual emancipation" in Delaware intended to attract a positive reception by slaveowners. The plan contemplated paying compensation from federal funds for the loss of wealth to slaveowners by freeing their slaves and offering freed slaves compensation if they chose voluntarily to go to another country.[411] He states that Lincoln sought to make his proposal attractive for slavery advocates and for whites who feared African-Americans:

> emphasiz[ing] the conservative nature of his proposal for gradual emancipation, and [holding] out the promise of colonization. "I do not speak of emancipation at once, but of a decision at once to emancipate gradually. Room in South America for colonization can be obtained cheaply and in abundance, and when numbers shall be large enough to be company and encouragement for one another, the freed people will not be so reluctant to go." The administration, at this time, had agents scouting the Mosquito Coast of Nicaragua as a possible destination for freed slaves.

---

410 "Baltimore Riot of 1861" at *www.historynet.com/baltimore-riot-of-1861.htm,* accessed Oct. 3, 2020; "Baltimore Riot (April 19,1861)" at *civilwarhome.com/baltimoreriot.htm,* accessed Oct. 3, 2020.

411 Harper, "Slavery in the North," at *slavenorth.com/delaware.htm,* accessed Oct. 3, 2020.

A precedent existed. In 1862, the District of Columbia had enacted a similar emancipation approach based upon what President Lincoln praised as "the two principles of compensation and colonization."[412]

The hope was that the Delaware proposal could become a template for freeing the slaves in other states. Lincoln was unpopular, however, in Delaware. Through the State Legislature, Delaware slaveholders strongly rejected his proposal.[413] Moreover, most African-Americans had no desire to leave the only country they knew. They sternly opposed colonization.

Unfortunately, there was not a clear path to resolution of the slavery issue. The result was, in the end, a terrible War of unimaginable destructive proportions.

Lincoln's Opposition to Slavery

President Lincoln's complexity as a human being dealing with a political-charged and highly-complex issue does not mean that he did not fundamentally oppose slavery—he did so consistently.

Illustrating Lincoln's early opposition to slavery, in 1849, then-Congressman Lincoln "attempted to introduce a bill for gradual emancipation of all slaves" in the District of Columbia. His efforts, however, were "aborted by Senator John C. Calhoun and others."[414]

Lincoln's very election as President contributed significantly to the South's secession. Earlier in his career, in 1854, he already had opposed the spread of slavery to new territories.[415] He continued to do so through his career on moral grounds.[416] In the famous Lincoln-Douglas debates, Lincoln opposed Mr. Douglas' proposal to allow slavery in the territories.[417] Mr. Douglas proposed "popular sovereignty," a local control concept.[418] "Popular sovereignty," which had formed the basis for the Kansas-Nebraska Act,[419] led, among other things to a local civil war in "Bleeding Kansas."[420]

President Lincoln's views evolved. Over time, he became even more adamantly opposed to slavery and racism. He believed that slavery would die out eventually, if it were not permitted to expand into new territories. In his view, as soil in existing slave states became less productive, new territories would provide markets in which slaveholders could sell their slaves.

---

412 "A Historical Overview of DC Emancipation" at *emancipation.dc.gov/node/105922,* accessed Oct. 3, 2020.

413 Harper, "Slavery in the North," at *slavenorth.com/delaware.htm,* accessed Oct. 3, 2020.

414 "Abolition in the District of Columbia" at *www.loc.gov/item/today-in-history/april-16,* accessed Oct. 3, 2020.

415 "Abraham Lincoln" at *www.history.com/topics/us-presidents/abraham-lincoln,* Oct. 3, 2020.

416 "The Cooper Union Address: The Making of a Candidate" at *www.nps.gov/liho/learn/historyculture/aboutcooper.htm#:~:text=The Cooper Union Address%3A The Making of a,Our Living Representative Men%2C Prepared for Presidential Purposes.,* accessed Oct. 3, 2020; "Lincoln's Cooper Union Address: New York City Speech Propelled Lincoln to the White House" at *www.thoughtco.com/lincolns-cooper-union-address-1773575,* accessed Oct. 3, 2020; "Cooper Union Speech (February 27, 1860)" at *housedivided.dickinson.edu/sites/lincoln/cooper-union-speech-february-27-1860/,* accessed Oct. 3, 2020.

417 "The Lincoln-Douglas Debates" at *www.ushistory.org/us/32b.asp#:~:text=The debates attracted tens of thousands of voters,was%2C he said%2C a sacred right of self-government,* accessed Oct. 3, 2020.

418 "Stephen A. Douglas (Updated Aug. 21, 2108)" at *www.history.com/topics/us-politics/stephen-a-douglas,* accessed Oct. 3, 2020.

419 "Kansas-Nebraska Act" at *www.britannica.com/topic/Kansas-Nebraska-Act,* accessed Oct. 3, 2020; "Kansas enters the Union" at *www.history.com/this-day-in-history/kansas-enters-the-union,* accessed Oct. 3, 2020; "Kansas-Nebraska Act" at *www.history.com/topics/19th-century/kansas-nebraska-act,* accessed Oct. 3, 2020.

420 "Kansas-Nebraska Act" at *www.history.com/topics/19th-century/kansas-nebraska-act,* accessed Oct. 3, 2020.

In 1860, in a key speech at the Cooper Union in New York City, an event that later proved to be pivotal in the Republican Party's selection of Lincoln as its nominee for President, Lincoln demonstrated thorough and careful research regarding the federal government's authority to regulate slavery in the territories. He based his analysis on the enactment of the Northwest Ordinance prohibiting slavery in potential territories and states.

In that connection:[421]

> Lincoln noted that of the 39 men who gathered to vote on the Constitution in the summer of 1787, four also served in Congress. Of those four, three voted in favor of the Northwest Ordinance, which, of course, contained the section prohibiting enslavement north of the Ohio River.
>
> He further noted that in 1789, during the first Congress to assemble following the ratification of the Constitution, a law was passed to enforce the provisions of the ordinance, including the prohibition of enslavement in the territory. That law passed through Congress without objection and was signed into law by President George Washington.[422]

The National Park Service's website summarizes the principal sections of the speech, as follows:[423]

> Lincoln's speech can be divided into three parts. In the first, he showed that twenty-one of the thirty-nine signers of the Constitution were on record that the Federal Government could prohibit slavery in the national territories. In the second, Lincoln explained to the South that Republicans were no threat to slavery where it already existed. Finally, Lincoln spoke to the North. They must fearlessly persist in excluding slavery from the national territories, and therefore, confine it to the states where it already existed.

President Lincoln's commitment to end slavery led to his assassination by John Wilkes Booth, "a vigorous supporter of the Southern cause [who] was outspoken in his advocacy of slavery and his hatred of Lincoln." Mr. Booth reportedly shouted after the deed, "Sic semper tyrannis!" (the motto of the state of Virginia, meaning "Thus always to tyrants!") or "The South is avenged!" or both."[424]

Lincoln's Evolution

President Lincoln's perspectives evolved on key issues associated with African-Americans.

One example is on the issue of colonization, which he favored "strongly" for a considerable time. He even proposed it to a group of African-Americans in a meeting during his first term in office. Their great hostility to the idea, as well as that of Frederick Douglass, persuaded President Lincoln to cease its pursuit.[425]

---

421 "Northwest Ordinance of 1787: Before the Constitution, an Early Federal Law Impacted Slavery" at *www.thoughtco.com/northwest-ordinance-of-1787-4177006*, accessed Oct. 3, 2020.

422 See "—Northwest Ordinance" above.

423 "The Cooper Union Address: The Making of a Candidate" at *www.nps.gov/liho/historyculture/aboutcooper.htm*, accessed Oct. 3, 2020.

424 "John Wilkes Booth: American actor and assassin" at *www.britannica.com/biography/John-Wilkes-Booth*, accessed Oct. 3, 2020.

425 "5 Things You May Not Know About Abraham Lincoln, Slavery and Emancipation" at *www.history.com/news/5-things-you-may-not-know-about-lincoln-slavery-and-emancipation*, accessed Oct. 3, 2020.

Another example is the issue of whether African-Americans should be granted rights of citizenship, such as the right to vote. In 1858, during one of his debates with Stephen Douglas, Mr. Lincoln made the following statements, which today would be quite offensive not only to African-Americans, but most whites:[426]

> I will say then … I am not, nor ever have been, in favor of bringing about in any way the social and political equality of the white and black races, [applause]—that I am not nor ever have been in favor of making voters or jurors of negroes, nor of qualifying them to hold office, nor to intermarry with white people; and I will say in addition to this that there is a physical difference between the white and black races which I believe will forever forbid the two races living together on terms of social and political equality. And inasmuch as they cannot so live, while they do remain together there must be the position of superior and inferior, and I as much as any other man am in favor of having the superior position assigned to the white race.

Lincoln believed, however, that slaves should be free:[427]

> What he did believe was that, like all men, black men had the right to improve their condition in society and to enjoy the fruits of their labor. In this way they were equal to white men, and for this reason slavery was inherently unjust.
>
> Like his views on emancipation, Lincoln's position on social and political equality for African Americans would evolve over the course of his presidency. …

Reflecting President Lincoln's changing perspectives, seven years later, in 1865, he spoke in favor of the new Louisiana State government and State constitution. The new Louisiana Constitution, which Lincoln favored, "declar[ed] emancipation for the whole State," "[gave] the benefit of public schools equally to black and white, and empower[ed] the Legislature to confer the elective process upon the coloured man."[428]

Demonstrating his evolution in thinking, Lincoln stated: "It is also unsatisfactory to some that the elective franchise is not given to the colored man. I would myself prefer that [it] were now conferred on the very intelligent, and on those who serve our cause as soldiers."[429]

That speech contributed directly to Lincoln's assassination:[430]

> One member of the crowd outside the White House that night was the handsome young actor John Wilkes Booth, who snarled to his companion about Lincoln's address: "That means n—- citizenship! Now, by God, I'll put him through. That is the last speech he will ever make."

---

426 "Lincoln Home—Fourth Debate: Charleston, Illinois" at *www.nps.gov/liho/learn/historyculture/debate4.htm*, accessed Oct. 3, 2020.

427 "5 Things You May Not Know About Abraham Lincoln, Slavery and Emancipation" at *www.history.com/news/5-things-you-may-not-know-about-lincoln-slavery-and-emancipation*, accessed Oct. 3, 2020.

428 "Last Public Address—Abe Lincoln" at *abelincolnhistory.com/speeches/last-public-address.htm#:~:text=Last%20 Public%20Address%20-% 20Abe%20Lincoln.%20After%20this,the%20United%20States%20after%20the%20 American%20Civil%20War%2C, accessed Oct. 3, 2020.*

429 "Last Public Address—Abe Lincoln" at *abelincolnhistory.com/speeches/last-public-address.htm#:~:text=Last%20 Public%20Address%20-%20Abe%20Lincoln.%20After%20this,the%20United%20States%20after%20the%20 American%20Civil%20War%2C*, accessed Oct. 3, 2020.

430 "What Lincoln Said in His Final Speech" at *www.history.com/news/what-lincoln-said-in-his-final-speech*, accessed Oct. 3, 2020.

Emancipation Proclamation

President Lincoln's Emancipation Proclamation, effective on January 1, 1863, did not declare all slaves to be free. Instead, it declared freedom for the slaves in the rebel states. The Proclamation did not free even those slaves, so long as they remained in enemy hands, although Union commanders frequently freed slaves in territories the Union army conquered and controlled and as slaves escaped to Union lines.

For example, after federal troops had landed at Galveston, on June 19, 1865, two-and-a-half years after the effectiveness of the Emancipation Proclamation, Major General Gordon Granger declared slavery to be abolished in Texas. The date is known and "celebrated annually in Texas and other states as 'Juneteenth.'"[431] Even then, word spread slowly across Texas. Dr. Randolph Campbell quotes one slave as stating, "When we all gits free, they's the long time letting us know."[432] By the ratification of the 13th Amendment, slaves knew they had been freed.[433]

Thus, the Emancipation Proclamation led at least indirectly to freedom for slaves in Union-occupied areas.

Aside from his proposal to Delaware slaveholders, however, President Lincoln did not attempt to free other slaves in the Union or border slave states.

The Emancipation Proclamation served as a strategic change in the purpose of the Civil War toward ending slavery. While the Emancipation Proclamation "was issued as a war measure and its legality under the Constitution was unsettled,"[434] Dr Peter Kolchin states that "the decree had enormous symbolic significance, transforming a conservative war to restore the Union into a revolutionary war to reconstruct it."[435]

Union states took positive steps. Maryland freed its slaves in 1864.[436] Missouri freed its slaves in January 1865,[437] before General Lee surrendered at the Appomattox Courthouse in 1865.

Nevertheless, the 13th Amendment was required in order to free all the slaves in all the states—both North and South. On January 31, 1865, Congress passed, and on February 1, 1865, President Lincoln approved, the 13th Amendment for the states to ratify. That process was completed on December 6, 1865.[438] The 13th Amendment freed all of America's slaves to an uncertain future.

---

431 Campbell, at 231; Campbell, "Slavery" at *tshaonline.org/handbook/online/articles/yps01*, accessed Oct. 3, 2020.

432 Campbell, at 249.

433 Campbell, at 249.

434 "Sept. 22, 1862: Preliminary Emancipation Proclamation Announced" at *learning.blogs.nytimes.com/2011/09/22/sept-22-1862-preliminary-emancipation-proclamation-announced/*, accessed Oct. 3, 2020.

435 Kolchin, at 207.

436 Slavery in Maryland, at 31.

437 "Slaves and Emancipation" at *civilwarmo.org/educators/resources/info-sheets/slaves-and-emancipation*, Oct. 3, 2020.

438 "13th Amendment to the U.S. Constitution: Abolition of Slavery (1865)" at *www.ourdocuments.gov/doc php?flash=true&doc=40,* accessed Oct. 3, 2020.

"Freed Slaves Cheering Lincoln's Emancipation Proclamation, 1863", *Slavery Images: A Visual Record of the African Slave Trade and Slave Life in the Early African Diaspora,* accessed November 15, 2020, *http://slaveryimages.org/s/slaveryimages/item/792*

"Celebration of the Abolition of Slavery in the District of Columbia by the Colored People", *Slavery Images: A Visual Record of the African Slave Trade and Slave Life in the Early African Diaspora,* accessed November 15, 2020, *http://slaveryimages.org/s/slaveryimages/item/535*

"The Effects of the Proclamation: Freed Negroes Coming into Our Lines at Newbern, North Carolina", *Slavery Images: A Visual Record of the African Slave Trade and Slave Life in the Early African Diaspora,* accessed November 15, 2020, *http://slaveryimages.org/s/slaveryimages/item/534*

"Fugitive Slaves Escaping to Union Lines, 1864", *Slavery Images: A Visual Record of the African Slave Trade and Slave Life in the Early African Diaspora,* accessed November 15, 2020, *http://slaveryimages.org/s/slaveryimages/item/794*

Gettysburg Address

The real Lincoln, the man, recognized explicitly the concepts of liberty and equality in his Gettysburg Address on November 19, 1863, when he echoed the words of the Declaration of Independence:

> Four score and seven years ago our fathers brought forth on this continent, a new nation, conceived in Liberty, and dedicated to the proposition that all men are created equal.

Those words speak for themselves. President Lincoln was committed to liberty and equality.

President Lincoln and Frederick Douglass

Lincoln's relationship with Frederick Douglass speaks volumes about Lincoln's racial perspectives as President.

Douglass and Lincoln interacted with each other both in person and through public statements. They variously disagreed and agreed and supported each other. Despite the closeness of their relationship, Douglass did not hesitate to criticize Lincoln, at times harshly.[439] Nevertheless, as meetings between them showed, Douglass and Lincoln respected and admired each other.[440] Biographers characterize the relationship between the two men as one of "friendship."[441] Russell Freedman states:[442]

> [T]hey shared a common purpose. Douglass needed Lincoln's help to rid the nation of slavery. Lincoln needed Douglass to help him end the war and reunite the nation.
>
> Lincoln "treated me as a man," Douglass told a friend . . . . "He did not let me feel for a moment that there was any difference in the color of our skins. The president is a most remarkable man."

Holland states that Douglass "decid[ed] to do what he could in his [newspaper] and on the platform to elect Lincoln; and he then threw himself into the contest 'with firmer faith and more ardent hope than ever before.'"[443]

President Lincoln's commitment to ending slavery is reflected by his substantial direct interaction with, and personal encouragement to, Douglass, a former slave. They met on three occasions.

First Meeting—Douglass' "Nerve"

In their first meeting, which occurred on August 10, 1863, Douglass went to the White House uninvited, and without an appointment.[444] Douglass describes his action as "requir[ing] ... nerve:"[445]

---

439 R. Freedman, ABRAHAM LINCOLN AND FREDERICK DOUGLASS: THE STORY BEHIND AN AMERICAN FRIENDSHIP at 73 (Houghton Mifflin Harcourt, 2012) ("Freedman").

440 Freedman at 84-85.

441 See generally, Freedman, J. Stauffer, GIANTS: THE PARALLEL LIVES OF FREDERICK DOUGLASS AND ABRAHAM LINCOLN (New York and Boston: Twelve, Hachette Book Group, 2008) ("Stauffer").

442 Freedman at 91-92.

443 F. Holland, FREDERICK DOUGLASS, THE COLORED ORATOR at 280 (London and Toronto: Funk & Wagnall's Co., 1895), available at the Academic Affairs Library, Univ. of North Carolina at Chapel Hill, *docsouth.unc.edu* ("Holland").

444 Stauffer at 3.

445 F. Douglass, LIFE AND TIMES OF FREDERICK DOUGLASS, WRITTEN BY HIMSELF at 421 (Boston: De Wolfe, Fiske & Co., 1892), available from the Library of Congress at *www.hathitrust.org/digital_library* ("Douglass, Life and Times").

> I need not say that at the time I undertook this mission it required much more nerve than a similar one would require now. The distance then between the black man and the white American citizen was immeasurable. I was an ex-slave, identified with a despised race, and yet I was to meet the most exalted person in this great republic. ... I could not know what kind of a reception would be accorded me.

Stopped at the White House gate, Douglass sent his card to Lincoln by a messenger. "He "expected to have to wait at least half a day." But once Douglass sent his card, a messenger came for him quickly.[446]

Douglass describes the meeting as lacking "pomp and ceremony" and portrays Lincoln as friendly, "with his feet extended on the floor:"[447]

> I was never more quickly or more completely put at ease in the presence of a great man than in that of Abraham Lincoln. ... Long lines of care were already deeply written on Mr. Lincoln's brow, and his strong face, full of earnestness, lighted up as soon as my name was mentioned.

Douglass continues his description of Lincoln as receptive and casual:[448]

> As I approached and was introduced to him he arose and extended his hand, and bade me welcome. I at once felt myself in the presence of an honest man—one whom I could love, honor, and trust without reserve or doubt. Proceeding to tell him who I was and what I was doing, he promptly, but kindly, stopped me, saying: "I know who you are, Mr. Douglass; Mr. Seward has told me all about you. Sit down. I am glad to see you."

Douglass presented his concerns:[449]

> I then told him the object of my visit: that I was assisting to raise colored troops; that several months before I had been very successful in getting men to enlist, but that now it was not easy to induce the colored men to enter the service, because there was a feeling among them that the government did not, in several respects, deal fairly with them. Mr. Lincoln asked me to state particulars. I replied that there were three particulars which I wished to bring to his attention. First, that colored soldiers ought to receive the same wages as those paid to white soldiers. Second, that colored soldiers ought to receive the same protection when taken prisoners, and be exchanged as readily and on the same terms as any other prisoners, and if Jefferson Davis should shoot or hang colored soldiers in cold blood the United States government should, without delay, retaliate in kind and degree upon Confederate prisoners in its hands. Third, when colored soldiers, seeking "the bubble reputation at the cannon's mouth," performed great and uncommon service on the battle-field, they should be rewarded by distinction and promotion precisely as white soldiers are rewarded for like services.

Lincoln made a favorable impression on Douglass. Douglass states: "Mr. Lincoln listened with patience and silence to all I had to say. He was serious and even troubled by what I had said and by what he himself had evidently before thought upon the same points. He, by his silent listening not less than by his earnest reply to my words, impressed me with the solid gravity of his character."[450]

---

446 Douglass, Life and Times at 421-24; Freedman at 83; Stauffer at 19; B.T. Washington, FREDERICK DOUGLASS at 229 (Philadelphia: George W. Jacobs & Co., 1907) ("Washington").

447 Douglass, Life and Times at 422.

448 Douglass, Life and Times at 422.

449 Douglass, Life and Times at 422-23.

450 Douglass, Life and Times at 423.

After the meeting Douglass met with the Secretary of War, who was "cordial" and listened.[451] Douglass was sufficiently satisfied with the meetings that he determined to continue recruiting back troops, stating, "Both the President and Secretary assured me that justice ultimately would be done to my race and I gave full faith and credit to their promises."[452]

Second Meeting—Lincoln's Antislavery Proposal Echoes Brown

Washington describes the second meeting between Douglass and Lincoln as occurring on the President's initiative. "[A]fter the [Emancipation] Proclamation was issued," Lincoln "summoned" Douglass to the White House for a meeting on August 18, 1864.[453] When Douglass "disembarked" from the train in Washington, "a White House messenger was there to meet him."[454] Stauffer states that, "by the end of their meeting," the two men "considered each other friends."[455]

Stauffer describes the President's disposition: "Douglass found Lincoln 'in an alarmed condition,'" concerned that he might be forced to settle for peace and abandon slaves.[456] Lincoln then asked Douglass to create a secret "elite" force of black scouts who could go into the South, informing slaves of emancipation and urging slaves to escape to Union lines.[457] Lincoln expressed concern that "the slaves in the South were not coming into the Union lines as fast as he expected and wished. He said that he might be forced into arrangements for peace before his purposes could be realized, and if so, he wanted the greatest possible number of slaves within the territory of freedom."[458]

As events developed, General Sherman's victory at Atlanta made Lincoln's plan unnecessary.

Third Encounter—Lincoln's Fateful Second Inauguration

Lincoln delivered his second inaugural address on March 4, 1865, as the Civil War was ending. It was "a month before he was assassinated."[459] "Frederick Douglass was a prominent figure at the inauguration ceremonies … ."[460]

Early in the proceedings, Douglass gained an adverse glimpse into the heart of Lincoln's Vice President, and eventual successor, Andrew Johnson:[461]

> On this inauguration day, while waiting for the opening of the ceremonies, I made a discovery in regard to the Vice President, Andrew Johnson. There are moments in the lives of most men when the doors of their souls are open, and, unconsciously to themselves, their true characters may be read by

---

451 Douglass, Life and Times at 421-25.

452 Douglass, Life and Times at 425.

453 Washington at 236.

454 Stauffer at 284. Note omitted.

455 Stauffer at 288.

456 Stauffer at 286-87.

457 Stauffer at 286-88; Freedman at 89-92, Washington at 236-37.

458 Washington at 236; Freedman at 89-92.

459 "Abraham Lincoln's Second Inaugural Address" at *www.loc.gov/rr/program/bib/ourdocs/lincoln2nd.html,* accessed Oct. 3, 2020.

460 Washington at 240; Freedman at 97-98.

461 Douglass, Life and Times at 442-43.

> the observant eye. It was at such an instant that I caught a glimpse of the real nature of this man, which all subsequent developments proved true. I was standing in the crowd by the side of Mrs. Thomas J. Dorsey, when Mr. Lincoln touched Mr. Johnson and pointed me out to him. The first expression which came to his face, and which I think was the true index of his heart, was one of bitter contempt and aversion. Seeing that I observed him, he tried to assume a more friendly appearance, but it was too late; it is useless to close the door when all within has been seen. His first glance was the frown of the man; the second was the bland and sickly smile of the demagogue. I turned to Mrs. Dorsey and said, "Whatever Andrew Johnson may be, he certainly is no friend of our race."
>
> No stronger contrast between two men could well be presented than the one exhibited on this day between President Lincoln and Vice-President Johnson. Mr. Lincoln was like one who was treading the hard and thorny path of duty and self-denial; Mr. Johnson was like one just from a drunken debauch. The face of the one was full of manly humility, although at the topmost height of power and pride; that of the other was full of pomp and swaggering vanity. The fact was, though it was yet early in the day, Mr. Johnson was drunk.

Following Lincoln's address, Douglass walked to the White House for the Inaugural Ball. By attending, Douglass once again was breaking a significant barrier for black Americans.[462] Douglass first confronted discrimination at the door: "two policemen stationed there took me rudely by the arm and ordered me to stand back[.] I told the officers I was quite sure there must be some mistake, for no such order could have emanated from President Lincoln; and that if he knew I was at the door he would desire my admission."[463]

The officers sought to guide Douglass away by deception, but Douglass persisted. Douglass continues, "At this moment a gentleman who was passing in recognized me, and I said to him: "Be so kind as to say to Mr. Lincoln that Frederick Douglass is detained by officers at the door."[464]

Douglass' firm resistance to discrimination once again produced positive results as he gained admission. Douglass describes the scene, when once more Lincoln honored Douglass, this time publicly referring to Douglass before gathered celebrities, as "my friend" and asking his opinion:[465]

> It was not long before … I walked into the spacious East Room, amid a scene of elegance such as in this country I had never before witnessed. Like a mountain pine high above all others, Mr. Lincoln stood, in his grand simplicity, and home-like beauty. Recognizing me, even before I reached him, he exclaimed, so that all around could hear him, "Here comes my friend Douglass." Taking me by the hand, he said, "I am glad to see you. I saw you in the crowd to-day, listening to my inaugural address; how did you like it?" I said, "Mr. Lincoln, I must not detain you with my poor opinion, when there are thousands waiting to shake hands with you." "No, no," he said, "you must stop a little, Douglass; there is no man in the country whose opinion I value more than yours. I want to know what you think of it?" I replied, "Mr. Lincoln, that was a sacred effort." "I am glad you liked it!" he said; and I passed on, feeling that any man, however distinguished, might well regard himself honored by such expressions, from such a man.

---

462 Douglass, Life and Times at 443-44; Freedman at 98-100. See also Stauffer at 295; Holland at 309-10; Washington at 241-42.

463 Douglass, Life and Times at 444.

464 Douglass, Life and Times at 444.

465 Douglass, Life and Times at 444-45.

Lincoln's Second Inaugural Address

President Lincoln delivered his second inaugural address on March 4, 1865, as the Civil War was ending. It was a month before he was assassinated.[466] Given the tremendous tragedy of the Civil War, it was a sorrowful speech.

President Lincoln spoke of how, at the time of his first inaugural address, war had been "dreaded" by all. No one wanted it, but both sides were willing to fight it:[467]

> On the occasion corresponding to this four years ago all thoughts were anxiously directed to an impending civil war. All dreaded it—all sought to avert it. ... Both parties deprecated war, but one of them would make war rather than let the nation survive, and the other would accept war rather than let it perish. And the war came.

President Lincoln described slavery as "the cause of the war:"[468]

> One-eighth of the whole population were colored slaves, not distributed generally over the Union, but localized in the Southern part of it. These slaves constituted a peculiar and powerful interest. All knew that this interest was, somehow, the cause of the war. To strengthen, perpetuate, and extend this interest was the object for which the insurgents would rend the Union, even by war; while the government claimed no right to do more than to restrict the territorial enlargement of it.

Quoting the Bible, President Lincoln spoke of slavery's retribution as the "woe" that caused the terrible disaster:[469]

> The Almighty has His own purposes. "Woe unto the world because of offenses! for it must needs be that offenses come; but *woe to that man by whom the offense cometh."* If we shall suppose that American slavery is one of those offenses which, in the providence of god, must needs come, but which, having continued through his appointed time, he now wills to remove, and that *he gives to both North and South this terrible war, as the woe due to those by whom the offense came,* shall we discern therein any departure from those divine attributes which the believers in a living God always ascribe to him? Fondly do we hope—fervently do we pray—that this mighty scourge of war may speedily pass away. Yet, if God wills that it continue *until all the wealth piled by the bondsman's two hundred and fifty years of unrequited toil shall be sunk, and until every drop of blood drawn with the lash shall be paid by another drawn with the sword,* as was said three thousand years ago, so still it must be said "The judgments of the Lord are true and righteous altogether."

Lincoln's phraseology demonstrated a deep animosity to slavery. That was especially true of his references to "all the wealth piled by the bondsman's two hundred and fifty years of unrequited toil" and to payment for "every drop of blood drawn with the lash ... by another drawn with the sword."

---

466 "Abraham Lincoln's Second Inaugural Address" at *www.loc.gov/rr/program/bib/ourdocs/lincoln2nd.html,* accessed Oct. 3, 2020.

467 "Text of Lincoln's Speech Delivered at Washington, D. C. March 4, 1865" at *www.owleyes.org/text/second-inaugural-address/read/text-of-lincolns-speech,* accessed Oct. 3, 2020.

468 "Text of Lincoln's Speech Delivered at Washington, D. C. March 4, 1865" at *www.owleyes.org/text/second-inaugural-address/read/text-of-lincolns-speech,* accessed Oct. 3, 2020.

469 "Text of Lincoln's Speech Delivered at Washington, D. C. March 4, 1865" at *www.owleyes.org/text/second-inaugural-address/read/text-of-lincolns-speech,* accessed Oct. 3, 2020. Emphasis added.

In the closing of his address, President Lincoln was a statesman, a peacemaker seeking reconciliation, not further hostility:[470]

> With malice toward none; with charity for all; with firmness in the right, as God gives us to see the right, let us strive on to finish the work we are in; to bind up the nation's wounds; to care for him who shall have borne the battle, and for his widow, and his orphan, to do all which may achieve and cherish a just, and a lasting peace, among ourselves, and with all nations.

President Lincoln had been a true leader, seeking to achieve workable goals to which the proponents of slavery would agree, as was necessary short of a bloody military victory.

Summary

Along the way, President Lincoln, bowing to political realities, undertook to preserve the Union, and also sought to develop a positive and realistic program to free the slaves.

President Lincoln was a man, a complex, well-motivated man, who opposed slavery, and who attempted to bring a workable solution into effect under extremely difficult circumstances.

Abraham Lincoln deserves to be viewed, like Thomas Jefferson, and George Washington, as a genuine, even if not perfect, American hero responding to then-prevailing societal conditions.

America's Slavery Heroes, who contributed so much to America's fundamental change in direction through their courageous and persistent battle against the pervasive scourge and terror of slavery, also deserve to be ranked and honored on a par with all of them.

Both President Lincoln and America's Slavery Heroes adamantly opposed the system of slavery created and promoted by the Duke of York, King Charles II, and their colleagues and successors.

Almost a century after the Declaration of Independence and the Constitution, President Lincoln, his successors, and America's Slavery Heroes re-made America into a new, much different, nation than the one created in 1776.

Yet, there remained, and still endure, important goals, not yet fully-achieved, in order to remedy the brutal enslavement of millions of Africans and African-Americans and to effectuate the true equality envisioned by the advocates of the 13th, 14th, and 15th Amendments.

---

470 "Abraham Lincoln's Second Inaugural Address" at *www.loc.gov/rr/program/bib/ourdocs/lincoln2nd.html*, accessed Oct. 3, 2020.

"Black Troops of the Union Army, Philadelphia, early 1864", *Slavery Images: A Visual Record of the African Slave Trade and Slave Life in the Early African Diaspora,* accessed November 15, 2020, *http://slaveryimages.org/s/slaveryimages/item/798*

"Black Soldiers in the Union/Federal Army, ca. 1863-64", *Slavery Images: A Visual Record of the African Slave Trade and Slave Life in the Early African Diaspora,* accessed November 27, 2020, *http://slaveryimages.org/s/slaveryimages/item/817*

CHAPTER FIVE: THE DUKE'S SLAVE TRADING LEGACY

AFRICANS IN TRANSITION: FROM PEOPLE TO THINGS

"slaves are like other people"[471]

Frederick Douglass

§ § §

African captives forced into slavery experienced at least three radical transitions:

- A geographical transition—The slave society transported them from Africa to the New World
- A lifestyle transition—The slave society transformed those who had not been slaves in Africa from freedom-loving independent individuals to captives
- An identity transition, an objectification—The slave society transformed them from human beings with minds of their own to the slave society's perspective that they were things compelled to be submissive and obedient

This section discusses the objectification transition.

It is easy to refer to the unfortunate people trapped in the slavery holocaust as "slaves."

That overlooks, however, the fundamental element that they were people, human beings.

Like the millions murdered by the Nazi's before and during World War II, like the Native Americans forced from their homes and their land, murdered, and marched to and confined in unwanted reservations in the American West, these Africans were human beings subjected to unimaginably merciless treatment.[472]

By the time they landed in America and elsewhere in the New World, the Africans already had been kidnapped in their native communities and separated from their families and friends. They had been chained, beaten, and starved. They had witnessed first-hand, and had experienced personally, ferocious cruelty.

They had survived months at sea, chained in cramped ship holds teeming with filth and disease. Lacking English language skills and coming from diverse cultures, they could not communicate either with their captors or, often, with each other. Even in the presence of others, they were alone.

They were depressed, often ill, angry, and confused. They knew not what slaveholders expected of them. It could not be communicated through language.

Having lived in freedom all their lives, they would have loathed their circumstances. Likely they were resistant at first until the beatings—the "seasoning"—began. The abuse was incessant and unrelenting. Hundreds of lashes with knotted whips were common. Whips ripped the flesh. Blood coursed down their bodies. Pain remained for days and even weeks. Scars survived a lifetime.

Beatings would have increased slaves' depression, weakness, and confusion—and their rage.

Can you imagine being trapped in this situation, not knowing what to do, infuriated and hostile, and thrashed at the whim of the master or overseer?

---

471 Douglass, Narrative at 19.

472 See "*—Genocide and Holocaust*" below.

"IDEA OF UTTER HELPLESSNESS"

"The term slave to this day sounds with terror to my soul—a word too obnoxious to speak—a system too intolerable to be endured. I know this from long and sad experience. I now feel as if I had just been aroused from sleep, and, looking back with quickened perception at the state of torment from whence I fled. I was there held and claimed as a slave; as such I was subjected to the will and power of my keeper, in all respects whatsoever. That the slave is a human being, no one can deny. It is his lot to be exposed in common with other men, to the calamities of sickness, death, and the misfortunes incident to life. But unlike other men, he is denied the consolation of struggling against external difficulties, such as destroy the life, liberty, and happiness of himself and family. A slave may be bought and sold in the market like an ox. He is be (sic) sold off to a distant land from his family. He is bound in chains hand and foot; and his sufferings are aggravated a hundred fold, by the terrible thought, that he is not allowed to struggle against misfortune, corporeal punishment, insults and outrages committed upon himself and family; and he is not allowed to help himself, to resist or escape the blow, which he sees impending over him. "This idea of utter helplessness, in perpetual bondage, is the more distressing, as there is no period even with the remotest generation when it shall terminate."

H. Bibb, Narrative of the Life and Adventures of Henry Bibb, An American Slave Written by Himself at 18-19 (1849), available at the Academic Affairs Library, Univ. of North Carolina at Chapel Hill, docsouth.unc.edu

Yet, resistance was useless. There was no escape.

The slave society made certain to communicate that message

Only when the human spirit had been crushed systematically and thoroughly, only when the human being became completely, one hundred percent submissive and obedient, would the lashes cease for a time until the former human, now an object, a chattel under the law, made a mistake or gave evidence of resentment or disobedience.

Then, the pitiless violence would be replicated.

The slave society's desired end result was a "thing"—no longer viewed as a human being—that would yield its personality simply to do precisely what it was told, and nothing more or less.

This is the merchandise produced by slavery.

It began in Africa with the hijacking, the loss of freedom, the separation from family and community, the weeks or months in an African slave prison, and the Middle Passage on the slave ship to a new continent.

Now, in America, it was "life."

Of course, we know that inside the outer shell sought by the slave society—the façade—those "things" were people. They were human beings, but they dared not give outward evidence of it.

GENOCIDE AND HOLOCAUST

Slavery in the New World, which included Brazil, the Caribbean, and America as willing participants, was a true genocide and a true holocaust.[473]

The death toll and the cruelty of the slave trade and slavery far exceed most modern genocides.

The deaths associated with the slave trade arose during three intervals for the African captives:

> **GENOCIDE**
>
> "the deliberate and systematic destruction of a racial, political, or cultural group"
>
> "Genocide" at *www.merriam-webster.com/dictionary/genocide,* accessed Oct. 31, 2020

- The time of kidnapping in Africa, travel to the African Coast, and imprisonment in coastal prisons and concentration camps awaiting shipment to the New World
- The time of encapsulation on the slave ships, *i.e.,* the Middle Passage
- The time shortly after arrival in the New World in a weakened and dazed condition, exposed to new diseases, and subjected to "seasoning"—a euphemism referring to ferocious abuse to turn the human Africans into slave merchandise, things, chattels, obedient and submissive farm animals[474]

Focusing upon the time of encapsulation on slave ships, Dr. Henry Gates states that, out of an estimated 12.5 million Africans shipped in the Middle Passage to the New World (approximately 380,000 directly to America), an estimated 10.7 million survived.[475] Dr. Gates' data thus indicate deaths during the Middle Passage alone of approximately 1.8 million.

After the Middle Passage, Dr. Beckles provides a "conservative estimate" of "about 15% of survivors of the passage" dying "within the first two years of arrival" in the New World.[476]

Additionally, large numbers died while still in Africa.[477]

Dr. Marcus Rediker agrees that, during the Middle Passage, "1.8 million of [the African captives] died, their bodies cast overboard to the sharks that followed the ships."[478]

Adding to that number estimates of death during the two other time periods, Dr. Rediker provides a "conservative" total estimate that "roughly 5 million men, women, and children died" in the international slave trade:[479]

---

473 See *"Chapter One: Meet America's Slave Society—An 'Actual Reign of Terror"* and *"—The Triangular Trade and the Middle Passage: Key Role in Genocide"* below.

474 See *"—Africans in Transition: From People to Things"* above.

475 Gates, "Slavery by the Numbers" at *www.theroot.com/slavery-by-the-numbers-1790874492,* accessed Oct. 5, 2020. See also "Slave Voyages" at *www.slavevoyages.org,* accessed Oct. 5, 2020.

476 Beckles, at 115.

477 Beckles, at 109-11.

478 Rediker, at 5.

479 Rediker, at 5. Emphasis added.

> A conservative estimate of 15 percent—which would include those who died in transit [from the African interior to the West African coast] and held in barracoons and factories on the coast—suggests another 1.8 million deaths in Africa. Another 15 percent (or more, depending on region), a million and a half would expire during the first year of laboring life in the New World. From stage to stage—expropriation in Africa, Middle Passage, initial exploitation in America—*roughly 5 million men, women, and children died.* Another way to look at the loss of life would be to say that an estimated 14 million people were enslaved to produce a "yield" of 9 million longer-surviving enslaved Atlantic workers.

HOLOCAUST

"a mass slaughter of people"

"Holocaust" at *www.merriam-webster.com/dictionary/holocaust,* accessed Oct. 31, 2020

To be clear, that is a conservative estimate. It does have broad support from other scholars, such as Dr. Herbert Klein, who presents data on the Middle Passage itself reflecting deaths approximating twenty percent of captives on slave ships in the Seventeenth Century declining to ten percent or even less by the late Eighteenth Century.[480] Those data are consistent with the numbers reflected above as stated by Dr. Gates and Dr. Rediker for the Middle Passage alone.

Dr. Klein states that even if the rate were "under ten percent by the late eighteenth and early nineteenth centuries, this seemingly 'low' rate produces a crude death rate for a healthy economically active population that is truly astronomical in its level."[481]

Dr. James Rawley and Dr. Stephen Behrendt cite widely varying estimates by different scholars of deaths in the Middle Passage from "traditional estimates" of "8 to above 30 percent" to other estimates by Thomas Clarkson of "mortality of enslaved Africans, under the most favorable circumstance, at 45 percent, and in many instances above 80 percent." Dr. Rawley and Dr. Behrendt conclude that death rates varied significantly among different ports of departure in Africa, reflecting prevalent local diseases, as well as the season of the year (Winter was worse) and current levels of market demand that might cause slavers to accept weaker captives.[482]

Less conservatively, Dr. David Stannard states that in the "African slave trade" there were "at least 30,000,000—and possibly as many as 40,000,000 to 60,000,000—Africans killed, most of them in the prime of their lives, before they even had a chance to begin working as human chattel on plantations in the Indies and the Americas."[483]

W.E.B. Du Bois suggests a number in the range of 50 million in Africa and on the high seas:[484]

> Certainly it seems that at least 10,000,000 Negroes were expatriated. Probably every slave imported represented on the average five corpses in Africa or on the high seas. The American slave trade, therefore, meant the elimination of at least 60,000,000 Negroes from their fatherland.

---

480 H. Klein, THE ATLANTIC SLAVE TRADE at 138-39, 141 (Cambridge Univ. Press, 2010) ("Klein").

481 Klein, at 160.

482 J. Rawley and S. Behrendt, THE TRANSATLANTIC SLAVE TRADE at 144-45, 247-50 (Univ. of Nebraska Press, 2005) ("Rawley and Behrendt").

483 D. Stannard, AMERICAN HOLOCAUST at 151 (Oxford Univ. Press, 1992).

484 W.E.B. Du Bois, THE NEGRO at 155 (Henry Holt and Co., Thornton Butterworth Ltd., 1915), available from the Library of Congress at *www.hathitrust.org/digital_library.*

Whatever the correct numbers, they were exceptionally large.

It is time for truly patriotic Americans to acknowledge the truth that America was involved knowingly, willingly in one of the most hideous genocides in the history of the World.[485] True patriotism admits to mistakes, and learns from them.

485 This is not intended to diminish the tragedy America forced on Native Americans, the tragedy of the Nazi Holocaust, or the tragedies of other holocausts.

THE TRIANGULAR TRADE AND THE MIDDLE PASSAGE: KEY ROLE IN GENOCIDE

> "[T]he cruelties and horrors of [the international slave trade] far surpass those described in any other branch of history. The soldiers who have looted cities, the pirates who have made passengers and sailors walk the plank, and the religious zealots who have burned their opponents at the stake, were more merciful than the slave-traders."
>
> **John R. Spears**[486]

> "European slave traders created shipping conditions, the sheer awfulness of which was unrivaled before, during, and after the era of the transatlantic slave trade."
>
> **Dr. David Eltis**[487]

§ § §

After the prologue of abduction in Africa and a deadly existence in coastal prisons, the Middle Passage from Africa to the New World was the next vision that African captives received of their future fates.[488]

Information regarding the Middle Passage and events on specific ships comes from British governmental investigations, including testimony before Parliamentary committees.[489]

Triangular Trade

The Middle Passage received its name as the middle component of a trading route called the "Triangular Trade."[490]

On one leg of the Triangular Trade, ships transported manufactured goods, for example, gunpowder, weapons, and cloth (made from New World cotton), from England to Africa, where slave traders, such as the Duke of York's Royal African Company, exchanged the products for African captives.[491] History.com describes "RAC ships sail[ing] from Bristol, Liverpool and London to West Africa … ."[492] Dr. Hilary Beckles opines that trading for slaves with "alcohol and firearms" increased the military power of "the participating African elites."[493]

---

486 J. Spears, THE AMERICAN SLAVE TRADE: AN ACCOUNT OF ITS ORIGINS, GROWTH AND SUPPRESSION at vii-viii (Scribner, 1907), available from the Library of Congress at *www.hathitrust.org/digital_library* ("Spears").

487 Eltis, at 117.

488 For an additional description of life on a slave ship from a captive's perspective, see Olaudah Equiano's book, THE INTERESTING NARRATIVE OF THE LIFE OF OLAUDAH EQUIANO OR, GUSTAVUS VASSA, THE AFRICAN, WRITTEN BY HIMSELF (T. Wilkins, 1789), available from the Library of Congress at *www.hathitrust.org/digital_library*

489 Thomas, at 301-02, 799.

490 Spears, at 68; "The Angolan Connection and Slavery in Virginia" at *www.historyisfun.org/learn/learning-center/the-angolan-connection-and-slavery-in-virginia/*, accessed Oct. 13, 2020.

491 Rediker, at 46-47; "Transatlantic Slave Trade" at *wayback.archive-it.org/10611/20180704133101/http://www.unesco.org/new/en/social-and-human-sciences/themes/slave-route/transatlantic-slave-trade*, accessed Oct. 6, 2020 ("Wayback"); "The trade triangle" at *liverpoolmuseums.org.uk/history-of-slavery/transatlantic-slave-trade*, accessed Oct. 6, 2020 ("Liverpool Trade Triangle").

492 "What was the Royal African Company?" at *www.history.com/news/what-was-the-royal-african-company*, accessed Sept. 28, 2020.

493 Beckles, at 17.

History.com then describes the next leg of the Royal African Company's voyages: "From 1680-86, the company transported an average of 5,000 slaves per year, most of which were shipped to the Caribbean and Virginia."[494] This was the "Middle Passage" from Africa to the New World.

In America and the Caribbean, the traders exchanged the Africans for commodities from the New World, such as sugar, tobacco, rice, and cotton, which slaves already in the New World had produced.[495] In New England, rum was an export.[496] Lord Hugh Thomas cites also the importance of metals, especially iron bars, weapons, shells, alcohol, and beads.[497]

Completing the Triangle, the traders then shipped those commodities to England. English companies converted American commodities to manufactured goods that traders would use to begin a new Triangle with shipments of the manufactured goods to Africa.[498]

According to Lord Thomas, "By the end of the eighteenth century, something approaching eighty thousand black African slaves were being carried every year across the Atlantic."[499]

Middle Passage

Dr. Beckles identifies "[s]ix distinct stages of the Middle Passage," as follows:[500]

- "capture and enslavement in Africa;
- "journey to the coast and other departure points;
- "storage and package for shipment;
- "transatlantic crossing;
- "sale and dispersion in the Americas;
- "seasoning/adjustment in the Americas"

He describes the international slave trade and the Middle Passage, as " the largest forced human migration in recorded history:" [501]

> [T]he trade undoubtedly constitutes the largest forced human migration in recorded history, and the true extent of human suffering associated with this involuntary relocation of men, women and children may never be known. Their shipment, packed and stored beneath the decks of ships like the commodity that they were considered to be, is one of the greatest horrors of modern times.

---

494 "What was the Royal African Company?" at *www.history.com/news/what-was-the-royal-african-company,* accessed Sept. 28, 2020.

495 Rediker, at 46-47; Wayback; Liverpool Trade Triangle.

496 McManus, Black Bondage in the North, at 9.

497 Thomas, at 322-31.

498 Rediker, at 46-47; Wayback; Liverpool Trade Triangle.

499 Thomas, at 370.

500 Beckles, at 106.

501 Beckles, at 16-17.

> During the "Middle Passage," … many Africans died as a result of punishment, hunger, disease, or trauma. Many others were thrown overboard if the slavers considered them sick and a threat to the health of others. …

Kidnapping, Purchase, and Storage in Africa

At the beginning of enslavement, the Africans' capture often came at the hands of African kings, warlords or hostile tribes in battles with and raids on rival tribes, as well as through outright capture by European kidnappers and slave traders. Some African traders, acting as middlemen, collected slaves beforehand to speed the process.[502]

Dr. Ira Berlin describes the impact the process had upon Africa, "as ambitious African merchants and politicos constructed dynasties from the profits of slave trading. In west Africa, new men rose to chiefdoms and paramountcies, creating states … . Farther to the south, … merchants subverted old kingdoms … . New states arose as these merchants and their mercenary allies pushed deeper into the interior of central Africa."[503]

"Goree," or Slave-stick.

"'Goree,' or Slave-Stick", *Slavery Images: A Visual Record of the African Slave Trade and Slave Life in the Early African Diaspora,* accessed November 16, 2020, *http://slaveryimages.org/s/slaveryimages/item/2653*

He adds that "[e]specially commissioned armies and freelancing gangs, driven by the possibility of political aggrandizement and great wealth, moved deep into the interior of Africa, kidnapping millions of men and women and killing millions of others. … It was a world in which no one was safe."[504]

Dr. Edgar McManus states that "[b]y 1770 the slave raids had depopulated whole regions of West Africa"[505]

Once kidnapped, Africans faced a dismal fate. Lord Thomas provides insights of American naval commodore, Henry Wise, about the capture and storage of Africans in Africa destined for slavery in America:[506]

> Another picture of slaves waiting in a barracoon was given by an American naval commodore, Henry Wise, who wrote from Cabinda, in July 1859, how, "in chained gangs, the unfortunate slaves

502 Thomas, at 343.

503 Berlin, at 100. Footnote omitted.

504 Berlin, at 100-01. Footnote omitted.

505 McManus, Black Bondage in the North, at 23.

506 Thomas, at 713.

> are driven by the lash from the interior to the barracoons on the beach; there the sea-air, insufficient diet, and dread of their approaching fate, produce the most fatal diseases: dysentery and fever [often] release them from their sufferings; the neighboring soil grows rich in the decaying remains of so many of their fellow creatures, and the tracks are thick-strewn with their bones … On a short march," he continued, "of 600 slaves, a few weeks back, intended for the Emma Lincoln [of the United States], 125 expired on the road. The mortality on these rapid marches is seldom less than 20 percent. Such, sir, is the slave trade under the American flag."

"A Captive", *Slavery Images: A Visual Record of the African Slave Trade and Slave Life in the Early African Diaspora,* accessed November 14, 2020, *http://slaveryimages.org/s/slaveryimages/item/1882*

According to Dr. Henry Gates, "Children typically comprised 26 percent or more of a slave ship's human cargo."[507]

John Spears states, with respect to illegal slave smuggling after the international trade was prohibited by Britain and America, that "in the nineteenth century, the slavers dealt in children as far as possible. Children did not bring as large a price as field hands, of course, but they cowered under torture, and there was no fear of their uprising against the crew."[508]

BARRACOON

"an enclosure or barracks formerly used for temporary confinement of slaves or convicts"

Barracoon at *www.merriam-webster.com/dictionary/barracoon,*
accessed Oct. 14, 2020

"A Slave-Shed", *Slavery Images: A Visual Record of the African Slave Trade and Slave Life in the Early African Diaspora,* accessed November 14, 2020, *http://slaveryimages.org/s/slaveryimages/item/1980*

Because the captives came from diverse African cultures, they did not have a common language. Ships' crews and officers often viewed that as an advantage reducing the odds of captives' coordination of a rebellion on-board.[509] It also would have added, however, to the captives' sense of isolation.

The process of negotiations with African captors and purchase of Africans from those captors was extremely degrading. Dr. Hilary Beckles quotes a

507 Gates, "Slavery by the Numbers" at *www.theroot.com/slavery-by-the-numbers-1790874492,* accessed Oct. 5, 2020. See also "Slave Voyages" at *www.slavevoyages.org,* accessed Oct. 5, 2020.

508 Spears, at 79.

509 Rediker, at 276.

description by an English captain of his inspection of potential purchases with the help of "a mulatto African who could tell an unsound slave at a glance."[510]

The mulatto scrutinized the African captives:[511]

> handling the "naked blacks from head to foot, squeezing their joints and muscles, twisting their arms and legs, and examining teeth, eyes, and chest, and pinching breasts and groin without mercy. The slaves stood in couples, stark naked, and were made to jump, cry out, lie down, and roll, and hold their breath for a long time."

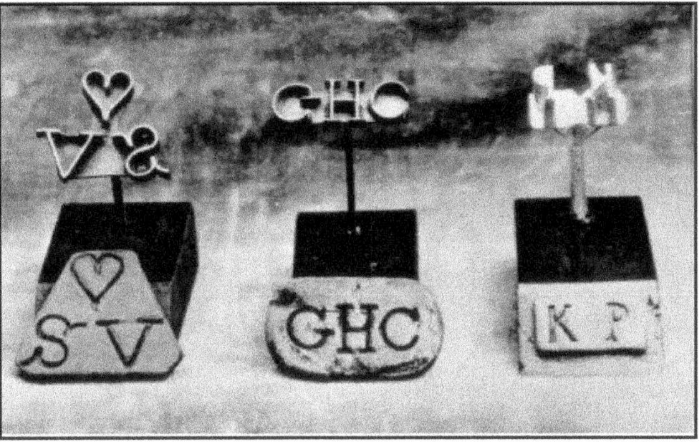

"Metal Branding Irons with Owners' Initials", *Slavery Images: A Visual Record of the African Slave Trade and Slave Life in the Early African Diaspora,* accessed November 14, 2020, *http://slaveryimages.org/s/slaveryimages/item/1975*

Dr. Beckles adds that "French merchants usually brought in the ship's surgeon to examine the female slaves, in order to estimate their reproductive capacities."

After the purchases, the captives were stored in warehouses, prisons, and forts,[512] at times for extensive periods "until the ships arrived." Dr. Rediker states that this period of confinement could last "six months and more."[513]

"During this process, the slaves were branded with hot irons on their shoulders, arms, or chest, in order to label them for transportation and storage."[514] Michael Cottman states that "branding was standard practice for all slavers."[515] Slaves purchased for the Royal African Company "were branded 'DY,' Duke of York."[516]

Lord Thomas describes the branding process:[517]

> Slaves were as always branded before their departure for the Americas. In this respect there was no difference between what happened in the legal, eighteenth century and the illegal, nineteenth: an iron with letters cut into it "is put into fire on the beach, and a small pot containing palm oil is always at hand; the iron is heated, and dipped into this palm oil, and dabbed on the hip [men] or [just above] the breast [women] or wherever the slave dealer may choose to have his slaves marked. The palm oil is to prevent the flesh adhering to the iron."

---

510 Beckles, at 85-86.

511 Beckles, at 85-86.

512 Rediker, at 212; "The Slave Ship" at *cbsnews.com/news/the-slave-ship-60-minutes/,* accessed Oct. 6, 2020 ("The Slave Ship"); Cottman, "The Ghosts of the Henrietta Marie" at *www.washingtonpost.com/wp-srv/national/daily/feb99/excerpt07.htm*, accessed Oct. 6, 2020 ("Cottman").

513 Rediker, at 212.

514 Beckles, at 86.

515 Cottman; Rediker, at 268.

516 Beckles, at 86; Rediker, at 268.

517 Thomas, at 715.

The Story of Ottobah Cugoano's Capture in Africa

In his narrative, a man named Ottobah Cugoano related his experience as an African captive from the time of his kidnapping to his life in England:[518]

A Slave Raid", *Slavery Images: A Visual Record of the African Slave Trade and Slave Life in the Early African Diaspora,* accessed November 16, 2020, http://slaveryimages.org/s/slaveryimages/item/2657

I was early snatched away from my native country, with about eighteen or twenty more boys and girls, as we were playing in a field. We lived but a few days' journey from the coast where we were kidnapped... .

Some of us attempted, in vain, to run away, but pistols and cutlasses were soon introduced, threatening, that if we offered to stir, we should all lie dead on the spot. ...

I was kept about six days at [a] man's house, and in the evening there was another man came, and talked with him a good while and I heard the one say to the other he must go, and the other said, the sooner the better; that man came out and told me that he knew my relations at Agimaque, and that we must set out to-morrow morning, and he would convey me there. Accordingly we set out next day, and travelled till dark, when we came to a place where we had some supper and slept. He carried a large bag, with some gold dust, which he said he had to buy some goods at the sea-side to take with him to Agimaque. Next day we travelled on, and in the evening came to a town, where I saw several white people, which made me afraid that they would eat me, according to our notion, as children, in the inland parts of the country. This made me rest very uneasy all the night, and next morning I had some victuals brought, desiring me to eat and make haste, as my guide and kidnapper told me that he had to go to the castle with some company that were going there, as he had told me before, to get some goods.

After I was ordered out, the horrors I soon saw and felt, cannot be well described; I saw many of my miserable countrymen chained two and two, some handcuffed, and some with their hands tied behind. We were conducted along by a guard, and when we arrived at the castle, I asked my guide what I was brought there for, he told me to learn the ways of the browfow, that is, the white-faced people. I saw him take a gun, a piece of cloth, and some lead for me, and then he told me that he must now leave me there, and went off. This made me cry bitterly, but I was soon conducted to a prison, for three days, where I heard the groans and cries of many, and saw some of my fellow-captives. But when

518 O. Cugoano, NARRATIVE OF THE ENSLAVEMENT OF OTTOBAH CUGOANO, A NATIVE OF AFRICA; PUBLISHED BY HIMSELF (James Bullock, 1787), Academic Affairs Library, UNC-CH, available at *docsouth.unc.edu*. The electronic edition has been transcribed from pages 120-127 of the Appendix to "THE NEGRO'S MEMORIAL; OR, ABOLITIONIST'S CATECHISM; BY AN ABOLITIONIST."

a vessel arrived to conduct us away to the ship, it was a most horrible scene; there was nothing to be heard but the rattling of chains, smacking of whips, and the groans and cries of our fellow-men. Some would not stir from the ground, when they were lashed and beat in the most horrible manner. I have forgot the name of this infernal fort; but we were taken in the ship that came for us, to another that was ready to sail from Cape Coast. When we were put into the ship, we saw several black merchants coming on board, but we were all drove into our holes, and not suffered to speak to any of them. In this situation we continued several days in sight of our native land; but I could find no good person to give any information of my situation to Accasa at Agimaque. And when we found ourselves at last taken away, death was more preferable than life; and a plan was concerted amongst us, that we might burn and blow up the ship, and to perish all together in the flames: but we were betrayed by one of our own countrywomen, who slept with some of the headmen of the ship, for it was common for the dirty filthy sailors to take the African women and lie upon their bodies; but the men were chained and pent up in holes. It was the women and boys which were to burn the ship, with the approbation and groans of the rest; though that was prevented, the discovery was likewise a cruel bloody scene.

But it would be needless to give a description of all the horrible scenes which we saw, and the base treatment which we met with in this dreadful captive situation, as the similar cases of thousands, which suffer by this infernal traffic, are well known. Let it suffice to say that I was thus lost to my dear indulgent parents and relations, and they to me. All my help was cries and tears, and these could not avail, nor suffered long, till one succeeding woe and dread swelled up another. Brought from a state of Innocence and freedom, and, In a barbarous and cruel manner, conveyed to a state of horror and slavery, this abandoned situation may be easier conceived than described. From the time that I was kidnapped, and conducted to a factory, and from thence in the brutish, base, but fashionable way of traffic, consigned to Grenada, the grievous thoughts which I then felt, still pant in my heart; though my fears and tears have long since subsided. And yet it is still grievous to think that thousands more have suffered in similar and greater distress, Under the hands of barbarous robbers, and merciless task-masters; and that many, even now, are suffering in all the extreme bitterness of grief and woe, that no language can describe. The cries of some, and the sight of their misery, may be seen and heard afar; but the deep-sounding groans of thousands, and the great sadness of their misery and woe, under the heavy load of oppressions and calamities inflicted upon them, are such as can only be distinctly known to the ears of Jehovah Sabaoth.

This Lord of Hosts, in his great providence, and in great mercy to me, made a way for my deliverance from Grenada. Being in this dreadful captivity and horrible slavery, without any hope of deliverance, for about eight or nine months, beholding the most dreadful scenes of misery and cruelty, and seeing my miserable companions often cruelly lashed, and, as it were, cut to pieces, for the most trifling faults; this made me often tremble and weep, but I escaped better than many of them. For eating a piece of sugar-cane, some were cruelly lashed, or struck over the face, to knock their teeth out. Some of the stouter ones, I suppose, often reproved, and grown hardened and stupid with many cruel beatings and lashings, or perhaps faint and pressed with hunger and hard labour, were often committing trespasses of this kind, and when detected, they met with exemplary punishment. Some told me they had their teeth pulled out, to deter others, and to prevent them from eating any cane in future. Thus seeing my miserable companions and countrymen in this pitiful, distressed, and horrible situation, with all the brutish baseness and barbarity attending it, could not but fill my little mind [with] horror and indignation. But I must own, to the shame of my own countrymen, that I was first kidnapped and betrayed by some of my own complexion, who were the first cause of my exile, and slavery; but if there were no buyers there would be no sellers. So far as I can remember, some of the Africans in my country keep slaves, which they take in war, or for debt; but those which they keep are well fed, and good care taken of them, and treated well; and as to their clothing, they differ according to the custom of the country. But I may safely say, that all the poverty and misery that any of the inhabitants of Africa meet with among themselves, is far inferior to those inhospitable regions of misery which they meet with in the West-Indies, where their hard-hearted overseers have neither Regard to the laws of God, nor the life of their fellow-men.

Thanks be to God, I was delivered from Grenada, and that horrid brutal slavery. A gentleman coming to England took me for his servant, and brought me away, where I soon found my situation become more agreeable. After coming to England, and seeing others write and read, I had a strong desire to learn, and getting what assistance I could, I applied myself to learn reading and writing, which soon became my recreation, pleasure, and delight; and when my master perceived that I could write some, he sent me to a proper school for that purpose to learn. Since, I have endeavoured to improve my mind in reading, and have sought to get all the intelligence I could, in my situation of life, towards the state of my brethren and countrymen in complexion, and of the miserable situation of those who are barbarously sold into captivity, and unlawfully held in slavery.

FINIS

SLAVERS REVENGING THEIR LOSSES.

"Slavers Revenging Their Losses", *Slavery Images: A Visual Record of the African Slave Trade and Slave Life in the Early African Diaspora,* accessed November 16, 2020, h*ttp://slaveryimages.org/s/slaveryimages/item/422*

"Captured Africans Taken to the Coast (either Nigeria, 1853 or Liberia/Sierra Leone, 1840)", *Slavery Images: A Visual Record of the African Slave Trade and Slave Life in the Early African Diaspora,* accessed November 16, 2020, *http://slaveryimages.org/s/slaveryimages/item/393*

"Slaves Abandoned", *Slavery Images: A Visual Record of the African Slave Trade and Slave Life in the Early African Diaspora,* accessed November 16, 2020, *http://slaveryimages.org/s/slaveryimages/item/2899*

Deaths and Floating Tombs

Dr. Beckles quotes historian Joseph Miller describing the Middle Passage as a "death journey." He states that "the Middle Passage … usher[ed] in an hitherto unimaginable level of human degradation,"[519] adding that "the slave ships were in effect 'floating tombs.'"[520]

Dr. Jill Lepore provides the following description of the occurrences and deaths:[521]

> Most of the West and Central Africans in early eighteenth-century New York had witnessed and endured extraordinary suffering. For every one hundred Africans seized in the African interior, only about sixty-four survived the journey to the coast and only about forty-eight or forty-nine made it across the Atlantic's Middle Passage. Of that forty-eight or forty-nine, only between twenty-eight and thirty were still alive after the three- to four-year period of "seasoning."

The specific experiences of particular slave ships varied, of course. Certain ships experienced far more death than did others. Dr. Berlin gives an illustrative example of the slave ship *Venus,* which brought slaves to Louisiana. Even after what would have been substantial deaths in Africa itself:[522]

> Of the 450 slaves loaded aboard the *Venus* in Africa in April 1729, only 363 reached the Mississippi River. Another forty-three succumbed before they disembarked in New Orleans. According to officials, the remaining slaves were so disease-ridden that "more than two-thirds of those who were sold at auction into the hands of the inhabitants … died" soon thereafter.

Dr. James Rawley and Dr. Stephen Behrendt cite a ship named the *Daniel and Henry,* which in 1700 experienced the following:[523]

> The ship's log describes slaving along the Gold Coast until 452 slaves had been acquired and suffering horrendous losses on the Middle Passage. One month out it recorded, "We have now throwne overbord 153 slaves"; and a month later, "wee have now att this day noone 183 slaves dead and many more very bad." At Jamaica the ship sold 246 slaves and six died in port.

The African captives died from disease, starvation, dehydration, abuse, murder, and suicide.

Dr. Herbert Klein cites another cause of death: "148 ships that were lost at sea and all of whose African slaves on board perished."[524]

Among the greatest terrors were the sharks trailing the ships "all the way across the Atlantic." "If the shark was the dread of sailors, it was the outright terror of the enslaved."

Speculum Oris

"The Speculum Oris was a scissor shaped instrument inserted into the mouth of a slave to force the jaws open. The crew of slave ships would force captive Africans to eat so that they couldn't escape servitude by starving themselves to death."

Patricia Smith, Speculum Oris, at *rattle.com/speculum-oris-by-patricia-smith/*, accessed Oct. 9, 2020

519 Beckles, at 105.

520 Beckles, at 116.
See "*—Genocide and Holocaust*" above.

521 Lepore, at 62.

522 Berlin, at 83.

523 Rawley and Behrendt, at 209. Footnote omitted.

524 Klein, at 161.

Nevertheless, despite the terror, jumping overboard was a common means of resistance and suicide. In order to protect their "investments," captains would dispatch crews to attempt "rescues," but many captives drowned or died in the teeth of the sharks.[525]

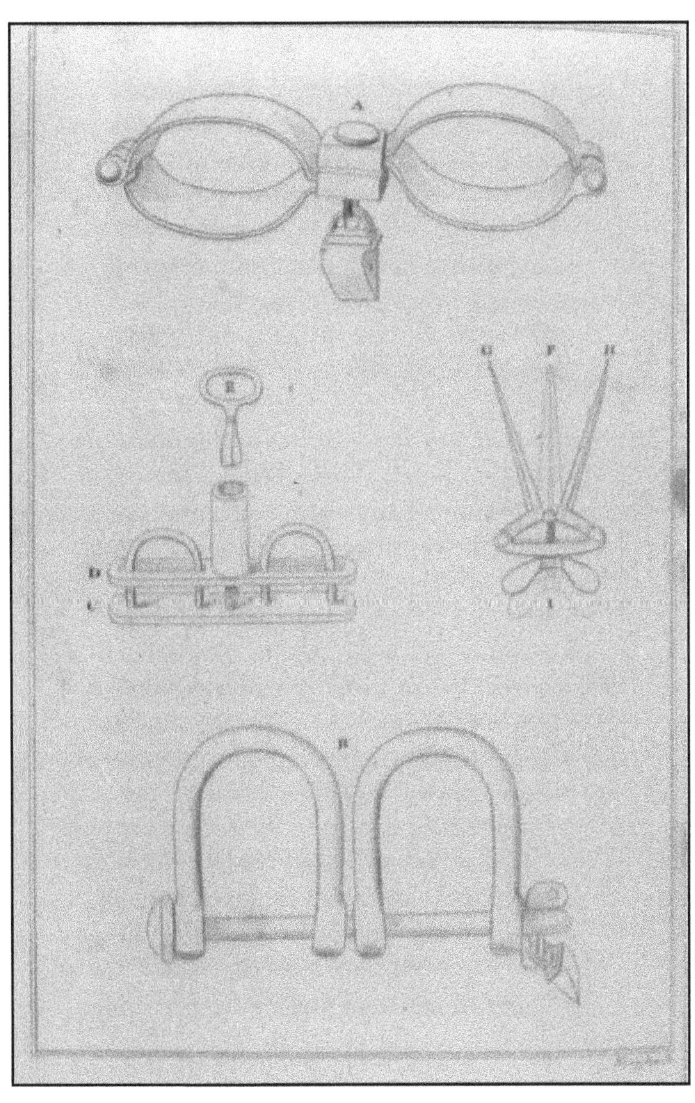

"Untitled Image (Iron Shackles)", *Slavery Images: A Visual Record of the African Slave Trade and Slave Life in the Early African Diaspora*, accessed November 13, 2020, *http://slaveryimages.org/s/slaveryimages/item/2619*

Packing the Ships

Slave traders loaded the ships with tools of terror: "manacles, shackles, neck rings, and chains, as well as the cat-o'-nine-tails, the *speculum oris*, and the thumbscrews … ." [526]

The traders, captains and crews regarded and treated the Africans as "cargo,"[527] not human beings. Crews managed the Africans humans only by assigned numbers.[528] "[M]any a slaver was without any sympathy for the unfortunates."[529]

Dr. Rediker describes the process of chaining the African captives: "[u]nder the direction of the captain and mate as well as the armorer or gunner, the sailors would hammer the cuffs into place, linking the men by twos, the left wrist and ankle of one to the right wrist and ankle of the other." He adds that "[t]he iron constraints excoriated the flesh. Even minimal movement could be painful."[530]

The slave traders wedged the chained Africans into specially constructed holds on the slave ships, frequently chained together, "packed like stones in a wall."[531]

Dr. Beckles describes two methods of storing the slaves in the ships' holds. One was "tight packing" involving alternating captives in a spooned manner, "locked to one another," one captive's head to the heels of the next captive, on the theory that approximately ten percent would be lost by death. The other, loose-packing, assumed

525 Rediker, at 37, 38-39, 288.

526 Rediker, at 202.

527 The Slave Ship.

528 Rediker, at 172.

529 Spears, at 72.

530 Rediker, at 234.

531 Beckles, at 113; Rediker, at 271.

that more captives would survive if treated less inhumanely. Nevertheless, "[o]vercrowding was the norm on all slave ships … ."[532]

Lord Thomas illustrates the available space for the captives by citing one captain who afforded captives on his ship as "a mere fifteenth of the space thought right for a British soldier when engaged in crossing an ocean."[533]

Joseph Kleinman and Eileen Kurtis-Kleinman cite a surgeon as stating that, on the ship *Brookes,* "The slaves were so crammed that they had no room to turn their bodies from one side to the other."[534]

They quote a seventeenth century slave trader as stating:[535]

> "Women who were pregnant were assembled in the back cabin, the children were huddled together … as if they were herrings in a barrel. If anyone wanted to sleep, they lay on top of each other. To satisfy their natural needs, they had bilge places … over the edge of the sea, but, as many feared to lose their place … they relieved themselves where they were, above all the men [who were] cruelly pushed together, in such a way that the heat and smell became intolerable."

<u>CAT O' NINE TAILS</u>

"a whip made of usually nine knotted lines or cords fastened to a handle"

"History and Etymology for *cat-o'-nine-tails*

"from the resemblance of its scars to the scratches of a cat"

"Cat-o'-nine-tails" at *www.merriam-webster.com/dictionary/cat-o'-nine-tails,* accessed Oct. 9, 2020

Dr. Peter Kolchin describes cramped ships with holds five feet high in which "slaves were often crammed together so closely they could barely move."[536]

In the early 1900s, John R. Spears described graphically the holds on a variety of slave ships. Despite minor variances, the result always was that the slave traders afforded the captives only miniscule spaces that the captives endured for months of intense suffering.

The following are John Spears' examples:[537]

> Most of the ships built for the trade in the eighteenth century had two decks. The space between the keel and the lower deck was called the lower hold, while the space between the two decks was sometimes called the upper hold, but was generally designated "'tween decks." The 'tween-deck space was reserved for the slaves. The new slaver built at "Warren in the county of Bristole, in the colony of Rhode Island," was to be "ten feet in the hold, with three feet ten inches betwixt decks." That is to say, the space between the decks where the slaves were to be kept during the time the cargo was accumulating (three to ten months) and while crossing the Atlantic (six to ten weeks) was a room as long and as wide as the

532 Beckles, at 109, 113.

533 Thomas, at 715.

534 J. Kleinman and E. Kurtis-Kleinman, LIFE ON AN AFRICAN SLAVE SHIP at 8 (Lucent Books, 2001) ("Kleinmans").

535 Kleinmans, at 49.

536 Kolchin, at 21.

537 Spears, at 68-71.

ship, but only three feet ten inches high—the space of an average Newport slaver in the days when the traffic was lawful and respected.

The men were ironed together, two and two by the ankles, but women and children were left unironed. They were then taken to the slave-deck, the males forward of a bulkhead built abaft the main hatch, and the women aft. There all were compelled to lie down with their backs on the deck and feet outboard. In this position the irons on the men were usually secured to chains or iron rods that were rove through staples in the deck, or the ceiling of the ship. The entire deck was covered with them lying so. They were squeezed so tightly together, in fact, that the average space allowed to each one was but sixteen inches wide by five and a half feet long.

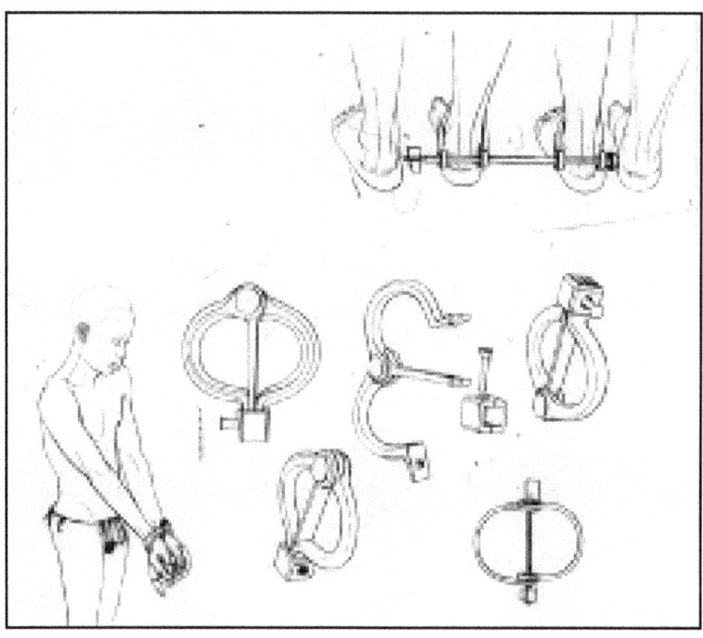

"Fers pour négres", *Slavery Images: A Visual Record of the African Slave Trade and Slave Life in the Early African Diaspora,* accessed November 13, 2020, *http://slaveryimages.org/s/slaveryimages/item/2063*

In the Liverpool ships in the latter part of the eighteenth century—ships that carried from three hundred to five hundred slaves at a load—the average height between the two decks was five feet two inches. This statement of the average distance between decks was proven by measuring many ships. But that is not to say that the slaves were more comfortable on the ships having greater space between decks. On the contrary, they were less so. Economy of space was studied with a sharp eye. It would never do to allow all that space between decks to remain unoccupied. So a shelf or gallery, usually six feet wide, was suspended midway between the two decks, and on this another layer of slaves was placed Of course the deck under the shelf or gallery was covered with slaves packed as closely together as possible. This shelf was made of unplaned lumber, and there was no effort to make tight the joints between the boards.

The smaller ships—the sloops and schooners that had no 'tween-decks—were arranged for stowing the slaves by building a temporary deck beneath the upper one. Having stowed the barrels of food and water in the hold so as to occupy as little space as possible, a row of stanchions, fore and aft on the keelson, and rising just above the barrels, was erected. These were connected by a ridge-pole, and from this ridgepole rafters were extended to the sides of the ship. On the rafters common unplaned boards were laid. Thus a deck was laid that could be easily removed on occasion.

The space between this deck and the upper one was rarely, if ever, more than three feet high, and cases are on record where it was considerably less than two feet—in this century even as little as eighteen inches.

Most of the vessels used after the trade was outlawed were of the small, single-decked class. Because the trade was unlawful these slavers had to be prepared to pass as palm-oil buyers when they were overhauled by a cruiser, and they could not do that if they had a slave-deck laid. Accordingly the slave deck was not laid until the slaves were on the beach ready to embark. Being then in great haste the slaver did not usually go to the trouble of erecting stanchions and building his deck substantially. He merely laid his rafters or timbers on the barrels, as best he might; spread the boards over them, with a nail driven in here and there, perhaps, but sometimes with never a nail to hold them in place, and then the slaves were brought on board and jammed into the thin space with less regard for their comfort than is shown now for hogs shipped in a two-deck stock-car.

"On Board a Slave Ship", *Slavery Images: A Visual Record of the African Slave Trade and Slave Life in the Early African Diaspora,* accessed November 14, 2020, *http://slaveryimages.org/s/slaveryimages/item/2559*

In fact, when the cruisers became at last somewhat vigilant, cargoes were shipped in vessels that had no slave-deck; the slaves were piled on the barrels of food and water until the barrels were blanketed out of sight.

But the limit of devilish ingenuity in stowing slaves was not reached until the trade was outlawed. To increase the number of slaves on the deck they were then compelled to lie on their sides, breast to back, "spoon fashion," to use the term then common. Where the 'tween-deck space was two feet high or more the slaves were stowed sitting up in rows, one crowded into the lap of another, and with legs on legs, like riders on a crowded toboggan. In storms the sailors had to put on the hatches, and seal tight the openings into the infernal cesspool.

In early days of slavery, the Middle Passage for the Africans packed tightly in this manner could require up to four months or even more,[538] depending upon weather and favorable winds. Later, with experience, trips still required six to eight weeks.[539]

Beginning in the 1660s, until the Duke of York's reign as King James II ended, the Royal African Company, under the Duke's control, would have operated in this manner with the benefit of his governmental sponsorship of the slave trade to America and of the Duke's control of African forts captured from the Dutch. After the English deposed King James II, the Royal African Company he founded continued to operate as a slave trader for decades, including but not limited to, during the reigns of his two daughters, Queen Mary and Queen Anne.[540]

538 Eltis, at 156-57; Rediker, at 212.; The Slave Ship; Cottman.

539 Eltis, at 156-57; Rediker, at 212; Liverpool Trade Triangle.

540 See *"Chapter One: Meet America's Slave Society—Why the Duke of York Is the Father of America's Slave Society," "Chapter Three: The Duke of York Promotes Slavery,"* and *"Appendix II: King Charles II's 1664 Charter Granting to the Duke of York Authority Over New York."*

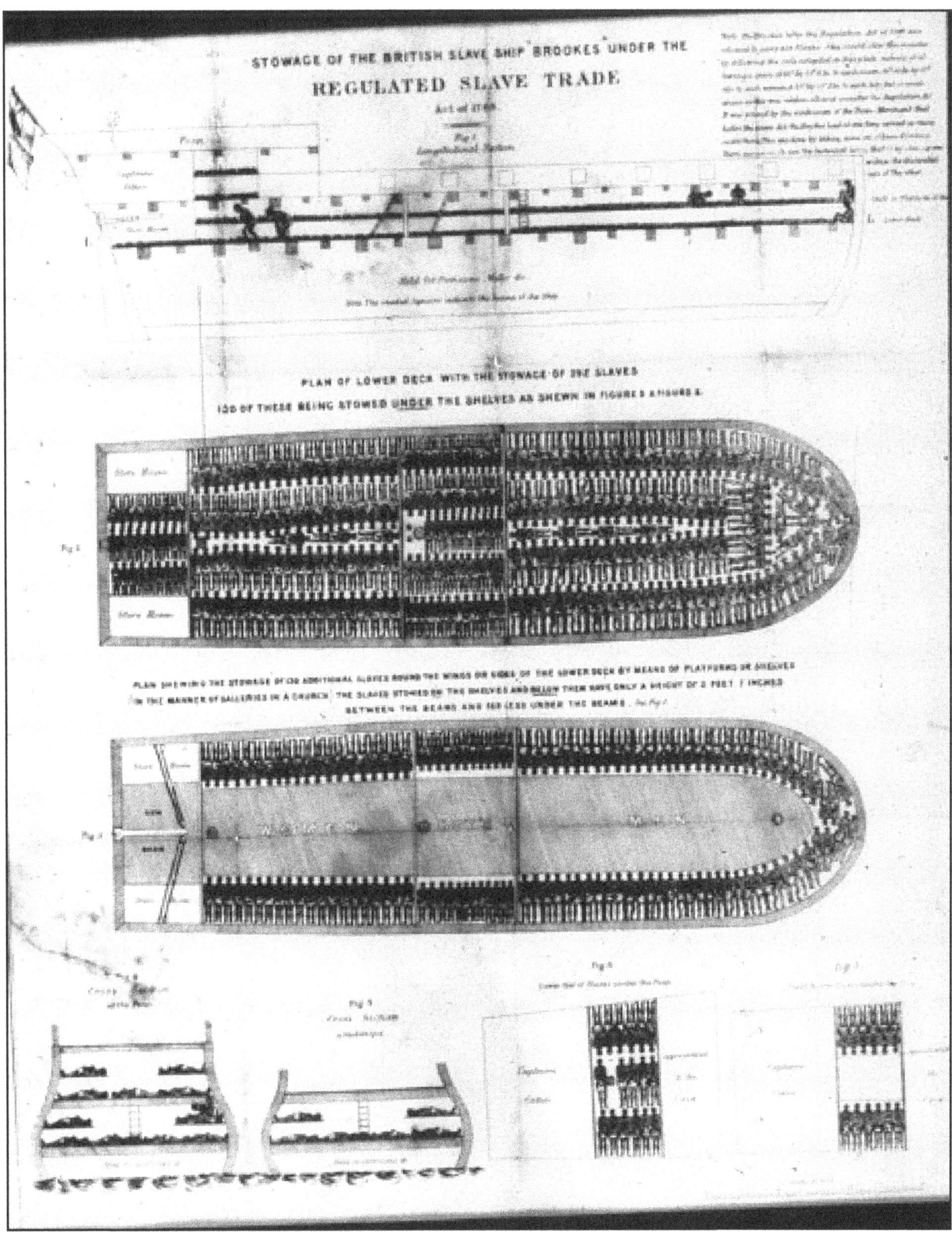

"Stowage of the British Slave Ship Brookes under the Regulated Slave Trade Act of 1788", *Slavery Images: A Visual Record of the African Slave Trade and Slave Life in the Early African Diaspora*, accessed November 13, 2020, ***http://slaveryimages.org/s/slaveryimages/item/2553***

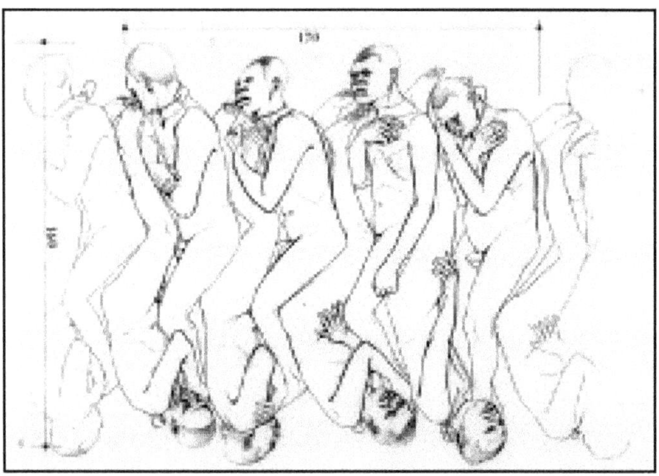

Untitled Image (Sleeping Positions of Captive Africans on the French Slave Ship L'Aurore)", *Slavery Images: A Visual Record of the African Slave Trade and Slave Life in the Early African Diaspora,* accessed November 13, 2020, *http://slaveryimages.org/s/slaveryimages/item/2552*

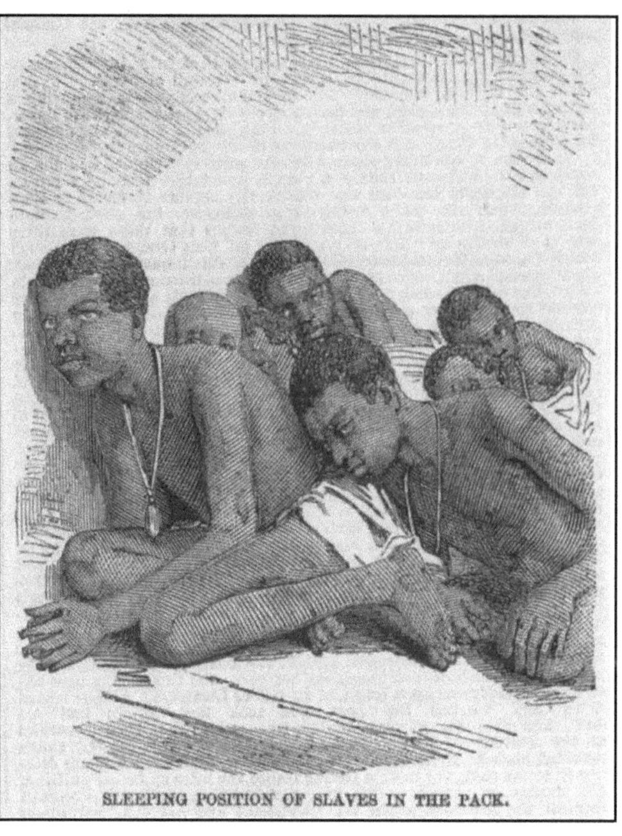

"Sleeping Position of Africans on Slave Ship, 1857," *Slavery Images: A Visual Record of the African Slave Trade and Slave Life in the Early African Diaspora*, accessed November 14, 2020, *http://slaveryimages.org/s/slaveryimages/item/2764*

"The Africans of the Slave Bark 'Wildfire'", *Slavery Images: A Visual Record of the African Slave Trade and Slave Life in the Early African Diaspora,* accessed November 14, 2020, *http://slaveryimages.org/s/slaveryimages/item/2575*

"Africans Rescued from a Slave Ship, East Africa, 1869", *Slavery Images: A Visual Record of the African Slave Trade and Slave Life in the Early African Diaspora,* accessed November 13, 2020, *http://slaveryimages.org/s/slaveryimages/item/2043*

Slaves as "Investments"

The bottom line was that "Slaves were a costly investment, and the slavers were concerned to maximize their profits, even if this meant losing quite a few slaves by doing so."[541] Dr. Beckles describes the slave trade as highly competitive and speculative, with individual voyages quite profitable, and others losing money. Thus, it was important to minimize costs and maximize revenues by whatever means possible.[542]

Dr. Beckles and Dr. Rediker describe average slave trade profits from six to eight percent up to nine or ten percent, with Dr. Beckles adding: "it was nevertheless possible to realize large profits on individual voyages, or on a small cluster of voyages."[543]

According to Lonnie Bunch, Secretary of the Smithsonian Institution, by the eighteenth century, sales of individual Africans as slaves could occur for prices equivalent to $9,000 to $15,000 today.[544]

Once the international slave trade became prohibited, smuggling profits rose considerably with the greater risks to the smugglers. John Spears describes the profits of one ship:[545]

> In an estimate of the steamer's profits ..., [the slave trader] placed the cost at $300,000, and the income—"1,200 negroes at $650, $780,000, which leaves net profit and steamer on hand, $480,000."

ACCOUNT OF A SLAVE SHIP DURING A RESCUE

"She had taken in, on the coast of Africa, 336 males and 226 females, making in all 562, and had been out seventeen days, during which she had thrown overboard fifty-five. The slaves were all inclosed under grated hatchways between decks. The space was so low that they sat between each other's legs and [were] stowed so close together that there was no possibility of their lying down or at all changing their position by night or day. As they belonged to and were shipped on account of different individuals, they were all branded like sheep with the owners' marks of different forms. These were impressed under their breasts or on their arms, and, as the mate informed me with perfect indifference 'burnt with the red-hot iron.' Over the hatchway stood a ferocious-looking fellow with a scourge of many twisted thongs in his hand...

"The heat of these horrid places was so great and the odor so offensive that it was quite impossible to enter them, even had there been room. ..."

"Aboard a Slave Ship: An Account by The Rev. Robert Walsh, 1829" at *www.thirteen.org/wnet/historyofus/web05/features/source/docs/C04.pdf,* accessed Oct. 5, 2020.

Using the inflation multiple of 33, the sale price of each slave at $650 would be equivalent to $21,450 today. The estimated net profit of $480,000 would be equivalent to $15,840,000.

Disease and Filth

Dr. Kolchin quotes Alexander Falconbridge, "a doctor on numerous slaving voyages," who cited unbearable heat in the ships' holds. Dr. Falconbridge added that: "The floor of their rooms, was so covered with the blood and mucus which had proceeded from them in consequence of the flux, that it resembled a slaughterhouse."[546]

541 Beckles, at 114.

542 Beckles, at 120-31.

543 Beckles, at 122; Rediker, at 50.

544 "The Slave Ship" at *cbsnews.com/news/the-slave-ship-60-minutes/,* accessed Oct. 6 2020.

545 Spears, at 198.

546 Kolchin, at 21.

Disease was rampant and, in the absence of sanitation, spread easily.[547] The National Museums Liverpool states: "Epidemics of fever, dysentery (the 'flux') and smallpox were frequent."[548] Of course, there was extensive death. "Sickness and death were central to the African experience aboard the slave ship."[549]

Dr. James Rawley and Dr. Stephen Behrendt state: "[w]ithout doubt disease was a relentless killer of slaves on shipboard." They enumerate "Dysentery, 'fever,' measles, smallpox, and scurvy. Dysentery, often called by contemporaries 'the flux,' was perhaps the most common disease." They also identify "ophthalmia, contagious and a cause of blindness" as "affict[ing] Africans in great number," the "yaws, a chronic, contagious tropical disease characterized by raspberry-like swellings," and intestinal worms, which "often began in childhood."[550]

According to Dr. Rediker, one sailor testified that: "Sickness was a big part of the experience. Breathing "infected air" amid "green contagion," the fevered lie "strew' o'er the filthy deck."[551]

Dr. Rediker states that health conditions on a "sickly" slave ship "everyone agreed, was a horror beyond imagination." Ships lacked room for hospitals. The sick lay on bare planks rubbing them raw. "A man below decks sometimes awoke in the morning and found himself shackled to a corpse."[552]

A doctor stated that "the stench and foul air were … intolerable."[553] According to John Spears:[554]

> It was asserted by the naval officers who were stationed on the coast to stop the traffic that in certain states of the weather they could detect the odor of a slaver further away than they could see her on a clear night. The odor was often unmistakable at a distance of five miles down wind.

Dr. Rediker provides a graphic and sickening description of the combination of the tight packing of the chained human beings and the need of human beings to "answer the call of nature." The tight packing of the captives could result in fights among them, especially[555]

> **"I CAN'T BREATHE"**
>
> In the context of the stench and filth on slave ships, the phrase "I can't breathe," disseminated recently, takes on a special and historic connotation.

> occasioned by the efforts of the captives to get through the mass of bodies to the necessary tubs to relieve themselves. …
>
> Any man who had to answer the call of nature had to coordinate the trip with his partner, who might not wish to be disturbed … . If the partner proved willing, two people then tried to make their way through the multitude of bodies, all the while negotiating the rolling motions of the ship. Inevitably, one person stepped or fell on another …

547 Beckles, at 107-09; "Life on board slave ships" at *www.liverpoolmuseums.org.uk/history-of-slavery/middle-passage#section--log-book-of-the-unity,-1769-1770*, accessed Oct. 6, 2020 ("Liverpool History").

548 Liverpool History.

549 Rediker, at 273.

550 Rawley and Behrendt, at 250, 252.

551 Rediker, at 150.

552 Rediker, at 274.

553 Rediker, at 274.

554 Spears, at 71.

555 Rediker, at 271-72.

> These difficulties pale, however, when compared to what happened when sickness—especially dysentery or any other malady that produced diarrhea—swept through the lower deck. Suddenly the afflicted could not always get to the tubs in time, or in some instances they were simply too weak to make the effort … . This … was a special torment to West Africans, who were known to pride themselves on personal cleanliness.

In one case, Dr. Rediker describes, and John Spears confirms, a crew's actions following the captain's directions, despite the mate's objections, that if the crew threw captives overboard so that the captives experienced a "natural death" then insurance underwriters would bear the loss:[556]

> The ship soon grew sickly: sixty Africans and seven members of the crew perished . …
>
> [T]hat evening the crew threw 54 slaves, hands bound, overboard. They threw another 42 over the side two days later, and 26 more soon after. Ten of the enslaved watched the hideous spectacle and jumped overboard of their own volition, committing suicide and bringing the number of deaths to 132.

John Spears cites the Captain on a ship named the *Gloria* who had underestimated the water needed. When the Captain discovered the mistake at sea, he prescribed strict water rations, with the result that slaves received no water at all. "Death followed so fast that in a short time at least a hundred men and women were shackled to dead partners."[557]

The witness describing the incident continued by stating that:[558]

> That night we caroused, and satisfied our thirst, whilst the negroes suffocated below. Next morning came a storm, which drove us on our course a hundred knots. Two days afterward, Ruiz and four of the men were taken suddenly ill with a disease that baffled my medical knowledge. Their tongues swelled, and grew black; their flesh turned yellow, and in six hours they were dead. The first mate went next, and then three others of the crew, and a black driver, whose body became leprous with yellow spots. I began to notice a strange, fetid smell pervading the vessel, and a low, heavy fog on deck, almost like steam. Then the horrid truth became apparent. Our rotting negroes under hatches had generated the plague, and it was a malaria or death-mist that I saw rising. At this time all our men but three and myself had been attacked; and we abandoned the *Gloria*, in her long boat, taking the remnant of water, a sack of biscuit, and a rum beaker, with what gold-dust and other valuables we could hastily gather up. We left nine of our late comrades dead and five dying on the *Gloria's* deck. After running for two days we struck a current, and in three more were drifted to the island of Tortola.

---

556 Rediker, at 240; Spears, at 72-74.

557 Spears, at 75.

558 Spears, at 75-76.

Suicide

Suicide was unexceptional. Dr. Beckles states that desperate slaves would commit suicide, which was "commonplace."[559]

Dr. Beckles cites an example provided by Hugh Thomas of "a case witnessed by slavers of the Dutch West India Company in 1767:"[560]

> "A harsh response followed a sale of Ashanti slaves in Elmina ... Six captives had been personal servants of a recently dead director-general of the ... company. and they would have been freed if the Asantehene had paid some debts which he owed the company. But he did not, and the Dutch decided to sell the men concerned to traders. "We put their feet in shackles", ... on the day that they were to be sold; the slave dungeons were thoroughly searched for knives and weapons, but apparently not enough..."
>
> "The result ... was that when the company slaves were ordered into yards to hold each other, they (the personal slaves) ... cut their own throats; one negro even cut the throat of his wife and then his own; the yard of the noble company's chief castle was thus turned into a bloodbath."

FORCED FEEDING

"Many others, to kill themselves, refused to eat. They were flogged to compel them to eat, but this failed so often that it was the custom for all slavers to carry a tube-like instrument used by surgeons to force food into the mouths of patients suffering from lockjaw. This was driven into the mouths of obstinate negroes, smashing lips and teeth, until food could be forced down the throat. Instances were described where the lips were burned with coals and hot irons to compel the negroes to open their mouths and swallow the food."

J. Spears, The American Slave Trade: An Account of Its Origins, Growth and Suppression at 77 (Scribner, 1907)

On slave ships, African captives choosing death over enslavement did so most commonly by jumping overboard or by self-starvation. Despite crews' efforts to preserve "cargo value," captives succeeded.

Dr. Rawley and Dr. Behrendt describe the feeding process:[561]

> The feeding of the slaves early in the trade became routinized. It was customary to give two meals a day, placing ten slaves about small tubs containing their victuals. Each slave was provided with a wooden spoon. A staple on English ships was horse beans, brought from England and stored in dry vats until they were boiled in lard until they formed a pulp. ... Rice, available both in Europe and Africa was a second staple; it was sometimes boiled with yams, available in Africa. Meat, whether beef or pork, was rarely offered. ... Palm oil, flour, water, and pepper mixed together produced *slabber-sauce.* Corn (wheat), vegetables, lemons, and limes from time to time appeared in this regimen.

When "some people refused to eat, willfully or because they were sick or depressed," "[v]iolence would force them." The crews accomplished this by utilizing the cat o' nine tails, thumbscrews, or other torture instruments, or the *speculum oris.*[562]

---

559 Beckles, at 140.

560 Beckles, at 140-41.

561 Rawley and Behrendt, at 256.

562 Rediker, at 238; Cottman.

Joseph Kleinman and Eileen Kurtis-Kleinman cite the doctor, Alexander Falconbridge as stating that "Upon the Negroes refusing to take sustenance, … I have seen coals of fire, glowing hot, put on a shovel and placed so near their lips to scorch and burn them."[563]

Dr. Rediker cites accounts, provided by ships' crews, officers, and doctors, of Africans who chose to end their lives by extraordinarily desperate means. The first account was related by a ship's doctor who had adjudged a man brought on board, to have "every symptom of a sullen melancholy:"[564]

> The man immediately refused all sustenance. From the beginning of his captivity aboard the ship, he simply would not eat. This reaction, too, was commonplace, but he went further. Early one morning, when sailors went below to check on the captives, they found the man a bloody mess. They urgently called the doctor. The man had attempted to cut his own throat and had succeeded in "dividing only the external jugular vein." He had lost more than a pint of blood. [The doctor] stitched up the wound and apparently considered force-feeding the man.

During the stitching procedure, the captive "declared simply and straightforwardly that 'he would never go with white men.'"

A search for weapons turned up nothing. Forced feeding was not a viable solution due to the neck wound. However, "[t]he following night the man made a second attempt on his own life. He tore out the sutures and cut his throat on the other side." Since the crew could find no tools that could have caused the wounds, the doctor finally concluded that the man "had ripped open his throat with his own fingernails." The crew tied the man's hands to prevent further efforts, but the man "refused all sustenance, and died in about a week or ten days afterwards of mere want of food."[565]

In another account, Dr. Rediker portrays suicide by female captives on a different ship:[566]

> Two women, who were among "the finest slaves on the ship," watched the violence and took rebellious action. They poignantly folded themselves in each other's arms and "plunged over the poop of the vessel into the sea." As they drowned, the other women "cried out in a most affecting manner, and many of them were preparing to follow their companions." They were locked belowdecks immediately to prevent mass suicide.

The sheer sadism, and the viciousness practiced against the African captives on board ships, could not be accentuated more than in the following account of a nine-month-old baby's "suicide" by starvation in 1765 on a ship named the *Black Joke:*[567]

> a small child, whose mother was also on board, "took sulk, and would not eat," refusing both the breast and standard fare of rice mixed with palm oil. Captain Thomas Marshall flogged the child with the cat [o' nine tails] as enslaved men looked on through the crevices of the barricado: they made "a great murmuring" in protest. Still the child refused to eat, and day after day the captain wielded the cat but also tied a mango log, eighteen to twenty inches long and twelve to thirteen pounds in weight, around its neck by a string. "The last time he took the child up and flogged it," … he "let it drop out of his

563 Kleinmans, at 52.

564 Rediker, at 17-18.

565 Rediker, at 17-18; Spears, at 77.

566 Rediker, at 151.

567 Rediker, at 286; Spears, at 77-78.

> hands" to the deck, saying "Damn you. … I will make you eat, or I will be the death of you." In less than an hour, the child died.

That was not, however, sufficient to satisfy the Captain:[568]

> In a final act of cruelty, the captain commanded the child's mother to throw the small corpse overboard. When she refused, he beat her. Eventually, she complied, and afterward, "she seemed very sorry, and cried for several hours." Even the smallest rebel, a nine-month-old child who refused to eat, could not be tolerated aboard the *Black Joke*."

John Spears adds to this story:[569]

> Of the truth of the story there is no doubt. It was told under oath before a committee of Parliament, and of all the tales of inhuman deeds perpetrated by the slavers, none had more effect in ridding the earth of the traffic than this.

"Traversée: Danse de négres", *Slavery Images: A Visual Record of the African Slave Trade and Slave Life in the Early African Diaspora,* accessed November 27, 2020, *http://slaveryimages.org/s/slaveryimages/item/2554*

The ships' crews not only forced African captives to eat, but they also forced the captives to exercise, despite their chains. Slavers called this "dancing." Ships' physicians considered exercise important to maintain the captives' health as an investment. As with refusals to eat, the ships' crews applied the instruments of torture to coerce the captives to move around.[570]

John Spears provides additional detail regarding the forced dancing:[571]

> From one point of view the picture of a gang of slaves when on deck for an airing was one of the most shocking known to the trade. For the slaver captain knew how much brooding over their wrongs tended to promote disease, and his chief object in bringing them on deck was to cheer them. He wanted them to sing and dance, and he saw that they did it too—he applied the lash not only to make them eat, but to make them sing. There they stood in rows and as the brawny slaver, whip in hand, paced to and fro, they sang their home-songs, and danced, each with his free foot slapping the deck.

Insurrection and Punishment

Insurrections were a serious threat to slavers. Dr. Beckles describes African resistance by attacking ships, and slaves revolting in bloody insurrections both before and during their voyages. He adds that "The records of the English Royal African Company are … replete with such incidents of protest and rebellion."[572]

---

568 Rediker, at 286; Spears, at 77-78.

569 Spears, at 78.

570 Rediker, at 237-38; Liverpool History.

571 Spears, at 78.

572 Beckles, at 137-43.

Dr. Herbert Klein states that "[s]laves rebelled—sometimes successfully—on a total of 313 voyages, and Africans on the coast cut off the slave ships or their small boats on another 70 voyages."[573]

Dr. David Eltis states that:[574]

> The vast majority of rebellions resulted in inordinate bloodletting, whatever the outcome. If the slaves got the upper hand, even temporarily, most of the crew could expect to be killed. If the crew retained control, the death of the rebel leaders was almost inevitable, and the actual numbers of slaves put to death would be limited only by the need to get enough slaves to the Americas to ensure a profit in what was a highly competitive business. Naked physical force determined who would be in control of a slave ship; any relaxation of vigilance or reduction in the amount of force available would mean rebellion.

Occasionally, when captives saw that a rebellion would fail, they chose to destroy the ship, including themselves and the entire crew. Dr. Rediker cites an instance in 1773 on the ship *New Britannia,* when rebelling captives "saw that defeat at the hands of the crew was inevitable," and then "they set fire to the magazine, and blowed the vessel up." The result was the death of "almost everyone on board, as many as three hundred altogether."[575]

"Punishment Aboard a Slave Ship, 1792", *Slavery Images: A Visual Record of the African Slave Trade and Slave Life in the Early African Diaspora,* accessed November 13, 2020, *http://slaveryimages.org/s/slaveryimages/item/2040*

He cites another instance described by a sailor, in which "all the slaves [locked belowdecks] unanimously… rush[ed] to leeward in a gale of wind, on purpose to upset the ship, choosing to drown themselves … ."[576]

Dr. Beckles affirms that Europeans would use "the most gruesome punishments" for rebellions by slaves, including "hang[ing] rebel leaders by their feet and whip[ping] them to death," and cutting off limbs, allowing leaders to bleed to death. In other cases, Europeans would behead bodies and throw them overboard.[577]

Dr. Rediker describes tortures of captives who had engaged in failed insurrections. Captains would engage in "exemplary public punishments" on the main deck using, among other weapons, the cat o' nine tails, thumbscrews, and "a large cook's fork, which was heated white hot and applied to the flesh of rebels."[578]

573 Klein, at 161.

574 Eltis, at 157.

575 Rediker, at 290.

576 Rediker, at 290.

577 Beckles, at 139.

578 Rediker, at 217.

Dr. Rediker supports Dr. Beckles' reference to "gruesome punishments" with an account by the first mate on the slave ship *Brownlow* based upon statements made by the ship's Captain, Richard Jackson:[579]

> After a failed insurrection, Jackson sentenced the rebellious slaves to die, then selected their mode of punishment. The first group
>
> > he jointed; that is, he cut off, with an axe, first their feet, then their legs below the knee, then their thighs; in like manner their hands, then their arms below the elbow, and then at their shoulders, till their bodies remained only like the trunk of a tree when all the branches are lopped away; and lastly their heads. And as he proceeded in his operation, he threw the reeking members and heads in the midst of the bulk of the trembling slaves, who were chained upon the main-deck.
>
> The terror so far was insufficient, so Captain Jackson then punished the second group:
>
> > He tied round the upper parts of the heads of others a small soft platted rope, which the sailors call a point, so loosely as to admit a short lever: by continuing to turn the lever, he drew the point more and more tight, till at length he forced their eyes to stand out of their heads; and when he had satiated himself with their torments, he cut off their heads.

"Africans Thrown Overboard from a Slave Ship, Early 19th cent.", *Slavery Images: A Visual Record of the African Slave Trade and Slave Life in the Early African Diaspora,* accessed November 14, 2020, *http://slaveryimages.org/s/slaveryimages/item/2011*

John Spears provides an account based upon testimony of a deponent regarding a smuggling ship, with the testimony then furnished to Congress and the President:[580]

> On the voyage there was an insurrection. It was quickly subdued by force, but, through fear of more trouble of the kind, the captain determined to punish the ringleaders. In all, forty-six men and one woman were hanged and shot to death.
>
> "They were ironed or chained, two together, and when they were hung, a rope was put round their necks and they drawn up to the yard-arm clear of the sail," said one of the crew when testifying under oath. "This did not kill them, but only choked or strangled them. They were then shot in the breast and the bodies thrown overboard. If only one of two that were ironed together was to be hung, the rope was

579 Rediker, at 218-19.

580 Spears, at 79-81.

put around his neck and he was drawn up clear of the deck, and his leg laid across the rail and chopped off to save the irons and release him from his companion, who at the same time lifted up his leg till the other was chopped off as aforesaid, and he released.

"The bleeding negro was then drawn up, shot in the breast, and thrown overboard as aforesaid. The legs of about one dozen were chopped off in this way.

"When the feet fell on deck they were picked up by the crew and thrown overboard, and sometimes they shot at the body while it still hung living, and all kinds of sport was made of the business.

"When the woman was hung up and shot, the ball did not take effect, and she was thrown overboard living, and was seen to struggle some time in the water before she sunk; and deponent further says, that after this was over they brought up and flogged about twenty men and six women. The flesh of some of them where they were flogged putrefied and came off in some cases six or eight inches in diameter, and in places half an inch thick."

SUICIDE BY PUNISHMENT

"How men and women were flogged to death; how they died smiling under the blows, saying, 'Soon we shall be free'; how they leaped overboard and exultingly bade farewell to friends who rejoiced in their escape—all that has been told over and again by the slaver captains themselves."

J. Spears, The American Slave Trade: An Account of Its Origins, Growth and Suppression at 77 (Scribner, 1907)

The Story of the Amistad

In August 1829, approximately 50 African captives led by a "Mende Tribesman, Joseph Cinque," plus one Cuban slave owned by the captain, rebelled aboard the slave ship *Amistad*.[581]

John Spears describes the revolt according to the description of one of two survivors allowed to remain on board, Jose Ruiz:[582]

> She had sailed from Havana on June 27th, bound for Guanaja, in the Cuban state of Puerto Principe, but on the night of June 30th the slaves on the ship had mutinied, killed the captain and cook, sent the two sailors ashore in the boat, and ordered him (Ruiz) and Pedro Montez to navigate the ship to Africa. Under fear of death the *Amistad* had been steered toward the east by day, but at night she had been headed for the United States. So it had happened that they had been for several days within a few miles of Long Island, and had finally anchored where found in order to get food and water.

The American government imprisoned the Africans, and an international controversy erupted between slavery advocates and abolitionists.[583]

John Spears describes the Spanish false claim on the Africans as based upon fraudulent translation of Spanish documentation, with the Spanish asserting that the Africans were actually Cuban slaves. The Spanish asserted

581 Kleinmans, at 72; Spears, at 184-93.

582 Spears, at 185-86.

583 Spears, at 187 *et seq.*

their claim pursuant to a treaty with the United States calling for the return of property taken by pirates. Thus, the Spanish claimed that the Africans on the ship effectively were pirates. American government officials sought to assist the Spanish in gaining control over the Africans.[584]

Abolitionists, however, entered the picture. As described by John Spears:[585]

> [T]he negroes, who were put in jail at New London, had found friends who were willing to spend money to see that they had a fair trial, were that possible in the existing state of civilization.

The abolitionists were able to expose the fraudulent translation of the Spanish documentation. Mr. Spears continues:[586]

> In short, the abolitionists said these negroes, that had been taken from their African homes and carried to Cuba, contrary to the laws of Spain, were not slaves but freemen, and when they were confined as slaves on the *Amistad* they had the natural right to rise against those who restrained them, and to regain liberty even if they had to kill two men to do it.

Although American officials sought to turn the Africans over to the Spanish, the courts intervened. The case reached the Supreme Court. John Quincy Adams argued successfully for the slaves' freedom.[587]

Justice Story wrote the Court's opinion:[588]

> He said that in order to sustain the claims of Ruiz and Montez [the two survivors on the Amistad] "it is essential to establish: 1st. That these negroes under all the circumstances fall within the description of merchandise in the sense of the treaty [between Spain and America]. 2d. That there has been a rescue of them on the high seas out of the hands of the pirates and robbers, which, in the present case, can only be by showing that they themselves are pirates and robbers. 3d. That Ruiz and Montez, the asserted proprietors, are the true proprietors, and have established their title by competent proof."
>
> As to the first point, if the negroes had been lawfully held as slaves under the Spanish law, said the Justice, "we see no reason why they may not justly be deemed, within the intent of the treaty, to be included under the denomination of merchandise. ... But admitting this, it is clear, in our opinion ... it is plain beyond controversy, if we examine the evidence, they never were the lawful slaves of Ruiz or Montez, or of any other Spanish subject. ... If, then, these negroes are not slaves ... there is no pretence to say they are pirates or robbers. But it is argued on behalf of the United States that the ship and cargo and negroes were duly documented as belonging to Spanish subjects, and this court has no right to look behind these documents. ... To this argument we can in nowise assent. ... The very language of the ninth article of the treaty of 1795 requires the proprietor to make due and sufficient proof of his property. And how can that proof be deemed either due or sufficient which is but a connected and stained tissue of fraud? Upon the whole, our opinion is ... that the said negroes be declared free, and be dismissed from the custody of the court, and go without date."

---

584 Spears, at 186-87.

585 Spears, 187.

586 Spears, at 187-88.

587 Kleinmans, at 72.

588 Spears, at 188-89. Footnote omitted.

In addition to the Africans, one captive on the Amistad had been a Cuban slave of the deceased captain. That slave, however, "simply disappeared," with the probable aid of the underground railroad.[589]

John Spears declares triumphantly that:[590]

> [T]he Supreme Court of the United States, when it heard the case, decided then, for the first time, that black men carried from their homes in Africa as slaves had the right, when seeking their liberty, to kill any who would deprive them of it.

In 1832, Mr. Cinque and several other Amistad survivors returned to Africa, settling in Liberia.[591]

Rape

Rape of enslaved women on the slave ships was common. Dr. Rediker provides the following description:[592]

> The cabin would ... be the place where the captain asserted his power over the bodies of enslaved women on board as he routinely took "wives" or "favorites" and forced them to stay in his chambers and provide for his sexual pleasure.

He then cites the *Charleston* on which "the captain and indeed all the officers took three to four 'wives' each and sold them for a 'good price' once they reached the New World."

Crew members did not have the same privileges, but regardless of how "consent" might have been obtained, "were allowed to have intercourse with such of the black women whose consent they can procure."[593]

Slave Society's Perspective

Although the slave trade had a terrible reputation, the slave society's perspectives on the Middle Passage were less grim than the preceding descriptions. Even then, however, there was grudging acknowledgement of horrible conditions.

Thomas R.R. Cobb, the prominent slavery legal advocate, while describing his perspective discounting the treatment of the captives, nevertheless confirms that the Middle Passage was a significantly undesirable experience for Africans:[594]

> The passage from Africa to the Colonies was the most trying period in the sufferings of the slaves. The "horrors of the middle passage" have been sung by poets, and minutely described by eye-witnesses. Nothing, added so much to the final prohibition of the trade. Yet doubtless these "horrors" have been exaggerated. The cupidity and avarice of the dealer tempted him to overload his small vessel. Yet experience soon taught that the consequent pestilence and decimation of his cargo, more than overbalanced his gains. Self-interest co-operated with humanity in demanding a proper regard to the health and comfort of the victims. The slaves were transported naked. Yet clothing was, to them, an unknown and unnecessary luxury. The males were secured with irons when put on board, but these were removed, unless they proved unruly and rebellious. The decks, between which they were stowed side

589 Spears, at 191.

590 Spears, at 193.

591 Kleinmans, at 72.

592 Rediker, at 203.

593 Rediker, at 242.

594 Cobb, Vol I, at clv-clvi. Footnotes omitted.

> by side like bales of goods, were only high enough to allow a sitting posture. Yet the day was spent on the upper deck, and ample provision made for ventilation; while cleanliness was enforced as a matter of necessity. Wholesome and bountiful food was provided, as a matter of calculation for the improvement of their appearance. While bathing and other sanitary regulations were of universal practice. (sic)
>
> While this is the general truth, instances existed of great wretchedness experienced during the voyage. And, even with all these precautions, disease frequently made sad havoc among the poor creatures. Avarice and cupidity too frequently drowned the voice of experience; and hence we find the British Parliament, by statute, restricting the number of slaves to be carried to *five* for every *three* tons, up to 201 tons, and to *one* for every additional ton. By the same act, a well-qualified surgeon was required on every vessel ...
>
> The profits of such a trade, notwithstanding the large percentage of deaths, are manifest.
>
> The negroes thus imported were generally contented and happy. ...

Arrival in the New World

Regardless of the conditions on a particular slave ship, which would have been brutal under any of the conditions described, by the time the slave ships finally reached the New World, the African captives— abused, terrified, angry, depressed, exhausted, and in a state of shock—had been subject to severe mistreatment for prolonged periods.

Arriving in port did not mean that the captives would disembark. Local authorities may have quarantined the ships. Dr. James Rawley and Dr. Stephen Behrendt state:[595]

> Postcrossing mortality before sale heightened the tragic loss of life in the passage from Africa to America. Here there was often a waiting period before disembarkation and perhaps another before sale.

Once on land, auctioneers and prospective buyers inspected the new slaves like the farm animals, domestic workers, or concubines they were to become—bodies scrutinized, muscles squeezed, and mouths forced open to inspect teeth prior to sale to new masters.

Their lives in America began at the slave auctions or another form of sale.

Slave auctions were extremely degrading. Solomon Northup provides the following description of his experience at a slave auction in New Orleans following his kidnapping in Washington, DC:[596]

> Next day many customers called to examine Freeman's "new lot." The latter gentleman was very loquacious, dwelling at much length upon our several good points and qualities. He would make us hold up our heads, walk briskly back and forth, while customers would feel of our hands and arms and bodies, turn us about, ask us what we could do, make us open our mouths and show our teeth, precisely as a jockey examines a horse which he is about to barter for or purchase. Sometimes a man or woman was taken back to the small house in the yard, stripped, and inspected more minutely. Scars upon a slave's back were considered evidence of a rebellious or unruly spirit, and hurt his sale.

Joseph Kleinman and Eileen-Kurtis-Kleinman describe two additional methods of sale. The slave society called one method a "scramble," in which "the merchant or slave ship captain assigned a price to each slave, and buyers agreed to pay the price. The merchant or captain then gave a signal ... and the scramble began." Buyers

595 Rawley and Behrendt, at 262.

596 Northup, at 79-81.

rushed into the assembled slaves, grabbing those they could. The process "could become violent." "[S]laves were terrified."[597]

The "least common" method was a private sale pursuant to an agreement made by a slave trader ahead of time with "a planter, group of planters, trading firm, or factor to buy the slaves he brought from Africa." This could "help[] fund the voyage."[598]

After they arrived in America or elsewhere in the New World, the slaves' lives continued to be harsh. Many slaves died quickly.[599]

"Deck of Slave Ship, Jamaica, 19th cent.", Slavery Images: *A Visual Record of the African Slave Trade and Slave Life in the Early African Diaspora,* accessed November 18, 2020, *http://slaveryimages.org/s/slaveryimages/item/2031*

Slavery.org quotes Mayne Reid, The maroon; or, planter life in Jamaica (New York, 1864): "the scene depicted here shows the deck of a slave ship as it anchors in Jamaica, when the slaves were being prepared for sale. They were brought up on the top deck. Each individual, as he came up the hatchway, was rudely seized by a sailor, who stood by with a soft brush in his hand and a pail at his feet; the latter containing a black composition of gunpowder, lemon-juice, and palm-oil. Of this mixture the unresisting captive received a coating which, by the hand of another sailor, was rubbed in the skin, and polished with a danby-brush until the sable epidermis glistened like a newly-blacked boot. … It was not the first time those unfeeling men had assisted at the spectacle of a slaver's cargo being made ready for market."

597 Kleinmans, at 88.

598 Kleinmans, at 89.

599 Beckles, at 115; Rediker, at 5.

Dr. Berlin states that "[t]he impact of disease was ... especially severe on newly imported African men and women, who had no exposure to the contagions of the New World ... ." He cites, among others, measles and whooping cough, "compounded by poor diet, insufficient clothing, and inadequate shelter."[600]

Slave Trading Continued

The international slave trade continued on a legal basis—explicitly contemplated in America's Constitution for another 20 years after ratification—until the legal international trade ended through British and American enactments in 1807 and 1808. Thereafter, the international trade continued through illegal smuggling. John Spears cites a Georgia Governor who resigned to engage in the illegal slave trade, and a famous American racing yacht used to smuggle slaves quickly and surreptitiously while flying the American flag.[601]

Mr. Spears discusses at length illegal smuggling as an activity well known to American government officials, including President Buchanan, who did little or nothing to stop it.[602]

Even apart from illegal international smuggling, slave trading did not end. The internal slave trade, yet another shameful, sadistic, and degrading experience for slaves, flourished openly in America on a fully legal basis until the Civil War.[603]

Summary

The international slave trade was a key element of a genocidal crime against humanity of unimaginable proportions. The genocide, which killed a conservatively estimated five million Africans on the basis of race, was comparable only to the worst genocide of the Twentieth Century, the Holocaust. The full extent of the slave society's sadism and terror are, however, infrequently discussed today in America, by politicians, in schools, or in polite society.

The international slave trade began in earnest with the Stuart family—King Charles II and the Duke of York acting specifically in America. It continued with the Duke's daughters, Queen Mary and especially Queen Anne.[604]

The American colonies and states consciously and deliberately continued the institution of slavery and the expanded slave trade that the Duke began.

There is an effort today—often deliberate and pre-meditated—to pretend that this was just "something that happened" long ago, and to hide, ignore or minimize America's significant role in that crime and genocide. Such assertions are a fraud perpetuated upon the American public.

600 Berlin, at 184.

601 Spears, at 125, 197.

602 Spears, at 122-26, 194-212.

603 See "*—The Internal Slave Trade: Coffles and Auctions*" below.

604 "Anne: Queen of Great Britain and Ireland" at *www.britannica.com/biography/Anne-queen-of-Great-Britain-and-Ireland.* Accessed Oct. 14, 2020; "Queen Anne" at *www.npg.org.uk/learning/digitalhistpry/abolition-of-slavery/queen-anne,* accessed Oct. 14, 2020; "The Business of Enslavement" at *www.bbc.co.uk/history/british/abolition/slavery_business_gallery_06.shtml,* accessed Oct. 14, 2020.

THE INTERNAL SLAVE TRADE: COFFLES AND AUCTIONS

> "The interstate slave trade had a devasting impact on black families. As the coffles trudged south, slave husbands and wives came to appreciate the fragility of the marriage bond and slave parents learned their children would disappear, never to be seen again. Sales south shattered approximately one slave marriage in three and separated one fifth of the children under fourteen from one or both of their parents. 'I have seen hundreds of cases where families were separated,' recalled one Maryland slave. 'I have heard them cry fit to break their hearts.'"[605]

§ § §

In addition to the slave society's other deliberate acts of terrorism, slave coffles graphically exposed the slave society's character as a Terrorist Society.

Few schools teach this. Few of America's politicians admit it. Polite society does not discuss it. There is an unspoken understanding to bury the evidence in a vault far underground, effectively as one would dispose of nuclear fuel rods. That way, through unyielding silence, through nearly-complete evasion of unpleasantness, future generations of "patriotic" Americans will not learn of it.

The legal international slave trade ended in 1808, although the slave society sustained smuggling. America's slave society then turned to the internal slave trade for its supply of human bodies.

COFFLE

"A line of animals or slaves fastened or driven along together."

"Coffle" at *www.lexico.com/en/definition/coffle,* accessed Sept. 29, 2020

In the Upper South, tobacco had depleted the soil, and was less profitable.[606] In the Deep South, however, the invention of the cotton gin created a new vast market for slaves on cotton plantations.[607]

More than a million slaves emigrated, although not voluntarily, to plantations in places like Mississippi, Alabama, Louisiana, and eventually, Texas.[608]

The slaves came from Virginia, Maryland, and the Eastern Seaboard to the Deep South plantations.[609] Edward Ball states that "The Slave Trail of Tears is the great missing migration—a thousand-mile-long river of people, all of them black, reaching from Virginia to Louisiana." It was a massive migration. Mr. Ball adds that "This movement lasted longer and grabbed up more people than any other migration in North America before 1900." The slave migration was greater than the Westward expansion in the wagon trains. It was "20 times larger than Andrew Jackson's 'Indian removal' campaigns of the 1830s."[610] Slave traders and migrating planters and farmers tore slaves from their spouses, children, friends, and communities to enter the abusive cotton plantation life, lonely and without means of psychological support.

---

605 Slavery in Maryland at 11.

606 Halpren and Dal Lago, at 123-24.

607 Torget, at 35.

608 Kolchin, at 96.

609 Halpern and Dal Lago, at 123.

610 Edward Ball.

Solomon Northup made his involuntary trip by ship down the East Coast.[611]

Alternatively, large numbers of slaves marched on foot in chains and under the whip for the 1,000 mile journey from Washington, DC and Alexandria, Virginia, to the New Orleans slave auction.[612] The droves of slaves often constituted multiple "coffles." This was not an infrequent occurrence. It was a routine event in America.

The extensive and public use of slave coffles in America is remarkable and shocking to someone, like me, who had never heard of them. Although deeply hidden from view today, it is one of the most reprehensible aspects of American history and of the shame of American slavery.

Outraged, Frederick Douglass spoke angrily about the inhumanity of slave coffles and their frequency:[613]

"Behold the practical operation of this internal slave trade—the American slave trade, sustained by American politics and American religion! Here you will see men and women reared like swine for the market. You know what is a swine-drover? I will show you a man-drover. They inhabit all our Southern States. They perambulate the country, and crowd the highways of the nation with droves of human stock. You will see one of these human-flesh-jobbers, armed with pistol, whip and bowie-knife, driving a company of a hundred men, women, and children, from the Potomac to the slave market at New Orleans. These wretched people are to be sold singly, or in lots, to suit purchasers. They are food

"Slave Coffle, Virginia, 1839", *Slavery Images: A Visual Record of the African Slave Trade and Slave Life in the Early African Diaspora*, accessed November 14, 2020, *http://slaveryimages.org/s/slaveryimages/item/1965*

611 See *"Chapter Six: The Duke of York's Creation on a Rampage—The Story of Eliza: Children Torn from a Mother's Arms"* below.

612 Sweig, "Alexandria to New Orleans: The Human Tragedy of the Interstate Slave Trade, Parts I-IV" (The Connection Newspapers, Oct. 8, 15, 23, 2014) at *connectionarchives.com/PDF/2014/Slave%20Trader/Slave%20Trader.PDF; www.alexandriagazette.com/news/2014/oct/08/alexandria-new-orleans-human-tragedy-interstate-sl/; www.alexandriagazette.com/news/2014/oct/15/alexandria-new-orleans/; www.connectionnewspapers.com/news/2014/oct/23/alexandria-new-orleans-human-tragedy-interstate-sl/,* accessed Oct. 12, 2020.

613 Douglass, "What to the Slave Is the Fourth of July?" (July 5, 1852), reprinted in part in F. Douglass, **MY BONDAGE AND MY FREEDOM** at 446-47 (1855), available from the Library of Congress at *www.hathitrust.org/digital_library.* See also "Text of Douglass's Speech" at *www.owleyes.org/text/what-to-the-slave-is-the-fourth-of-july/read/text-of-douglasss-speech#root-162*, accessed Nov. 5, 2020.

for the cotton-field, and the deadly sugar-mill. Mark the sad procession, as it moves wearily along, and the inhuman wretch who drives them. Hear his savage yells and his blood-chilling oaths, as he hurries on his affrighted captives. There, see the old man, with locks thinned and gray. Cast one glance, if you please, upon that young mother, whose shoulders are bare to the scorching sun, her briny tears falling on the brow of the babe in her arms. See, too, that girl of thirteen, weeping, yes, weeping, as she thinks of the mother from whom she has been torn. The drove moves tardily. Heat and sorrow have nearly consumed their strength. Suddenly you hear a quick snap, like the discharge of a rifle; the fetters clank, and the chain rattles simultaneously; your ears are saluted with a scream, that seems to have torn its way to the center of your soul. The crack you heard, was the sound of the slave whip; the scream you heard, was from the woman you saw with the babe. Her speed had faltered under the weight of her child and her chains; that gash on her shoulder tells her to move on. Follow this drove to New Orleans. Attend the auction; see men examined like horses; see the forms of women rudely and brutally exposed to the shocking gaze of American slave-buyers. See this drove sold and separated forever; and never forget the deep, sad sobs that arose from that scattered multitude. Tell me, citizens, where, under the sun, can you witness a spectacle more fiendish and shocking. Yet this is but a glance at the American slave trade, as it exists, at this moment, in the ruling part of the United States.

"I was born amid such sights and scenes. To me the American slave trade is a terrible reality. …"

SLAVE COFFLES WITNESSED

"About five years ago, I remember to have passed in a single day four droves of slaves for the south west; the largest drove had 350 slaves in it, and the smallest upwards of 200, I counted 68 or 70 in a single coffle. The 'coffle chain' is a chain fastened at one end to the centre of the bar of a pair of hand cuffs, which are fastened to the right wrist of one, and the left wrist of another slave, they standing abreast, and the chain between them. These are the head of the coffle. The other end is passed through a ring in the bolt of the next handcuffs, and the slaves being manacled thus, two and two together, walk up, and the coffle chain is passed, and they go up towards the head of the coffle, Of course they are closer or wider apart in the coffle, according to the number to be coffled, and to the length of the chain. I have seen Hundreds of droves and chain-coffles of this description, and every coffle was a scene of misery and wo, of tears and brokenness of heart."

T. Weld, American Slavery As It Is: Testimony of a Thousand Witnesses at 76-77 (American Anti-Slavery Society, 1839), available from the Library of Congress at *www.hathitrust.org/digital_library*

The coffles, consisted of up to hundreds of men, women and children chained together by their arms or necks, or in the cases of women, at times by rope, with even children. Small children and injured slaves might ride in wagons.

Slave traders paraded these coffles on their marches South in full view of thousands upon thousands of people in town after town, state after state.

They forded rivers, and slogged on foot, with or without shoes, in chains through streams and mud.

SLAVE COFFLE EVEN IN THE NATION'S CAPITAL

"On the beautiful avenue in front of the Capitol, members of Congress, during this session, have been compelled to turn aside from their path, to permit a coffle of slaves, males and females, chained to each other by their necks, to pass on their way to this national slave market."

T. Weld, American Slavery As It Is: Testimony of a Thousand Witnesses at 76-77 (American Anti-Slavery Society 1839), available from the Library of Congress at *www.hathitrust.org/digital_library*

They trudged over dirt paths, plodded across mountains, and struggled over rocky slopes. Regardless of hunger or thirst, water and food would not have been readily available when desired while the slaves marched. Those necessities would have to be delayed until rest periods and night, even for children.

The marches occurred in all types of weather—heat, cold, rain, snow, sun, and wind—with limited clothing, shoes, hats, and other protections against the elements.

When they died *en route,* slave traders left their bodies in shallow graves, or in more isolated locations, simply along the side of the road.

Why are not these horrible occurrences acknowledged today in America? Is it simply too reprehensible? Would it interfere with the squeaky clean "patriotism" we are supposed to imbibe? How could schools and politicians simply ignore a mass migration that "was 20 times larger than Andrew Jackson's 'Indian removal' campaigns of the 1830s?"[614]

How could anyone dismiss these events as "something that happened 150 years ago?"

The record of this terror thankfully is still accessible in old books, even if obscure for, and unknown to, most Americans.

In **AMERICAN SLAVERY AS IT IS,** Theodore Weld quotes one newspaper reporting on coffles:[615]

> The Western Luminary, a religious paper published at Lexington, Kentucky, in an editorial article, in the summer of 1833, says:
>
> > "A few weeks since we gave an account of a company of men, women and children, part of whom were manacled, passing through our streets. Last week, a number of slaves were driven through the main street of our city, among whom were *a number manacled together,* two abreast, *all connected by, and supporting a heavy iron chain,* which extended the whole length of the line."

Mr. Weld presents another description:

> Mr. GEORGE P.C. HUSSEY, of Fayetteville, Franklin county, Pennsylvania, writes thus:
>
> > "I was born and raised in Hagerstown, Washington county, Maryland, where slavery is perhaps milder than in any other part of the slave states; and yet I have seen

"Coffle of Enslaved, Washington, D.C., 1840s", *Slavery Images: A Visual Record of the African Slave Trade and Slave Life in the Early African Diaspora,* accessed November 14, 2020, *http://slaveryimages.org/s/slaveryimages/item/1939*

614 Edward Ball.

615 Weld, at 75-77.

> hundreds of colored men and women chained together, two by two, and driven to the south. I have seen slaves tied up and lashed till the blood ran down to their heels."

The following are brief glimpses provided in an article written by Edward Ball published by the Smithsonian Institution regarding slave coffles and regarding the slave auctions awaiting the victims when they reached New Orleans or other destinations:[616]

- "[S]eamstresses, nurses, valets, field hands, hostlers, carpenters, cooks, houseboys, coachmen, laundresses, boatmen. There were so-called fancy girls, young women who would work mainly as concubines. And, always, children.
- "Bill Keeling, male, age 11, height 4'5" | Elisabeth, female, age 10, height 4'1" | Monroe, male, age 12, height 4'7" | Lovey, female, age 10, height 3'10" | Robert, male, age 12, height 4'4" | Mary Fitchett, female, age 11, height 4'11"
- "In 1834, Armfield [a particularly active Alexandria, Virginia, slave trader] sat on his horse in front of the procession, armed with a gun and a whip. Other white men, similarly armed, were arrayed behind him."
- "Sometimes, as in [Charles] Ball's case, the chain ran through an iron neck collar. 'I could not shake off my chains, nor move a yard without the consent of my master.'"[617]
- "The coffles moved along at three miles an hour. Caravans like Armfield's covered about 20 miles a day."

MORE SLAVE COFFLES WITNESSED

"I have seen at least fifteen droves of 'human cattle,' passing by us on their way to the south; and I do not recollect an exception, where there were not more or less of them chained together."

T. Weld, American Slavery As It Is: Testimony of a Thousand Witnesses at 76-77 (American Anti-Slavery Society 1839), available from the Library of Congress at *www.hathitrust.org/digital_library*

- "[B]ad habits concerning sex were rampant among some of those men. You know they took advantage of the black women, and there were no repercussions there."
- "In Virginia, the coffles marched from town to town."
- "At the village of Benton a week before Christmas 1847, Waller [another slave trader] huddled with his gang in a ferocious storm. "Exceedingly heavy and continued rains have stopped our progress," he told his wife. "We have been stopped for two days by the breaking up of turnpikes and bridges."
- At the auction, "They were sorted by sex and size and made to stand in sequence. Men on one side, in order of height and weight, women on the other. A typical display placed an 8-year-old girl on the left end of a line… This sorting arrangement meant that it was more likely children would be sold from their parents."

---

616 Edward Ball.

617 See also C. Ball, **SLAVERY IN THE UNITED STATES, A NARRATIVE OF THE LIFE AND ADVENTURES OF CHARLES BALL** at 37-38 (John S. Taylor, 1837), Davis Library, Univ. of North Carolina at Chapel Hill, available at available at *docsouth.unc.edu.*

- "At the Forks, there were no auctions, only haggling. Buyers looked at the people, took them inside, made them undress, studied their teeth, told them to dance, asked them about their work, and, most important, looked at their backs. The inspection of the back made or broke the deal. Many people had scars from whipping. For buyers, these were interpreted not as signs of a master's cruelty, but of a worker's defiance. A 'clean back' was a rarity, and it raised the price."
- "'On the block was one of the most beautiful young women I ever saw. She was about sixteen, dressed in a cheap striped woolen gown, and bareheaded.' Her name was Hermina. 'She was sold for $1250 to one of the most lecherous-looking old brutes I ever set eyes on,' the reporter noted. That is the equivalent of $35,000 today."

Slaves separated forcefully from their loved ones never forgot them. Once slavery ended, they sought desperately to reunite:[618]

- "The first polite questions appeared in newspapers in the summer of 1865, right after the Civil War and Emancipation. Former slaves—there were four million—asked by word of mouth, but that went nowhere, and so they put announcements in the papers, trying to find mothers and sisters, children and husbands swept away from them by the Slave Trail."
- "The black churches picked it up. Every Sunday, preachers around the South looked out at congregations and read announcements from 'Lost Friends' and columns like it."
- "Year after year the notices spread—hundreds, and then thousands. They continued in black newspapers until World War I, fully 50 years after Emancipation."

This was "something that happened 150 years ago." It happened in America during the 1800s up to the time of the Civil War, almost a century after the Declaration of Independence. It had the blessing of the Constitution and the Fugitive Slave Laws the Constitution fathered. It occurred in the full view of Congress, Presidents, and Supreme Court Justices.

Let the old dusty record speak loudly!

---

618 Edward Ball.

Searching for Family

Miss Elizabeth Powell of Sacramento, wishes information of her relatives. consisting of her father, mother, three brothers and two sisters. Her father's name was Sam. Mosely ; he was owned by a man named Joe. Powell, who lived in Kentucky at a place called Amandy, Furnace, about two miles from Ohio River. Elizabeth belonged to the same man. and was sold to speculator Ellis of Louisiana. Her mother's name was Elizabeth ; her brothers, Harry Amos and Isaac, and her sisters, Rebecca and Lucretia. Any information of the above parties will be thankfully received. Address Elizabeth Powell, care of P. A. Bell, editor ELEVATOR, San Francisco.

"Elizabeth Powell is searching for her relatives," Information Wanted Ad, The Elevator (San Francisco, CA), May 27, 1870, *Last Seen: Finding Family After Slavery,* accessed November 18, 2020, *http://www.informationwanted.org/items/show/3704.*

Searching for Family

INFORMATION WANTED.

By Isaac Moore of his parents and relatives. He was born in Clay County, Missouri, about 12 miles north-east of a small town called Liberty. His father's name was Abraham, he belonged to a man named Joel Moore. His mother's name was Toner, she first belonged to a man named Mike Wellton, who sold her to Dave Crockett. While with Mike Wellton she had six children named Jerry, Louisa, 'Liza, Martha, Ellen and Isaac. After his mother was sold to Dave Crockett, she had four more children named 'Merica, Paulina, Jane and William. Isaac left Missouri via Under-ground Railroad in 1850, and has not heard of his relations since. Any information which can be given of the above parties will be thankfully received. Address Isaac Moore, in care of P. A. Bell, editor ELEVATOR, San Francisco.

"Isaac Moore is searching for his parents and relatives," Information Wanted Ad, *The Elevator* (San Francisco, CA), December 29,1871, *Last Seen: Finding Family After Slavery,* accessed November 18, 2020, *http://www.informationwanted.org/items/show/3689.*

CHAPTER SIX: THE DUKE OF YORK'S CREATION ON A RAMPAGE

THE SLAVE SOCIETY'S REIGN OF TERROR PROSPERS

As the American colonies grew and became states, the form of slavery given birth by the English government in the 1660s through the fatherhood of the Duke of York and the motherhood of the American colonies persevered. Moreover, the slave society's oppression became even more intense.

Once the American nation created itself, once the Founding Fathers acted or failed to act, with all their contradictions in the Declaration of Independence and the Constitution, slavery grew rapidly. The horror of what I call Phase 1 of the Reign of Terror continued unabated. Then, it expanded in what I call Phase 2 of the Reign of Terror.

Suddenly, a new significant proslavery development appeared—the cotton gin triggered an explosion of slavery. The invention served as the vehicle for far greater atrocities within the new nation than had existed in the colonies before America's founding. Although the legal international slave trade had ended, the new atrocities included slave coffles, the "Trail of Tears,"[619] and the associated heart-wrenching destruction of slave families on a much greater scale than had transpired previously. Meanwhile, smuggling continued the international slave trade illegally.

ANTISLAVERY "GAG RULE"

[On May 26, 1836,] "during the 24th Congress (1835–1837), the U.S. House of Representatives instituted the 'gag rule,' the first instance of what would become a traditional practice forbidding the House from considering anti-slavery petitions. ... [John Quincy] Adams shouted during the roll call vote, 'I hold the resolution to be a direct violation of the Constitution of the United States.' For the next four Congresses, Adams fervently fought against the gag rule, declaring it a restriction on free speech. Despite his efforts, the House successfully reintroduced the gag rule each Congress until Adams finally mustered enough votes to repeal it on December 3, 1844."

"The House 'Gag Rule'" at *history.house.gov/Historical-Highlights/1800-1850/The-House-of-Representatives-instituted-the-"gag-rule"/*, accessed Nov. 1, 2020

As these events emerge, we no longer read of slaves gibbeted or broken on the wheel. We do read, however, about slaves burned at the stake more than half a century after the Declaration of Independence. We also read of slaves' heads posted still later along public roads in the slave society's conscious, deliberate efforts to inflict terror upon slaves and their children.

Today, we are able to read the narratives of America's Slavery Heroes describing their firsthand experiences during Phase 2 involving unrelenting violence against slaves. This Chapter relates such experiences in the form of "Stories" written in the slaves' and former slaves' own words, and abolitionists' words, speaking directly to you in the 2020s.

We also read about the slave society's callous and persistent disregard of supposed constitutional rights in the first ten Amendments—the Bill of Rights.[620]

619 Edward Ball.
See *"Chapter Five: The Duke's Slave Trading Legacy—The Internal Slave Trade: Coffles and Auctions."*

620 See "—The Slave Society's War on Abolitionists" below.

Under the Constitution, with its Three-Fifths Compromise, the slave society gained an exaggerated influence over America's political life, and through the government, over American society.[621]

With the Three-Fifths Compromise, the slave society was highly confident for decades of its power, through the electoral college, to elect slave-holding and otherwise compliant Presidents and to dominate a proslavery Congress. Given the Presidency and Congress, the slave society also controlled the Supreme Court.[622] The slave society's power was so strong that, for years, it enforced a "gag rule" in Congress preventing discussion of antislavery proposals.

With that extensive power, the slave society simply chose to ignore the Bill of Rights and other supposed constitutional guarantees of liberty applicable only to the federal government—the right of free speech, the right of a free press, freedom of religion, the right to due process, the right to a fair trial by a jury of one's peers, and the prohibition of cruel and unusual punishment.[623]

In brief, the especially dehumanizing form of slavery that the English had legislated, promoted, and incentivized in the American colonies did not miss a beat after America became a nation. Instead, the Reign of Terror grew into an even greater monster.

No longer were slaves numbered in the hundreds of thousands, now they became millions, and after that, even more millions.

Now, the slave society tore the slaves from their friends and families and transported them far away from one heartless region where they no longer were profitable to another, still more pitiless, region demanding their unceasing services.

It is not hyperbole to declare straightforwardly that this was one of the greatest crimes against humanity in the history of the World!

Yet, much of America refuses to concede that information.

---

621 See *"Chapter Four: America's Slavery Contradictions—The Constitution Contemplated and Protected Slavery."*

622 See *"Chapter Four: America's Slavery Contradictions—George Washington, Thomas Jefferson, John Adams, and Other Founding Fathers—Supreme Court Justices."*

623 See *"—The Slave Society's War on Abolitionists"* below.

WHO WERE THE SLAVES?

The captives who became slaves in America were Africans.[624]

Above all, they were people, human beings. It is crucial to keep this in mind.

To the slave society's members, however, slaves were things, chattels.

As the Duke of York and his colleagues constructed American slavery based upon that sadistic concept, a primary perceived difficulty of the English colonialists was a serious shortage of inexpensive labor. The colonists had sought to fill this need by whatever resources could become available. That included free white workers, indentured servants and, later, as promoted by the English government, slaves.

Labor by free whites was in short supply. Dr. Leslie Harris states that "wars in Europe hampered the flow of European immigrants."[625] Individuals who came to early America did not need to work for wages in order to make a living. Plenty of land was available for one to become independent and to have a decent life through farming, hunting and fishing. Douglas Harper states: "So much land was available, so cheaply, that no one was willing to come to America and sign on as a laborer. ... Because of this acute labor shortage, all the American colonies turned to compulsory labor."[626] Dr. Harris adds that "many [Europeans] attempted to establish independent farms or businesses."[627]

Indentured servants were fine, but they did not always fill the need. Work for them was available in Europe. The numbers of indentured servants in the American colonies declined in the late 1600s, making heavy reliance upon them difficult. Since prices for slaves were declining at the time, it was more costly to replace existing indentured servants with new indentured servants when contracts ended.[628] Moreover, being white, indentured servants could blend easily into the population, if they sought to escape their contracts.

At first, the colonialists were not particular about whom they enslaved. They enslaved whites, Native Americans and Africans. Like indentured servants, however, white slaves could blend into the population upon escaping.

The colonialists could purchase African slaves from two sources: One source was Africans directly from Africa. The second source was slaves that had previously worked in the Caribbean on large plantations. That experience provided them a degree of acculturation and understanding of the work expected, *i.e.,* "seasoning."

The need for labor was so great that the Massachusetts General Court "voted to reimburse the man who had purchased ... Africans [in Bermuda] for his expense; he was to repay the colony from the proceeds when he sold the slaves."[629]

624 See *"Chapter Five: The Duke's Slave Trading Legacy —Africans in Transition: From People to Things."*

625 Harris, at 29.

626 Harper, "Slavery in the North," at *slavenorth.com/slavenorth.htm,* accessed Oct. 5, 2020.

627 Harris, at 27.

628 Kolchin, at 11,12.

629 "February 26, 1638, First Slaves Arrive in Massachusetts" at *www.massmoments.org/moment-details/first-slaves-arrive-in-massachusetts.html,* accessed Oct. 5, 2020.

New Englanders also justified slaves taken captive in wars. Douglas Harper quotes a New Englander who desired a "juste warre" with the Pequot tribe, "so the colonists might capture enough Indian men, women and children to exchange in Barbados for black slaves," concluding that "the colony would never thrive 'untill we get … a stock of slaves sufficient to doe all our business.'"[630]

A problem with Native Americans was that the men might be warriors, who could fight back, making them especially dangerous. They also could escape into Native territory, which they knew geographically, and where they had friends and families. So, as indicated, Massachusetts slaveowners who owned or captured Native Americans traded them in the Caribbean for African-Americans.[631]

Escape for Africans was more challenging. Being readily visible, Africans had greater difficulty with blending in. In addition, unlike whites, and Native Americans in their tribal settings, Africans, not being fluent in English, could not easily communicate. They had their own native African languages, the variety of which inhibited communication even among slaves. That made it easier for slave masters to utilize harsh punishments with fewer defections.

The prevailing conditions led eventually to a greater dependence upon African slavery. Thus, the Duke of York was able to promote and exploit the slave trade.

As time passed, pursuant to laws promoted by the Duke of York, King Charles II, and their colleagues, followed by their English government successors, the colonialists began to restrict slavery to Africans. This occurred by prohibiting enslavement of whites ("Christians," but of course excluding African Christians) and eventually by prohibiting enslavement of Native Americans.

Yet, the Africans themselves were human beings who came from diverse cultures and societies.[632] In A **GUIDE TO THE HISTORY OF SLAVERY IN MARYLAND**, the Maryland State Archives and University of Maryland describe the African multi-cultural context relevant to the slaves:[633]

> The men and women dragged across the Atlantic were called "Africans." But they were not Africans when they boarded the slave ships. Rather, they were members of particular nations—Angolans, Igbos, and Mande, for example—each with its own political hierarchy, social structure, traditions, and culture. Some were matriarchal and others patriarchal. Some Africans labored as farmers, worked as village-based artisans or merchants, or served as soldiers. Most had been free, but some had been slaves. They wove different kinds of cloth, made different kinds of pottery, smelted different kinds of metal, sang different songs, and worshipped different gods.

LANGUAGE ISSUES

"Only the 30 percent of the newest arrivals who came directly from Africa could 'scarce speak a word of English,' speaking, instead, one of their native tongues—Kikongo, Gã, Mandinga, Soninke, Temne, Fulbe, and Sere—or any of the many other African languages heard on the streets of New York, and, most of all, a lingua franca in West Africa."

J. Lepore, "Chapter 2: The Tightening Vise: Slavery and Freedom in British New York" in I. Berlin and L. Harris, ed., Slavery in New York at 68 (The New Press, 2005). Footnote omitted.

630 Harper, "Slavery in the North" at *slavenorth.com/massachusetts.htm*, accessed Oct. 5, 2020.

631 Harper, "Slavery in the North" at *slavenorth.com/massachusetts.htm*, accessed Oct. 5, 2020.

632 "The Angolan Connection and Slavery in Virginia" at *www.historyisfun.org/learn/learning-center/the-angolan-connection-and-slavery-in-virginia/*, accessed Oct. 13, 2020.

633 Slavery in Maryland, at 4.

Thomas R.R. Cobb, the proslavery advocate, provides the following information regarding the African origins of slaves:[634]

> The immense supply of slaves (near 75,000 annually), necessarily caused most wretched cruelties to be practiced by the petty kings and slave-dealers on the African coast. From the great river Senegal to the farther limits of Angola, a distance of many thousand miles, the entire coast was visited to furnish this supply. The interior, especially along the banks of the rivers, yielded its quota to the general demand. Numerous tribes inhabited this vast extent of country, and consequently great differences existed in the color, nature, habits, and dispositions of the negroes exported. Prominent among these were the Mandingoes, Koromantyns, Whidahs or Fidahs, Eboes, and Congoes. The first were considered the most elevated and farthest removed from the pure type. The second, from the Gold Coast, were the most stubborn, unruly, rebellious, and intrepid. The Whidahs were the most thievish; and the Eboes from Benin, the most timid and dejected. Their peculiarities were soon discovered; and hence, upon the arrival of a slave-ship, the advertisement always gave notice of the tribes from which they were purchased.

It must be recalled that Mr. Cobb was a blatant racist. Demonstrating that aspect of his character, he provides the following views, which I include so that you are able to gain insight into the thinking of proslavery Americans (including Northerners) at the time of slavery's Reign of Terror:[635]

> The negroes thus introduced into America, were gross and stupid, lazy and superstitious. With an occasional exception of a captive warrior, they were only transferred from the slavery of a savage to that of a civilized and Christian master. ... To the fact of their improved condition, as well as their natural constitution and habit, the want of a common language, a common sympathy, and a common grief, may be attributed the absence of any concerted attempt at rebellion, even in those colonies where they outnumbered the white population.

Once the slaves reached America, masters assigned them to diverse activities. Slaves lived in a variety of circumstances. You will see descriptions of different professional skills developed by slaves (which in turn, at times, gave some slaves a degree of negotiating ability), as well as increasing the fears of white workers with whom slaves competed. There were slaves serving in skilled professions, especially in cities or on large plantations where specialization was more feasible. Having said that, the vast majority of male slaves were field hands on large and small farms and on plantations, while women worked as domestics, but also as field hands.[636]

Dr. Henry Gates, citing the Gilder Lehrman Institute of American History, states that, in 1860, 31 percent of American slaves worked "on plantations of 40 or more slaves, while a majority (53 percent) were held on farms of between 7 and 39 slaves." He adds that "almost 'a third of slave laborers were children and an eighth were elderly or crippled.'"[637]

634 Cobb, Vol I, at cliv-clv. Footnote omitted.

635 Cobb, Vol I, at cli-clii.

636 Kolchin, at 105; Hodges and Brown, at xxii.

637 Gates, "Slavery by the Numbers" at *www.theroot.com/slavery-by-the-numbers-1790874492*, accessed Oct. 5, 2020.

Dr. Peter Kolchin and Dr. Ira Berlin describe slaves working in circumstances varying by region, type and size of farm or plantation, rural versus urban demographic settings, and time frame, especially early colonial versus the antebellum South with its "paternalism."[638]

Following the prohibition of the international slave trade in 1808 and the growth of the internal slave trade, characteristics of slaves began to change. After 1808, the number of slaves in America continued to increase from natural births.[639] One result was that America became, by a considerable margin, the largest slave-owning country in the New World.[640] Another result was that the slave population changed its character by attrition to one that became heavily American-born, with decreasing numbers having been born in Africa.[641]

The emergence of a substantial number of slaves who had been slaves their entire lives, rather than captives from Africa, had its impact, which fed the concept of Southern paternalism. Slave children had never known another life. Masters and slaves knew each other for extended periods, and developed relationships over that time. It does not mean, however, that slaves accepted their fates, as evidenced by substantial numbers of runaway slaves, incidents of resistance, and the zealous efforts of America's Slavery Heroes.[642]

Thus, slaves were diverse people, both at the time of their capture and sale in Africa and, in America, in their lives as slaves. The fundamental message, however, is that, within that diversity, as Frederick Douglass and William Wells Brown, asserted repeatedly, in reality the slaves were not "things" at all, they were living, breathing people, human beings.

---

638 See generally P. Kolchin, **AMERICAN SLAVERY 1619-1877** (Hill and Wang, 2003) and I. Berlin, **MANY THOUSANDS GONE: THE FIRST TWO CENTURIES OF SLAVERY IN NORTH AMERICA** (Harvard Univ. Press 1998).

639 "The President's House in Philadelphia" at *www.ushistory.org/presidentshouse/plans/eisterhold/04-Systems-and-Methods-of-Slavery.php*, accessed Oct. 5, 2020.

640 Kolchin, at 94.

641 Kolchin, at 34, 37-38.

642 See "*—Slaveholder Advertisements for Runaway Slaves*" below.

A BILL OF SALE

Slavery involved treating slaves as chattels—things, animals. The slave society sold, leased, mortgaged, inherited, and managed slaves, just as any other property. The beginning of a human being's life as a slave after reaching America was to experience sale, commonly at an auction.

Chattel

1: an item of tangible movable or immovable property except real estate and things (such as buildings) connected with real property

2: slave, bondman // slaveholders who were determined to hold on to their human chattel

What is the Difference Between chattel and slave?

The word *chattel* is encountered in two main senses. The earlier of the two is primarily technical and refers to property, specifically property that is distinct from real estate holdings. The second meaning of *chattel* can excite considerable emotion, as it refers to humans as property, *i.e.*, slaves. *Chattel, slave* and the less common *bondman* and *thrall* are all synonyms for a person held in servitude by another. *Chattel* and *cattle* both come to English from the same source: each is descended from the Medieval Latin word *capitale,* which itself traces to the Latin *caput* meaning "head."

"Chattel" at *www.merriam-webster.com/dictionary/chattel#note-1,* accessed Oct. 6, 2020. Emphasis in original.

It is appropriate to show you at the beginning of this discussion of slavery in practice how a Bill of Sale for a slave appeared. In this case, it is a Bill of Sale granting a specific slave, William Wells Brown, his freedom—the end of his slavery.

Like Frederick Douglass and other fugitive slaves, William Wells Brown fled to Europe to escape the dangers posed by the Fugitive Slave Law of 1850. As also occurred in the case of Mr. Douglass, English friends obtained a Bill of Sale upon their purchase of Mr. Brown's freedom from his slaveowner in Missouri. Due to white fear of "free" African-Americans, Missouri law, as with the law in other slave states, required a judicial approval for Mr. Brown's manumission.

Josephine Brown, a daughter of Mr. Brown, provides the Bill of Sale (and her perspectives about it):[643]

> In the spring of 1854, a few ladies, personal friends of Mr. Brown, in England, wishing to secure to him the right of returning to the United States at any time that he might feel inclined, without the liability of being arrested as a fugitive slave, negotiated with his old master for the purchase of his freedom. As it may be interesting to the reader to know how an American disposes of his neighbors, we give below the *Bill of Sale,* called a *Deed of Emancipation:* —

643 J. Brown, at 96-99. Emphasis in original.

"*Know all men by these presents,* That I, Enoch Price, of the city and county of St. Louis, and State of Missouri, for and in consideration of the sum of three hundred dollars, to be paid to Joseph Greely, my agent in Boston, Mass., by Miss Ellen Richardson, or her agent, on the delivery of this paper, do emancipate, set free, and liberate from slavery, a mulatto man named Sanford Higgins, alias Wm. Wells Brown, that I purchased of Samuel Willi on the 2d October, 1833. Said Brown is now in the fortieth year of his age, and I do acknowledge that no other person holds any claim on him as a slave but myself.

PRICE FOR
WILLIAM WELLS BROWN

The sum of $300 in the 1850s would approximate $9,900 today.

"In witness whereof, I hereunto set my hand and seal, this 24th day of April, 1854.

"ENOCH PRICE.

"Witness, OLIVER HARRIS,
JOHN A. HASSON."

"STATE OF MISSOURI, COUNTY OF ST. LOUIS, s. s.

"*In the St. Louis Circuit Court,*
April Term, 1854. April 25th.

"Be it remembered, that on this 25th day of April, eighteen hundred and fifty-four, in the open Court, came Enoch Price, who is personally known to the Court to be the same person whose name is subscribed to the foregoing instrument of writing as a party thereto, and he acknowledged the same to be his act and deed, for the purposes therein mentioned; — which said acknowledgment is entered on the record of the Court of that day.

MANUMISSION

"the act or process of manumitting especially: formal emancipation from slavery"

"Manumission" at *www.merriam-webster.com/dictionary/ manumission,* accessed Oct. 6, 2020. Emphasis in original.

"In testimony whereof, I hereto set my hand and affix the seal of said Court, at office in the city of St. Louis, the day and year last aforesaid.

"WM. J. HAMMOND, Clerk."

"STATE OF MISSOURI, COUNTY OF ST. LOUIS, s. s.

"I, Wm. J. Hammond, Clerk of the Circuit Court in and for the county aforesaid, certify the foregoing to be a true and correct copy of the Deed of Emancipation from Enoch Price to Sanford Higgins, (*alias* Wm. Wells Brown,) as fully as the same remains in my office.

"In testimony whereof, I hereto set my hand and affix the seal of said Court, at office in the city of St. Louis, this 25th day of April, eighteen hundred and fifty-four.

"WM. J. HAMMOND, Clerk."

WHY RESTRICTIONS ON MANUMISSION

- Fear of dependency by uneducated former slaves
- Fear of crime by former slaves who could not earn a living
- "Free" African-Americans, by example or speech, might encourage slaves to escape
- "Free" African-Americans might actively assist slaves in escaping

"STATE OF MISSOURI, COUNTY OF ST. LOUIS, s. s.

"I, Alexander Hamilton, sole Judge of the Circuit Court within and for the Eighth Judicial Circuit of the State of Missouri, (composed of the County of St. Louis,) certify that William J. Hammond, whose name is subscribed to the foregoing certificate, was at the date thereof, and now is, Clerk of the Circuit Court within and for the County of St. Louis, duly elected and qualified; that his said certificate is in due form of law, and that full faith and credit are and should be given to all such his official acts.

"Given under my hand, at the city of St. Louis, this 26th day of April, eighteen hundred and fifty-four.

"A. HAMILTON, Judge"

"July 7th, 1854. I have received this day Wm. I. Bowditch's check on the Globe Bank for three hundred dollars, in full for the consideration of the foregoing instrument of emancipation.

"JOSEPH GREELY,

"By THOMAS PAGE'S authority."

Ms. Brown concluded with her view of the Bill of Sale:[644]

The foregoing, reader, is a true copy of the bill of sale by which a democratic, Christian American sells his fellow-countryman for *British gold*. Let this paper be read and the fact rung in the ears of our nervous *negro aristocracy* who are upholding an institution which withers and curses the land, which blasts every thing that it touches, which lies like an incubus on the nation's breast, which overshadows the Genius of the American Revolution, and makes our countrymen the scorn and by-word of the inhabitants of monarchical Europe.

644 J. Brown, at 99. Emphasis in original.

CERTIFICATE OF MANUMISSION

"Recorded in Book 0, of DEEDS, page 735, in the Clerk's Office, at Burlington,—J. MCILVAINE, Clerk:"

"BURLINGTON COUNTY COURT—We do hereby certify, that on this twenty-fifth day of September, in the year of our Lord, one thousand eight hundred and six, William Griffith, Esquire, of the township and city of Burlington, in the said county of Burlington, brought before us, two of the Overseers of the Poor of said township, and two of the Justices of the Peace of the said county, his slaves, named Quamino and Sarah, man and wife; who, on view and examination, appear to us to be in sound mind, and not under any bodily incapacity of obtaining a support—and are, also, not under the age of twenty-one years, nor above the age of forty years: In witness whereof we have hereto set our hands, the day and year above written.

THOMSON NEALE,
JOHN HOSKINS, JR.
Overseers of the Poor of the said township of Burlington.

THOMAS ADAMS,
WILLIAM HYER.
Justices of the Peace, in and for said county of Burlington."

W. Allinson, Memoir of Quamino Buccau, a Pious Methodist at 14-15 (Henry Longstreth, 1851), Academic Affairs Library, University of North Carolina at Chapel Hill, available at *docsouth.unc.edu*

THE MYTH OF THE "KIND" SLAVEHOLDER

"Is there not some chosen curse,
Some hidden thunder in the stores of heaven,
Red with uncommon wrath, to blast the man
Who gains his fortune from the blood of souls?"

William Cowper[645]

"Tell me not of kind masters under slavery's hateful rule! There is no such thing as a person of that description; for, as you will see, my master, one of the most distinguished of this uncommon class of slaveholders, hesitated not to allow the wife of my love to be torn from my fond embrace, and the darling idols of my heart, my little children, to be snatched from my arms, and thus to doom them to a separation from me, more dreadful to all of us than a large number of lashes, inflicted on us daily."

Henry "Box" Brown[646]

§ § §

Toward the end of slavery, Southerners, especially, began to advocate myths about slavery.

One myth was that slaves were better off as slaves than as "free" African-Americans, that African-Americans could not live well in freedom.

Another myth strongly advocated by Southerners during the antebellum South was that slaveholders were "paternalistic," they "loved" their slaves, and they were kind to their slaves. They argued that it was to the slaveholders' benefit to be "kind" to slaves and to "take care" of the slaveholders' "property" as an investment. That myth continued to have advocates for decades, even after slavery ended. People today continue to argue the myth.[647]

In the final analysis, however, while particular masters were not as brutal or violent toward their slaves as were others, it also was a uniform belief that masters must always be in control and that slaves must always be submissive and dependent upon their masters and must obey the masters' wishes. In order to enforce slaves' obedience and submissiveness and to underscore the masters' ever-present dominance and power, the slave society considered it not only to be appropriate, but absolutely necessary, for masters to utilize discipline in brutal forms within the masters' discretion.

While there are advocates expressing the view that "paternalistic" slavery was not really so bad, the American public rarely directly hears the views of slaves regarding such arguments.

---

645 Quoted on Cover of W. Brown, **NARRATIVE OF WILLIAM W. BROWN, A FUGITIVE SLAVE, WRITTEN BY HIMSELF** at 116-17 (Anti-Slavery Office, 2nd ed. 1848), available from the Library of Congress at *www.hathitrust.org/digital_library* ("W. Brown, Narrative").

646 Dictated by H. Brown, written and edited by C. Stearns, **NARRATIVE OF HENRY BOX BROWN, WHO ESCAPED FROM SLAVERY** at 13 (Brown and Stearns, 1849), Academic Affairs Library, Univ. of North Carolina at Chapel Hill, available at *docsouth.unc.edu.*

647 See "*—Sanitizing History Is Fraudulent Education*" below.

William Wells Brown relates the slave's perspective in his book, **NARRATIVE OF WILLIAM W. BROWN, A FUGITIVE SLAVE**, as follows:[648]

> In giving a history of my own sufferings in slavery, as well as the sufferings of others with which I was acquainted, or which came under my immediate observation, I have spoken harshly of slaveholders, in church and state.
>
> Nor am I inclined to apologize for anything which I have said. There are exceptions among slaveholders, as well as among other sinners; and the fact that a slaveholder feeds his slaves better, clothes them better, than another, does not alter the case; he is a slaveholder. I do not ask the slaveholder to feed, clothe, or to treat his victim better as a slave. I am not waging a warfare against the collateral evils, or what are sometimes called the abuses, of slavery. I wage a war against slavery itself, because it takes man down from the lofty position which God intended he should occupy, and places him upon a level with the beasts of the field. It decrees that the slave shall not worship God according to the dictates of his own conscience; it denies him the word of God; it makes him a chattel, and sells him in the market to the highest bidder; it decrees that he shall not protect the wife of his bosom; it takes from him every right which God gave him. Clothing and food are as nothing compared with liberty. What care I for clothing or food, while I am the slave of another? You may take me and put cloth upon my back, boots upon my feet, a hat upon my head, and cram a beef-steak down my throat, and all of this will not satisfy me as long as I know that you have the power to tear me from my dearest relatives. All I ask of the slaveholder is to give the slave his liberty. It is freedom I ask for the *slave*.

"NO FREEMAN COULD ENDURE"

"Heaven save me from kind masters, as well as from those called more cruel; for even their 'tender mercies are cruel,' and what no freeman could endure for a moment."

Dictated by H. Brown, written and edited by C. Stearns, Narrative of Henry Box Brown, Who Escaped from Slavery at 13 (Brown and Stearns, 1849), Academic Affairs Library, Univ. of North Carolina at Chapel Hill, available at *docsouth.unc.edu*

---

648 W. Brown, Narrative at 116-17. Emphasis in original.

SLAVE COFFLE ON A RIVER BOAT

"When I learned the fact of my having been hired to a negro speculator, or a "soul-driver" as they are generally called among slaves, no one can tell my emotions. Mr. Walker had offered a high price for me, as I afterwards learned, but I suppose my master was restrained from selling me by the fact that I was a near relative of his. On entering the service of Mr. Walker, I found that my opportunity of getting to a land of liberty was gone, at least for the time being. He had a gang of slaves in readiness to start [on a river boat from Missouri] for New Orleans, and in a few days we were on our journey. I am at a loss for language to express my feelings on that occasion. Although my master had told me that he had not sold me, and Mr. Walker had told me that he had not purchased me, I did not believe them; and not until I had been to New Orleans, and was on my return, did I believe that I was not sold.

"There was on the boat a large room on the lower deck, in which the slaves were kept, men and women, promiscuously—all chained two and two, and a strict watch kept that they did not get loose; for cases have occurred in which slaves have got off their chains, and made their escape at landing places, while the boats were taking in wood;—and with all our care, we lost one woman who had been taken from her husband and children, and having no desire to live without them, in the agony of her soul jumped overboard, and drowned herself. She was not chained.

"It was almost impossible to keep that part of the boat clean.

"On landing at Natchez, the slaves were all carried to the slave-pen, and there kept one week, during which time, several of them were sold."

W. Brown, Narrative of William W. Brown, A Fugitive Slave, Written by Himself at 39-41 (Anti-Slavery Office, 2nd ed. 1848), available from the Library of Congress at *www.hathitrust.org/digital_library*

STILL MORE MYTHS ABOUT SLAVERY

The Washington Post published an article[649] by Daina Ramey Berry, a history professor at the University of Texas, and Talitha L. LeFlouria, an African-American studies professor at the University of Virginia, on slavery myths presenting myths I reinforce throughout this book.

The "Five Myths" identified in the article are:

- "The first Africans came to America in 1619"
- "Enslaved people who worked in the house had easier lives"
- "Slavery was limited to the South"
- "Women were not as involved in slave-owning as men were"
- "The Civil War ended slavery"

In this book, I have sought to provide ample support for defining and explaining, among others, all of the foregoing as "myths" regarding slavery in America, as well as additional myths, including the following:

- *America's slavery was not unusual in the context of the time*—ignoring the less inhumane systems of slavery practiced in other significant contemporary cultures, and ignoring America's status as one of the last, and by far the largest, slave society remaining in the New World at the time of the Civil War
- *Slavery in America was bad, but not inhumane or brutal*—ignoring sadistic cruelty inherent in American slavery
- *America has washed slavery from its culture by the Civil War, by the 13th, 14th, and 15th Amendments to the Constitution, and by civil rights legislation; consequently slavery does not affect American society significantly today;* America effectively can disregard slavery—ignoring today's extreme denial of equal educational opportunity for African-Americans by thousands of local, as well as state governments
- *Slavery was committed only by white people*—failing to recognize that, as Dr. Henry Gates describes, there were some African-Americans who owned slaves; Dr. Gates states that 3,776 "free" African-Americans (about 1% of the black population) owned 12,907 slaves, out of the millions of slaves in America (a significant proportion, 42%, of the black slaveholders owned only one slave, suggesting that the "ownership" was for the protection of family members, but yet there were others who owned many slaves for economic reasons, including for example, John Carruthers Stanly, who owned 163 slaves in North Carolina, William Ellison, who owned 63 slaves in South Carolina and who provided strong material support to the Confederate cause, and multiple Louisiana black slaveholders)[650]

---

649 Berry and LeFlouria, "Five Myths—Slavery" (Wash. Post, Feb. 9, 2020, at B3) at *www.washingtonpost.com/outlook/five-myths/five-myths-about-slavery/2020/02/07/d4cb0e6a-42e0-11ea-b503-2b077c436617_story.html*, accessed Oct. 6, 2020.

650 Gates, "Did Black People Own Slaves?" (March 4, 2013) at *www.africanamerica.org/topic/did-black-people-own-slaves*, accessed Nov. 21, 2020.

- *Slavery in America was a "capitalist conspiracy"*—ignoring the fundamental and pervasive role of centralized English government in the promotion of slavery in the American colonies specifically as a means to increase tax and other revenues and the dominant role of America's own federal government, especially, but not solely, through the Fugitive Slave Laws
- *Slavery was "something that happened 150 years ago"*—sanitizing the true horror of slavery and the high degree of significance slavery still represents, even today, as a core feature of America's economy, culture, society, politics, and national development

Actually, while America has made important progress in its race relations through the ending of official segregation in the 1960s, remnants of slavery are very much still present as an important influence in today's America.

One of the most obvious "Badges of Slavery" still existent in America is the outrageous discrimination in educational opportunities provided by governmental entities—thousands of public school districts—for many African-Americans and other disadvantaged youth. Those government policies are a prime direct cause of poverty, and of income and wealth disparities, in America. Capitalists do not cause the educational inequality. It is a failure of government and, at times, of intentional governmental actions and policies.

SLAVES' DAILY LIVES

"Reader, believe me when I say that no tongue, nor pen ever has or can express the horrors of American Slavery."

Henry Bibb[651]

§ § §

I thought you would like to know how slaves lived from day to day in terms of the necessities of life—food, clothing, housing and medical care. In this connection, you should keep in mind that America was diverse, both in the colonial period and after the Revolution. Likewise, slavery was diverse.

From the slave narratives and interviews, we learn that there was differentiation in slaves' lives, that slaves led a variety of lives. As Dr. Peter Kolchin states, there was an "extraordinary diversity present under slavery."[652] Urban slaves—who were largely domestic servants, laborers and skilled craftsmen—led lives that were different from the lives of slaves in rural areas. Rural slaves constituted the vast majority of the slave population. Rural slaves were predominantly agricultural field hands and domestic servants. Those two groups themselves often led quite different lives.

Of course, the temperament of the masters and mistresses is an important consideration. In general, urban slaves had better food and housing than rural slaves. Skilled craftsmen tended to benefit from better conditions.[653] Domestic slaves, however, while having some benefits, also were constantly on call and under direct supervision, even on weekends, during holidays, and at night, while field slaves often were able to escape constant interference when away from overseers in the fields.

Even in rural areas, there was diversity. Large plantations often had labor forces consisting of

A YOUNG BOY'S DAILY LIFE

"I was taken away from my mother, and hired out to labor for various persons, eight or ten years in succession; and all my wages were expended for the education of Harriet White, my playmate. It was then my sorrows and sufferings commenced. It was then I first commenced seeing and feeling that I was a wretched slave, compelled to work under the lash without wages and often, without clothes enough to hide my nakedness. I have often worked without half enough to eat, both late and, early, by day and by night. I have often laid my wearied limbs down at night to rest upon a dirt floor, or a bench, without any covering at all, because I had no where else to rest my wearied body, after having worked hard all the day. I have also been compelled in early life, to go at the bidding of a tyrant, through all kinds of weather, hot or cold, wet or dry, and without shoes frequently, until the month of December, with my bare feet on the cold frosty ground, cracked open and bleeding as I walked."

H. Bibb, Narrative of the Life and Adventures of Henry Bibb, An American Slave Written by Himself at 14-15 (1849), available at the Academic Affairs Library, Univ. of North Carolina at Chapel Hill, *docsouth.unc.edu*

---

651 H. Bibb, Narrative of the Life and Adventures of Henry Bibb, An American Slave Written by Himself at 15 (1849), available at the Academic Affairs Library, Univ. of North Carolina at Chapel Hill, *docsouth.unc.edu*

652 Kolchin, at 244.

653 Kolchin, at 53, 178.

hundreds of slaves, even a thousand or more. Smaller farms and plantations may have had as few as one or two slaves who labored closely with their masters.

Slaves' food, clothing and housing varied considerably. Frederick Douglass lived on large plantations, where food and accommodations were sparse, and in a Baltimore household, where food was so plentiful he could trade tidbits to poor white boys in exchange for forbidden reading lessons.[654]

On the larger plantations, slaves had their own social lives in small communities of huts distant from masters' houses. On small enterprises, slaves experienced not only the disadvantages of slaves on larger plantations, but also loneliness and an absence of opportunities to form friendships and families, except with slaves of neighbors who may have been miles away.

Even in the South, there were distinctions between the Upper South—Maryland (where slavery occurred "in its mildest form"[655]) and Virginia—thought to have been a bit less brutal than the Deep South.

In the Deep South, there were still more distinctions. Dr. Peter Kolchin describes how, in the "low country" along the Carolina coast, absentee owners relied upon a "task" system in which masters assigned slaves daily chores. Those slaves were able to rest when their daily tasks were complete.[656] The owners had little interaction with their slaves, retaining overseers to manage their plantations. Elsewhere, slaveholders employed the "gang" system," often, but not always, working groups of slaves under the direct supervision of overseers.

In the Deep South away from the "low country," owners lived on their plantations and were familiar with their slaves and, in later years, became much involved in the slaves' lives. This led to an asserted "paternalistic" approach in which professedly the slaveowners cared somewhat for their slaves,[657] but also exercised "an extraordinary amount of interference in their daily lives."[658] Further, despite the asserted "paternalism," there was also the ultimate control of the masters and the underlying violence and threat of violence to keep control in place.

Frederick Douglass and Harriet Tubman lived on large plantations in Maryland, while Solomon Northup worked on smaller estates in Louisiana. Sojourner Truth came from upstate New York, where large plantations were few or nonexistent. Harriet Jacobs, in contrast to agricultural slaves, had the perspective of a domestic slave living in a community. William Wells Brown worked in a wide variety of jobs in domestic positions and in fields, in businesses in the City of St. Louis, and on river boats transporting other slaves from Missouri for sale in the Deep South.

In terms of specific descriptions of slaves' lives, importantly, we have the first-hand narratives of America's Slavery Heroes. Theodore Weld's **AMERICAN SLAVERY AS IT IS** also provides a wealth of observations by eyewitnesses who reported what they saw to the American Anti-Slavery Society.

There are other examples consistent with those below. I have selected but a few.

654 Douglass, My Bondage and My Freedom, at 155.

655 Douglass, My Bondage and My Freedom, at 61.

656 Kolchin, at 31-32.

657 Kolchin, at 111-35.

658 Kolchin, at 118.

Slaves' Work Days

To introduce the subject of field slaves' daily lives, Solomon Northup provides a description of the constant fear of lashings experienced by slaves on plantations on which Mr. Northup labored:[659]

> An hour before day light the horn is blown. Then the slaves arouse, prepare their breakfast, fill a gourd with water, in another deposit their dinner of cold bacon and corn cake, and hurry to the field again. It is an offence invariably followed by a flogging, to be found at the quarters after daybreak. Then the fears and labors of another day begin; and until its close there is no such thing as rest. He fears he will be caught lagging through the day; he fears to approach the gin-house with his basket-load of cotton at night; he fears, when he lies down, that he will oversleep himself in the morning. Such is a true, faithful, unexaggerated picture and description of the slave's daily life, during the time of cotton-picking, on the shores of Bayou Boeuf.

SNAPSHOTS OF NORMAL WORK DAYS

"At the rolling of sugars, an interval of from two to three months, they *work both night and day*. Abridged of their sleep, they *scarce retire to rest during the whole period*."

"Every body here knows *overdriving* to be one of the most common occurrences, the planters do not deny it, except, perhaps, to northerners."

"During the cotton-picking season they usually labor in the field during the whole of the daylight, and then spend a good part of the night in ginning and baling. The labor required is very frequently excessive, and speedily impairs the constitution. ..."

"It is the common rule for the slaves to be kept at work *fifteen hours in the day*, and in the time of picking cotton a certain number of pounds is required of each. If this amount is not brought in at night, the slave is whipped, and the number of pounds lacking is added to the next day's job; this course is often repeated from day to day."

"It was customary for the overseers to call out the gangs *long before day*, say three o'clock, in the winter, while dressing out the crops; such work as could be done by fire light (pitch pine was abundant,) was provided."...

"The slaves had to cook and eat their breakfast and be in the field by *daylight, and continue there till dark*."

T. Weld, American Slavery As It Is: Testimony of a Thousand Witnesses at 35-36 (American Anti-Slavery Society 1839), available from the Library of Congress at *www.hathitrust.org/digital_library*. Emphasis added.

Mr. Northup describes the routine for slaves in the evening after working in the fields all day, as follows:[660]

> [T]he labor of the day is not yet ended, by any means. Each one must then attend to his respective chores. One feeds the mules, another the swine—another cuts the wood, and so forth; besides, the packing is all done by candle light. Finally, at a late hour, they reach the quarters, sleepy and overcome with the long day's toil. Then a fire must be kindled in the cabin, the corn ground in the small hand-mill, and supper, and dinner for the next day in the field, prepared. ...
>
> The same fear of punishment with which they approach the gin-house, possesses them again on lying down to get a snatch of rest. It is the fear of oversleeping in the morning. Such an offence would certainly be attended with not less than twenty lashes. With a prayer that he may be on his feet and wide awake at the first sound of the horn, he sinks to his slumbers nightly. ...

659 Northup, at 171.

660 Northup, at 168, 170.

Frederick Douglass describes the beginnings of slaves' days on a plantation where he was held, and significantly, provides further information regarding the whips used by slave masters and overseers:[661]

> More slaves are whipped for oversleeping than for any other fault. Neither age nor sex finds any favor. The overseer stands at the quarter door, armed with stick and cowskin, ready to whip any who may be a few minutes behind time. When the horn is blown, there is a rush for the door, and the hindermost one is sure to get a blow from the overseer. Young mothers who worked in the field, were allowed an hour, about ten o'clock in the morning, to go home to nurse their children. Sometimes they were compelled to take their children with them, and to leave them in the corner of the fences, to prevent loss of time in nursing them. The overseer generally rides about the field on horseback. A cowskin and a hickory stick are his constant companions. … I think this whip worse than the "cat-o'nine-tails." It condenses the whole strength of the arm to a single point, and comes with a spring that makes the air whistle. It is a terrible instrument, and is so handy, that the overseer can always have it on his person, and ready for use. The temptation to use it is ever strong; and an overseer can, if disposed, always have cause for using it. With him, it is literally a word and a blow, and, in most cases, the blow comes first.

Mr. Douglass describes the lunch break for slaves, followed by an afternoon's labor:[662]

> Soon, however, the overseer comes dashing through the field. *"Tumble up! Tumble up*, and to *work, work,"* is the cry; and, now, from twelve o'clock (mid-day) till dark, the human cattle are in motion, wielding their clumsy hoes; hurried on by no hope of reward, no sense of gratitude, no love of children, no prospect of bettering their condition; nothing, save the dread and terror of the slave-driver's lash. So goes one day, and so comes and goes another.

William Wells Brown describes hearing his mother's screams, when he was a house servant able to sleep later than field hands, as the overseer whipped his mother for being minutes late into the field:[663]

> I have often laid and heard the crack of the whip, and the screams of the slave. My mother was a field hand, and one morning was ten or fifteen minutes behind the others in getting into the field. As soon as she reached the spot where they were at work, the overseer commenced whipping her. She cried, "Oh! pray—Oh! pray—Oh! Pray"—these are generally the words of slaves, when imploring mercy at the hands of their oppressors. I heard her voice, and knew it, and jumped out of my bunk, and went to the door. Though the field was some distance from the house, I could hear every crack of the whip, and every groan and cry of my poor mother. I remained at the door, not daring to venture any farther. The cold chills ran over me, and I wept aloud. After giving her ten lashes, the sound of the whip ceased, and I returned to my bed, and found no consolation but in my tears. It was not yet daylight.

---

661 Douglass, My Bondage and My Freedom, at 102-03.

662 Douglass, My Bondage and My Freedom, at 104-05.

663 W. Brown, Narrative at 15-16.

A Gallery of Slave Labor

"Scene on a Cotton Plantation: Gathering Cotton", Slavery Images: A Visual Record of the African Slave Trade and Slave Life in the Early African Diaspora, accessed November 16, 2020, *http://slaveryimages.org/s/slaveryimages/item/1059*

"Picking Cotton, Georgia, 1858", Slavery Images: A Visual Record of the African Slave Trade and Slave Life in the Early African Diaspora, accessed November 16, 2020, *http://slaveryimages.org/s/slaveryimages/item/1149*

"Hauling Cotton Bales, U.S. South, 1850s", Slavery Images: A Visual Record of the African Slave Trade and Slave Life in the Early African Diaspora, accessed November 19, 2020, *http://slaveryimages.org/s/slaveryimages/item/1171*

"Hauling and Shipping Cotton, Savannah, Georgia, 1871", Slavery Images: A Visual Record of the African Slave Trade and Slave Life in the Early African Diaspora, accessed November 19, 2020, *http://slaveryimages.org/s/slaveryimages/item/1063*

"Gathering the Cane", *Slavery Images: A Visual Record of the African Slave Trade and Slave Life in the Early African Diaspora,* accessed November 19, 2020, *http://slaveryimages.org/s/slaveryimages/item/1082*

"Cutting Timber, Virginia, 1850s", *Slavery Images: A Visual Record of the African Slave Trade and Slave Life in the Early African Diaspora,* accessed November 21, 2020, *http://slaveryimages.org/s/slaveryimages/item/932*

"Indigo Production, South Carolina, 1757", *Slavery Images: A Visual Record of the African Slave Trade and Slave Life in the Early African Diaspora,* accessed November 19, 2020, *http://slaveryimages.org/s/slaveryimages/item/1084*

"Stacking Wheat, Culpeper, Virginia, 1863", *Slavery Images: A Visual Record of the African Slave Trade and Slave Life in the Early African Diaspora,* accessed November 19, 2020, *http://slaveryimages.org/s/slaveryimages/item/1145*

"Represents Our next door neighbor, A little black girl spinning wool", *Slavery Images: A Visual Record of the African Slave Trade and Slave Life in the Early African Diaspora*, accessed November 21, 2020, *http://slaveryimages.org/s/slaveryimages/item/959*

"Weeding Rice Field, U.S. South, 19th cent.", *Slavery Images: A Visual Record of the African Slave Trade and Slave Life in the Early African Diaspora*, accessed November 16, 2020, *http://slaveryimages.org/s/slaveryimages/item/1151*

"Planting Rice, U.S. South, 1859", *Slavery Images: A Visual Record of the African Slave Trade and Slave Life in the Early African Diaspora*, accessed November 19, 2020, *http://slaveryimages.org/s/slaveryimages/item/1169*

"Rice Harvesting, U.S. South, 1859", *Slavery Images: A Visual Record of the African Slave Trade and Slave Life in the Early African Diaspora,* accessed November 16, 2020, *http://slaveryimages.org/s/slaveryimages/item/1168*

"The Droves", *Slavery Images: A Visual Record of the African Slave Trade and Slave Life in the Early African Diaspora*, accessed November 21, 2020, *http://slaveryimages.org/s/slaveryimages/item/900*

Heading Herring", *Slavery Images: A Visual Record of the African Slave Trade and Slave Life in the Early African Diaspora*, accessed November 21, 2020, *http://slaveryimages.org/s/slaveryimages/item/953*

"Tobacco Production, Virginia, 18th cent.", *Slavery Images: A Visual Record of the African Slave Trade and Slave Life in the Early African Diaspora*, accessed November 19, 2020, *http://slaveryimages.org/s/slaveryimages/item/1118*

"Barber Shop, Richmond, Virginia, 1853", *Slavery Images: A Visual Record of the African Slave Trade and Slave Life in the Early African Diaspora*, accessed November 21, 2020, *http://slaveryimages.org/s/slaveryimages/item/2724*

Food

Frederick Douglass describes the food deprivation he suffered when a young boy:[664]

> We were not regularly allowanced. Our food was coarse corn meal boiled. This was called mush. It was put into a large wooden tray or trough, and set down upon the ground. The children were then called, like so many pigs, and like so many pigs they would come and devour the mush; some with oyster-shells, others with pieces of shingle, some with naked hands, and none, with spoons. He that ate fastest got most; he that was strongest secured the best place; and few left the trough satisfied.

Mr. Douglass describes his experiences at one plantation:[665]

> As a general rule, slaves do not come to the quarters for either breakfast or dinner, but take their "ash cake" with them, and eat it in the field. This was so on the home plantation; probably, because the distance from the quarter to the field, was sometimes two, and even three miles.
>
> The dinner of the slaves consisted of a huge piece of ash cake, and a small piece of pork, or two salt herrings. Not having ovens, nor any suitable cooking utensils, the slaves mixed their meal with a little water, to such thickness that a spoon would stand erect in it; and, after the wood had burned away to coals and ashes, they would place the dough between oak leaves and lay it carefully in the ashes, completely covering it; hence, the bread is called ash cake. The surface of this peculiar bread is covered with ashes, to the depth of a sixteenth part of an inch, and the ashes, certainly, do not make it very grateful to the teeth, nor render it very palatable. The bran, or coarse part of the meal, is baked with the fine, and bright scales run through the bread. This bread, with its ashes and bran, would disgust and choke a northern man, but it is quite liked by the slaves. They eat it with avidity, and are more concerned about the quantity than about the quality. They are far too scantily provided for, and are worked too steadily, to be much concerned for the quality of their food.

Douglass then describes his experiences at another plantation that drove him to steal food:[666]

> [At another plantation,] [t]here were eight persons in the family. There was, each week, one half bushel of corn-meal brought from the mill; and in the kitchen, corn-meal was almost our exclusive food, for very little else was allowed us. Out of this half bushel of corn-meal, the family in the great house had a small loaf every morning; thus leaving us, in the kitchen, with not quite a half a peck of meal per week, apiece. This allowance was less than half the allowance of food on Lloyd's plantation. It was not enough to subsist upon; and we were, therefore, reduced to the wretched necessity of living at the expense of our neighbors. We were compelled either to beg, or to steal, and we did both. I frankly confess, that while I hated everything like stealing, as such, I nevertheless did not hesitate to take food, when I was hungry, wherever I could find it. Nor was this practice the mere result of an unreasoning instinct; it was, in my case, the result of a clear apprehension of the claims of morality. I weighed and considered the matter closely, before I ventured to satisfy my hunger by such means. Considering that my labor and person were the property of Master Thomas, and that I was by him deprived of the necessaries of life—necessaries obtained by my own labor—it was easy to deduce the right to supply myself with what was my own. It was simply appropriating what was my own to the use of my master, since the health and strength derived from such food were exerted in his service.

---

664 Douglass, Narrative, at 27.

665 Douglass, My Bondage and My Freedom, at 103-04. Emphasis in original.

666 Douglass, My Bondage and My Freedom, at 188-89. Emphasis in original.

PECK

"Peck, unit of capacity in the U.S. Customary and the British Imperial Systems of measurement. In the United States the peck is used only for dry measure and is equal to 8 dry quarts, or 537.6 cubic inches (8.810 litres)."

"Peck" at *www.britannica.com/science/peck,* accessed Oct. 10, 2020

> To be sure, this was stealing, according to the law and gospel I heard from St. Michael's pulpit; but I had already begun to attach less importance to what dropped from that quarter, on that point, while, as yet, I retained my reverence for religion. It was not always convenient to steal from master, and the same reason why I might, innocently, steal from him, did not seem to justify me in stealing from others. In the case of my master, it was only a question of *removal*—the taking his meat out of one tub, and putting it into another; the ownership of the meat was not affected by the transaction. At first, he owned it in the tub, and last, he owned it in *me.*

Mr. Douglass contrasts his experience living for a time as an urban slave boy in a household in Baltimore:[667]

> Instead of the cold, damp floor of my old master's kitchen, I found myself on carpets; for the corn bag in winter, I now had a good straw bed, well furnished with covers; for the coarse corn-meal in the morning, I now had good bread, and mush occasionally; for my poor tow-linen shirt, reaching to my knees, I had good, clean clothes. I was really well off.

Solomon Northup describes the food allowed on his Master Epps' Louisiana plantation[668]

> All that is allowed them is corn and bacon, which is given out at the corncrib and smoke-house every Sunday morning. Each one receives, as his weekly allowance, three and a half pounds of bacon, and corn enough to make a peck of meal. That is all—no tea, coffee, sugar, and with the exception of a very scanty sprinkling now and then, no salt. I can say, from a ten years' residence with Master Epps, that no slave of his is ever likely to suffer from the gout, superinduced by excessive high living. Master Epps' hogs were fed on shelled corn—it was thrown out to his "niggers" in the ear. The former, he thought, would fatten faster by shelling, and soaking it in the water—the latter, perhaps, if treated in the same manner, might grow too fat to labor. Master Epps was a shrewd calculator, and knew how to manage his own animals ...
>
> I kept my corn in a small wooden box, the meal in a gourd; and, by the way, the gourd is one of the most convenient and necessary utensils on a plantation. Besides supplying the place of all kinds of crockery in a slave cabin, it is used for carrying water to the fields. Another, also, contains the dinner. It dispenses with the necessity of pails, dippers, basins, and such tin and wooden superfluities altogether.
>
> When the corn is ground, and fire is made, the bacon is taken down from the nail on which it hangs, a slice cut off and thrown upon the coals to broil. The majority of slaves have no knife, much less a fork. They cut their bacon with the axe at the wood-pile. The com meal is mixed with a little water, placed in the fire, and baked. When it is "done brown," the ashes are scraped off, and being placed upon a chip, which answers for a table, the tenant of the slave hut is ready to sit down upon the ground to supper. By this time it is usually midnight.

667 Douglass, My Bondage and My Freedom, at 144.

668 Northup, at 168-70. Emphasis in original.

AMERICAN SLAVERY AS IT IS contains the following examples regarding slaves' food:[669]

WILLIAM LADD, Esq., of Minot, Me., president of the American Peace Society, and formerly a slaveholder of Florida, gives the following testimony as to the allowance of food to slaves.

"The usual food of the slaves was *corn,* with a modicum of salt. In some cases the master allowed no salt, but the slaves boiled the sea water for salt in their little pots. For about eight days near Christmas, i.e., from the Saturday evening before, to the Monday evening after Christmas day, they were allowed some *meat.* They always with one single exception ground their corn in a hand-mill, and cooked their food themselves."

§ § §

Extract of a letter from Rev. D.C. EASTMAN, a preacher of the Methodist Episcopal church, in Fayette county, Ohio.

"In March, 1838, Mr. Thomas Larrimer, a deacon of the Presbyterian church in Bloomingbury, Fayette county, Ohio, Mr. G.S. Fullerton, merchant, and member of the same church, and Mr. William A. Ustick, an elder of the same church, spent a night with a Mr. Shepherd, about 30 miles North of Charleston, S.C., on the Monk's corner road. He owned five families of negroes, who, he said, were fed from the same meal and meat tubs as himself, but that 99 out of a 100 of all the slaves in that county *saw meat but once a year,* which was on Christmas holidays."

As an illustration of the inhuman experiments sometimes tried upon slaves, in respect to the *kind* as well as the quality and quantity of their food, we solicit the attention of the reader to the testimony of the late General Wade Hampton, of South Carolina. General Hampton was for some time commander in chief of the army on the Canada frontier during the last war, and at the time of his death, about three years since, was the largest slaveholder in the United States. The General's testimony is contained in the following extract of a letter, just received from a distinguished clergyman in the west, extensively known both as a preacher and a writer. His name is with the executive committee of the American Anti-Slavery Society. ...

"I received my information from a lady in the west of high respectability and great moral worth,—but think it best to withhold her name, although the statement was not made in confidence.

"My informant stated that she sat at dinner once in company with General Wade Hampton, and several others; that the conversation turned upon the treatment of their servants, &c.; when the General undertook to entertain the company with the relation of an experiment he had made in the feeding of his slaves on cotton seed. He said that he first mingled one-fourth cotton seed with three-fourths corn, on which they seemed to thrive tolerably well; that he then had measured out to them equal quantities of each, which did not seem to produce any important change; afterwards he increased the quantity of cotton seed to three-fourths, mingled with one-fourth corn, and then he declared, with an oath, that 'they died like rotten sheep!'"

AMERICAN SLAVERY AS IT IS continues with the following examples:[670]

"On my uncle's plantation, the food of the slaves, was corn pone and a small allowance of meat."

"The quantity allowed by custom is a *peck of corn a week!*"

669 Weld, at 28-31.

670 Weld, at 28-31.

"A *single peck of corn a week, or the like measure of rice,* is the *ordinary* quantity of provision for a *hard-working slave;* to which a small quantity of meat is occasionally, though *rarely*, added. ..."

"The slaves are generally allowanced a pint of corn meal and a salt herring is the allowance, or in lieu of the herring a 'dab' of fat meat of about the same value. I have known the sour milk, and clauber to be served out to the hands, when there was an abundance of milk on the plantation. This is a luxury not often afforded."

"The food, or 'feed' of slaves is generally of the *poorest* kind."

"They live on a coarse, *crude, unwholesome diet.*"

"I have myself known numerous instances of large families of *badly fed* negroes swept off by a prevailing epidemic; and it is well known to many intelligent planters in the south, that the best method of preventing that horrible malady, *Chachexia Africana,* is to feed the negroes with *nutritious* food." ...

"The slaves got to the field in the morning; they carry with them corn meal wet with water, and at *noon* build a fire on the ground and bake it in the ashes. After the labors of the day are over, they take their *second* meal of ash-cake."

"The slaves eat *twice* during the day."

"The slaves received two meals during the day. Those who have their food cooked for them get their breakfast about eleven o'clock, and their other meal *after night.*"

CLAUBER

"Scottish variant of clabber"

"Clauber" at *www.merriam-webster.com/dictionary/clauber,* accessed Oct. 10, 2020

CLABBER

"sour milk that has thickened or curdled"

"Clabber" at *www.merriam-webster.com/dictionary/clabber,* accessed Oct. 10, 2020

§ § §

AMERICAN SLAVERY AS IT IS then provides yet additional examples:[671]

Testimony of Angelina Grimke Weld

Mrs. Weld is the youngest. daughter of the late Judge Grimke, of the Supreme Court of South Carolina, and a sister of the late Hon. Thomas S. Grimke, of Charleston.[She testified as follows:] ...

"Only two meals a day are allowed the house slaves—the *first at twelve* o'clock. If they eat before this time, it is by stealth, and I am sure there must be a good deal of suffering among them from *hunger*, and particularly by children. Besides this, they are often kept from their meals by way of punishment. No table is provided for them to eat from. ... I *never* saw slaves seated round a *table* to partake of any meal."

§ § §

Mr. [Joseph] IDE is a respected member of the Baptist Church in Sheffield, Caledonia county, Vt.; and recently the Postmaster in that town. He spent a few months at the south in the years 1837 and 8. In a letter to the Rev. Wm. Scales of Lyndon, Vt. written a few weeks since, Mr. Ide writes as follows...[672]

"[My informant] has often told me of the cruel treatment of the slaves on a plantation adjoining her father's in the low country of South Carolina. She says she has often seen them driven to the necessity of eating frogs and lizards to sustain life."

671 Weld, at 52, 55-56, 101. Emphasis in original.

672 Weld, at 101. Emphasis in original.

CONTRASTING STANDARDS

"My brother and myself, were in the practice of carrying grain to mill, a few times a year, which was the means of furnishing us with some information respecting other slaves. We often went twenty miles, to a mill owned by a Col. Ambler, in Yansinville county, and used to improve our opportunities for gaining information. Especially desirous were we, of learning the condition of slaves around us, for we knew not how long we should remain in as favorable hands as we were then. On one occasion, while waiting for our grain, we entered a house in the neighborhood, and while resting ourselves there, we saw a number of forlorn-looking beings pass the door, and as they passed, we noticed that they turned and gazed earnestly upon us. Afterwards, about fifty performed the same act, which excited our minds somewhat, as we overheard some of them say, "Look there, and see those two colored men with shoes, vests and hats on," and we determined to obtain an interview with them. Accordingly, after receiving some bread and meat from our hosts, we followed these abject beings to their quarters;—and such a sight we had never witnessed before, as we had always lived on our master's plantation, and this was about the first of our journeys to the mill. They were dressed with shirts made of coarse bagging, such as coffee-sacks are made from, and some kind of light substance for pantaloons, and no other clothing whatever. They had on no shoes, hats, vests, or coats, and when my brother asked them why they spoke of our being dressed with those articles of clothing, they said they had "never seen negroes dressed in that way before." They looked very hungry, and we divided our bread and meat among them, which furnished them only a mouthful each. They never had any meat, they said, given them by their masters. My brother put various questions to them, such as, "if they had wives?" "did they go to church?" "had they any sisters?" &c. The one who gave us the information, said they had wives, but were obliged to marry on their own plantation. Master would not allow them to go away from home to marry, consequently he said they were all related to each other, and master made them marry, whether related or not. My brother asked this man to show him his sisters; he said he could not tell them from the rest, they were all his sisters; and here let me state, what is well known by many people, that no such thing as real marriage is allowed to exist among the slaves. ...

"But we were obliged to cut short our conversation with these slaves, by beholding the approach of the overseer, who was directing his steps towards us, like a bear seeking its prey. We had only time to ask this man, "if they were often whipped?" to which he replied, that not a day passed over their heads, without some of their number being brutally punished; "and," said he, "we shall have to suffer for this talk with you." He then told us, that many of them had been severely whipped that very morning, for having been baptized the night before. After we left them, we looked back, and heard the screams of these poor creatures, suffering under the blows of the hard-hearted overseer, for the crime of talking with us;—which screams sounded in our ears for some time. We felt thankful that we were exempted from such terrible treatment; but still, we knew not how soon we should be subject to the same cruel fate. By this time we had returned to the mill, where we met a young man, (a relation of the owner of this plantation,) who for some time appeared to be eyeing us quite attentively. At length he asked me if I had "ever been whipped," and when I told him I had not, he replied, "Well, you will neither of you ever be of any value, then;" so true is it that whipping is considered a necessary part of slavery. Without this practice, it could not stand a single day. He expressed a good deal of surprise that we were allowed to wear hats and shoes,—supposing that a slave had no business to wear such clothing as his master wore. We had brought our fishing-lines with us, and requested the privilege to fish in his stream, which he roughly denied us, saying, "we do not allow niggers to fish." Nothing daunted, however, by this rebuff, my brother went to another place, and was quite successful in his undertaking, obtaining a plentiful supply of the finny tribe; but as soon as this youngster perceived his good luck, he ordered him to throw them back into the stream, which he was obliged to do, and we returned home without them."

Dictated by H. Brown, written and edited by C. Stearns, Narrative of Henry Box Brown, Who Escaped from Slavery at 21-22, 24-25 (Brown and Stearns, 1849), Academic Affairs Library, Univ. of North Carolina at Chapel Hill, available at *docsouth.unc.edu*

Clothing

Frederick Douglass describes slaves' clothing allowance on a plantation:[673]

> The yearly allowance of clothing for the slaves on this plantation, consisted of two tow-linen shirts—such linen as the coarsest crash towels are made of; one pair of trowsers of the same material, for summer, and a pair of trowsers and a jacket of woolen, most slazily put together, for winter; one pair of yarn stockings, and one pair of shoes of the coarsest description. The slave's entire apparel could not have cost more than eight dollars per year. The allowance of food and clothing for the little children, was committed to their mothers, or to the older slavewomen having the care of them. Children who were unable to work in the field, had neither shoes, stockings, jackets nor trowsers given them. Their clothing consisted of two coarse tow-linen shirts—already described—per year; and when these failed them, as they often did, they went naked until the next allowance day. Flocks of little children from five to ten years old, might be seen on Col. Lloyd's plantation, as destitute of clothing as any little heathen on the west coast of Africa; and this, not merely during the summer months, but during the frosty weather of March. The little girls were no better off than the boys; all were nearly in a state of nudity.

Mr. Douglass further describes the deprivation of clothing he suffered when a young boy:[674]

> I was seldom whipped by my old master, and suffered little from anything else than hunger and cold. .... I had no bed. I must have perished with cold, but that, the coldest nights, I used to steal a bag which was used for carrying corn to the mill. I would crawl into this bag, and there sleep on the cold, damp, clay floor, with my head in and feet out. My feet have been so cracked with the frost, that the pen with which I am writing might be laid in the gashes.

AMERICAN SLAVERY AS IT IS provides these examples, among others, regarding slaves' clothing:[675]

> Mr. NEHEMIAH CAULKINS, of Waterford, New London Co., Connecticut, has furnished the Executive Committee of the American Anti-Slavery Society, with the following statements relative to the condition and treatment of slaves, in the south eastern part of North Carolina. Most of the facts related by Mr. Caulkins fell under his personal observation. The air of candor and honesty that pervades the narrative, the manner in which Mr. C. has drawn it up, the good sense, just views, conscience and heart which it exhibits, are sufficient of themselves to recommend it to all who have ears to hear.[676] ...
>
> "The allowance of clothing on this plantation to each slave, was given out at Christmas for the year, and consisted of one pair of coarse shoes, and enough coarse cloth to make a jacket and trowsers. If the man has a wife she makes it up; if not, it is made up in the house. The slaves on this plantation, being near Wilmington, procured themselves extra clothing by working Sundays and moonlight nights,

OSNABURG

"A rough coarse durable cotton fabric in plain weave made originally of flax and used in the gray for bagging and industrial purposes and in various finishes usually for upholstery, sportswear, and curtains"

"Osnaburg" at *www.merriam-webster.com/dictionary/osnaburg*, accessed Oct. 10, 2020

673 Douglass My Bondage and My Freedom, at 101.

674 Douglass, Narrative, at 26-27.

675 Weld, at 10, 11, 13, 16. Emphasis in original.

676 Weld, at 10-11, 13, 16. Emphasis in original.

cutting cord-wood in the swamps, which they had to back about a quarter of a mile to the river; they would then get a permit from their master, and taking the wood in their canoes, carry it to Wilmington, and sell it to the vessels, or dispose of it as they best could, and with the money buy an old jacket of the sailors, some coarse cloth for a shirt, &c. They sometimes gather the moss from the trees, which they cleanse and take to market. The women receive their allowance of the same kind of cloth which the men have. This they make into a frock; if they have any under garments *they must procure them for themselves.* ..."

"I knew one young man seventeen years of age, by the name of Dave, on Mr. J. Swan's plantation, worked day after day in the rice machine as naked as when he was born. The reason of his being so, his master said in my hearing, was, that he could not keep clothes on him—he would get into the fire and burn them off."

§ § §

This testimony is communicated in a letter from Mr. Cyrus Pierce, a respectable and well known citizen of Nantucket, Mass. Of the witnesses, Messrs. T. D. M. and F. C. Macy, Mr. Pierce says, "They are both inhabitants of this island, and have resided at the south; they are both worthy men whose integrity and intelligence I can vouch unqualifiedly; the former has furnished me with the following statement...[677]

"Their supply of clothing is scanty each slave being allowed a Holland coat and pantaloons, of the coarsest manufacture, and one pair of cowhide shoes. The women, enough of the same kind of cloth for one frock. They have also one pair of shoes. Shoes are given to the slaves in the winter only. In summer, their clothing is composed of osnaburgs."

§ § §

Narrative and Testimony of Rev. Horace Moulton[678]

Mr. Moulton is an esteemed minister of the Methodist Episcopal Church, in Marlborough, Mass. He spent five years in Georgia between 1817 and 1824. The following communication has been recently received from him.

Marlborough, Mass., Feb. 18, 1839. ...

"The masters [in Georgia] make a practice of getting two suits of clothes for each slave per year, a thick suit for winter, and a thin one for summer. They provide also one pair of northern made sale shoes for each slave in *winter.* These shoes usually begin to rip in a few weeks. The negroes' mode of mending them is, to *wire* them together, in many instances. ... The males and females have their suits from the same cloth for their winter dresses. These winter garments appear to be made of a mixture of cotton and wool, very coarse and *sleazy.* The whole suit for the men consists of a pair of pantaloons and a short sailor-jacket, *without shirt, vest, hat, stockings, or any kind of loose garments!* These, if worn steadily when at work, would not probably last more than one or two months; therefore, for the sake of saving them, many of them work, especially in the summer, with no clothing on them except a cloth tied round their waist, and *almost all* with nothing more on them than pantaloons, and these frequently so torn that they do not serve the purposes of common decency. The women have for clothing a short petticoat, and a short loose gown, something like the male's sailor-jacket, *without any under garment, stockings, bonnets, hoods, caps, or any kind of over-clothes.* When at work in warm weather, they usually strip off the

677 Weld, at 106-06.

678 Weld, at 17, 19. Emphasis in original.

loose gown, and have nothing on but a short petticoat with some kind of covering over their breasts. Many children may be seen in the summer months *as naked as they came into the world.* I think, as a whole, they suffer more for the want of comfortable bed-clothes, than they do for wearing apparel. It is true, that some by begging or buying, have more clothes than above described, but the *masters provide them with no more.* They are miserable objects of pity. …"

Housing

Solomon Northup describes slaves' housing conditions in Louisiana:[679]

> The softest couches in the world are not to be found in the log mansion of the slave. The one whereon I reclined year after year, was a plank twelve inches wide and ten feet long. My pillow was a stick of wood. The bedding was a coarse blanket, and not a rag or shred beside. Moss might be used, were it not that it directly breeds a swarm of fleas.
>
> The cabin is constructed of logs, without floor or window. The latter is altogether unnecessary, the crevices between the logs admitting sufficient light. In stormy weather the rain drives through them, rendering it comfortless and extremely disagreeable. The rude door hangs on great wooden hinges. In one end is constructed an awkward fire-place.

Mr. Douglass describes the slaves' housing conditions in Maryland:[680]

"Negro Village in Georgia", *Slavery Images: A Visual Record of the African Slave Trade and Slave Life in the Early African Diaspora*, accessed November 15, 2020, *http://slaveryimages.org/s/slaveryimages/item/1362*

> As to beds to sleep on, they were known to none of the field hands; nothing but a coarse blanket—not so good as those used in the north to cover horses—was given them, and this only to the men and women. The children stuck themselves in holes and corners, about the quarters; often in the corner of the huge chimneys, with their feet in the ashes to keep them warm. The want of beds, however, was not considered a very great privation. Time to sleep was of far greater importance, for, when the day's work is done, most of the slaves have their washing, mending and cooking to do; and, having few or none of the ordinary facilities for doing such things, very many of their sleeping hours are consumed in necessary preparations for the duties of the coming day.
>
> The sleeping apartments—if they may be called such—have little regard to comfort or decency. Old and young, male and female, married

679 Northup, at 170-71.

680 Douglass, My Bondage and My Freedom, at 101-02.

and single, drop down upon the common clay floor, each covering up with his or her blanket,—the only protection they have from cold or exposure. …

AMERICAN SLAVERY AS IT IS provides these examples, among others, regarding slaves' housing:

Mr. NEHEMIAH CAULKINS, of Waterford, New London Co., Connecticut, has furnished the Executive Committee of the American Anti-Slavery Society, with the following statements … .[681]

"Follow them next to their huts; some with and some without floors:—Go at night, view their means of lodging, see them lying on benches, some on the floor or ground, some sitting on stools, dozing away the night;—others, of younger age, with a bare blanket wrapped about them; and one or two lying in the ashes. These things *I have often seen with my own eyes.*"

§ § §

Testimony of Angelina Grimke Weld[682]

"Slave Houses on a Rice Plantation, U.S. South, 1859", *Slavery Images: A Visual Record of the African Slave Trade and Slave Life in the Early African Diaspora*, accessed November 15, 2020, http://slaveryimages.org/s/slaveryimages/item/1426

"The utter disregard of the comfort of the slaves, in *little* things, can scarcely be conceived by those who have not been a *component part* of slaveholding communities, Take a few particulars out of hundreds that might be named. In South Carolina musketoes (sic) swarm in myriads, more than half the year—they are so excessively annoying at night, that no family thinks of sleeping without nets or "musketoe-bars" hung over their bedsteads, yet slaves are never provided with them, unless it be the favorite old domestics who get the cast-off pavilions; and yet these very masters and mistresses will be so kind to their *horses* as to provide them with *fly nets.* Bedsteads and bedding too, are rarely provided for any of the slaves—if the waiters and coachmen, waiting maids, cooks, washers, &c., have beds at all, they must generally get them for themselves. Commonly they lie down at night on the bare floor, with a small blanket wrapped round them in winter, and in summer a coarse osnaburg sheet, or nothing. Old slaves generally have beds, but it is because when younger they have provided them for themselves."

§ § §

Mr. [Joseph] IDE is a respected member of the Baptist Church in Sheffield, Caledonia County, Vt., and recently the Postmaster in that town. He spent a few months at the south in the years 1837

681 Weld, at 10-11, 13, 16. Emphasis in original.

682 Weld, at 52, 55. Emphasis in original.

and 8. In a letter to the Rev. Wm. Scales of Lyndon, Vt. written a few weeks since, Mr. Ide writes as follows...[683]

"In relation to negro huts, I will say that planters usually own large tracts of land. They have extensive clearings and a beautiful mansion house—and generally some forty or fifty rods from the dwelling are situated the negro cabins, or huts, built of logs in the rudest manner. Some consist of poles rolled up together and covered with mud or clay—many of them not as comfortable as northern pig-sties."

§ § §

"A Planter's Mansion", *Slavery Images: A Visual Record of the African Slave Trade and Slave Life in the Early African Diaspora*, accessed November 15, 2020, *http://slaveryimages.org/s/slaveryimages/item/1373*

This testimony is communicated in a letter from Mr. Cyrus Pierce, a respectable and well known citizen of Nantucket, Mass. Of the witnesses, Messrs. T. D. M. and F. C. Macy, Mr. Pierce says, "They are both inhabitants of this island, and have resided at the south; they are both worthy men whose integrity and intelligence I can vouch unqualifiedly; the former has furnished me with the following statement. ...[684]

"When it rained, the slaves were allowed to collect under a tree until the shower had passed. Seldom, on a week day, were they permitted to go to their huts during rain; and even had this privilege been granted, many of those miserable habitations were in so dilapidated a condition, that they would afford little or no protection. Negro huts are built of logs, covered with boards or thatch, having no *flooring,* and but one apartment, serving all the purposes of sleeping, cooking, &c. Some are furnished with a temporary loft. I have seen a whole family herded together in a loft ten feet by twelve. In cold weather, they gather around the fire, spread their blankets *on the ground,* and keep as comfortable as they can."

In the North, in contrast to plantation housing in "lines of slave cabins," Dr. Ira Berlin describes slaves "reduced to near invisibility by being stuffed into garrets, back rooms, closets, and outbuildings." He quotes Sojourner Truth's recollection of a "cellar" where "the 'inmates, of both sexes and all ages' slept on 'damp boards, like the horse, with a little straw and a blanket.'"[685]

Medical Care

At the time of slavery, medicine, medical knowledge, and medical ethics were not as refined as they are today. Consequently, we cannot expect practices in the first half of the nineteenth century to have been up to today's standards. Whites also experienced medical issues confronting the slaves.

683 Weld, at 101.

684 Weld, at 105, 106. Emphasis in original.

685 Berlin, at 56.

Further, there also should be recognition in this area, just as in other areas relating to care of slaves, such as food, housing, family, clothing, labor expectations, and the like, that there were masters and mistresses who were less inhumane or brutal than were other masters and mistresses.

Likewise, individual doctors would have been concerned for the health interests of the slaves. The following anecdotes reflect certain doctors with that perspective.

In the end, however, the parties paying the bill—masters and mistresses—often would have had a significant influence on a slave's medical treatment. Further, other doctors, regarding the slaveholders as their effective patients, would have placed the slaves' best interests low on the list of priorities.

The bottom line is that, in America, in contrast to other cultures, slave masters were not required by law or practice to treat slaves' medical conditions in any particular manner. The assumption was that masters would treat their property well in order to receive the benefits of the slaves' forced labor. Having said that, however, since the masters were the parties weighing their own economic priorities in the light of competing benefits and costs, the slaves' personal interests often fell in line behind the master's monetary interests.

<u>LIVING CONDITIONS IMPACTED HEALTH</u>

"Enslaved African Americans were more vulnerable than whites to respiratory infections, thanks to poorly constructed slave shacks that admitted winter cold and summer heat. Slaves' immune systems were unfamiliar with, or naïve to, microbes that caused various pneumonias and tuberculosis. Parasitic infections and abysmal nutrition also undermined blacks' immunological rigor."

H. Washington, Medical Apartheid: The Dark History of Medical Experimentation on Black Americans from Colonial Times to the Present at 29 (Anchor Books, 2006)

It did not need to be that way. Americans easily could have given slaves the benefits of stronger protection in the event of illness than merely the unregulated discretion of slave masters. The Spanish in Florida did so. The French *Code Noir* purported to do so.

In the following passage involving a deeply religious master, Frederick Douglass describes common brutality against slaves through denial of medical care:[686]

> I have said my master found religious sanction for his cruelty. As an example, I will state one of many facts going to prove the charge. I have seen him tie up a lame young woman, and whip her with a heavy cowskin upon her naked shoulders, causing the warm red blood to drip; and, in justification of the bloody deed, he would quote this passage of Scripture—"He that knoweth his master's will, and doeth it not, shall be beaten with many stripes."
>
> Master would keep this lacerated young woman tied up in this horrid situation four or five hours at a time. I have known him to tie her up early in the morning, and whip her before breakfast; leave her, go to his store, return at dinner, and whip her again, cutting her in the places already made raw with his cruel lash. The secret of master's cruelty toward "Henny" is found in the fact of her being almost helpless. When quite a child, she fell into the fire, and burned herself horribly. Her hands were so burnt that she never got the use of them. She could do very little but bear heavy burdens. She was to master a bill of expense; and as he was a mean man, she was a constant offence to him. He seemed desirous

686 Douglass, Narrative, at 55-56.

of getting the poor girl out of existence. He gave her away once to his sister; but, being a poor gift, she was not disposed to keep her. Finally, my benevolent master, to use his own words, "set her adrift to take care of herself." Here was a recently-converted man, holding on upon the mother, and at the same time turning out her helpless child, to starve and die!

MASTER PAYS THE BILL

"Ominously for blacks, the owners, not the enslaved workers, determined safety and rationed medical care, deciding when and what type of care was to be given. Because professional attention was expensive, most owners dosed their own slaves as long as they could before calling in physicians, who usually saw slaves only in extremis, as a last resort. … Physician records also expressed disgust at the conditions in which enslaved workers were kept."

H. Washington, Medical Apartheid: The Dark History of Medical Experimentation on Black Americans from Colonial Times to the Present at 30 (Anchor Books, 2006)

Mr. Douglass describes the heartless treatment of another handicapped young girl by a planter:[687]

[Another] young woman was the daughter of Milly, an own aunt of mine. The poor girl on arriving at our house, presented a pitiable appearance. She had left in haste, and without preparation; and, probably, without the knowledge of Mr. Plummer [the overseer]. She had traveled twelve miles, bare-footed, bare-necked and bare-headed. Her neck and shoulders were covered with scars, newly made; and not content with marring her neck and shoulders, with the cowhide, the cowardly brute had dealt her a blow on the head with a hickory club, which cut a horrible gash, and left her face literally covered with blood. In this condition, the poor young woman came down, to implore protection at the hands of my old master. I expected to see him boil over with rage at the revolting deed, and to hear him fill the air with curses upon the brutal Plummer; but I was disappointed. He sternly told her, in an angry tone, he "believed she deserved every bit of it," and, if she did not go home instantly, he would himself take the remaining skin from her neck and back. Thus was the poor girl compelled to return, without redress, and perhaps to receive an additional flogging for daring to appeal to old master against the overseer.

Solomon Northup provides the following description of his masters' low level of concern regarding Mr. Northup's health:[688]

It was now the season of hoeing. I was first sent into the corn-field, and afterwards set to scraping cotton. In this employment I remained until hoeing time was nearly passed, when I began to experience the symptoms of approaching illness. I was attacked with chills, which were succeeded by a burning fever. I became weak and emaciated, and frequently so dizzy that it caused me to reel and stagger like a drunken man. Nevertheless, I was compelled to keep up my row. When in health I found little difficulty in keeping pace with my fellow-laborers, but now it seemed to be an utter impossibility. Often I fell behind, when the driver's lash was sure to greet my back, infusing into my sick and drooping body a little temporary energy. I continued to decline until at length the whip became entirely ineffectual. The sharpest sting of the rawhide could not arouse me. Finally, in September, when the busy season of cotton picking was at hand, I was unable to leave my cabin. Up to this time I had received no medicine, nor any attention from my master or mistress. The old cook visited me occasionally, preparing me corn coffee, and sometimes boiling a bit of bacon, when I had grown too feeble to accomplish it myself.

687 Douglass, Douglass, My Bondage and My Freedom, at 82-83.

688 Northup, at 176-78.

When it was said that I would die, Master Epps, unwilling to bear the loss, which the death of an animal worth a thousand dollars would bring upon him, concluded to incur the expense of sending to Holmesville for Dr. Wines. He announced to Epps that it was the effect of the climate, and there was a probability of his losing me. He directed me to eat no meat, and to partake of no more food than was absolutely necessary to sustain life. Several weeks elapsed, during which time, under the scanty diet to which I was subjected, I had partially recovered. One morning, long before I was in a proper condition to labor, Epps appeared at the cabin door, and, presenting me a sack, ordered me to the cotton field. …

AMERICAN SLAVERY AS IT IS adds the following descriptions of slave medical care:

Mr. [Philemon] Bliss is a highly respectable member of the bar, in Elyria, Lorain Co. Ohio, and member of the Presbyterian church, in that place. He resided in Florida during the years 1834 and 5.[689]

The following extracts are from letters written by Mr. B, in 1835, while residing on a plantation near Tallahassee, and published soon after in the Ohio Atlas; also from letters written in 1836, and published in the New York Evangelist.

"In case of sickness, if the master or overseer thinks them seriously ill, they are taken care of, but their complaints are usually not much heeded. A physician told me that he was employed by a planter last

PROVISION OF MEDICAL CARE?

"At one time a colored man, who had been in the habit of singing religious songs quite often, was taken sick and did not make his appearance at the factory. For two or three days no notice whatever was taken of him, no medicine provided for him, and no physician sent to heal him. At the end of that time, Mr. Allen ordered three strong men to go to the man's house, and bring him to the factory. This order being obeyed, the man, pale and hardly able to stand, was stripped to his waist, his hands tied together, and the rope fastened to a large post. The overseer then questioned him about his singing, told him that it consumed too much time, and that he was going to give him some medicine which would cure him. The poor trembling man made no reply, when the pious Mr. Allen, for no crime except that of sickness, inflicted 200 lashes upon the quivering flesh of the invalid, and he would have continued his 'apostolic blows,' if the emaciated form of the languishing man, had not sunken under their heavy weight, and Mr. Allen was obliged to desist.

"I witnessed this transaction with my own eyes; but what could I do, for I was a slave, and any interference on my part would only have brought the same punishment upon me. This man was sick a month afterwards, during which time the weekly allowance of seventy-five cents for the hands to board themselves with, was withheld from him, and his wife was obliged to support him by washing for others; and yet Northern people tell me that a slave is better off than a free man, because when he is sick his master provides for him! Master knew all the circumstances of this case, but never uttered one word of reproof to the overseer, that I could learn; at any rate, he did not interfere at all with this cruel treatment of him, as his motto was, 'Mr. Allen is always right.'"

Dictated by H. Brown, written and edited by C. Stearns, Narrative of Henry Box Brown, Who Escaped from Slavery at 43-44 (Brown and Stearns, 1849), Academic Affairs Library, Univ. of North Carolina at Chapel Hill, available at *docsouth.unc.edu*

689 Weld, at 102, 104-05. Emphasis in original.

winter to go to a plantation of his in the country, as many of the negroes were sick. Says he—'I found them in a most miserable condition. The weather was cold, and the negroes were barefoot, with hardly enough of *cotton* clothing to cover their nakedness. Those who had huts to shelter them were obliged to build them nights and Sundays. Many were sick and some had died. I had the sick taken to an older plantation of their masters where they could be made comfortable and they recovered, I directed that they should not go to work till after sunrise, and should not work in the rain till their health became established. But the overseer refusing to permit it, I declined attending on them farther. I was called,' continued he, 'by the overseer of another plantation to see one of the men. I found him lying by the side of a log in great pain. I asked him how he did, 'O,' says he, 'I'm most dead, can live but little longer.' How long have you been sick 'I've felt for more than six weeks as though I could hardly stir.' Why didn't you tell your master, you was sick? 'I couldn't see my master, and the overseer always whips us when we complain, I could not stand a whipping,' I did all I could for the poor fellow, but *his lungs were rotten.* He died in three days from the time he left off work.' The cruelty of that overseer is such that the negroes almost tremble at his name. Yet he gets a high salary, for he makes the largest crop of any other man in the neighborhood, though none but the hardiest negroes can stand it under him. 'That man,' says the Doctor, 'would be hung in my country.' He was a German."

<u>A BLIND BABY</u>

"Walker bought a woman who had a blind child; it being considered worthless, it was given to the trader by the former owner of the woman on the score of humanity, he saying that he wished to keep mother and child together. At first Walker declined taking the child, saying that it would be too much trouble, but the mother wishing to have her boy with her, begged him to take it, promising to carry it the whole distance in her arms. Consequently he took the child, and the gang started on their route to the nearest steamboat landing, which was above one hundred miles. As might have been expected, the woman was unable to carry the boy and keep up with the rest of the gang. They put up at night at a small town, and the next morning, when about to start, Walker took the little boy from its mother and sold it to the innkeeper for the small sum of one dollar. The poor woman was so frantic at the idea of being separated from her only child, that it seemed impossible to get her to leave it. Not until the chains were put upon her limbs, and she fastened to the other slaves, could they get her to leave the spot. By main force this slave mother was compelled to go on and leave her child behind. Some days after, a lady from one of the free states was travelling the same road and put up at the same inn: she saw the child the morning after her arrival, and heard its history from one of the slaves, which was confirmed by the innkeeper's wife."

W. Brown, Clotel, or, The President's Daughter: A Narrative of Slave Life in the United States, with a Sketch of the Author's Life at 7-8 (London, Partridge & Oakey, 1853), Academic Affairs Library, Univ. of North Carolina at Chapel Hill, available at *docsouth.unc.edu*

§ § §

This testimony is communicated in a letter from Mr. Cyrus Pierce, a respectable and well known citizen of Nantucket, Mass. Of the witnesses, Messrs. T. D. M. and F. C. Macy, Mr. Pierce says, "They are both inhabitants of this island, and have resided at the south; they are both worthy men whose integrity and intelligence I can vouch unqualifiedly; the former has furnished me with the following statement. ...[690]

690 Weld, at 105-06.

"'Ocra,' said the overseer, one evening, to the driver, 'if any pretend to be sick, send me word—allow no lazy wench or fellow to skulk in the negro house.' Next morning, a few minutes after the departure of the hands to the field, Ocra was seen hastening to the house of the overseer. He was soon in his presence. 'Well, Ocra, what now?' Nothing, sir, only Rachel says she sick—can't go to de field to-day.' 'Ah, sick, is she? I'll see to her; you may be off. She shall see if I am longer to be fooled with in this way. Here, Christmas, mix these salts—bring them to me at the negro house.' And seizing his whip, he made off to the negro settlement. Having a strong desire to see what would be the result, I followed him. As I approached the negro house, I heard high words, Rachel was stating her complaint—children were crying from fright—and the overseer threatening. Rachel.—'I can't work to-day—I'm sick.' Overseer.—"But you shall work, if you die for it. Here, take these salts. Now move off—quick—let me see your face again before night, and, by G_d, you shall smart for it. Be off—no begging-not a word;' and he dragged her from the house, and followed her 20 or 30 rods, threatening. The woman did not reach the field. Overcome by the exertion of walking, and by agitation, she sunk down exhausted by the road side—was taken up, and carried back to the house, where an *abortion* occurred, and her life was greatly jeoparded."

§ § §

Rev. Dr. CHANNING of Boston, who once resided in Virginia, relates the following fact in his work on slavery, page 163, 1st edition.[691]

"I cannot forget my feelings on visiting a hospital belonging to the plantation of a gentleman *highly esteemed for his virtues,* and whose manners and conversation expressed much *benevolence and conscientiousness.* When I entered with him the hospital, the first object on which my eye fell was a young woman, very ill, probably approaching death. She was stretched on the floor. Her head rested on something like a pillow; but *her body and limbs were extended on the hard boards.* The owner, I doubt not, had at least as much kindness as myself; but he was so used to see the slaves living without common comforts, that the idea of unkindness in the present instance did not enter his mind." ...

FOOT-BALL

"Of the cruelty of one Hasbrouck. He had a sick slave-woman, who was lingering with a slow consumption, whom he made to spin, regardless of her weakness and suffering; and this woman had a child, that was unable to walk or talk, at the age of five years, neither could it cry like other children, but made a constant, piteous moaning sound. This exhibition of helplessness and imbecility, instead of exciting the master's pity, stung his cupidity, and so enraged him, that he would kick the poor thing about like a foot-ball.

"Isabella's [Sojourner's Truth's original name] informant had seen this brute of a man, when the child was curled up under a chair, innocently amusing itself with a few sticks, drag it hence, that he might have the pleasure of tormenting it. She had seen him, with one blow of his foot, send it rolling quite across the room, and down the steps at the door. Oh, how she wished it might instantly die! "But," she said, "it seemed as tough as a moccasin." Though it *did* die at last, and made glad the heart of its friends; and its persecutor, no doubt, rejoiced with them, but from very different motives. ..."

Dictated by S. Truth, written and edited by O. Gilbert, Sojourner Truth's Narrative and Book of Life at 83 (1875), available from the Library of Congress at *www.hathitrust.org/digital_library*

691 Weld, at 44-45. Emphasis in original.

THE EVIL OF READING AND WRITING

Judge Stroud quotes a Virginia law applicable to the education of "negros," not limited to slaves. The law required officers to "seize any negro" receiving an education, and imposed jail terms and substantial fines on whites instructing "negros:"[692]

> In Virginia, according to the Code of 1849, "Every assemblage of negroes for the purpose of instruction in reading or writing shall be an unlawful assembly. Any justice may issue his warrant to any officer or other person, requiring him to enter any place where such assemblage may be, and seize any negro therein; and he or any other justice may order such negro to be punished *with stripes.*
>
> "If a white person assemble with negroes for the purpose of instructing them to read or write, he shall be confined to jail not exceeding six months, and fined not exceeding one hundred dollars."

§ § §

The slave society forbade Frederick Douglass—as a slave—to learn to read and write. Yet, with luck, ingenuity, persistence, and sheer willpower, he not only managed to do so, but he also became one of America's greatest orators and authors, able to express himself in a brilliantly sophisticated manner. Douglass made the crucial discovery that education was the door through which he could cease to be a slave.

As with the vast majority of slaves, education was completely unavailable to Douglass. While still a young boy in Baltimore, he sought on his own initiative, upon hearing the Bible read, to obtain his initial lessons in the alphabet and rudimentary reading from a mistress to whose Baltimore family he had been transferred from plantations on the Maryland Eastern Shore. The master of the family, Hugh Auld, however, quickly and vehemently forbade his wife to provide such education on the grounds that it was both illegal and likely to motivate Douglass to seek freedom. Quoting Douglass as he describes his master's aggressive racist perspective, highly-offensive today, but quite typical of Douglass' time: "A nigger should know nothing but to obey his master—to do as he is told to do. … [I]f you teach that nigger (speaking of myself) how to read, there would be no keeping him. It would forever unfit him to be a slave."[693]

Frederic May Holland explains that "The owners of slaves dread nothing more than that any of their slaves should learn to read."[694]

Booker T. Washington states "it was too late. The precocious young slave had acquired a taste for book-learning."[695]

Hugh Auld's unwitting key message—that slaves must be kept in ignorance to remain subservient—stirred an ardent desire for freedom in the boy's heart. Douglass states:[696]

---

692 Stroud, at 60-61. Citations omitted. Emphasis in original.
See also *"Chapter Seven: Moving Forward?—Remnants of Slavery: Intolerable Discrimination in Education—The Slave Society Forbade Education."*

693 Douglass, Narrative at 33.

694 Holland at 177.

695 Washington at 25.

696 Douglass, Narrative at 33. See also Washington at 25.

> These words sank deep into my heart, stirred up sentiments within that lay slumbering, and called into existence an entirely new train of thought. It was a new and special revelation, explaining dark and mysterious things with which my youthful understanding had struggled, but struggled in vain. I now understood what had been to me a most perplexing difficulty—to wit, the white man's power to enslave the black man. It was a grand achievement, and I prized it highly. From that moment, I understood the pathway from slavery to freedom.

The "almost intolerable burden of the thought" that "I am a slave for life" provided substantial motivation to prepare himself to escape. "It was a terrible reality."[697]

In Baltimore, Mr. Douglass was so fortunate as to be able to use the more plentiful food to which he had access in that household to gain the benefit of forbidden reading lessons:[698]

> Seized with a determination to learn to read, at any cost, I hit upon many expedients to accomplish the desired end. The plea which I mainly adopted, and the one by which I was most successful, was that of using my young white playmates, with whom I met in the street, as teachers. I used to carry, almost constantly, a copy of Webster's spelling book in my pocket; and, when sent of errands, or when play time was allowed me, I would step, with my young friends, aside, and take a lesson in spelling. I generally paid my tuition fee to the boys, with bread, which I also carried in my pocket. For a single biscuit, any of my hungry little comrades would give me a lesson more valuable to me than bread. Not every one, however, demanded this consideration, for there were those who took pleasure in teaching me, whenever I had a chance to be taught by them.

<u>THE CRIME OF EDUCATION</u>

"INDICTMENT.

"COMMONWEALTH OF VIRGINIA, NORFOLK COUNTY, ss. In the Circuit Court. The Grand Jurors empannelled and sworn to inquire of offences committed in the body of the said County on their oath present, that Margaret Douglass being an evil disposed person, not having the fear of God before her eyes, but moved and instigated by the devil, wickedly, maliciously, and feloniously, on the fourth day of July, in the year of our Lord one thousand eight hundred and fifty-four, at Norfolk, in said County, did teach a certain black girl named Kate to read in the Bible, to the great displeasure of Almighty God, to the pernicious example of others in like case offending, contrary to the form of the statute in such case made and provided, and against the peace and dignity of the Commonwealth of Virginia."

W. Craft, Running a Thousand Miles for Freedom; or, the Escape of William and Ellen Craft from Slavery at 32-33 (London, William Tweedie, 1860), Academic Affairs Library, Univ. of North Carolina at Chapel Hill, available at *docsouth.unc.edu*

With the knowledge that he would need a written "pass" from his master in order to move about more freely, and perhaps to use in an escape, he also learned to write. He asked workmen at a shipyard about the identities of handwritten letters they used to identify ship parts. He then would use those letters to challenge his street friends, practicing the letters on "the board fence, brick wall, and pavement."[699]

697 Douglass, My Bondage and My Freedom at 156.

698 Douglass, My Bondage and My Freedom at 155.

699 Douglass, Narrative at 43-44; Washington at 27.

He also received advice from "a good colored man, named Charles Johnson," who befriended the young Douglass and taught him about religion and to pray.[700] Douglass read pages from the Bible discarded into "filthy street gutters."[701] He "began to copy from the Bible and the Methodist hymn-books at night when he was supposed to be asleep."[702]

After his escape, Douglass worked long hours at a foundry in New Bedford, Massachusetts, but found a way to educate himself in the process. At the foundry, he not only worked, but also pursued knowledge, nailing newspapers up on a post to read while he worked the bellows:[703]

> My next place of work was at the brass-foundry owned by Mr. Richmond. My duty here was to blow the bellows, swing the crane and empty the flasks in which castings were made; and at times this was hot and heavy work. The articles produced here were mostly for shipwork, and in the busy season the foundry was in operation night and day. I have often worked two nights and each working day of the week. My foreman, Mr. Cobb, was a good man, and more than once protected me from abuse that one or more of the hands were disposed to throw upon me. While in this situation I had little time for mental improvement. Hard work, night and day, over a furnace hot enough to keep the metal running like water, was more favorable to action than thought, yet here I often nailed a newspaper to the post near my bellows, and read while I was performing the up and down motion of the heavy beam by which the bellows was inflated and discharged. It was the pursuit of knowledge under difficulties, and I look back to it now after so many years with some complacency and a little wonder that I could have been so earnest and persevering in any pursuit other than for my daily bread.

Thus, Douglass escaped not only physical slavery, but slavery of the mind, to become a celebrated author and orator.

---

700 F. Douglass, MY BONDAGE AND MY FREEDOM at 166 (New York : Miller, Orton & Mulligan, 1855)), available from the Library of Congress at *www.hathitrust.org/digital_library* ("Douglass, My Bondage and My Freedom").

701 Douglass, My Bondage and My Freedom at 167.

702 Washington at 30.

703 Douglass, Life and Times at 262-63.

THE STORY OF HENRIETTA'S AND MARY'S DAILY LIVES

Frederick Douglass provides an exception to the less undesirable lives of urban slaves—*The Story of Henrietta's and Mary's Daily Lives.* The *Story* delivers insight into how, even despite social disapproval, slaveowners could continue in abusive treatment of their slaves because i*t was their legal right to do so:*[704]

> An instance of this sort is furnished in the case of a family who lived directly opposite to our house, and were named Hamilton. Mrs. Hamilton owned two slaves. Their names were Henrietta and Mary. They had always been house slaves. One was aged about twenty-two, and the other about fourteen. They were a fragile couple by nature, and the treatment they received was enough to break down the constitution of a horse. Of all the dejected, emaciated, mangled and excoriated creatures I ever saw, those two girls—in the refined, church going and Christian city of Baltimore—were the most deplorable. Of stone must that heart be made, that could look upon Henrietta and Mary, without being sickened to the core with sadness. Especially was Mary a heart-sickening object. Her head, neck and shoulders, were literally cut to pieces. I have frequently felt her head, and found it nearly covered over with festering sores, caused by the lash of her cruel mistress. I do not know that her master ever whipped her, but I have often been an eye witness of the revolting and brutal inflictions by Mrs. Hamilton; and what lends a deeper shade to this woman's conduct, is the fact, that, almost in the very moments of her shocking outrages of humanity and decency, she would charm you by the sweetness of her voice and her seeming piety. She used to sit in a large rocking chair, near the middle of the room, with a heavy cowskin, such as I have elsewhere described; and I speak within the truth when I say, that those girls seldom passed that chair, during the day, without a blow from that cowskin, either upon their bare arms, or upon their shoulders. As they passed her, she would draw her cowskin and give them a blow, saying, "*move faster, you black jip!*" and, again, "*take that, you black jip!*" continuing, "*if you don't move faster, I will give you more.*" Then the lady would go on, singing her sweet hymns, as though her *righteous* soul were sighing for the holy realms of paradise.
>
> Added to the cruel lashings to which these poor slave-girls were subjected—enough in themselves to crush the spirit of men—they were, really, kept nearly half starved; they seldom knew what it was to eat a full meal, except when they got it in the kitchens of neighbors, less mean and stingy than the psalm-singing Mrs. Hamilton. I have seen poor Mary contending for the offal, with the pigs in the street. So much was the poor girl pinched, kicked, cut and pecked to pieces, that the boys in the street knew her only by the name of "*pecked,*" a name derived from the scars and blotches on her neck, head and shoulders.

CRUEL AND BARBAROUS

"we Coloured People of these United States, are, the most wretched, degraded and abject set of beings that ever lived since the world began, down to the present day, and ... the white Christians of America, who hold us in slavery, (or, more properly speaking, pretenders to Christianity,) treat us more cruel and barbarous than any Heathen nation did any people whom it had subjected, or reduced to the same condition ... ."

D. Walker, Appeal to the Colored People of the World at 2 (1829), Academic Affairs Library, Univ. of North Carolina at Chapel Hill, available at available at *docsouth.unc.edu*

704 Douglass, My Bondage and My Freedom, at 148-50. Emphasis in original.

It is some relief to this picture of slavery in Baltimore, to say—what is but the simple truth—that Mrs. Hamilton's treatment of her slaves was generally condemned, as disgraceful and shocking; but while I say this, it must also be remembered, that the very parties who censured the cruelty of Mrs. Hamilton, would have condemned and promptly punished any attempt to interfere with Mrs. Hamilton's *right* to cut and slash her slaves to pieces. There must be no force between the slave and the slaveholder, to restrain the power of the one, and protect the weakness of the other; and the cruelty of Mrs. Hamilton is as justly chargeable to the upholders of the slave system, as drunkenness is chargeable on those who, by precept and example, or by indifference, uphold the drinking system.

THE STORY OF LUKE'S DAILY LIFE

Slave women were not the only victims of sexual exploitation by slaveholders. Harriet Jacobs describes the following treatment of a slave named "Luke," who was forced to endure constant beatings and to perform acts "of a nature too filthy to be repeated":[705]

> I was somewhat acquainted with a slave named Luke, who belonged to a wealthy man in our vicinity. His master died, leaving a son and daughter heirs to his large fortune. In the division of the slaves, Luke was included in the son's portion. This young man became a prey to the vices growing out of the "patriarchal institution," and when he went to the north, to complete his education, he carried his vices with him. He was brought home, deprived of the use of his limbs, by excessive dissipation. Luke was appointed to wait upon his bed-ridden master, whose despotic habits were greatly increased by exasperation at his own helplessness. He kept a cowhide beside him, and, for the most trivial occurrence, he would order his attendant to bare his back, and kneel beside the couch, while he whipped him till his strength was exhausted. Some days he was not allowed to wear anything but his shirt, in order to be in readiness to be flogged. A day seldom passed without his receiving more or less blows. If the slightest resistance was offered, the town constable was sent for to execute the punishment, and Luke learned from experience how much more the constable's strong arm was to be dreaded than the comparatively feeble one of his master. The arm of his tyrant grew weaker, and was finally palsied; and then the constable's services were in constant requisition. The fact that he was entirely dependent on Luke's care, and was obliged to be tended like an infant, instead of inspiring any gratitude or compassion towards his poor slave, seemed only to increase his irritability and cruelty. As he lay there on his bed, a mere degraded wreck of manhood, he took into his head the strangest freaks of despotism; and if Luke hesitated to submit to his orders, the constable was immediately sent for. Some of these freaks were of a nature too filthy to be repeated. When I fled from the house of bondage, I left poor Luke still chained to the bedside of this cruel and disgusting wretch.

705 Jacobs, at 288-89.

THE STORY OF HARRIET JACOBS' LIFE IN AN ATTIC

Harriet Jacobs found herself under constant pressure from her master, Dr. Flint, to submit to his sexual aggressions. To escape him, she took refuge for seven years, living in a tiny attic space. Ms. Jacobs' experiences demonstrate dramatically the inequality of slave women against the power of their exploitive masters.

Dr. Flint relentlessly pursued Ms. Jacobs, who was decades younger than he. He sought to entice her. He even offered to build a home for her. He threatened her. The following conversation illustrates the master's sheer power over the slave. The conversation occurred when Dr. Flint learned that Ms. Jacobs loved a black man:[706]

> "So you want to be married, do you?" said he, "and to a free nigger."
>
> "Yes, sir."
>
> "Well, I'll soon convince you whether I am your master, or the nigger fellow you honor so highly. If you *must* have a husband, you may take up with one of my slaves."
>
> What a situation I should be in, as the wife of one of *his* slaves, even if my heart had been interested! I replied, "Don't you suppose, sir, that a slave can have some preference about marrying? Do you suppose that all men are alike to her?"
>
> "Do you love this nigger?" said he, abruptly.
>
> "Yes, sir."
>
> "How dare you tell me so!" he exclaimed, in great wrath. After a slight pause, he added, "I supposed you thought more of yourself; that you felt above the insults of such puppies." I replied, "If he is a puppy I am a puppy, for we are both of the negro race. It is right and honorable for us to love each other. The man you call a puppy never insulted me, sir; and he would not love me if he did not believe me to be a virtuous woman."
>
> He sprang upon me like a tiger, and gave me a stunning blow. It was the first time he had ever struck me; and fear did not enable me to control my anger. When I had recovered a little from the effects, I exclaimed, "You have struck me for answering you honestly. How I despise you!"
>
> There was silence for some minutes. Perhaps he was deciding what should be my punishment; or, perhaps, he wanted to give me time to reflect on what I had said, and to whom I had said it. Finally, he asked, "Do you know what you have said?"
>
> "Yes, sir; but your treatment drove me to it."
>
> "Do you know that I have a right to do as I like with you,—that I can kill you, if I please?"
>
> "You have tried to kill me, and I wish you had; but you have no right to do as you like with me."
>
> "Silence!" he exclaimed, in a thundering voice. "By heavens, girl, you forget yourself too far! Are you mad? If you are, I will soon bring you to your senses. Do you think any other master would bear what I have borne from you this morning? Many masters would have killed you on the spot. How would you like to be sent to jail for your insolence?"

706 Jacobs, at 61-63. Emphasis in original.

> "I know I have been disrespectful, sir," I replied; "but you drove me to it; I couldn't help it. As for the jail, there would be more peace for me there than there is here."
>
> "You deserve to go there," said he, "and to be under such treatment, that you would forget the meaning of the word *peace*. It would do you good. It would take some of your high notions out of you. But I am not ready to send you there yet, notwithstanding your ingratitude for all my kindness and forbearance. You have been the plague of my life. I have wanted to make you happy, and I have been repaid with the basest ingratitude; but though you have proved yourself incapable of appreciating my kindness, I will be lenient towards you. I will give you one more chance to redeem your character. If you behave yourself and do as I require, I will forgive you and treat you as I always have done; but if you disobey me, I will punish you as I would the meanest slave on my plantation. Never let me hear that fellow's name mentioned again. If I ever know of your speaking to him, I will cowhide you both, and if I catch him lurking about my premises, I will shoot him as soon as I would a dog. Do you hear what I say? I'll teach you a lesson about marriage and free niggers! Now go, and let this be the last time I have occasion to speak to you on this subject."
>
> Reader, did you ever hate? I hope not. I never did but once; and I trust I never shall again. Some body has called it "the atmosphere of hell;" and I believe it is so.

Due to her circumstances, Ms. Jacobs went to extraordinary lengths to remove herself from Dr. Flint's grasp, first hiding in a snake-filled swamp and then in the attic. The attic was in her grandmother's house. In the attic, she remained close to her children, but for security, they did not know of her presence. A citizen in the town had purchased Ms. Jacob's grandmother when Dr. Flint had attempted to sell her. None of the townspeople, who loved her and her baking, would bid another price. The winning bidder promptly had granted Ms. Jacob's grandmother her freedom.

In order to disguise her hiding place in the neighborhood, Ms. Jacob's family arranged for messengers to mail letters under her name from Northern cities to her grandmother, knowing that Dr. Flint would read them.[707] Once he did, he traveled North more than once in search of her.[708]

Ms. Jacobs relates the story of her life in a three-foot high sloped attic space—"only nine feet long and seven wide"—for almost seven years to avoid Dr. Flint:[709]

> A small shed had been added to my grandmother's house years ago. Some boards were laid across the joists at the top,

HARRIET JACOBS ON
<u>SEXUAL EXPLOITATION OF SLAVE WOMEN</u>

"I turned from him with disgust and hatred. But he was my master. I was compelled to live under the same roof with him—where I saw a man forty years my senior daily violating the most sacred commandments of nature. He told me I was his property; that I must be subject to his will in all things. My soul revolted against the mean tyranny. But where could I turn for protection? No matter whether the slave girl be as black as ebony or as fair as her mistress. In either case, there is no shadow of law to protect her from insult, from violence, or even from death; all these are inflicted by fiends who bear the shape of men. The mistress, who ought to protect the helpless victim, has no other feelings towards her but those of jealousy and rage."

H. Jacobs, Incidents in the Life of a Slave Girl at 44-45 (1861), available from the Library of Congress at *www.hathitrust.org/digital_library.*

707 Jacobs, at 193-98.

708 See. e.g., Jacobs, at 159, 160, 176, 189.

709 Jacobs, at 173-78. Emphasis in original

and between these boards and the roof was a very small garret, never occupied by any thing but rats and mice. It was a pent roof, covered with nothing but shingles, according to the southern custom for such buildings. The garret was only nine feet long and seven wide. The highest part was three feet high, and sloped down abruptly to the loose board floor. There was no admission for either light or air. My uncle Philip, who was a carpenter, had very skilfully made a concealed trap-door, which communicated with the storeroom. He had been doing this while I was waiting in the swamp. The storeroom opened upon a piazza. To this hole I was conveyed as soon as I entered the house. The air was stifling; the darkness total. A bed had been spread on the floor. I could sleep quite comfortably on one side; but the slope was so sudden that I could not turn on the other without hitting the roof. The rats and mice ran over my bed; but I was weary, and I slept such sleep as the wretched may, when a tempest has passed over them. Morning came. I knew it only by the noises I heard; for in my small den day and night were all the same. I suffered for air even more than for light. But I was not comfortless. I heard the voices of my children. There was joy and there was sadness in the sound. It made my tears flow. How I longed to speak to them! I was eager to look on their faces; but there was no hole, no crack, through which I could peep. This continued darkness was oppressive. It seemed horrible to sit or lie in a cramped position day after day, without one gleam of light. Yet I would have chosen this, rather than my lot as a slave, though white people considered it an easy one; and it was so compared with the fate of others. I was never cruelly over-worked; I was never lacerated with the whip from head to foot; I was never so beaten and bruised that I could not turn from one side to the other; I never had my heel-strings cut to prevent my running away; I was never chained to a log and forced to drag it about, while I toiled in the fields from morning till night; I was never branded with hot iron, or torn by bloodhounds. On the contrary, I had always been kindly treated, and tenderly cared for, until I came into the hands of Dr. Flint. I had never wished for freedom till then. But though my life in slavery was comparatively devoid of hardships, God pity the woman who is compelled to lead such a life!

My food was passed up to me through the trap-door my uncle had contrived; and my grandmother, my uncle Phillip, and aunt Nancy would seize such opportunities as they could, to mount up there and chat with me at the opening. But of course this was not safe in the daytime. It must all be done in darkness. It was impossible for me to move in an erect position, but I crawled about my den for exercise. One day I hit my head against something, and found it was a gimlet. My uncle had left it sticking there when he made the trap-door. I was as rejoiced as Robinson Crusoe could have been at finding such a treasure. It put a lucky thought into my head. I said to myself, "Now I will have some light. Now I will see my children." I did not dare to begin my work during the daytime, for fear of attracting attention. But I groped round; and having found the side next the street, where I could frequently see my children, I stuck the gimlet in and waited for evening. I bored three rows of holes, one above another; then I bored out the interstices between. I thus succeeded in making one hole about an inch long and an inch broad. I sat by it till late into the night, to enjoy the little whiff of air that floated in. In the morning I watched for my children. The first person I saw in the street was Dr. Flint. I had a shuddering, superstitious feeling that it was a bad omen. Several familiar faces passed by. At last I heard the merry laugh of children, and presently two sweet little faces were looking up at me, as though they knew I was there, and were conscious of the joy they imparted. How I longed to *tell* them I was there!

My condition was now a little improved. But for weeks I was tormented by hundreds of little red insects, fine as a needle's point, that pierced through my skin, and produced an intolerable burning. The good grandmother gave me herb teas and cooling medicines, and finally I got rid of them. The heat of my den was intense, for nothing but thin shingles protected me from the scorching summer's sun. But I had my consolations. Through my peeping-hole I could watch the children, and when they were near enough, I could hear their talk. …

Autumn came, with a pleasant abatement of heat. My eyes had become accustomed to the dim light, and by holding my book or work in a certain position near the aperture I contrived to read and sew. That was a great relief to the tedious monotony of my life. But when winter came, the cold penetrated through the thin shingle roof, and I was dreadfully chilled. The winters there are not so long, or so severe, as in northern latitudes; but the houses are not built to shelter from cold, and my little den was peculiarly comfortless. The kind grandmother brought me bed-clothes and warm drinks. Often I was obliged to lie in bed all day to keep comfortable; but with all my precautions, my shoulders and feet were frostbitten. O, those long, gloomy days, with no object for my eye to rest upon, and no thoughts to occupy my mind, except the dreary past and the uncertain future! I was thankful when there came a day sufficiently mild for me to wrap myself up and sit at the loophole to watch the passers by. Southerners have the habit of stopping and talking in the streets, and I heard many conversations not intended to meet my ears. I heard slave-hunters planning how to catch some poor fugitive. Several times I heard allusions to Dr. Flint, myself, and the history of my children, who, perhaps, were playing near the gate. One would say, "I wouldn't move my little finger to catch her, as old Flint's property." Another would say, "I'll catch any nigger for the reward. A man ought to have what belongs to him, if he is a damned brute." The opinion was often expressed that I was in the Free States. Very rarely did any one suggest that I might be in the vicinity. Had the least suspicion rested on my grandmother's house, it would have been burned to the ground. But it was the last place they thought of. Yet there was no place, where slavery existed, that could have afforded me so good a place of concealment.

Dr. Flint and his family repeatedly tried to coax and bribe my children to tell something they had heard said about me. One day the doctor took them into a shop, and offered them some bright little silver pieces and gay handkerchiefs if they would tell where their mother was. Ellen shrank away from him, and would not speak; but Benny spoke up, and said, "Dr. Flint, I don't know where my mother is. I guess she's in New York; and when you go there again, I wish you'd ask her to come home, for I want to see her; but if you put her in jail, or tell her you'll cut her head off, I'll tell her to go right back."

During Ms. Jacob's long self-imprisonment, she witnessed family events, such as Christmas celebrations:[710]

CHRISTMAS was approaching. Grandmother brought me materials, and I busied myself making some new garments and little playthings for my children. Were it not that hiring day is near at hand [traditionally in the slave society at the New Year, when individual

A SLAVEHOLDER ON RAPE

"The law, by recognizing the existence of the slave as a person, thereby confers no rights or privileges except such as are necessary to protect that existence. All other rights_ must be granted specially. Hence, the penalties for rape would not and should not, by such implication, be made to extend to carnal forcible knowledge of a slave, the offense not affecting the existence of the slave, and that existence being the extent of the right which the implication of the law grants. ... [I]t is clearly against the policy of the law to extend over this class of the community, that character of protection which many of the penal statutes are intended to provide for the citizen. ...

"The occurrence of such an offense is almost unheard of; and *the known lasciviousness of the negro, renders the possibility of its occurrence very remote.* Yet, for the honor of the statute-book, if it does occur, there should be adequate punishment."

Slavery advocate, T. Cobb, An inquiry into the law of Negro slavery in the United States of America, Vol I, at 86, 100 (T. & J. W. Johnson & Co., 1858), available from the Library of Congress at *www.hathitrust.org/digital_library*. Emphasis added.

710 Jacobs, at 179.

> slaves would be hired out to others for the next year], and many families are fearfully looking forward to the probability of separation in a few days, Christmas might be a happy season for the poor slaves. Even slave mothers try to gladden the hearts of their little ones on that occasion. Benny and Ellen [Ms. Jacob's children] had their Christmas stockings filled. Their imprisoned mother could not have the privilege of witnessing their surprise and joy. But I had the pleasure of peeping at them as they went into the street with their new suits on. I heard Benny ask a little playmate whether Santa Claus brought him any thing. "Yes," replied the boy; "but Santa Claus ain't a real man. It's the children's mothers that put things into the stockings." "No, that can't be," replied Benny," for Santa Claus brought Ellen and me these new clothes, and my mother has been gone this long time."
>
> How I longed to tell him that his mother made those garments, and that many a tear fell on them while she worked !

For a seven-year period, Ms. Jacobs continued to hide in the attic:[711]

> I don't know what kept life within me. Again and again, I thought I should die before long; but I saw the leaves of another autumn whirl through the air, and felt the touch of another winter. In summer the most terrible thunder storms were acceptable, for the rain came through the roof, and I rolled up my bed that it might cool the hot boards under it. Later in the season, storms sometimes wet my clothes through and through, and that was not comfortable when the air grew chilly. Moderate storms I could keep out by filling the chinks with oakum.

From her vantage point, she observed the degradations of other slaves' lives:[712]

But uncomfortable as my situation was, I had glimpses of things out of doors, which made me thankful for my wretched hiding-place. One day I saw a slave pass our gate, muttering," It's his own, and he can kill it if he will." My grandmother told me that woman's history. Her mistress had that day seen her baby for the first time, and in the lineaments of its fair face she saw a likeness to her husband. She turned the bondwoman and her child out of doors, and for bade her ever to return. The slave went to her master, and told him what had happened. He promised to talk with her mistress, and make it all right. The next day she and her baby were sold to a Georgia trader.

Another time I saw a woman rush wildly by, pursued by two men. She was a slave, the wet nurse of her mistress's children. For some trifling offence her mistress ordered her to be stripped and whipped. To escape the degradation and the torture, she rushed to the river, jumped in, and ended her wrongs in death.

This continued season after season, year after year. Eventually, after years of living voluntarily in such extreme circumstances to avoid Dr. Flint, through family arrangements Ms. Jacobs was able to escape to the North on a ship with a sympathetic captain.[713]

In the North—New York and Boston—Ms. Jacobs continuously experienced fear of recapture under the Fugitive Slave Law through continued active pursuits by Dr. Flint and his heirs.[714] Eventually, a friend purchased Ms. Jacobs' freedom.[715]

---

711 Jacobs, at 183-84.

712 Jacobs, at 183-84.

713 Jacobs, at 231-40.

714 See, *e.g.*, Jacobs, at 258-63, 271-73, 274, 285-92.

715 Jacobs, at 301-03.

THE STORY OF ELIZA: CHILDREN TORN FROM A MOTHER'S ARMS

"Remote as is the City of Philadelphia from those slave-holding states in which the introduction of slaves from places within the territory of the United States is freely permitted, and *where also the market is tempting,* it has been ascertained that *more than thirty* free coloured persons, mostly children, have been kidnapped here and carried away within the last two years. Five of these, through the kind interposition of several humane gentlemen, have been restored to their friends, though not without great expense and difficulty; the others are still retained in bondage, and if rescued at all it must be by sending *white* witnesses a journey of more than a thousand miles. The costs attendant upon law-suits under such circumstances, will probably fall but little short of the estimated value, as slaves, of the individuals kidnapped. That very many free negroes have been kidnapped in non-slave-holding states admits of but little doubt. Within the last few years *two* notorious cases—those of *Rachel and Elizabeth Parker,* sisters, born and brought up to full womanhood in Chester county, Pennsylvania—may be mentioned. With what difficulty and expense were they at length rescued and restored to freedom!

"The interesting book, *Twelve Years a Slave, &c. of Solomon Northup*, who was kidnapped at Washington City, furnishes another most memorable example."[716]

§ § §

Although a "free" man from New York, unknown parties drugged and kidnapped Solomon Northup on a visit to Washington, DC. Slave traders housed him in a slave pen in what is now Alexandria, Virginia. He says his ultimate captor was named "Burch," which fits with a notorious Alexandria slave trader. "Burch" then shipped Mr. Northup to the New Orleans slave auction, where he sold Mr. Northup.

Kidnapping. Page 120.

"Kidnapping", *Slavery Images: A Visual Record of the African Slave Trade and Slave Life in the Early African Diaspora,* accessed November 14, 2020, *http://slaveryimages.org/s/slaveryimages/item/2479*

After re-gaining his freedom, Mr. Northup described in his narrative what I call the *Story of Eliza*. It is a story of the special horrors of slavery for women and men with spouses and children. It illustrates the terrible consequences of the destruction of slave families. This was a common occurrence with the forced migration of slaves from the Upper South to New Orleans and elsewhere for purchase by cotton planters.

716 Stroud, at 50, footnote. Emphasis in original.

The *Story of Eliza* portrays the strong family bonds between slave parents and their children, and the intense efforts slave parents often made to preserve as much of family structures as possible under exceedingly adverse conditions. The *Story of Eliza* further demonstrates the over-whelming grief slave parents experienced when slave masters and slave traders forcibly took the slaves' children from them.

This was "something that happened 150 years ago."

Mr. Northup provides the following descriptions of Eliza's loss of her children and consequent personal devastation. I have excerpted, and assembled sequentially as the *Story of Eliza,* Mr. Northup's descriptions of the scenes he witnessed as years passed, of the destruction of Eliza's family and the unspeakable personal outcome for Eliza. Mr. Northup, like Eliza herself, did not have knowledge of what became of Eliza's children after the destruction of her family.[717]

Mr. Northup describes his first meeting with Eliza and her family, consisting of her son, Randall and her daughter Emily, during which he learned about the sudden unexpected and disturbing turn of events leading them to be in the slave pen with him:

> In the course of several days the outer door [of the slave pen in Washington, DC, where Mr. Northup had been held after his kidnapping] was thrown open, allowing me the liberty of the yard. There I found three slaves—one of them a lad of ten years, the others young men of about twenty and twenty-five. I was not long in forming an acquaintance, and learning their names and the particulars of their history.
>
> § § §
>
> The lad was a sprightly child, that answered to the name of Randall. Most of the time he was playing about the yard, but occasionally would cry, calling for his mother, and wondering when she would come. His mother's absence seemed to be the great and only grief in his little heart. He was too young to realize his condition, and when the memory of his mother was not in his mind, he amused us with his pleasant pranks.
>
> § § §
>
> I remained in Williams' slave pen about two weeks. The night previous to my departure a woman was brought in, weeping bitterly, and leading by the hand a little child. They were Randall's mother and half-sister. On meeting them he was overjoyed, clinging to her dress, kissing the child, and exhibiting every demonstration of delight. The mother also clasped him in her arms, embraced him tenderly, and gazed at him fondly through her tears, calling him by many an endearing name.

Eliza was deeply in love with her children and made earnest efforts to comfort them:

> Emily, the child, was seven or eight years old, of light complexion, and with a face of admirable beauty. Her hair fell in curls around her neck, while the style and richness of her dress, and the neatness of her whole appearance indicated she had been brought up in the midst of wealth. She was a sweet child indeed. The woman also was arrayed in silk, with rings upon her fingers, and golden ornaments suspended from her ears. Her air and manners, the correctness and propriety of her language—all showed, evidently, that she had sometime stood above the common level of a slave. She seemed to be amazed at finding herself in such a place as that. It was plainly a sudden and unexpected turn of fortune that had brought her there. Filling the air with her complainings, she was hustled, with the children and myself, into the cell. Language can convey but an inadequate impression of the lamentations to

717 Northup, at 48, 49, 50-53, 54-57, 58, 59-60, 63, 75-76, 78, 80-83, 83-84, 84-88, 89, 92, 96, 106-07, 122, 151, 159-60.

which she gave incessant utterance. Throwing herself upon the floor, and encircling the children in her arms, she poured forth such touching words as only maternal love and kindness can suggest. They nestled closely to her, as if *there* only was there any safety or protection. At last they slept, their heads resting upon her lap. While they slumbered, she smoothed the hair back from their little foreheads, and talked to them all night long. She called them her darlings—her sweet babes—poor innocent things, that knew not the misery they were destined to endure. Soon they would have no mother to comfort them—they would be taken from her. What would become of them? Oh! she could not live away from her little Emmy and her dear boy. They had always been good children, and had such loving ways. It would break her heart, God knew, she said, if they were taken from her; and yet she knew they meant to sell them, and, may be, they would be separated, and could never see each other anymore. It was enough to melt a heart of stone to listen to the pitiful expressions of that desolate and distracted mother. Her name was Eliza; and this was the story of her life, as she afterwards related it.

Eliza had been sold surreptitiously from a happy life through trickery:

She was the slave of Elisha Berry, a rich man, living in the neighborhood of Washington. She was born, I think she said, on his plantation. Years before, he had fallen into dissipated habits, and quarreled with his wife. In fact, soon after the birth of Randall, they separated. Leaving his wife and daughter in the house they had always occupied, he erected a new one nearby, on the estate. Into this house he brought Eliza; and, on condition of her living with him, she and her children were to be emancipated. She resided with him there nine years, with servants to attend upon her, and provided with every comfort and luxury of life. Emily was his child! Finally, her young mistress, who had always remained with her mother at the homestead, married a Mr. Jacob Brooks. At length, for some cause, (as I gathered from her relation,) beyond Berry's control a division of his property was made. She and her children fell to the share of Mr. Brooks. During the nine years she had lived with Berry, in consequence of the position she was compelled to occupy, she and Emily had become the object of Mrs. Berry and her daughter's hatred and dislike. Berry himself she represented as a man of naturally a kind heart, who always promised her that she should have her freedom, and who, she had no doubt, would grant it to her then, if it were only in his power. As soon as they thus came into the possession and control of the daughter, it became very manifest they would not live long together. The sight of Eliza seemed to be odious to Mrs. Brooks; neither could she bear to look upon the child, half-sister, and beautiful as she was!

"Holding Pen or Cells for Slaves Awaiting Sale, Alexandria, Virginia, 1863", *Slavery Images: A Visual Record of the African Slave Trade and Slave Life in the Early African Diaspora,* accessed November 14, 2020, *http://slaveryimages.org/s/slaveryimages/item/1967*

The day she was led into the pen, Brooks had brought her from the estate into the city, under pretence that the time had come when her free papers were to be executed, in fulfillment of her master's promise. Elated at the prospect of immediate liberty, she decked herself and little Emmy in their best apparel, and accompanied him with a joyful heart. On their arrival in the city, instead of being baptized into the family of freemen, she was delivered to the trader Burch. The paper that was executed was a bill of sale. The hope of years was blasted in a moment. From the height of most exulting happiness to the utmost depths of wretchedness, she had that day descended. No wonder that she wept, and filled the pen with wailings and expressions of heart-rending woe.

Understandably, Eliza was deeply upset about her new fate:

> At intervals during the first night of Eliza's incarceration in the pen, she complained bitterly of Jacob Brooks, her young mistress' husband. She declared that had she been aware of the deception he intended to practice upon her, he never would have brought her there alive. They had chosen the opportunity of getting her away when Master Berry was absent from the plantation. He had always been kind to her. She wished that she could see him; but she knew that even he was unable now to rescue her. Then would she commence weeping again—kissing the sleeping children—talking first to one, then to the other, as they lay in their unconscious slumbers, with their heads upon her lap. So wore the long night away; and when the morning dawned, and night had come again, still she kept mourning on, and would not be consoled.

Suddenly, during the night the slave traders chained and marched them in a slave coffle to a steamship during the night in full view of the national capitol:

> About midnight following, the cell door opened, and Burch and Radburn [Burch's assistant] entered, with lanterns in their hands. Burch, with an oath, ordered us to roll up our blankets without delay, and get ready to go on board the boat. He swore we would be left unless we hurried fast. He aroused the children from their slumbers with a rough shake, and said they were d—d sleepy, it appeared. Going out into the yard, he called Clem Ray [another slave in the pen], ordering him to leave the loft and come into the cell, and bring his blanket with him. When Clem appeared, he placed us side by side, and fastened us together with hand-cuffs—my left hand to his right. John Williams [another slave] had been taken out a day or two before, his master having redeemed him, greatly to his delight. Clem and I were ordered to march, Eliza and the children following. We were conducted into the yard, from thence into the covered passage, and up a flight of steps through a side door into the upper room, where I had heard the walking to and fro. Its furniture was a stove, a few old chairs, and a long table, covered with papers. It was a white-washed room, without any carpet on the floor, and seemed a sort of office. By one of the windows, I remember, hung a rusty sword, which attracted my attention. Burch's trunk was there. In obedience to his orders, I took hold of one of its handles with my unfettered hand, while he taking hold of the other, we proceeded out of the front door into the street in the same order as we had left the cell.

"Untitled Image (Slave Dealer, Virginia)", Slavery Images: A Visual Record of the African Slave Trade and Slave Life in the Early African Diaspora, accessed November 14, 2020, *http://slaveryimages.org/s/slaveryimages/item/2998*

> It was a dark night. All was quiet. I could see lights, or the reflection of them, over towards Pennsylvania Avenue, but there was no one, not even a straggler, to be seen. I was almost resolved to attempt to break away. Had I not been hand-cuffed the attempt would certainly have been made, whatever consequence might have followed. Radburn was in the rear, carrying a large stick, and hurrying up the children as fast as the little ones could walk. So we passed, hand-cuffed and in silence, through the streets of Washington—through

> the Capital of a nation, whose theory of government, we are told, rests on the foundation of man's inalienable right to life, LIBERTY, and the pursuit of happiness! Hail! Columbia, happy land, indeed!
>
> Reaching the steamboat, we were quickly hustled into the hold, among barrels and boxes of freight. A colored servant brought a light, the bell rung, and soon the vessel started down the Potomac, carrying us we knew not where. The bell tolled as we passed the tomb of Washington! Burch, no doubt, with uncovered head, bowed reverently before the sacred ashes of the man who devoted his illustrious life to the liberty of his country.

On board the steamship, Eliza was polite:

> None of us slept that night but Randall and little Emmy. For the first time Clem Ray was wholly overcome. To him the idea of going south was terrible in the extreme. He was leaving the friends and associations of his youth—every thing that was dear and precious to his heart—in all probability never to return. He and Eliza mingled their tears together, bemoaning their cruel fate. For my own part, difficult as it was, I endeavored to keep up my spirits. I resolved in my mind a hundred plans of escape, and fully determined to make the attempt the first desperate chance that offered. I had by this time become satisfied, however, that my true policy was to say nothing further on the subject of my having been born a freeman. It would but expose me to mal-treatment, and diminish the chances of liberation.
>
> After sunrise in the morning we were called up on deck to breakfast. Burch took our hand-cuffs off, and we sat down to table. He asked Eliza if she would take a dram. She declined, thanking him politely. …

The traders transferred the group at various times and kept them in a slave pen in Richmond, where they learned more about each other:

> At Fredericksburg we were transferred from the stage coach to a car, and before dark arrived in Richmond, the chief city of Virginia. At this city we were taken from the cars, and driven through the street to a slave pen, between the railroad depot and the river, kept by a Mr. Goodin. This pen is similar to Williams' in Washington, except it is somewhat larger; and besides, there were two small houses standing at opposite comers within the yard. These houses are usually found within slave yards, being used as rooms for the examination of human chattels by purchasers before concluding a bargain. Unsoundness in a slave, as well as in a horse, detracts materially from his value. If no warranty is given, a close examination is a matter of particular importance to the negro jockey.

HARRIET TUBMAN LOSES TWO SISTERS

"[Harriet Tubman] had … seen two older sisters taken away as part of a chain gang, and they had gone no one knew whither; she had seen the agonized expression on their faces as they turned to take a last look at their 'Old Cabin Home'; and had watched them from the top of the fence, as they went off weeping and lamenting, till they were hidden from her sight forever."

K. Larson, Bound for the Promised Land—Harriet Tubman, Portrait of an American Hero at 32 (Ballantine Books, 2003)

§ § §

> Goodin … turned to Clem, and then to Eliza and the children, examining them severally, and asking various questions. He was pleased with Emily, as was every one who saw the child's sweet countenance. She was not as tidy as when I first beheld her; her hair was now somewhat disheveled; but through its unkempt and soft profusion there still beamed a little face of most surpassing loveliness. …

§ § §

While we were … learning the history of each other's wretchedness, Eliza was seated in a corner by herself, singing hymns and praying for her children. …

The ultimate goal was the New Orleans slave auction:

[The slave traders transported the slaves on a slave ship to New Orleans.] Very soon traders and consignees came on board [the slave ship at the wharf]. One, a tall, thin-faced man, with light complexion and a little bent, made his appearance, with a paper in his hand. Burch's gang, consisting of myself, Eliza and her children, Harry, Lethe, and some others, who had joined us at Richmond, were consigned to him. This gentleman was Mr. Theophilus Freeman. … Lethe was called, then Eliza, then Harry, until the list was finished, each one stepping forward as his or her name was called.

§ § §

The very amiable, pious-hearted Mr. Theophilus Freeman, partner or consignee of James H. Burch, and keeper of the slave pen in New Orleans, was out among his animals early in the morning. With an occasional kick of the older men and women, and many a sharp crack of the whip about the ears of the younger slaves, it was not long before they were all astir, and wide awake. Mr. Theophilus Freeman bustled about in a very industrious manner, getting his property ready for the sales-room, intending, no doubt, to do that day a rousing business. …

At the slave auction, the trader sold Randall, Eliza's son, despite her desperate pleadings that he not be sold away from her:

Lethe was sold to a planter of Baton Rouge, her eyes flashing with anger as she was led away.

The same man also purchased Randall. The little fellow was made to jump, and run across the floor, and perform many other feats, exhibiting his activity and condition. All the time the trade was going on, Eliza was crying aloud, and wringing her hands. She besought the man not to buy him, unless he also bought herself and Emily. She promised, in that case, to be the most faithful slave that ever lived. The man answered that he could not afford it, and then Eliza burst into a paroxysm of grief, weeping plaintively. Freeman turned round to her, savagely, with his whip in his uplifted hand, ordering her to stop her noise, or he would flog her. He would not have such work—such sniveling; and unless she ceased that minute, he would take her to the yard and give her a hundred lashes. Yes, he would take the nonsense out of her pretty quick—if he didn't, might he be d—d. Eliza shrunk before him, and tried to wipe away her tears, but it was all in vain. She wanted to be with her children, she said, the little time she had to live. All the frowns and threats of Freeman, could not wholly silence the afflicted mother. She kept on begging and beseeching them, most piteously, not to separate the three. Over and over again she told them how she loved her boy. A great many times she repeated her former promises—how very faithful and obedient she would be; how hard she would labor day and night, to the last moment of her life, if he would only buy them all together. But it was of no avail; the man could not afford it. The bargain was agreed upon, and Randall must go alone. Then Eliza ran to him; embraced him passionately; kissed him again and again; told him to remember her—all the while her tears falling in the boy's face like rain.

The slave trader threatened Eliza viciously for her pleadings on behalf of Randall:

Freeman damned her, calling her a blubbering, bawling wench, and ordered her to go to her place, and behave herself, and be somebody. He swore he wouldn't stand such stuff but a little longer. He would soon give her something to cry about, if she was not mighty careful, and *that* she might depend upon.

The planter from Baton Rouge, with his new purchases, was ready to depart.

"Don't cry, mama. I will be a good boy. Don't cry," said Randall, looking back, as they passed out of the door.

What has become of the lad, God knows. It was a mournful scene indeed. I would have cried myself if I had dared.

Next, an illness, likely smallpox delayed further events at the auction:

That night, nearly all who came in the brig Orleans, were taken ill. They complained of violent pain in the head and back. Little Emily—a thing unusual with her—cried constantly. In the morning a physician was called in, but was unable to determine the nature of our complaint. While examining me, and asking questions touching my symptoms, I gave it as my opinion that it was an attack of small-pox—mentioning the fact of Robert's death [on board the slave ship] as the reason of my belief. It might be so indeed, he thought, and he would send for the head physician of the hospital. Shortly, the head physician came—a small, light-haired man, whom they called Dr. Carr. He pronounced it small-pox, whereupon there was much alarm throughout the yard. Soon after Dr. Carr left, Eliza, Emmy, Harry and myself were put into a hack and driven to the hospital—a large white marble building, standing on the outskirts of the city. Harry and I were placed in a room in one of the upper stories. I became very sick. …

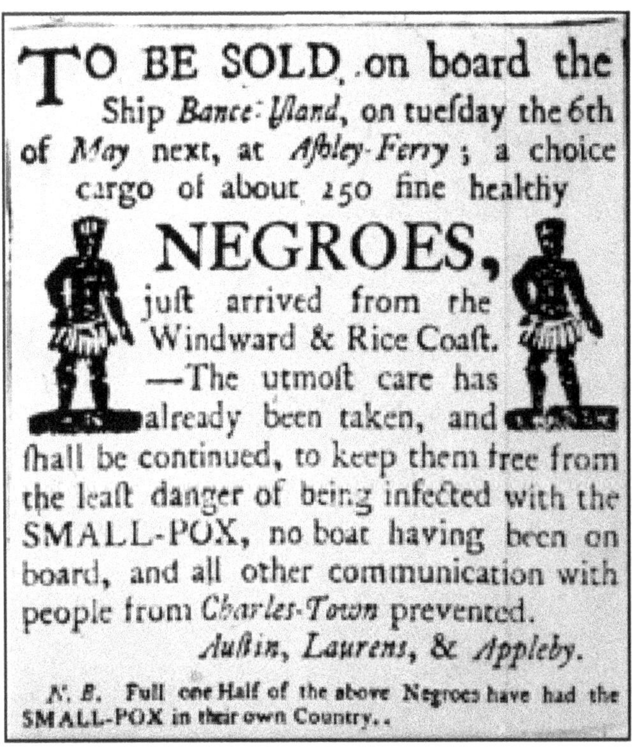
TO BE SOLD, on board the Ship *Bance-Island*, on tuesday the 6th of *May* next, at *Ashley-Ferry*; a choice cargo of about 250 fine healthy

NEGROES,

just arrived from the Windward & Rice Coast. —The utmost care has already been taken, and shall be continued, to keep them free from the least danger of being infected with the SMALL-POX, no boat having been on board, and all other communication with people from *Charles-Town* prevented.

Austin, Laurens, & Appleby.

N. B. Full one Half of the above Negroes have had the SMALL-POX in their own Country.

"To be sold on board the ship Bance-Island … a choice cargo of about 250 fine healthy Negroes. ", *Slavery Images: A Visual Record of the African Slave Trade and Slave Life in the Early African Diaspora*, accessed November 14, 2020, *http://slaveryimages.org/s/slaveryimages/item/1913*

§ § §

The crisis having passed, I began to revive, and at the end of two weeks and two days, returned with Harry to the pen, bearing upon my face the effects of the malady, which to this day continues to disfigure it. Eliza and Emily were also brought back next day in a hack, and again were we paraded in the sales-room, for the inspection and examination of purchasers. …

After the bout with smallpox, the auctioneer sold Eliza along with Mr. Northup, but refused to sell Emily:

At length, one day, while we were in the yard, Freeman came out and ordered us to our places, in the great room. A gentleman was waiting for us as we entered … .

He was a man above the ordinary height, somewhat bent and stooping forward. He was a good looking man, and appeared to have reached about the middle age of life. There was nothing repulsive in his presence; but on the other hand, there was something cheerful and attractive in his face, and in his tone of voice. The finer elements were all kindly mingled in his breast, as anyone could see. He moved about among us, asking many questions, as to what we could do, and what labor we had been accustomed to; if we thought we would like to live with him, and would be good boys if he would buy us, and other interrogatories of like character.

> After some further inspection, and conversation touching prices, he finally offered Freeman one thousand dollars for me, nine hundred for Harty, and seven hundred for Eliza. Whether the small pox had depreciated our value, or from what cause Freemen had concluded to fall five hundred dollars from the price I was before held at, I cannot say. At any rate, after a little shrewd reflection, he announced his acceptance of the offer.

Eliza's sale without Emily resulted in inconsolable grief, leading the slave trader to strike her violently. The purchaser then offered to purchase Emily, as well:

> As soon as Eliza heard it, she was in an agony again. By this time she had become haggard and hollow-eyed with sickness and with sorrow. It would be a relief if I could consistently pass over in silence the scene that now ensued. It recalls memories more mournful and affecting than any language can portray. I have seen mothers kissing for the last time the faces of their dead offspring; I have seen them looking down into the grave, as the earth fell with a dull sound upon their coffins, hiding them from their eyes forever; but never have I seen such an exhibition of intense, unmeasured, and unbounded grief, as when Eliza was parted from her child. She broke from her place in the line of women, and rushing down where Emily was standing, caught her in her arms. The child, sensible of some impending danger, instinctively fastened her hands around her mother's neck, and nestled her little head upon her bosom. Freeman sternly ordered her to be quiet. but she did not heed him. He caught her by the arm and pulled her rudely, but she only clung the closer to the child. Then, with a volley of great oaths, he struck her such a heartless blow, that she staggered backward, and was like to fall. Oh! how piteously then did she beseech and beg and pray that they might not be separated. Why could they not be purchased together? Why not let her have one of her dear children? "Mercy, mercy, master!" she cried, falling on her knees. "Please, master, buy Emily. I can never work any if she is taken from me: I will die."
>
> Freeman interfered again, but, disregarding him, she still plead most earnestly, telling how Randall had been taken from her—how she never would see him again, and now it was too bad—oh, God! it was too bad, too cruel, to take her away from Emily—her pride—her only darling, that could not live, it was so young, without its mother!
>
> Finally, after much more of supplication, the purchaser of Eliza stepped forward, evidently affected, and said to Freeman he would buy Emily, and asked him what her price was.
>
> "What is her *price? Buy* her?" was the responsive interrogatory of Theophilus Freeman. And instantly answering his own inquiry, he added, "I won't sell her. She's not for sale."
>
> The man remarked he was not in need of one so young—that it would be of no profit to him, but since the mother was so fond of her, rather than see them separated, he would pay a reasonable price.

"FANCY GIRLS"

"There also was lascivious demand for attractive young female slaves with light brown skin. These 'fancy maids' or 'fancy girls' often were raped by traders and sold in New Orleans to work as sex slaves—either in brothels or for exclusive exploitation by owners who paid up to $7,000 to flaunt their wealth, power, and audacity."

Rhodes, "Mother of the Domestic Slave Trade" at 36-37 Econ Focus, Richmond Federal Reserve (2nd Quarter, 2013) at Rhodes, Mother of the Domestic Slave Trade, Econ Focus, Richmond Federal Reserve (2nd Quarter, 2013) at *www.richmondfed.org/~/media/richmondfedorg/publications/research/econ_focus/2013/q2/pdf/economic_history.pdf, accessed Oct. 18, 2020*

Note: Using the inflation multiplier of 33, the sum of $7,000 at the time of slavery is the equivalent of approximately $230,000 today.

The slave trader refused to sell Emily in view of the extraordinary price he anticipated that he could get for her in the future. That led to a terrible scene and to Emily's being torn forcefully from Eliza's arms:

> But to this humane proposal Freeman was entirely deaf. He would not sell her then on any account whatever. There were heaps and piles of money to be made of her, he said, when she was a few years older. There were men enough in New-Orleans who would give five thousand dollars for such an extra, handsome, fancy piece as Emily would be, rather than not get her. No, no, he would not sell her then. She was a beauty—a picture—a doll—one of the regular bloods—none of your thick-lipped, bullet-headed, cotton-picking niggers—if she was might he be d—d.
>
> When Eliza heard Freeman's determination not to part with Emily, she became absolutely frantic.
>
> "I will *not* go without her. They shall *not* take her from me," she fairly shrieked, her shrieks commingling with the loud and angry voice of Freeman, commanding her to be silent.
>
> Meantime Harry and myself had been to the yard and returned with our blankets, and were at the front door ready to leave. Our purchaser stood near us, gazing at Eliza with an expression indicative of regret at having bought her at the expense of so much sorrow. We waited some time, when, finally, Freeman, out of patience, tore Emily from her mother by main force, the two clinging to each other with all their might.

Emily was terrified, but Eliza was powerless:

> "Don't leave me, mama—don't leave me," screamed the child, as its mother was pushed harshly forward; "Don't leave me—come back, mama," she still cried, stretching forth her little arms imploringly. But she cried in vain. Out of the door and into the street we were quickly hurried. Still we could hear her calling to her mother, "Come back—don't leave me—come back, mama," until her infant voice grew faint and still more faint, and gradually died away, as distance intervened, and finally was wholly lost.

That was the last time that Eliza saw her children:

> Eliza never after saw or heard of Emily or Randall. Day nor night, however, were they ever absent from her memory. In the cotton field, in the cabin, always and everywhere, she was talking of them—often to them, as if they were actually present. Only when absorbed in that illusion, or asleep, did she ever have a moment's comfort afterwards.
>
> She was no common slave, as has been said. To a large share of natural intelligence which she possessed, was added a general knowledge and information on most subjects. She had enjoyed opportunities such as are afforded to very few of her oppressed class. She had been lifted up into the regions of a higher life. Freedom—freedom for herself and for her offspring, for many years had been her cloud by day, her pillar of fire by night. In her pilgrimage through the wilderness of bondage, with eyes fixed upon that hope-inspiring beacon, she had at length ascended to "the top of Pisgah," and beheld "the land of promise." In an unexpected moment she was utterly overwhelmed with disappointment and despair. The glorious vision of liberty faded from her sight as they led her away into captivity. Now "she weepeth sore into the night, and tears are on her cheeks—all her friends have dealt treacherously with her: they have become her enemies."

§ § §

> On leaving the New-Orleans slave pen, Harry and I followed our new master through the streets, while Eliza, crying and turning back, was forced along by Freeman and his minions, until we found ourselves on board the steamboat Rodolph, then lying at the levee. In the course of half an hour we were moving briskly up the Mississippi, bound for some point on Red River. …

The slaves purchased at the auction, including Eliza and Mr. Northup reached their destination:

> **PISGAH**
>
> 1. Attributive Designating a faint view or glimpse of something unobtainable or distant, especially in "Pisgah sight," "Pisgah view."
> 2. A point affording an overview or glimpse of a current or future situation. Also in "Pisgah-hill."
>
> "Pisgah" at *www.lexico.com/en/definition/pisgah.*, accessed Oct, 18, 2020

At length we left the steamboat Rodolph at a place called Alexandria, several hundred miles from New-Orleans. It is a small town on the southern shore of Red River. Having remained there over night, we entered the morning train of cars, and were soon at Bayou Lamourie, a still smaller place, distant eighteen miles from Alexandria. At that time it was the termination of the railroad. Ford's plantation was situated on the Texas road, twelve miles from Lamourie, in the Great Pine Woods. This distance, it was announced to us, must be traveled on foot, there being public conveyances no farther. Accordingly we all set out in the company of Ford. It was an excessively hot day. Harry, Eliza, and myself were yet weak, and the bottoms of our feet were very tender from the effects of the small-pox. ...

In subsequent encounters, Eliza continuously talked about her children:

Eliza was still ringing her hands and deploring the loss of her children. Ford tried as much as possible to console her—told her she need not work very hard; that she might remain with Rose, and assist the madam in the house affairs.

§ § §

[After the passage of time—] On my arrival at Bayou Boeuf, I had the pleasure of meeting Eliza, whom I had not seen for several months. She had not pleased Mrs. Ford, being more occupied in brooding over her sorrows than in attending to her business, and had, in consequence, been sent down to work in the field on the plantation. She had grown feeble and emaciated, and was still mourning for her children. She asked me if I had forgotten them, and a great many times inquired if I still remembered how handsome little Emily was—how much Randall loved her—and wondered if they were living still, and where the darlings could then be. She had sunk beneath the weight of an excessive grief. Her drooping form and hollow cheeks too plainly indicated that she had well nigh reached the end of her weary road.

Despite her grief, Eliza showed kindness to others:

[After Mr. Northup's undeserved beating by a master—] I was in great misery—all sore and swollen—the slightest movement producing excruciating suffering. Soon the hands came in from the field. Rachel, when she went after Lawson, had told them what had happened. Eliza and Mary broiled me a piece of bacon, but my appetite was gone. Then they scorched some corn meal and made coffee. It was all that I could take. Eliza consoled me and was very kind. It was not long before the cabin was full of slaves. ...

§ § §

[After another passage of time—] On reaching the plantation they entered the great house, while I repaired to Eliza's cabin. The slaves were astonished to find me there, on returning from the field, supposing I was drowned [after escaping another beating]. That night, again, they gathered about the cabin to listen to the story of my adventure. They took it for granted I would be whipped, and that it would be severe, the well-known penalty of running away being five hundred lashes.

"Poor fellow," said Eliza, taking me by the hand, "it would have been better for you if you had drowned. You have a cruel master, and he will kill you yet, I am afraid."

Over time, Eliza gradually wasted away in deep inconsolable sorrow:

I arrived at Ford's plantation towards the close of the afternoon, passing the evening in Eliza's cabin, with Lawson, Rachel, and others of my acquaintance. When we left Washington Eliza's form was round and plump. She stood erect, and in her silks and jewels, presented a picture of graceful strength and elegance. Now she was but a thin shadow of her former self. Her face had become ghastly haggard, and the once straight and active form was bowed down, as if bearing the weight of a hundred years. Crouching on her cabin floor, and clad in the coarse garments of a slave, old Elisha Berry would not have recognized the mother of his child. I never saw her afterwards. Having become useless in the cotton-field, she was bartered for a trifle, to some man residing in the vicinity of Peter Compton's. Grief had gnawed remorselessly at her heart, until her strength was gone; and for that, her last master, it is said, lashed and abused her most unmercifully. But he could not whip back the departed vigor of her youth, nor straighten up that bended body to its full height, such as it was when her children were around her, and the light of freedom was shining on her path.

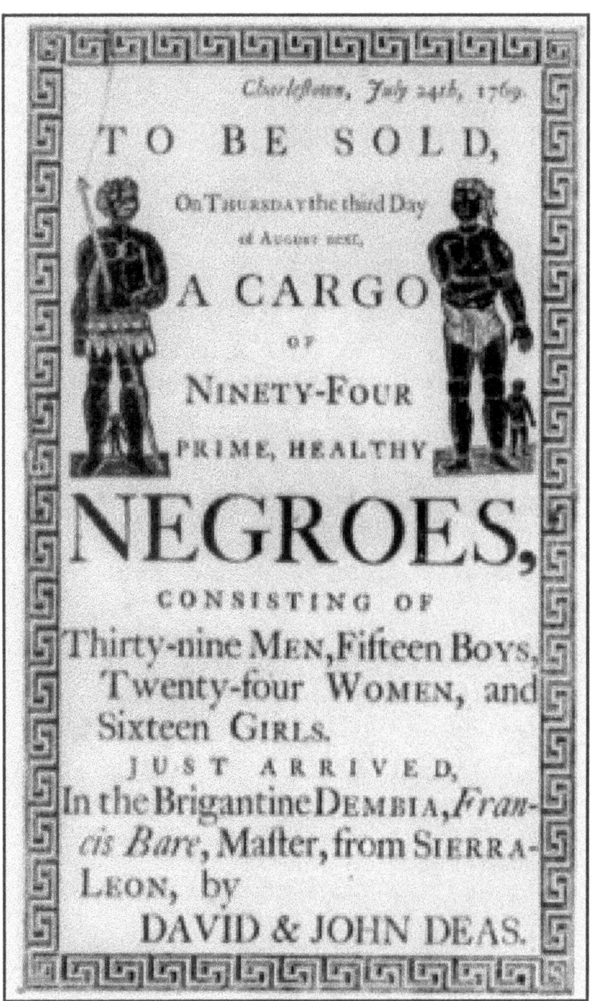

"Advertisement for Sale of Newly Arrived Africans, Charleston, July 24, 1769", *Slavery Images: A Visual Record of the African Slave Trade and Slave Life in the Early African Diaspora,* accessed November 14, 2020, *http://slaveryimages.org/s/slaveryimages/item/1971*

Eliza eventually died of anguish:

I learned the particulars relative to [Eliza's] departure from this world, from some of Compton's slaves, who had come over Red River to the bayou, to assist young Madam Tanner during the "busy season." She became at length, they said, utterly helpless, for several weeks lying on the ground floor in a dilapidated cabin, dependent upon the mercy of her fellow-thralls for an occasional drop of water, and a morsel of food. Her master did not "knock her on the head," as is sometimes done to put a suffering animal out of misery, but left her unprovided for, and unprotected, to linger through a life of pain and wretchedness to its natural close. When the hands returned from the field one night they found her dead! During the day, the Angel of the Lord, who moveth invisibly over all the earth, gathering in his harvest of departing souls, had silently entered the cabin of the dying woman, and taken her from thence. She was *free* at last!

"Inspection and Sale of a Negro", *Slavery Images: A Visual Record of the African Slave Trade and Slave Life in the Early African Diaspora,* accessed November 14, 2020, *http://slaveryimages.org/s/slaveryimages/item/1909*

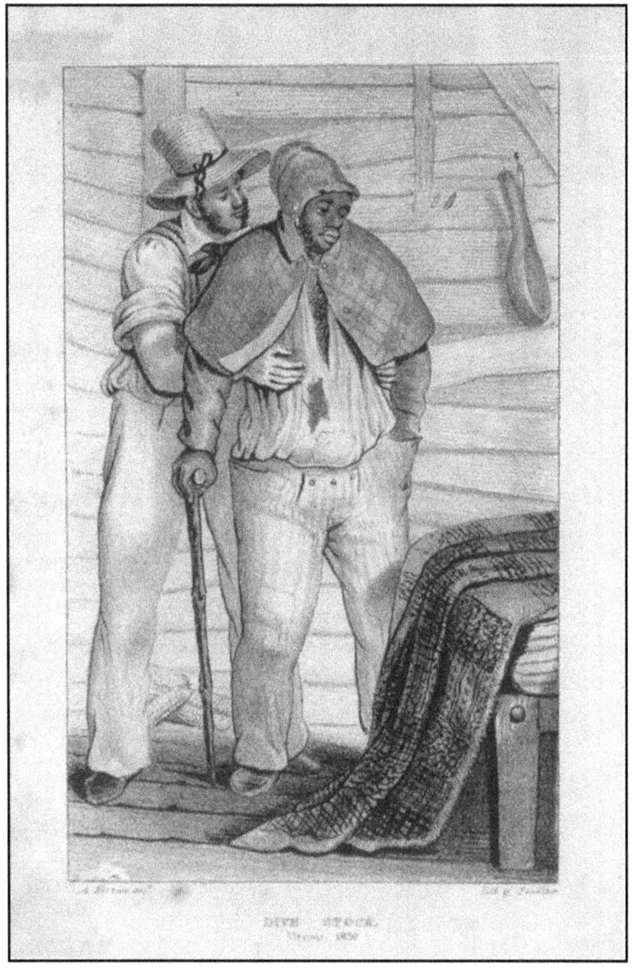

"Examining a Slave for Sale, Virginia, 1830", *Slavery Images: A Visual Record of the African Slave Trade and Slave Life in the Early African Diaspora,* accessed November 14, 2020, *http://slaveryimages.org/s/slaveryimages/item/1941*

"A Slave Auction in Virginia", *Slavery Images: A Visual Record of the African Slave Trade and Slave Life in the Early African Diaspora,* accessed November 14, 2020, *http://slaveryimages.org/s/slaveryimages/item/2226*

"A Slave Auction", *Slavery Images: A Visual Record of the African Slave Trade and Slave Life in the Early African Diaspora*, accessed November 14, 2020, *http://slaveryimages.org/s/slaveryimages/item/1878*

THE STORY OF PATSEY: UNCONTROLLED WHIPPING FOR NOTHING

The *Story of Patsey* demonstrates, in Solomon Northup's words, even casual use of extreme violence against a defenseless slave. The violence befell the slave even in the absence of resistance or incitement.

The *Story* incorporates the elements of an attractive, lively and hardworking slave with superior capabilities; the lasciviousness and extreme sadism of a slave master; the boundless jealousy and cruelty of a slave mistress; and the reprehensible destruction of the very vitality of life.

The *Story* has other values for us today looking back, knowing that the slave society was relentless in arguing that a slave master or mistress would always be moderate in his or her treatment of slaves because the master or mistress would not wish to damage their "property." The *Story of Patsey* exposes the untruth of that claim. It demonstrates the lack of concern that slave masters and mistresses had for any legal or social consequences from inhumane actions toward their slaves.

This was "something that happened 150 years ago."

Solomon Northup's book, **TWELVE YEARS A SLAVE**, describes Patsey's experiences, which I have excerpted from Mr. Northup's book and have assembled sequentially in the *Story of Patsey.* Patsey was an extraordinary young woman, full of life, with a pleasant attitude and remarkable skills:[718]

> An ordinary day's work [picking cotton] is two hundred pounds. A slave who is accustomed to picking, is punished, if he or she brings in a less quantity than that. There is a great difference among them as regards this kind of labor. Some of them seem to have a natural knack, or quickness, which enables them to pick with great celerity, and with both hands, while others, with whatever practice or industry, are utterly unable to come up to the ordinary standard. Such hands are taken from the cotton field and employed in other business. Patsey, of whom I shall have more to say, was known as the most remarkable cotton picker on Bayou Boeuf. She picked with both hands and with such surprising rapidity, that five hundred pounds a day was not unusual for her.
>
> Each one is tasked, therefore, according to his picking abilities, none, however, to come short of two hundred weight. I, being unskillful always in that business, would have satisfied my master by bringing in the latter quantity, while on the other hand, Patsey would surely have been beaten if she failed to produce twice as much.

Mr. Northup describes his lack of skill at picking cotton, which stands in sharp contrast to Patsey's outstanding talent:

> After a most laborious day I arrived at the gin-house with my load. When the scale determined its weight to be only ninety-five pounds, not half the quantity requited of the poorest picker, Epps threatened the severest flogging, but in consideration of my being a "raw hand," concluded to pardon me on that occasion. The following day, and many days succeeding, I returned at night with no better success—I was evidently not designed for that kind of labor. I had not the gift—the dexterous fingers and quick motion of Patsey, who could fly along one side of a row of cotton, stripping it of its undefiled and fleecy whiteness miraculously fast. Practice and whipping were alike unavailing, and Epps, satisfied of it at last, swore I was a disgrace—that I was not fit to associate with a cotton-picking "nigger"— that I could not pick enough in a day to pay the trouble of weighing it, and that I should go into the cotton

718 Northup at 166, 178-79, 184-86, 188-89, 197-200, 213-14, 227-29, 253-59, 260, 308. Emphasis in original.

> field no more. I was now employed in cutting and hauling wood, drawing cotton from the field to the gin-house, and performed whatever other service was required. Suffice to say, I was never permitted to be idle. …
>
> The number of lashes is graduated according to the nature of the case. Twenty-five are deemed a mere brush, inflicted, for instance, when a dry leaf or piece of boll is found in the cotton, or when a branch is broken in the field; fifty is the ordinary penalty following all delinquencies of the next higher grade; one hundred is called severe: it is the punishment inflicted for the serious offence of standing idle in the field; from one hundred and fifty to two hundred is bestowed upon him who quarrels with his cabin-mates, and five hundred, well laid on, besides the mangling of the dogs, perhaps, is certain to consign the poor, unpitied runaway to weeks of pain and agony.

PUNISHMENT IN STOCKS

"A slave who had been separated from his wife, because it best suited the convenience of his owner, ran away. He was taken up on the plantation where his wife, to whom he was tenderly attached, then lived. His only object in running away was to return to her—no other fault was attributed to him. For this offence he was confined in the stocks six weeks, in a miserable hovel, not weather-tight. He received fifty lashes weekly during that time, was allowed food barely sufficient to sustain him, and when released from confinement, was not permitted to return to his wife. His master, although himself a husband and a father, was unmoved by the touching appeals of the slave, who entreated that he might only remain with his wife, promising to discharge his duties faithfully; his master continued inexorable, and he was torn from his wife and family. The owner of this slave was a professing Christian, in full membership with the church, and this circumstance occurred when he was confined to his chamber during his last illness. …"

T. Weld, American Slavery As It Is: Testimony of a Thousand Witnesses at 23 (American Anti-Slavery Society 1839), available from the Library of Congress at *www.hathitrust.org/digital_library*

Mr. Northup describes the slaves owned by Master Epps, including Patsey, whose beauty and attitude distinguished her:

> [Master] Epps remained on Huff Power two years, when, having accumulated a considerable sum of money, he expended it in the purchase of the plantation on the east bank of Bayou Boeuf, where he still continues to reside. He took possession of it in 1845, after the holidays were passed. He carried thither with him nine slaves, all of whom, except myself, and Susan, who has since died, remain there yet. He made no addition to this force, and for eight years the following were my companions in his quarters, viz: Abram, Wiley, Phebe, Bob, Henry, Edward, and Patsey. …
>
> Patsey is twenty-three-… . She is in no wise connected with the others, but glories in the fact that she is the offspring of a "Guinea nigger," brought over to Cuba in a slave ship, and in the course of trade transferred to Buford, who was her mother's owner.
>
> § § §
>
> Patsey was slim and straight. She stood erect as the human form is capable of standing. There was an air of loftiness in her movement, that neither labor, nor weariness, nor punishment could destroy. Truly, Patsey was a splendid animal, and were it not that bondage had enshrouded her intellect in utter and everlasting darkness, would have been chief among ten thousand of her people. She could leap the highest fences, and a fleet hound it was indeed, that could outstrip her in a race. No horse could fling her from his back. She was a skillful teamster. She turned as true a furrow as the best, and at splitting rails there were none who could excel her. When the order to halt was heard at night, she would have her mules at the crib, unharnessed, fed and curried, before Uncle Abram had found his hat. Not, however, for all or any of these, was she chiefly famous. Such lightning-like motion was in her fingers

as no other fingers ever possessed, and therefore it was, that in cotton picking time, Patsey was queen of the field.

She had a genial and pleasant temper, and was faithful and obedient. Naturally, she was a joyous creature, a laughing, light-hearted girl, rejoicing in the mere sense of existence. Yet Patsey wept oftener, and suffered more, than any of her companions. She had been literally excoriated. Her back bore the scars of a thousand stripes; not because she was backward in her work, nor because she was of an unmindful and rebellious spirit, but because it had fallen to her lot to be the slave of a licentious master and a jealous mistress. She shrank before the lustful eye of the one, and was in danger even of her life at the hands of the other, and between the two, she was indeed accursed. In the great house, for days together, there were high and angry words, poutings and estrangement, whereof she was the innocent cause. Nothing delighted the mistress so much as to see her suffer, and more than once, when Epps had refused to sell her, has she tempted me with bribes to put her secretly to death, and bury her body in some lonely place in the margin of the swamp. Gladly would Patsey have appeased this unforgiving spirit, if it had been in her power, but not like Joseph, dared she escape from Master Epps, leaving her garment in his hand. Patsey walked under a cloud. If she uttered a word in opposition to her master's will, the lash was resorted to at once, to bring her to subjection; if she was not watchful when about her cabin, or when walking in the yard, a billet of wood, or a broken bottle perhaps, hurled from her mistress' hand, would smite her unexpectedly in the face. The enslaved victim of lust and hate, Patsey had no comfort of her life.

<u>EARS NAILED IN STOCKS</u>

Punishment for Hog Stealing by any "negro or slave"—first offense "on his bare back thirty nine lashes well laid on" and for the second offense, he "shall stand two hours in the pillory and have both his eares nailed thereto and at the expiration of the said two hours have his ears cut off close by the nailes"

"Virtual Jamestown: Laws on Slavery" at *www.virtualjamestown.org/laws1.html,* accessed Nov. 10, 2020

FATAL PUNISHMENT
<u>WITHOUT CONSEQUENCES</u>

"Mrs. Weld is the youngest. daughter of the late Judge Grimke, of the Supreme Court of South Carolina, and a sister of the late Hon. Thomas S. Grimke, of Charleston. [She states:]...

"A slaveholder, after flogging a little girl about thirteen years old, set her on a table with her feet fastened in a pair of stocks. He then locked the door and took out the key. When the door was opened she was found dead, having fallen from the table. When I asked a prominent lawyer, who belonged to one of the first families in the State, whether the murderer of this helpless child could not be indicted, he coolly replied, that the slave was Mr. —'s property, and if he chose to suffer the loss, no one else had any thing to do with it. The loss of human life, the distress of the parents and other relatives of the little girl, seemed utterly out of his thoughts: it was the loss of property only that presented itself to his mind."

T. Weld, American Slavery As It Is: Testimony of a Thousand Witnesses at 52, 54 (American Anti-Slavery Society 1839), available from the Library of Congress at *www.hathitrust.org/digital_library*

As occurred on other plantations when a slave master was attracted to a female slave, Mistress Epps was extremely jealous:

> [After an absence,] I learned from Aunt Phebe and Patsey, that the latter had been getting deeper and deeper into trouble. The poor girl was truly an object of pity. "Old Hogjaw," the name by which Epps was called, when the slaves were by themselves, had beaten her more severely and frequently than ever. As surely as he came from Holmesville, elated

with liquor—and it was often in those days—he would whip her, merely to gratify the mistress; would punish her to an extent almost beyond endurance, for an offence of which he himself was the sole and irresistible cause. In his sober moments he could not always be prevailed upon to indulge his wife's insatiable thirst for vengeance.

To be rid of Patsey—to place her beyond sight or reach, by sale, or death, or in any other manner, of late years, seemed to be the ruling thought and passion of my mistress. Patsey had been a favorite when a child, even in the great house. She had been petted and admired for her uncommon sprightliness and pleasant disposition. She had been fed many a time, so Uncle Abram said, even on biscuit and milk, when the madam, in her younger days, was wont to call her to the piazza, and fondle her as she would a playful kitten. But a sad change had come over the spirit of the woman. Now, only black and angry fiends ministered in the temple of her heart, until she could look on Patsey but with concentrated venom.

The jealousy of a slave mistress changed the personality of Mistress Epps when matters came to Patsey, which in turn caused Master Epps to brutalize Patsey in order to please his wife:

Mistress Epps was not naturally such an evil woman, after all. She was possessed of the devil, jealousy, it is true, but aside from that, there was much in her character to admire. Her father, Mr. Roberts, resided in Cheneyville, an influential and honorable man, and as much respected throughout the parish as any other citizen. She had been well educated at some institution this side the Mississippi; was beautiful, accomplished, and usually good-humored. She was kind to all of us but Patsey—frequently, in the absence of her husband, sending out to us some little dainty from her own table. In other situations—in a different society from that which exists on the shores of Bayou Boeuf, she would have been pronounced an elegant and fascinating woman. An ill wind it was that blew her into the arms of Epps.

He respected and loved his wife as much as a coarse nature like his is capable of loving, but supreme selfishness always overmastered conjugal affection.

"He loved as well as baser natures can,

But a mean heart and soul were in that man."

WHAT'S IN A SLAVE'S NAME?

As William Wells Brown illustrates, slaveholders assigned names to slaves, first names only. They did not permit last names.

"[M]y old master, Dr. Young, had no children of his own, but had with him a nephew, the son. of his brother, Benjamin Young. When this boy was brought to Doctor Young, his name being William, the same as mine, my mother was ordered to change mine to something else. This, at the time, I thought to be one of the most cruel acts that could be committed upon my rights; and I received several very severe whippings for telling people that my name was William, after orders were given to change it. Though young, I was old enough to place a high appreciation upon my name. It was decided, however, to call me "Sandford," and this name I was known by, not only upon my master's plantation, but up to the time that I made my escape. I was sold under the name of Sandford.

"But as soon as the subject came to my mind, I resolved on adopting my old name of William, and let Sandford go by the board, for I always hated it."

W. Brown, Narrative of William W. Brown, A Fugitive Slave, Written by Himself at 97-98 (Anti-Slavery Office, 2nd ed. 1848), available from the Library of Congress at www.hathitrust.org/digital_library

> He was ready to gratify any whim—to grant any request she made, provided it did not cost too much. Patsey was equal to any two of his slaves in the cotton field. He could not replace her with the same money she would bring. The idea of disposing of her, therefore, could not be entertained. The mistress did not regard her at all in that light. The pride of the haughty woman was aroused; the blood of the fiery southern boiled at the sight of Patsey, and nothing less than trampling out the life of the helpless bondwoman would satisfy her.
>
> Sometimes the current of her wrath turned upon him whom she had just cause to hate. But the storm of angry words would pass over at length, and there would be a season of calm again. At such times Patsey trembled with fear, and cried as if her heart would break, for she knew from painful experience, that if mistress should work herself to the red-hot pitch of rage, Epps would quiet her at last with a promise that Patsey should be flogged—a promise he was sure to keep. Thus did pride, and jealousy, and vengeance war with avarice and brute-passion in the mansion of my master, filling it with daily tumult and contention. Thus, upon the head of Patsey—the simple-minded slave, in whose heart God had implanted the seeds of virtue—the force of all these domestic tempests spent itself at last.

Nevertheless, Master Epps continued to pursue Patsey, and Mistress Epps continued to feel jealousy. The following incident occurred in an open field. Mr. Northup did what he could to shield Patsey:

> [Master Epps] had been absent at Holmesville, in attendance at a shooting-match, and none of us were aware of his return. While hoeing by the side of Patsey, she exclaimed, in a low voice, suddenly, "Platt [Solomon Northup's slave name], d'ye see old Hog-Jaw beckoning me to come to him?"
>
> Glancing sideways, I discovered him in the edge of the field, motioning and grimacing, as was his habit when half-intoxicated. Aware of his lewd intentions, Patsey began to cry. I whispered her not to look up, and to continue at her work, as if she had not observed him. Suspecting the truth of the matter, however, he soon staggered up to me in a great rage.
>
> "What did you say to Pats?" he demanded, with an oath. I made him some evasive answer, which only had the effect of increasing his violence.
>
> "How long have you owned this plantation, *say*, you d—d nigger?" he inquired, with a malicious sneer, at the same time taking hold of my shirt collar with one hand, and thrusting the other into his pocket. "Now I'll cut your black throat; that's what I'll do," drawing his knife from his pocket as he said it. But with one hand he was unable to open it, until finally seizing the blade in his teeth, I saw he was about to succeed, and felt the necessity of escaping from him, for in his present reckless state, it was evident he was not joking, by any means. My shirt was open in front, and as I turned round quickly and sprang from him, while he still retained his gripe, it was stripped entirely from my

MISTAKES NOT TOLERATED

"Dr. DAVID NELSON, late president of Marion College, Missouri, a native of Tennessee, and till forty years old a slaveholder, said in an Anti-Slavery address at Northampton, Mass. Jan. 1839—

"I have not attempted to harrow your feelings with stories of cruelty. I will, however, mention one or two among the many incidents that came under my observation as family physician. I was one day dressing a blister, and the mistress of the house sent a little black girl into the kitchen to bring me some warm water. She probably mistook her message; for she returned with a bowl full of boiling water; which her mistress no sooner perceived, than she thrust her hand into it, and held it there till it was half cooked."

T. Weld, American Slavery As It Is: Testimony of a Thousand Witnesses at 86 (American Anti-Slavery Society 1839), available from the Library of Congress at *www.hathitrust.org/digital_library*

> back. There was no difficulty now in eluding him. He would chase me until out of breath, then stop until it was recovered, swear, and renew the chase again. Now he would command me to come to him, now endeavor to coax me, but I was careful to keep at a respectful distance. In this manner we made the circuit of the field several times, he making desperate plunges, and I always dodging them, more amused than frightened, well knowing that when his sober senses returned, he would laugh at his own drunken folly. At length I observed the mistress standing by the yard fence, watching our half-serious, half comical manoeuvres. Shooting past him, I ran directly to her. Epps, on discovering her, did not follow. He remained about the field an hour or more, during which time I stood by the mistress, having related the particulars of what had taken place. Now, she was aroused again, denouncing her husband and Patsey about equally.

The combination of emotions led to an extremely brutal whipping of Patsey for a nonexistent, or at most a minor, violation of purported rules. When Patsey returned from a visit to a neighboring plantation, Master Epps' own jealousy aroused him at his neighbor:

> It was no uncommon thing with [Master Epps] to prostrate Aunt Phebe with a chair or stick of wood; but the most cruel whipping that ever I was doomed to witness—one I can never recall with any other emotion than that of horror—was inflicted on the unfortunate Patsey.
>
> It has been seen that the jealousy and hatred of Mistress Epps made the daily life of her young and agile slave completely miserable. I am happy in the belief that on numerous occasions I was the means of averting punishment from the inoffensive girl. In Epps' absence the mistress often ordered me to whip her without the remotest provocation. I would refuse, saying that I feared my master's displeasure, and several times ventured to remonstrate with her against the treatment Patsey received. I endeavored to impress her with the truth that the latter was not responsible for the acts of which she complained, but that she being a slave, and subject entirely to her master's will, he alone was answerable.
>
> At length "the green-eyed monster" crept into the soul of Epps also, and then it was that he joined with his wrathful wife in an infernal jubilee over the girl's miseries.
>
> On a Sabbath day in hoeing time, not long ago, we were on the bayou bank, washing our clothes, as was our usual custom. Presently Patsey was missing. Epps called aloud, but there was no answer. No one had observed her leaving the yard, and it was a wonder with us whither she had gone. In the course of a couple of hours she was seen approaching from the direction of Shaw's. This man … was a notorious profligate, and withal not on the most friendly terms with Epps. Harriet, his black wife, knowing Patsey's troubles, was kind to her, in consequence of which the latter was in the habit of going over to see her every opportunity. Her visits were prompted by friendship merely, but the suspicion gradually entered the brain of Epps, that another and a baser passion led her thither—that it was not Harriet she desired to meet, but rather the unblushing libertine, his neighbor. Patsey found her master in a fearful rage on her return. His violence so alarmed her that at first she attempted to evade direct answers to his questions, which only served to increase his suspicions. She finally, however, drew herself up proudly, and in a spirit of indignation boldly denied his charges.
>
> "Missus don't give me soap to wash with, as she does the rest," said Patsey, "and you know why. I went over to Harriet's to get a piece," and saying this, she drew it forth from a pocket in her dress and exhibited it to him. "That's what I went to Shaw's for, Massa Epps," continued she; "the Lord knows that was all."
>
> "You lie, you black wench!" shouted Epps.
>
> "I *don't* lie, massa. If you kill me, I'll stick to that."
>
> "Oh! I'll fetch you down. I'll learn you to go to Shaw's. I'll take the starch out of ye," he muttered fiercely through his shut teeth.

Master Epps ordered that Patsey be stripped of all clothing and, naked and spread-eagled, be staked by both wrists and both legs to the ground face down. He ordered Mr. Northup to whip Patsey, which Mr. Northup did as lightly as he could:

> [T]urning to me, he ordered four stakes to be driven into the ground, pointing with the toe of his boot to the places where he wanted them. When the stakes were driven down, he ordered her to be stripped of every article of dress. Ropes were then brought, and the naked girl was laid upon her face, her wrists and feet each tied firmly to a stake. Stepping to the piazza, he took down a heavy whip, and placing it in my hands, commanded me to lash her. Unpleasant as it was, I was compelled to obey him. Nowhere that day, on the face of the whole earth, I venture to say, was there such a demoniac exhibition witnessed as then ensued.
>
> Mistress Epps stood on the piazza among her children, gazing on the scene with an air of heartless satisfaction. The slaves were huddled together at a little distance, their countenances indicating the sorrow of their hearts. Poor Patsey prayed piteously for mercy, but her prayers were vain. Epps ground his teeth, and stamped upon the ground, screaming at me, like a mad fiend, to strike *harder.*
>
> "Strike harder, or *your* turn will come next, you scoundrel," he yelled.
>
> "Oh, mercy, massa!—oh! have mercy, *do.* Oh, God! pity me," Patsey exclaimed continually, struggling fruitlessly, and the flesh quivering at every stroke.

"Whipping of a Fugitive Slave, French West Indies, 1840s", *Slavery Images: A Visual Record of the African Slave Trade and Slave Life in the Early African Diaspora,* accessed November 15, 2020, *http://slaveryimages.org/s/slaveryimages/item/3107*

It was not enough to satisfy Master Epps, who then assumed the flogging role:

> When I had struck her as many as thirty times, I stopped, and turned round toward Epps, hoping he was satisfied; but with bitter oaths and threats, he ordered me to continue. I inflicted ten or fifteen blows more. By this time her back was covered with long welts, intersecting each other like net work. Epps was yet furious and savage as ever, demanding! if she would like to go to Shaw's again, and swearing he would flog her until she wished she was in h—l. Throwing down the whip, I declared I could punish her no more. He ordered me to go on, threatening me with a severer flogging than she had received, in case of refusal. My heart revolted at the inhuman scene, and risking the consequences, I absolutely refused to raise the whip. He then seized it himself, and applied it with ten-fold greater force than I had. The painful cries and shrieks of the tortured Patsey, mingling with the loud and angry curses of Epps, loaded the air. She was terribly lacerated—I may say, without exaggeration, literally flayed.

The lash was wet with blood, which flowed down her sides and dropped upon the ground. At length she ceased struggling. Her head sank listlessly on the ground. Her screams and supplications gradually decreased and died away into a low moan. She no longer writhed and shrank beneath the lash when it bit out small pieces of her flesh. I thought that she was dying!

It was the Sabbath of the Lord. The fields smiled in the warm sunlight—the birds chirped merrily amidst the foliage of the trees—peace and happiness seemed to reign everywhere, save in the bosoms of Epps and his panting victim and the silent witnesses around him. The tempestuous emotions that were raging there were little in harmony with the calm and quiet beauty of the day. I could look on Epps only with unutterable loathing and abhorrence, and thought within myself—"Thou devil, sooner or later, somewhere in the course of eternal justice, thou shalt answer for this sin!"

Patsey's condition was distressing after the whipping:

Finally, he ceased whipping from mere exhaustion, and ordered Phebe to bring a bucket of salt and water. After washing her thoroughly with this, I was told to take her to her cabin. Untying the ropes, I raised her in my arms. She was unable to stand, and as her head rested on my shoulder, she repeated many times, in a faint voice scarcely perceptible, "Oh, Platt—oh, Platt!" but nothing further. Her dress was replaced, but it clung to her back, and was soon stiff with blood. We laid her on some boards in the hut, where she remained a long time, with eyes closed and groaning in agony. At night Phebe applied melted tallow to her wounds, and so far as we were able, all endeavored to assist and console her. Day after day she lay in her cabin upon her face, the sores preventing her resting in any other position.

The whipping was so brutal that it changed Patsey's once happy demeanor to sadness;

A blessed thing it would have been for her—days and weeks and months of misery it would have saved her—had she never lifted up her head in life again. Indeed, from that time forward she was not what she had been. The burden of a deep melancholy weighed heavily on her spirits. She no longer moved with that buoyant and elastic step—there was not that mirthful sparkle in her eyes that formerly distinguished her. The bounding vigor—the sprightly, laughter-loving spirit of her youth, were gone. She fell into a mournful and desponding mood, and often-times would start up in her sleep, and with raised hands, plead for mercy. She became more silent than she was, toiling all day in our midst, not uttering a word. A care-worn, pitiful expression settled on her face, and it was her humor now to weep, rather than rejoice. If ever there was a broken heart—one crushed and blighted by the rude grasp of suffering and misfortune—it was Patsey's.

She had been reared no better than her master's beast—looked upon merely as a valuable and handsome animal—and consequently possessed but a limited amount of knowledge. And yet a faint

ANOTHER PUNISHMENT FOR NOTHING

"I was passing through a piece of timbered land, and on a sudden I heard a sound as of murder; I rode in that direction, and at some distance discovered a naked black man, hung to the limb of a tree by his hands, his feet chained together, and a pine rail laid with one end on the chain between his legs, and the other upon the ground, to steady him; and in this condition the overseer gave him *four hundred lashes*. The miserably lacerated slave was then taken down, and put to the care of a physician. And what do you suppose was the offence for which all this was done? Simply this: his owner, observing that he laid off corn rows too crooked, he replied, "Massa, much corn grow on crooked row as on straight one." This was it—this was enough. His overseer, boasting of his skill in managing a nigger, he was submitted to him and treated as above."

T. Weld, American Slavery As It Is: Testimony of a Thousand Witnesses at 85, 90 (American Anti-Slavery Society 1839), available from the Library of Congress at *www.hathitrust.org/digital_library.* Emphasis in original.

> light cast its rays over her intellect, so that it was not wholly dark. She had a dim perception of God and of eternity, and a still more dim perception of a Saviour who had died even for such as her. She entertained but confused notions of a future life—not comprehending the distinction between the corporeal and spiritual existence. Happiness, in her mind, was exemption from stripes—from labor—from the cruelty of masters and overseers. Her idea of the joy of heaven was simply rest, and is fully expressed in these lines of a melancholy bard:
>
> "I ask no paradise on high,
> With cares on earth oppressed,
> The only heaven for which I sigh,
> Is rest, eternal rest."
>
> § § §
>
> Patsey's life, especially after her whipping, was one long dream of liberty. Far away, to her fancy an immeasurable distance, she knew there was a land of freedom. A thousand times she had heard that somewhere in the distant North there were no slaves—no masters. In her imagination it was an enchanted region, the Paradise of the earth. To dwell where the black man may work for himself—live in his own cabin—till his own soil, was a blissful dream of Patsey's—a dream, alas! the fulfillment of which she can never realize.

At long last, Mr. Northup was able to smuggle a letter out from the plantation to his family in New York informing them of his location. That resulted in his gaining his freedom.

Patsey expressed deep sadness at Mr. Northup's leaving, knowing that she was losing a friend and an ally:

> [Upon my rescue,] [o]n my way back to the carriage, Patsey ran from behind a cabin and threw her arms about my neck.
>
> "Oh! Platt," she cried, tears streaming down her face, "you're goin' to be free—you're goin' way off yonder where we'll neber see ye any more. You've saved me a good many whippins, Platt; I'm glad you're goin' to be free—but oh! de Lord, de Lord! What'll become of me?"
>
> I disengaged myself from her, and entered the carriage. The driver cracked his whip and away we rolled. I looked back and saw Patsey, with drooping head, half reclining on the ground; Mrs. Epps was on the piazza; Uncle Abram, and Bob, and Wiley, and Aunt Phebe stood by the gate, gazing after me. I waved my hand, but the carriage turned a bend of the bayou, hiding them from my eyes forever.

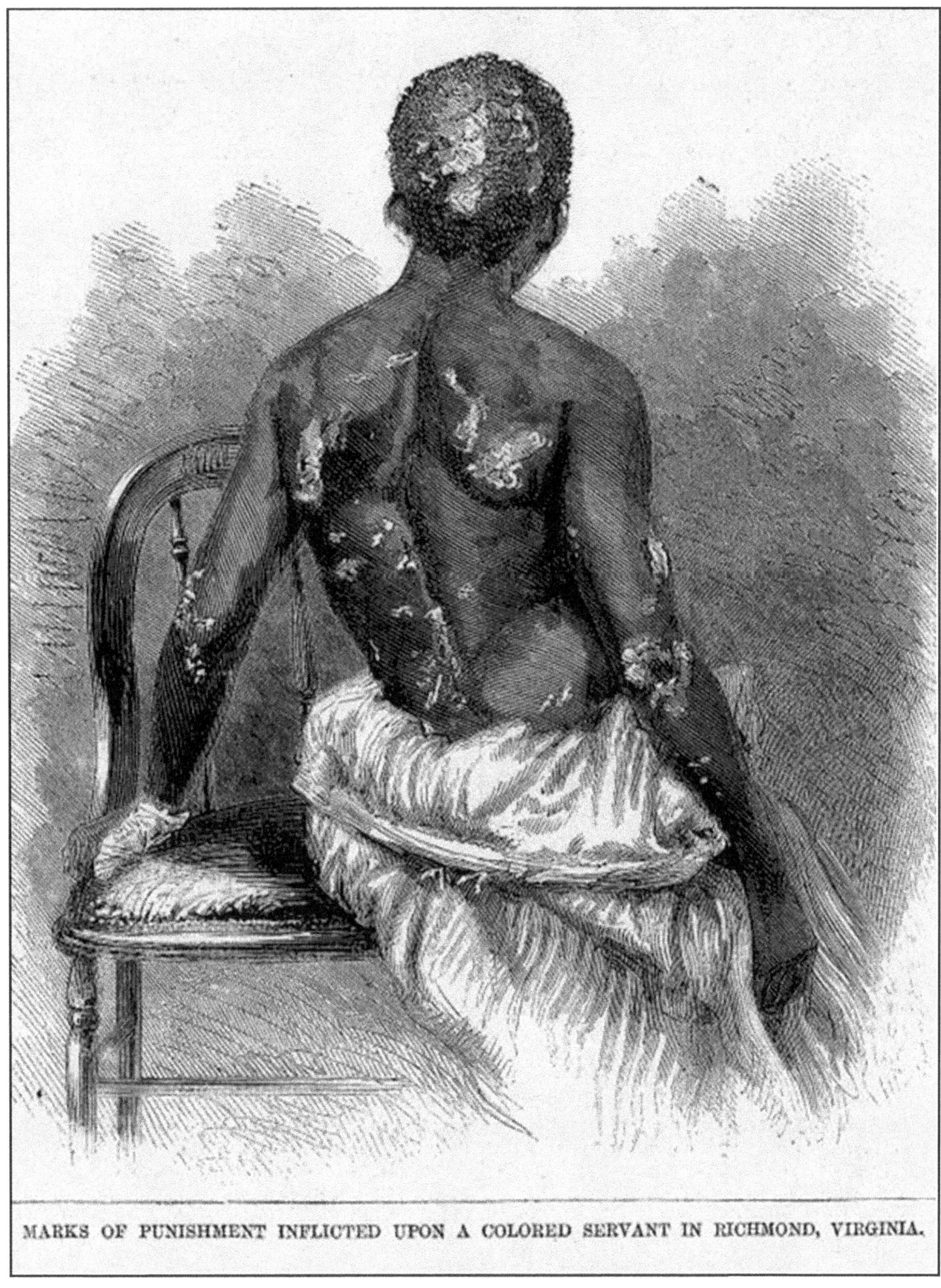

MARKS OF PUNISHMENT INFLICTED UPON A COLORED SERVANT IN RICHMOND, VIRGINIA.

"Marks of Punishment Inflicted upon a Colored Servant in Richmond, Virginia", *Slavery Images: A Visual Record of the African Slave Trade and Slave Life in the Early African Diaspora,* accessed November 15, 2020, *http://slaveryimages.org/s/slaveryimages/item/1325*

PUNISHMENT FOR "STEALING" A PIECE OF CANDY

"Well, she got her rawhide down from de nail by de fire place, an' she grabbed me by de arm an' she try to turn me 'cross her knees whilst she set in de rocker so's she could hol' me. I twisted an' turned till finally she called her daughter. De gal come an' took dat strap like her mother tole her an' commence to lay it on real hard whilst Missus holt me. I twisted 'way so dere warn't no chance o' her gittin' in no solid lick. Den ole Missus lif' me up by de legs, an' she stuck my haid under de bottom of her rocker, an' she rock forward so's to hol' my haid an' whup me some mo'. I guess dey must of whupped me near a hour wid dat rocker leg a-pressin' down on my haid.

"Nex' thing I knew de ole Doctor was dere, an' I was lyin' on my pallet in de hall, an' he was a-pushin' an' diggin' at my face, but he couldn't do nothin' at all wid it. Seem like dat rocker pressin' on my young bones had crushed 'em all into soft pulp. De nex' day I couldn' open my mouf an' I feel it an' dey warn't no bone in de lef' side at all. …

"I ain't never growed no mo' teef on dat side[.] … "Been eatin' liquid, stews, an' soup ever since dat day, an' dat was eighty-six years ago."

"Henrietta King"; an excerpt from "Weevils in the Wheat" (1976) at *www.encyclopediavirginia.org/_Henrietta_King_an_excerpt_from_Weevils_in_the_Wheat_1976, accessed Oct. 18, 2020*

THE STORY OF AUNT ESTHER'S WRETCHED EXISTENCE

Lest you might suppose that Patsey's fate was exceptional, Frederick Douglass provides the following *Story* of the treatment of his Aunt Esther, and then again a *Story* about an "impudent" slave named Nelly. The *Stories* exemplify the slave society's interpretation of statutory provisions allowing masters to apply "moderate punishment" to slaves.

In *The Story of Aunt Esther's Wretched Existence,* Douglass illuminates the extreme brutality in slavery against women, as well as how lecherous masters, desiring concubines, would seek to dominate their slave women's romantic relationships:[719]

> Howsoever the slaveholder may allow himself to act toward his slave, and, whatever cruelty he may deem it wise, for example's sake, or for the gratification of his humor, to inflict, he cannot, in the absence of all provocation, look with pleasure upon the bleeding wounds of a defenseless slave-woman. When he drives her from his presence without redress, or the hope of redress, he acts, generally, from motives of policy, rather than from a hardened nature, or from innate brutality. Yet, let but his own temper be stirred, his own passions get loose, and the slave-owner will go *far beyond* the overseer in cruelty. He will convince the slave that his wrath is far more terrible and boundless, and vastly more to be dreaded, than that of the underling overseer. What may have been mechanically and heartlessly done by the overseer, is now done with a will. The man who now wields the lash is irresponsible. He may, if he pleases, cripple or kill, without fear of consequences; except in so far as it may concern profit or loss. To a man of violent temper—as my old master was—this was but a very slender and inefficient restraint. I have seen him in a tempest of passion, such as I have just described—a passion into which entered all the bitter ingredients of pride, hatred, envy, jealousy, and the thirst for revenge.
>
> The circumstances which I am about to narrate, and which gave rise to this fearful tempest of passion, are not singular nor isolated in slave life, but are common in every slaveholding community in which I have lived. They are incidental to the relation of master and slave, and exist in all sections of slaveholding countries.

AN OFFER YOU CAN'T REFUSE

"[A] planter had a female slave who was a member of the Methodist Church; for a slave she was intelligent and conscientious. He proposed a criminal intercourse with her. She would not comply. He left her and sent for the overseer, and told him to have her flogged. It was done. Not long after, he renewed his proposal. She again refused. She was again whipped. He then told her why she had been twice flogged, and told her he intended to whip her till she should yield. The girl, seeing that her case was hopeless, her back smarting with the scourging she had received, and dreading a repetition, gave herself up to be the victim of his brutal lusts."

T. Weld, American Slavery As It Is: Testimony of a Thousand Witnesses at 15 (American Anti-Slavery Society 1839) (Narrative of Mr. Nehemiah Caulkins), available from the Library of Congress at *www.hathitrust.org/digital_library*

---

719 Douglass, My Bondage and My Freedom at 84-88. Emphasis in original. See also Douglass, Narrative at 6-8.

BREEDING SLAVES

"The following was told me by an intimate friend; it took place on a plantation containing about one hundred slaves. One day the owner ordered the women into the barn, he then went in among them, whip in hand, and told them he meant to flog them all to death; they began immediately to cry out "What have I done Massa? What have I done Massa!" He replied; "D—n you, I will let you know what you have done, you don't breed, I haven't had a young one from one of you for several months." They told him they could not breed while they had to work in the rice ditches. (The rice grounds are low and marshy, and have to be drained, and while digging or clearing the ditches, the women had to work in mud and water from one to two feet in depth; they were obliged to draw up and secure their frocks about their waist, to keep them out of the water, in this manner they frequently had to work from daylight in the morning till it was so dark they could see no longer.) After swearing and threatening for some time, he told them to tell the overseer's wife, when they got in that way, and he would put them upon the land to work."

T. Weld, American Slavery As It Is: Testimony of a Thousand Witnesses at 15-16 (American Anti-Slavery Society 1839), available from the Library of Congress at *www.hathitrust.org/digital_library*

The reader will have noticed that, in enumerating the names of the slaves who lived with my old master, *Esther* is mentioned. This was a young woman who possessed that which is ever a curse to the slave-girl; namely,—personal beauty. She was tall, well formed, and made a fine appearance. The daughters of Col. Lloyd could scarcely surpass her in personal charms. Esther was courted by Edward Roberts, and he was as fine looking a young man, as she was a woman. He was the son of a favorite slave of Col. Lloyd. Some slaveholders would have been glad to promote the marriage of two such persons; but, for some reason or other, my old master took it upon him to break up the growing intimacy between Esther and Edward. He strictly ordered her to quit the company of said Roberts, telling her that he would punish her severely if he ever found her again in Edward's company. This unnatural and heartless order was, of course, broken. A woman's love is not to be annihilated by the peremptory command of any one, whose breath is in his nostrils. It was impossible to keep Edward and Esther apart. Meet they would, and meet they did. Had old master been a man of honor and purity, his motives, in this matter, might have been viewed more favorably. As it was, his motives were as abhorrent, as his methods were foolish and contemptible. It was too evident that he was not concerned for the girl's welfare. It is one of the damning characteristics of the slave system, that it robs its victims of every earthly incentive to a holy life. The fear of God, and the hope of heaven, are found sufficient to sustain many slave-women, amidst the snares and dangers of their strange lot; but, this side of God and heaven, a slave-woman is at the mercy of the power, caprice and passion of her owner. Slavery provides no means for the honorable continuance of the race. Marriage—as imposing obligations on the parties to it—has no existence here, except in such hearts as are purer and higher than the standard morality around them. It is one of the consolations of my life, that I know of many honorable instances of persons who maintained their honor, where all around was corrupt.

Esther was evidently much attached to Edward, and abhorred—as she had reason to do—the tyrannical and base behavior of old master. Edward was young, and fine looking, and he loved and courted her. He might have been her husband, in the highest sense just alluded to; but who and *what* was this old master? His attentions were plainly brutal and selfish, and it was as natural that Esther should loathe him, as that she should love Edward. Abhorred and circumvented as he was, old master, having the power, very easily took revenge. I happened to see this exhibition of his rage and cruelty toward Esther. The time selected was singular. It was early in the morning, when all besides was still, and before any of the family, in the house or kitchen, had left their beds. I saw but few of the shocking preliminaries, for the cruel work had begun before I awoke. I was probably

MORE ON BREEDING SLAVES

"One of the slaves on another plantation, gave birth to a child which lived but two or three weeks. After its death the planter called the woman to him, and asked how she came to let the child die; said it was all owing to her carelessness, and that he meant to flog her for it. She told, him with all the feeling of a mother, the circumstances of its death. But her story availed her nothing against the savage brutality of her master. She was severely whipped. A healthy child four months old was then considered worth $100 in North Carolina."

T. Weld, American Slavery As It Is: Testimony of a Thousand Witnesses at 15-16 (American Anti-Slavery Society 1839), available from the Library of Congress at *www.hathitrust.org/digital_library*

awakened by the shrieks and piteous cries of poor Esther. My sleeping place was on the floor of a little, rough closet, which opened into the kitchen; and through the cracks of its unplaned boards, I could distinctly see and hear what was going on, without being seen by old master. Esther's wrists were firmly tied, and the twisted rope was fastened to a strong staple in a heavy wooden joist above, near the fireplace. Here she stood, on a bench, her arms tightly drawn over her breast. Her back and shoulders were bare to the waist. Behind her stood old master, with cowskin in hand, preparing his barbarous work with all manner of harsh, coarse, and tantalizing epithets. The screams of his victim were most piercing. He was cruelly deliberate, and protracted the torture, as one who was delighted with the scene. Again and again he drew the hateful whip through his hand, adjusting it with a view of dealing the most pain-giving blow. Poor Esther had never yet been severely whipped, and her shoulders were plump and tender. Each blow, vigorously laid on, brought screams as well as blood. *"Have mercy; Oh! Have mercy"* she cried; *"I won't do so no more;"* but her piercing cries seemed only to increase his fury. His answers to them are too coarse and blasphemous to be produced here. The whole scene, with all its attendants, was revolting and shocking, to the last degree; and when the motives of this brutal castigation are considered, language has no power to convey a just sense of its awful criminality. After laying on some thirty or forty stripes, old master untied his suffering victim, and let her get down. She could scarcely stand, when untied. From my heart I pitied her, and— child though I was—the outrage kindled in me a feeling far from peaceful; but I was hushed, terrified, stunned, and could do nothing, and the fate of Esther might be mine next. The scene here described was often repeated in the case of poor Esther, and her life, as I knew it, was one of wretchedness.

THE STORY OF NELLY'S "IMPUDENCE"

In *The Story of Nelly's "Impudence,"* Frederick Douglass provides another description of severe brutality against a female slave. Mr. Douglass also provides, however, a lesson in the value of African-Americans asserting themselves against oppression:[720]

> [A]fter the whipping of Aunt Esther, I saw many cases of the same shocking nature, not only in my master's house, but on Col. Lloyd's plantation. One of the first which I saw, and which greatly agitated me, was the whipping of a woman belonging to Col. Lloyd, named Nelly. The offense alleged against Nelly, was one of the commonest and most indefinite in the whole catalogue of offenses usually laid to the charge of slaves, viz; "impudence." This may mean almost anything, or nothing at all, just according to the caprice of the master or overseer, at the moment. But, whatever it is, or is not, if it gets the name of "impudence," the party charged with it is sure of a flogging. This offense may be committed in various ways; in the tone of an answer; in answering at all; in not answering; in the expression of countenance; in the motion of the head; in the gait, manner and bearing of the slave. In the case under consideration, I can easily believe that, according to all slaveholding standards, here was a genuine instance of impudence. In Nelly there were all the necessary conditions for committing the offense. She was a bright mulatto, the recognized wife of a favorite "hand" on board Col. Lloyd's sloop, and the mother of five sprightly children. She was a vigorous and spirited woman, and one of the most likely, on the plantation, to be guilty of impudence. My attention was called to the scene, by the noise, curses and screams that proceeded from it; and, on going a little in that direction, I came upon the parties engaged in the skirmish. Mr. Sevier, the overseer, had hold of Nelly, when I caught sight of them; he was endeavoring to drag her toward a tree, which endeavor Nelly was sternly resisting; but to no purpose, except to retard the progress of the overseer's plans. Nelly—as I have said—was the mother of five children; three of them were present, and though quite small, (from seven to ten years old, I should think,) they gallantly came to their mother's defense, and gave the overseer an excellent pelting with stones. One of the little fellows ran up, seized the overseer

SLAVE DISCIPLINE

"[Sarah] Grimke is a daughter of the late Judge Grimke, of the Supreme Court of South Carolina, and sister of the late Hon. Thomas S. Grimke. [She provides the following testimony.]
"I heard [a female acquaintance of mine in Charleston] say, that she had the ears of her waiting maid slit for some petty theft. This she told me in the presence of the girl, who was standing in the room. She often had the helpless victims of her cruelty severely whipped, not scrupling herself to wield the instrument of torture, and with her own hands inflict severe chastisement. Her husband was less inhuman than his wife, but he was often goaded on by her to acts of great severity. ...

T. Weld, American Slavery As It Is: Testimony of a Thousand Witnesses at 22, 23 (American Anti-Slavery Society 1839) (Narrative of Mr. Nehemiah Caulkins), available from the Library of Congress at *www.hathitrust.org/digital_library*

720 Douglass, My Bondage and My Freedom at 92-95. Emphasis in original.

by the leg and bit him; but the monster was too busily engaged with Nelly, to pay any attention to the assaults of the children. There were numerous bloody marks on Mr. Sevier's face, when I first saw him, and they increased as the struggle went on. The imprints of Nelly's fingers were visible, and I was glad to see them. Amidst the wild screams of the children—*"Let my mammy go"—"let my mammy go"*—there escaped, from between the teeth of the bullet-headed overseer, a few bitter curses, mingled with threats, that "he would teach the d—d b—h how to give a white man impudence." There is no doubt that Nelly felt herself superior, in some respects, to the slaves around her. She was a wife and a mother; her husband was a valued and favorite slave. Besides, he was one of the first hands on board of the sloop, and the sloop hands—since they had to represent the plantation abroad—were generally treated tenderly. The overseer never was allowed to whip Harry; why then should he be allowed to whip Harry's wife? Thoughts of this kind, no doubt, influenced her; but, for what ever reason, she nobly resisted, and, unlike most of the slaves, seemed determined to make her whipping cost Mr. Sevier as much as possible. The blood on his (and her) face, attested her skill, as well as her courage and dexterity in using her nails. Maddened by her resistance, I expected to see Mr. Sevier level her to the ground by a stunning blow; but no; like a savage bull-dog—which he resembled both in temper and appearance—he maintained his grip, and steadily dragged his victim toward the tree, disregarding alike her blows, and the cries of the children for their mother's release. He would, doubtless, have knocked her down with his hickory stick, but that such act might have cost him his place. It is often deemed advisable to knock a man slave down, in order to tie him, but it is considered cowardly and inexcusable, in an overseer, thus to deal with a *woman*. He is expected to tie her up, and to give her what is called, in southern parlance, a "genteel flogging," without any very great outlay of strength or skill. I watched, with palpitating interest, the course of the preliminary struggle, and was saddened by every new advantage gained over her by the ruffian. There were times when she seemed likely to get the better of the brute, but he finally overpowered her, and succeeded in getting his rope around her arms, and in firmly tying her to the tree, at which he had been aiming. This done, and Nelly was at the mercy of his merciless lash; and now, what followed, I have no heart to describe. The cowardly creature made good his every threat; and wielded the lash with all the hot zest of furious revenge. The cries of the woman, while undergoing the terrible infliction, were mingled with those of the children, sounds which I hope the reader may never be called upon to hear. When Nelly was untied, her back was covered with blood. The red stripes were all over her shoulders. She was whipped—severely whipped; but she was not subdued, for she continued to denounce the overseer, and to call him every vile name. He had bruised her flesh, but had left her invincible spirit undaunted. Such floggings are seldom repeated by the same overseer. They prefer to whip those who are most easily whipped. …

STILL MORE ON BREEDING SLAVES

"A planter offered a white man of my acquaintance twenty dollars for every one of his female slaves, whom he would get in the family way. This offer was no doubt made for the purpose of improving the stock, on the same principle that farmers endeavor to improve their cattle by crossing the breed."

T. Weld, American Slavery As It Is: Testimony of a Thousand Witnesses at 15-16 (American Anti-Slavery Society 1839), available from the Library of Congress at *www.hathitrust.org/digital_library*

"Whipping Slaves, Missouri, 1856", *Slavery Images: A Visual Record of the African Slave Trade and Slave Life in the Early African Diaspora,* accessed November 15, 2020, *http://slaveryimages.org/s/slaveryimages/item/1284*

THE STORY OF FED'S HEAT-STROKE EXPERIMENT AND OTHER TRIALS

"To Planters and Others.—Wanted, fifty negroes. Any person, having sick negroes, considered incurable by their respective physicians, and wishing to dispose of them, Dr. S. will pay cash for negroes affected with scrofula, or king's evil, confirmed hypochondriasm, apoplexy, diseases of the liver, kidneys, spleen, stomach and intestines, bladder and its appendages, diarrhoea, (sic) dysentery, &c. The highest cash price will be paid, on application as above,' (viz., 'Medical Infirmary, No.110 Church Street, Charleston.')"[721]

§ § §

Dr. Stephen Kenny cites a circular published by Charleston's Medical College of South Carolina:[722]

"No place in the United States offers as great opportunities for the acquisition of Anatomical knowledge, subjects being obtained from among the colored population in sufficient number for every purpose, and proper dissection carried on without offending any individual in the community. Those impediments which exist in so many other places, to the prosecution of this study, are not here thrown in the path of the Student, public feeling being rather favourable than hostile to the advancement of the Science of Anatomy."

§ § §

Dr. Todd Savitt provides the following example of unconsented (except by the slave's master) medical experimentation upon a slave, named Fed, after the doctor had treated the master successfully as a patient:[723]

There lived in Clinton, seat of Jones County, Georgia, during the 1820s and early 1830s, a physician-planter who was attempting to discover the best remedies for heat stroke. This man, Dr. Thomas Hamilton, borrowed the slave Fed from a grateful patient in order to test some of his medications on a human subject. He had a hole dug in the ground which he then had heated with fire to a high temperature. Fed sat naked on a stool on a platform placed within this ovenlike pit with only his head above ground level. To retain the heat Hamilton fastened wet blankets over the hole. Fed took a different medicine each of the five or six times he entered the pit over a period of two or three weeks, so that Hamilton could determine which preparation best enabled the slave to

"Untitled Image (Portrait of John Brown)", *Slavery Images: A Visual Record of the African Slave Trade and Slave Life in the Early African Diaspora,* accessed November 15, 2020, *http://slaveryimages.org/s/slaveryimages/item/2512*

721 Goodell, at 86-87.

722 Kenny, "'I can do the child no good': Dr. Sims and the Enslaved Infants of Montgomery, Alabama, Social History of Medicine" at 4 (2007), available at *www.researchgate.net/publication/5246334_'I_can_do_the_child_no_good'_Dr_Sims_and_the_Enslaved_Infants_of_Montgomery_Alabama, accessed Oct. 10, 2020.* Footnotes omitted.

723 Savitt, "The Use of Blacks for Medical Experimentation and Demonstration in the Old South" at 344, Jour. Of Southern History, Vol. 48, No. 3 (Aug. 1982).
See also Washington at 52-55.

withstand high temperatures. Fed fainted each time from the heat and from exhaustion (he had put in a full day's work before each experiment). According to Fed's account of the proceedings the doctor found cayenne pepper to be the most effective preparation. ...

Hamilton's crude experiments did little to advance medical knowledge. ...

Harriet Washington quotes Fed as stating:[724]

I was, it seems a strong and likely subject to be experimented upon, and the Doctor having fixed the thing in his mind, asked [my master] to lend me to him. This he did at once, never caring to inquire what was going to be done with me. I myself did not know. Even if I had been made aware of the nature of the trials I was about to undergo, I could not have helped myself. There was nothing for it but passive resignation, and I gave myself up in ignorance and in much fear.

Fed later adopted the name "John Brown," which was a name used on a forged pass he was given by a man assisting Fed in his successful escape (after several failures). Using the name John Brown, Fed published his slave narrative.[725]

In his narrative, Mr. Brown states that, following the first experiment:[726]

Three or four days afterwards, the experiment was repeated, and so on for five or six times, the Doctor allowing me a few days' rest between each trial. His object was to ascertain which of the medicines he administered to me on these occasions, enabled me to withstand the greatest degree of heat. He found that cayenne-pepper tea accomplished this object; and a very nice thing he made of it.

Mr. Brown also describes how Dr. Hamilton marketed his "findings" from the heat-stroke experiments:[727]

As soon as he got back home, he advertised that he had discovered a remedy for sun-stroke. It consisted of pills, which were to be dissolved in a dose of cayenne-pepper tea, without which, he said, the pills would not produce any effect. Nor do I see how they should have done so, for they were only made of common flour. However, he succeeded in getting them into general use, and as he asked a good price, he soon realized a large fortune.

Dr. Hamilton then conducted yet additional experiments on Mr. Brown (Fed) to test a diet and to discover how deep Mr. Brown's black skin was:[728]

Having completed his series of experiments upon me, in the heated pit, and allowed me some days' rest, I was put on a diet, and then, during a period of about three weeks, he bled me every other day. At the end of that time he found I was failing, so he left off, and I got a month's rest, to regain a little strength. At the expiration of that time, he set to work to ascertain how deep my black skin went. This he did by applying blisters to my hands, legs and feet, which bear the scars to this day. He continued until he drew up the dark skin from between the upper and the under one. He used to blister me at intervals of about two weeks. He also tried other experiments upon me, which I cannot dwell upon.

---

724 Washington at 53.

725 J. Brown, **SLAVE LIFE IN GEORGIA: A NARRATIVE OF THE LIFE, SUFFERINGS, AND ESCAPE OF JOHN BROWN, A FUGITIVE SLAVE, NOW IN ENGLAND** at 149 (1855), Academic Affairs Library, Univ. of North Carolina at Chapel Hill, available at *docsouth.unc.edu/neh/jbrown/jbrown.html* ("J. Brown").

726 J. Brown, at 47.

727 J. Brown, at 49.

728 J. Brown, at 47-48.

> Altogether, and from first to last, I was in his hands, under treatment, for about nine months, at the end of which period I had become so weak, that I was no longer able to work in the fields.

Eventually, Mr. Brown, following his escape and being at risk due to the Fugitive Slave Law, "fled to England."[729]

As the advertisements at the beginning of this section by medical institutions bragging about access to African-Americans for experimentation demonstrate, medical experimentation on slaves was not uncommon.

Dr. Kenny provides the following description of the medical abuse of a small child by two physicians. This description suggests a willingness to undertake completely unnecessary, painful, and potentially dangerous experimentation on a slave—an infant—without parental consent.

Describing this incident, Dr. Stephen Kenny states:[730]

> The [slave] child had great difficulty feeding and had been sick for four or five months—"more or less all its life". Finding the child incapacitated by involuntary muscular contractions—"a regular gyration"—Vickers initially placed the child on its side and in "one hour the spasmodic action … began to subside". But, it then occurred to Vickers to indulge in some speculative physical investigations, "with the view of observing the symptoms of … a trismal character". This involved aggravating and reproducing the painful paralysis, by pressurizing the parietal and occipital bones. Vickers occupied himself in this way "for nearly half an hour … alternately producing and relieving the symptoms of *lock-jaw;* in the first instance by *displacing* the occiput and, in the next, by *replacing* it" …
>
> Eleven days later, Vickers returned with Sims, who wanted "the satisfaction of fully verifying" these "observations on the trismal symptoms in connection with the displaced occiput". Sims saw that the child's cranial bones were still "movable by pressure", and through "the use of considerable force", succeeded in emulating Vickers by again displacing the occiput … .

GRAVE ROBBING

"[C]onstruction sites throughout the country have yielded evidence of medical grave robbing. The largest and earliest African burial site in the nation was revealed in June 1991 during preparations to build on the lower Manhattan site of what is now the Foley Square Federal Office Tower Building in New York City. Construction workers unearthed 427 skeletons in what had been consecrated as the 'Negros Burying Ground' in the eighteenth century. In 1992, the team of Michael Blakely, director of Howard University's W. Montague Cobb Biological Anthropology Laboratory, found widespread evidence of grave robbing, including missing coffins, as well as bodies and skulls that displayed anatomists marks."

H. Washington, Medical Apartheid: The Dark History of Medical Experimentation on Black Americans from Colonial Times to the Present at 123 (Anchor Books, 2006)

729 J. Brown, at 135 *et seq.*

730 Kenny, "'I can do the child no good': Dr. Sims and the Enslaved Infants of Montgomery, Alabama, Social History of Medicine" at 12 (2007) *www.researchgate.net/publication/5246334_'I_can_do_the_child_no_good'_Dr_Sims_and_the_Enslaved_Infants_of_Montgomery_Alabama,* accessed Oct. 10, 2020. Footnotes omitted. Emphasis in original.

REST IN PIECES

"Construction workers renovating a stately 154-year old Greek revival structure that once housed the Medical College of Georgia (MCG) stumbled upon a nightmare cached beneath the building. Strewn beneath its concrete floor lay a chaos of desiccated body parts and nearly ten thousand human bones and skulls, many bearing the marks of nineteenth-century anatomy tools or numbered with India ink. …

"The bodies in the basement had been spirited by night from the graveyard—but not from just any graveyard: Most were taken from Cedar Grove Cemetery, an African-American burial ground. … Since its founding, black Augusta residents had consistently complained of grave robbing there. Also, the college's four or five porters had all named the black cemetery in their periodic reports on the provenance of the cadavers they provided to students each term. …"

H. Washington, Medical Apartheid: The Dark History of Medical Experimentation on Black Americans from Colonial Times to the Present at 120-22 (Anchor Books, 2006). See also Savitt, *The Use of Blacks for Medical Experimentation and Demonstration in the Old South* at 339, Jour. Of Southern History, Vol. 48, No. 3 (Aug. 1982).

THE STORY OF SAM'S GRIN

Harriett Washington provides a particularly graphic example of the helplessness of slaves under the control of certain slave doctors. The doctor in this case was the famous Dr. Marion Sims, who reported on the procedure, with the medical journal remarking that it was "pleased to record this highly creditable achievement of a Southern surgeon."[731]

Sam was a slave. Sam had "an incessant racking pain in his jaw," which distracted him and kept him up at night. Sam's owner tried "a homemade concoction" that "produce[d] a painful boil on Sam's gums." Sam "became worthless in the fields." Sam's owner called in a doctor, who concluded that Sam had "a cancer of his lower jawbone."

The doctor turned to Dr. Sims, as a surgeon. Sam, however, "stonily declared himself 'determined not to be foiled in the attempt' by Dr. Sims to operate."

Ms. Washington states that, unfortunately for Sam, Dr. Sims had already decided not only that he would operate on Sam, but would do so "in a teaching clinic for a medical audience of students and potential proteges." Sims "hoped to immortalize the operation in a medical publication … ."

When the two met, Dr. Sims greeted Sam with "all smiles." "He kindly inquired into the slave's health and graciously invited Sam to have a seat." Dr. Sims had rigged the seat "surreptitiously" with planks. "[A]s soon as Sam was seated, five young physicians bounded forward to restrain him with straps" on Sam's head, body and extremities. "Sam, Sims noted, 'appeared to be very much alarmed!'"

"Sims operated for forty minutes to remove a large section of Sam's lower jawbone, sans anesthesia." Sims declared "with satisfaction" that "his surgical innovation" had proved itself regardless of "whether the patient is willing or not."

The medical report stated that "Sam's mouth is always open in a wide grin."

731 Washington, at 101-03.

THE STORY OF BOMEFREE: DEATH OF A LONELY LOYAL SERVANT

In theory, slave masters had a societal obligation to provide for the care of their "helpless" slaves. Excluded from earning income, slaves could not save money for retirement or health care for themselves or their families. Slavery was their "social security." That created a tension, however. Masters were making economic decisions. Slaves wanted food, clothing, housing and medical care, for which masters must pay.

Masters responded in a variety of ways. Some were more conscientious than others. The slave society asked few, if any, questions.

The tension became especially obvious when slaves were ill or old. Under those conditions, the slaves were not producing income for the masters. They were simply an expense. As a result, while there were masters who would provide a degree of support for the slaves they "loved," other masters focused more on the bottom line, often viewing the slaves simply as a financial drain.

Since life does not last forever, not only slaves, but masters died. When that occurred, even a considerate, but dead, master could do nothing for the slaves. Others who may have no feelings for the slaves would settle the estates and divide the "property," including slaves. Slave families easily could be, and were, separated. The heirs could be the masters' children or other relatives who had more interest in avoiding obligations ("burdens") to care for non-producing slaves. A potentially less pecuniary master's gratuitous motivation to provide care no longer existed.

Keeping those observations in mind, the *Story of Bomefree* describes Sojourner Truth's memories of her father, whose name was James, but whom she called "Bomefree." Bomefree's *Story*, assembled sequentially from Ms. Truth's recollections, illustrates the fate older loyal slaves could endure after having served masters for decades, even for life:[732]

> Isabella's [Sojourner's earlier name] father was very tall and straight, when young, which gave him the name of "Bomefree,"—low Dutch for tree—at least, this is Sojourner's pronunciation of it and by this name 'he usually went. The most familiar appellation of her mother was "Mau-mau Bett." She was the mother of some ten or twelve children; though Sojourner is far from knowing the exact number of her brothers and sisters; she being the youngest, save one, and all older than herself having been sold before her remembrance. She was privileged to behold six of them while she remained a slave.
>
> Of the two that immediately preceded her in age, a boy of five years, and a girl of three, who were sold when she was an infant, she heard much; and she wishes that all who would fain believe that slave parents have not natural affection for their offspring could have listened as she did, while Bomefree and Mau-mau Bett,—their dark cellar lighted by a blazing pine-knot,—would sit for hours, recalling and recounting every endearing, as well as harrowing circumstance that taxed memory could supply, from the histories of those dear departed ones, of whom they had been robbed, and for whom their hearts still bled. ...
>
> § § §
>
> At length, the never-to be-forgotten day of the terrible auction arrived, when the "slaves, horses, and other cattle" of Charles Ardinburgh, deceased, were to be put under the hammer, and again change

732 Dictated by S. Truth, written and edited by O. Gilbert, at 15-16, 18-25. Emphasis in original.

masters. Not only Isabella and Peter, but their mother, was now destined to the auction block, and would have been struck off with the rest to the highest bidder, but for the following circumstance: A question arose among the heirs, "Who shall be burdened with Bomefree, when we have sent away his faithful Mau-mau Bett?" He was becoming weak and infirm; his limbs were painfully rheumatic and distorted—more from exposure and hardship than from old age, though he was several years older than Mau-mau Bett: he was no longer considered of value, but must soon be a burden and care to some one. After some contention on the point at issue, none being willing to be burdened with him, it was finally agreed, as most expedient for the heirs, that the price of Mau-mau Bett should be sacrificed, and she receive her freedom, on condition that she take care of and support her faithful James,—faithful, not only to her as a husband, but proverbially faithful as a slave to those who would not willingly sacrifice a dollar for *his* comfort, now that he had commenced his descent into the dark vale of decrepitude and suffering. This important decision was received as joyful news indeed to our ancient couple, who were the objects of it, and who were trying to prepare their hearts for a severe struggle, and one altogether new to them, as they had never before been separated; for, though ignorant, helpless, crushed in spirit, and weighed down with hardship and cruel bereavement, they were still human, and their human hearts beat within them with as true an affection as ever caused a human heart to beat. And their anticipated separation now, in the decline of life, after the last child had been torn from them, must have been truly appalling. Another privilege was granted them—that of remaining occupants of the same dark, humid cellar I have before described: otherwise, they were to support themselves as they best could. And as her mother was still able to do considerable work, and her father a little, they got on for some time very comfortably. The strangers who rented the house were humane people, and very kind to them; they were not rich, and owned no slaves. How long this state of things continued, we are unable to say, as Isabella had not then sufficiently cultivated her organ of time to calculate years, or even weeks or hours. But she thinks her mother must have lived several years after the death of Master Charles. She remembers going to visit her parents some three or four times before the death of her mother, and a good deal of time seemed to her to intervene between each visit.

At length her mother's health began to decline—a fever-sore made its ravages on one of her limbs, and the palsy began to shake her frame; still, she and James tottered about, picking up a little here and there, which, added to the mites contributed by their kind neighbors, sufficed to sustain life, and drive famine from the door.

§ § §

One morning, in early autumn, (from the reason above mentioned, we cannot tell what year,) Mau-mau Bett told James she would make him a loaf of rye-bread, and get Mrs. Simmons, their kind neighbor, to bake it for them, as she would bake that forenoon. James told her he had engaged to rake after the cart for his neighbors that morning; but before he commenced, he would pole off some apples from a tree near, which they were allowed to gather; and if she could get some of them baked with the bread, it would give it a nice relish for their dinner. He beat off the apples, and soon after, saw Mau-mau Bett come out and gather them up.

At the blowing of the horn for dinner, he groped his way into his cellar, anticipating his humble, but warm and nourishing meal; when, lo! instead of being cheered by the sight and odor of fresh-baked bread and the savory apples, his cellar seemed more cheerless than usual, and at first neither sight nor sound met eye or ear. But, on groping his way through the room, his staff, which he used as a pioneer to go before, and warn him of danger, seemed to be impeded in its progress, and a low, gurgling, choking sound proceeded from the object before him, giving him the first intimation of the truth as it was, that Mau-mau Bett, his bosom companion, the only remaining member of his large family, had fallen in a fit of the palsy, and lay helpless and senseless on the earth! Who among us, located in pleasant homes, surrounded with every comfort, and so many kind and sympathizing friends, can picture to ourselves the dark and desolate state of poor old James—penniless, weak, lame, and nearly blind, as he was at the moment he found his companion was removed from him, and he was left alone in the world, with no one to aid, comfort, or console him? for she never revived again, and lived only a few hours after being discovered senseless by her poor bereaved James.

§ § §

Isabella and Peter were permitted to see the remains of their mother laid in their last narrow dwelling, and to make their bereaved father a little visit, ere they returned to their servitude. And most piteous were the lamentations of the poor old man, when, at last, *they* also were obliged to bid him "Farewell!" Juan Fernandes, on his desolate island, was not so pitiable an object as this poor lame man. Blind and crippled, he was too superannuated to think for a moment of taking care of himself, and he greatly feared no persons would interest themselves in his behalf. "Oh," he would exclaim, "I had thought God would take me first,—Mau-mau was so much smarter than I, and could get about and take care of herself;—and I am *so old*, and so *helpless*. What is to become of me? I can't do any thing more—my children are all gone, and here I am left helpless and alone." "And then, as I was taking leave of him," said his daughter, in relating it, "he raised his voice, and cried aloud like a child.—*Oh, how he* DID *cry!* I HEAR it *now* and remember it as well as if it were but yesterday—*poor old man!!!* He thought God had done it all—and my heart bled within me at the sight of his misery. He begged me to get permission to come and see him sometimes, which I readily and heartily promised him." But when all had left him, the Ardinburghs, having some feeling left for their faithful and favorite slave, "took turns about" in keeping him—permitting him to stay a few weeks at one house, and then a while at another, and so around. If, when he made a removal, the place where he was going was not too far off, he took up his line of march, staff in hand, and asked for no assistance. If it was twelve or twenty miles, they gave him a ride. While he was living in this way, Isabella was twice permitted to visit him. Another time she walked twelve miles, and carried her infant in her arms to see him, but when she reached the place where she hoped to find him, he had just left for a place some twenty miles distant, and she never saw him more. The last time she did see him, she found him seated on a rock, by the-road side, alone, and far from any house. He was then migrating from the house of one Ardinburgh to that of another, several miles distant. His hair was white like wool—he was almost blind—and his gait was more a creep than a walk—but the weather was warm and pleasant, and he did not dislike the journey. When Isabella addressed him, he recognized her voice, and was exceeding glad to see her. He was assisted to mount the wagon, was carried back to the famous cellar of which we have spoken, and there they held their last earthly conversation. He again, as usual, bewailed his loneliness,—spoke in tones of anguish of his many children, saying, "They are all taken away from me! I have now not one to give me a cup of cold water—why should I live and not die?" Isabella, whose heart yearned over her father, and who would have made any sacrifice to have been able to be with, and take care of him, tried to comfort, by telling him that "she had heard the white folks say, that all the slaves in the State would be freed in ten years, and that then she would come and take care of him." "I would take just as good care of you as Mau-mau would, if she was here"—continued Isabel. "Oh, my child." replied he, "I cannot live that long." "Oh do, daddy, do live, and I will take such good care of you," was her rejoinder. She now says, "Why, I thought then, in my ignorance, that he could live, if he would. I just as much thought so, as I ever thought any thing in my life—and I insisted on his living: but he shook his head, and insisted he could not."

SLAVERY WAS "SOCIAL SECURITY"

Virginia Eleventh Grade Textbook:
"the slave enjoyed what we might call comprehensive social security."

Dean, "'Who Controls the Past Controls the Future:' The Virginia History Textbook Controversy at 334 (Virginia Magazine of History and Biography, vol 17, no. 4, 2009)

But before Bomefree's good constitution would yield either to age, exposure, or a strong desire to die, the Ardinburghs again tired of him, and offered freedom to two old slaves—Caesar, brother of Mau-mau Bett, and his wife Betsey—on condition that they should take care of James. (I was about to say, "their brother-in-law"—but as slaves are neither *husbands* nor wives in law the idea of their being brothers-in-law is truly ludicrous.) And although they were too old and infirm to take care of themselves, (Caesar having been afflicted for a long time with fever-sores, and his wife with the jaundice,) they eagerly accepted the boon of freedom, which had been the life-long desire of their souls—though at a time when emancipation was to them little more than destitution, and was a freedom more to be desired by the master than the slave. Sojourner declares of the slaves in their ignorance, that "their thoughts are no longer than her finger."

§ § §

A rude cabin, in a lone wood, far from any neighbors, was granted to our freed friends, as the only assistance they were now to expect. Bomefree, from this time, found his poor needs hardly supplied, as his new providers were scarce able to administer to their own wants. However, the time drew near when things were to be decidedly worse rather than better; for they had not been together long, before [Betsey] died, and shortly after, Caesar followed her to "that bourne from whence no traveller returns"—leaving poor James again desolate, and more helpless than ever before; as, this time, there was no kind family in the house, and the Ardinburghs no longer invited him to their homes. Yet, lone, blind and helpless as he was, James for a time lived on. One day, an aged colored woman, named Soan, called at his shanty, and James besought her, in the most moving manner, even with tears, to tarry awhile and wash and mend him up, so that he might once more be decent and comfortable; for he was suffering dreadfully with the filth and vermin that had collected upon him.

Soan was herself an emancipated slave, old and weak, with no one to care for her; and she lacked the courage to undertake a job of such seeming magnitude, fearing she might herself get sick, and perish there without assistance; and with great reluctance, and a heart swelling with pity, as she afterwards declared, she felt obliged to leave him in his wretchedness and filth. And shortly after her visit, this faithful slave, this deserted wreck of humanity, was found on his miserable pallet, frozen and stiff in death. The kind angel had come at last, and relieved him of the many miseries that his fellow-man had heaped upon him. Yes, he had died, chilled and starved, with none to speak a kindly word, or do a kindly deed for him, in that last dread hour of need!

The news of his death reached the ears of John Ardinburgh, a grandson of the old Colonel; and he declared that "Bomefree, who had ever been a kind and faithful slave, should now have a good funeral." And now, gentle reader, what think you constituted a good funeral? Answer—some black paint for the coffin, and a jug of ardent spirits! What a compensation for a life of toil, of patient submission to repeated robberies of the most aggravated kind, and, also, far more than murderous neglect!! Mankind often vainly attempt to atone for unkindness or cruelty to the living, by honoring the same after death; but John Ardinburgh undoubtedly meant *his* pot of paint and jug of whisky should act as an opiate on his slaves, rather than on his own seared conscience.

AUNTY, IN THE HOUSE

"A. GUTHRIE, Esq., elder in the Presbyterian church at Putnam, Muskingum county, Ohio, furnishes the testimony which follows.

"A near female friend of mine in company with another young lady, in attempting to visit a sick woman on Washington's Bottom, Wood county, Virginia, missed the way, and stopping to ask directions of a group of colored children on the outskirts of the plantation of Francis Keen, Sen., they were told to ask 'aunty, in the house.' On entering the hut, says my informant, I beheld such a sight as I hope never to see again; its sole occupant was a female slave of the said Keen—her whole wearing apparel consisted of a frock, made of the coarsest tow cloth, and so scanty, that it could not have been made more tight around her person. In the hut there was neither table, chair, nor chest—a stool and a rude fixture in one corner, were all its furniture, On this last were a little straw and a few old remnants of what had been bedding—all exceedingly filthy.

"The woman thus situated *had been for more than a day in travail, without any assistance, any nurse, or any kind of proper provision*—during the night she said some fellow slave woman would stay with her, and the aforesaid children through the day. From a woman, who was a slave of Keen's at the same time, my informant learned, that this poor woman suffered for three days, and then died—when too late to save her life her master sent assistance. It was understood to be a rule of his, to neglect his women entirely in such times of trial, unless they previously came and informed him, and asked for aid."

T. Weld, American Slavery As It Is: Testimony of a Thousand Witnesses at 15-16 (American Anti-Slavery Society 1839), available from the Library of Congress at *www.hathitrust.org/digital_library*

DENIAL OF RELIGIOUS FREEDOM

"In a law enacted by the state of Georgia, December 13th, 1792, with the title, 'To protect religious societies in the exercise of their religious duties,' it is required of every justice of the peace, &c., and every civil officer of a county being present, &c. &c, to take into custody any person who shall interrupt or disturb a congregation of *white persons* assembled at any church, &c., and to impose a fine on the offender; and in default of payment he may be imprisoned, &c. &c.; yet the same law concludes in these words:—'No congregation or company *of negroes* shall, under pretence of divine worship, assemble themselves contrary to the act regulating patrols.'"

G. Stroud, A Sketch of the Laws Relating to Slavery in the Several States of the United States of America at 64 (H. Longstreth, 1856), available from the Library of Congress at *www.hathitrust.org/digital_library.* Emphasis in original.

"Prayer Meeting, Georgia, 1873-74", *Slavery Images: A Visual Record of the African Slave Trade and Slave Life in the Early African Diaspora,* accessed November 27, 2020, *http://slaveryimages.org/s/slaveryimages/item/1852*

THE STORY OF DEMBY'S DEMISE AND OTHER MURDERS

Frederick Douglass provides the following episode demonstrating dramatically the sheer power of the master and the overseer over their slaves. Although there were laws against abuse of slaves that was not "moderate," the laws were rarely, if ever, enforced.

Mr. Douglass' account is yet another illustration of white fear of African-Americans. The philosophy was that, without complete repression, no matter how brutal, the slaves would refuse to submit to their fate and might rise against their masters.

Frederick Douglass describes the following:[733]

> Mr. Gore [an overseer] once undertook to whip one of Colonel Lloyd's slaves, by the name of Demby. He had given Demby but few stripes, when, to get rid of the scourging, [Demby] ran and plunged himself into a creek, and stood there at the depth of his shoulders, refusing to come out. Mr. Gore told him that he would give him three calls, and that, if he did not come out at the third call, he would shoot him. The first call was given. Demby made no response, but stood his ground. The second and third calls were given with the same result. Mr. Gore then, without consultation or deliberation with any one, not even giving Demby an additional call, raised his musket to his face, taking deadly aim at his standing victim, and in an instant poor Demby was no more. His mangled body sank out of sight, and blood and brains marked the water where he had stood.
>
> A thrill of horror flashed through every soul upon the plantation, excepting Mr. Gore. He alone seemed cool and collected. He was asked by Colonel Lloyd and my old master, why he resorted to this extraordinary expedient. His reply was, (as well as I can remember,) that Demby had become unmanageable. He was setting a dangerous example to the other slaves,—one which, if suffered to pass without some such demonstration on his part, would finally lead to the total subversion of all rule and order upon the plantation. He argued that if one slave refused to be corrected, and escaped with his life, the other slaves would soon copy the example; the result of which would be, the freedom of the slaves, and the enslavement of the whites. Mr. Gore's defence was satisfactory. He was continued in his station as overseer upon the home plantation. His fame as an overseer went abroad. His horrid crime was not even submitted to judicial investigation. It was committed in the presence of slaves, and they of course could neither institute a suit, nor testify against him … .

SLAVE STARVATION

"[Sarah] Grimke [provides the following additional testimony.] "A friend of mine, in whose veracity I have entire confidence told me that about two years ago, a woman in Charleston with whom I was well acquainted, had starved a female slave to death. She was confined in a solitary apartment, kept constantly tied, and condemned to the slow and horrible death of starvation. This woman was notoriously cruel. …"

T. Weld, American Slavery As It Is: Testimony of a Thousand Witnesses at 22, 23 (American Anti-Slavery Society 1839) (Narrative of Mr. Nehemiah Caulkins), available from the Library of Congress at *www.hathitrust.org/digital_library*

733 Douglass, Narrative at 22-23.

Mr. Douglass, recounting details of incidents in which slaveholders had killed slaves without punishment, states as another example that:[734]

> As an evidence of the reckless disregard of human life—where the life is that of a slave—I may state the notorious fact, that the wife of Mr. Giles Hicks, who lived but a short distance from Col. Lloyd's, with her own hands murdered my wife's cousin, a young girl between fifteen and sixteen years of age—mutilating her person in a most shocking manner. The atrocious woman, in the paroxysm of her wrath, not content with murdering her victim, literally mangled her face, and broke her breast bone. Wild, however, and infuriated as she was, she took the precaution to cause the slave-girl to be buried; but the facts of the case coming abroad, very speedily led to the disinterment of the remains of the murdered slave-girl. A coroner's jury was assembled, who decided that the girl had come to her death by severe beating. It was ascertained that the offense for which this girl was thus hurried out of the world, was this: she had been set that night, and several preceding nights, to mind Mrs. Hicks's baby, and having fallen into a sound sleep, the baby cried, waking Mrs. Hicks, but not the slave-girl. Mrs. Hicks, becoming infuriated at the girl's tardiness, after calling her several times, jumped from her bed and seized a piece of fire-wood from the fire-place; and then, as she lay fast asleep, she deliberately pounded in her skull and breast-bone, and thus ended her life. I will not say that this most horrid murder produced no sensation in the community. It did produce a sensation; but, incredible to tell, the moral sense of the community was blunted too entirely by the ordinary nature of slavery horrors, to bring the murderess to punishment. A warrant was issued for her arrest, but, for some reason or other, that warrant was never served....

INABILITY TO TESTIFY

"Slavery is upheld by suppressing the testimony of its Victims."

W. Goodell, The American slave code in theory and practice at 300 (American and Foreign Anti-Slavery Society 1853), available from the Library of Congress at *www.hathitrust.org/digital_library*

Mr. Douglass describes other ghastly murders of slaves in Maryland, a border State in which there was represented to be less brutality against slaves than in the deep South:[735]

> I speak advisedly when I say this,—that killing a slave, or any colored person, in Talbot county, Maryland, is not treated as a crime, either by the courts or the community. Mr. Thomas Lanman, ship carpenter, of St. Michael's, killed two slaves, one of whom he butchered with a hatchet, by knocking his brains out. He used to boast of the commission of the awful and bloody deed. I have heard him do so laughingly saying, among other things, that he was the only benefactor of his country in the company, and that when "others would do as much as he had done, we should be relieved of the d—d niggers."

Harriet Jacobs describes murders by another master in North Carolina:[736]

> If a slave stole from him even a pound of meat or a peck of corn, if detection followed, he was put in chains and imprisoned, and so kept till his form was attenuated by hunger and suffering.
>
> A freshet once bore his wine cellar and meat house miles away from the plantation. Some slaves followed, and secured bits of meat and bottles of wine. Two were detected; a ham and some liquor being

734 Douglass, My Bondage and My Freedom at 125-26.

735 Douglass, My Bondage and My Freedom at 124-25.

736 Jacobs at 72.

found in their huts. They were summoned by their master. No words were used, but a club felled them to the ground. A rough box was their coffin, and their interment was a dog's burial. Nothing was said.

HOW GEORGE LOST HIS HEAD

The *Story of George* has differing versions, one more hideous than the other. Note, however, that I didn't say that the second version was not "horrible."

You might keep in mind as you read the *Story, IF* you chose to do so (and you might wish to avoid this one, even if you have made it this far in the book), that in either case the events establish certain key principles:

- Laws in Kentucky prohibited murdering slaves
- Despite the slave society's protests to the contrary, masters could, and would, take action that would damage their "property"
- In one way or another, despite the laws against and widespread societal disapproval of truly murderous violence against slaves, offending masters could find a way to escape punishment

Theodore Weld's book, **AMERICAN SLAVERY AS IT IS: TESTIMONY OF A THOUSAND WITNESSES**[737] contains extracts regarding *The Story of George* by citizens reporting the events.

The Story of George is one of the most spectacular incidents described in Mr. Weld's book. In this case, the perpetrators were nephews of President Thomas Jefferson. A minister, Rev. William Dickey, provided the information in a letter. Rev. Dickey relied on court proceedings in Kentucky and testimony therein and through meeting personally with the defendant Isham Lewis.[738]

According to Mr. Weld's book, a journal titled Human Rights (Aug. 1837) had first published the letter, including remarks regarding the incident and Rev. Dickey, stating, in part:

Hundreds of people around the mouth of Cumberland River are personally knowing to these facts. There are records of the court that tried the wretches. ... It ls quite needless, perhaps, to add, that the Rev. Wm. Dickey is a Presbyterian clergyman, one of the oldest members of the Chilicothe Presbytery, and greatly respected and beloved by the churches in Southern Ohio. He was born in South Carolina, and was for many years pastor of a church in Kentucky.

The following is Rev. Dickey's letter as published in **AMERICAN SLAVERY AS IT IS:**

> In the county of Livingston, Ky. near the mouth of Cumberland River, lived Lilburn Lewis, a sister's son of the celebrated Jefferson. He was the wealthy owner of a considerable gang of negroes, whom he drove constantly, fed sparingly, and lashed severely. The consequence was, that they would run away. Among the rest was an ill-thrived boy of about seventeen, who, having just returned from a skulking spell, was sent to the spring for water, and in returning let fall an elegant pitcher: it was dashed to shivers upon the rocks. This was made the occasion for reckoning with him. It was night, and the slaves were all at home. The master had them all collected in the most roomy negro-house, and a rousing fire put on. When the door was secured, that none might escape, either through *fear of him* or *sympathy with George,* he opened to them the design of the interview, namely, that they might be effectually advised to *stay at home* and *obey his orders.* All things now in train, he called up George, who approached his master with

737 T. Weld, **AMERICAN SLAVERY AS IT IS: TESTIMONY OF A THOUSAND WITNESSES** (American Anti-Slavery Society 1839), available from the Library of Congress at *www.hathitrust.org/digital_library* ("Weld").

738 Weld at 93-94. Emphasis in original.

SHOCK

"The following was written by a sister-in-law of Gerrit Smith, Esq., Peterboro. She is married to the son of a North Carolinian:

"In North Carolina, some years ago, several slaves were arrested for committing serious crimes and depredations, in the neighborhood of Wilmington, among other things, burning houses, and, in one or more instances, murder.

"It happened that the wife of one of these slaves resided in one of the most respectable families in W. in the capacity of nurse. Mr. J. *the first lawyer in the place,* came into the room, where the lady of the house was sitting, with the nurse, who held a child in her arms, and, addressing the nurse, said, Hannah! would you know your husband if you should see him ?—Oh, yes, sir, she replied—when HE DREW FROM BENEATH HIS CLOAK THE HEAD OF THE SLAVE, at the sight of which the poor woman immediately fainted. The heads of the others were placed upon poles, in some part of the town, afterwards known as 'Negro Head Point.'"

T. Weld, American Slavery As It Is: Testimony of a Thousand Witnesses at 161 (American Anti-Slavery Society 1839), available from the Library of Congress at *www.hathitrust.org/digital_library.* Emphasis in original.

unreserved submission. He bound him with cords; and by the assistance of Isham Lewis, his youngest brother, laid him on a broad bench, the *meat-block.* He then proceeded to *hack off George at the ankles!* It was with the *broad axe!* In vain did the unhappy victim *scream and roar!* for he was completely in his master's power; not a hand among so many durst interfere: casting the feet into the fire, he lectured them at some length.— He next *chopped him off below the knees!* George *roaring out* and praying his master to begin at the *other* end! He admonished them again, throwing the legs into the fire— then, above the knees, tossing the joints into the fire—the next stroke severed the thighs from the body; these were also committed to the flames—and so it may be said of the arms, head, and trunk, until all was in the fire! He threatened any of them with similar punishment who should in future disobey, run away, or disclose the proceedings of that evening. Nothing now remained but to consume the flesh and bones; and for this purpose the fire was brightly stirred until two hours after midnight; when a coarse and heavy back-wall, composed of rock and clay, covered the fire and the remains of George. It was the Sabbath—this put an end to the *amusements* of the evening. The negroes were now permitted to disperse, with charges to keep this matter among themselves, and never to whisper it in the neighborhood, under the penalty of a like punishment.

When he returned home and retired, his wife exclaimed, "Why, Mr. Lewis, where have you been, and what were you doing?" She had heard a strange *pounding* and dreadful *screams,* and had smelled something like fresh meat *burning.* The answer he returned was, that he had never enjoyed himself at a ball so well as he had enjoyed himself that night.

Next morning he ordered the hands to rebuild the back-wall, and he himself superintended the work, throwing the pieces of flesh that still remained, with the bones, behind, as it went up—thus hoping to conceal the matter. But it *could not be hid*—much as the negroes seemed to hazard, they did *whisper the horrid deed.* The neighbors came, and in his presence tore down the wall; and finding the remains of the boy, they apprehended Lewis and his brother, and testified against them. They were committed to jail that they might answer at the coming court for this shocking outrage; but finding security for their appearance at court, THEY WERE ADMITTED TO BAIL!

In the interim, other articles of evidence leaked out. That of Mrs. Lewis hearing a pounding, and screaming, and her smelling fresh meat burning, for not till now had this come out. He was offended with her for disclosing these things, alleging that they might have some weight against him at the pending trial.

In connection with this is another item, full of horror. Mrs. Lewis, or her girl, in making her bed one morning after this, found, under her bolster, *a keen* BUTCHER KNIFE! The appalling discovery forced from her the confession that she considered her life in jeopardy. Messrs. Rice and Philips, whose wives were her sisters, went to see her and to bring her away if she wished it. Mr. Lewis received them with all the expressions of *Virginia hospitality.* As soon as they were seated, they said, "Well, Letitia, we supposed that you might be unhappy here, and afraid for your life; and we have come to-day to take you to your father's, if you desire it." She said, "Thank you, kind brothers, I am indeed afraid for my life."—We need not interrupt the story to tell how much surprised he affected to be with this strange procedure of his brothers-in-law, and with this declaration of his wife. But all his professions of fondness for her, to the contrary notwithstanding, they rode off with her before his eyes.—He followed and overtook, and went with them to her father's; but she was locked up from him, with her own consent, and he returned home.

Now he saw that his character was gone, his respectable friends believed that he had massacred George; but, worst of all, he saw that they considered the life of the harmless Letitia was in danger from his perfidious hands. It was too much for his chivalry to sustain. The proud Virginian sunk under the accumulated load of public odium. He proposed to his brother Isham, who had been his accomplice in the George affair, that they should finish the play of life with a still deeper tragedy. The plan was, that they should shoot one another. Having made the hot-brained bargain, they repaired with their guns to the grave-yard, which was on an eminence in the midst of his plantation. It was inclosed with a railing, say thirty feet square. One was to stand at one railing, and the other over against him at the other. They were to make ready, take aim, and count deliberately 1, 2, 3, and then fire, Lilburn's will was written, and thrown down open beside him. They cocked their guns and raised them to their faces; but the peradventure occurring that, one of the guns might miss fire, Isham was sent for a rod, and when it was brought, Lilburn cut it off at about the length of two feet, and was showing his brother how the survivor might do, provided one of the guns should fail; (for they were determined upon going together;) but forgetting, perhaps, in the perturbation of the moment that the gun was cocked, when he touched the trigger with the rod the gun fired, and he fell, and died in a few minutes—and was with George in the eternal world, where the slave is free from his master. But poor Isham was so terrified with this unexpected occurrence and so confounded by the awful contortions of his brother's face, that he had not nerve enough to follow up the play, and finish the plan as was intended, but suffered Lilburn to go alone. The negroes came running to see what it meant that a gun should be fired in the grave-yard. There lay their master, dead! They ran for the neighbors. Isham still remained on the spot. The neighbors at the first charged him with the murder of his brother. But he, though as if he had lost more than half his mind, told the whole story; and the course or range of the ball in the dead man's body agreeing with his statement, Isham was not farther charged with Lilburn's death.

A DEATH FOR NO OFFENSE

"A negro was tied up, and flogged until the blood ran down and filled his shoes, so that when he raised either foot and set it down again, the blood would run over their tops. I could not look on any longer, but turned away in horror; the whipping was continued to the number of 500 lashes, as I understood; a quart of spirits of turpentine was then applied to his lacerated body. The same negro came down to my boat, to get some apples, and was so weak from his wounds and loss of blood, that he could not get up the bank, but fell to the ground. The crime for which the negro was whipped, was that of telling the other negroes, that the overseer had lain with his wife."

T. Weld, American Slavery As It Is: Testimony of a Thousand Witnesses at 69 (American Anti-Slavery Society 1839), available from the Library of Congress at *www.hathitrust.org/digital_library.*

> The Court sat—Isham was judged to be guilty of a capital crime in the affair of George He was to be hanged at Salem. The day was set. My good old father visited him in the prison—two or three times talked and prayed with him; I visited him once myself. We fondly hoped that he was a sincere penitent. Before the day of execution came, by some means, I never knew what, Isham was missing, About two years after, we learned that he had gone down to Natchez, and had married a lady of some refinement and piety. I saw her letters to his sisters, who were worthy members of the church of which I was pastor. The last letter told of his death. He was in Jackson's army, and fell in the famous battle of New Orleans.
>
> I am, sir, your friend,
>
> Wm. Dickey.

I found another, rather different, telling of this Story in **A HISTORY OF BLACKS IN KENTUCKY: FROM SLAVERY TO SEGREGATION, 1760-1891** by Dr. Marion B. Lucas.

It conforms more or less to many, but not all, of the details presented in Rev. Dickey's letter. The incident occurred on December 15-16, 1811, which can be determined by the timing of the major earthquake known as the New Madrid earthquake.

That appends an element of heavenly intervention.

The following is Dr. Lucas' description of the incident:[739]

> The most shocking incident of premeditated, barbarous cruelty occurred in isolated Livingston County one Sunday night in December 1811. Lilburn and Isham Lewis, nephews of Thomas Jefferson, became incensed at George, an unruly slave, after he dropped a pitcher of water. Later, in a drunken rage, they seized the slave and tied him to the floor of the kitchen cabin. The brothers assembled their seven slaves and ordered them to build a large fire in the fireplace. Lilburn locked the door and informed his slaves that he intended to end their insolence once and for all. While the terrified slaves stood against the wall, Lilburn struck George in the neck with a single blow from an axe, probably killing him instantly.
>
> The two brothers then compelled one of the slaves to dismember the body of the murdered bondsman. The remains of George's body were burned in the fireplace piecemeal until about 2:00 A.M. when an earthquake hit western Kentucky, causing the chimney to collapse and smother the fire. The next day, during aftershocks, the Lewis brothers forced their slaves to clean the remains of the body out of the fireplace and begin rebuilding it. They concealed the unburned portions of George's body among the rocks of the reconstructed chimney.
>
> The demise of Lilburn and Isham began when new earthquakes struck Livingston County in early 1812. The rebuilt chimney fell, exposing the unburned remains of the body. A dog dragged the skull to the house of a neighbor who took it to county authorities.

Dr. Lucas confirms the brothers' release on bail, Lilburne's death, Isham's conviction and subsequent escape, and Isham's death in the Battle of New Orleans.

In the end, regardless of how precisely the brothers murdered George for the misbehaviors of "skulking" and dropping a pitcher, he suffered a horrible fate. Moreover, Isham went unpunished for his participation. I have not seen any theories as to how Isham came to escape, although one may speculate.

---

739 M. Lucas, **A HISTORY OF BLACKS IN KENTUCKY: FROM SLAVERY TO SEGREGATION, 1760-1891** at 47-48 (Kentucky Historical Society, 2nd ed. 2003).

"BUCKING" IN KENTUCKY

"'Bucking' was one of the more punishing methods of whipping bondsmen, both children or adults. After tying a slave's hands together in front, his master forced him to sit down and draw his knees toward his chest. The slave's arms were then forced around his knees and pushed down far enough to allow a stick to slide under his knees but above his arms. A stick of three-and-one-half feet or longer, prevented rolling to either side, thus locking the bondsman in a position that completely exposed his back. Owners particularly upset with their slaves left them 'bucked' after the whipping, prolonging the agony."

M. Lucas, A History of Blacks in Kentucky: From Slavery to Segregation, 1760-1891 at 45 (Kentucky Historical Society, 2nd ed. 2003). Footnote omitted.

MOB JUSTICE

On the 28th, of April 1836 [more than half a century after the Declaration of Independence], in the city of St. Louis, Missouri, a black man, named McIntosh, who had stabbed an officer, that had arrested him, was seized by the multitude, fastened to a tree *in the midst* of the city, wood piled around him, and in open day and in the presence of an immense throng of citizens, he was burned to death. The Alton (Ill.) Telegraph, in its account of the scene says:

> "All was silent as death while the executioners were piling wood around their victim. He said not a word, until feeling that the flames had seized upon him. He then uttered an awful howl, attempting to sing and pray, then hung his head, and suffered in silence, except in the following instance:—After the flames had surrounded their prey, his eyes burnt out of his head, and his mouth seemingly parched to a cinder, some one in the crowd, more compassionate than the rest, proposed to put an end to his misery by shooting him, when it was replied, 'that would be of no use, since he was already out of pain.' 'No, no,' said the wretch, 'I am not, I am suffering as much as ever; shoot me, shoot me.' 'No, no,' said one of the fiends who was standing about the sacrifice they were roasting, 'he shall not be shot. *I would sooner slacken the fire, if that would increase his misery;*' and the man who said this was, as we understand, an OFFICER OF JUSTICE!"

"The St. Louis correspondent of a New York paper adds,

> "The shrieks and groans of the victim were loud and piercing, and to observe one limb after another drop into the fire was awful indeed. He was about fifteen minutes in dying."

T. Weld, American Slavery As It Is: Testimony of a Thousand Witnesses at 156-57 (American Anti-Slavery Society 1839), available from the Library of Congress at *www.hathitrust.org/digital_library;* see also C. Ball, Slavery in the United States, A Narrative of the life and Adventures of Charles Ball at vi-viii (John S. Taylor, 1837), Davis Library, Univ. of North Carolina at Chapel Hill, available at available at *docsouth.unc.edu.* Emphasis in original.

THE BURNING OF JERRY: ATTENDING HIS OWN FUNERAL

In 1828, "a group of four black slave artisans were on a … journey by ship from Charleston to New Orleans. Before leaving South Carolina, they vowed they would never be slaves in New Orleans. By the time the boat docked, they all had committed suicide."[740]

Vincent Harding

§ § §

Until my research, I never learned that America's slave society burned slaves at the stake or otherwise burned slaves alive. I did learn that, centuries ago, the English, and during the Inquisition, the Spanish burned religious and political enemies at the stake, but I never imagined that, in the 1800s, American officials burned anyone, including slaves, alive. In South Carolina, however, there had been instances of burning criminals at the stake in the 1700s and 1800s.[741] In this case, the flames burned in the Nineteenth Century.

In 1990, the South Carolina Historical Society published the information appearing below.

More than 50 years after the Declaration of Independence, in 1830 South Carolina found a slave named Jerry to be guilty of "rape with intent to murder the white wife of his employer."[742]

No one seems to have been concerned about the Constitution's prohibition of cruel and unusual punishment. Perhaps that is because it was not "unusual."

A "citizen" provided one recollection of the dramatic episode:

SLAVE PUNISHMENT IN NEW YORK

"After the slave revolt in 1712, slaves were broken on the wheel, burnt alive, or gibbeted. In the aftermath of the failed 1741 conspiracy, dozens of slaves were burnt at the stake, hanged, or gibbeted."

G. Hodges and E. Brown ed., "Pretends to Be Free"—Runaway Slave Advertisements from Colonial and Revolutionary New York and New Jersey at xx (Fordham Univ. Press 2019)

> The first [reference to the case] was in the Abbeville *Medium* in 1872 when "Citizen" recalled, "I once saw a Negro burned at the stake, for attempting to commit a most horrid crime on a lady. This was an awful sight, and I recollect that Rev. J. T. Pressly stated in his sermon he preached at the stake, prior to the burning, that the punishment was 'a relic of Barbarism:' and well might he have made that statement, for it was one of the most heart rending sights I ever witnessed, and I am sure I shall never witness such a scene again."

740 Harding, "Symptoms of Liberty and Blackhead Signposts: David Walker and Nat Turner" in K. Greenberg, ed, **NAT TURNER: A SLAVE REBELLION IN HISTORY AND MEMORY** (Oxford Univ. Press, 2003).

741 Ware, "The Burning of Jerry: The Last Slave Execution by Fire in South Carolina?" The South Carolina Historical Magazine, Vol. 91, 100-06 (Apr. 1990).
See also "1830: The slave Jerry, the last American execution by burning?" at *www.executedtoday.com/2011/05/01/1830-the-slave-jerry-the-last-american-execution-by-burning/*, accessed Oct. 20, 2020.

742 See the preceding note. The summary of Jerry's fate is derived from those sources.

The Court convicted Jerry on the testimony of one witness. He offered no evidence in defense. An account of Jerry's execution, recollected years later by a Presbyterian minister (supported by news articles at the time of the event), described the following scene:

> thousands of men, women and children, both white and colored, assembled together in an old field ... to witness the execution of a beastly criminal by burning alive at the stake. ... [T]here sat the prisoner, the waiting impatient crowd, the immense pile of pitch pine logs and kindling wood scattered around ... .

The perpetrators forced Jerry to hear his own funeral sermon delivered before the execution. He "covered his face during the whole service." Thereafter:

> As the poor doomed man ascended the pile, he began to pray audibly and this was kept up continuously during the process of chaining him to the stake, and until the mounting flames deprived him of a wretched life.

Significantly, the transcript of the hearing of Jerry's trial reflects that the Court "previous to awarding and ordering said sentence to be executed[,] appraised and valued said Negro slave man named Jerry at four hundred dollars." From the perspective of the slave society, Jerry, although a convicted criminal, was still "property."

After receipt of the trial transcript, the State Legislature, having sympathy for the slaveholder's loss of value as a result of the execution, authorized a payment of $122.45. The State paid half of that sum to the slaveholder, and the balance to the victim of the crime.

THE STORY OF WILEY: GOTTA HAVE A "PASS"

Part of the slave society's repression was the mandate that slaves have "passes" or "licenses" from their masters in order to leave their masters' premises.

As part of the requirement, any white could stop a black and demand to see the pass. If the black were a slave, and resisted, the white could administer punishment, usually lashes. The number of lashes would be in the discretion of the white. If the slave sought to escape, the white often could kill the slave. Such activities provided poor whites a sense of power.

Care might be necessitated. If a white wrongfully killed a slave, the master could sue for damages to his "property." There was no protection, however, for the slave as a human being.

In addition, in some states pursuant to law, or pursuant to local practice, slave "patrols," consisting of local citizens, could be appointed (and state law sometimes required that patrols be maintained by local jurisdictions).

WHY REQUIRE PASSES?

- Fear of loss of valuable "property," if slaves should run away
- Runaway slaves might steal food (including farm animals) or other property in order to sustain life
- Slaves may assemble to plot insurrections

The pass requirement has a tie to the denial of education for slaves in reading and writing. An educated slave might forge a pass, thereby frustrating the slave society's smothering tyranny.

T*he Story of Wiley* illustrates, in Solomon Northup's words, how the "pass" requirement operated to prevent slaves even from visiting their friends. The *Story* further illustrates how whites, in this case a "slave patrol" with bloodhounds, would catch potential "runaway" slaves, demanding to see their passes, as well as the severe consequences of not having a "pass:"[743]

> The year 1850, down to which time I have now arrived, omitting many occurrences uninteresting to the reader, was an unlucky year for my companion Wiley, the husband of Phebe, whose taciturn and retiring nature has thus far kept him in the background. Notwithstanding Wiley seldom opened his mouth, and revolved in his obscure and unpretending orbit without a grumble, nevertheless the warm elements of sociality were strong in the bosom of that silent "nigger." In the exuberance of his self-reliance, disregarding the philosophy of Uncle Abram, and setting the counsels of Aunt Phebe utterly at naught, he had the fool-hardiness to essay a nocturnal visit to a neighboring cabin without a pass.
>
> So attractive was the society in which he found himself, that Wiley took little note of the passing hours, and the light began to break in the east before he was aware. Speeding homeward as fast as he could run, he hoped to reach the quarters before the horn would sound; but, unhappily, he was spied on the way by a company of patrollers.
>
> How it is in other dark places of slavery, I do not know, but on Bayou Boeuf there is an organization of patrollers, as they are styled, whose business it is to seize and whip any slave they may find wandering from the plantation. They ride on horseback, headed by a captain, armed, and accompanied by dogs. They have the right, either by law, or by general consent, to inflict discretionary chastisement upon a

743 Northup, at 236-40.

black man caught beyond the boundaries of his master's estate without a pass, and even to shoot him, if he attempts to escape. Each company has a certain distance to ride up and down the bayou. They are compensated by the planters, who contribute in proportion to the number of slaves they own. The clatter of their horses' hoofs dashing by can be heard at all hours of the night, and frequently they may be seen driving a slave before them, or leading him by a rope fastened around his neck, to his owner's plantation.

Wiley fled before one of these companies, thinking he could reach his cabin before they could overtake him; but one of their dogs, a great ravenous hound, griped him by the leg, and held him fast. The patrollers whipped him severely, and brought him, a prisoner, to [Master] Epps. From him he received another flagellation still more severe, so that the cuts of the lash and the bites of the dog rendered him sore, stiff and miserable, insomuch he was scarcely able to move. It was impossible in such a state to keep up his row, and consequently there was not an hour in the day but Wiley felt the sting of his master's rawhide on his raw and bleeding back. His sufferings became intolerable, and finally he resolved to run away. Without disclosing his intentions to run away even to his wife Phebe, he proceeded to make arrangements for carrying his plan into execution. Having cooked his whole week's allowance, he cautiously left the cabin on a Sunday night, after the inmates of the quarters were asleep. When the horn sounded in the morning, Wiley did not make his appearance. Search was made for him in the cabins, in the corn-crib, in the cotton-house, and in every nook and corner of the premises. Each of us was examined, touching any knowledge we might have that could throw light upon his sudden disappearance or present whereabouts. Epps raved and stormed, and mounting his horse, galloped to neighboring plantations, making inquiries in all directions. The search was fruitless. Nothing whatever was elicited, going to show what had become of the missing man. The dogs were led to the swamp, but were unable to strike his trail. They would circle away through the forest, their noses to the ground, but invariably returned in a short time to the spot from whence they started.

Wiley had escaped, and so secretly and cautiously as to elude and baffle all pursuit. Days and even weeks passed away, and nothing could be heard of him. Epps did nothing but curse and swear. It was the only topic of conversation among us when alone. We indulged in a great deal of speculation in regard to him, one suggesting he might have been drowned in some bayou, inasmuch as he was a poor swimmer; another, that perhaps he might have been devoured by alligators, or stung by the venomous

CALL OUT THE DOGS

"Permit me then to relate what I have seen; and do not imagine that these are all exceptions to the general treatment, but rather believe that thousands of cruelties are practised in this Christian land, every year, which no eye that ever shed a tear of pity could look upon. ...

"At length I arrived at the dwelling of a planter of my acquaintance, with whom I passed the night. At about eight o'clock in the evening I heard the barking of several dogs; mingled with the most agonizing cries that I ever heard from any human being. Soon after the gentleman came in, and began to apologize, by saying that two of his runaway slaves had just been brought home; and as he had previously tried every species of punishment upon them without effect, he knew not what else to add, except to set his blood hounds upon them. 'And,' continued he, 'one of them has been so badly bitten that he has been trying to die. I am only sorry that he did not; for then I should not have been further troubled with him. If he lives I intend to send him to Natchez or to New Orleans to work with the ball and chain.'"

T. Weld, American Slavery As It Is: Testimony of a Thousand Witnesses at 107, 108 (American Anti-Slavery Society 1839), available from the Library of Congress at *www.hathitrust.org/digital_library*

ENFORCEMENT FOR PASSES

"South Carolina and Georgia—'any person finding more than seven slaves together in the highway without a white person, may give each one twenty lashes;' 'If any slave shall be out of the house, &c, or off the plantation, &c, of his master, &c, and shall refuse to submit to an examination by any white person, &c, such white person may apprehend and moderately correct him; and if he shall assault or strike such white person, he may be lawfully killed'"

W. Goodell, The American slave code in theory and practice at 226-32 (American and Foreign Anti-Slavery Society 1853), available from the Library of Congress at *www.hathitrust.org/digital_library*

EXAMPLE OF A PASS

"The [pass] I now received was dated, and read as follows:

> 'Platt has permission to go to Ford's plantation, on Bayou Boeuf, and return by Tuesday morning.
> 'John M. Tibeats.'"

S. Northup, Twelve Years a Slave at 157-58 (1853), available from the Library of Congress at *www.hathitrust.org/digital_library*

moccasin, whose bite is certain and sudden death. The warm and hearty sympathies of us all, however, were with poor Wiley, wherever he might be. Many an earnest prayer ascended from the lips of Uncle Abram, beseeching safety for the wanderer.

In about three weeks, when all hope of ever seeing him again was dismissed, to our surprise, he one day appeared among us. On leaving the plantation, he informed us, it was his intention to make his way back to South Carolina—to the old quarters of Master Buford. During the day he remained secreted, sometimes in the branches of a tree, and at night pressed forward through the swamps. Finally, one morning, just at dawn, he reached the shore of Red River. While standing on the bank, considering how he could cross it, a white man accosted him, and demanded a pass. Without one, and evidently a runaway, he was taken to Alexandria, the shire town of the parish of Rapides, and confined in prison. It happened several days after that Joseph B. Roberts, uncle of Mistress Epps, was in Alexandria, and going into the jail, recognized him. Wiley had worked on his plantation, when Epps resided at Huff Power. Paying the jail fee, and writing him a pass, underneath which was a note to Epps, requesting him not to whip him on his return, Wiley was sent back to Bayou Boeuf. It was the hope that hung upon this request, and which Roberts assured him would be respected by his master, that sustained him as he approached the house. The request, however, as may be readily supposed, was entirely disregarded. After being kept in suspense three days, Wiley was stripped, and compelled to endure one of those inhuman floggings to which the poor slave is so often subjected. It was the first and last attempt of Wiley to run away. The long scars upon his back, which he will carry with him to the grave, perpetually remind him of the dangers of such a step.

"Fugitive Slave Trapped, U.S. South, 19th cent.", *Slavery Images: A Visual Record of the African Slave Trade and Slave Life in the Early African Diaspora*, accessed November 30, 2020, *http://slaveryimages.org/s/slaveryimages/item/1293*

THE STORY OF AUGUSTUS AND THE BLOODHOUNDS

The following Story provided by Solomon Northup illustrates the high degree of risks for slaves in running away, including in this case, the viciousness of slave masters' bloodhounds:[744]

> Not unfrequently the runaway loses his life in the attempt to escape. Epps' premises were bounded on one side by Carey's, a very extensive sugar plantation. He cultivates annually at least fifteen hundred acres of cane, manufacturing twenty-two or twenty-three hundred hogsheads of sugar; an hogshead and a half being the usual yield of an acre. Besides this he also cultivates five or six hundred acres of corn and cotton. He owned last year one hundred and fifty three field hands, besides nearly as many children, and yearly hires a drove during the busy season from this side the Mississippi.

"Fugitive Slaves and Bloodhounds, U.S. South, 1850s", Slavery Images: A Visual Record of the African Slave Trade and Slave Life in the Early African Diaspora, accessed November 30, 2020, *http://slaveryimages.org/s/slaveryimages/item/1292*

> One of his negro drivers, a pleasant, intelligent boy, was named Augustus. During the holidays, and occasionally while at work in adjoining fields, I had an opportunity of making his acquaintance, which eventually ripened into a warm and mutual attachment. Summer before last he was so unfortunate as to incur the displeasure of the overseer, a coarse, heartless brute, who whipped him most cruelly. Augustus ran away. Reaching a cane rick on Hawkins' plantation, he secreted himself in the top of it. All Carey's dogs were put upon his track—some fifteen of them—and soon scented his footsteps to the hiding place. They surrounded the rick, baying and scratching, but could not reach him. Presently, guided by the clamor of the hounds, the pursuers rode up, when the overseer, mounting on to the rick, drew him forth. As he rolled down to the ground the whole pack plunged upon him, and before they could be beaten off, had gnawed and mutilated his body in the most shocking manner, their teeth having penetrated to the bone in an hundred (sic) places. He was taken up, tied upon a mule, and carried home. But this was Augustus' last trouble. He lingered until the next day, when death sought the unhappy boy, and kindly relieved him from his agony.

744 Northup at 243-44.

"A Slave-Hunt", *Slavery Images: A Visual Record of the African Slave Trade and Slave Life in the Early African Diaspora,* accessed November 15, 2020, *http://slaveryimages.org/s/slaveryimages/item/1212*

"Fugitive Slave Attacked by Dogs, 19th cent. (?)", *Slavery Images: A Visual Record of the African Slave Trade and Slave Life in the Early African Diaspora,* accessed November 15, 2020, *http://slaveryimages.org/s/slaveryimages/item/1294*

TERRIBLE FIGHT WITH BLOODHOUNDS.

"Bloodhounds Being Killed by Black Union Soldiers, 1862", *Slavery Images: A Visual Record of the African Slave Trade and Slave Life in the Early African Diaspora,* accessed November 15, 2020, *http://slaveryimages.org/s/slaveryimages/item/820*

SLAVES' DESIRE FOR FREEDOM: BY A SC SUPREME COURT JUSTICE'S DAUGHTER

In AMERICAN SLAVERY AS IT IS, Theodore Weld provides the following accounts:[745]

Miss Grimke is a daughter of the late Judge Grimke, of the Supreme Court of South Carolina, and sister of the late Hon. Thomas S. Grimke. [She states:]

> "As I left my native state on account of slavery, and deserted the home of my fathers to escape the sound of the lash and the shrieks of tortured victims, I would gladly bury in oblivion the recollection of those scenes with which I have been familiar; but this may not, cannot be; they come over my memory like gory spectres, and implore me with resistless power, in the name of a God of mercy, in in the name of a crucified Savior, in the name of humanity; for the sake of the slaveholder, as well as the slave, to bear witness to the horrors of the southern prison house. I feel impelled by a sacred sense of duty, by my obligations to my country, by sympathy for the bleeding victims of tyranny and lust, to give my testimony respecting the system of American slavery,—to detail a few facts, most of which came under my personal observation. And here I may premise, that the actors in these tragedies were all men and women of the highest respectability, and of the first families in South Carolina, and, with one exception, citizens of Charleston; and that their cruelties did not in the slightest degree affect their standing in society.
>
> "A handsome mulatto woman, about 18 or 20 years of age, whose independent spirit could not brook the degradation of slavery, was in the habit of running away: for this offence she had been repeatedly sent by her master and mistress to be whipped by the keeper of the Charleston work-house. This had been done with such inhuman severity as to lacerate her back in a most shocking manner; a finger could not be laid between the cuts. But the love of liberty was too strong to be annihilated by torture; and, as a last resort, she was whipped at several different times, and kept a close prisoner. A heavy iron collar, with three long prongs projecting from it, was placed round her neck, and a strong and sound front tooth was extracted, to serve as a mark to describe her, in case of escape. Her sufferings at this time were agonizing; she could lie in no position but on her back, which was sore from scourgings, as I can testify, from personal inspection, and her only place of rest was the floor, on a blanket. These outrages were committed in a family

INSTRUMENT OF TORTURE USED BY SLAVEHOLDERS.

"Instrument of Torture Used by Slaveholders", *Slavery Images: A Visual Record of the African Slave Trade and Slave Life in the Early African Diaspora*, accessed November 15, 2020, *http://slaveryimages.org/s/slaveryimages/item/1235*

745 Weld at 22-23. Emphasis in original.

where the mistress daily read the scriptures, and assembled her children for family worship. She was accounted, and was really, so far as alms-giving was concerned, a charitable woman, and tender hearted to the poor; and yet this suffering slave, who was the seamstress of the family, was continually in her presence, sitting in her chamber to sew, or engaged in her other household work, with her lacerated and bleeding back, her mutilated mouth, and heavy iron collar, without, so far as appeared, exciting any feelings of compassion.

§ § §

"A highly intelligent slave, who panted after freedom with ceaseless longings, made many attempts to get possession of himself. For every offence he was punished with extreme severity. At one time he was tied up by his hands to a tree, and whipped until his back was one gore of blood. To this terrible infliction he was subjected at intervals for several weeks, and kept heavily ironed while at his work. His master one day accused him of a fault, in the usual terms dictated by passion and arbitrary power; the man protested his innocence, but was not credited. He again repelled the charge with honest indignation. His master's temper rose almost to frenzy; and seizing a fork, he made a deadly plunge at the breast of the slave. The man being far his superior in strength, caught his arm, and dashed the weapon on the floor. His master grasped at his throat, but the slave disengaged himself, and rushed from the apartment. Having made his escape, he fled to the woods; and after wandering about for many months, living on roots and berries, and enduring every hardship, he was arrested and committed to jail. Here he lay for a considerable time, allowed scarcely food enough to sustain life, whipped in the most shocking manner, and confined in a cell so loathsome, that when his master visited him, he said the stench was enough to knock a man down. The filth had never been removed from the apartment since the poor creature had been immured in it. Although a black man, such had been the effect of starvation and suffering, that his master declared he hardly recognized him—his complexion was so yellow, and his hair, naturally thick and black, had become red and scanty; an infallible sign of long continued living on bad and insufficient food. Stripes, imprisonment, and the gnawings of hunger, had broken his lofty spirit for a season; and, to use his master's own exulting expression, he was "as humble as a dog." After a time he made another attempt to escape, and was absent so long, that a reward was offered for him, *dead or alive.* He eluded every attempt to take him, and his master, despairing of ever getting him again, offered to pardon him if he would return home. It was always understood that such intelligence will reach the runaway; and accordingly, at the entreaties of his wife and mother, the fugitive once more consented to return to his bitter bondage. I believe this was the last effort to obtain his liberty. His heart became touched with the power of the gospel; and the spirit which no inflictions could subdue, bowed at the cross of Jesus, and with the language on his lips—"the cup that my father hath given me, shall I not drink it?" submitted to the yoke of the oppressor, and wore his chains in unmurmuring patience

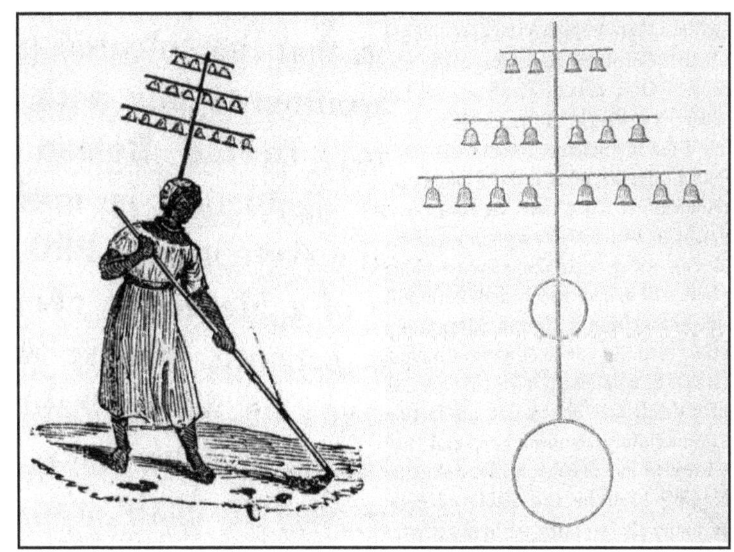

"Metal Collar to Prevent Running Away, South Carolina, 1830s", *Slavery Images: A Visual Record of the African Slave Trade and Slave Life in the Early African Diaspora*, accessed November 15, 2020, *http://slaveryimages.org/s/slaveryimages/item/1207*

till death released him. The master who perpetrated these wrongs upon his slave, was one of the most influential and honored citizens of South Carolina, and to his equals was bland, and courteous, and benevolent even to a proverb. …

§ § §

"As I was traveling in the lower country in South Carolina, a number of years since, my attention was suddenly arrested by an exclamation of horror from the coachman, who called out, "Look there, Miss Sarah, don't you see?"—I looked in the direction he pointed, and saw a human head stuck up on a high pole. On inquiry, I found that a runaway slave, who was outlawed, had been shot there, his head severed from his body, and put upon the public highway, as a terror to deter slaves from running away."

THE STORY OF HENRY "BOX" BROWN: SHIPPING HIMSELF TO FREEDOM

Perhaps, following such depressing information, it is time to take a bit of a break to relate a slave's outstanding success exercising considerable ingenuity and determination.

"Interior of the Seabrook Tobacco Warehouse at Richmond, Virginia", *Slavery Images: A Visual Record of the African Slave Trade and Slave Life in the Early African Diaspora,* accessed November 21, 2020, *http://slaveryimages.org/s/slaveryimages/item/2988*

Henry Brown was a slave in Virginia. A family asserted to be less inhumane than were other slaveholders owned Brown.

At the time of the Story, Mr. Brown worked in a tobacco company in Richmond, 14 to 16 hours per day. He was able to retain a portion of his wages.

Mr. Brown fell in love with a slave named Nancy. A neighboring planter named Lee owned Nancy. Mr. Brown states that:[746]

> I went to Mr. Lee, and made known to him my wishes, when he told me, he never meant to sell Nancy, and if my master would agree never to sell me, then I might marry her. This man was a member of a Presbyterian church in Richmond, and pretended to me, to believe it wrong to separate families; but after I had been married to my wife one year, his conscientious scruples vanished, and she was sold to a saddler living in Richmond … .

So, Henry and Nancy, his love, were married, although, of course, in accord with the laws of slavery, the slave society did not provide their marriage legal status. Eventually, they had three children, and Nancy was pregnant with their fourth.[747]

Slaveholders sold and resold Nancy thereafter. Brown states:[748]

> The last purchaser of my wife, was Mr. Samuel S. Cartrell, also a member of Dr. Plummer's church.
>
> He induced me to pay him $50.00 in order to assist him in purchasing my companion, so as

$50 IN TODAY'S MONEY

Using the inflation factor of 33, the $50 Mr. Brown paid Mr. Cartrell was the approximate equivalent of $1,650 in today's money.

746 Dictated by H. Brown, written and edited by C. Stearns, **NARRATIVE OF HENRY BOX BROWN, WHO ESCAPED FROM SLAVERY** at 47-48 (Brown and Stearns, 1849), Academic Affairs Library, Univ. of North Carolina at Chapel Hill, available at *docsouth.unc.edu* ("H. Brown").

747 "Henry 'Box' Brown" at *www.biography.com/activist/henry-box-brown,* accessed Oct. 20, 2020; "Henry 'Box' Brown: A Slave Signed, Sealed and Delivered" at *www.historynet.com/henry-box-brown-a-slave-signed-sealed-and-delivered.htm,* accessed Oct. 20, 2020; "Henry 'Box' Brown" at *www.pbs.org/black-culture/shows/list/underground-railroad/stories-freedom/henry-box-brown/,* accessed Oct. 20, 2020.

748 H. Brown, at 49-50. Footnote omitted.

> to prevent her being sold away from me. I also paid him $50 a year, for her time, although she would have been of but little value to him, for she had young children and could not earn much for him,— and rented a house for which I paid $72, and she took in washing, which with the remainder of my earnings, after deducting master's "lion's share," supported our family. Our bliss, as far as the term bliss applies to a slave's situation, was now complete in this respect, for a season; for never had we been so pleasantly situated before; but, reader, behold its cruel termination. O the harrowing remembrance of those terrible, terrible scenes! May God spare you from ever enduring what I then endured.

Mr. Cartrell chose to violate their agreement. As a result, a Methodist minister purchased Mr. Brown's family and took them to North Carolina. Mr. Brown's last vision of his family was as they marched away in a slave coffle of 350 slaves. He said good-bye to his children "with tears in his eyes on the side of the street." Mr. Brown states:[749]

> Pretty soon five wagon-loads of little children passed, and looking at the foremost one, what should I see but a little child, pointing its tiny hand towards me, exclaiming, "There's my father; I knew he would come and bid me good-bye." It was my eldest child! Soon the gang approached in which my wife was chained. I looked, and beheld her familiar face; but O, reader, that glance of agony! may God spare me ever again enduring the excruciating horror of that moment! She passed, and came near to where I stood. I seized hold of her hand, intending to bid her farewell; but words failed me; the gift of utterance had fled, and I remained speechless. I followed her for some distance, with her hand grasped in mine, as if to save her from her fate, but I could not speak, and I was obliged to turn away in silence.

At that point, Mr. Brown became determined to escape from slavery. He conceived an escape by "shutting myself up in a box, and getting myself conveyed as dry goods to a free state."[750] Not Amazon, Federal Express, or UPS, but close.

Mr. Brown enlisted the aid of others in accomplishing his scheme. One was a "free" African-American named James Smith, who was a friend from church. A second Smith, although not related, was a white storekeeper named Samuel Smith. Mr. Samuel Smith agreed to assist Mr. Brown for $86.[751]

Samuel Smith made contact with abolitionists in Philadelphia, including among others, William Still, a "free" African-American known as the Father of the Underground Railroad, as well as other abolitionists. They agreed to receive Mr. Brown shipped to them in a freight box from Richmond.[752]

In March 1849, Mr. Brown first created a reason for absence from work:[753]

> I went to Mr. Allen, and requested of him permission to refrain from labor for a short time, in consequence of a disabled finger; but he refused to grant me this permission, on the ground that my

749 H. Brown, at 50-55; "Henry 'Box' Brown" at *www.pbs.org/black-culture/shows/list/underground-railroad/stories-freedom/henry-box-brown/,* accessed Oct. 20, 2020.

750 "Henry 'Box' Brown: A Slave Signed, Sealed and Delivered" at *www.historynet.com/henry-box-brown-a-slave-signed-sealed-and-delivered.htm,* accessed Oct. 20, 2020.

751 "Henry 'Box' Brown: A Slave Signed, Sealed and Delivered" at *www.historynet.com/henry-box-brown-a-slave-signed-sealed-and-delivered.htm,* accessed Oct. 20, 2020; "Henry 'Box' Brown" at *www.biography.com/activist/henry-box-brown,* accessed Oct. 20, 2020.

752 "Henry 'Box' Brown" at *www.biography.com/activist/henry-box-brown,* accessed Oct. 20, 2020; "Henry 'Box' Brown: A Slave Signed, Sealed and Delivered" at *www.historynet.com/henry-box-brown-a-slave-signed-sealed-and-delivered.htm,* accessed Oct. 20, 2020.

753 H. Brown, at 58.

> hand was not lame enough to justify him in so doing. Nothing daunted by this rebuff, I took some oil of vitriol, intending to pour a few drops upon my finger, to make it sufficiently sore, to disable me from work, which I succeeded in, beyond my wishes; for in my hurry, a larger quantity than it was my purpose to apply to my finger, found its way there, and my finger was soon eaten through to the bone. The overseer then was obliged to allow me to absent myself from business, for it was impossible for me to work in that situation. But I did not waste my precious furlough in idle mourning over my fate.

Samuel Smith executed Mr. Brown's plan, using a box marked "dry goods:"[754]

> Samuel Alexander Smith shipped Henry by Adams Express Company on March 23, 1849, in a box 3 feet long by 2 feet 8 inches deep by 2 feet wide, and sent the box as "dry goods." Henry Brown traveled in the box lined with baize, a coarse woollen cloth, carrying with him only one bladder of water and a few biscuits. There was a hole cut in the box for air, and it was nailed and tied with straps; in large words, "This side up" was written on the box. Brown traveled by a variety of wagons, railroads, steamboats, ferries, and finally, for added safety, a delivery wagon that brought the box to the Philadelphia Anti-Slavery Society before daybreak.

The trip lasted 27 hours, during which Mr. Brown experienced a bumpy ride:[755]

> During the 27-hour journey, the box was turned upside down on several occasions and handled roughly. Henry wrote that he "was resolved to conquer or die … ." At one point, Henry thought that he might die, but fortunately two men needed a place to sit down and, "so perceiving my box, standing on end, one of the men threw it down and the two sat upon it. I was thus relieved from a state of agony which may be more imagined than described."

Positioned upside down, he felt his eyes "swelling as if they would burst from their sockets; and the veins on my temples were dreadfully distended with pressure of blood upon my head."[756] He had endured for an hour and a half until two men flipped the box on its side to sit on it. The swelling subsided; his head cleared."[757]

When the shipment (i.e., Mr. Brown) arrived in Philadelphia, one of the men recalled Mr. Brown's first words were "How do you do, gentlemen?" Then, "he sang a psalm from the Bible."[758]

Henry "Box" Brown and his escape became a cause celebre in the North, but Southerners saw his escape as more Yankee meddling with their "property." The slave society pressed even more fiercely for passage of the Fugitive Slave Act, which would force the federal government to help return escaped slaves. When that act passed in 1850, Brown fled to England.[759]

754 "Henry 'Box' Brown" at *www.pbs.org/black-culture/shows/list/underground-railroad/stories-freedom/henry-box-brown/*, accessed Oct. 20, 2020.

755 "Henry 'Box' Brown" at *www.pbs.org/black-culture/shows/list/underground-railroad/stories-freedom/henry-box-brown/*, accessed Oct. 20, 2020.

756 "Henry 'Box' Brown" at *www.pbs.org/black-culture/shows/list/underground-railroad/stories-freedom/henry-box-brown/*, accessed Oct. 20, 2020.

757 "Henry 'Box' Brown: A Slave Signed, Sealed and Delivered" at *www.historynet.com/henry-box-brown-a-slave-signed-sealed-and-delivered.htm*, accessed Oct. 20, 2020.

758 "Henry 'Box' Brown" at *www.pbs.org/black-culture/shows/list/underground-railroad/stories-freedom/henry-box-brown/*.

759 "Henry 'Box' Brown" at *www.biography.com/activist/henry-box-brown*, accessed Oct. 20, 2020.

While in America, Mr. Brown spoke actively against slavery, although he did not purchase the freedom of his wife or children. He became a professional entertainer, devising a panorama during which he would climb into his original box. He presented the panorama first in America, and then in England. He married an English woman, had a family, and remained in England until 1875. He then returned to America, but migrated to Canada in 1889.[760]

The authorities arrested the two Mr. Smiths after they attempted to use the strategy again. Samuel Smith was convicted and sentenced to six-and-a-half years in the State Penitentiary. James Smith's trial resulted in a divided panel. He was released, and later freed.[761]

---

760 "Henry 'Box' Brown" at *www.biography.com/activist/henry-box-brown,* accessed Oct. 20, 2020; "Henry 'Box' Brown" at *www.pbs.org/black-culture/shows/list/underground-railroad/stories-freedom/henry-box-brown/,* accessed Oct. 20, 2020.

761 "Henry 'Box' Brown" at *www.biography.com/activist/henry-box-brown,* accessed Oct. 20, 2020; "Henry 'Box' Brown" at *www.pbs.org/black-culture/shows/list/underground-railroad/stories-freedom/henry-box-brown/,* accessed Oct. 20, 2020.

THE GENDER-BENDING 1,000-MILE PUBLIC ESCAPE

William and Ellen Craft, slaves in Georgia, conducted one of the most daring and imaginative escapes in the history of American slavery. William Craft describes their adventure—for that is what it was—in his book.[762]

The Crafts developed an escape plan constructed around Ellen Craft's assumption of the role of a white slaveholder, with William as her devoted slave. This required imaginative disguises. Their plan relied in important respects upon Ellen's white skin. William states in the book:[763]

> Notwithstanding my wife being of African extraction on her mother's side, she is almost white—in fact, she is so nearly so that the tyrannical old lady to whom she first belonged became so annoyed, at finding her frequently mistaken for a child of the family, that she gave her when eleven years of age to a daughter, as a wedding present. This separated my wife from her mother, and also from several other dear friends.

The existence of white-skinned slaves is a feature of American slavery that many people fail to understand. Despite laws against miscegenation, slaveholders often engaged in sexual relations with slave women. It occurred frequently against the will of the slave women, but they had no ability to resist.

One result of these sexual encounters—at times bald rapes—was that slaves became not only light-skinned, but from generation to generation, ever lighter until there were many slaves, like Ellen, who could not be distinguished from other white people. Ellen was a quadroon, meaning that she had only one ancestor among her parents and grandparents who was black.

The following are excerpts from William's narrative describing the disguise Ellen adopted for their escape:[764]

> Knowing that slaveholders have the privilege of taking their slaves to any part of the country they think proper, it occurred to me that, as my wife was nearly white, I might get her to disguise herself as an invalid gentleman, and assume to be my master, while I could attend as his slave, and that in this manner we might effect our escape. After I thought of the plan, I suggested it to my wife, but at first she shrank from the idea. She thought it was almost impossible for her to assume that disguise, and travel a distance of 1,000 miles across the slave States. However, on the other hand, she also thought of her condition. She saw that the laws under which we lived did not recognize her to be a woman, but a mere chattel, to be bought and sold, or otherwise dealt with as her owner might see fit. Therefore the more she contemplated her helpless condition, the more anxious she was to escape from it. So she said, "I think it is almost too much for us to undertake; however, I feel that God is on our side, and with his assistance, notwithstanding all the difficulties, we shall be able to succeed. Therefore, if you will purchase the disguise, I will try to carry out the plan."
>
> But after I concluded to purchase the disguise, I was afraid to go to any one to ask him to sell me the articles. It is unlawful in Georgia for a white man to trade with slaves without the master's consent. But, notwithstanding this, many persons will sell a slave any article that he can get the money to buy. Not

---

762 W. Craft, **RUNNING A THOUSAND MILES FOR FREEDOM; OR, THE ESCAPE OF WILLIAM AND ELLEN CRAFT FROM SLAVERY** (London, William Tweedie, 1860), Academic Affairs Library, Univ. of North Carolina at Chapel Hill, available at *docsouth.unc.edu* ("Craft").

763 Craft at 2.

764 Craft at 29-31.

> that they sympathize with the slave, but merely because his testimony is not admitted in court against a free white person. Therefore, with little difficulty I went to different parts of the town, at odd times, and purchased things piece by piece, (except the trowsers which she found necessary to make,) and took them home to the house where my wife resided. She being a ladies' maid, and a favourite slave in the family, was allowed a little room to herself; and amongst other pieces of furniture which I had made in my overtime, was a chest of drawers; so when I took the articles home, she locked them up carefully in these drawers. No one about the premises knew that she had anything of the kind.

The Crafts were able to obtain passes to leave their masters' premises for a few days over the Christmas holidays when they would not be missed. They made further plans for Ellen's disguise:[765]

> [W]hen the thought flashed across my wife's mind, that it was customary for travellers to register their names in the visitors' book at hotels, as well as in the clearance or Custom-house book at Charleston, South Carolina—it made our spirits droop within us.
>
> So, while sitting in our little room upon the verge of despair, all at once my wife raised her head, and with a smile upon her face, which was a moment before bathed in tears, said, "I think I have it!" I asked what it was. She said, "I think I can make a poultice and bind up my right hand in a sling, and with propriety ask the officers to register my name for me." I thought that would do.
>
> It then occurred to her that the smoothness of her face might betray her; so she decided to make another poultice, and put it in a white handkerchief to be worn under the chin, up the cheeks, and to tie over the head. This nearly hid the expression of the countenance, as well as the beardless chin. ...
>
> My wife, knowing that she would be thrown a good deal into the company of gentlemen, fancied that she could get on better if she had something to go over the eyes; so I went to a shop and bought a pair of green spectacles. This was in the evening.
>
> We sat up all night discussing the plan, and making preparations. Just before the time arrived, in the morning, for us to leave, I cut off my wife's hair square at the back of the head, and got her to dress in the disguise and stand out on the floor. I found that she made a most respectable looking gentleman.

Ellen added another element of the disguise when a man sat next to her on a train and sought to strike up a conversation. Fearing a conversation might betray her voice, Ellen "feign[ed] deafness as the only means of self-defense."[766]

The Crafts rode on trains and steamers as they travelled over four days from the Deep South to Philadelphia. They spent the night in a hotel in Savannah, and passed through Charleston, Wilmington, Richmond, Fredericksburg, Washington, and Baltimore. Along the way, others ate dinner with them and spoke with them. Throughout their journey, William refers to Ellen as his "master." She used the name "Mr. Johnson."

The disguise worked wonderfully. To illustrate this, in one incident on a train in Virginia, the following occurred when they met a gentleman traveling with his daughters:[767]

> [While the gentleman was absent,] the ladies and my master had a little cosy chat. But on his return, he said, "You seem to be very much afflicted, sir." "Yes, sir," replied the gentleman in the poultices. "What seems to be the matter with you, sir; may I be allowed to ask?" "Inflammatory rheumatism, sir."

---

765 Craft at 34-35.

766 Craft at 44.

767 Craft at 59-61.

> "Oh! that is very bad, sir," said the kind gentleman: "I can sympathise with you; for I know from bitter experience what the rheumatism is." If he did, he knew a good deal more than Mr. Johnson.
>
> The gentleman thought my master would feel better if he would lie down and rest himself; and as he was anxious to avoid conversation, he at once acted upon this suggestion. The ladies politely rose, took their extra shawls, and made a nice pillow for the invalid's head. My master wore a fashionable cloth cloak, which they took and covered him comfortably on the couch. After he had been lying a little while the ladies, I suppose, thought he was asleep; so one of them gave a long sigh, and said, in a quiet fascinating tone, "Papa, he seems to be a very nice young gentleman." But before papa could speak, the other lady quickly said, "Oh! dear me, I never felt so much for a gentleman in my life!" To use an American expression, "they fell in love with the wrong chap."
>
> After my master had been lying a little while he got up, the gentleman assisted him in getting on his cloak, the ladies took their shawls, and soon all were seated. They then insisted upon Mr. Johnson [Ellen's assumed name] taking some of their refreshments, which of course he did, out of courtesy to the ladies. All went on enjoying themselves until they reached Richmond, where the ladies and their father left the train. But, before doing so, the good old Virginian gentleman, who appeared to be much pleased with my master, presented him with a recipe, which he said was a perfect cure for the inflammatory rheumatism. But the invalid not being able to read it, and fearing he should hold it upside down in pretending to do so, thanked the donor kindly, and placed it in his waistcoat pocket. My master's new friend also gave him his card, and requested him the next time he travelled that way to do him the kindness to call; adding, "I shall be pleased to see you, and so will my daughters." Mr. Johnson expressed his gratitude for the proffered hospitality, and said he should feel glad to call on his return.

The following is another illustration occurring shortly after the Crafts arrived in Philadelphia and went to a boarding house recommended by a black man for the evening:[768]

> After my wife had a little recovered herself, she threw off the disguise and assumed her own apparel. We then stepped into the sitting-room, and asked to see the landlord. The man came in, but he seemed thunderstruck on finding a fugitive slave and his wife, instead of a "young cotton planter and his nigger." As his eyes travelled round the room, he said to me. "Where is your master?" I pointed him out. The man gravely replied, "I am not joking, I really wish to see your master." I pointed him out again, but at first he could not believe his eyes; he said "he knew that was not the gentleman that came with me."
>
> But, after some conversation, we satisfied him that we were fugitive slaves, and had just escaped in the manner I have described. We asked him if he thought it would be safe for us to stop in Philadelphia. He said he thought not, but he would call in some persons who knew more about the laws than himself. He then went out, and kindly brought in several of the leading abolitionists of the city, who gave us a most hearty and friendly welcome amongst them.

The Crafts settled in Boston, from which they lectured with William Wells Brown.

After the enactment of the Fugitive Slave Law of 1850, their masters sent slave catchers to Boston and a warrant was issued to the federal Marshall for their arrest. Consequently, they went to England. In England, they once again joined forces with Mr. Brown.

768 Craft at 81-82.

THE STORY OF JOSIAH'S JOYOUS ESCAPE

As described by Dr. Kate Larson in **BOUND FOR THE PROMISED LAND—HARRIET TUBMAN, PORTRAIT OF AN AMERICAN HERO,** Harriett Tubman, popularly known as "Moses," not only escaped to freedom herself, but over eleven years, "returned to the Eastern Shore of Maryland approximately thirteen times to liberate family and friends; in all, she personally brought away about seventy former slaves … . She also gave instructions to approximately fifty more slaves who found their way to freedom independently."[769]

Ms. Tubman was a firm and fearless leader. A friend, Thomas Garret related the following incident, which occurred as Ms. Tubman was leading a group of fugitives to freedom:[770]

> The date of the commencement of her labors, I cannot certainly give; but I think it must have been about 1845; from that time till 1860, I think she must have brought from the neighborhood where she had been held as a slave. from 60 to 80 persons, from Maryland, some 80 miles from here. No slave who placed himself under her care, was ever arrested that I have heard of; she mostly had her regular stopping places on her route; but in one instance, when she had several stout men with her, some 30 miles below here, she said that God told her to stop, which she did; and then asked him what she must do. He told her to leave the road, and turn to the left; she obeyed, and soon came to a small stream of tide water; there was no boat, no bridge; she again inquired of her Guide what she was to do. She was told to go through. It was cold, in the month of March; but having confidence in her Guide, she went in; the water came up to her armpits; the men refused to follow till they saw her safe on the opposite shore. They then followed, and, if I mistake not, she had soon to wade a second stream; soon after which she came to a cabin of colored people, who took them all in, put them to bed, and dried their clothes, ready to proceed next night on their journey. Harriet had run out of money, and gave them some of her underclothing to pay for their kindness. When she called on me two days after, she was so hoarse she could hardly speak, and was also suffering with violent toothache.

NEVER LOST A PASSENGER

"I was the conductor on the Underground Railroad for eight years, and I can say what most conductors can't say—I never ran my train off the track and I never lost a passenger."

Harriet Tubman, as quoted in K. Larson, Bound for the Promised Land—Harriet Tubman, Portrait of an American Hero at 276 (New York: Ballantine Books, 2003).

---

769 See, *e.g.*, Larson at xvii.

770 S. Bradford, **HARRIETT, THE MOSES OF HER PEOPLE** at 85-86 (George R. Lockwood & Son, 1886), Academic Affairs Library, Univ. of North Carolina at Chapel Hill Libraries at *docsouth.unc.edu/neh/harriet/harriet.html,* accessed Oct. 21, 2020.

"Fugitive Slaves, U.S. South, 1861", *Slavery Images: A Visual Record of the African Slave Trade and Slave Life in the Early African Diaspora,* accessed November 15, 2020, *http://slaveryimages.org/s/slaveryimages/item/1210*

Ms. Tubman would hide the escaping slaves she was assisting and would signal them by singing coded religious songs that she sang. Usually, they traveled by night, often on foot, heading North to Pennsylvania, but even there, they were not safe from slave masters who came North to recapture them. Black and white citizens assisted the fugitives in Maryland, Pennsylvania, New York, and New England. After the passage of the Fugitive Slave Law of 1850, escaping fugitives went to Canada on trains over Niagara Falls.

The following is a description of a slave named Josiah "Joe" or "Joseph" Bailey, whom Harriet Tubman rescued and transported to Canada on the Underground Railroad. Mr. Bailey had been "hired out" to a farmer named Hughlett for a period of six years and had provided excellent services, as shown by the fact that Mr. Bailey had "supervised the overall operations of Hughlett's land."[771]

After the six years of meritorious service, Mr. Hughlett purchased Mr. Bailey, and promptly insisted on whipping Mr. Bailey to ensure Mr. Bailey's submission. Mr. Bailey determined to run away. Sarah Bradford states:[772]

> On her seventh or eighth journey, [Tubman] brought with her a band of fugitives, among whom was a very remarkable man, whom I knew only by the name of "Joe." Joe was a noble specimen of a

771 S. Bradford, **HARRIETT, THE MOSES OF HER PEOPLE** at 39-42 (George R. Lockwood & Son, 1886), Academic Affairs Library, Univ. of North Carolina at Chapel Hill Libraries at *docsouth.unc.edu/neh/harriet/harriet.html,* accessed Oct. 21, 2020.
See also Archives of Maryland (Biographical Series), "Josiah 'Joe' Bailey (b. 1828-d.?)" at *msa.maryland.gov/megafile/msa/speccol/sc5400/sc5496/001500/001535/html/001535bio.html,* accessed Nov. 7, 2020.

772 S. Bradford, **HARRIETT, THE MOSES OF HER PEOPLE** at 39-42 (George R. Lockwood & Son, 1886), Academic Affairs Library, Univ. of North Carolina at Chapel Hill Libraries at *docsouth.unc.edu/neh/harriet/harriet.html,* accessed Oct. 21, 2020.
See also Archives of Maryland (Biographical Series), "Josiah 'Joe' Bailey (b. 1828-d.?)" at msa.maryland.gov/megafile/msa/speccol/sc5400/sc5496/001500/001535/html/001535bio.html, accessed Nov. 7, 2020.

negro, enormously tall, and of splendid muscular development. He had been hired out by his master to another planter, for whom he had worked for six years, saving him all the expense of an overseer, and taking all trouble off from his hands. He was such a very valuable piece of property, and had become so absolutely necessary to the planter to whom he was hired, that he determined to buy him at any cost. His old master held him proportionately high. But by paying one thousand dollars down, and promising to pay another thousand in a certain time, the purchase was made, and this chattel passed over into the hands of a new owner.

The morning after the purchase was completed, the new master came riding down on a tall, powerful horse into the negro quarter, with a strong new rawhide in his hand, and stopping before Joe's cabin, called to him to come out. Joe was just eating his breakfast, but with ready obedience, he hastened out at the summons. Slave as he was, and accustomed to scenes of brutality, he was surprised when the order came, "Now, Joe, strip, and take a licking." Naturally enough, he demurred at first, and thought of resisting the order; but he called to mind a scene he had witnessed a few days before in the field, the particulars of which are too horrible to be given here, and he thought it the wisest course to submit; but first he tried a gentle remonstrance.

> "Mas'r," said he, "habn't I always been faithful to you? Habn't I worked through sun an' rain, early in de mornin' an' late at night; habn't I saved you an oberseer by doin' his work? hab you anything to complain agin me?"
>
> "No, Joe, I have no complaint to make of you. You're a good nigger, an' you've always worked well. But you belong to me now; you're my nigger, and the first lesson my niggers have to learn is that I am master and they belong to me, and are never to resist anything I order them to do. So I always begin by giving them a good licking. Now strip and take it."

Joe saw that there was no help for him, and that for the time he must submit. He stripped off his clothing, and took his flogging without a word, but as he drew his shirt up over his torn and bleeding back, he said to himself: "Dis is de first an' de last." As soon as he was able he took a boat, and under cover of the night, rowed down the river, and made his way to the cabin of "Old Ben," Harriet's father, and said to him: "Nex' time Moses comes, let me know."

It was not long after this time, that the mysterious woman appeared—the woman on whom no one could lay his finger—and men, women, and children began to disappear from the plantations. One fine morning Joe was missing, and call as loud as he might, the master's voice had no power to bring him forth. Joe had certainly fled; and his brother William was gone, and Peter and Eliza. From other plantations other slaves were missing, and before their masters were awake to the fact, the party of fugitives, following their intrepid leader, were far on their way towards liberty.

As Ms. Tubman led the slaves North, Josiah was constantly terrified of recapture. The excerpts describe Ms. Tubman's rescue of this group:[773]

Their adventures were enough to fill a volume; they were pursued; they were hidden in "potato holes," while their pursuers passed within a few feet of them; they were passed along by friends in various disguises; they scattered and separated, to be led by guides by a roundabout way, to a meeting-place again. They were taken in by Sam Green, the man who was afterwards sent to State Prison for ten years for having a copy of "Uncle Tom's Cabin" in his house; and so, hunted and hiding and wandering, they came at last to the long bridge at the entrance of the city of Wilmington, Delaware. The rewards posted up everywhere had been at first five hundred dollars for Joe, if taken within the limits of the

---

773 Bradford at 29-35. This incident is also described in Larson at 133-36.

United States; then a thousand, and then fifteen hundred dollars, "an' all expenses clar an' clean, for his body in Easton Jail." Eight hundred for William, and four hundred for Peter, and twelve thousand for the woman who enticed them away. The long Wilmington Bridge was guarded by police officers, and the advertisements were everywhere. The party were scattered, and taken to the houses of different colored friends, and word was sent secretly to Thomas Garrett, of Wilmington, of their condition, and the necessity of their being taken across the bridge. Thomas Garrett is a Quaker, and a man of a wonderfully large and generous heart, through whose hands, Harriet tells me, two thousand self-emancipated slaves passed on their way to freedom. He was always ready, heart and hand and means, in aiding these poor fugitives, and rendered most efficient help to Harriet on many of her journeys back and forth. …

As soon as Thomas Garrett heard of the condition of these poor people, his plan was formed. He engaged two wagons, filled them with bricklayers, whom of course he paid well for their share in the enterprise, and sent them across the bridge. They went as if on a frolic, singing and shouting. The guards saw them pass, and of course expected them to re-cross the bridge. After nightfall (and fortunately it was a dark night) the same wagons went back, but with an addition to their party. The fugitives were on the bottom of the wagons, the bricklayers on the seats, still singing and shouting; and so they passed by the guards, who were entirely unsuspicious of the nature of the load the wagons contained, or of the amount of property thus escaping their hands. And so they made their way to New York. When they entered the antislavery office there, Joe was recognized at once by the description in the advertisement. "Well," said Mr. Oliver Johnson, "I am glad to see the man whose head is worth fifteen hundred dollars." At this Joe's heart sank. If the advertisement had got to New York, that place which it had taken them so many days and nights to reach, he thought he was in danger still. "And how far is it now to Canada?" he asked. When told how many miles, for they were to come through New York State, and cross the Suspension Bridge, he was ready to give up. "From dat time Joe was silent," said Harriet; he sang no more, he talked no more; he sat wid his head on his hand, and nobody could 'muse him or make him take any interest in anyting." They passed along in safety, and at length found themselves in the cars, approaching Suspension Bridge. The rest were very joyous and happy, but Joe sat silent and sad. …

"Negroes Escaping Out of Slavery", *Slavery Images: A Visual Record of the African Slave Trade and Slave Life in the Early African Diaspora,* accessed November 28, 2020, *http://slaveryimages.org/s/slaveryimages/item/1326*

The cars began to cross the bridge. Harriet was very anxious to have her companions see the Falls. William, Peter, and Eliza came eagerly to look at the wonderful sight; but Joe sat still, with his head upon his hand.

"Joe, come look at de Falls! Joe, you fool you, come see de Falls! its your last chance." But Joe sat still and never raised his head. At length Harriet knew by the rise in the center of the bridge, and the descent on the other side, that they had crossed "the line." She sprang across to Joe's seat, shook him with all her might, and shouted, "Joe, you've shook de lion's paw!" Joe did not know what she meant. "Joe, you're free!" shouted Harriet. Then Joe's head went up, he raised his hands on high, and his face, streaming with tears, to heaven, and broke out in loud and thrilling tones:

"Glory to God and Jesus too,
One more soul is safe!
Oh, go and carry de news,
One more soul got safe."

"Joe, come and look at de Falls!" called Harriet.

"Glory to God and Jesus too,
One more soul got safe."

was all the answer. The cars stopped on the other side. Joe's feet were the first to touch British soil, after those of the conductor. …

"The ladies and gentlemen gathered round him," said Harriet, "till I couldn't see Joe for the crowd, only I heard 'Glory to God and Jesus too!' louder than ever." William went after him, and pulled him, saying, "Joe, stop your noise! you act like a fool!" Then Peter ran it, and jerked him mos' off his feet,—"Joe, stop your hollerin'! Folks'll think you're crazy!" But Joe gave no, heed. The ladies were crying, and the tears like rain ran down Joe's sable cheeks. A lady reached over her fine cambric handkerchief to him. Joe wiped his face, and then he spoke.

"Oh! If I'd felt like dis down South, it would hab taken nine men to take me; only one more journey for me now, and dat is to Hebben!" "Well, you ole fool you," said Harriet, with whom there seems but one step from the sublime to the ridiculous, "you might a' looked at de Falls fust, and den gone to Hebben afterwards." She has seen Joe several times since, a happy and industrious freeman in Canada.

THE STORY OF CHARLES NALLE'S NARROW ESCAPE: THE FUGITIVE SLAVE LAW IN ACTION

In another famous incident illustrating her strong determination, persistence, and immense physical strength, Harriet Tubman was instrumental in saving a recaptured slave in New York from return to his master under the Fugitive Slave Law of 1850.[774]

The Supreme Court already had held in *Prigg v. Pennsylvania*[775] that slaveowners had the right under the 1793 Fugitive Slave Law to enter into free states to recapture slaves, even when state law prohibited the recapture. The Court overturned, as unconstitutional under the Supremacy Cause of the Constitution, Pennsylvania's conviction of a slave hunter who, in Pennsylvania, recaptured a slave and her children (one of whom was "free"). Thus, the federal law in favor of slaveholders reigned supreme.

The following are a summary and excerpts from **SCENES IN THE LIFE OF HARRIET TUBMAN**. In reading the narrative, you may wish to keep in mind that Ms. Tubman was only five feet tall. She suffered severe injury early in her life when an iron weight thrown at another slave struck her in the head. The injury caused her to experience frequent seizures.

While in Troy, New York, Ms. Tubman learned that an escaped slave named Charles Nalle, was held by the U.S. Commissioner and was to be returned to his master in Virginia. Mr. Nalle "had been followed by his master (who was his younger brother and not one grain whiter than he)." After escaping, and before his recapture, Mr. Nalle had lived for two years in Columbia, Pennsylvania, and had a wife and five children. He worked as a coachman.

Like other Stories, *Charles Nalle's Narrow Escape* depicts aspects of the slave society. For example, notice that Mr. Nalle was "a tall, handsome, intelligent *white* man, with his wrists manacled together, walking between the U. S. Marshal and another officer, and behind him his brother and his master." In other words, Mr. Nalle's father was also the father of Mr. Nalle's "master," who was his half-brother. As masters had sexual relations with slave women, their offspring would then be slaves for life to the fathers-masters.

Confusing?

A second area illuminated by *Charles Nalle's Narrow Escape* is the operation of the Fugitive Slave Law. The officials arresting Mr. Nalle included New York officials. The federal government could and would punish them if they did not pursue and capture the fugitive. The slaveholder could file charges against them. So, the officials were not only performing their "duty" under the federal law, but they also were protecting themselves from liability.

Once Harriet Tubman learned about Mr. Nalle's arrest, she "forced her way, and rushed up the stairs to the door of the [court] room" holding Mr. Nalle. She positioned herself next to a window from which the rapidly gathering and very sizable crowd in the street could see her. To the officers, she appeared as an old "decrepit" woman wearing a bonnet. The crowd, however, watched her in the window for a signal when the officers would attempt to move Mr. Nalle.

---

774 This incident is described in detail in Bradford at 88-91; and Larson at 179-83. Emphasis in original.

775 *Prigg v. Pennsylvania*, 41 U.S. 539 (1842).

At that point—

> Harriet, now seeing the necessity for a tremendous effort for his rescue, sent out some little boys to cry fire. The bells rang, the crowd increased, till the whole street was a dense mass of people. Again and again the officers came out to try and clear the stairs, and make a way to take their captive down; others were driven down, but Harriet stood her ground, her head bent down, and her arms folded. "Come, old woman, you must get out of this," said one of the officers; "I must have the way cleared; if you can't get down alone, someone will help you." Harriet, still putting on a greater appearance of decrepitude, twitched away from him, and kept her place. ... At length the officers appeared, and announced to the crowd that if they would open a lane to the wagon, they would promise to bring the man down the front way.
>
> The lane was opened, and the man was brought out—a tall, handsome, intelligent white man, with his wrists manacled together, walking between the U. S. Marshal and another officer, and behind him his brother and his master, so like him that one could hardly be told from the other. The moment they appeared, Harriet roused from her stooping posture, threw up a window, and cried to her friends: "Here he comes—take him!" and then darted down the stairs like a wild-cat. She seized one officer and pulled him down, then another, and tore him away from the man; and keeping her arms about the slave, she cried to her friends: "Drag us out! Drag him to the river! Drown him! but don't let them have him!" They were knocked down together, and while down she tore off her sunbonnet and tied it on the head of the fugitive [so the crowd could identify him].

The crowd separated Mr. Nalle from the officers, and loaded him, still manacled, on a ferry. On the other side of the river, however, a constable, who had been notified by telegram, arrested Mr. Nalle and took him to a house. Then,

> Harriet rushed up to the place. Some men were attempting to make their way up the stairs. The officers were firing down, and two men were lying on the stairs, who had been shot. Over their bodies our heroine rushed, and with the help of others burst open the door of the room, dragged out the fugitive, whom Harriet carried down stairs in her arms. A gentleman who was riding by with a fine horse, stopped to ask what the disturbance meant; and on hearing the story, his sympathies seemed to be thoroughly aroused; he sprang from his wagon, calling out, "That is a blood-horse, drive him till he drops." The poor man was hurried in; some of his friends jumped in after him, and drove at the most rapid rate to Schenectady.

Mr. Nalle escaped. Later, antislavery advocates purchased his freedom.

In covering the incident,[776]

The Troy [NY] *Daily News* reported that 'the most conspicuous person opposed to the legal course was the venerable old colored woman, who exclaimed "Give us liberty or give us death!"

776 Larson at 181. Footnotes omitted

THE JERRY RESCUE

Northerners rebelled against the Fugitive Slave Law. There were dramatic fugitive rescues. In Christiana, Pennsylvania, a large crowd of blacks, killed a Virginia slaveholder seeking the arrest of fugitives.[777] The State could not convict any of the perpetrators despite charges of treason. In Boston, sympathizers rescued another slave, Shadrach Minkins.[778]

Shortly thereafter, another dramatic rescue, known as the "Jerry Rescue," occurred in Syracuse, led in part by Rev. Jermain Loguen, himself a fugitive.

On October 1, 1851, Federal Marshals arrested a fugitive named "William Henry, known generally as "Jerry."[779] The arrest occurred during a Liberty Party convention in Syracuse.[780] A crowd reported to be "nearly two thousand" persons[781] grew outside the jail imprisoning Jerry.

The Syracuse Vigilance Committee met to determine what to do. "Loguen saw this meeting as the time to test whether whites 'have courage only to make speeches and resolutions when there is no danger.' Clearly he was prepared to fight regardless of the committee's decision, avowing '... if white men won't fight, let fugitives and black men smite down the Marshals and Commissioner—anybody who holds Jerry—and rescue him or perish.'"[782]

At one point, Jerry broke free and made a run for freedom, but was captured in the street, shackled roughly, and hauled back to court. An eye witness stated:[783]

> I saw this fugitive from, not justice, but injustice, dragged through the streets like a dog, every rag of clothes stripped from his back, hauled upon a cart like a dead carcass and driven away to a police office, for a mock trial.

---

777 The Christiana Riot: Violent Resistance to Fugitive Slave Law at *www.thoughtco.com/the-christiana-riot-1773557,* accessed Aug. 15. 2022.

778 "Rescued from the Fangs of the Slave Hunter:" The Case of Shadrach Minkins at *www.nps.gov/articles/-rescued-from-the-fangs-of-the-slave-hunter-the-case-of-shadrach-minkins.htm,* accessed Aug. 15, 2022.

779 J. Loguen, **THE REV. J. W. LOGUEN, AS A SLAVE AND AS A FREEMAN, A NARRATIVE OF REAL LIFE** at 398-425 (Syracuse: J.G.K. Truair & Co., 1859), Academic Affairs Library, Univ. of North Carolina at Chapel Hill, available at *docsouth.unc.edu* ("Loguen Narrative"); C. Hunter, **TO SET THE CAPTIVES FREE: REVEREND JERMAIN WESLEY LOGUEN AND THE STRUGGLE FOR FREEDOM IN CENTRAL NEW YORK,** 1835-1872 at 117-24 (Hyrax Publishing, 2013) ("Hunter"); Dearstyne, "Syracuse Hero Jermain Loguen, Abolition and The Jerry Rescue" at *www.newyorkalmanack.com/2022/02/syracuse-hero-jermain-loguen-abolition-the-jerry-rescue/,* accessed March 14, 2022.

780 Loguen Narrative at 399.

781 Hunter at 126.

782 Hunter at 120. Footnote omitted. See also Loguen Narrative at 402.

783 Hunter at 119. Footnote omitted.

Rev. Loguen and other Syracuse blacks, accompanied by whites, rescued Jerry.[784] In doing so, they used rocks, axes, iron bars, clubs, and a battering ram breaking down windows and doors to enter the building.[785] The Marshals fled.[786] The acting members of the crowd removed Jerry from his jail cell in chains, transporting him to a hidden location, and eventually to Canada.[787]

Loguen and other leaders of the rescue also went to Canada to escape prosecution.[788] Authorities indicted a total of 27 defendants for violating the 1850 Law, but only one was convicted. He died while his case was on appeal. Juries acquitted the other defendants or failed to reach verdicts.[789] Loguen eventually came back to Syracuse. Although authorities indicted him, they never tried him.[790]

News media publicized the event across the country to the consternation of slaveholders who had counted upon the Law, if needed, to retrieve their escaped slaves from "free" states.[791] The expense of the trials "convinced many who supported it that the law was unenforceable."[792]

---

784 Hunter at 120-23. Footnote omitted. "Jermain Wesley Loguen" at *www.nationalabolitionhalloffameandmuseum.org/jermain-wesley-loguen.html*, accessed March 14, 2022.

785 Loguen Narrative at 411-14, 416; Hunter at 121-22.

786 Loguen Narrative at 413, 417 note; Hunter at 122.

787 Loguen Narrative at 419-24; Hunter at 122-23.

788 Loguen Narrative at 427-29; Hunter at 133-34.

789 Hunter at 136.

790 Loguen Narrative at 433-37, 442; Hunter at 135-36.

791 Loguen Narrative at 425.

792 Hunter at 136. Footnote omitted.

SLAVEHOLDER ADVERTISEMENTS FOR RUNAWAY SLAVES

Until my research, I did not learn about the frequency of runaway slaves or their conditions evidencing their significant abuse and mistreatment. I did not learn about the horrifying retributions that awaited slaves in the frequent event of their recapture.

Desperation could overcome the fear of retribution, if caught. Not uncommonly, slaves left to search for family members after one or more were sold away. Other times, slaves hoped to escape to freedom—North to a "free" state or, after the enactment of the Fugitive Slave Act of 1850, to Canada, especially from the Upper South. Others escaped from North Carolina or Southern Virginia to surreptitious maroon communities deep in the Great Dismal Swamp or in the Appalachian Mountains. Still others fled to Florida from South Carolina, Georgia, Alabama, or Tennessee. In Louisiana, slaves could escape into maroon communities deep in bayou country. Slaves from Texas and Louisiana escaped to Mexico.

Often, when slaves escaped, their masters would advertise for them in newspapers, handbills, and posters. Following the invention of the telegraph, it became possible to disseminate information widely and quickly. It also became viable to apprehend slaves far from the masters' plantations.

Runaway slave advertisements were a common feature of life in both colonial America and in America following the Revolution.

In order to provide identifying information, the masters would, of course, describe the slaves. That did not stop, however, with typical features, such as height, weight, and skin color.

The runaway slave advertisements were, in effect, open admissions by slaveholders of the highly-abusive treatment to which they had subjected their slaves. Slaveholders did not hesitate to describe for identification of their slaves in this public manner the slaves' injuries resulting from slaveholder abuse.

If you ponder it, you may also realize that those unashamed advertisements provide pointed evidence of the extent to which the slave society dominated American life and public opinion. Slaveholders believed they had done nothing wrong, and had no qualms in letting the World know about their abusive characters. Rather than protecting slaves from abuse, the slave society closed ranks to assist slaveholders by pursuing runaway slaves.

As expressed in **"PRETENDS TO BE FREE"—RUNAWAY SLAVE ADVERTISEMENTS FROM COLONIAL AND REVOLUTIONARY NEW YORK AND NEW JERSEY**, "First and foremost, runaway notices are evidence of slave resistance. … Above all, flight was the most effective individual means of struggle against slavery … ."[793]

PRETENDS TO BE FREE contains "662 notices describ[ing] 753 fugitive slaves, an average of more than eleven per year between 1716 and 1783. Yet the advertisements published in [the] book do not constitute all the fugitive bondspeople of early New York and New Jersey. … Moreover, published runaway advertisements, as Peter Wood has explained, 'represent little more than the top of an ill-defined iceberg.'"[794] The book cites an advertisement in New Jersey "as late as 1840."[795]

---

793 Hodges and Brown, at xiv.

794 Hodges and Brown, at xv.

795 Hodges and Brown, at xxxv.

Illustrating the direct involvement of legal authorities and the law in the protection of slave masters' "property," the advertisements re-published in **PRETENDS TO BE FREE** often warn against provision of aid to fugitive slaves:[796]

> By mid-century [1700s], warnings to masters of vessels against harboring fugitives were standard clauses in runaway advertisements.

The same can be said for general warnings to the population as a whole. A common clause in a runaway slave advertisement stated in substance, for example, "All persons at their Peril, are forewarned from harboring or carrying her off."[797] New York and New Jersey "laws penalized anyone who harbored runaways with a £5 fine and made those who caused a loss of a slave liable for full value."[798] In *Jones v. Van Zandt,*[799] the Supreme Court upheld financially-ruinous monetary liability of an Ohio abolitionist to a Kentucky slaveowner for assisting the owner's slaves in escaping through the Underground Railroad.

Escaping slaves often showed evidence of considerable abuse, such as "his great toes have been froze, and have only little Pieces of Nails on them."[800]

The following are further examples:[801]

> [One slave] master reported that his slave went from "work at his plough and was without shoe or stocking and no other clothes but an Oznabrig (sic) Shirt and Trowsers, an Old ragged waistcoat and an old hat." Bondsmen escaped despite drastic measures by their masters. Caesar ran away from Isaac Freeman of Woodbridge, New Jersey in February, 1756, then escaped again in August, 1756. Caesar wore a "pair of iron pothooks around his neck with a chain fastened to it that reached his feet." Quaco fled in 1761 wearing an "iron collar with two hooks to it, round his neck, a pair of Handcuffs with a chain to them, six feet long."
>
> § § §
>
> The comments masters made about physical characteristics are testimony to the injury, disease, and rough usage of slaves. During the 1740s and 1750s slaves were commonly described as "pock-marked," showing scars of smallpox epidemics. Others showed signs of physical abuse. Ralph, who fled from a sloop in New York harbor, had many dents in the top of his head, possibly caused by the "Ward-end of a key." Others showed the traditional marks of bondage. Scipio, who fled with his arms pinioned behind him, had "Buttocks pretty well marked with the Lash." Even more common were the scars or evidence of such injuries as broken legs and arms, missing teeth, lameness, partial blindness or verbal tics such as stuttering.

The following are examples cited by Charles Dickens in his **AMERICAN NOTES**[802] of runaway slave advertisements by slaveholders. The advertisements openly described the brutality with which masters maltreated their slaves:

---

796 Hodges and Brown, at xxi.

797 Hodges and Brown, at 130.

798 Hodges and Brown, at xix-xx.

799 *Jones v. Van Zandt,* 46U.S. 215 (1847),

800 Hodges and Brown, at xxvii. Footnote omitted.

801 Hodges and Brown, at xxv-xxvi, xxxi. Footnotes omitted.

802 C. Dickens, **AMERICAN NOTES,** Ch. 17, at 184-87 (Hazell, Watson & Viney, 187?), available from the Library of Congress at *www.hathitrust.org/digital_library.* Emphasis in original.

Let us try this public opinion by another test, which is important in three points of view: first, as showing how desperately timid of the public opinion slave-owners are, in their delicate descriptions of fugitive slaves in widely circulated newspapers; secondly, as showing how perfectly contented the slaves are, and how very seldom they run away; thirdly, as exhibiting their entire freedom from scar, or blemish, or any mark of cruel infliction, as their pictures are drawn, not by lying abolitionists, but by their own truthful masters.

The following are a few specimens of the advertisements in the public papers. It is only four years since the oldest among them appeared; and others of the same nature continue to be published every day, in shoals.

> "Ran away, a black woman, Betsy. Had an iron bar on her right leg."
>
> "Ran away, the negro Manuel. Much marked with irons."
>
> "Ran away, a negro boy about twelve years old. Had round his neck a chain dog-collar with 'De Lampert' engraved on it."
>
> "Ran away, the negro Hown. Has a ring of iron on his left foot. Also, Grise, his wife, having a ring and chain on the left leg."
>
> "Ran away, a negro boy named James. Said boy was ironed when he left me."
>
> "Committed to jail, a man who calls his name John. He has a clog of iron on his right foot which will weigh four or five pounds."
>
> "Detained at the police jail, the negro wench, Myra. Has several marks of LASHING, and has irons on her feet."
>
> "Ran away, a negro man named Henry; his left eye out, some scars from a dirk on and under his left arm, and much scarred with the whip."
>
> "Committed to jail, a negro man. Has no toes on the left foot."
>
> "Ran away, a negro woman named Rachel. Has lost all her toes except the large one."
>
> "Ran away, Sam. He was shot a short time since through the hand, and has several shots in his left arm and side."
>
> "Ran away, my negro man Dennis. Said negro has been shot in the left arm between the shoulder and elbow, which has paralysed the left hand."
>
> "Ran away, my negro man named Simon. He has been shot badly, in his back and right arm."
>
> "Ran away, a negro named Arthur. Has a considerable scar across his breast and each arm, made by a knife; loves to talk much of the goodness of God."
>
> "Twenty-five dollars reward for my man Isaac. He has a scar on his forehead, caused by a blow; and one on his back, made by a shot from a pistol."
>
> "Ran away, a negro girl called Mary. Has a small scar over her eye, a good many teeth missing, the letter A is branded on her cheek and forehead."
>
> "Ran away, negro Ben. Has a scar on his right hand; his thumb and forefinger being injured by being shot last fall. A part of the bone came out. He has also one or two large scars on his back and hips."

"Detained at the jail, a mulatto, named Tom. Has a scar on the right cheek, and appears to have been burned with powder on the face."

"Ran away, a negro man named Ned. Three of his fingers are drawn into the palm of his hand by a cut. Has a scar on the back of his neck, nearly half round, done by a knife."

"Fifty dollars reward, for my fellow Edward. He has a scar on the corner of his mouth, two cuts on and under his arm, and the letter E on his arm."

"Ran away, negro boy Ellie. Has a scar on one of his arms from the bite of a dog."

"Ran away, from the plantation of James Surgette, the following negroes: Randal, has one ear cropped; Bob, has lost one eye; Kentucky Tom, has one jaw broken."

"Ran away, Anthony. One of his ears cut off, and his left hand cut with an axe."

"Fifty dollars reward for the negro Jim Blake. Has a piece cut out of each ear, and the middle finger of the left hand cut off to the second joint."

"Ran away, a negro woman named Maria. Has a scar on one side of her cheek, by a cut. Some scars on her back."

RUNAWAY SLAVE DESCRIPTIONS

"Ran away, Negress Caroline. Had on a collar with one prong turned down." ...

"Ran away, the negress Fanny. Had on an iron band about her neck." ...

"Ran away, a negro woman and two children. A few days before she went off, I burnt her with a hot iron, on the left side of her face. I tried to make the letter M."...

"One hundred dollars reward, for a negro fellow, Pompey, 40 years old. He is branded on the left jaw." ...

"Was committed to jail, a negro man. Says his name is Josiah. His back very much scarred by the whip; and branded on the thigh and hips in three or four places, thus (J M). The rim of his right ear has been bit or cut off."

C. Dickens, American Notes, Ch. 17, at 184-87 (Hazell, Watson & Viney, 187?), available from the Library of Congress at *www.hathitrust.org/digital_library*

Mr. Dickens continued:

"Ran away, the Mulatto wench Mary. Has a cut on the left arm, a scar on the left shoulder, and two upper teeth missing."

I should say, perhaps, in explanation of this latter piece of description, that among the other blessings which public opinion secures to the negroes, is the common practice of violently punching out their teeth. To make them wear iron collars by day and night, and to worry them with dogs, are practices almost too ordinary to deserve mention.

"Ran away, my man Fountain. Has holes in his ears, a scar on the right side of his forehead, has been shot in the hind parts of his legs, and is marked on the back with the whip."

"Two hundred and fifty dollars reward for my negro man Jim. He is much marked with shot in his right thigh. The shot entered on the outside, halfway between the hip and knee joints."

"Brought to jail, John. Left ear cropt."

"Taken up, a negro man. Is very much scarred about the face and body, and has the left ear bit off."

"Ran away, a black girl, named Mary. Has a scar on her cheek, and the end of one of her toes cut off."

> "Ran away, my Mulatto woman, Judy. She has had her right arm broke."
>
> "Ran away, my negro man, Levi. His left hand has been burnt, and I think the end of his forefinger is off."
>
> "Ran away, a negro man, NAMED WASHINGTON. Has lost a part of his middle finger, and the end of his little finger."
>
> "Twenty-five dollars reward for my man John. The tip of his nose is bit off."
>
> "Twenty-five dollars reward for the negro slave, Sally. Walks as though crippled in the back."
>
> "Ran away, Joe Dennis. Has a small notch in one of his ears."
>
> "Ran away, negro boy, Jack. Has a small crop out of his left ear."
>
> "Ran away, a negro man, named Ivory. Has a small piece cut out of the top of each ear."
>
> While upon the subject of ears, I may observe that a distinguished abolitionist in New York once received a negro's ear, which had been cut off close to the head, in a general post letter. It was forwarded by the free and independent gentleman who had caused it to be amputated, with a polite request that he would place the specimen in his "collection."

In summary, despite the slave society's claims of "loving" and "caring for" their slaves, in the bright light of day, we can see readily that the slave society was sadistic and abusive to slaves, even more than to farm animals. There can be little better evidence of the extreme ill-treatment of slaves than the masters' own brazen public confessions of mistreatment in their own runaway slave advertisements.

THE SLAVE SOCIETY'S WAR ON ABOLITIONISTS

Slave Society's Repression

America's repressive dictatorship over millions of people—slaves—also spread a blanket of fear and repression over other Americans. When it came to Americans who opposed slavery—abolitionists—the guarantees in the Bill of Rights of freedom of speech, freedom of the press, and freedom of religion were meaningless. The slave society also often disregarded the prohibition of cruel and unusual punishment, as well as the constitutional rights to a fair trial by jury and due process.

Abolitionists, both African-American and white, were at risk of federal and state governmental prosecution and of mob rule. Despite the risks, there were courageous "free" African-Americans and whites who spoke and published against slavery and who actively assisted fugitive slaves. The slaves were not alone.

Illustrating the strength and reach of the American slave society, the Fugitive Slave Law of 1850 prohibited citizens in non-slave states from assisting fugitives and made them subject to prosecution and liable to slaveholders for doing so.

In the slave states, the Constitution—which protected slavery—was useless. The federal Bill of Rights was useless. The slave society flouted the ideals of the Declaration of Independence. Indeed, at times it would appear to have been a violation of law simply to read the Declaration of Independence to slaves and even to "free" African-Americans. As Pennsylvania Judge George Stroud states in his highly-respected 1856 treatise: "It is quite obvious that particular parts, if not the whole, of the Declaration of Independence are proscribed by [Louisiana] statutes."[803]

William Jay describes how proslavery advocates regarded abolitionists:[804]

> One of the most usual terms by which Abolitionists are designated by their opponents is, "the fanatics." It seems they are fanatics, because they believe slavery to be sinful.

During slavery, there was an open war in the slave states upon any person who dared to speak out against slavery, or even who may not simply have been sufficiently proslavery. In Texas, the Galveston News Weekly proclaimed, "Those who are not for us, must be against us."[805] There was no room for disagreement on the subject.

The Terror—and that is what it was for many—reached across state lines to businesses and business people who might conduct business in slave states. Slavery advocates even crossed state lines to launch physical attacks against abolitionists, even murdering Elijah Lovejoy, an abolitionist publisher in Illinois mobs previously had driven from Missouri.[806] State officials offered rewards for outspoken Northern abolitionists' capture or death.

---

803 Stroud, at 106.

804 W. Jay, **AN INQUIRY INTO THE CHARACTER AND TENDENCY OF THE AMERICAN COLONIZATION, AND AMERICAN ANTI-SLAVERY SOCIETIES** at 145 (Leavitt, Lord & Co., 1835) available from the Library of Congress at *www.HathiTrust.org/digital_library.*

805 Campbell, at 219-20. Emphasis added.

806 "Elijah Lovejoy, American Abolitionist" at *www.britannica.com/biography/Elijah-P-Lovejoy,* accessed June 9, 2022.

The slave society offered a bounty of $4,000 for William Lloyd Garrison.[807]

At the same time, slave state laws demonstrated how despicably so-called "free" African-Americans were regarded and treated by white proslavery devotees, such as pursuant to Louisiana law, being "commanded" to show respect to whites. A prescribed punishment for sowing "discontent" among "free" African-Americans was either "hard labour" for life or death.

CORNERSTONE SPEECH

"The new constitution has put at rest, forever, all the agitating questions relating to our peculiar institution—African slavery as it exists amongst us—the proper status of the negro in our form of civilization. This was the immediate cause of the late rupture and present revolution. …

"Our new government is founded upon … ideas; its foundations are laid, its corner-stone rests upon the great truth, that the negro is not equal to the white man; that slavery—subordination to the superior race—is his natural and normal condition. This, our new government, is the first, in the history of the world, based upon this great physical, philosophical, and moral truth. … Those at the North, who still cling to these errors, with a zeal above knowledge, we justly denominate fanatics."

"Alexander Stephens, Vice President of the Confederacy, The Cornerstone Speech" (1861) at *www.owleyes.org/search?q=cornerstone%20speech,* accessed Oct. 22, 2020

The Ineffectual Bill of Rights

The slave society cared little for freedoms for abolitionists. Judge Stroud cites "restraints upon freedom of speech and of the press:"[808]

> Besides the laws which affect *slaves only,* the statute-books of the slave-holding states exhibit degrading and despotic enactments growing out of the institution of slavery, which bear directly upon the *free white* population.
>
> Those to which I particularly allude are restraints upon freedom of speech and of the press.
>
> I pass over all statutable efforts to prevent the circulation of publications designed to excite insurrection among the slaves. I regard the distribution of all such publications as utterly indefensible.

He quotes the Louisiana law against literature with intent "to diminish that respect which is commanded to free people of colour for the whites by law, or to destroy that line of distinction which the law has established between the several classes of this community:" [809]

> In the *Revised Statutes of Louisiana* are these enactments:—"If any white person shall be convicted of being the author, printer or publisher of any written or printed paper or papers within this state, or shall use any language with the intent to disturb the peace or security of the same, in relation to the slaves of the people of this state, or TO DIMINISH THAT RESPECT *which is commanded to free people of colour for the whites by law, or to destroy that line of distinction which the law has established between the several classes of this community,* such person shall be adjudged guilty of high misdemeanour, and shall *be fined in* a sum not less than three hundred dollars nor exceeding one thousand dollars, and, moreover, *imprisoned* for a term not less than *six months* nor exceeding *three years.*" …

807 "William Lloyd Garrison and the Liberator" at *www.ushistory.org/US/28a.asp,* accessed June 9, 2022.

808 Stroud, at 104-06. Emphasis in original. Citations omitted.

809 Stroud, at 104-06. Emphasis in original.

For literature "having a tendency to produce discontent among the free coloured population of the state," Judge Stroud cites the punishment as being "hard labour for life" or "death at the discretion of the court:"[810]

> "Whosoever shall write, print, publish or distribute any thing having a tendency to produce *discontent* among the *free coloured population* of the state, shall, on conviction thereof before any court of competent jurisdiction, be sentenced *to imprisonment at hard labour for life, or suffer death*, at the discretion of the court."

The Louisiana law even reached sentiments "having a tendency to produce discontent" voiced "from … the pulpit," thus overriding the guarantee of freedom of religion, with punishment "at hard labour" up to 21 years or, in the discretion of the court, "death:"[811]

> "Whosoever shall make use of language in any public discourse from the bar, the bench, the stage, the pulpit, or in any place whatsoever, or whoever shall make use of language in private discourses or conversations, or shall make use of signs or actions, *having a tendency to produce discontent* among the *free coloured* population of this state, or to excite insubordination among the slaves, or whosoever shall knowingly be instrumental in bringing into this state any paper, pamphlet or book having such tendency as aforesaid, shall, on conviction thereof before any court of competent jurisdiction, suffer *imprisonment at hard labour* not less *than three years nor more than twenty-one years,* or DEATH, at the discretion of the court." …

Judge Stroud then expresses concern that it would be illegal in Louisiana to quote the Declaration of Independence:[812]

> It is quite obvious that particular parts, if not the whole, of the *Declaration of Independence* are proscribed by these statutes. What words can be named more likely *"to produce discontent"* or *"diminish the respect,"* &c., or *"destroy the line of distinction*

MISSISSIPPI DECLARATION OF CAUSES FOR SECESSION

"Our position is thoroughly identified with the institution of slavery—the greatest material interest of the world. Its labor supplies the product which constitutes by far the largest and most important portions of commerce of the earth. These products are peculiar to the climate verging on the tropical regions, and by an imperious law of nature, none but the black race can bear exposure to the tropical sun. These products have become necessities of the world, and a blow at slavery is a blow at commerce and civilization. That blow has been long aimed at the institution, and was at the point of reaching its consummation. There was no choice left us but submission to the mandates of abolition, or a dissolution of the Union, whose principles had been subverted to work out our ruin. …

"Utter subjugation awaits us in the Union, if we should consent longer to remain in it. It is not a matter of choice, but of necessity. We must either submit to degradation, and to the loss of property worth four billions of money, or we must secede from the Union framed by our fathers, to secure this as well as every other species of property."

"A Declaration of the Immediate Causes which Induce and Justify the Secession of the State of Mississippi from the Federal Union" at *www.battlefields.org/learn/articles/declarations-causes#mississippi,* accessed Oct. 22, 2020

810 Stroud, at 104-06. Emphasis in original.

811 Stroud, at 104-06. Emphasis in original.

812 Stroud, at 104-06. Emphasis in original.

> *between the several classes of the community,"* than—"ALL MEN ARE BORN FREE AND EQUAL," which this imperishable document declares is a *self-evident truth?* It says too that "*life,* LIBERTY, and *the pursuit of happiness,* are *inalienable rights* of man;" and it denominates this declaration also a *self-evident truth.*
>
> But to utter these sentiments or any thing equivalent, even in *private conversation,* within the territorial boundaries of *Louisiana,* is punishable with *"imprisonment at hard labour* not less than *three* years," and it may be with *twenty-one years* or DEATH, at the discretion of the court; while for the more deliberate crime of *printing* or *publishing* the same, nothing will expiate but such *imprisonment* FOR LIFE, or the infliction of DEATH! ...

Judge Stroud cites similar prohibitions in other states:[813]

> In *Alabama* there are kindred laws, but less exceptionable, because in these a guilty *intent* is requisite to constitute crime. As, however, *intent* is always a question for a jury, this tribunal, composed of the same people who make the laws, will have no difficulty in imagining an intent wherever a *distasteful* publication is charged upon a prisoner. ...
>
> The Code of Virginia of 1849 contains the following:—"If a free person by speaking or writing maintain that owners have not right of property in their slaves, he shall be confined in jail not more than one year and fined not exceeding five hundred dollars. He may be arrested and carried before a justice by any white person." ...

Again, illustrating the serious risks for the white and "free" African-American abolitionists in slave states, in Virginia not only did law forbid abolitionist "propaganda," but abolitionists were indicted for "printing and circulating" abolitionist literature.[814]

In Maryland, the State convicted Sam Green, a "free" African-American, who had aided Harriet Tubman. The State sentenced him to ten years in prison for possessing a copy of Uncle Tom's Cabin.[815]

In 1837, the Missouri General Assembly "prohibit[ed] the publication, circulation and promulgation of the abolition doctrines" in the State. The first offense was subject to a $1,000 fine (approximately $33,000 in today's money) and two years in the penitentiary; the second to 20 years; and the third to a life sentence.[816]

Attacks on Abolitionists Even Across State Lines

The slave society not only attacked abolitionists by disagreeing with them. The slave society also prohibited them to speak about or possess abolitionist literature by attacking them physically.

The federal courts participated in actions against abolitionists who assisted fugitive slaves. The Supreme Court held in *Jones v. Van Zandt*[817] that a white abolitionist in Ohio was liable to a Kentucky slaveowner for assisting the owner's slave in escaping. The abolitionist suffered financial ruin.

---

813 Stroud, at 104-06. Emphasis in original.

814 "West Virginia History" at *www.wvculture.org/history/journal_wvh/wvh21-1.html,* accessed Oct. 22, 2020.

815 Bradford, at 30.

816 Missouri State Archives—"Missouri's Early Slave Laws: A History in Documents, Laws Concerning Slavery in Missouri Territorial to 1850s" at *www.sos.mo.gov/archives/education/aahi/earlyslavelaws/slavelaws.asp,* Accessed Oct. 22, 2020.

817 *Jones v. Van Zandt,* 46 U.S. 215 (1847).

William Lloyd Garrison, a leading, abolitionist, cited a State law in Virginia prohibiting postmasters from delivering newspapers and other mail expressing abolitionist views. He quotes the Virginia Attorney General, who declared the enforceability of Virginia law against postmasters as to items in the mail, such as newspapers or books from other states:[818]

Richmond, Nov. 26th, 1859.

Sir,—The question is submitted to me for an opinion as to the effect of the law of Virginia upon the distribution of mail matter when it is of an incendiary character. A newspaper, printed in the State of Ohio, propagating abolition doctrines, is sent to a person through a post office in Virginia. What is the duty of the Postmaster in the premises?

The law of Virginia (Code of' Va., chap. 198, sec. 24) provides that "If a Postmaster or Deputy Postmaster know that any such book or writing (referring to such as advise or incite negroes to rebel or make insurrection, or inculcate resistance to the right of property of masters in their slaves) has been received at his office in the mail, he shall give notice thereof to some Justice, who shall inquire into the circumstances, and have such book or writing burned in his presence; if it appear to him that the person to whom it was directed subscribed therefor, knowing its character, or agreed to receive it for circulation to aid the purposes of abolitionists, the Justice shall commit such person to jail. If any Postmaster or Deputy Postmaster violate this section, he shall be fined not exceeding two hundred dollars."

This law is obligatory upon every Postmaster and Deputy Postmaster in the Commonwealth; and it is his duty, upon being aware that such book or writing is received at his office, to notify a Justice of the fact) that he may take the proceedings prescribed in the section quoted.

This State law is entirely constitutional, and does not, properly considered, conflict with the Federal authority in the establishment of post offices and post roads. This Federal power to transmit and carry mail matter does not carry with it the power to publish or to circulate. This last is a great State power, reserved and absolutely necessary to be maintained as a security to its citizens and to their rights. If the States had surrendered this power, it would, in these important particulars, have been at the mercy of the Federal authorities.

With the transmission of the mail matter to the point of its reception, the Federal power ceases. At that point, the power of the State becomes exclusive. Whether her citizens shall receive the mail matter is a question exclusively for her determination. Whatever her regulation upon the subject, is for her decision alone, and no one can gainsay it. Her sovereign right to make it closes the door to cavil and objection.

It is true the Postmaster is an officer of the Federal Government, but it is equally true he is a citizen of the State. By taking the Federal office, he cannot avoid his duty as a citizen; and the obligation to perform the duty of his office cannot absolve him from obedience to the laws of his Commonwealth nor will they be found to conflict. The State, in the case supposed, holds the hand of her citizen from receiving what is sent to him, and takes it herself. No citizen has the right to receive an invitation to treason against the commands of his State, and her law forbidding it and commanding it to be burned, refers to the right of the citizen to receive, not to the right of the Federal power to transmit and carry mail matter intended for him, which he does not receive, only because the law of the State forbids it.

818 W. Garrison, **THE NEW REIGN OF TERROR IN THE SLAVEHOLDING STATES, FOR 1859-60** at 5-7 (American Anti-Slavery Society, 1860) ("Garrison").

I have no hesitation in saying that any law of Congress, impairing directly or indirectly this reserved right of the State, is unconstitutional, and that the penalty of the State law would be imposed upon a Postmaster offending against it, though he should plead his duty to obey such unconstitutional act of Congress.

If there be a conflict, therefore, between the postal regulations of Congress and this law of Virginia, it is because the former have transcended their true constitutional limits, and have trenched upon the reserved rights of the State. In such a case the citizen, though a Postmaster, must take care to obey the legitimate authority, and will not be exempt from the penalty of the State law by reason of any obligation to perform the duties of a Federal office, which are made to invade the reserved jurisdiction of the State in matters involving her safety and her peace.

It is eminently important that the provisions of the law in question should be rigidly adhered to by all the Postmasters in the State, and that the Justices to whose notice the matter may be brought should firmly execute the law, whenever a proper case presents itself for their decision.

With high respect, your obedient servant,

J.R. TUCKER.

For the Governor.

The war on abolitionists did not end only with enforcement of State law, but extended also to refusal to enforce State law in order to protect abolitionists, their families, and their property from harm. The Governor of Kentucky informed citizens threatened with violent removal from the State that:[819]

> the public mind was deeply moved by the events in Virginia [Nat Turner's insurrection], and that until the excitement subsided, their presence in the State would be dangerous, and he could not engage to protect them from their fellow-citizens who had resolved that they must go.

Thus, law and trials were unnecessary for proslavery forces to attack abolitionists physically. In Texas, mobs forced abolitionists out of the State, killing some. Texas vigilantes hunted a Methodist minister who had gone to Missouri, captured him, and brought him back to Texas, where they hung him.[820]

Abolitionists also suffered from mob rule in Missouri. Mobs drove them from one county to another. They threw a publisher's printing press into a river, and drove him out of the State.[821]

Even in the North, Mr. Garrison himself "in Boston, ... was dragged through the streets and nearly killed. A bounty of $4000 was placed on his head."[822]

Virginia indicted Horace Greeley, the editor of the New York Tribune, for statements he had made in his newspaper.[823]

819 Garrison, at 15.

820 Campbell, at 224-28.

821 "Slavery in Missouri" at *centerplace.org/history/misc/soc/soc14.htm*, accessed Oct. 22, 2020.

822 "William Lloyd Garrison and the Liberator" at *www.ushistory.org/US/28a.asp*, accessed Oct. 22, 2020.

823 "West Virginia History" at *www.wvculture.org/history/journal_wvh/wvh21-1.html*, accessed Oct. 22, 2020.

TEXAS DECLARATION OF CAUSES FOR SECESSION

"In all the non-slave-holding States, in violation of that good faith and comity which should exist between entirely distinct nations, the people have formed themselves into a great sectional party, now strong enough in numbers to control the affairs of each of those States, based upon the unnatural feeling of hostility to these Southern States and their beneficent and patriarchal system of African slavery, proclaiming the debasing doctrine of the equality of all men, irrespective of race or color—a doctrine at war with nature, in opposition to the experience of mankind, and in violation of the plainest revelations of the Divine Law."

"A declaration of the causes which impel the State of Texas to secede from the Federal Union" at *www.tsl.texas.gov/ref/abouttx/secession/2feb1861.html,* accessed Oct. 22, 2020

After David Walker published his widely-distributed **APPEAL,**[824] urging slaves to be ready to revolt and criticizing their passivity, the slave society placed a bounty on his head:[825]

> The Governor of Georgia wrote to the Hon. Harrison Grey Otis, the Mayor of Boston, requesting him to suppress the Appeal. His Honor replied to the Southern Censor, that he had no power nor disposition to hinder Mr. Walker from pursuing a lawful course in the utterance of his thoughts. A company of Georgia men then bound themselves by an oath, that they would eat as little as possible until they had killed the youthful author. They also offered a reward of a thousand dollars for his head, and ten times as much for the live Walker.

Mr. Walker died under mysterious circumstances, possibly murder, possibly tuberculous, at a relatively young age.[826]

Underscoring the reach of proslavery forces across state lines to stifle speech, Mr. Garrison provides the following example of strong proslavery pressures brought upon Northern businesses conducting business in slave states:[827]

> Northern merchants who sell goods for Southern consumption are called upon to square their opinions according to the plantation standard, and any recusancy on their part is visited with the discipline of the loss of trade. Editors of petty Southern newspapers hardly capable of forming an intelligent notion upon any subject, and quite incapable of writing two consecutive sentences of even tolerable English, form their Black Lists and White Lists, and compel the obedience and subsidy of large commercial houses of a great, and wealthy, and powerful city, a thousand miles distant. And, worst of all this state of things seems accepted rather as in the natural order of events, than as a monstrous growth of an insolent tyranny on the one hand, and the subserviency of an infinitely mean, and sordid, and peddling poltroonery on the other.

---

824 D. Walker, **APPEAL TO THE COLORED PEOPLE OF THE WORLD, BUT IN PARTICULAR, AND VERY EXPRESSLY, TO THOSE OF THE UNITED STATES OF AMERICA, WRITTEN IN BOSTON, STATE OF MASSACHUSETTS** (1829), Academic Affairs Library, Univ. of North Carolina at Chapel Hill, available at docsouth.unc.edu.

825 "History Is a Weapon: David Walker's Appeal" at *www.historyisaweapon.com/defcon1/walkerappeal.html,* accessed Oct. 22, 2020.

826 "History Is a Weapon: David Walker's Appeal" at www.historyisaweapon.com/defcon1/walkerappeal.html, accessed Oct. 22, 2020.

827 Garrison, at iii-iv.

> And here is its latest development. A morning paper of yesterday publishes 'a card,' signed 'James P. Hambleton, editor of the *Southern Confederacy.*' The Black List of the *Confederacy* had included the name of Davis, Noble & Co., No, 87 Chambers street, and the purpose of the card is to exonerate this firm from the charge implied in that publication, the editor being now satisfied, on 'the best evidence that the aforesaid firm are true, constitutional men, having never been tainted with any of the Anti-Slavery isms of the day, either directly or indirectly, and that we hereby recommend them to their former patrons at the South, as a concern in every respect deserving their continued patronage and support.' ...

Trial in North Carolina for Religious Speech

Mr. Garrison provides a news report of a trial in North Carolina against Rev. Daniel Worth, a minister, for speaking against slavery and circulating a book, **HELPER'S IMPENDING CRISIS.** Among other things, the book discussed how slavery disadvantaged the South economically and made suggestions on ending slavery. The slave society's insecurity was so great that it could not tolerate such a book. In opposing any form of literature questioning slavery, like the Duke of York's despotic disregard for a "Charter of Liberties" requested by the people under his rule,[828] the slave society simply ignored the freedoms of speech, press, and religion.

The following are excerpts from the news report of charges against Rev. Worth for "uttering language in the pulpit calculated to make slaves and free negroes dissatisfied with their condition:"[829]

> On Friday, the 23d inst., Daniel Worth, a Wesleyan Methodist preacher, a native of this State, but who had been residing until within two years past in Indiana, where he was formerly a member of the

GEORGIA DECLARATION OF CAUSES FOR SECESSION

"For the last ten years we have had numerous and serious causes of complaint against our non-slave-holding confederate States with reference to the subject of African slavery. They have endeavored to weaken our security, to disturb our domestic peace and tranquility, and persistently refused to comply with their express constitutional obligations to us in reference to that property ... .

"The prohibition of slavery in the Territories, hostility to it everywhere, the equality of the black and white races, disregard of all constitutional guarantees in its favor, were boldly proclaimed by [anti-slavery] leaders and applauded by its followers. ...

"[B]y their declared principles and policy they have outlawed $3,000,000,000 of our property in the common territories of the Union; put it under the ban of the Republic in the States where it exists and out of the protection of Federal law everywhere; because they give sanctuary to thieves and incendiaries who assail it to the whole extent of their power, in spite of their most solemn obligations and covenants; because their avowed purpose is to subvert our society and subject us not only to the loss of our property but the destruction of ourselves, our wives, and our children, and the desolation of our homes, our altars, and our firesides. To avoid these evils we resume the powers which our fathers delegated to the Government of the United States, and henceforth will seek new safeguards for our liberty, equality, security, and tranquility. ..."

"Georgia Declaration of Causes for Secession" at *www.battlefields.org/learn/articles/declarations-causes#georgia,* accessed Oct. 22, 2020

828 See *"Chapter Three: The Duke of York Promotes Slavery—The 'Duke's Laws' and His Opposition to Representative Government."*

829 Garrison, at 23-24.

> Legislature of that State, was arrested by the Sheriff of this county on a charge of selling and circulating "Helper's Impending Crisis," and also of uttering language in the pulpit calculated to make slaves and free negroes dissatisfied with their condition, thereby offending against the laws of the State. He was brought before the magistrates of the town, and a partial hearing had, when the case was adjourned until the following afternoon at one o'clock, for the purpose of procuring the attendance of witnesses for the prosecution. The prisoner was taken to jail, bail having been refused by the magistrates.
>
> On Saturday, at the appointed hour, the Court met. The examination was held in the old Court-House, which was crowded. …

From the news account cited by Mr. Garrison, Rev. Worth did indeed circulate literature and suggest a means by which slavery could be ended. He also made comments critical of North Carolina State legislators:[830]

> Worth acknowledged during the examination that he had been engaged in circulating Helper's book, and also a work on the "War in Kansas," but that he did not consider it any harm to circulate them … .
>
> During the examination, various extracts were read from "Helper's Impending Crisis," some showing the *modus operandi* by which slavery was to be got rid of in the South, and others pretending to give facts, all of which were commented on by the various counsel for the State.
>
> It was also proved that Worth had, in the pulpit, on the Sabbath day, applied the most opprobrious epithets to the legislators of the State of North Carolina, saying that the laws ought not to be obeyed; that "they were made by a set of drunkards, gamblers and whoremongers."

Rev. Worth's prosecutors appealed to the passions of the jury and those in attendance in the courtroom:[831]

> The prosecution was opened by Wm. Scott, Esq. … . He read many extracts from the book, and showed how grossly perverted were the facts pretended to be therein set forth—that they were base lies and calumnies on the South.
>
> Robert P. Dick, Esq., made some highly effective and stirring remarks … . He spoke of Helper as a traitor to the State that had once claimed him as a North Carolinian, adding that this man who sought, in his "Impending Crisis," to array the South against slavery, and bring about bloodshed and anarchy, and to desolate and lay waste the beautiful South, to dissolve the glorious Union, which had been given us by the wisdom of our forefathers, was obnoxious to the law under other criminal charges. He prayed and trusted that the Union would never be dissolved.
>
> Robert McLean, Esq., took up the question at issue. The very doctrines that the prisoner had been disseminating in his remarks from the pulpit, and which were contained in "Helper's Impending Crisis," which book he had been proved to have circulated, were at utter variance with the laws of the State of North Carolina, and it was upon this charge that he was now undergoing his examination. …

A website and paper published by the Wesleyan Methodist Church provides additional information regarding the incidents surrounding, and the trials of, Rev. Worth, as well as regarding actions taken against others who opposed slavery:[832]

---

830 Garrison, at 23-24.

831 Garrison, at 23-24.

832 Hamm, "Daniel Worth: Persistent Abolitionist, A Thesis Presented to the Department of History and The University Honors Committee, Butler University" (1979), at 120-131, republished at "Antislavery Roots: A Call to end Slavery—The Wesleyan Methodist Church 1843-1865" at *www.wesleyan.org/wp-content/uploads/2020/06/Daniel-Worth-Persistent-Abolitionist-Hamm.pdf*, accessed Oct. 22, 2020 ("Hamm"). Footnotes omitted.

The website states:

> As fugitive slaves made their way north, sixty-two-year-old Daniel Worth was heading south to replace expelled Wesleyan Methodist ministers. Arrested in December 1859, he spent the winter in an unheated cell, causing permanent disability. Worth became a hero in abolitionist circles and a celebrated speaker in some of the nation's largest churches. …

The paper describes the courtroom scene, stating that "the mood in the crowded courtroom grew ugly" when Rev. Worth discussed his views, including "sentiments of the rankest abolitionism:"[833]

> Never one to shrink from a battle, Worth did not mince words. He denied categorically any intention of inciting a slave revolt. He then went on to utter "sentiments of the rankest abolitionism." Apparently Worth intended to defend both his intentions and The Impending Crisis. Quoting extensively from the work and making antislavery statements, he denied that he was a disunionist or had attempted to provoke violence, citing the Wesleyans' opposition to war. His real motives for taking up residence in the state, he claimed, were to minister to the scattered Wesleyan congregations and attempt to improve his wife's health. Worth nonetheless drew a warning from the bench to confine himself to the matter at hand, while the mood in the crowded courtroom grew ugly. Ralph Gorrell, a prominent Greensboro attorney, addressed the crowd urging them to allow the law to take its course, and calm soon returned…

The paper indicates that Rev. Worth declined bail, knowing that a mob was outside the courthouse and that additional State officials were waiting to serve him with yet more warrants. The paper continues by describing the "ugly" mood in North Carolina. One newspaper opined that Rev. Worth "should have been taken out and swung to the nearest tree."

Elsewhere, proslavery forces advocated death for Rev. Worth's expression of his perspectives:[834]

> In North Carolina the popular mood was ugly. A reporter for the *New York Tribune* later wrote that the state's "50,000 square miles of stagnation had been stirred to action," while a member of one of Worth's congregations told *The Wesleyan* that the entire state was convulsed with hysteria. The New Bern *Daily Progress* editorialized. "We still think that Worth, when arrested, should have been taken out and swung to the nearest tree. Folly to talk about letting the law take its course in such cases." The usually reserved *Greensboro Patriot* repeated this sentiment, echoed as far away as New Orleans … . William W. Holden, the fiery editor of the state leading newspaper, the *Weekly Standard* of Raleigh, editorialized that Worth had "offended both man and God" and concluded: "We regret that the only legal punishment in his case is whipping, the pillory, and imprisonment. It is far better that one man should die than that the peace of whole communities should be endangered." …

In addition to Rev. Worth, a North Carolina schoolteacher lost his job when he "had publicly proclaimed himself an abolitionist." The State arrested others for circulating the book, "while authorities reluctantly released an old Quaker named Jonathan Harris who was known to have abolitionist sympathies." When proslavery forces found copies of the book in a box, "the books were burned in the town square."[835]

For months, Rev. Worth remained in jail in a deteriorating mood. A second trial found him guilty, but the Judge reduced Rev. Worth's bail to $3,000 (approximately $99,000 today). That provided the opportunity Rev. Worth needed:[836]

---

833 Hamm.

834 Hamm.

835 Hamm.

836 Hamm.

> Late in the evening of April 27 the bond was posted by five men, one of whom, James Davis, was a planter who supposedly said that he would sell a slave if necessary to raise the money needed. Aaron Worth [Rev. Worth's nephew] is the only source for the rest of the story.
>
> > The bonds were signed late in the evening, and he was placed in a closed carriage with two friends, one a slaveholder well-armed (without [Rev. Worth's] knowledge, however) and driven over unfrequented roads in a direction unexpected by his enemies. The following day was a drizzling one and but few people were on the road, and they were not recognized by anyone, and they soon succeeded in putting him on a train in Virginia, where he was soon north of the Mason-Dixon line.
>
> ... Thus with the aid of a slaveholder riding shotgun, the pacifist abolitionist Daniel Worth arrived in New York City May 5.

Other abolitionists were not so fortunate. The Wesleyan website provides the following further example of proslavery mob violence against an abolitionist:

> Micajah McPherson—A member of Freedom's Hill, Micajah was hung from a dogwood tree by a lynch mob for his anti-slavery activities. Thinking he was dead, the lynch mob returned for the rope to hang others. Micajah survived to continue his active role among the Wesleyans well after slavery was abolished.

Summary

The foregoing examples demonstrate in stark terms both that there were whites, as well as "free" African-Americans, willing to take substantial risks to aid and assist slaves.

The examples also demonstrates that there were aggressive proslavery forces waiting to impose brutal punishments upon them for doing so—often with full governmental support under color of law.

They establish the slave society's blatant disregard of freedoms set forth in the Constitution's Bill of Rights.

SLAVERY WAS A NATIONAL INSTITUTION: NORTH AND SOUTH

"In the South … slavery stood at the heart of the economic and social system … ."

"The colonial era saw the emergence in America of a true slave society … in which slave labor formed the basis of the economy and social order."

Dr. Peter Kolchin[837]

"For portions of the seventeenth and eighteenth centuries, New York City housed the largest urban slave population in mainland North America, with more slaves than any other city on the continent. During those years, slaves composed more than one quarter of the labor force in the city and perhaps as much as one half of the workers in many of its outlaying districts. Slavery died with glacial slowness; slave could be found in New York into the fifth decade of the eighteenth century."

Dr. Ira Berlin and Dr. Leslie Harris[838]

"For much of the eighteenth century, New York City was second only to Charleston, South Carolina, in its proportion of slaves in an urban population. It was a fact about New York that nearly always elicited comment from European visitors. 'It rather hurts a European eye to see so many negro slaves upon the streets,' one Scottish traveler complained.'"

Dr. Jill Lepore[839]

"To claim that the colonies would not have survived without slaves would be a distortion, but there can be no doubt that development was significantly speeded by their labor. They provided the basic working force that transformed shaky outposts of empire into areas of permanent settlement."

Dr. Edgar McManus[840]

"In several states, this trade [in slaves] is a chief source of wealth."

Frederick Douglass[841]

§ § §

Until my research, I did not learn that the English form of slavery practiced in America had its origins in New York. I did not learn that "New England had formal, legal slavery a full generation before it was established in the South."[842] I did not learn that, until the Civil War, Northern business interests and the North's economy supported slavery and conducted significant business with slaveowners and other slavery business interests.

---

837 Kolchin, at 27-28.

838 Berlin and Harris, at 4.

839 Lepore, at 60. Footnote omitted.

840 McManus, Black Bondage in the North at 17.

841 Douglass, "What to the Slave Is the Fourth of July?" (July 5, 1852) at "Text of Douglass's Speech" at *www.owleyes.org/text/what-to-the-slave-is-the-fourth-of-july/read/text-of-douglasss-speech#root-162,* accessed Nov. 5, 2020.

842 Harper, "Slavery in the North," at *slavenorth.com/slavenorth.htm,* accessed Oct. 23, 2020.

I did not learn that Maryland,[843] Delaware[844] and New Jersey[845] (and Union Border slave states Kentucky and Missouri) continued to practice slavery, even after the issuance of the Emancipation Proclamation and—except for Maryland, which ended slavery in 1864[846]—after the Civil War until the adoption of the 13th Amendment. Delaware declined to ratify the Amendment for decades, "calling it an illegal extension of federal powers over the states."[847] I did not learn that the District of Columbia not only had slaves until 1862, but was an important center of the slave trade until the Compromise of 1850.

NEW YORK'S GRADUAL ABOLITION

"[I]n 1817, New York enacted a second momentous piece of abolition legislation, stipulating that enslaved African Americans born before July 4, 1799—the portion of the slave population neglected by the 1799 law—would become free on July 4, 1827. By establishing a precise date on which the last slaves in New York would be freed, the law effectively abolished slavery in New York. It also accelerated the work of the 1799 law by shortening the period of apprenticeship required of African Americans emancipated under the 1799 law, to twenty-one years for both men and women. Since children born to slave mothers on the eve of July 4, 1827 could be apprenticed to the age of twenty-one, African Americans would remain unfree until 1848."

"The final nail in the coffin of slavery was not hammered in until 1841, when the state finally revoked the right of travelers to reside in New York for up to nine months with their slaves."

Rael, "Chapter 4: The Long Death of Slavery," in I. Berlin and L. Harris, ed., Slavery in New York at 132-33 (The New Press, 2005)

New York's Gradual Emancipation Law

"Emancipation" in the North generally assumed the form of "gradual" freedom, but it usually affected only future children of slaves, not existing slaves. In New York, existing slaves continued to labor in servitude until the mid-1800s.

Dr. Ira Berlin and Dr. Leslie Harris explain the operation of New York's 1799 gradual emancipation law:[848]

> The Gradual Emancipation Law freed not a single New York slave. It promised to free their children, but not until after they had served a long apprenticeship, until age twenty-eight for men and twenty-five for women—time enough for slaveholders to appropriate their most productive years. No slave needed to be freed under the law until well into the third decade of the nineteenth century, and slavery—in the person of those who were slaves in 1799—could conceivably survive until the brink of the twentieth century. ... [S[laveholders were not above selling would-be freed people to the slave states to the south.
>
> The 1799 law, in short, did not end slavery ... [In] 1817, at the urging of Governor Daniel Tomkins, the legislature agreed that on July 4, 1827, all those promised freedom by the Gradual Emancipation Law would be free. Still, those black men and women not covered by the 1799 law remained in bondage, and slavery survived in New York for another two decades.

---

843 Slavery in Maryland, at 31.

844 Harper, "Slavery in the North," at *slavenorth.com/delaware.htm*, accessed Oct. 23, 2020.

845 Hodges and Brown, at xxxiv.

846 Slavery in Maryland, at 31.

847 Harper, "Slavery in the North," at *slavenorth.com/delaware.htm*, accessed Oct. 23, 2020.

848 Berlin and Harris, at 16.

New York Was the Financial and Business Center of Slavery

Dr. Berlin and Dr. Harris describe how New York became the financial and commercial key to, and also became dependent upon, the success of the slave society, even after slavery's gradual abolition in the State:[849]

> The staggered emancipation set in motion in 1799 by [New York's] Gradual Emancipation Law also affected white New Yorkers. While Northern slavery was a diminishing presence, the presence of Southern slavery was strengthened and enlarged in the years that followed. During the nineteenth century, slavery was not so much abolished in New York as transformed. ... [The new order deepened—not dissolved—the commitment of many white New Yorkers to chattel bondage.
>
> Perhaps the most important element of this transformation was New York's increasing intimacy with the Southern economy. Following the War of 1812, New York City became the primary port for the shipment of raw cotton from the South to the textile mills of Europe. With the growth of the cotton trade, New York bankers, factors, and brokers became the chief financiers of slavery's expansion, which pushed the plantation westward from upcountry South Carolina into the black belt of Georgia, Alabama, and Mississippi and then across the Mississippi River. In bankrolling the cotton economy, New York businessmen assisted planters in purchasing the land slaves worked, the tools with which they labored, and—most importantly—the clothes they wore. New York's textile industry specialized in "negro cloth." But the connections did not stop there. New Yorkers manufactured the whips that overseers wielded, the books that planters read, and the finery plantation mistresses prized. Money borrowed from New York lenders allowed planters to buy slaves, and insurance purchased from New York brokers protected the planters' investments. White New Yorkers lubricated the Southern economy and became rich in the process. Even as the number of slaves in New York shrank, New York's links to—even dependence upon—slavery grew.

Citing the practice of Southern planters to visit New York on business and to enjoy its high life, bringing their slaves with them, Dr. Berlin and Dr. Harris opine that "such connections literally made New York an outpost of Southern culture."[850]

Dr. Patrick Rael states that "The only Northern state to outlast New York in preserving slavery was New Jersey; the last slaves were freed there in 1865."[851]

All Americans Benefited from Slavery

President Lincoln described the North's—and all Americans'—benefits from slavery in his 1862 State of the Union address:[852]

> It is no less true for having been often said that the people of the South are not more

SLAVES BUILT WHITE HOUSE, CAPITOL

"The D.C. commissioners, charged by Congress with building the new city under the direction of the president, initially planned to import workers from Europe to meet their labor needs. However, response to recruitment was dismal and soon they turned to African Americans—both enslaved and free—to provide the bulk of labor that built the White House, the United States Capitol, and other early government buildings."

"Q&A: Did Slaves Build the White House?" at *www.whitehousehistory.org/questions/did-slaves-build-the-white-house*, accessed Oct. 23, 2020

849 Berlin and Harris, at 22.

850 Berlin and Harris, at 23.
See also Rael, at 122-25, 132.

851 Rael, at 114.

852 President Lincoln's address is available at "Abraham Lincoln, Second Annual Message" at *www.presidency.ucsb.edu/documents/second-annual-message-9*, accessed Oct. 23, 2020. Emphasis added.

> responsible for the original introduction of this property than are the people of the North; and *when it is remembered how unhesitatingly we all use cotton and sugar and share the profits of dealing in them,* it may not be quite safe to say that the South has been more responsible than the North for its continuance.

In the North, textile mills, shipping and financial companies, and insurers, and the service businesses supporting them, profited and kept American slavery viable. As Abraham Lincoln stated, all Americans willingly bought and used cotton clothing, sugar, rice, tobacco and other products having origins as commodities produced by slaves. Thus, all Americans were able to purchase those items at less expensive prices because the slave laborers who produced the commodities received no pay.

The notion that slavery was solely a Southern institution, and that the North had little involvement in slavery, is fiction—a fantasy of certain Northerners who, to put it bluntly, often dislike Southerners and view Southerners with disdain and arrogance. To the contrary, slavery "played a central role in the economy of colonial New England."[853]

Douglas Harper discusses a tendency by Northerners to deny the North's involvement with slavery and to blame the South:[854]

> As the reality of slavery in the North faded, and a strident anti-Southern abolitionism arose, the memory of Northern slaves, when it surfaced at all, tended to focus on how happy and well-treated they had been … .
>
> Yet the petitions for freedom from New England and Mid-Atlantic blacks, and the numbers in which they ran off from their masters to the British during the Revolution, suggest rather a different picture. …
>
> The attempt to force blame for all America's ills onto the South led the Northern leadership to extreme twists of logic. …

PRETENDS TO BE FREE demonstrates the frequency with which slaves in New York and New Jersey ran away. The compilation contains hundreds of slaveholder advertisements seeking the capture and return of fugitive slaves.[855]

Northerners Discriminated Extensively *Against African-Americans*

While criticizing the South, Northerners discriminated extensively against African-Americans, including "free" African-Americans, who were not truly "free" due to the extensive oppression. In some

VOTER RESTRICTIONS

"In 1811, the [New York] state legislature required black men to present a government-endorsed certificate of freedom in order to vote; in 1815, the law was strengthened with a comprehensive registration system for black voters that placed significant barriers between black men and the ballot. Ostensibly designed to help reduce the electoral fraud rampant in early national New York, these laws scapegoated African Americans as special threats to democracy while saying nothing of the far more widespread problem of white voter fraud."

Rael, "Chapter 4: The Long Death of Slavery," in I. Berlin and L. Harris, ed., Slavery in New York at 131(The New Press, 2005)

---

853 "February 26, 1638, First Slaves Arrive in Massachusetts" at *www.massmoments.org/moment-details/first-slaves-arrive-in-massachusetts.html,* accessed Oct. 23, 2020.

854 Harper, "Slavery in the North," at *slavenorth.com/denial.htm*, accessed Oct. 23, 2020.

855 G. Hodges and E. Brown ed., **"PRETENDS TO BE FREE—RUNAWAY SLAVE ADVERTISEMENTS FROM COLONIAL AND REVOLUTIONARY NEW YORK AND NEW JERSEY"** (Fordham Univ. Press 2019).

states, even purportedly "free" African-Americans could not vote. They could not testify. They could not serve in militias.

The following are additional examples.

David Walker points out that African-Americans could not serve on juries and argues that the State compelled their children "to attend inferior schools."[856] Mr. Walker provides the following description of education discrimination in Massachusetts:[857]

> I must close this article by relating the very heart-rending fact, that I have examined school-boys and young men of colour in different parts of the country, in the most simple parts of Murray's English Grammar, and not more than one in thirty was able to give a correct answer to my interrogations. If any one contradicts me, let him step out of his door into the streets of Boston, New-York, Philadelphia, or Baltimore, (no use to mention any other, for the Christians are too charitable further south or west!)—I say, let him who disputes me, step out of his door into the streets of either of those four cities, and promiscuously collect one hundred school-boys, or young men of colour, *who have been to school,* and who are considered by the coloured people to have received an excellent education, because, perhaps, some of them can write a good hand, but who, notwithstanding their neat writing, may be almost as ignorant, in comparison, as a horse.—And, I say it, he will hardly find (in this enlightened day, and in the midst of this *charitable* people) five in one hundred, who, are able to correct the false grammar of their language.—The cause of this almost universal ignorance among us, I appeal to our school-masters to declare. Here is a fact, which I this very minute take from the mouth of a young coloured man, who has been to school in this state (Massachusetts) *nearly* nine years, and who knows grammar this day, nearly as well as he did the day he first entered the school-house, under a white master. This young man says: "My master would never allow me to study grammar." I asked him, why? "The school committee," said he "forbid the coloured children learning grammar"—they would not allow any but the white children "to study grammar." It is a notorious fact, that the major part of the white Americans, have, ever since we have been among them, tried to keep us ignorant, and make us believe that God made us and our children to be slaves to them and theirs. *Oh! my God, have mercy on Christian Americans!!!*

Northerners also discriminated against African-Americans in the use of transportation.

Douglass, who was biracial like countless other slaves and former slaves, encountered predictable reactions on a train:[858]

> Attempting to start from Lynn, one day, for Newburyport, on the Eastern railroad, I went, as my custom was, into one of the best railroad carriages on the road. The seats were very luxuriant and beautiful. I was soon waited upon by the conductor, and ordered out; whereupon I demanded the reason for my invidious removal. After a good deal of parleying, I was told that it was because I was black. This I denied, and appealed to the company to sustain my denial; but they were evidently unwilling to commit themselves, on a point so delicate, and requiring such nice powers of discrimination, for they remained as dumb as death. I was soon waited on by half a dozen fellows of the baser sort (just such as would volunteer to take a bull-dog out of

856 "David Walker Biography (c. 1796-c. 1830)" at *www.biography.com/writer/david-walker,* accessed Oct. 23, 2020.

857 Walker, at 38-39.

858 F. Douglass, **LIFE AND TIMES OF FREDERICK DOUGLASS, WRITTEN BY HIMSELF** at 399 (Boston: De Wolfe, Fiske & Co., 1892), available from the Library of Congress at *www.hathitrust.org/digital_library* ("Douglass, Life and Times").

a meeting-house in time of public worship), and told that I must move out of that seat, and if I did not, they would drag me out. I refused to move, and they clutched me, head, neck, and shoulders.

The outcome of the dispute was not entirely favorable to the railroad:[859]

[I]n anticipation of the stretching to which I was about to be subjected, I had interwoven myself among the seats. In dragging me out, on this occasion, it must have cost the company twenty-five or thirty dollars, for I tore up seats and all.

He then found that the train company dealt with him by stopping service entirely at the station:[860]

the superintendent ... ordered the trains to run through Lynn without stopping, while I remained in that town; and this ridiculous farce was enacted. For several days the trains went dashing through Lynn without stopping. At the same time that they excluded a free colored man from their cars, this same company allowed slaves, in company with their masters and mistresses, to ride unmolested.

In the end, after substantial controversy, Mr. Douglass succeeded: The train company allowed him to ride trains.

In Ohio, a train conductor forced William Wells Brown to ride in a baggage car. His daughter, Josephine, relates the following comical, if it were not so sad, story:[861]

[P]retended fastidiousness on the part of the whites has produced some of the most ridiculous scenes. WILLIAM WELLS BROWN, while travelling through Ohio in 1844, went from Sandusky to Republic, on the Mad River and Lake Erie Railroad. On arriving at Sandusky, he learned that colored people were not allowed to take seats in the cars with whites; and that, as there was no *Jim Crow car* on that road, blacks were generally made to ride in the baggage-car. Mr. Brown, however, went into one of the best passenger cars, seated himself, crossed his legs, and looked as unconcerned as if the car had been made for his sole use. At length, one of the railway officials entered the car, and asked him what he was doing there. "I am going to Republic," said Mr. Brown. "You can't ride here," said the conductor. "Yes I can," returned the colored man. "No you can't," rejoined the railway man. "Why?" inquired Mr. Brown. "Because we don't allow *niggers* to ride with white people," replied the conductor. "Well, I shall remain here," said Mr. Brown. "You will see, pretty soon, whether you will or not," retorted the railway man, as he turned to leave the car. By this time, the passengers were filling up the seats, and every thing being made ready to start. After an absence of a few minutes, the conductor again entered the car, accompanied by two stout men, and took Mr. Brown by the collar and pulled him out. Pressing business demanded that Mr. Brown should go, and by that train; he therefore got into the freight car, just as the train was moving off. Seating himself on a flour barrel, he took from his pocket the last number of the *Liberator* [published by abolitionist, William Lloyd Garrison], and began reading it. On went the train, making its usual stops, until within four or five miles of Republic, when the conductor, (who, by-the-by, was the same man who had moved Mr. Brown from the passenger car) demanded his ticket. "I have no ticket," returned he. "Then I will take your fare," said the conductor. "How much is it?" inquired Mr. Brown. "One dollar and a quarter," was the answer. "How much do you charge those who ride in the passenger cars?" inquired the colored man. "The same," said the conductor. "Do you suppose that I will pay the same price for riding up here in the freight car, that those do who are

859 Douglass, My Bondage and My Freedom at 399-400.

860 Douglass, My Bondage and My Freedom at 399-400 (1855).

861 J. Brown, at 56-58. Emphasis in original.

> in the passenger car?" asked Mr. Brown. "Certainly," replied the conductor. "Well, you are very much mistaken, if you think any such thing," said the passenger. "Come, black man, out with your money, and none of your nonsense with me," said the conductor. "I won't pay you the price you demand, and that's the end of it," said Mr. Brown. "Don't you intend paying your fare?" inquired the conductor. "Yes," replied the colored man; "but I won't pay you a dollar and a quarter." "What do you intend to pay, then?" demanded the official. "I will pay what's right, but I don't intend to give you all that sum." "Well, then," said the conductor, "as you have had to ride in the freight car, give me one dollar and you may go." "I won't do any such thing," returned Mr. Brown. "Why won't you?" inquired the railway man. "If I had come in the passenger car, I would have paid as much as others do; but I won't ride up here on a flour barrel, and pay you a dollar." "You think yourself as good as white people, I suppose?" said the conductor; and his eyes flashed as if he meant what he said. "Well, being you seem to feel so bad because you had to ride in the freight car, give me seventy-five cents, and I'll say no more about it," continued he. "No, I won't. If I had been permitted to ride with the other passengers, I would pay what you first demanded; but I won't pay seventy-five cents for riding up here, astride a flour barrel, in the hot sun." "Don't you intend paying any thing at all?" asked the conductor. "Yes, I will pay what is right." "Give me half a dollar, and I will say no more about it." "No, I won't," returned the other; "I shall not pay fifty cents for riding in a freight car." "What will you pay, then?" demanded the conductor. "What do you charge per hundred on this road?" asked Mr. Brown. "Twenty-five cents," answered the conductor. "Then I will pay you thirty-seven and a half cents," said the passenger, "for I weigh just one hundred and fifty pounds." "Do you expect to get off by paying that trifling sum?" "I have come as freight, and I will pay for freight, and nothing more," said Mr. Brown. The conductor took the thirty-seven and a half cents, declaring, as he left the car, that that was the most impudent negro that ever travelled on that road.

Even Harriet Tubman, a Civil War hero traveling on a military discount pass, suffered abusive on a train from Philadelphia to New York:[862]

> When the conductor ordered her to the smoking car, she refused. She explained that she was working for the government and was entitled to ride wherever she liked. "Come, hustle out of here! We don't carry niggers for half fare," the conductor yelled at her. He physically struggled with her, but Tubman's strength apparently outmatched him. ... He called upon two other men to help; they pried her fingers loose ..., then wrenched her arm and broke it. She was thrown violently into the smoking car, further injuring her shoulder and possibly breaking several of her ribs. No one on the car came to her aid; in fact, several passengers shouted epithets and encouraged the conductor to toss her off the train.

Sojourner Truth battled discrimination on public transportation in Washington, DC. A century before Rosa Parks refused to move to the back of a bus in Montgomery, Alabama, Ms. Truth fought the District of Columbia public transit system, especially the racist employees of the system. Until Truth's aggressive actions, system employees ignored the law.

The following anecdotes describe Truth's running battles with street car conductors and drivers of the streetcars:[863]

---

862 Larson, at 232. Footnotes omitted.

863 Dictated by S. Truth, written, compiled, and edited by O. Gilbert and F. Titus, **SOJOURNER TRUTH'S NARRATIVE AND BOOK OF LIFE** at 184-87 (1875), available from the Library of Congress *www.hathitrust.org/digital_library* ("Truth's Narrative and Book of Life"). Emphasis in original.

Unwilling to submit to this state of things, [Truth] complained to the president of the street railroad, who ordered the Jim Crow car to be taken off. A law was now passed giving the colored people equal car privileges with the white.

Not long after this, Sojourner, having occasion to ride, signaled the car, but neither conductor nor driver noticed her. Soon another followed, and she raised her hand again, but they also turned away. She then gave three tremendous yelps, "I want to ride! I want to ride!! I WANT TO RIDE!!!" Consternation seized the passing crowd—people, carriages, go-carts of every description stood still. The car was effectually blocked up, and before it could move on, Sojourner had jumped aboard. Then there arose a great shout from the crowd, "Ha! ! ha! ha!! She has beaten him," &c. The angry conductor told her to go forward where the horses were, or he would put her out. Quietly seating herself, she informed him that she was a passenger. "Go forward where the horses are, or I will throw you out," said he in a menacing voice. She told him that she was neither a Marylander nor a Virginian to fear his threats; but was from the Empire State of New York, and knew the laws as well as he did.

Several soldiers were in the car, and when other passengers came in, they related the circumstance and said, "You ought to have heard that old woman talk to the conductor." Sojourner rode farther than she needed to go; for a ride was so rare a privilege that she determined to make the most of it. She left the car feeling very happy, and said, "Bless God! I have had a ride." …

Mrs. Laura Haviland, a widely known philanthropist, spent several months in the same hospital [where Truth worked] and sometimes went about the city with Sojourner to procure necessaries for the invalids. Returning one day, being much fatigued, Mrs. Haviland proposed to take a car although she was well aware that a white person was seldom allowed to ride if accompanied by a black one. "As Mrs. Haviland signaled the car," says Sojourner, "I stepped one side as if to continue my walk and when it stopped I ran and jumped aboard. The conductor pushed me back, saying, 'Get out of the way and let this lady come in.' 'Whoop!' said I, 'I am a lady too.' We met with no further opposition till we were obliged to change cars. A man coming out as we were going into the next car, asked the conductor if 'niggers were allowed to ride.' The conductor grabbed me by the shoulder and jerking me around, ordered me to get out. I told him I would not. Mrs. Haviland took hold of my other arm and said, 'Don't put her out.' The conductor asked if I belonged to her. 'No,' replied Mrs. Haviland, 'She belongs to humanity.' 'Then take her and go,' said he, and giving me another push slammed me against the door. I told him I would let him know whether he could shove me about like a dog, and said to Mrs. Haviland, 'Take the number of this car.'

"At this, the man looked alarmed, and gave us no more trouble. When we arrived at the hospital, the surgeons were called in to examine my shoulder and found that a bone was misplaced. I complained to the president of the road, who advised me to arrest the man for assault and battery. The Bureau furnished me a lawyer, and the fellow lost his situation. It created a great sensation, and before the trial was ended, the inside of the cars looked like pepper and salt; and I felt, like Poll Parrot, 'Jack, I am riding.'" A little circumstance will show how great a change a few weeks had produced: A lady saw some colored women looking wistfully toward a car, when the conductor, halting, said, "Walk in, ladies." Now they who had so lately cursed me for wanting to ride, could stop for black as well as white, and could even condescend to say, 'Walk in, ladies.'"

Similarly, in Philadelphia, William Still fought public transit for years over discrimination requiring blacks to ride on street car running boards regardless of weather and danger. In an 1863 letter to *The Press,* Still cited inconveniences, and worse consequences to Philadelphia blacks who were compelled to ride on streetcar running boards:[864]

> A venerable old minister of the Gospel, in going from here to his home at Frankford, one dark, cold, and rainy night last winter, while occupying the only place on the platform assigned for colored people, was killed. Who has forgotten this fact?
>
> ... One evening, in going home from a lecture, two elegantly dressed young women stepped into a car and took seats. The conductor courageously brought the rules forward, and one of them instantly stepped out, while the other remained. The car was stopped, and the conductor seized her, and actually, by physical force, thrust her out of the car. The father of this young woman pays several hundred dollars taxes annually, keeps his horse and carriage, and lives as nicely as most respectable citizens. But the God-given hue of the skin of his daughter rendered her obnoxious to the rules of the railway company, and she had to meekly submit to the outrage.

Mr. Douglass reports still more discrimination in the North regarding employment, when white workers, who often feared competition from African-Americans, refused to work alongside him:[865]

> Once assured of my safety in New Bedford, I put on the habiliments of a common laborer, and went on the wharf in search of work. I had no notion of living on the honest and generous sympathy of my colored brother, Johnson, or that of the abolitionists. My cry was like that of Hood's laborer, "Oh! Only give me work." Happily for me, I was not long in searching. I found employment, the third day after my arrival in New Bedford, in stowing a sloop with a load of oil for the New York market. It was new, hardy and dirty work, even for a calker, but I went at it with a glad heart and a willing; hand. I was now my own master—a tremendous fact—and the rapturous excitement with which I seized the job, may not easily be understood, except by some one with an experience something like mine. The thoughts—"I can work! I can work for a living; I am not afraid of work; I have no Master Hugh to rob me of my earnings"—placed me in a state of independence, beyond seeking friendship or support of any man. That day's work I considered the real starting point of something like a new existence. Having finished this job and got my pay for the same, I went next in pursuit of a job at calking. It so happened that Mr. Rodney French, late mayor of the city of New Bedford, had a ship fitting out for sea, and to which there was a large job of calking and coppering to be done. I applied to that noble hearted man for employment, and he promptly told me to go to work; but going on the float-stage for the purpose, I was informed that every white man would leave the ship if I struck a blow upon her.

After moving North, Frances Ellen Watkins Harper could not return to Maryland. Foster states: "About 1853, Maryland passed a law that forbid free blacks from the North to enter the state. The penalty was enslavement."[866] Harper was aware that a "free" black man who entered Maryland innocently had been sold

864 J. Boyd, "William Still: His Life and Work to This Time" in W. Still, **STILL'S UNDERGROUND RAIL ROAD RECORDS** at lii (Philadelphia: Wm Still, 1886), available from the Library of Congress at *www.hathitrust.org/digital_library.*

865 Douglass, My Bondage and My Freedom, at 348-49.

866 F. Foster, ed., **A BRIGHTER COMING DAY: A FRANCES ELLEN HARPER READER** Introduction at 10 (New York: The Feminist Press at the City University of New York, 1990) ("Foster"); W. Still, **THE UNDERGROUND RAILROAD: A RECORD** at 757 (Philadelphia: Porter & Coates, 1872) ("Still, 1872 Edition"), available from the Library of Congress at *www.hathitrust.org/digital_library*; "Frances Ellen Watkins Harper" at *www.africanamericanpoetry.org/frances-e-w-harper*, accessed March 1, 2022.

into slavery in Georgia. He escaped, and but after recapture soon died. "Her reaction to this incident was both personal and philosophical. Coming at a moment when she was searching for a way to contribute to the general welfare of her race, it became a major turning point in her life."[867] She devoted her life to opposing slavery.[868]

Ironically, while Maryland was a slave state, certain "free" states would not readily admit "free" African-Americans. Douglas Harper describes how "Ohio, with slave-state Kentucky across the river, took the lead in aggressively barring black immigration."[869] Ohio required African-Americans to post bonds and provide judicial evidence that they were free. When African-Americans petitioned the State legislature, the legislature "denied they had the right to petition the government 'for any purpose whatsoever.'"[870] Mobs of white citizens in Cincinnati attacked an African-American ghetto, burning homes and beating residents. The mobs forced "about half" of the African-American residents to emigrate to Canada. Ohio did not permit African-American children to attend schools with whites. Ohio courts upheld the practice, citing "an almost invincible repugnance to such communion and fellowship."[871]

Douglas Harper also describes how, although Illinois and Indiana had abolished slavery in their state constitutions, Indiana in 1816 and Illinois in 1818, Illinois required "free" African-Americans moving into the State to produce legal documents establishing their freedom and to post prohibitive bonds. African-Americans violating the Illinois law could be "advertised and sold at public auction."[872] Michigan, Iowa, and Oregon enacted similar laws. Illinois required African-Americans already living in the State to register with a court, show evidence of their freedom, and obtain a certificate. Violators of that law could be sentenced to indentured servitude for a year.[873]

Harper states that Indiana used its anti-immigration law to convict an African-American who brought his future wife into the State to marry her. The State Supreme Court upheld the law as having the purpose of preventing entry of African-Americans into Indiana and "to remove those already among us as speedily as possible." He continues his summary: There was no legal segregation in Indiana's public schools. None was necessary. The white citizens of the state would keep the schools racially pure more thoroughly than any legal provision could. A court upheld the white-only Indiana public schools in 1850, finding that, in the eyes of the state, "black children were deemed unfit associates of whites, as school companions."[874]

Sojourner Truth experienced the Indiana prohibition. Violent proslavery mobs frequently interrupted events and threatened the safety of antislavery participants. "The slave-holding spirit was now fully aroused in Indiana, and very bitter toward the negro. A law had been passed forbidding their entering the State or remaining in it. This law was unconstitutional, nevertheless the democrats had enforced it and endeavored to enforce it in Sojourner's case. A warrant was made out and she was arrested for both offenses. After Mrs. Griffing undertook Truth's defense alone, she outwitted and beat the enemy. Sojourner, nothing daunted, determined to remain and carry out the programme."[875]

---

867 Foster, Introduction at 10.

868 Foster, Introduction, at 10. Citation omitted. See also Still, 1872 edition at 757-58.

869 Harper, "Slavery in the North" at *slavenorth.com/ohio.htm,* accessed Oct. 23, 2020.

870 Harper, "Slavery in the North" at *slavenorth.com/ohio.htm,* accessed Oct. 23, 2020.

871 Harper, "Slavery in the North" at *slavenorth.com/ohio.htm,* accessed Oct. 23, 2020.

872 Harper, "Slavery in the North" at *slavenorth.com/northwest.htm,* accessed Oct. 23, 2020.

873 Harper, "Slavery in the North" at *slavenorth.com/northwest.htm,* accessed Oct. 23, 2020.

874 Harper, "Slavery in the North" at *slavenorth.com/northwest.htm,* accessed Oct. 23, 2020.

875 Truth's Narrative and Book of Life at 139-40.

There were plentiful instances of rowdy mobs along the abolitionists' paths disrupting meetings, and even attacking Frederick Douglass and other speakers physically, of which the following is an example:[876]

> When the party of reformers reached Indiana, where the pro-slavery spirit was always strong, the State having been settled largely by Southerners, their campaign of education became a running fight, in which Douglass, whose dark skin attracted most attention, often got more than his share. His strength and address brought him safely out of many an encounter; but in a struggle with a mob at Richmond, Indiana, he was badly beaten and left unconscious on the ground. A good Quaker took him home in his wagon, his wife bound up Douglass's wounds and nursed him tenderly,—the Quakers were ever the consistent friends of freedom, but for the lack of proper setting he carried to the grave a stiff hand as the result of this affray.

Fugitive Slave Laws Were National Laws

Not only did the Constitution protect slavery, but it was a fundamental national American government policy. As the Constitution contemplated, the federal government enacted and enforced the Fugitive Slave Laws of 1793 and 1850. The 1850 Law required the capture of escaped slaves anywhere in America and their return to their masters by government officials, and even by citizens, as if the slaves were criminals. The Law rewarded judges for returning slaves. The federal law applied even in states that had enacted emancipation laws.

As Tony Horwitz describes in his book about John Brown, **MIDNIGHT RISING**, in May 1854, President Franklin Pierce, *a Northerner from New Hampshire,* ordered federal troops to take a fugitive slave from Boston—removing him from the reach of abolitionists attempting to free him—and to transport the slave on a U.S. Navy vessel to his Virginia owner.[877]

In addition to the Fugitive Slave Law, Frederick Douglass, speaking in 1850, viewed slavery as a national shame penetrating New York and Boston (where race riots had occurred), as well as the North in general:[878]

> The evils resulting from this huge system of iniquity are not confined to the states south of Mason and Dixon's line. Its noxious influence can easily be traced throughout our northern borders. It comes even as far north as the state of New York. Traces of it may be seen even in Rochester; and travelers have told me it casts its gloomy shadows across the lake, approaching the very shores of Queen Victoria's dominions.
>
> The presence of slavery may be explained by—as it is the explanation of—the mobocratic violence which lately disgraced New York, and which still more recently disgraced the city of Boston. These violent demonstrations, these outrageous invasions of human rights, faintly indicate the presence and power of slavery here. It is a significant fact, that while meetings for almost any purpose under heaven may be held unmolested in the city of Boston, that in the same city, a meeting cannot be peaceably held for the purpose of preaching the doctrine of the American Declaration of Independence, "that all men are created equal." The pestiferous breath of slavery taints the whole moral atmosphere of the north, and enervates the moral energies of the whole people.

---

876 C. Chesnutt, **FREDERICK DOUGLASS** at 42-43 (Boston: Small, Maynard & Co., 1899), available from the Library of Congress at *www.hathitrust.org/digital_library.*

877 T. Horowitz, **MIDNIGHT RISING** at 39-40 (Picador, 2011) ("Horowitz").

878 Douglass, "Inhumanity of Slavery—Extract from a Lecture on Slavery at Rochester, December 1, 1850" contained in Douglass, My Bondage and My Freedom at 437.

Early Northern History of Slavery

The North's extensive involvement with slavery began in America's earliest days. Early in New England's history, settlers enslaved captured Native Americans. Dr. Edgar J. McManus describes how "Northern colonial progress" was hampered by "an acute labor shortage that everywhere retarded growth and hobbled the economy."[879]

According to Dr. McManus, "chattel bondage" began in New England using Native Americans captured in wars with local tribes. Native American warriors, however, were a dangerous threat, so the settlers traded the Native Americans to the Caribbean for Africans. Such exchanges became common, and "The use of black labor soon became general throughout New England."[880]

Due to the perceived essential necessity for labor, the Massachusetts General Court even advanced money ("a public investment") to fund a shipment of slaves.[881]

Dr. McManus cites, as the "first official recognition of chattel slavery as a legal institution," Massachusetts' ironic adoption of its "Body of Liberties" in 1641, legalizing ownership of slaves taken in wars and "the enslavement of 'such strangers as … are sold to us.'"[882] The "Articles of the New England Confederation" contained those principles, to which Connecticut and New Plymouth also subscribed. Rhode Island, which was not a member of the Confederation, enacted a similar law in 1652.[883]

By 1639, New Englanders used slaves in Connecticut and by 1645 in New Hampshire.[884]

Although some assert that slavery began in Port Comfort Virginia, near Jamestown, in 1619,[885] that is not entirely accurate in terms of true American slavery. The 1619 incident in Virginia involved a form of slavery similar to indentured servitude with servants who eventually gained their freedom, raised families, and owned property.[886]

Moreover, genuine slaves in Spanish colonies had existed in what is now America—Florida and Texas—for almost 100 years by the time the English brought captives into Virginia in 1619. The first recorded slave revolt in what is now America was against the Spanish in 1526.[887]

In New England, however, slavery—as opposed to indentured servitude—spread from the inception. Dr. McManus states[888] that New England's "[d]ependence on black labor drew the North into the overseas slave trade." He adds[889] that Rhode Island agriculture made "[s]lavery particularly suitable." Further, "Rhode Island's

---

879 McManus, Black Bondage in the North, at 1, 6-7, 10-11, 17, 42-43, 59. Footnotes omitted.

880 McManus, Black Bondage in the North, at 6.

881 "February 26, 1638, First Slaves Arrive in Massachusetts" at *www.massmoments.org/moment-details/first-slaves-arrive-in-massachusetts.html,* accessed Oct. 23, 2020.

882 McManus, Black Bondage in the North, at 59.

883 McManus, Black Bondage in the North, at 59.

884 McManus, Black Bondage in the North, at 6.

885 See "Project 1619" at *project1619.org,* accessed Oct. 23, 2020.

886 Brewer, at 1048-49; Berlin, at 30-31.

887 Deagan and MacMahon, at 13, 16.

888 McManus, Black Bondage in the North, at 7.

889 McManus, Black Bondage in the North, at 7.

heavy traffic in Negroes, together with that of Massachusetts, made New England the leading slave-trading region in America. The heavy profits of the slave trade stimulated the growth of other industries," such as shipbuilding, distilleries, molasses and agriculture.[890] He states that, in the early eighteenth century, the "great New York City merchants imported whole cargoes [of slaves], sometimes directly from Africa."[891]

Dr. McManus describes diverse elements of the New England economy relying upon slavery:[892]

> large numbers of artisans, sailors, and farmers were all dependent upon the traffic in Negroes. It became the hub of New England's economy.

He continues that, without slavery, key New England industries:[893]

> would have been wiped out, and large numbers of artisans, farmers, distillery workers, and sailors thrown out of work.

Dr. McManus continues that "The slave traffic quickly became one of the cornerstones of New England's commercial prosperity"[894] and that "The slave force everywhere made a vital contribution to the Northern economy."[895]

It is fiction that slavery was brutal only in the South. As described throughout this book, Northern slaveowners frequently were extremely sadistic, and many Northerners were blatantly racist.

SLAVE PUNISHMENT
AFTER DUKE OF YORK DEFEATS DUTCH

"English-owned slaves could be gibbeted, castrated, branded with hot irons, dismembered, or locked in dungeons for unlimited periods as punishment for insubordination."

Beckles, *Slave Voyages—The Transatlantic Trade in Enslaved Africans* at 67 (United Nations Educational, Scientific and Cultural Organization)

The website, MassMoments, states:[896]

> while in some cases conditions were less harsh in New England than on southern plantations, in reality slavery in the North was no less brutal. The Puritan missionary John Eliot "lamented ... with a bleeding and burning passion, that the English used their Negroes but as their Horses or the Oxen, and that so little care was taken about their immortal Souls."

In addition, the laws promoting slavery in New York led to significant restrictions on Africans, reflecting white fear and a perception that Africans must be repressed brutally.

Dr. McManus describes how "[s]tatutory recognition of slavery began in the Middle colonies with the English occupation of New Netherland."[897]

---

890 McManus, Black Bondage in the North, at 10.

891 McManus, Black Bondage in the North, at 12-13.

892 McManus, Black Bondage in the North, at 10.

893 McManus, Black Bondage in the North, at 10.

894 McManus, Black Bondage in the North, at 9.

895 McManus, Black Bondage in the North, at 17.

896 "February 26, 1638, First Slaves Arrive in Massachusetts" at *www.massmoments.org/moment-details/first-slaves-arrive-in-massachusetts.html,* accessed Oct. 23, 2020.

897 McManus, Black Bondage in the North, at 59.

"Sunday Meeting of Colored People at Chicago", *Slavery Images: A Visual Record of the African Slave Trade and Slave Life in the Early African Diaspora,* accessed November 15, 2020, *http://slaveryimages.org/s/slaveryimages/item/2272*

In outlining the enactment of slave laws in New York after the Duke of York conquered the Dutch, Dr. Alan Singer contrasts Dutch law in New Netherland, pursuant to which "permanent, racially based, hereditary slavery was not a clearly established institution." Dr. Singer describes the pivotal role of the English under the Duke in weaving the English form of slavery into the fabric of the New York colony, with a specific focus on Africans "once the British took control:"[898]

> British authorities acknowledged the titles of Dutch settlers to the people they claimed to own and, in 1665, a law recognized the legal status of slavery in the colony. Twelve years later, in 1677, a court ruled that any person of African ancestry who was brought to trial was presumed to be a slave unless they could establish that they were free. The racial basis of enslavement was further reinforced through an edict issued by British Governor Edmund Andros in 1679. Andros forbade settlers from enslaving local Indians, but confirmed the legality of African enslavement. …

Dr. Singer describes how, under the Duke, the English systematically enacted laws that placed restrictions on Africans, citing:[899]

> a series of measures designed to formalize the slave system. In 1682, local officials recognized the right of slaveholders to use physical violence, short of lethal force, to punish people they claimed as slaves. In 1684, a city ordinance prohibited more than four Africans and Native Americans from meeting together and Africans and Native Americans from possessing guns.

Even after the English ended the reign of the Duke as King James II, his successors were William

EVEN FUNERALS

"Slaves also gathered to bury their dead. … Slaves gathered at the end of the day, after their work was done, to escort the body to the grave. Whites reported hearing drumming and chanting, no doubt African derived, at these independent ceremonies late into the night. By the 1720s, whites had become concerned about these unsupervised gatherings. The [New York City] Common Council first ruled that funerals had to occur before sunset and then limited the number of mourners who could attend a slave's funeral to twelve, plus pallbearers and gravediggers.

L. Harris, In the Shadow of Slavery—African Americans in New York City, 1626-1863 at 41 (Univ. of Chicago Press 2003). Footnote omitted.

898 Singer, at 53. Emphasis added. Citations omitted.

899 Singer, at 53.

and Mary, a daughter, from 1689 to 1702, and Queen Anne, another daughter who came to power in 1702. Under James' daughters, the English continued to impose constantly increasing restrictions on Africans:[900]

> In 1702, a curfew was imposed on enslaved men and women over the age of fourteen, and New York's first comprehensive slave code was adopted which equated slave status with being African. The 1702 act approved by the governor and council forbade "Trade with any slave either in buying or selling, without leave and Consent of the Master or Mistress"; reiterated the restrictions on assembly except "when it shall happen they meet in some servile employment for their Master's or Mistress's profit"; and confirmed the right of "any Master or Mistress of slaves to punish their slaves for their Crimes and offenses." In 1706, a New York court ruled that conversion to Christianity did not change the legal status of enslaved Africans, and in 1711 the city's Common Council established the Wall Street waterfront "Meal Market" as the official location for the hiring of all slave labor. ...

Dr. Edgar McManus states[901] that "[t]he racial uniqueness of the Negro encouraged a trend toward special treatment which in the end reduced the bondsmen to chattels completely under the power of the masters." He adds that "New York City slaves were legally subject to an elaborate body of public controls." Dr. McManus expresses a view similar to that of Dr. Singer that, from 1682, the English government in New York enacted a variety of statutes that legalized brutal treatment of African-American slaves. These statues, among other things, "subjected Negro bondsmen to special public controls, disqualified them as witnesses, and recognized the complete power of the masters over them."[902]

"Funeral, Antebellum U.S. South, 19th cent.", *Slavery Images: A Visual Record of the African Slave Trade and Slave Life in the Early African Diaspora*, accessed November 15, 2020, *http://slaveryimages.org/s/slaveryimages/item/1854*

Dr. Jill Lepore cites a lengthy set of later repressive prohibitions and regulations enacted in 1730 and 1731 restricting slaves in New York, such as among others:[903]

- Limiting the number of slaves who could meet to three (up to 40 lashes on the "naked back" for violations)
- A requirement to carry a lantern and lighted candle when out at night "so as the light may be plainly seen"
- Making excessive noise, especially on Sundays
- Gambling
- Riding a horse too swiftly or in a disorderly manner
- Vending corn, peaches, or other fruit

Yet, the development of the severe English form of slavery did not end there.

900 Singer, at 53-54.

901 McManus, Slavery in New York, at 80-82, 86. Footnotes omitted.

902 McManus, Slavery in New York, at 80. Footnotes omitted.

903 Lepore, at 78.

Northern Slavery's Violence Grows

During the reign of the Duke of York, including in his role as King James II, New York amplified slavery's violence against slaves. The violence increased under his successors.

In New York, slaves no longer could gather, subject to a punishment of "flogging." The Colony required towns to have official "Negro whippers" for the purpose:[904]

> As early as 1682, it was a misdemeanor, punishable by flogging for more than four slaves to meet together on their own time. In 1702 the number permitted to meet together was reduced to three and, in order to insure uniform enforcement, each town was required to maintain a "Negro whipper" to flog violators. Gambling was strictly prohibited and slaves over the age of fourteen had to be off the streets by sunset unless they were accompanied by a member of the master's family.

Dr. Leslie Harris describes an incident in which the government made its control over slaves abundantly clear for all slaves:[905]

> On an August evening in 1696, the mayor of New York attempted to disperse a group of slaves. When he threatened to take them into custody, one of them, Prince, struck him in the face. The mayor quickly made Prince an example: The next day, the slave was stripped, tied to a cart, and dragged around the perimeter of the city. At each street corner, he received eleven lashes.

New York law granted masters the rights to sell and lease their slaves and to punish slaves severely:[906]

> Legally the slaves were chattels which the masters might lend, lease, sell or otherwise dispose of at any time. Short of death and mutilation, the law unconditionally upheld the right of the master to punish private offenses committed by his bondsmen and to use whatever force was needed to compel obedience. The ultimate sanction of slavery was force, and the law supported it completely in this respect. … [W]hether the master was cruel or kind was his own affair … .

New York citizens committed heinous acts against slaves, as described by Dr. McManus. He states that slaves who killed white people "could expect no mercy" in New York, with the courts empowered to impose whatever punishment the courts deemed appropriate under the circumstances. He states that "[f]or more serious offenses punishment was frankly terroristic and brutal."[907] Given that New York was barbarous in colonial times, this resulted in terrible and sickening brutality, as evidenced by the following examples:[908]

- When "two slaves were sentenced to death by torture for murdering a white family," according to a witness, the slaves "were put to all manner of torment possible" "One of the culprits was hung alive in chains and partially impaled so that his death pains were prolonged for hours."
- In another case, "when a slave killed another slave," thus costing the master who owned the deceased slave, "the court sentenced him 'to be hanged by the neck till he shall be dead, and to be cut with a knife in his throat and after to be hanged in a chain for an example of others'"
- "The normal punishment for [rape] would have been burning at the stake."

---

904 McManus, Slavery in New York, at 80-81. Footnotes omitted.

905 Harris, at 37. Footnote omitted.

906 McManus, Slavery in New York, at 81-82. Footnotes omitted.

907 McManus, Slavery in New York, at 94. Footnotes omitted.

908 McManus, Slavery in New York, at 94-97. Footnotes omitted.

Dr. McManus states that a New Jersey court "sentenced a slave convicted of murder to have his hand 'cut off and burned before thine eyes'" before hanging.[909]

He describes a slave in New York "sentenced to 'be hung up in chains alive and so to continue without any sustenance until he be dead.'"[910] He further cites slaves who "had their ears cut off."[911]

Expansion of Slavery in the North

The English government officially backed the slave trade,[912] evidenced especially by the "Duke's Laws" "recogniz[ing] slavery as a legal institution" in New York after England defeated the Dutch. He adds that "Slavery in New Jersey [which had been part of New Netherland] obtained legal sanction for the first time under the [English] proprietary regime of Berkeley and Carteret." In 1700, legislation "made Pennsylvania the last Northern colony to legitimize the institution."[913]

Dr. McManus illustrates the importance of slavery in Pennsylvania: "The colonial iron industry depended heavily upon black labor," citing a petition from Pennsylvania ironmasters to reduce the import duty on slaves because of an insufficiency of white workers "for the hard conditions that prevailed in the bloomeries and mills repelled free workers."[914]

TheRoot.com states, regarding New York City, that:[915]

> Enslaved and free Africans were largely responsible for the construction of the early city, first by clearing land, then by building a fort, mills, bridges, stone houses, the first city hall, the docks, the city prison, Dutch and English churches, the city hospital and Fraunces Tavern. At the corner of Wall Street and Broadway, they helped erect Trinity Church.

The website also describes the auctions of slaves at the Meal Market at Wall and Water Streets after unloading at the New York port from their voyages from Africa.

WALL STREET

"In March 1653, [Peter Stuyvesant] ordered [Dutch West India] Company slaves to build a barricade with logs 'twelve feet long, eighteen inches in circumference, sharpened at the upper end" from river to river across Manhattan Island. 'The Wall'—Wall Street—was added to the slaves' workload."

C. Moore "Chapter 1, A World of Possibilities: Slavery and Freedom in Dutch New Amsterdam," in I. Berlin and L. Harris, ed. Slavery in New York at 51 (The New Press, 2005)

In 1702, even after the Duke of York's reign as King James II had ended, the promotion of slavery by the English government included instruction to New York's Governor "to see to it that New Yorkers had a steady supply of Negroes at reasonable prices."[916]

---

909 McManus, Black Bondage in the North, at 85.

910 McManus, Black Bondage in the North, at 129-30. Footnotes omitted.

911 McManus, Black Bondage in the North, at 132.

912 See *"Chapter Three: The Duke of York Promotes Slavery—Duke of York as Key Governmental Slave Trader: Royal African Company."*

913 McManus, Black Bondage in the North, at 59-60.

914 McManus, Black Bondage in the North, at 42-43..

915 Harper, "How Slave Labor Made New York" at *www.theroot.com/how-slave-labor-made-new-york-1790895122,* accessed Oct. 24, 2020.

916 McManus, Black Bondage in the North, at 11.

"The Cook", *Slavery Images: A Visual Record of the African Slave Trade and Slave Life in the Early African Diaspora,* accessed November 16, 2020, *http://slaveryimages.org/s/slaveryimages/item/520*

Dr. Leslie Harris states that "the British continued the reliance on African slave labor as the foundation of New York's colonial working class."[917]

She describes how, once the English gained control of New York:[918]

> [O]wnership of slaves in British New York spread widely among the white population. From the merchant elite to small businessmen, owning slaves was a profitable enterprise. Overall in Manhattan, 40 percent of European households owned slaves, averaging 2.4 slaves per household.

Dr. Singer describes the great extent of New York City's reliance upon slavery, with slaves "ma[king] up as much as 30 percent of the population in some counties near New York."[919]

Dr. Harris adds:[920]

> After 1737, the Manhattan port experienced a large increase in trade, generating a need for unskilled labor. ... The importation of slaves escalated to meet the city's demand for unskilled labor. ... By the mid-eighteenth century, New York held the largest number of slaves of any colony north of Maryland, and Manhattan held the third largest concentration of slaves in a North American city, after Charleston and New Orleans.

Dr. Berlin and Dr. Harris add that, because slaveholders in New York discouraged slave marriage and families, including domestic female slaves having children, there was an increased emphasis upon direct importation of Africans. In turn, susceptibility to disease and abuse led to "increased ... mortality rates of the slave population. The vicious cycle made New York into a death factory for black people."[921]

Although the revolutionary War gave slaves an opportunity to escape, many through defection to British lines, following the War, Dr. Patrick Rael states that the black population had recovered in New York City, and "New York City became a haven for slavery."[922]

Before the Revolution, as America moved to the mid- and late-1700s, in addition to New York, slavery remained vital to the entire Northern economy.

917 Harris, at 27.

918 Harris, at 29-30. Footnotes omitted.

919 Singer, at 9.

920 Harris, at 29-30. Footnotes omitted.

921 Berlin and Harris, at 12.

922 Rael, at 126.

Dr. Greg Grandin states[923]:

> Even before the expansion of slave labor in the South and into the West, slavery was already an important source of northern profit … . Banks capitalized the slave trade and insurance companies underwrote it. Covering slave voyages helped start Rhode Island's insurance industry, while in Connecticut, some of the first policies written by Aetna were on slave lives. In turn, profits made from loans and insurance policies were plowed into other northern businesses.

In Slavery in the North, Douglas Harper states: "African slavery is so much the outstanding feature of the South, in the unthinking view of it, that people often forget there had been slaves in all the old colonies." He adds that slavery—[924]

> wove itself into the entire regional economy of New England. The Massachusetts slave trade gave work to coopers, tanners, sailmakers, and ropemakers. Countless agents, insurers, lawyers, clerks, and scriveners handled the paperwork for slave merchants. Upper New England loggers, Grand Banks fishermen, and livestock farmers provided the raw materials shipped to the West Indies on that leg of the slave trade. Colonial newspapers drew much of their income from advertisements of slaves for sale or hire. New England-made rum, trinkets, and bar iron were exchanged for slaves.

He cites objections by "Massachusetts merchants" to British rum and molasses taxes. In addition, he cites rum as an important article of trade used to purchase slaves in Africa:[925]

> When the British in 1763 proposed a tax on sugar and molasses, Massachusetts merchants pointed out that these were staples of the slave trade, and the loss of that would throw 5,000 seamen out of work in the colony and idle almost 700 ships.
>
> The connection between molasses and the slave trade was rum. Millions of gallons of cheap rum, manufactured in New England, went to Africa and bought black people.

BABIES LESS DESIRABLE

"Slaves' low fertility failed to concern their owners. On the contrary, female sterility became a selling point in a city with limited housing. … One owner sold his female slave in 1756 'because she breeds too fast for her owner to put up with such inconvenience.' Infant mortality was high, and infanticide not uncommon, although it is unclear who was committing infanticide—mothers or masters."

J. Lepore, "Chapter 2: The Tightening Vise: Slavery and Freedom in British New York" in I. Berlin and L. Harris, ed., Slavery in New York at 64 (The New Press, 2005)

IN FACT, BABIES ARE SO ANNOYING

"[Sojourner Truth] had often heard her father repeat a thrilling story of a little slave-child, which, because it annoyed the family with its cries, was caught up by a white man, who dashed its brains out against the wall. An Indian (for Indians were plenty in that region then) passed along as the bereaved mother washed the bloody corpse of her murdered child, and learning the cause of its death, said, with characteristic vehemence, 'If I had been here, I would have put my tomahawk in his head!' meaning the murderer's."

Dictated by S. Truth, written and edited by O. Gilbert, Sojourner Truth's Narrative and Book of Life at 82-83 (1875), available from the Library of Congress at www.hathitrust.org/digital_library

---

923 Grandin, "Capitalism and Slavery" (The Nation, May 1, 2015) at *www.thenation.com/article/archive/capitalism-and-slavery/*, accessed Oct. 24, 2020.

924 Harper, "Slavery in the North, Northern Profits from Slavery" at *slavenorth.com/profits.htm*, accessed Oct. 24, 2020.

925 Harper, "Slavery in the North, Northern Profits from Slavery" at *slavenorth.com/profits.htm,* accessed Oct. 24, 2020.

North's Role in the Slave Trade

The North's active involvement in slavery and the slave trade continued well into the mid-1800s. Dr. Alan Singer states that, in the 1800s, "the port of New York functioned as a major international center for financing the slave trade and the trade in goods produced by slave labor."[926]

Dr. Ira Berlin and Dr. Leslie Harris point to New York's large slave population even well after the Declaration of Independence:[927]

> For portions of the seventeenth and eighteenth centuries, New York City housed the largest urban slave population in mainland North America, with more slaves than any other city on the continent. During those years, slaves composed more than one quarter of the labor force in the city and perhaps as much as one half of the workers in many of its outlying districts. Slavery died with glacial slowness; slaves could be found in New York into the fifth decade of the nineteenth century. As slavery atrophied, however, its place in New York's commerce, politics, and culture increased in tandem with the city's connections with the slave South.

Douglas Harper emphasizes New England shipping's involvement in the infamous slave trade, with New England shippers earning plentiful profits and colonial governments receiving considerable taxes from active slave trading with the South. He states: "On the eve of the Revolution, the slave trade 'formed the very basis of the economic life of New England.'"[928]

He adds that: "Some 156,000 slaves were brought to the United States in the period 1801-08, almost all of them on ships that sailed from New England ports that had recently outlawed slavery."[929]

Mr. Harper continues that "New England was by far the leading slave merchant of the American colonies." He explains why that occurred: "After the Revolution, Rhode Island merchants had no serious American competitors. They controlled between 60 and 90 percent of the U.S. trade in African slaves."[930]

Lord Hugh Thomas cites the special role that slave traders from Newport, Rhode Island, played in the supply of rum to Africa ("Rum was an immediate success in Africa"), as well as participating actively in the slave trade beginning in 1725. He states that "Newport became a major commercial port, and her captains were selling slaves all over the British empire, particularly to planters in the Caribbean."[931]

RHODE ISLAND SLAVE TRADERS

"After the re-opening of the South Carolina market in 1804 and continuing until its closing in 1807 Rhode Island vessels accounted for nearly three-fifths of the American-borne trade."

J. Rawley and S. Behrendt, THE TRANSATLANTIC SLAVE TRADE at 326 (Univ. of Nebraska Press, 2005)

926 Singer, at 25.

927 Berlin and Harris, at 4.

928 Harper, "Slavery in the North" at *slavenorth.com/profits.htm,* accessed Oct. 24, 2020.

929 Harper, "Slavery in the North" at *slavenorth.com/profits.htm,* accessed Oct. 24, 2020.

930 Harper, "Slavery in the North" at *slavenorth.com/profits.htm,* accessed Oct. 24, 2020.

931 Thomas, at 236-61.

Dr. McManus, continues that "[t]he slave force everywhere made a vital contribution to the Northern economy." He continues that "[b]esides the great merchants," other New York professionals benefited from slavery, adding:[932]

> Many of the vendue houses drew a considerable part of their income from slave transactions. Even Quakers had no apparent qualms about selling slaves openly in the public marketplaces of Philadelphia. In New York City slave auctions were held weekly, sometimes daily, at the Merchant's Coffee House, the Fly Market, and Proctor's Vendue House. Virtually all the commission houses were involved in the trade, and some like the Meal Market, were almost exclusively places for the sale or hire of slaves.

Describing the attractiveness of the slave trade, Dr. McManus states that it "was so lucrative," that "disreputable" men turned to it readily, citing Captain William Kidd, the notorious pirate, for "carr[ying] slaves to New York."[933]

Dr. Singer portrays the importance of slavery in New York until its abolition in 1827:[934]

> Slavery, until its abolition in New York State in the beginning of the nineteenth century, the trans-Atlantic slave trade, even after it was declared illegal in 1808, the financing of slave plantations in the South and the Caribbean, the shipping of slave-produced products, and the manufacture of goods using the commodities of slavery, were all integral to the prosperity of New Netherland, the British Colony of New York, and New York State.

NEW YORK SLAVE TRADERS

"Aggregating a fuller body of data than ever previously used, the historian James G. Lydon has estimated that between 1715 and 1774 New Yorkers made at least 151 slaving voyages to Africa."

J. Rawley and S. Behrendt, THE TRANSATLANTIC SLAVE TRADE at 333 (Univ. of Nebraska Press, 2005)

He then discusses the key roles that slavery played in the success of businesses in New York, even decades following the State's abolition of slavery in 1827:[935]

> In the nineteenth century, New York City merchants and bankers financed illegal trans-Atlantic trade and trafficked in goods produced by human beings living and working under dire circumstances in the South and the Caribbean.

Vitality of North's Slavery Business Relationships with the South

Throughout American history, the arms and legs of slavery were in the South, but its heart and brain were in New York City.

---

932 McManus, Black Bondage in the North, at 12-13, 17, 19. Footnotes omitted.

933 McManus, Black Bondage in the North, at 20.

934 Singer, at 24; Harper, "How Slave Labor Made New York" at *www.theroot.com/how-slave-labor-made-new-york-1790895122,* accessed Oct. 24, 2020.

935 Singer, at 9. Citations omitted.

Identifying slavery's role in the national and international financial markets, Karl Rhodes, writing in a publication for the Richmond Federal Reserve, describes how slaves became the substance of nationally- and even internationally-sold mortgage-backed securities:[936]

> Deep South planters also viewed slaves as objects of finance. They frequently secured loans with human collateral, as did planters in the upper South. After the demise of the Second Bank of the United States, which had provided substantial funding for slave trading and cotton expansion, upstart banks in the Southwest offered easy credit to planters based on the number of slaves they could mortgage. The banks packaged these loans into mortgage-backed securities that they sold to banks in London, Amsterdam, and New York. London-based Baring Brothers, the leading merchant bank of the day, even persuaded the Louisiana legislature to guarantee the bonds.

"House Servant, Baltimore, 1861", *Slavery Images: A Visual Record of the African Slave Trade and Slave Life in the Early African Diaspora,* accessed November 16, 2020, *http://slaveryimages.org/s/slaveryimages/item/2727*

The national and international commodity markets likewise were deeply implicated in slavery. As Dr. Andrew Torget describes, with the rise of cotton as a valuable crop, at the New Orleans cotton exchange, "[a]gents from Liverpool, England, and New York City (representing the two centers of global cotton manufacturing) competed for the best bales."[937]

Dr. Singer discusses the active open involvement—until the Civil War—of New York City bankers, merchants, shippers, and commodity traders and businesses serving them:[938]

> Evidence shows that New York's merchants knew exactly what was happening. A New York Times editorial on December 7, 1860, bragged that the city's role in the cotton trade and its economic superiority were the result of its "position, skill, industry and wealth."
>
> The city's involvement in the slave trade was also well known. ... Between 1857 and 1860 alone, fifty-six ships were purchased in the port of New York for use in the illegal trans-Atlantic slave trade. ...
>
> The companies founded by New York City merchants and bankers during [the period around 1860], and the businesses they nurtured, all directly or indirectly benefited from slavery and the slave trade.

New York's close business relationships with slavery had a powerful effect upon the City's politics. According to Dr. Singer,[939]

---

936 Rhodes, "Mother of the Domestic Slave Trade" at 35, 37 Econ Focus, Richmond Federal Reserve (2nd Quarter, 2013) at *www.richmondfed.org/~/media/richmondfedorg/publications/research/econ_focus/2013/q2/pdf/economic_history.pdf,* accessed Oct. 18. 2020.

937 Torget, at 88-89. 125-26.

938 Singer, at 96-98.

939 Singer, at 24; Harper, "How Slave Labor Made New York" at *www.theroot.com/how-slave-labor-made-new-york-1790895122,* accessed Oct. 24, 2020.

> Many New Yorkers implicated in the slave system were politically influential and economically powerful. …
>
> In order to preserve the Union and protect their own profits from products produced by enslaved workers, many New Yorkers … were willing to compromise with Southern slave owners and support the slave system in the South even after the outbreak of the Civil War.

Dr. Peter Kolchin expresses a similar view:[940]

> Northern bankers, insurers, and shippers provided most of the credit and transportation that greased the wheels of the cotton economy.

Tony Horowitz describes the Northern mood after John's Brown's execution for his Harper's Ferry raid. Abolitionists become energized. Southerners were angry and fearful. However—[941]

> many Northerners, particularly businessmen who had commercial ties to the South feared the country's breakup. They organized enormous "Union meetings," to denounce Brown and declare allegiance to the Fugitive Slave Law and other Southern totems. "FANATICISM REBUKED," read a flyer for a Union meeting in Philadelphia on December 7, [1859,] which attracted six thousand people. There were similar rallies in Boston and New York, where speakers, including New York's mayor, hailed "the bond of commerce" between North and South.

The close New York business ties to slavery continued despite abolition. According to Dr. Singer, New York profited immensely from slavery in the South and the Caribbean, even decades after slavery was abolished in the State in 1827.

In that connection, he quotes[942] a Southern journalist, who cited a—

> fact known to every intelligent Southerner that we are compelled to go to the North for almost every article of utility … that, owing to the absence of a proper system of business amongst us, *the North becomes, in one way or another, the proprietor and dispenser of all our floating wealth.*

Slavery was so important to the City of New York, that according to Dr. Berlin, Dr. Harris, and Dr. Singer, Fernando Wood, the City's Mayor from 1855-58 and again from 1860-62, proposed New York's secession.[943] Dr. Singer adds that later, as a Congressman, Mayor Wood opposed the 13th Amendment.[944]

---

940 Kolchin, at 176.

941 Horowitz, at 261.

942 Singer, at 90. Emphasis added.

943 Berlin and Harris, at 23; "New York History Blog, Historical Views and News from The Empire State—Reckoning with Our Legacy of Slavery" (Oct. 21, 2019), Comment by Alan J. Singer, at *www.newyorkalmanack.com/2019/10/reckoning-with-our-legacy-of-slavery/*, accessed Oct. 24, 2020.

944 Berlin and Harris, at 23; "New York History Blog, Historical Views and News from The Empire State—Reckoning with Our Legacy of Slavery" (Oct. 21, 2019), Comment by Alan J. Singer, at *www.newyorkalmanack.com/2019/10/reckoning-with-our-legacy-of-slavery/*, accessed Oct. 24, 2020.

The website *history.com* agrees that, in New York, an "illicit slave market thrived" "long after" the 1808 law prohibiting the international slave trade. "When the war broke out ..., there was ... talk of New York seceding from the Union itself, so entwined were the city's business interests with the Confederate States."[945]

EXECUTION IN POUGHKEEPSIE

"A young slave, about twenty years of age, ('as nice a coloured man,' said Quamino, 'as you would wish to look at.') fired his master's barn and outbuildings, and thus destroyed much grain, together with live-stock. He was detected by the smoke issuing from his pocket, (into which he had thrust some combustibles,) imprisoned, tried, and on his confession, condemned to be burned to death. He was fastened to a stake, and when the pile was fired, the dense crowd excluded the air, so that the flames kindled but slowly, and the dreadful screams of the victim were heard at a distance of three miles. His master, who had been fond of him, wept aloud, and called to the Sheriff to put him out of his misery This officer then drew his sword; but the master, still crying like a child, exclaimed, 'Oh, don't run him through!' The Sheriff then caused the crowd to separate, so as to cause a current of air; and when the flame burst out fiercely he called to the sufferer to 'swallow the blaze;' which he did, and immediately he sunk dead."

W. Allinson, Memoir of Quamino Buccau, a Pious Methodist at 5 (Henry Longstreth, 1851), Academic Affairs Library, University of North Carolina at Chapel Hill, available at *docsouth.unc.edu*

New York's Sympathy for the South

Numerous Northerners objected when Lincoln introduced the military draft to bolster Union forces during the Civil War. The draft "made all male citizens between 20 and 35 and all unmarried men between 35 and 45 subject to military duty." Men "could buy their way out of harm's way, however, by hiring a substitute or paying $300 to the government (roughly $5,800 today)," which was "the yearly salary for the average American worker."[946]

History.com continues that:[947]

> As the war progressed, New York's anti-war politicians and newspapers kept warning its working class white citizens, many of them Irish or German immigrants, that emancipation would mean their replacement in the labor force by thousands of freed black slaves from the South.
>
> In September 1862, President Abraham Lincoln announced the Emancipation Proclamation (which would take effect early the following year), confirming the workers' worst fears.

In 1863, white New York workers rioted against the draft. Dr. Alan Singer states that the New York draft riots were inflamed in part due to fears by Irish workers of competition from African-Americans. Thousands of rioters threatened to burn factories that employed African-American workers "to replace White workers."[948]

945 "New York Draft Riots" at www.history.com/topics/american-civil-war/draft-riots, accessed Oct. 24, 2020; "New York History Blog, Historical Views and News from The Empire State—Reckoning with Our Legacy of Slavery" (Oct. 21, 2019), Comment by Alan J. Singer, at *www.newyorkalmanack.com/2019/10/reckoning-with-our-legacy-of-slavery/*, accessed Oct. 24, 2020.

946 "New York Draft Riots" at *www.history.com/topics/american-civil-war/draft-riots,* accessed Oct. 24, 2020.

947 "New York Draft Riots" at *www.history.com/topics/american-civil-war/draft-riots,* accessed Oct. 24, 2020.

948 Singer, at 86-87.

New York experienced the "the deadliest riots in U.S. history," including the 1967 Detroit riots and the 1992 Los Angeles riots. Riots also occurred in Detroit and Boston.[949] The Civil War draft riots in New York occurred especially among lower income Irish unable to make an alternative payment to the government to avoid the draft.[950]

The rioters also "vented their wrath on the homes and businesses of innocent African-Americans."[951] Among other things, rioters lynched and beat African-Americans in the street, and ransacked the Colored Orphan Asylum.[952] The rioters also attacked "military and government buildings," as well as "white abolitionists and women who were married to black men.[953]

Dr. Leslie Harris states that "In all, rioters lynched eleven black men over the five days of mayhem. The riots forced hundreds of blacks out of the city. ... During the riots, landlords drove blacks from their residences, fearing destruction of their property. After the riots, when the Colored Orphan Asylum attempted to rebuild on the site of its old building, neighboring property owners asked them to leave."[954]

NEW YORKERS FOR THE SOUTH

"A group of white men and boys mortally attacked black sailor William Williams—jumping on his chest, plunging a knife into him, smashing his body with stones—while a crowd ... watched. ... A white laborer, George Glass, rousted black coachman Abraham Franklin from his apartment and dragged him through the streets. A crowd gathered and hanged Franklin from a lamppost as they cheered for Jefferson Davis, the Confederate president. After the mob pulled Franklin's body from the lamppost, a sixteen-year-old Irish man, Patrick Butler, dragged the body through the streets by its genitals."

L. Harris, In the Shadow of Slavery—African-Americans in New York City, 1626-1863 at 283-84 (Univ. of Chicago Press 2003)

The "published death toll" was 119, though there were estimates as high as 1,200. There also were "millions of dollars in property damage" and 3,000 homeless African-Americans.[955]

That New York riot—a white riot lasting four days, the worst riot in American history—is "something that happened 150 years ago."

Summary

In summary, the North—where the English form of slavery practiced in America originated as an English government program—was heavily involved in, dependent upon, and profited from, the slave trade. The North's integral involvement with slavery began with the earliest days of the American colonies and, after the Revolutionary War, continued until the adoption of the 13th Amendment ended legal slavery in America. Even then, pervasive discrimination continued against blacks.

---

949 "New York Draft Riots" at *www.history.com/topics/american-civil-war/draft-riots,* accessed Oct. 24, 2020.

950 Singer, at 86 *et seq.*

951 "Draft Riot of 1863" at *www.britannica.com/event/Draft-Riot-of-1863,* accessed Oct. 24, 2020; "New York Draft Riots" at *www.history.com/topics/american-civil-war/draft-riots,* accessed Oct. 24, 2020.

952 "New York Draft Riots" at *www.history.com/topics/american-civil-war/draft-riots,* accessed Oct. 24, 2020.

953 "New York Draft Riots" at *www.history.com/topics/american-civil-war/draft-riots,* accessed Oct. 24, 2020.

954 Harris, at 285.

955 "New York Draft Riots" at *www.history.com/topics/american-civil-war/draft-riots,* accessed Oct. 24, 2020; "Draft Riot of 1863" at *www.britannica.com/event/Draft-Riot-of-1863,* accessed Oct. 24, 2020.

SANITIZING HISTORY IS FRAUDULENT EDUCATION

"Reject a book that says the South fought to hold her slaves. ...

"Reject a book that speaks of the slaveholder of the South as cruel and unjust to his slaves."

From an Educational Guide by Mildred Lewis Rutherford, Educator and Historian, Daughters of the Confederacy[956]

"While there were cruel masters who maimed or even killed their slaves (although killing and maiming were against the law in every state), there were also kind and generous owners ... Many [enslaved people] may not have even been terribly unhappy with their lot, for they knew no other."

Texas Charter School Book, quoted in Washington Post[957]

"Trump said he would create a national commission to promote a 'pro-American curriculum that celebrates the truth about our nation's great history,' which he said would encourage educators to teach students about the 'miracle of American history.'"

U.S. President Donald Trump, quoted in Washington Post[958]

"[P]lanters provided for their slaves as carefully as they did for members of their own families and in turn won the love of slaves."

Textbook Criticized by Michigan Committee[959]

"I never learned about the Elaine Race Massacre during my school days in history classes, even in Arkansas history instruction; I never heard it discussed in family circles or in casual conversations at local restaurants or coffee shops or at church and social gatherings."

Chester Johnson[960]

---

956 M. Rutherford, **A MEASURING ROD TO TEST TEXT BOOKS, AND REFERENCE BOOKS IN SCHOOLS, COLLEGES AND LIBRARIES** at 5 (1919) (reprinted by Forgotten Books, 2018), also available at *archive.org/details/measuringrodtot00ruth/page/n3/mode/2up,* accessed Oct. 26, 2020 ("Rutherford"); Heim, "Teaching America's Truth" (Wash. Post Online, Aug.28, 2019) at *www.washingtonpost.com/education/2019/08/28/teaching-slavery-schools/?arc404=true,* accessed Oct. 25, 2020 ("Heim").

957 Heim

958 Balingit and Meckler, "Trump alleges 'left-wing indoctrination' in schools, says he will create national commission to push more 'pro-American' history" (Wash. Post, Sept. 17, 2020) at *www.washingtonpost.com/education/trump-history-education/2020/09/17/f40535ec-ee2c-11ea-ab4e-581edb849379_story.html,* accessed Sept. 21, 2020.

959 Dean, "'Who Controls the Past Controls the Future:' The Virginia History Textbook Controversy" at 346 (Virginia Magazine of History and Biography, vol 17, no. 4, 2009) ("Dean").

960 C. Johnson, **DAMAGED HERITAGE: THE ELAINE RACE RIOT AND A STORY OF RECONCILIATION** at 6 (Pegasus Books, 2020) ("Johnson").

"I don't remember ever going into any depth about slavery other than that there was slavery. The textbooks were pretty whitewashed. We never talked about the conditions of slavery or why it persisted."

Philip Jackson, American history teacher in Montgomery County, Md.[961]

§ § §

SCHOOL BOOK FALSEHOODS "TO BUILD PATRIOTISM"

"My fourth-grade edition included this: 'Some of the Negro servants left the plantations because they heard President Lincoln was going to set them free. But most of the Negroes stayed on the plantations and went on with their work. Some of them risked their lives to protect the white people they loved.'"

"The lead historian for the seventh-grade edition was Francis Simkins, of Longwood College in Farmville. His 1947 book, 'The South Old and New,' was an articulation of the Lost Cause. Slavery was 'an educational process which transformed the black man from a primitive to a civilized person endowed with conceits, customs, industrial skills, Christian beliefs, and ideals, of the Anglo-Saxon of North America,' he wrote in that book. During the Civil War, enslaved people 'remained so loyal to their masters [and] supported the war unanimously.' ... Spotswood Hunnicutt, a co-author, believed that as a result of post-bellum interpretations, students were 'confused' that 'slavery caused a war in 1861.' The commission was 'looking after the best interest of the students.' The 'primary function of history,' she concluded, was 'to build patriotism.'"

Minton, "The lies our textbooks told my generation of Virginians about slavery," at B4 (Wash. Post, July 31, 2020) and at *www.washingtonpost.com/outlook/slavery-history-virginia-textbook/2020/07/31/d8571eda-d1f0-11ea-8c55-61e7fa5e82ab_story.html,* accessed Oct. 25, 2020

Educational Sanitization

How many school districts in America teach the bitter truth that slavery and the slave trade not only were a genocide, but one of the worst holocausts in World history, in which America's slave society—as official government policy—was a willing participant?

How many school districts in America teach that the slave trade led to more than five million cruel deaths of Africans based upon their race?

How many school districts in America teach the horrors of slave coffles, which dehumanized and brutalized slaves as they marched in chains on foot, like farm and ranch animals in Western cattle drives, the 1,000 miles from America's Capital to the slave auctions in New Orleans? How many teach about the destruction of families and communities?

How many school districts in America teach that disobedient slaves received hundreds of lashes with knotted whips designed to tear flesh, while blood ran down the slaves' bodies?

How many school districts in America teach that the slave society engaged in conscious and deliberate

---

961 Heim, "Teaching America's Truth" (Wash. Post Online, Aug.28, 2019) at *www.washingtonpost.com/education/2019/08/28/teaching-slavery-schools/?arc404=true,* accessed Nov. 7, 2020.

terrorism, among other things posting the heads of rebellious slaves on spikes along public roads to threaten both adult slaves and slave children?

Maybe somewhere.

It certainly was not my schools.

America's politicians do not dare to utter such messages. Polite American society does not discuss these subjects. Those truths may be too horrible to acknowledge.

AVOIDING REALITY

Textbook author:

"The realistic version would put our ancestors in too severe a light and would moreover be an unpleasant story, which is ... contrary to Virginia custom."

Dean, "'Who Controls the Past Controls the Future:' The Virginia History Textbook Controversy" at 328 (Virginia Magazine of History and Biography, vol 17, no. 4, 2009)

My high school education was a typical education for a young man in a large metropolitan area six decades ago. The schools I attended were not particularly better or worse than the schools in other school districts. Although the Supreme Court had ruled years earlier that school segregation violated the Constitution, my schools remained completely segregated. I had no African-American classmates.

My schools concentrated on teaching me what a wonderful and great country America is, with a proud, largely unblemished history. Indeed, it is true that America has wonderful characteristics. It also has, however, a dark and shameful history kept carefully under wraps.

American schools teach poorly not only math and reading skills, but also history. That is why so many of us—certainly me—have known so little about slavery. Schools deny valuable information to African-Americans—and all Americans—regarding the importance of slavery to America, the rich heritage of the African-American Slavery Heroes in fighting slavery, and their significant contributions to America.

When I attended school, there was no mention that the slave society simply ignored fundamental federal rights contained in the Bill of Rights.

Even today, when America is held up to students as a "free" country, there is no suggestion that, during much of America's history, it was actually a brutal dictatorship over millions of people, that America's slave society subjected those millions to terror through cruel and unusual, often medieval, punishments, or that many millions more—both "free" African-Americans and whites—were unable to express their opinions freely.[962]

The deliberate teaching of blatantly fraudulent history was especially prominent at least into the 1970s and often later years. While schools began moderating that approach over time, Americans in older generations—like me—often received a deeply flawed version of American history relating to slavery.

By manufacturing our imitation "knowledge," the willingness of thousands of school districts simply to lie in the cause of faux "patriotism" contributes directly to the substantial racial divide today. That is why so many white Americans and African-Americans cannot communicate with or understand each other.

Even after "moderating," many of America's schools continue to teach what might be termed "toned down," i.e., sanitized—and highly inaccurate—versions of history that reduce, and even eliminate, the pervasive role of slavery in virtually every significant event in America's history before slavery's demise. The sanitization

962 See *"Chapter Two: America's Slave Society Was a Terror Society"* and *"Chapter Six: The Duke of York's Creation on a Rampage—The Slave Society's War on Abolitionists."*

extends to omission of the key role of slavery in American history—presidential and congressional elections, formation and demise of political parties, conduct of wars, writing and interpretation of the Constitution, settling the West, admission of states to the Union, the Civil War, and decades upon decades of unremedied discrimination.

My Deceptive Education

For my own part, slavery was taught in passing, with only brief acknowledgement that it had existed. Slavery's role as only one of the factors in the South's role in the Civil War (as opposed to the central driving force) was mentioned, as were briefly the Underground Railroad, the Emancipation Proclamation, and the 13th Amendment to the Constitution.

Unmistakably, "Throughout the 20th century, textbooks often glossed over slavery, treating it not as central to the American story but as an unfortunate blemish washed away by the blood of the Civil War."[963]

In my case, my schools taught me nothing about the prevalence of slavery in America for more than 200 years. My schools did not teach me about the significant contribution that slavery made to America's growth, wealth, culture and economic success. My schools did not teach me about slavery's origination in the American colonies as an official English government program or about how slavery thrived in America both before and after the Revolution. They did not teach me that the Constitution protected slavery. My teachers never mentioned the name of the Duke of York or discussed his key role in the promotion, legalization, incentivization, and rapid growth of slavery.

Although I certainly understood that slavery was not a "nice" experience for slaves, I received no indication of the devastating reality of the English form of slavery practiced in the colonies and early America. I was taught little about the terrible suffering of the slaves.

TERRORISTIC JUSTICE

"They took the negro, mounted him on a horse, led the horse under a tree, put a rope around his neck, raised him up by throwing the rope over a limb; they then got into a quarrel among themselves; some swore that he should be burnt alive; the rope was cut and the negro dropped to the ground. He immediately jumped to his feet; they then made him walk a short distance to a tree; he was then tied fast and a fire kindled, when another quarrel took place; the fire was pulled away from him when about half dead, and a committee of twelve appointed to say in what manner he should be disposed of. They brought in that he should then be cut down, his head cut off, his body burned, and his head stuck on a pole at the corner of the road in the edge of the town. That was done and all parties satisfied!

"G______ *owned the negro's wife, and was in the habit of sleeping with her!* The negro said he had killed him, and he believed he should be rewarded in heaven for it."

T. Weld, American Slavery As It Is: Testimony of a Thousand Witnesses at 157 (American Anti-Slavery Society 1839), available from the Library of Congress at *www.hathitrust.org/digital_library.* Emphasis added.

My schools did not teach me about the compulsion of slaves to work long hours at arduous tasks through routine beatings, mutilations, and, often, worse; how the original slaves lost their cultures, friends, and families; how the slave society destroyed families of slaves and stole their labor to increase the wealth of their masters.

963 Heim.

My schools failed to mention the deep constant fear that whites had of slaves, and especially of runaway slaves, and rebellious slaves.

I never heard the term "slave coffle" or learned how that normal practice destroyed slaves' families and lives.

My teachers did not discuss the frequency of slaves running away or why they ran away. My teachers did not mention the requirements that slaves have "passes" to leave their masters' premises and submit to all whites, or the laws and social customs permitting whites to beat slaves into submission and even kill them if they resisted capture, or the terrible punishments administered if they were caught.

TERROR FOR A REBEL SLAVE LEADER

"Charles [Deslondes, a rebel leader] had his Hands chopped off then shot in one thigh & then the other, until they were both broken—then shot in the Body and before he had expired was put into a bundle of straw and roasted!

"The blacks sent to New Orleans, were convicted and executed. Their heads were placed on high poles, above and below the city, and along the river as far as the plantation on which the revolt began, and on those on which they had committed devastation."

"1811 German Coast Slave Uprising" at *genealogytrails.com/main/events/slavery_1811uprising.html,* accessed Oct. 25, 2020.

My schools did not teach me about revolts by desperate slaves, except for brief mention of Nat Turner. My schools did not explain to me about the incredibly extreme punishments meted out to suspected rebellious slaves. My schools carefully omitted that slaves had been burned at the stake, broken on the wheel, mutilated, roasted over a fire for hours, or gibbeted.

My schools did not mention or acknowledge that the slave society posted rebellious slaves' heads on posts along public roads as pre-meditated terrorism.

My schools said nothing about less inhumane forms of slavery practiced in other cultures. My schools did not contrast American slavery with less inhumane Dutch, Spanish, French, and West African forms of slavery.

Further, my schools ignored the key supportive role of the North. My schools did not teach me that slavery "had for a time been prevalent in the North or that the economy of the North was long reliant on, and provided significant support for, the South's slave-labor production."[964] My teachers, ignoring the pervasive role of slavery throughout all of America, failed to talk about the heavy involvement in slavery of the Northern colonies and states. They did not tell me about New York's key financial and commercial roles in support of the slave trade until the Civil War, the active Northern markets for slave-produced commodities, or the vital shipping and trading assistance that Northern businesses provided to the slave trade and Southern plantations.

Remarkably, my schools completely neglected to tell me that almost four million people were slaves in America at the time of the Civil War. My schools, of course, did not acknowledge that slaves had constituted a majority of the population in some states, even more commonly on a county level, and close to a majority in others.

Inexplicably, my schools did not teach me that America had more slaves at the time of the Civil War than any other country in the New World, or for that matter, more than all of those other countries combined. No one told me that America was one of the last New World slave societies then in existence.[965]

964 Heim.
See "*Chapter Six: The Duke of York's Creation on a Rampage—Slavery Was a National Institution: North and South.*"

965 Kolchin, at 94.

My schools did not teach me about Frederick Douglass' unbelievable achievements, although I heard his name. My schools did not teach me about Harriet Tubman's phenomenal bravery or significance. I heard nothing about Sojourner Truth, Harriet Jacobs, Solomon Northup, William Wells Brown, Lt. Prince Witten, David Walker, or other African-American heroes.

True to form, my schools told me the name of William Lloyd Garrison, a white man, as the leading abolitionist, and about John Brown, another white man, but not information regarding William Stills, the Father of the Underground Railroad, African-American slave rebels, or heroic slaves and former slaves.

No one told me that entire towns of truly free blacks had existed in Spanish Florida, while supposed "free" blacks in America had few rights. No one told me that the Spanish government relied on an army of free black warriors, while "free" blacks in America could not serve in militias or even possess any weapon of any kind. No one told me that slaveholders in Georgia and South Carolina and their mercenaries, *supported by American troops,* attacked free blacks in Florida—outside America's borders—capturing and enslaving free Florida blacks, or that the free black warriors defeated American troops in battle.

One must ask how African-American students can be proud of heroes whose names they seldom or never hear and whose significant achievements are not highlighted or held up as positive models for emulation.

My experiences do not appear to have been unique. There is a growing recognition that some of America's schools have been, and some still are, inadequate in teaching the history of slavery and the significance of slavery to America and its culture.[966]

<u>Deliberate Falsification</u>

Dr. Adam Dean discusses how segregationist government officials in Virginia took over, for decades, the writing of Virginia's school books to expunge adverse references to slavery and to pretend that the South fought the Civil War due to the North's desire to infringe on the "property" rights of Virginians. The officials, for example, State Attorney General, J. Lindsay Almond, Jr., who "defied court-ordered integration, calling himself 'the most massive of all resisters,'" could, through State Commissions, alter the content of books and designate which authors' works could be presented.[967]

Thus, since school districts are government agencies, the history of slavery often was (and at times still is) falsified intentionally as a matter of government policy.

To the extent that this serious educational deficiency was not intentional, it was at least grossly negligent or reckless on the part of school districts, teachers, book publishers, and authors. In any case, it was a fraudulent education. It was a massive lie in the interest of promotion of a fictional sense of "patriotism."

<u>SLAVES WERE "BETTER OFF"</u>

"Many baby boomers were fed tales in school that masked the reality of slavery. Some teaching even emphasized the idea that Africans brought here in chains were actually better off."

Heim, "Teaching America's Truth" (Wash. Post Online, Aug.28, 2019) at *www.washingtonpost.com/education/2019/08/28/teaching-slavery-schools/?arc404=true,* accessed Nov. 7, 2020

966 See, *e.g.*, the books cited herein by Dr. Alan Singer, Dr. Edgar McManus, Dr. Leslie Harris and Dr. Peter Kolchin and others.
See also Heim.

967 Dean, at 324-31.

Underscoring intent, in 1919 at the height of the Jim Crow era, Mildred Lewis Rutherford provided the following strict guidance, endorsed by the United Confederate Veterans, to schools, colleges, and libraries regarding acceptable literature and text books discussing slavery and the Civil War:[968]

> [R]eject a book that speaks of the Constitution other than a Compact between Sovereign States.
>
> Reject a text-book that does not give the principles for which the South fought in 1861 … .
>
> Reject a book that calls the Confederate soldier a traitor or rebel, and the war a rebellion.
>
> Reject a book that says the South fought to hold her slaves.
>
> Reject a book that speaks of the slaveholder of the South as cruel and unjust to his slaves.
>
> Reject a text-book that glorifies Abraham Lincoln and vilifies Jefferson Davis … .

NAT TURNER

Textbook author:

"Rebellious blacks, such as Nat Turner, 'must be severely condemned[.]'"

Dean, "'*Who Controls the Past Controls the Future:*" The Virginia History Textbook Controversy at 328 (Virginia Magazine of History and Biography, vol 17, no. 4, 2009)

As Mildred Rutherford urged, Southern schools complied with the sanitization of history. A Washington Post article quotes the Texas charter school textbook cited above as recently as the 2000s, stating that "Many [enslaved people] may not have even been terribly unhappy with their lot, for they knew no other."[969]

In other words, even more than a century after the ratification of the 13th Amendment, the remaining supporters of America's slave society in the 20th Century sought through school systems to bury its past by deception. All-too-willing school systems complied.

Southampton, Virginia, White Bicentennial

The following is an account reflecting Virginia schools' grossly negligent, if not intentional, participation in casual, but nevertheless extreme, sanitization of American history. It was as if slavery had never existed or, at least, was not important to America.

An African-American named James McGee in Southampton County, Virginia, the location of Nat Turner's rebellion, provides the account. As an African-American, Mr. McGee could not attend school with white children, but he and others could observe from outside a fence a white bicentennial celebration and associated educational portrayal at a white school's athletic field. The program and script of the event are located at the Library of Virginia.[970]

Dr. Kenneth Greenberg describes the events, based upon Mr. McGee's recollection:[971]

> James McGee tells of a chilling boyhood memory … . In 1949, in a still-segregated world, in a state still uncomfortable with a full presentation of its racial past, Southampton County was celebrating the bicentennial of its founding with a gala celebration at the athletic field of the white high school in

968 Rutherford, at 5.

969 Heim.

970 Greenberg, "Name, Face, Body" in K. Greenberg, ed., **NAT TURNER: A SLAVE REBELLION IN HISTORY AND MEMORY** at 19-20 (Oxford Univ. Press, 2003) ("Greenberg"). Footnotes omitted.

971 Greenberg, at 19-20. Footnotes omitted.

the Town of Franklin. The main event was an extraordinary historical pageant organized by the Junior Chamber of Commerce and the Woman's Club.

Dr. Greenberg describes the content of the program, which completely omitted mention of the famous and tumultuous local slave rebellion led by Nat Turner that killed 55 to 60 whites, severely disrupting American society, especially across the South.

The bicentennial program failed even to acknowledge that slavery had been a key element of the County's history for more than 200 years:[972]

> As the young James McGee and other black children watched a history of the county unfold before them from a vantage point literally and symbolically outside the fence that surrounded the field, they were treated to a series of displays and tableaux depicting an early Indian Village, pioneers, "the gentlemen of '76," the coming of the railroad, the "War Between the States," the Gay Nineties, Iwo Jima and much more. What they did not see at this celebration was a depiction of Nat Turner or any mention at all of the existence of slavery.

Dr. Greenberg describes, however, at another location, one of the slave society's most inhumane criminal reminders conceivable:

> As James McGee remembers it, there was only one small hint of the terrible memories that lay buried in the county. A table of historical artifacts had been placed at the armory nearby. And on the table, McGee later recalled, amidst a variety of artifacts associated with the 1831 rebellion, he saw a purse with a label stating that it had been made from the skin of Nat Turner.

WHITE REACTION TO NAT TURNER

"I did not then know precisely what was the cause of these scenes, for I could not get any very satisfactory information concerning the matter from my master, only that some of the slaves had undertaken to kill their owners; but I have since learned that it was the famous Nat Turner's insurrection that caused all the excitement I witnessed. Slaves were whipped, hung, and cut down with swords in the streets, if found away from their quarters after dark. The whole city was in the utmost confusion and dismay; and a dark cloud of terrific blackness, seemed to hang over the heads of the whites. So true is it, that 'the wicked flee when no man pursueth.' Great numbers of the slaves were locked in the prison, and many were 'half hung,' as it was termed; that is, they were suspended to some limb of a tree, with a rope about their necks, so adjusted as not to quite strangle them, and then they were pelted by the men and boys with rotten eggs. This half-hanging is a refined species of cruelty, peculiar to slavery, I believe."

Dictated by H. Brown, written and edited by C. Stearns, Narrative of Henry Box Brown, Who Escaped from Slavery at 38 (Brown and Stearns, 1849), Academic Affairs Library, Univ. of North Carolina at Chapel Hill, available at *docsouth.unc.edu*

Dr. Greenberg adds:

> William S. Drewry [who wrote a dissertation about the rebellion after interviewing county residents] had described this object in 1900, and James Mc Gee saw it nearly 50 years later.

972 Greenberg, at 19-20. Footnotes omitted.

Deliberate Falsification in Virginia Education

Schools in Virginia, like schools in other states, minimized the brutality of slavery and the importance of slavery to America. To the 1970s and even in later years, segregationist State officials portrayed slaves as happy, contented and in love with their masters.

Bennett Minton states:[973]

> "Chapter 29 of [a] seventh-grade edition, titled 'How the Negroes Lived Under Slavery,' included these sentences: 'A feeling of strong affection existed between masters and slaves in a majority of Virginia homes.' The masters 'knew the best way to control their slaves was to win their confidence and affection.' ... Color illustrations featured masters and slaves all dressed smartly, shaking hands amiably."

Virginia schools did not hesitate to criticize basic rights granted in the Constitution or to make blatantly racist statements. Dr. Adam Dean describes an eleventh grade text book:[974]

> The book justified the black codes [enacted by Southern states following Reconstruction], claiming that "wandering, pillaging Negroes ... misunderstood freedom from slavery to mean freedom from any obligation to earn a living." Unfortunately, the Radical Republicans took power and "sacrifice[ed] the welfare of the nation to the advantage of their political party." They passed the Fourteenth Amendment, which led to the supposedly egregious situation where "illiterate Negroes in Virginia could serve as jurors and voters." The amendment, the authors continued, was illegitimate because it was "proclaimed [as] part of the Constitution" without the consent of the majority of the nation. By claiming that the Fourteenth Amendment was spurious, segregationists insinuated that continued resistance to its provisions was justified.

That is the deliberate, and fraudulent, sanitization of history committed by so many of America's schools, politicians, social organizations, and others who believe slavery was merely "something that happened 150 years ago."

There is little, if any, indication they taught about the strict slave laws enacted beginning in the 1660s with the restoration of the English Monarchy, the international slave trade, repeated slave uprisings, slave coffles, violence and terror against slaves, or slave breeding for resale.

There is little, if any, indication they taught about the Alexandria and Louisville slave markets that functioned as points of departures for hundreds of thousands of slaves shipped to the cotton South, often marching in coffles from Alexandria by foot or, from Louisville, being "sold down the river."

There is little, if any, indication they taught about the heart-wrenching destruction of slave families—spouses and children taken forcibly, never to be seen again.

False Education and Faux Patriotism Contribute to America's Racial Divide

This is the false "education" that millions of middle-aged and older Americans received and that forms a basis for their political and racial perspectives. Confronted by vocal opposition, some schools today perpetuate the falsehoods.

---

973 Minton, "The lies our textbooks told my generation of Virginians about slavery," (Wash. Post, July 31, 2020) at B4 and at *www.washingtonpost.com/outlook/slavery-history-virginia-textbook/2020/07/31/d8571eda-d1f0-11ea-8c55-61e7fa5e82ab_story.html,* accessed Oct. 25, 2020.

974 Dean, at 335. Footnote omitted.

Teaching the truth is not "critical race theory." It is honesty.

Unfortunately, "The failure to educate students about slavery prevents a full and honest reckoning with its ongoing cost in America." To teach honestly, "The difficult truth means explaining to students not just how this practice of institutionalized evil came to be but also how it was accepted, embraced and inculcated in American daily life ..." and that slavery was "reinforced by practice and justified or excused in all corners of the country."[975]

Despite the widespread failings of school systems, African-American children hear unsanitized information from their parents, grandparents, aunts, uncles, and others around the dinner table and at family and community gatherings.

White children, in contrast, are unlikely to have the same experience. Consequently, they are far more likely to believe the sanitized versions of history taught in the schools.

The result is an inability to communicate.

Dr. Alan Singer states:[976]

> Part of the problem is that the historical narrative in American history is distorted to give the impression that the United States was always destined to triumph as a land of the free. ...
>
> New York, the North, and the nation certainly need to confront the actual history of slavery in this country.
>
> A reevaluation of the history of slavery will challenge some of our country's most sacred myths.

SECESSION TO PROTECT "RIGHTS"

Virginia Fourth Grade Textbook:

"[T]he people of all the states had certain rights under the United States Constitution, but the people in the South believed that their rights were being taken away from them [and they decided] to leave the United States and start a new nation."

Dean, "'*Who Controls the Past Controls the Future:*" The Virginia History Textbook Controversy at 331 (Virginia Magazine of History and Biography, vol 17, no. 4, 2009)

Fortunately, there may be a degree of hope for some schools. There are calls to provide students with more accurate and complete information. If so, that will better inform future students. Unfortunately, political opposition discourages honesty.

A danger is a tendency to allow another form of falsification by those who, going to the opposite extreme, do not honestly teach how slavery began, the vital role of government in the creation and promotion of American slavery. They minimize the key positive roles of the Declaration of Independence and how a sometimes hesitant, but nevertheless constructive, Abraham Lincoln contributed significantly to the end of slavery and the ratification of the 13th Amendment.

What America needs is a sense of perspective and balance, a sense of patriotism founded upon a balanced rendition of history. I fear, however, that is unachievable.

For those of us who attended school in the past, the sole remedy appears to be to gain information through books like this and the books and other sources I cite herein. They are readily available. I encourage you to engage in your own independent research.

975 Heim.

976 Singer, at 16, 36.

Students today may receive more accurate information, but don't count on it. Powerful forces actively oppose the teaching of accurate information about slavery that does not seek to instill an unquestioning "patriotism."[977] Formidable opposition seeks to deny, ignore, or hide the significant role of government in the creation and promotion of, and support for, slavery and today's remnants of slavery.

SOUTH CAROLINA CAUSES FOR SECESSION

"The ends for which this Constitution was framed are declared by itself to be 'to form a more perfect union, establish justice, insure domestic tranquility, provide for the common defence, promote the general welfare, and secure the blessings of liberty to ourselves and our posterity.'

"These ends it endeavored to accomplish by a Federal Government, in which each State was recognized as an equal, and had separate control over its own institutions. The right of property in slaves was recognized by giving to free persons distinct political rights, by giving them the right to represent, and burthening them with direct taxes for three-fifths of their slaves; by authorizing the importation of slaves for twenty years; and by stipulating for the rendition of fugitives from labor.

"We affirm that these ends for which this Government was instituted have been defeated, and the Government itself has been made destructive of them by the action of the non-slaveholding States. Those States have assumed the right of deciding upon the propriety of our domestic institutions; and have denied the rights of property established in fifteen of the States and recognized by the Constitution; they have denounced as sinful the institution of Slavery; they have permitted the open establishment among them of societies, whose avowed object is to disturb the peace and to eloign the property of the citizens of other States. They have encouraged and assisted thousands of our slaves to leave their homes; and those who remain, have been incited by emissaries, books and pictures to servile insurrection.

"For twenty-five years this agitation has been steadily increasing, until it has now secured to its aid the power of the Common Government. Observing the forms of the Constitution, a sectional party has found within that article establishing the Executive Department, the means of subverting the Constitution itself. A geographical line has been drawn across the Union, and all the States north of that line have united in the election of a man to the high office of President of the United States whose opinions and purposes are hostile to slavery. He is to be entrusted with the administration of the Common Government, because he has declared that that 'Government cannot endure permanently half slave, half free,' and that the public mind must rest in the belief that Slavery is in the course of ultimate extinction."

"Declaration of the Immediate Causes Which Induce and Justify the Secession of South Carolina from the Federal Union" (Dec. 20, 1860) at *teachingamericanhistory.org/library/document/south-carolina-declaration-of-causes-of-secession/*, accessed Oct. 25, 2020

---

977 Balingit and Meckler, "Trump alleges 'left-wing indoctrination' in schools, says he will create national commission to push more 'pro-American' history" (Wash. Post, Sept. 17, 2020) at *www.washingtonpost.com/education/trump-history-education/2020/09/17/f40535ec-ee2c-11ea-ab4e-581edb849379_story.html*, accessed Sept. 21, 2020.

WHO WAS THE PATRIOT? WHO WAS THE TRAITOR?

With the sanitization in education, it seems appropriate to ask:

What is "patriotism"?

What is "treason"?

Following his raid on the federal armory at Harper's Ferry to capture weapons for use in freeing slaves, Virginia accused John Brown, among other things, of treason.[978]

The following "patriots" were present at Mr. Brown's capture, trial, or his execution for "treason:"

- Virginia Governor Henry Wise, who rushed to Harper's Ferry while the fighting was still in progress, wishing to be a leader in Mr. Brown's capture and fate[979]
- Edmund Ruffin, a "Fire-Eater," a fierce proslavery advocate who, after Harper's Ferry, supported secession even more strongly and vigorously than before[980]
- John Wilkes Booth, an actor, who was able to don a soldier's uniform and join troops for the event[981]
- Robert E. Lee, who led the federal troops capturing Mr. Brown and met with him in jail[982]
- J.E.B. Stuart, who led the federal troops under General Lee, captured Mr. Brown, and met with him in jail[983]
- Stonewall Jackson, who was present for Mr. Brown's execution[984]
- Senator James Mason of Virginia, who had drafted the Fugitive Slave Law, met with Mr. Brown in jail, and questioned him[985]

JOHN BROWN

"[I]t is unjust that I should suffer such a penalty. Had I interfered in the manner which I admit, and which I admit has been fairly proved (for I admire the truthfulness and candor of the greater portion of the witnesses who have testified in this case)—had I so interfered in behalf of the rich, the powerful, the intelligent, the so-called great, or in behalf of any of their friends—either father, mother, brother, sister, wife, or children, or any of that class—and suffered and sacrificed what I have in this interference, it would have been all right; and every man in this court would have deemed it an act worthy of reward rather than punishment."

"John Brown's Speech to the Court at His Trial (Nov. 2, 1859)," available at *"John Brown's Speech to the Court at his Trial"* at *nationalcenter.org/JohnBrown'sSpeech.html,* accessed Oct. 26, 2020

978 Horowitz, at 185.

979 Horowitz, at 184-85.

980 Horowitz, at 254-55.

981 Horowitz, at 254.

982 Horowitz, at 187, 276.

983 Horowitz, at 187, 276.

984 Horowitz, at 276.

985 Horowitz, at 186.

The Harper's Ferry raid changed everything. It energized abolitionists. It gravely distressed slaveholders and the South in general. Shortly afterward, the "patriots" began to take far different courses of action, at times quite ironic.

Within 16 months after Virginia accused John Brown of treason, the seceding States formed the Confederacy and elected Jefferson Davis as President.[986]

Within 18 months after Mr. Brown's capture and trial, the following occurred:

- Henry Wise, no longer Governor, "convened a band of conspirators, appointing himself as commander" and led that force in an attack on the same federal armory that Mr. Brown had attacked, seizing weapons for the Confederacy on the same day that Virginia voted to secede and six days after South Carolina attacked Fort Sumpter[987]
- Edmund Ruffin, the devout "Fire-Eater" secessionist, "revived a dormant secessionist group … declar[ing] Harpers Ferry the 'last and crowning aggression of Northern usurpation and hatred,'" and advocating secession even more strongly and vigorously[988]

Thereafter, Robert E. Lee led the Confederate troops against the Union. J.E.B. Stuart and Stonewall Jackson served as key Confederate Generals. James Mason supported the Confederacy.

Of course, in 1865, Mr. Booth assassinated President Lincoln for ending slavery and favoring voting rights for freed slaves.

---

986 Horowitz, at 275.

987 Horowitz, at 275.

988 Horowitz, at 262.

SLAVERY AFTER SLAVERY

America's Reign of Terror technically ended for a time with the ratification in 1865 to 1870 of the 13th, 14th, and 15th Amendments to the Constitution. In form, the Amendments radically restructured the Constitution, ending its protection for slavery, granting citizenship to all persons born or naturalized in the United States, and adding the central freedom and equality principles of the Declaration of Independence. The end of the Civil War, strengthened by those Amendments, introduced the period known as "Reconstruction," lasting approximately a decade. During Reconstruction, African-Americans had the right to vote, and served in political offices at both state and federal levels.[989]

"Slave Quarters, Kingsley Plantation, Duval County, Florida, ca. 1870", *Slavery Images: A Visual Record of the African Slave Trade and Slave Life in the Early African Diaspora,* accessed November 15, 2020, *http://slavery-images.org/s/slaveryimages/item/1404*

Nevertheless, African-Americans remained impoverished. Most lacked professional skills. They did not have assets to build businesses, other than from menial labor. Despite the availability of land taken from the Native Americans that whites readily occupied and settled with government encouragement, it did not occur to the government to assist African-Americans in obtaining their own land. They only could work on land owned by whites.

The end of Reconstruction initiated what I am calling Phase 3 of the Reign of Terror. The relentless slave society re-asserted itself. African-Americans suffered greatly. The slave society continued to disregard the Bill of Rights as during slavery, and in addition, came to ignore the Amendments. That did not occur only for African-Americans. Just as the slave society had conducted a war against abolitionists,[990] it extended its brutality against whites seeking to assist African-Americans. As a personal note, in the 1950s, white supremacists in Mississippi beat a friend of my father for attempting to open an African-Americans school. That did not occur 150 years ago. It was only 65 years ago, and was during my teen age years.

It is beyond the scope of this book to describe the chamber of horrors in which former slaves existed following Reconstruction. That would require another book.

989 "Reconstruction" at *www.history.com/topics/american-civil-war/reconstruction,* accessed Oct. 26, 2020.

990 See "*—The Slave Society's War on Abolitionists*" above.

Black Codes

To summarize briefly a subject that, in many respects, is as horrible as slavery itself, once Reconstruction ended, whites once again furiously attacked and subjected African-Americans. Even before Reconstruction, states had already enacted "Black Codes" imposing slavery-like conditions upon the "freed" slaves:[991]

> The Black Codes were a series of statutes and laws enacted in 1865 and 1866 by the legislatures of the Southern states of Mississippi, Alabama, Georgia, Louisiana, Virginia, Florida, Tennessee, and North Carolina following the end of the Civil War at the beginning of the Reconstruction Era. The Black Codes were created to restrict the freedom of ex-slaves in the South.

"Marketplace, Lynchburg, Virginia, 1870s", *Slavery Images: A Visual Record of the African Slave Trade and Slave Life in the Early African Diaspora*, accessed November 15, 2020, *http://slaveryimages.org/s/slaveryimages/item/755*

After Reconstruction, the slave society enforced the Black Codes with a vengeance and immense hatred. The Codes imposed discriminatory requirements and prohibitions, including conditions modeled on slavery, reflecting the continuance of substantial white fear of African-Americans, such as:[992]

- Enacting laws applicable to African-Americans differing from laws for whites, with greater restrictions and harsher punishments
- Legalizing segregation, ultimately endorsed by the Supreme Court in *Plessy v. Ferguson,*[993] under the doctrine of "separate but equal" (although in reality, not only was there no equality, but the segregated facilities and programs, including education, were sadly inadequate)
- As during slavery, restricting African-American ownership or rental of land

991 "Black Codes" at *www.american-historama.org/1866-1881-reconstruction-era/black-codes.htm#:~:text=The%20 Black%20Codes%20were%20laws%20that%20were%20introduced,of%20ex-slaves%20was%20restricted%20in%20 numerous%20ways%20including%3A*, accessed Oct. 26, 2020.

992 See, e.g., "'Black Codes' of Mississippi" at *www.thirteen.org/wnet/slavery/experience/legal/docs6.html, accessed Oct. 26, 2020; "Black Codes" at www.american-historama.org/1866-1881-reconstruction-era/black-codes.htm#:~:text=The%20 Black%20Codes%20were%20laws%20that%20were%20introduced,of% 20ex-slaves%20was%20restricted%20in%20 numerous%20ways%20including%3A*, accessed Oct. 26, 2020; Reconstruction at *www.history.com/topics/american-civil-war/reconstruction.*, accessed Oct. 26, 2020.

993 *Plessy v. Ferguson,* 163 U.S. 537 (1896).

- Requiring African-Americans to have "contracts" "employing" them for work, which often forced African-Americans into "share-cropping" arrangements, discussed below, in which white land owners took advantage of black farmers
- Imposing "apprenticeships" upon young African-Americans lacking visible means of support, with the courts determining who the "employers" would be
- Prohibiting African-Americans from leaving their work "contracts," thereby also limiting their ability to travel and to move about freely
- Authorizing the capture and return of African-Americans to their "employers," just as white citizens and slave patrols had been able to capture and return slaves to their masters
- Prohibiting "loitering" and "vagrancy," just as the slave society had restricted slaves from gathering with their friends
- Prohibiting racial intermarriage (in Mississippi, a felony punishable by life in prison)
- As during slavery, prohibiting African-Americans from bearing arms

"Separating White Cotton from Yellow (Long Staple), South Carolina, 1880", Slavery Images: A Visual Record of the African Slave Trade and Slave Life in the Early African Diaspora, accessed November 19, 2020, *http://slaveryimages.org/s/slaveryimages/item/3111*

President Woodrow Wilson

Reflecting the unrelenting power of the slave society half a century following the Civil War, President Woodrow Wilson, raised in the South and the first Southern President since Reconstruction, moved federal government agencies back to segregation and discrimination. The segregation encompassed work areas, lunch rooms, and restrooms. Few schools teach that the President known for advocating the League of Nations "was also a segregationist who wrote a history textbook praising the Confederacy and, in particular, the Ku Klux Klan."[994]

Those events were contemporaneous with the 1919 publication of Mildred Lewis Rutherford's guide promoting the rejection of books teaching that the South fought the Civil War to protect slavery or that slave holders were "cruel and unjust."[995]

The occurrences also were contemporaneous with events discussed below, including the Tulsa Massacre, the Elaine, Arkansas, Massacre, the Rosewood, Florida, Massacre, and lynchings, burnings, shootings and other violence against African-Americans. All of those took place contemporaneously with the Wilson Administration.

994 Little, "How Woodrow Wilson Tried to Reverse Black American Progress" at *www.history.com/news/woodrow-wilson-racial-segregation-jim-crow-ku-klux-klan, accessed Oct. 26, 2020.*

995 Rutherford; Heim.

Sharecropping and the Elaine, Arkansas Massacre

Sharecropping

Sharecropping practices trapped African-American farmers in a state of virtual slavery.[996]

After black farmers had raised their cotton crops on land owned by plantation owners, white owners would sell the crops, deduct charges for supplies provided to the farmers, pay the farmers an amount determined by the land owners (supposedly "sharing" the proceeds), and retain the balance. Because the land owners underpaid the farmers for the crops and overcharged the farmers for the supplies, and because land owners denied the farmers access to itemized statements, there was a remaining balance that the land owners claimed for the supplies. The farmers could "pay" that "debt" only by continuing to work the land.

Walter White, an NAACP lawyer, quotes "A white Southerner writing in *The Memphis Commercial Appeal* of January 26, 1919," as stating:[997]

> In certain parts of the South men who consider themselves men of honor and would exact a bloody expiation of one who should characterize them as common cheats do not hesitate to boast that they rob the Negroes by purchasing their cotton at prices that are larcenous, by selling goods to them at extortionate figures and even by padding their accounts with a view of keeping them always in debt. Men of this stripe have been known to lament that in the last two years the Negroes have been so prosperous that it has not been possible to filch from them all they make.

SHARECROPPER

"a tenant farmer especially in the southern U.S. who is provided with credit for seed, tools, living quarters, and food, who works the land, and who receives an agreed share of the value of the crop minus charges"

"Sharecropper" at *www.merriam-webster.com dictionary/sharecropper,* accessed Nov. 22, 2020

Mr. White adds that "A protest from a Negro against tactics of this kind is met with a threat of force. Justice at the hands of a white jury in regions where this practice obtains is inconceivable. Even an attempt to carry the matter into the courts is usually provocative of violence."

According to practice, the farmers could not leave the land while owing money to the land owners.[998] In effect, through sharecropping, the farmers continued to live, in important respects, in enslaved servitude with little hope of escaping their predicament.

---

996 See generally, C. Johnson, **DAMAGED HERITAGE: THE ELAINE RACE RIOT AND A STORY OF RECONCILIATION** (Pegasus Books, 2020); I. Wells-Barnett, **THE ARKANSAS RACE RIOT** (1920), available at archive.org/details/TheArkansasRaceRiot/page/n1/mode/2up, accessed Nov. 22, 2020; White, "'Massacring Whites' in Arkansas" at 715-16 (The Nation, Dec. 6, 1919); Uenuma, "The Massacre of Black Sharecroppers That Led the Supreme Court to Curb the Racial Disparities of the Justice System" (Smithsonian Magazine, Aug. 2, 2018) at www.smithsonianmag.com/history/death-hundreds-elaine-massacre-led-supreme-court-take-major-step-toward-equal-justice-african-americans-180969863/, accessed Nov. 22, 2020); Stockley, "Elaine Massacre of 1919" at encyclopediaofarkansas.net/entries/elaine-massacre-of-1919-1102/, accessed Nov. 22, 2010.
The discussion in this subsection is based upon the foregoing resources.

997 White, "'Massacring Whites' in Arkansas" at 715-16 (The Nation, Dec. 6, 1919).

998 White, "'Massacring Whites' in Arkansas" at 715-16 (The Nation, Dec. 6, 1919).

The Elaine, Arkansas, Massacre

In Elaine, Phillips County, Arkansas, African-Americans outnumbered whites, constituting 78.6 percent of the population. There were 25,354 African-Americans compared to 7,176 whites.[999]

Elaine is the site of a little-known massacre of a substantial number of African-Americans. It is the subject of a book by Chester Johnson.[1000] The Elaine Massacre occurred during the presidency of segregationist Woodrow Wilson. The Tulsa Race Massacre occurred not long after. In the "Red Summer" of 1919, race riots occurred against blacks in dozens of cities. Another contemporaneous massacre occurred in Rosewood, Florida, extending over a week in 1923. In Rosewood, white mobs destroyed a small African-American town and hunted blacks hiding in the woods, killing many in vicious attacks.[1001]

"Hoeing and Planting Cotton Seeds, South Carolina, 1880", *Slavery Images: A Visual Record of the African Slave Trade and Slave Life in the Early African Diaspora,* accessed November 16, 2020, *http://slaveryimages.org/s/slaveryimages/item/3108*

Those occurrences transpired more than half a century after ratification of the 13th Amendment, and almost a century and a half after the Declaration of Independence.

On September 30, 1919, a group of approximately 100 African-American sharecropping farmers in Phillips County, Arkansas, met in a church to pursue organization as the Progressive Farmers and Household Union and to retain a lawyer to represent them in challenging land owner practices through the judicial process. Those actions represented a significant direct threat to the land owners. The farmers had arranged for armed guards to protect their meeting.

As a result of the presence of whites in an automobile outside the church, one or the other side fired shots. Exchanges of additional gun fire followed. One white was killed, and another injured.

The next day, the County Sheriff investigated. An estimated 500 to 1,000 armed whites from the surrounding area, as well as from nearby Tennessee and Mississippi, gathered. More than 500 federal troops sent by the Governor to maintain peace arrested hundreds of blacks, housing them in a stockade.[1002] Although the Governor failed to take the "required step" of first calling out the Arkansas National Guard, the Wilson Administration's War Department "quickly consented to the request" for federal troops.[1003]

999 White, "'Massacring Whites' in Arkansas" at 715-16 (The Nation, Dec. 6, 1919); Stockley, "Elaine Massacre of 1919" at *encyclopediaofarkansas.net/entries/elaine-massacre-of-1919-1102/*, accessed Nov. 22, 2010.

1000 C. Johnson, **DAMAGED HERITAGE: THE ELAINE RACE RIOT AND A STORY OF RECONCILIATION** (Pegasus Books, 2020) ("Johnson").

1001 "Rosewood Massacre" at *www.history.com/topics/early-20th-century-us/rosewood-massacre,* accessed Nov. 27, 2020.

1002 Stockley, "Elaine Massacre of 1919" at *encyclopediaofarkansas.net/entries/elaine-massacre-of-1919-1102/,* accessed Nov. 22, 2010.

1003 Johnson, at 11.

Whites began killing African-Americans randomly. People who had not even been in the vicinity at the time of the church meeting met their deaths when they returned from hunting.[1004] The federal troops killed African-Americans.[1005]

The white mob attacked even returning World War I veterans. Francine Uenuma states in the Smithsonian Magazine that "During the massacre, Arkansan Leroy Johnston, who had had spent nine months recovering in a hospital from injuries he suffered in the trenches of France—was pulled from a train shortly after returning home and was shot to death alongside his three brothers."[1006]

Estimates of African-American deaths range from 25 to 100, while five whites died.[1007] There are other, much higher estimates of the number of African-American deaths. Chester Johnson, who grew up in a neighboring county, discusses the varying estimates, in a context in which an accurate number of deaths is difficult to determine today. Mr. Johnson cites one estimate by a reporter for the *Arkansas Gazette* of more than 850 deaths, but states that "this figure is uniformly discredited as being too high." He adds that an estimate of 14 deaths also was "discredited as being too low."[1008]

Mr. Johnson quotes Robert Whitaker, who authored a book titled **THE KILLING FIELDS**, as follows:[1009]

> The local posses out of Helena, which came that first morning, probably did kill only 15 to 20 blacks. And that became the number they reported in the news, as though that were the total number killed. The killing by the groups that came across from Memphis and other surrounding areas is much harder to count. There are sporadic accounts from whites that tell of various killing events, and I mapped out those best I could. But this part is indeed murky, and this killing went mostly unreported by the white press. Finally, there is the killing by the soldiers called out to put down the "riot." The white newspapers told at the time that the soldiers restored the peace. But if you look at their own reports, they tell of opening fire with machine guns and of a significant number of blacks killed.
>
> ... [I]n my opinion, ... the total number killed was above 100. ... I personally believe 300 is too high, however.

Grif Stockley, of the Butler Center for Arkansas Studies, states that the soldiers imprisoned hundreds of African-Americans "in makeshift stockades until they could be questioned," and refers to "anecdotal evidence" that soldiers "also engaged in torture of African Americans to make them confess and give information."[1010]

1004 Stockley, "Elaine Massacre of 1919" at *encyclopediaofarkansas.net/entries/elaine-massacre-of-1919-1102/*, accessed Nov. 22, 2010.

1005 Johnson, at 11.

1006 Uenuma, "The Massacre of Black Sharecroppers That Led the Supreme Court to Curb the Racial Disparities of the Justice System" (Smithsonian Magazine, Aug. 2, 2018) at *www.smithsonianmag.com/history/death-hundreds-elaine-massacre-led-supreme-court-take-major-step-toward-equal-justice-african-americans-180969863/*, accessed Nov. 22, 2020).

1007 White, "'Massacring Whites' in Arkansas" at 715-16 (The Nation, Dec. 6, 1919).

1008 Johnson, at 12.

1009 Johnson, at 13.

1010 Stockley, "Elaine Massacre of 1919" at *encyclopediaofarkansas.net/entries/elaine-massacre-of-1919-1102/*, accessed Nov. 22, 2010.

Local whites formed a "Committee of Seven" to question blacks. The questioning occurred with blacks seated in an electrified chair to compel them to be forthcoming.[1011] The whites alleged that the African-Americans were planning an insurrection. The African-Americans' version, supported by the union's literature,[1012] was that they had been forming a labor union to pursue remedies peacefully in court.

Grif Stockley states that:[1013]

> The Elaine Massacre was by far the deadliest racial confrontation in Arkansas history and possibly the bloodiest racial conflict in the history of the United States. While its deepest roots lay in the state's commitment to white supremacy, the events in Elaine (Phillips County) stemmed from tense race relations and growing concerns about labor unions.

He adds:

> Evidence shows that the mobs of whites slaughtered African Americans in and around Elaine. For example, H. F. Smiddy, one of the white witnesses to the massacre, swore in an eye-witness account in 1921 that "several hundred of them... began to hunt negroes and shotting [sic] them as they came to them." Anecdotal evidence also suggests that the troops from Camp Pike engaged in indiscriminate killing of African Americans in the area, which, if true, was a replication of past militia activity to put down perceived black revolts. In 1925, Sharpe Dunaway, an employee of the *Arkansas Gazette,* alleged that soldiers in Elaine had "committed one murder after another with all the calm deliberation in the world, either too heartless to realize the enormity of their crimes, or too drunk on moonshine to give a continental darn."

RAMPANT RACIST VIOLENCE

Chester Johnson cites the following racist violence in America at the time of the Elaine Massacre and during the pendency of the legal proceedings against Elaine African-Americans:

"[I]n early 1919 ... lynchings, shootings, or the burning alive of African-American veterans and other blacks in places like Star City and El Dorado, Arkansas, and in the nearby states of Louisiana and Mississippi"

"Over the previous several months, lynchings and mob violence against African-Americans had been widespread throughout the nation. In Arkansas alone during the first months of 1921, there had been in late January the burning alive of a black man in Nodena; in March, lynchings in both Hope and Monticello; and in early May the lynching of another African-American in McGhee."

"Only a few days before the Supreme Court hearing, a race battle broke out in Rosewood, Florida with numerous blacks being killed and white posses hunting down African-Americans hiding in the woods"

C. Johnson, **DAMAGED HERITAGE: THE ELAINE RACE RIOT AND A STORY OF RECONCILIATION** at 8, 20, 22 (Pegasus Books, 2020)

An all-white jury convicted twelve African-Americans of murder, and sentenced them to death, after considering the case for seven minutes.[1014] The defense did not interview any witnesses, seek a change of

---

1011 White, "'Massacring Whites' in Arkansas" at 715-16 (The Nation, Dec. 6, 1919).

1012 White, "'Massacring Whites' in Arkansas" at 715-16 (The Nation, Dec. 6, 1919).

1013 Stockley, "Elaine Massacre of 1919" at *encyclopediaofarkansas.net/entries/elaine-massacre-of-1919-1102/*, accessed Nov. 22, 2010.

1014 White, "'Massacring Whites' in Arkansas" at 716 (The Nation, Dec. 6, 1919).

venue, challenge any jurors (simply accepting the first twelve called), question prosecution witnesses, or call any defense witnesses.[1015]

BOLSHEVISM

"The colored farmers combined, counseled together, employed counsel to present their plea. They did not threaten to strike, did not strike, menaced nothing, injured nobody, and yet;

"Hundreds of them today are penniless, 'Refugees from pillaged homes;'

"More than a hundred were killed by white mobs, for which not one white man has been arrested;
"Seventy-five men are serving life sentences in the penitentiary, and

"Twelve men are sentenced to die. If this is democracy, what is bolshevism?"

I. Wells-Barnett, **THE ARKANSAS RACE RIOT** at 55 (1920), available at *archive.org/details/TheArkansasRaceRiot/page/n1/mode/2up*, accessed Nov. 29, 2020. Emphasis in original.

The Governor and the appellate courts prevented executions. Six defendants received new trials. After years of wrangling, the prosecution obtained plea bargained "confessions" from 65 others of guilt to lesser charges, resulting in sentences up to 21 years for second degree murder.[1016]

In 1923, the Supreme Court changed its past practice of ignoring such matters. The Court held in, *Moore v. Dempsey*,[1017] a case brought by the NAACP with the active leadership of a former sharecropper turned lawyer named Scipio Africanus Jones, that the procedures had violated the 14th Amendment rights of the six remaining first degree murder defendants.[1018]

The decision stands as a landmark in its recognition of the application of the 14th Amendment protections to African-Americans in state court proceedings.[1019]

In 2019, a memorial was dedicated to the twelve murder defendants in downtown Elaine, and the Arkansas Civil Rights Heritage Trail in Little Rock memorialized them.[1020]

1015 White, "'Massacring Whites' in Arkansas" at 716 (The Nation, Dec. 6, 1919); Stockley, "Elaine Massacre of 1919" at *encyclopediaofarkansas.net/entries/elaine-massacre-of-1919-1102/*, accessed Nov. 22, 2010; Uenuma, "The Massacre of Black Sharecroppers That Led the Supreme Court to Curb the Racial Disparities of the Justice System" (Smithsonian Magazine, Aug. 2, 2018) at *www.smithsonianmag.com/history/death-hundreds-elaine-massacre-led-supreme-court-take-major-step-toward-equal-justice-african-americans-180969863/*, accessed Nov. 22, 2020).

1016 Stockley, "Elaine Massacre of 1919" at *encyclopediaofarkansas.net/entries/elaine-massacre-of-1919-1102/*, accessed Nov. 22, 2010.

1017 Moore v. Dempsey, 261 U.S. 86 (1923).
See Riva, "Moore v. Dempsey" at *encyclopediaofarkansas.net/entries/moore-v-dempsey-5200/* (Last Updated 11/19/20), accessed Nov. 23, 2020.

1018 Uenuma, "The Massacre of Black Sharecroppers That Led the Supreme Court to Curb the Racial Disparities of the Justice System" (Smithsonian Magazine, Aug. 2, 2018) at *www.smithsonianmag.com/history/death-hundreds-elaine-massacre-led-supreme-court-take-major-step-toward-equal-justice-african-americans-180969863/*, accessed Nov. 22, 2020).

1019 Johnson, at 23-25.

1020 Stockley, "Elaine Massacre of 1919" at *encyclopediaofarkansas.net/entries/elaine-massacre-of-1919-1102/*, accessed Nov. 22, 2010.

Lynchings and Denial of Justice

Thus, in the 150 to 200 years after the Declaration of Independence, African-Americans still did not have the "unalienable Rights [of] Life, Liberty, and the Pursuit of Happiness." Brutality against African-Americans resulted in a perpetuation of the Reign of Terror.

Only 100 years ago, through Black Codes, sharecropping, and similar arrangements, many African-Americans remained effectively in a state of servitude from which they were unable to extricate themselves.

Despite purported constitutional guarantees in the 13th, 14th, and 15th Amendments, through social pressures and threats of violence, and even death as late as 1964,[1021] by organizations such as the Ku Klux Klan, African-Americans no longer could vote. In addition, legal restrictions on voting embraced "discriminatory poll taxes, whites-only primaries, and targeted literacy tests."[1022] The slave society excluded African-Americans from most juries.

Vigilantes, such as the Ku Klux Klan, lynched thousands of African-Americans. As during slavery, the slave society dispensed with the constitutional right to a trial by jury. One calculation states that, from 1882 to 1968, there were 3,445 lynchings of African-Americans, as well as 1,297 lynchings of whites.[1023] The Washington Post reported that researchers had identified additional lynchings of African-Americans, citing an estimate by the Equal Justice Initiative, an Alabama-based organization, of 6,500 lynchings between 1865 and 1950. It included 2,000 lynchings during Reconstruction, which was outside the period covered in the first calculation above.[1024]

As examples of lynchings, in the capitol of Maryland, Annapolis, Henry Davis was lynched in 1906,[1025] and decades later, still in Maryland, this time in Princess Anne, George Armwood was lynched in 1933.[1026]

Mr. Davis was accused of assaulting a white woman, who reportedly defended herself with a horsewhip. He fled. The penalty for attempted assault was ten years in the penitentiary, and for actual assault, death by hanging. After Mr. Davis' capture, he was placed in the custody of the Sheriff's staff at County jail.[1027]

1021 See, e.g., "The KKK kills three civil rights workers" at *www.history.com/this-day-in-history/the-kkk-kills-three-civil-rights-activists,* accessed Oct. 28, 2020.

1022 Bordewich, "'Wilmington's Lie' Review: An American Tragedy" (Wall St. J., Jan. 3, 2020) at *www.wsj.com/articles/wilmingtons-lie-review-an-american-tragedy-11578067530*, accessed Oct. 26, 2020.

1023 "Lynchings by Year and Race" at *law2.umkc.edu/Faculty/projects/ftrials/shipp/lynchingyear.html,* accessed Oct. 26, 2020.

1024 Rosenwald, "At least 2,000 more black people were lynched by white mobs than previously reported, new research finds" at *www.washingtonpost.com/history/2020/06/16/lynchings-report-equal-justice-initiative-reconstruction-racial-terror/,* accessed Oct. 26, 2020.

1025 "Henry Davis, Lynched in Annapolis, Maryland, December 21, 1906," Archives of Maryland (Biographical Series) at *msa.maryland.gov/megafile/msa/speccol/sc3500/sc3520/013600/013635/html/13635bio.html#:~:text=Lynched in Annapolis%2C Maryland%2C December 21%2C 1906. Biography%3A,store in Iglehart Station in Anne Arundel County.,* accessed Oct. 26, 2020.

1026 "George Armwood, Lynched in Princess Anne, October 18, 1933," Archives of Maryland (Biographical Series) at *msa.maryland.gov/megafile/msa/speccol/sc3500/sc3520/013700/013750/html/13750bio.html,* accessed Oct. 26, 2020.

1027 "Henry Davis, Lynched in Annapolis, Maryland, December 21, 1906," Archives of Maryland (Biographical Series) at *msa.maryland.gov/megafile/msa/speccol/sc3500/sc3520/013600/013635/html/13635bio.html#:~:text=Lynched in Annapolis%2C Maryland%2C December 21%2C 1906. Biography%3A,store in Iglehart Station in Anne Arundel County.,* accessed Oct. 26, 2020. Footnote omitted.

The Maryland Archives describes his lynching:[1028]

> Davis was removed from the jail on Calvert Street and paraded through the town, before being shot numerous times and hanged in a tree along College Creek. As the guards stood their posts at the jail house, a mob of dozens simply overpowered the men, and were able to reach their target with little delay.

"Sugar Plantation, Louisiana, 1873-74", *Slavery Images: A Visual Record of the African Slave Trade and Slave Life in the Early African Diaspora,* accessed November 15, 2020, *http://slaveryimages.org/s/slaveryimages/item/2893*

Following the lynching, the victim's "daughter Lillian read a statement thanking those who were able to reach Davis and punish him for his crime. She continued to thank those involved for also sparing her mother, or any mother, daughter, sister or wife for that matter, of having to approach the witness stand and relive such a terrible event." After an investigation, the jury of inquest "was unable to 'fix' the lynching to any one person or persons."[1029]

Authorities accused Mr. Armwood of assaulting and raping an elderly woman. Mr. Armwood was "described as 'feeble-minded.'" At the age of 15, he had been taken into the custody of a Mr. John Richardson, for whom he worked thereafter, allegedly at low wages. Mr. Richardson attempted to hide Mr. Armwood. Nevertheless, armed men located Mr. Armwood at Mr. Richardson's home. Mr. Armwood "was dragged across the field and beaten as he was taken into custody."[1030]

At one point, Mr. Armwood was moved to Baltimore to protect him from a mob that had gathered in the rural community to lynch him. Local pressure, however, led to his return to the Cecil County jail.[1031]

1028 "Henry Davis, Lynched in Annapolis, Maryland, December 21, 1906," Archives of Maryland (Biographical Series) at *msa.maryland.gov/megafile/msa/speccol/sc3500/sc3520/013600/013635/html/13635bio.html#:~:text=Lynched in Annapolis%2C Maryland%2C December 21%2C 1906. Biography%3A,store in Iglehart Station in Anne Arundel County.*, accessed Oct. 26, 2020. Footnote omitted.

1029 "Henry Davis, Lynched in Annapolis, Maryland, December 21, 1906," Archives of Maryland (Biographical Series) at *msa.maryland.gov/megafile/msa/speccol/sc3500/sc3520/013600/013635/html/13635bio.html#:~:text=Lynched in Annapolis%2C Maryland%2C December 21%2C 1906. Biography%3A,store in Iglehart Station in Anne Arundel County.*, accessed Oct. 26, 2020. Footnote omitted.

1030 "George Armwood, Lynched in Princess Anne, October 18, 1933," Archives of Maryland (Biographical Series) at *msa.maryland.gov/megafile/msa/speccol/sc3500/sc3520/013700/013750/html/13750bio.html,* accessed Oct. 26, 2020. Footnote omitted.

1031 "George Armwood, Lynched in Princess Anne, October 18, 1933," Archives of Maryland (Biographical Series) at *msa.maryland.gov/megafile/msa/speccol/sc3500/sc3520/013700/013750/html/13750bio.html,* accessed Oct. 26, 2020. Footnote omitted.

Despite officials' promises to protect Mr. Armwood, and their attempts to do so using tear gas against a gathering mob, the Maryland Archives describes the following events:[1032]

> As the smoke cleared, the lynch mob used two fifteen-foot timbers as battering rams to breach the jailhouse doors. Captain Johnson was reportedly knocked unconscious and Deputy Dryden was forced to hand over the keys to the cells.
>
> Armwood hid under his mattress but was dragged out of his cell by the mob and a noose was placed around his neck. He was beaten, stabbed, and kicked, before he was tied to the back of a truck and driven to the place he would be hanged. … Before he was hanged, Armwood's ears were cut off and his gold teeth were ripped out. Armwood was reportedly dead by the time the mob raised and dropped his body from a tree branch.
>
> The lynch mob dragged George Armwood's corpse back to the courthouse on the corner of Prince and William Street in downtown Princess Anne. His body was hanged from a telephone pole and burned. His corpse was dumped in Hayman's Lumber Yard, to be gathered by the authorities in the morning.

"View of Darlington Courthouse and the Sycamore Tree Where Amy Spain, the Negro Slave, Was Hung by the Citizens of Darlington, South Carolina", *Slavery Images: A Visual Record of the African Slave Trade and Slave Life in the Early African Diaspora,* accessed November 28, 2020, *http://slaveryimages.org/s/slavery-images/item/1324*

In a habeas corpus trial, the jury released the defendants, to the cheers of a mob of a thousand white supporters.

In a particularly heinous example, strongly reminiscent of slavery, in 1918 in Georgia, after a young African-American man killed a planter, white mobs killed "at least 13 people." One lynching victim was the husband of a pregnant teenage woman named Mary Turner. Ms. Turner "became distraught," denying that her husband had anything to do with the planter's death, and "threatened to have members of the mob arrested." The mob turned on her to "teach her a lesson."[1033]

This is how they "taught her a lesson:"[1034]

> [T]hey hung her upside down from a tree, doused her in gasoline and motor oil, and set her on fire. While Turner was still alive, a member of the mob split her abdomen open with a knife. Her unborn child fell on the ground, where it cried before it was stomped on and crushed. Finally, Turner's

1032 "George Armwood, Lynched in Princess Anne, October 18, 1933," Archives of Maryland (Biographical Series) at *msa.maryland.gov/megafile/msa/speccol/sc3500/sc3520/013700/013750/html/13750bio.html,* accessed Oct. 26, 2020. Footnote omitted.

1033 "Lynching of Pregnant 19-Year-Old Mary Turner" at *blackthen.com/lynching-of-pregnant-19-year-old-mary-turner/,* accessed Oct. 26, 2020.

1034 "Lynching of Pregnant 19-Year-Old Mary Turner" at *blackthen.com/lynching-of-pregnant-19-year-old-mary-turner/,* accessed Oct. 26, 2020.

> body was riddled with hundreds of bullets. Mary Turner and her child were cut down and buried near the tree. A whiskey bottle marked the grave.

Racial Massacres

In addition to the Elaine, Arkansas Massacre in 1919, there were a substantial number of other devasting race riots resulting in hundreds of African-American deaths. All of these massacres, as well as many lynchings, occurred less than 150 years ago, even in some cases 100 hundred years or less ago.

The 1921 Tulsa Race Riot, "one of the deadliest riots in U.S. history,"[1035] occurred shortly after President Woodrow Wilson left office. The Riot began following an erroneous a report that a young African-American man named Dick Rowland had assaulted a young white elevator operator named Page. The local newspaper, the *Tulsa Tribune,* reported that Mr. Rowland "had tried to rape" Page, "with an accompanying editorial stating that a lynching was planned for that night."[1036] According to *History.com,* after a police investigation, however, "all charges against Dick Rowland were dropped. The police concluded that Rowland had most likely stumbled into Page, or stepped on her foot."[1037]

African-American men, including World War I veterans, formed a group to protect the young man in jail against a gathering mob of whites calling for his lynching. The white mob retaliated by days of rioting. The Riots—which became a massacre—led to attacks on African-Americans and to the burning of African-American businesses in a thriving business district known as "Black Wall Street." The massacre extended over 35 City blocks. It resulted in estimates of up to 300 deaths, with 6,000 African-Americans held under an armed guard at a fairgrounds, 1,200 to 1,400 homes burned, more than 200 homes looted, and 8,000 to 10,000 homeless.[1038] The rioters included "groups of white Tulsans—some of whom were deputized and given weapons by city officials."[1039]

Illustrating fraudulent educations in America's schools and the unwillingness of America's politicians to acknowledge the truth about the treatment of African-Americans, despite the widespread scope and severity of the massacre, the events simply disappeared from history. *History.com* states that "there was a deliberate effort to cover them up:"[1040]

> News reports were largely squelched, despite the fact that hundreds of people were killed and thousands left homeless. ...
>
> The *Tulsa Tribune* removed the front-page story of May 31 that sparked the chaos from its bound volumes, and scholars later discovered that police and state militia archives about the riot were missing as well. As a result, until recently the Tulsa Race Massacre was rarely mentioned in history books, taught in schools or even talked about.

1035 "Tulsa Race Massacre" at *www.history.com/topics/roaring-twenties/tulsa-race-massacre,* accessed Oct. 26, 2020.

1036 "Tulsa race massacre of 1921" at *www.britannica.com/event/Tulsa-race-riot-of-1921,* accessed Oct. 26, 2020.

1037 "Tulsa Race Massacre" at *www.history.com/topics/roaring-twenties/tulsa-race-massacre,* accessed Oct. 26, 2020.

1038 "Tulsa Race Massacre" at *www.history.com/topics/roaring-twenties/tulsa-race-massacre,* accessed Oct. 26, 2020; "Tulsa race massacre of 1921" at *www.britannica.com/event/Tulsa-race-riot-of-1921,* accessed Oct. 26, 2020; "Investigators find a mass grave while searching for 1921 Tulsa race massacre victims" at *www.cnn.com/2020/10/21/us/tulsa-massacre-excavation/index.html,* accessed Oct. 26, 2020.

1039 "Tulsa Race Massacre" at *www.history.com/topics/roaring-twenties/tulsa-race-massacre,* accessed Oct. 26, 2020.

1040 "Tulsa Race Massacre" at *www.history.com/topics/roaring-twenties/tulsa-race-massacre,* accessed Oct. 26, 2020.

Other such events occurred. Another episode was a "coup" in 1898 by marauding whites against the elected government of Wilmington, North Carolina, which included both white and African-American officials. As a result:[1041]

> Every official of the city's fusion government, white and black, elected and appointed, from the mayor on down, was forced to resign. An impromptu "election" was held, and eight white supremacists, including two men who had directed the rioters, were chosen as alderman. Col. Waddell—who had called for black voters to be shot in their tracks—was then selected as Wilmington's mayor.

The Wilmington white rioters rode through African-American neighborhoods killing people randomly, and seeking to kill any who attempted to vote. The Jim Crow society charged no whites with a crime. Also citing the Tulsa massacre and other white mobs, the Wall Street Journal states:[1042]

> What happened in Wilmington was not the first deliberate massacre of black Americans. In the late 1860s, white race riots killed scores of blacks in Memphis, New Orleans and upcountry Louisiana. Nor was it the last. Dozens of blacks were systematically slaughtered in Tulsa, Okla., and Ocoee, Fla., in the 1920s.

Conditions Today

Despite the discrimination, individual African-Americans are able to achieve success, but without education, marketable skills, access to decent jobs, wealth, land, or other assets upon which to live and to pass to their children, generation after generation the conditions of slavery—poverty—haunt many African-Americans and their children and grandchildren.

Most importantly for economic equality, there remains a pervasive, systematic failure in America to provide decent education to most African-American youth due to dependence by public officials upon political contributions from opponents of fundamental school reform, including school choice.[1043]

1041 Bordewich, "'Wilmington's Lie' Review: An American Tragedy" (Wall St. J., Jan. 3, 2020) at *www.wsj.com/articles/wilmingtons-lie-review-an-american-tragedy-11578067530;* accessed Oct. 26, 2020.

1042 Bordewich, "'Wilmington's Lie' Review: An American Tragedy" (Wall St. J., Jan. 3, 2020) at *www.wsj.com/articles/wilmingtons-lie-review-an-american-tragedy-11578067530;* accessed Oct. 26, 2020.

1043 See *"Chapter Seven: Moving Forward??—Remnants of Slavery: Severe Discrimination in Education."*

CHAPTER SEVEN: MOVING FORWARD??

"What's in your hand?! George Washington Carver!

"Who was so frail that he was traded for a broken down horse as a slave boy …

"… and George Washington Carver sitting in the science laboratory at Tuskegee told me, he said, "Dr. Powell," he said, "I just go out into the fields each morning at 5 o'clock, and I let God guide me …

"… and I bring back these little things and work them with my laboratory."

"And that man did more to revolutionize the agricultural science of peanuts, and of cotton, and sweet potatoes than any other human being in the field of agricultural science.

"What's in your hand? Just let God use you, that's all.

"What's in your hand?!"[1044]

Adam Clayton Powell

§ § §

1960S CIVIL RIGHTS LAWS AND DISCRIMINATION TODAY

Another century after the ratification of the 13th Amendment, African-American issues once again emerged with the Freedom Rider bus rides across the South, lunch counter sit-ins, voter registration efforts, the murders of civil rights workers, church bombings, and other brutal incidents.

Martin Luther King, Jr. became the recognized spokesperson for African-Americans, leading the march on Washington, and conducting peaceful demonstrations across the country, and delivering his famous "I Have a Dream" speech at the Lincoln Memorial.

His assassination produced untold anger, despair, and violence, as American cities burned.

Yet, in the decade of the 1960s, there was progress. Congress enacted voter laws increasing African-American participation in political affairs. Congress also prohibited discrimination by businesses engaged in interstate commerce. African-Americans at last could participate in modern life. Legal segregation ended in schools, employment, and public accommodations.

That was Phase 4, which significantly eased the Reign of Terror.

Yet, despite the end of legal segregation, there is a new Phase—Phase 5—*de facto* housing segregation remains through economics and severe inequality of income and wealth. That, in turn, leads to extensive educational segregation in neighborhood schools. In a circular manner, that reinforces housing discrimination

1044 Adam Clayton Powell, Jr., "What's in Your Hand Speech, 1967?" at *www.allreadable.com/2979EmEx,* accessed Sept. 27, 2020.

by the consequent operation of economics. In addition, there still are plentiful individuals who evidence blatant racism through their speech and actions.

As this Chapter discusses, there is scandalous inequality for black Americans in education and educational opportunity.

Additionally, the rate of police killings of African-Americans is seriously disproportionate to the rate of police killings of whites—more than double ("They account for less than 13 percent of the U.S. population, but are killed by police at more than twice the rate of White Americans.").[1045]

Some African-Americans express increasing frustration and anger focused on the police. Curiously, however, protesters do not mention educational discrimination. Yet, that is the root cause of a host of ills affecting countless African-Americans—poverty, a lack of access to high-paying jobs, income and wealth disparities, and an inability to advance in American society.

1045 "Fatal Force: 1,010 people have been shot and killed by police in the past year" (Wash. Post Online, Sept. 23, 2020) (Updated Nov. 11, 2020) at *www.washingtonpost.com/graphics/investigations/police-shootings-database/*, accessed Nov. 12, 2020.

SLAVERY'S FATHER, DUKE OF YORK: STILL HONORED TODAY

The Duke of York truly was the Father of America's Slave Society.

The Duke promoted—and profited from—a particularly heinous form of improvised English slavery that did not even meet the standards of the time set by the Dutch, Spanish, French, West Africans, and pre-1660 Virginians. All of those slave cultures at least recognized slaves' humanity.

The Duke's legal enactments were part of a body of laws known as "the Duke's Laws." The Duke created a form of slavery mandating that children of slave mothers be slaves for life.

In addition, the Duke focused slavery specifically upon Africans, presuming them to be slaves, while denying them an ability to prove a "free" status. The Duke and his colleagues and successors allowed masters to punish slaves with little restraint and without recourse by slaves. They denied slaves the right to have families protected against destruction, the right to gather with their friends, the right to conduct business and earn income, the right to own property, the right to testify in court against whites, the right to move about freely, and the right to achieve freedom. Government officials administered sickening punishments against rebellious slaves.

The Duke's form of slavery was shockingly brutal and inhumane. The Duke, a governmental official with a pivotal role, used his power to enact, incentivize, and promote slavery in the American colonies.

Courageous African-Americans—America's Slavery Heroes who escaped from slavery or whose parents were slaves—fought relentlessly against the Duke's form of slavery. With the inspiration provided by the Declaration of Independence and support of abolitionists, both African-American and white, they succeeded in bringing about slavery's end. Those courageous Heroes, who contributed momentously to America, deserve special recognition on a par with America's Founding Fathers and Abraham Lincoln.

America's imperfect Founding Fathers gave America the Declaration of Independence—a fundamental document inspiring the end of slavery after decades. They also gave America the Constitution that, in its original form, while recognizing and protecting slavery, created a system of checks and balances to inhibit governance by another tyrant, such as the Duke of York, and they added a Bill of Rights.

In contrast, the Duke, as a "top down" absolutist ruler, steadfastly opposed representative government and a Charter of Liberties sought by the people.

This is the Duke of York America chooses to "honor" in the names of America's leading financial city, county, and State and the name of the State Capital.

The name of the Duke of York continues with prominence and honor in America today.

REMNANTS OF SLAVERY: INTOLERABLE DISCRIMINATION IN EDUCATION

Remnants of slavery remain in America today. They endure despite official segregation's end with the Civil Rights Laws of the 1960s and the decision of the Supreme Court in *Brown v. Board of Education* holding that segregated schools violated the Constitution.[1046]

One of the most significant remnants of slavery, a "badge" of slavery—continued outrageous discrimination in education—still lies at the core of America's severe racial inequalities.

Today's vigilantes attacking protestors against police killings are descendants of the slave society. So are those who—while convincing themselves, as did abolitionists, of their deep sympathy for African-Americans—refuse to consider the destructive impacts of the denial of adequate education to many African-Americans. They continuously fail to act against it.

BADGE OF SLAVERY

"Any visible trace of slavery, such as racial discrimination in public education."

"Badge of Slavery definitions," Webster's New World Law Dictionary Copyright© 2010 by Wiley Publishing, Inc., Hoboken, New Jersey, quoted at www.yourdictionary.com/badge-of-slavery, accessed Sept. 16, 2020

The dismal performance of America's schools for disadvantaged youth translates directly into rampant employment, income, and wealth inequities for African-Americans. In turn, those provide the origins of enormous housing, health care, retirement, and other inequities.

For emphasis, *the bedrock of all of those injustices is profound racial inequality in education.*

From the time that captive Africans came to America on slave ships through more than 200 years of slavery, through the period of explicit school segregation, through the period after *Brown v. Board of Education,* through the enactment of the 1960s Civil Rights Laws, to the present, African-Americans have never—never—had anything approaching equal access to education.

The Slave Society Forbade Slave Education

During slavery, it was illegal in slave states to teach slaves to read or write. Sometimes the prohibition extended even to "free" African-Americans.

White Americans feared educated slaves. Slaveholders harbored numerous concerns about slaves who could read and write: Slaves might forge "passes" allowing them to venture from their masters' premises; educated slaves might be more likely to run away, especially since, being able to read, they could function better in society; after reading "subversive literature," educated slaves might be more inclined to desire freedom and less inclined to submit to their fate or their masters' commands; and educated slaves might be inclined to revolt—the greatest white fear of all!

Illustrating the extensive denial of education to slaves, and even "free" African-Americans, in his 1856 legal treatise on slave laws, Philadelphia Judge George Stroud cites and quotes statutes.[1047]

1046 *Brown v. Board of Education,* 347 U.S. 483 (1954).

1047 See also *"Chapter Six: The Duke of York's Creation on a Rampage—The Evil of Reading and Writing."*

The following are excerpts of statutory provisions Judge George Stroud offers from laws in South Carolina:[1048]

> Legislation on this subject began in South Carolina at a comparatively early date. By act of 1740 it was enacted as follows:—"Whereas the having of slaves taught to write, or suffering them to be employed in writing, may be attended with great inconveniences, *Be it enacted,* That all and every person and persons whatsoever who shall hereafter teach or cause any slave or slaves to be taught to write, or shall use or employ any slave as a scribe in any manner of writing hereafter taught to write, every such person or persons shall for every such offence forfeit the sum of one hundred pounds current money." …

Demonstrating slaveholders' seriousness in preventing slaves from learning to read or write, Judge Stroud continues by citing later laws prohibiting slaves from gathering for the purpose of "mental instruction," to the extent of *requiring* magistrates "to break doors," if necessary, in order to terminate slave education sessions:[1049]

> This was followed, in 1800, (leaving the act of 1740 also in force,) by this enactment:—"Assemblies of slaves, free negroes, mulattoes and mestizoes, whether composed of all or any of such description of persons, or of all or any of the same and of a proportion of white persons, met together for the purpose of mental instruction in a confined or secret place, &c. &c., are declared to be an *unlawful meeting;* and magistrates are hereby required, &c., to enter into such confined places, &c. &c., to break doors, &c. if resisted, and to disperse such slaves, free negroes, &c. &c.; and the officer dispersing such unlawful assemblage *may inflict such corporal punishment, not exceeding twenty lashes upon such*

NORTH CAROLINA LAW

"Any free person who shall hereafter teach, or *attempt* to teach, any slave within this state to *read* or *write,* the use of figures excepted, or shall give or sell to such slave or slaves *any books* or *pamphlets,* shall be liable to indictment, &c.; and upon conviction shall, at the discretion of the court, if a *white* man or woman, be fined not less than *one hundred* dollars, nor more than *two hundred* dollars, or imprisoned; and if a free person of colour, shall be *fined, imprisoned* or *whipped,* at the discretion of the court, not exceeding *thirty-nine* lashes, nor less than *twenty* lashes. … And for a similar offence *as to instruction,* a slave shall receive *thirty-nine* lashes on his or her *bare* back."

G. Stroud, A sketch of the laws relating to slavery in the several states of the United States of America at 61 (H. Longstreth, 1856), available from the Library of Congress at *www.hathitrust.org/digital_library.* Emphasis in original.

SLAVEOWNER OPPOSITION TO EDUCATION

"While I lived with my master in St. Michael's, there was a white young man, a Mr. Wilson, who proposed to keep a Sabbath school for the instruction of such slaves as might be disposed to learn to read the New Testament. We met but three times, when Mr. West and Mr. Fairbanks … with many others, came upon us with sticks and other missiles, drove us off, and forbade us to meet again. Thus ended our little Sabbath school in the pious town of St. Michael's."

F. Douglass, The Narrative of the Life of Frederick Douglass at 55 (1845), available from the Library of Congress at www.hathitrust.org/digital_library.

1048 Stroud, at 60. Citations omitted. Emphasis in original.

1049 Stroud, at 60. Citations omitted. Emphasis in original.

> *slaves, free negroes,* &c., as they may judge necessary for DETERRING THEM FROM THE LIKE UNLAWFUL ASSEMBLAGE IN FUTURE." ...

Judge Stroud then cites a prohibition against slaves gathering for "mental instruction," "even in company with white persons:"[1050]

> another section of the same act declares "That it shall not be lawful for any number of slaves, free negroes, mulattoes or mestizoes, even in company with white persons, to meet together for the purpose of *mental instruction,* either before the rising of the sun, or after the going down of the same." ...

Judge Stroud cites additional laws in Georgia, North Carolina, Louisiana, and Alabama imposing a variety of punishments against whites and "free" African-Americans, including fines of hundreds of dollars (in today's money, thousands) or imprisonment up to a year or both for teaching slaves to read or write. "Free" African-Americans and slaves receiving instruction were subject to additional punishments, such as up to 39 lashes.[1051]

FINES IN CURRENT DOLLARS

Using the inflation conversion rate of 33, a fine of $100 for teaching a slave to read would be the equivalent of $3,300 today.

Black abolitionist, David Walker, described the denial of education to slaves, as follows:[1052]

> It is a fact, that in our Southern and Western States, there are millions who hold us in chains or in slavery, whose greatest object and glory, is centered in keeping us sunk in the most profound ignorance and stupidity, to make us work without remunerations for our services. Many of whom if they catch a coloured person, whom they hold in unjust ignorance, slavery and degradation, to them and their children, with a book in his hand, will beat him nearly to death. I heard a wretch in the state of North Carolina said, that if any man would teach a black person whom he held in slavery, to spell, read or write, he would prosecute him to the very extent of the law.—Said the ignorant wretch, "a Nigar, ought not to have any more sense than enough to work for his master."

William Goodell states that basic principle, as follows:[1053]

> The Slave not being regarded as a member of Society, nor as a human being, the Government, instead of providing for his education, takes care to forbid it, as being inconsistent with the condition of chattelhood.

America's Educational Emergency

Maintaining slaves in an uneducated state was official government policy during slavery.

Educational inequality remains America's effective official governmental policy today at the federal, state and local levels.

Of course, that statement will give birth to great cries of wounded rage. Yet, examine the facts. Then, consider where and when you have heard anyone propose to undertake fundamental change of America's

1050 Stroud, at 60. Citations omitted. Emphasis in original.

1051 Stroud, at 60-63. Citations omitted. Emphasis in original.

1052 Walker, at 59.

1053 Goodell, at 319.

U.S. EDUCATION'S FAILING GRADES

The following information is derived from data reported for 2019 in student reading achievement (2015 for high school students), reflecting worsening scores from 2017 for 4th and 8th grade students:

4th Grade—65% below proficient

8th Grade—66% below proficient

12th Grade—63% below proficient

The 4th and 8th grade levels were slightly better than in 1992. High school levels were "not measurably different from 2013," but were lower than in 1992.

Levels for black students not only were lower than levels for white students, but were even lower than for "High Poverty" households overall.

National Assessment of Educational Progress, Institute of Education Sciences, "The Condition of Education 2020" (May 2020) at 69-70, 80-81 at *nces.ed.gov/pubs2020/2020144.pdf,* accessed Sept. 16, 2020

education system other than to heave yet more dollars to incompetent and wasteful school districts that have never performed satisfactorily.

There is a true national educational emergency, except that no one declares it, and it has been in effect for more than 350 years. Given its heavy impact throughout the daily lives of millions of African-Americans, it is the most serious civil rights issue confronting America today, but it remains virtually unacknowledged at official government levels. In that vein, the Sixth Circuit Court of Appeals ruled in 2020 that "a basic minimum education" giving access to literacy is a fundamental right protected by the Constitution.[1054]

America has diminished education as an issue in the face of police violence protests. Those certainly are important. Yet, without taking away from the significance of the protests, they will not create jobs for African-Americans. They will not eradicate income or wealth disparities. They will not improve access to decent housing, adequate health care, or sufficient retirement programs.

Education has the potential to do all of that.

If America were to "pay reparations," educational reform is the place to spend the money. It would create viable futures for millions of black children who now face dark lives in poverty. Managed responsibly, it also would provide remedial assistance to the current victims of active discrimination—those black adults who already are suffering genuine harm today.

The educational emergency begins with the extremely low proficiencies of African-American students in reading and math at levels far below the proficiencies of white students. Even white students, however, fare poorly. *Staggeringly, far fewer than half* of American students are proficient in those subject areas[1055]—a shocking statistic that should be ringing alarm bells loudly. Yet, the "bells" are simply tinkling.

1054 *Gary B., et al., v. Whitmer,* Case No. 18-1855/1871 (Sixth Cir., 2020). The State of Michigan settled the litigation with the Plaintiffs. Strauss, "Michigan settles historic lawsuit after court rules students have a constitutional right to a 'basic' education, including literacy" (Wash. Post, May 14, 2020) at *www.washingtonpost.com/education/2020/05/14/michigan-settles-historic-lawsuit-after-court-rules-students-have-constitutional-right-basic-education-including-literacy/,* accessed Sept. 28, 2020.

1055 Bloomberg.com Editorial Board, "Biden Shouldn't Let Teachers Unions Hold Students Back" (July 16, 2020) at *www.bloomberg.com/opinion/articles/2020-07-16/biden-shouldn-t-let-teachers-unions-dictate-education-policy,* accessed Sept. 27, 2020 ("Bloomberg Editorial Board"); "The Nation's Report Card: How Did U.S. Students Perform on the Most Recent Assessment?" (Public Schools Only vs. Private Schools Only) at *www.nation's reportcard.gov,* accessed Sept. 16, 2020.

African-American students fare far worse than do white students. The following table compares white and black percentages of 4th and 8th grade students at or above proficiency levels in reading in 2015:[1056]

READING

Grade	White	Black
4	46	18
8	44	16

MATH

Grade	White	Black
4	51	19
8	43	13

How can American schools claim validity when only 16% of 8th grade African-American students—less than one out of six—are proficient in reading, and only 13%—less than one out of seven—are proficient in math?

Public schools' response to the covid 19 pandemic made matters worse. Michael Bloomberg states that "By one analysis, the first year of the pandemic left students an average of five months behind in math and four months behind in reading."[1057]

SHOCKING WEALTH DISPARITY

"The typical black household headed by someone with an advanced degree has less wealth than a white household with only a high school diploma."

Long and Van Dam, "The black-white economic divide is as wide as it was in 1968" (Wash. Post, June 4, 2020) at *www.washingtonpost.com/business/2020/06/04/economic-divide-black-households,* accessed Nov. 12, 2020

The educational inadequacy for African-American students cannot be more dire. It is not possible for employment, income, and wealth for many African-Americans to be acceptable in the face of such extreme school failures!

There is a reason why disadvantaged families are unable to provide the same level of student support as are other families—the schools badly discriminated against the parents and grandparents in those disadvantaged families when the parents and grandparents attended school in the past. As a result, families lack the background necessary to provide full educational support to their children. The disadvantage of educational discrimination is transmitted from one generation to the next, and then to the next.

1056 "The Nation's Report Card, National Results Overview," at *www.nationsreportcard.gov/reading_math_2015/#?grade=4,* accessed Sept. 14, 2020. See also "Black Students in the Condition of Education 2020" at *nsba.org/Perspectives/2020/black-students-condition-education,* accessed June 10, 2022.

1057 Bloomberg, "A Wake-Up Call for Public Education: Falling Enrollment in America's schools is a sign of a system in crisis" at *www.bloomberg.com/opinion/articles/2022-06-02/declining-school-enrollment-signals-challenge-for-us-public-education,* accessed June 10, 2022 ("Bloomberg, Wake-Up Call").

District school apologists often use that past discrimination against earlier generations as yet another excuse for the district school failures. The claim is that the families, not the schools, are at fault for the low test scores of African-American children. Using that excuse, district schools discriminate against the current generation of students.

America must break the pattern. Otherwise, the disadvantage will be transferred indefinitely, just as it has been for hundreds of years past.

The record of significant success in certain urban charter schools demonstrates that, with appropriate fundamental changes in educational curricula and teaching techniques, the performance of African-American children can be enhanced considerably and the gap in test scores can be minimized or potentially even eliminated.[1058]

To help the families, action should extend as well to remedial education for parents of disadvantaged students who were themselves denied adequate educations.

The problem is magnified by the prominent level of single-parent families in the African-American community, constituting two-thirds of African-Americans households, according to the Annie E. Casey Foundation.[1059] That means many students have even less support as single parents, often having experienced teen pregnancies, struggle to earn a living. This is another remnant of slavery, as slaveholders both encouraged, even pressured, young slave girls to breed and destroyed slave families, disregarding the important value of two-parent families.

How is it possible that America can remain silent in the face of such educational failures? How can America's politicians, schools, and educators remain so unresponsive?

Yet, there is a significant unwillingness—including by activists who proudly flaunt their sympathies for African-Americans and for Black Lives Matter—to do what is necessary to remedy the cavernous educational gap.

That ignores the strong hunger of the African-Americans community for school choice. Repeatedly, polls of African-Americans have shown that substantial majorities, both nationally and in specific states, consistently favor school choice through charter schools and vouchers, by poll majorities approaching or exceeding, 60%.[1060]

When it comes to making a choice between, on one hand, supporting teachers' unions, which provide a largesse in the form of political contributions for the benefit of district board members and other politicians at all levels of government, and on the other hand, supporting African-Americans who vote, the unions win every time. School districts and politicians would throw African-American voters under the bus at the snap of the fingers rather than offend teachers' unions.

1058 See "*—Charter Schools' Competition Is Constructive Disruptive Innovation*" below.

1059 "Children in single-parent families by race in the United States" at *datacenter.kidscount.org/data/tables/107-children-in-single-parent-families-by#detailed/1/any/false/37,871,870,573,869,36,868,867,133,38/10,11,9,12,1,185,13/432,431,* accessed Sept. 16, 2020.

1060 "African-American support of charter schools" at *www.federationforchildren.org/african-american-support-charter-schools,* accessed Sept. 27, 2020; "African Americans Speak for Themselves: Most Want School Choice" at *www.cato.org/blog/african-americans-speak-themselves-most-want-school-choice,* accessed Sept. 27, 2020; "Poll: Support for School Choice Spiked 10 Percent among Public School Families during Covid Shutdown" at *www.nationalreview.com/news/poll-support-for-school-choice-spiked-10-percent-among-public-school-families-during-covid-shutdown,* accessed Sept. 27, 2020.

As a result, day after day, bit by bit, the lives and futures of millions of African-American children are steadily destroyed. It happened to their parents. It happened to their grandparents. It happened to their great grandparents and to others before them. Now, it is happening to today's children.

Money Alone Is Not the Answer

It is time for concerned Americans to press for meaningful change and to end educational racism in America as a remnant of slavery.

The answer is not more money alone. It requires genuine fundamental educational reform.

As Bloomberg.com's Editorial Board states:[1061]

> The need for reform is clear—and lack of money, overall, is not the main impediment. Per-pupil spending in the U.S. is among the highest in the world, but the country is getting a very poor return. …

Michael Bloomberg observes that "Charter schools educate 7% of all public-school students, yet they receive less than 1% of total federal spending on K-12 education." Bloomberg cites a "nationwide analysis [that] found that districts with a higher share of charters yield higher reading and math scores as well as graduation rates on average. … [The benefits are especially pronounced for Black, Latino and low-income students."[1062]

U.S. STUDENT PERFORMANCE—
INTERNATIONAL COMPARISONS

U.S Rank Range:

Reading: 12

Math: 25

Science: 20

Examples of countries ranking in 2003 higher than, or on a par with, the U.S. in all three subject areas include: Macao, Lichtenstein, Finland, South Korea, Japan, Canada, Australia, Switzerland, New Zealand, Ireland, France, Sweden, and Poland. Countries so ranking in at least one subject area include: Hungary, Czech Republic, Slovak Republic, Germany, Iceland, Spain, Luxembourg, Norway, Austria, Denmark, and Latvia.

"International Comparison of Math, Reading, and Science Skills Among 15-Year-Olds" at *www.infoplease.com/us/education/international-comparison-math-reading-and-science-skills,* accessed Sept. 16, 2020.

According to Dr. Patrick Wolf of the University of Arkansas and Dr. Anna Egalite of North Carolina State University, on a "[r]eal, inflation-adjusted" basis, spending in America "on K-12 education has increased almost 300 percent since 1971." Nevertheless, despite that enormous increase in expenditures, student test scores on the National Assessment of Education Progress have been primarily stagnant. Drs. Wolf and Egalite state: "Over the past 30 years, … 17-year olds, who are nearer to the end of the knowledge production process, have gained very little … ."[1063]

Naomi Schaefer Riley states in a Wall Street Journal commentary that:[1064]

> On the International Adult Literacy Survey, Americans went from being No. 1 for children who were educated in the 1950s to fifth for those in the '70s and 14th in the '90s. And things have only gotten

1061 Bloomberg.com Editorial Board. See also Bloomberg, Wake-Up Call.

1062 Bloomberg, Wake-Up Call.

1063 Wolf and Egalite, "Pursuing Innovation: How Can Educational Choice Transform K-12 Education in the U.S.?" at 3 (Friedman Foundation for Educational Choice, Apr. 2016) at *eric.ed.gov/?id=ED570184,* accessed Sept. 16, 2020) "Wolf and Egalite").

1064 Riley, "Bad Teaching Is Tearing America Apart" (Wall St. J., Sept. 11, 2020) at *www.wsj.com/articles/bad-teaching-is-tearing-america-apart-11599857351.*

worse. Between 2002 and 2015, American schoolchildren went from a ranking of 15th to 24th in reading on the Program for International Student Assessment.

In summary, simply spending more money, by itself, has proved to be ineffective without fundamental structural changes in the education system. Incompetent and wasteful school boards do not suddenly become more competent and effective when they receive more money. Money has not brought about the needed transformations, after decades of inadequate performance.

Wealth Inequality Has Increased Since Enactment of the Civil Rights Laws

Despite the progress accomplished through the Civil Rights Laws enacted in the 1960s, racial income and wealth inequality have increased in America. That has occurred despite five decades of legislation, affirmative action, and prosecution of discrimination cases in the courts.

The Washington Post reports that "In many ways, the gap between the finances of blacks and whites is still as wide in 2020 as it was in 1968." The Post adds that "In 1968, a typical middle-class black household had $6,674 in wealth compared with $70,786 for the typical middle-class white household, according to data from the historical Survey of Consumer Finances adjusted for inflation. In 2016, the typical middle-class black household had $13,024 in wealth versus $149,703 for the median white household, an even larger gap in percentage terms."[1065] The Urban Institute reports similar wealth disparity data, adding that "Income inequality can worsen wealth inequality because the income people have available to save and invest matters. Focusing on private income, such as earnings and dividends, plus cash government benefits, we see that the income of families near the top increased roughly 90 percent from 1963 to 2016, while the income of families at the bottom increased less than 10 percent."[1066]

EXPANDING SCHOOL CHOICE OPTIONS

- Charter Schools
- Home Schooling with Online Courses
- Home Schooling without Online Courses
- Home Schooling for Combined Families with Professional Teachers
- Private Schools with Vouchers
- Section 529 and Similar Plans

Forbes.com states that "The wealth gap in America has been growing since at least the 1970s as income levels stagnated for lower and middle class households while continuing to grow for households at the top of the spectrum." Forbes summarizes with the observation that "in 1968, the median black household had just 9.4% of the wealth of the median white household, according to Fed data. Yet by 2016, that ratio had fallen to just 8.7%."[1067]

While individuals are able to escape poverty, without access to equality in education and in the absence of improvements in education, most African-Americans are hampered in seeking better lives.

1065 Long and Van Dam, "The black-white economic divide is as wide as it was in 1968" (Wash. Post, June 4, 2020) at *www.washingtonpost.com/business/2020/06/04/economic-divide-black-households,* accessed Sept. 27, 2020.

1066 "Nine Charts about Wealth Inequality in America" (Updated) at *apps.urban.org/features/wealth-inequality-charts/,* accessed Sept. 16, 2020.

1067 Hansen, "Here's What The Racial Wealth Gap In America Looks Like Today" at *www.forbes.com/sites/sarahhansen/2020/06/05/heres-what-the-racial-wealth-gap-in-america-looks-like-today/#3be6c333164c,* accessed Sept.16, 2020.

School Competition Is Constructively Disruptive Innovation

Competition promotes innovation as the competitors seek advantages against their rivals. That general principle operates in education, as well as across the board in professional activities. Competitors will experiment to improve their services.

Without competition, district schools are *governmental* monopolies lacking motivation to make fundamental changes.

Just as government, through the Duke of York, enacted and promoted American slavery, America's school districts, as near monopolistic governmental entities, are preserving inequality as a critical remnant of slavery.

The goal of encouraging competing educational approaches is to encourage innovation leading to educational improvement. This is known as "disruptive innovation." It is extremely valuable.

Nongovernmental competitors who fail to innovate, and to adopt successful innovation originating elsewhere, will fail and will exit business. In the case of failing district schools, however, politicians provide continued funding from governmental resources enabling even failing schools to remain in operation to the great disadvantage of African-American students who do not have access to school choice. A preferable alternative is to turn to competing alternatives.

DISRUPTIVE INNOVATION

"Disruptive Innovation refers to a technology whose application significantly affects the way a market or industry functions. An example of modern disruptive innovation is the Internet, which significantly altered the way companies did business and which negatively impacted companies that were unwilling to adapt to it."

"Disruptive Innovation" at *www.investopedia.com/terms/d/disruptive-innovation.asp,* accessed Sept. 14, 2020.

Smartphones are an example of constructive disruption. Until smartphones emerged only about 15 years ago, the Blackberry was the dominant mobile communication device. Smartphones, however, introduced innovative ideas, such as internet access and a wide variety of personal convenience tools and apps, that quickly became the technology of choice.

The same principle operates in education in those instances when politicians allow competition. Charter schools and vouchers usable at private schools can facilitate students' moves to superior alternatives.

Although district schools and charter schools *overall* produce similar achievement results,[1068] the competition is constructive. Specific charter schools are beginning to produce remarkably positive innovative results specifically for African-American children.

Evidence shows that those charter schools are accomplishing this by creating original approaches to education that district schools will not, or due to regulatory restrictions and teachers' union contracts, are prohibited from adopting.

A key reason for charter school existence is to escape teachers' union dominance and political restrictions on experimentation.

1068 Cohodes, "Charter Schools and the Achievement Gap" at 4 (The Future of Children, Princeton-Brookings, Winter 2018) at *futureofchildren.princeton.edu/news/charter-schools-and-achievement-gap#:~:text=Charter Schools and the Achievement Gap,* accessed Sept. 27, 2020 ("Cohodes").

The mere availability of competition can induce district schools to make certain beneficial changes. Dr. Patrick Wolf of the University of Arkansas and Dr. Anna Egalite of North Carolina State University summarize the results of "42 evaluations of the effects of school-choice competition on the performance of affected public schools." They conclude that 30 of the studies found "that increased competitive pressure results in statistically significant achievement gains for at least some district schools in some subject areas" when competition occurred primarily through charter schools, vouchers, or tax-credit scholarships.[1069] They also found that "the positive effect of competition from charters, vouchers, and tax-credit scholarship programs on public school performance has been the strongest when the intensity of competition has increased dramatically."[10701071]

That is yielding positive results for African-American children. In a study titled "Charter Schools and the Achievement Gap," Dr. Sarah Cohodes of Teachers College at Columbia University notes that "charter schools have flexibility in regulation."[1072] Dr. Cohodes states that "a subset of charter schools has significant positive impacts on student outcomes. *These are typically urban charter schools serving minority and low income students that use a no excuses curriculum.*[1073]

Dr. Cohodes points out that charter school students in urban areas where attendance rolls are over-subscribed are selected by lottery, not by student selectivity.[1074] Dr. Cohodes concludes that charter schools did not achieve superior student performance as a result of either manipulation of admission lotteries or differences in the characteristics of student bodies.[1075]

"NO EXCUSES" CURRICULUM FACTORS IN NYC

- Intensive teacher observation
- Intensive teacher training
- Data-driven instruction
- Increased instructional time
- Intensive tutoring during the school day
- Culture of high expectations

Cohodes, "Charter Schools and the Achievement Gap" at 8, 10 (The Future of Children, Princeton-Brookings, Winter 2018) at *futureofchildren.princeton.edu/news/charter-schools-and-achievement-gap#:~:text=Charter Schools and the Achievement Gap*, accessed Sept. 27, 2020

FACTORS NOT POSITIVELY CORRELATED WITH EFFECTIVENESS

- Per-pupil spending
- Student-teacher ratios

Cohodes, "Charter Schools and the Achievement Gap" at 8 (The Future of Children, Princeton-Brookings, (Winter 2018) at *futureofchildren.princeton.edu/news/charter-schools-and-achievement-gap#:~:text=Charter Schools and the Achievement Gap,* Sept. 27, 2020

1069 Wolfe and Egalite, at 1, 18-22, 32.

1070 Wolfe and Egalite, at 23.

1071 See, however, "—School Districts, Teachers' Unions, and Politicians Block Progress" below.

1072 Dr. Cohodes is quoted in Anderson, "Harvard EdCast: Replicating Effective Charter School Practice" (Feb. 20, 2019) at *www.gse.harvard.edu/news/19/02/harvard-edcast-replicating-effective-charter-school-practice,* accessed Sept. 27, 2020. See also Cohodes and Parham, "Charter School' Effectiveness, Mechanisms, and Competitive Influence" (Nat. Bur. Of Econ. Research, Working Paper, May 2021).

1073 Cohodes, at 3.

1074 Cohodes, at 2. Emphasis added.

1075 Cohodes, at 4, 11.

She adds that, with the improvement in achievement, longer-term results also are emerging: "Where it's possible to look at longer-term outcomes, the same schools that have beneficial impacts on test scores also boost college preparation and college-going outcomes."[1076]

Innovations by urban charter schools in Boston that produced "positive school impacts" through a "no excuses" approach to education were: "discipline, uniforms and student participation."[1077]

She describes greater teacher oversight and higher expectations for both teachers and students:[1078]

> No excuses schools emphasize high expectations for both academics and behavior, longer school days and years, and frequent observations of teachers to give feedback, tutoring, and data-driven instruction that uses assessment to frequently update teachers.

Thus, innovations by urban charter schools in New York City that apply a "no excuses" approach to education were: "intensive teacher observation and training, data-driven instruction, increased instructional time, intensive tutoring, and a culture of high expectations."[1079]

She adds:[1080]

> One charter school practice stood out: high-quality tutoring. Many high-quality charter schools require intensive tutoring as a means of remediation and learning, often incorporating one-on-one or small group tutoring into the school day rather than as an add-on or optional activity.

In effect, it appears that, by intensive tutoring during the school day or otherwise, the charter schools are serving as the support that many parents, having been denied educations themselves and often working two jobs, are unable to provide.

Dr. Cohodes concludes that the charter school improvements "can have transformative effects on individual students' lives" and "reduce achievement gaps."[1081]

SIGNIFICANT BENEFITS OF
"NO EXCUSES CURRICULUM"

"Three years attending one of these high performing charter schools produces test-score gains about the size of the black-white test-score gap. The best evidence we have so far suggests that these test-score gains will translate into beneficial effects on outcomes like college-going, teen pregnancy, and incarceration."

Cohodes, "Charter Schools and the Achievement Gap" at 14 (The Future of Children, Princeton-Brookings, Winter 2018) at *futureofchildren.princeton.edu/news/charter-schools-and-achievement-gap#:~:text=Charter Schools and the Achievement Gap,* accessed Sept. 27, 2020

1076 Cohodes, at 7.

1077 Cohodes, at 8.

1078 Cohodes, at 6.

1079 Cohodes, at 8, 10.

1080 Cohodes, at 10.

1081 Cohodes, at 14.

Dr. Anna Egalite concludes in "The National Charter School Landscape" that:[1082]

> The vast majority of lottery-based studies have been conducted in urban centers, where the number of student applications to charter schools far exceeds the number of seats available. This generates a treatment group and a comparison group that are identical, on average, in terms of both observable (e.g., family background) and unobservable (e.g., motivation) characteristics. Studies from these locations have revealed statistically significant, large, and educationally meaningful achievement gains for lottery winners. *Particularly dramatic gains have been observed for disadvantaged students, students of color, and English language learners.*

Dr. M. Danish Shakeel and Dr. Paul E. Peterson of Harvard University report charter school achievement gains in a paper titled "Charter Schools Show Steeper Upward Trend in Student Achievement than District Schools." They state that:[1083]

> *The biggest gains are for African Americans and for students of low socioeconomic status attending charter schools.* When we adjust for changes in student background characteristics, we find that two-thirds of the relative gain in the charter sector cannot be explained by demography. In other words, the pace of change is more rapid either because the charter sector, relative to the district sector, is attracting a more proficient set of students in ways that cannot be detected by demographic characteristics, or because charter schools and their teachers are doing a better job of teaching students.

Shakeel and Peterson add that "Test performance for African Americans improved over time at both district and charter schools, but the trend was far more dramatic at charters. This is especially noteworthy as one in three charter students is African American."[1084]

LARGEST CHARTER SCHOOL GAINS ARE FOR <u>DISADVANTAGED STUDENTS</u>

"[A] subset of charter schools has significant positive impacts on student outcomes. These are typically urban charter schools serving minority and low income students that use a no excuses curriculum."

Dr. Sarah Cohodes quoted in Anderson, "Harvard EdCast: Replicating Effective Charter School Practice" at 19 *www.gse.harvard.edu/news/19/02/harvard-edcast-replicating-effective-charter-school-practice* (Feb. 20, 2019)

"Particularly dramatic gains have been observed for disadvantaged students, students of color, and English language learners."

Egalite, "The National Charter School Landscape" (Hoover Institution, July 1, 2020) at *www.hoover.org/research/national-charter-school-landscape*

"The biggest gains are for African Americans and for students of low socioeconomic status attending charter schools."

Shakeel and Peterson, "Charter Schools Show Steeper Upward trend in Student Achievement that District Schools" at *www.educationnext.org/charter-schools-show-steeper-upward-trend-student-achievement-first-nationwide-study/* (updated Sept. 8, 2020)

1082 Egalite, "The National Charter School Landscape" at 19 (Hoover Institution, July 1, 2020) at *www.hoover.org/research/national-charter-school-landscape*, accessed Sept. 27, 2020 ("Egalite"). Footnote omitted. Emphasis added.

1083 Shakeel and Peterson, "Charter Schools Show Steeper Upward Trend in Student Achievement than District Schools" (updated Sept. 8, 2020) at *www.educationnext.org/charter-schools-show-steeper-upward-trend-student-achievement-first-nationwide-study/*, accessed Sept. 27, 2020 ("Shakeel and Peterson"). Emphasis added.

1084 Shakeel and Peterson

District Schools, Teachers' Unions, and Politicians Block Progress

Although Dr. Cohodes suggests that district schools should adopt the "no excuses curriculum" innovations,[1085] and of course they should, there is little evidence that a significant number of district schools actually would do so.

The political resistance is adamant against providing equitable access to educational choice.

Much resistance derives from teachers' unions,[1086] which are able to dominate school boards through the electoral process. Schools governed by elected school boards are vulnerable to political dominance by substantial political contributors. Few public citizens contribute significantly to the election of school board members. Instead, teachers' unions and other parties seeking contracts, are often the primary sources of those political contributions. The elected board members then are less likely to negotiate diligently with those parties in entering into contracts.

RACIAL EDUCATIONAL DISPARITY EXAMPLES

- "African American students are often located in schools with less qualified teachers, teachers with lower salaries and novice teachers."
- "Research has shown evidence of systematic bias in teacher expectations for African American students and non-black teachers were found to have lower expectations of black students than black teachers."
- "African-American students are less likely than white students to have access to college-ready courses."
- "African American students are less likely to be college-ready."
- "Students of color are often concentrated in schools with fewer resources."
- "The 12th grade assessment also show[s] alarming disparities ..., with only seven percent of black students performing at or above proficient on the math exam in 2015, compared to 32 percent for white students."
- "There is a clear lack of black representation in school personnel."

"K-12 Disparity Facts and Statistics" at uncf.org/pages/K-12-Disparity-Facts-and-stats, accessed Sept. 14, 2020

Teachers unions often resist educational improvements, such as greater accountability and charter schools.[1087] Yet, those lead to enhanced student performance.

During the pandemic, a new form of home schooling spread. The approach combines home schooling students, such as five to ten, in one location with professional teachers. The funding comes from funding to cooperative charter schools. Because of the reduced overhead costs, it is possible to pay teachers more than in traditional schools. Teachers unions felt threatened, however, warning ironically that the improved education the students received would widen the education gap.[1088] The logical response for a successful innovation would seem to be to extend it also to disadvantaged students.

1085 Cohodes, at 14.

1086 Bloomberg.com Editorial Board.

1087 Bloomberg.com Editorial Board.

1088 Kaufman, "The Teacher Union's Tiny New Enemy: The behemoth National Education Association seeks to squash popular pandemic microschools" (Wall St. J., Oct. 14, 2020) at *www.wsj.com/articles/the-teachers-unions-tiny-new-enemy-11602709305*, accessed Oct. 17, 2020.

Teachers' unions are likely to object strongly to factors contributing to charter schools' success—intensive teacher oversight, incentive pay for excellent teachers, intensive teacher training,[1089] incentive pay for specially-trained teachers working in disadvantaged schools,[1090] longer teaching hours, and intensive tutoring during the school day or after school hours in addition to other teaching duties. That is why district schools do not use these common sense techniques in the first place and why the source of innovation is not the district school sector.

SCHOOL CHOICE POPULATION PROPORTIONS

- Charter schools—5%
- Homeschooling—3%
- Private schools—10%

Cohodes, "Charter Schools and the Achievement Gap" at 1 (The Future of Children, Princeton-Brookings, Winter 2018) at *futureofchildren.princeton.edu/news/charter-schools-and-achievement-gap#:~:text=Charter Schools and the Achievement Gap,* accessed Sept. 27, 2020

Dr. Cohodes describes politicians' focus on benefits for adults—teachers and school managers—as opposed to educational growth for children:[1091]

> It's a situation where we know more about how charters are doing, but a lot of what politics are about is not about the educational experiences of children in school[.] It's about what's happening for adults in terms of teachers, what's happening in terms of funding, what's happening in terms of unionization, what's happening in terms of support or lack of support for traditional public school districts . ... I think we've seen a lot of change. A lot of information but think there is still not a settled political question. A lot is about politics and not what's happening in school.

Dr. Egalite agrees:[1092]

> Political resistance to charter schools is fueled, in part, by teachers' unions. Labor unions often work in tandem with other organizations and groups, including school districts, as political opponents fighting charter school expansion on four fronts: in the legislature, in the courts, in the battle to influence public opinion, and by attempting to unionize charter school teachers.

Shakeel and Peterson cite a slowing of charter school growth beginning in 2016 due to regulatory restrictions:[1093]

1089 See, e.g., Morrar and Reese, "Inexperienced teachers are often sent to low-income schools in Sacramento. Why that Matters" (Sacramento Bee, Feb.13, 2020) at *www.sacbee.com/ article239922318.html* (printed copy).

1090 See, e.g., "Our Say: Everybody's wrong in Anne Arundel County teachers union dispute" (Capital Gazette, Oct. 2, 2017) at *www.capitalgazette.com/opinion/our-say/ac-ce-our-say-20171002-story.html,* accessed Sept. 17, 2020, stating: "Expelled from the Teachers Association of Anne Arundel County in May, the outspoken Annapolis High School teacher wants a state labor board to overturn her union's rare decision to throw her out. The union claims Moesel used her position as an association representative at Annapolis High to further her 'personal agenda.' This included 'ingratiating' herself with County Executive Steve Schuh and negotiating to keep incentives for teachers at Annapolis High that the union and the county school system had agreed to end."

1091 Dr. Cohodes is quoted in Anderson, "Harvard EdCast: Replicating Effective Charter School Practice" (Feb. 20, 2019) at *www.gse.harvard.edu/news/19/02/harvard-edcast-replicating-effective-charter-school-practice,* accessed Sept. 27, 2020.

1092 Egalite, at 2.

1093 Shakeel and Peterson.

> The rate of states passing charter laws declined after 1999, and many of the laws passed since 2000 have included provisions that can stymie growth: caps on the number of schools allowed, arcane application requirements, and land-use and other regulations. In addition, a political backlash is slowing charter expansion in some states.

They add that district school management and teachers' unions, fearing innovation, are "more likely" the cause of a recent slowdown in charter school growth:

> Given the rising achievement levels at charter schools, the slowdown in the sector's growth rate cannot be attributed to declining quality. It is more likely that political resistance to charters is increasing as both the management and labor sides of the district sector become increasingly concerned that charters might prove to be as disruptive an innovation as the transistor.

Bloomberg agrees, noting declining public school enrollments during the covid-19 pandemic, accompanied by increases in charter school enrollments and home schooling:[1094]

> The idea that we would allow public charter-school students from disadvantaged backgrounds to be deprived of great teachers so that we can staff schools with declining enrollments as though they were full makes no sense whatsoever — until factoring in politics. And then it makes perfect sense, because so many elected officials are beholden to union leaders who oppose charters.

DISTRICT SCHOOL ACCOUNTABILITY MATTERS

"School districts that have coupled higher pay with greater accountability for results have seen sustained improvement. But the unions resist greater accountability."

Bloomberg.com Editorial Board, "Biden Shouldn't Let Teachers Unions Hold Students Back" (July 16, 2020) at *www.bloomberg.com/opinion/articles/2020-07-16/biden-shouldn-t-let-teachers-unions-dictate-education-policy*, accessed Sept. 27, 2020

In other words, just as *government*—the Duke of York and King Charles II beginning in the 1660s—created, incentivized, and promoted America's slave society, today *government again*—America's district schools and politicians—is the cause of the deep racial disparities in education—a key remnant of the slave society. In turn, educational inadequacy lies at the heart of racial disparities in access to quality jobs, income and wealth for African-Americans.

Once more, *government,* through excessive and unwise regulation, is able to inhibit, and even prevent, needed school competition and the innovation competition fosters.

Private Schools Are Superior for African-American Children

Given the stubborn intransigence of America's educational system, it is time to bypass the system in order to offer genuine school choice to African-American and other disadvantaged families. That means access to private schools, as well as district schools, charter schools, and home schooling. Vouchers can accomplish this.

The following table provides 2019 student proficiency data for all students reflecting dramatic differences for public vs. private schools:[1095]

1094 Bloomberg, Wake-Up Call.

1095 "The Nation's Report Card: How Did U.S. Students Perform on the Most Recent Assessment?" (Public Schools Only vs. Private Schools Only)" at *www.nation's reportcard.gov,* accessed Sept. 16, 2020.

READING PROFICIENCY: ALL STUDENTS

Grade	Public	Private
4	34%	49%
8	32	57
12	36	54

Thus, for all students, private schools are head and shoulders above public schools in terms of student performance.

Let's focus specifically upon African-American performance in the different types of schools. The following table provides contrasting student reading scores for African-American students for public, public: charter, and private Catholic schools:[1096]

READING SCORES: AFRICAN-AMERICAN STUDENTS

School Type	Grade 4	Grade 8	Grade 12
Public	203	244	265
Public: Charter	206	247	256
Private Catholic	212	258	298
Private Catholic Over Public	9	14	33

Thus, in terms specifically of African-American student performance, private Catholic schools outrank both charter schools and district schools. The differences become greater as students graduate to higher grades.

Decades ago, some private schools grew as a means for wealthy white families to keep their children out of integrated district schools. In large part, that action was due to a desire to avoid the dismal performance of the district schools. At times, it was a racist response.

It is possible, however, for African-American children to gain access to those private schools through vouchers.

There is a reason why private schools attract the best students—overall, the schools simply are far superior to district schools. Excellent students and their families do not want to suffer the inadequacies of district schools. They want better educations, and when they can afford it, through the competition provided by private schools, are able to obtain it. It is immoral to hold excellent students back from the best educations available.

Yet, few African-American families are able to afford private schools. Without vouchers, only students from families with a degree of wealth, which most African-Americans lack due to past discrimination, are

1096 "The Nation's Report Card: Public, Private, and Charter Schools Dashboard (Average scores in NAEP reading for Black Students by grade and type of school: 2019 (grade 4), 2019 (grade 8), and 2015 (grade 12)" at *www.nation's reportcard.gov*, accessed Sept. 16, 2020.

able financially to take advantage of a superior education. That is inequitable for American students and families who do not have those resources. Federal, state, and local governments have resources to overcome the discrimination and to correct these inequitable circumstances.

To be clear, despite the desperate protests by those who favor rigid, exclusive government control of providing K-12 education—a failed approach that has seriously harmed African-Americans—the use of vouchers does not amount to public funding of private schools.

Instead, it is a mechanism for equitable government funding for the individual students themselves and a means to equalize student funding. States and local school boards should provide, through vouchers, equal educational dollars to each student at each level. The students and their families then would be able to choose for themselves which schools to attend using their vouchers. It is possible to condition vouchers upon the agreement of public schools, charter schools, or private schools to accept the vouchers, without additional student resources, in full payment of tuition.

That is not using government funding for private schools. It is using government funding for the students themselves and their families to spend in their discretion.

Greater reliance on charter schools and vouchers would not remove one cent on a per pupil basis from district schools. Those schools would continue to receive full payment for the pupils they would be able to attract. To attract those students, district schools would be compelled to adopt excellence standards and educational techniques and innovations originated by charter schools and private schools.

What vouchers, as well as charter schools, accomplish is the creation of an important missing ingredient in K-12 education—competition through choice. If district schools want to attract more students, they should not do it through a continuance of the underperforming strategy of government compulsion, but by improving their schools.

Politicians' Self-Interests Prevent Equality of Education

After decades of living in America and observing its politicians and district school boards, I do not believe they have the courage or selflessness to turn their backs on their political contributors to do what is right.

As with police unions, powerful public employee unions are at center stage, this time teachers' unions that adamantly oppose the reforms necessary to overcome educational racism in America. Politicians are terrified not only of police unions; they are like deer in the headlights when it comes to teacher unions.

Like slave masters providing slaves meager food and clothing, some politicians arrogantly collect votes from poorly-educated poverty-stricken African-Americans by offering desperate people government bread crumbs (as Joe Biden expressed, if they don't vote "our way," they "ain't black").

Fortunately, there are African-Americans who are able to break free from the systematic educational discrimination. As slaveholders feared, the more education people have, the more they think for themselves, the more questions they ask, the more diverse their opinions become, and the more they seek new ways of improving their lives. They may not be the submissive voters politicians expect.

America's schools for disadvantaged students have failed over and over for decades, even centuries. District schools have lost their credibility and forfeited the right to any benefit of the doubt. America's public schools simply are unable, and unwilling, to compete as is necessary in order to bring educational standards to the level they should reach. They need to be confronted with a new fully-competitive environment.

It is not in the self-interest of politicians—regardless of their political philosophy—to do what is needed. After all, they would lose valuable political contributions from special interests.

This is not "something that happened 150 years ago."

Due to the inability of politicians to take appropriate action, I do not believe it is possible for America's racial disparities to be resolved. It is "something" that is "happening" today. It is a colossal failure of *government,* not a capitalist conspiracy.

REMNANTS OF SLAVERY: WHITE FEAR, AFRICAN-AMERICAN DISTRUST, "OBEDIENCE," AND ENFORCEMENT

Two important remnants of slavery—white fear of African-Americans and African-American distrust of whites—remain endemic in today's America. They are virtually impossible to eradicate without good faith efforts advocated by people like Martin Luther King, Jr.

While there are those on both sides who wish, and work, to overcome ingrained racial attitudes, there are individuals who continue to hold deep animosity toward each other on racial grounds.

Violence against blacks is a genuine issue. Still, its resolution will do nothing to remedy the core issue of vital importance to overcoming racial wealth inequality and poverty—America's sadly deficient educational system.

That key perspective should be kept firmly in mind in the following discussion.

Violence Against African-Americans Today

White fear pervaded American slavery. Whites, surrounded by gigantic populations of angry slaves, constantly feared disobedient slaves, runaway slaves, and slave revolts. Remnants of that fear, transmitted through generations, remain in evidence today.

Research confirms black concerns. African-Americans are killed by police at a rate far in excess of police killings of whites.[1097]

Just as America's police kill far too often today, to maintain their dominance slave masters beat slaves mercilessly, and sometimes to death, for minor offenses, including insolence, for which white citizens received little or no punishment. This arose, and continues to arise, from the deep-seated white fear of badly mistreated African-Americans. A man accused of passing a counterfeit $20 bill suffers vicious public execution, without trial, by a poorly-trained police tyrant, undisciplined after numerous complaints.

COMPARATIVE RATES OF POLICE KILLINGS

"The rate at which black Americans are killed by police is more than twice as high as the rate for white Americans."

Fatal Force: 1,010 people have been shot and killed by police in the past year (Wash. Post Online, Sept. 23, 2020) (Updated Nov. 11, 2020) at *www.washingtonpost.com/graphics/investigations/police-shootings-database/*, accessed Nov. 12, 2020

Sometimes, whites who are not law enforcement officials consider themselves justified in killing African-Americans without the victim committing any crime. Self-appointed white patrollers in trucks pursue a black man jogging in a white Georgia neighborhood, and shoot him as he takes evasive action. Especially that incident provides a strong echo of slave laws authorizing patrols to capture slaves off their masters' premises and, if the slaves resisted, to kill them.

1097 "Fatal Force: 1,010 people have been shot and killed by police in the past year" (Wash. Post Online, Sept. 23, 2020) (Updated Nov. 11, 2020) at *www.washingtonpost.com/graphics/investigations/police-shootings-database/*, accessed Nov. 12, 2020.

Not all is negative. Positive signs have emerged in recent years. Some police, as in the example above, have been convicted for use of excessive force. The Court convicted the Georgia vigilantes who murdered the black jogger and sentenced them to long prison terms.

America deserves credit for those developments.

Slave Society Laws Repressing Slaves

Slave laws created the power not only of public officials, but also of slave masters and white society in general, to discipline slaves at will, with unchecked discretion.

Dr. Randolph Campbell quotes a Texas Supreme Court Justice as expressing "reluctan[ce] to interfere" in "the delicate and responsible relation of master and slave," leaving "[m]uch … to the master's judgment, discretion, and humanity."[1098]

William Goodell states that "It would not do to allow the rights of the master to be brought into discussion in the courts of justice. The slave, to REMAIN a slave, must be sensible that there is NO APPEAL from his master."[1099]

Philadelphia Judge George Stroud quotes the Supreme Court of North Carolina as stating in 1829, more than half a century after the Declaration of Independence:[1100]

> The end (of slavery) is the profit of the master, his security, and the public safety. The subject is one doomed in his own person and his posterity to live without knowledge and without the capacity to make any thing his own, and to toil that another may reap the fruits. Such services can only be expected from one who has no will of his own; who surrenders his will in implicit obedience to that of another. *Such obedience is the consequence only of uncontrolled authority over the body. There is nothing else which can operate to produce the effect. The power of the master must be absolute to render the submission of the slave perfect. In the actual condition of things it must be so. There is no remedy.* This discipline belongs to the state of slavery.

In contrast, Spanish Florida provided a mechanism for slaves to bring legal actions against their masters for abuse.[1101] The French *Code Noir* stated: "We enjoin our officers to criminally prosecute the masters, or their foremen, who have killed a slave under their auspices or control, and to punish the master according to the circumstances of the atrocity."[1102]

As if dominance by slave masters were insufficient, in America, the slave society gave not merely masters, but all whites, the right to challenge slaves off their masters' premises to demand to see a "pass" or "license." Slaves had no right to resist.[1103]

1098 Campbell, at 151-52.

1099 Goodell, at 126.

1100 Stroud, at 10. Emphasis added.

1101 Deagan and MacMahon, at 7.

1102 "Le Code Noir" at *thelouvertureproject.org/index.php?title=Le_Code_Noir,* accessed Sept. 27, 2020.

1103 See *"Chapter Six: The Duke of York's Creation on a Rampage—The Story of Wiley: Gotta Have a "Pass."*

Judge Stroud illustrates those laws in the following excerpt from his legal treatise:[1104]

> My chief objection to these laws is, that they furnish a *pretext*, and (may I not say ?) *an inducement,* to an ignoble mind to oppress and to tyrannize over the defenceless slave. He must patiently endure every species of personal injury which a white person, however brutal and ferocious his disposition... may choose to offer.
>
> Several of the slave-holding states have adopted laws which are highly objectionable for the reason just given. The subjoined may be taken as a specimen:— [In Maryland,] "If any slave shall happen to be slain for refusing to surrender him or herself, contrary to law, or in unlawful resisting any officer or *other person* who shall apprehend or endeavour to apprehend such slave or slaves, &c., such officer or *other person so killing such slave as aforesaid,* making resistance, shall be and he is by this act indemnified from any prosecution for such killing aforesaid, &c."

That law, enacted in 1751, was 270 years ago.

Judge Stroud adds:[1105]

> Strict subordination must be exacted from the slave, or bloodshed and murders will unavoidably ensue. The laws of the slave-holding states demand ... a much larger concession of power to the master ...: they demand that the life of the slave shall be in the master's keeping; that the slave, having the physical ability to avoid the infliction of a barbarous and vindictive punishment by his master, shall not be permitted to do so. They go, indeed, *even beyond this:* they place the slave under the like restriction in relation to *every white* person, without discrimination as to character, and with but little consideration as to motives. ...

Thomas R.R. Cobb, a slaveowner and slavery advocate, a highly-respected Georgia lawyer in the slave society, and key drafter of the Confederate Constitution, justifies laws sustaining police and white citizen patrol violence in his often cited 1859 legal treatise. In doing so, Mr. Cobb effectively acknowledges deep white fear of blacks:[1106]

> If the slave feels that he is solely under the power and control of his immediate master, he will soon become insolent and ungovernable to all others. *If the white man had, then, no right by law to control, the result would be, the excitement of angry passions, broils, and bloodshed.* Hence have arisen, in the States, the various police and patrol regulations, *giving to white persons other than the master,* under certain circumstances, the right of controlling, and, in some cases, correcting slaves.

MARYLAND LAW

"[F]or 'rambling, riding or going abroad in the night, or riding horses in the daytime without leave, a slave may be whipt, cropped, or branded on the cheek with the letter R, or otherwise punished, not extending to life, or so as to unfit him for labor."

W. Goodell, The American slave code in theory and practice at 229 (American and Foreign Anti-Slavery Society 1853), available from the Library of Congress at *www.hathitrust.org/digital_library.* Emphasis in original.

1104 Stroud, at 69. Emphasis in original.

1105 Stroud, at 67-68. Emphasis in original.

1106 Cobb, Vol. I, at 106. Emphasis added.

Judge Stroud provides examples of punishment of not only resistant slaves, but even supposedly "free" African-Americans, for resistance:[1107]

> In Maryland, … a justice of the peace … may direct the offender's ears to be cropped—and this, though he be a *free black.* [In Kentucky,] as in Maryland, *free* coloured persons are included:—"If any negro, mulatto or Indian, bond or free, shall, at any time, lift his or her hand in opposition to any person not being a negro, mulatto or Indian, he or she so offending shall for every such offence… receive thirty lashes on his or her bare back, well laid on, by order of such justice."

Stroud cites Virginia law providing up to 39 "stripes" for a "negro" "if he use[s] provoking language or menacing gestures to a white person."

He also quotes a Georgia statute:[1108]

> If any slave shall *presume* to strike a*ny white person,* such slave … shall, for the first offense, suffer such punishment as the said Justice or Justices shall, in his or their discretion, think fit, not extending to life or limb; and for the second offence, suffer *death.*

A History of Disrespect and Violence

Black distrust of whites stems from experience. As the quoted laws demonstrate, America has a long history of treating African-Americans with brutality and disrespect. As sometimes occurs today, troublesome slaves were treated with terrifying inhumanity. As thousands of runaway slave advertisements demonstrate dramatically in describing fugitive slaves, at the hands of slave masters slaves had ears cropped, noses split, teeth knocked out for identification, brands on their faces and bodies, and limbs mutilated like Kunta Kinte.[1109] Government officials willingly participated in the violence against slaves.

In 1712, New York officials burned four slaves at the stake and broke one on the wheel. In 1741, they burned more than a dozen ostensibly rebellious slaves at the stake on the basis of highly-questionable evidence that a conspiracy to revolt even existed.[1110] Dr. Jill Lepore describes similarities between New York's persecution of slaves in 1741 and the Salem witch trials and executions.[1111]

Thomas Archdeacon describes this period in New York, as follows:[1112]

MARYLAND AND DC LAWS

[S]laves "absenting themselves from their master's service, running out into the woods and there remaining, killing hogs and cattle" and "refus[ing] to surrender themselves, and mak[ing] resistance," may be pursued and captured and "it shall be lawful for such pursuers, when resistance is made, to shoot, kill, and destroy" the slaves"

W. Goodell, The American slave code in theory and practice at 230-31 (American and Foreign Anti-Slavery Society 1853), available from the Library of Congress at *www.hathitrust.org/digital_library.* Emphasis in original.

1107 Stroud, at 68.

1108 Stroud, at 68.

1109 See *"Chapter Six: The Duke of York's Creation on a Rampage—Slaveholder Advertisements for Runaway Slaves."*

1110 Singer, at 32-33, 59, 60-61.
See also Lepore, at 78-79, 85.

1111 Lepore, at 86.

1112 Archdeacon, at 145. Footnotes omitted.

> In the early years of the eighteenth century New Yorkers became unusually concerned about the dangers posed by their bondsmen. The murder of a Queens County family in 1708 led to the execution of four Negroes with "all the torment possible for a terror to others," and to the enactment of "An Act for Preventing the Conspiracy of Slaves." In the same period the courts heard a large number of cases concerning individuals accused of illegally entertaining slaves in their homes or ale houses.
>
> April 1712 brought to a climax the festering relations of white New Yorkers and their bondsmen. In the early hours of April 6, a group of slaves set fire to a house in the East Ward and then murdered 9 whites and wounded 12 others who came to help put out the blaze. Within two weeks, the courts indicted 43 Negroes and Indians of murder or attempted murder, convicted 25, and summarily executed 18. The ghastliness of some of the executions, including the eight-to-ten hour roasting of Nicholas Roosevelt's slave Tom, indicates the hysterical quality of the community's desire for revenge.

Dr. Ira Berlin and Leslie Harris cite a description by an adult New Yorker who wrote, describing his recollection from in 1741 when he was four years old: "I have a perfect idea of seeing the Negroes chained to a stake, and there burned to death."[1113]

That was before the Declaration of Independence. The violence continued long after the Declaration, as well.

As an example, more than half a century following 1776, in 1827, South Carolina burned a slave at the stake after compelling him to attend his own funeral.[1114]

Still later, in 1831, Virginians posted heads of slaves who dared to revolt with Nat Turner on spikes on a public road (known as "Blackhead Signpost Road").[1115] Likewise, in Louisiana in 1811.[1116] In 1831, North Carolinians marched slaves—including slave children—along a head-lined road known as "N____ Head Road" as warning to be submissive.[1117]

Today, cell phone imagery displays George Floyd's head.

Today's Remnants of the Slave Society's Violence

Ingrained harmful cultural patterns are difficult to expunge. Thankfully, the most extreme brutality of the past is not in evidence today.

Still, the Georgia case involving a killing of an African-American for jogging in a white neighborhood reflects long-standing fearful attitudes and behaviors of American whites toward African-Americans. Those attitudes date back hundreds of years. This has occurred ever since the Duke of York's time in the 1660s, not merely "150 years ago." It did not end with the Declaration of Independence. It did not end with the Constitution. It did not end with the Civil War. It did not end with the ratification of the 13th, 14th, and 15th Amendments to the Constitution. It did not end with the enactment of the Civil Rights Laws in the 1960s.

1113 Lepore, at 60.

1114 See *"Chapter Six: The Duke of York's Creation on a Rampage—The Burning of Jerry: Attending His Own Funeral."*

1115 "Blackhead Signpost Road needs another sign" at *www.thetidewaternews.com/2015/08/15/blackhead-signpost-road-needs-another-sign/#:~:text=In Southampton County%2C the scene of the 1831,black as a warning against any future outrage."*., accessed Sept. 28, 2020.

1116 "1811 German Coast Slave Uprising" at *genealogytrails.com/main/events/slavery_1811uprising.html*, accessed Sept. 25, 2020.

1117 "Negro Head Road" at *www.ncpedia.org/negro-head-road,* accessed Sept. 28, 2020.

Today, sometimes juries, dominated by whites, are unwilling to find a police officer guilty of a crime. Appropriate police training often is lacking. The Supreme Court provides police significant immunity protection. Police unions and union contracts protect them. Police maintain complaint and discipline records in secrecy or expunge the records within brief time frames. Close-knit police cultures protect violent officers. Although there are many conscientious police officers—and we very much do need and appreciate them—they too often are overridden internally by union officials and other officers.

What is different today? Widespread accessibility of camera-ready smartphones to citizens willing and able to use them, combined with police body cameras and private cameras. Suddenly, police behavior has become a matter of public record! And a good thing it is!

SAMPLE POLICE KILLING RATES/ TEN MILLION RESIDENTS

United States—28.40

Bangladesh—28.30

Pakistan—25.20

Egypt—21.20

Canada—9.70

Sweden—6.00

France—3.80

Netherlands—2.30

New Zealand—2.10

Norway—1.90

Nepal—1.70

Australia—1.70

Germany—1.30

United Kingdom—0.50

Poland—0.50

Japan—0.20

"Police killings by country 2020" at *worldpopulationreview.com/country-rankings/police-killings-by-country,* accessed Sept. 28, 2020

Re-Examination of Police Practices

It is time for a change.

This is not, however, a call to "defund" police, whatever that means. I don't know about you, but I certainly want police protection for my family, myself, and my property. I have had encounters with police over my life. Some angered me. I felt disrespected. I very much appreciated other contacts with helpful officers. I certainly want police protection for my family, our home, and myself.

African-Americans report similar reactions. According to a Gallup Poll conducted June 23 to July 6, 2020, when asked whether they want "the police to spend more time, the same amount of time or less time than they currently do in their area," a substantial majority of African-Americans—61%—answered that they "want the police presence to remain the same." Another 20% want the police to spend "more time" in their area. That cannot happen if police are "de-funded." In response to another question, 61% of African-Americans answered that they were "very confident" (18%) or "somewhat confident" (43%) of receiving "positive treatment by police." As a wake-up call to America's police and local governments, however, another 27% were "not too confident," while 12% were "not confident at all."[1118]

So, it must be said honestly and straightforwardly that "de-funding" the police makes little sense. Adverse experience in self-selected communities that have tried that approach underscores the conclusion.

1118 "Black Americans Want Police to Retain Local Presence" at *news.gallup.com/poll/316571/black-americans-police-retainlocal-presence.aspx,* accessed Sept. 28, 2020.

This is a call instead for careful and methodical planning and action—local jurisdiction by local jurisdiction—about how to restructure police training, administration, tactics, and discipline and how to negotiate union contracts that protect the public. The goal should be to enhance the police function through more refined reactions to difficult situations, rather than by reflexive and excessive violence.

Current American police tactics in certain jurisdictions are excessively focused on use of violent force, rather than on skillful and effective policing. Given white fear, this may result in the disproportionate police violence against African-Americans cited above. Individual police officers principally follow their training, which is where tactics should be reconsidered.

Indicating a need for re-examination of police training and tactics, America's police have a significantly more violent record than in most Western and numerous other countries.

Among other things, America's police kill civilians at rates far exceeding those of other Western and many other countries.[1119]

According to World Population Review, countries with low rates of police killings rank as among the safest countries in the world:[1120]

> Police killings are much less common or virtually nonexistent in some European countries. Denmark, Iceland, and Switzerland have all reported zero police killings. Both Denmark and Iceland are among the top ten safest countries in the world. Additionally, police in Iceland do not carry firearms.
>
> Other countries have very low numbers as well. Hong Kong, Luxembourg, Malta, New Zealand, Norway, Portugal, and Saint Lucia all have one police killing in a year. Of these, Portugal and New Zealand are considered to be among the ten safest countries in the world as well.

African-Americans should be able to respect, trust, and rely upon the police in their neighborhoods, and should feel comfortable assisting well-meaning police with information regarding crimes. African-Americans, just like everyone else, need strong police protection. This is especially true in large cities with high rates of crime—murders, gang violence, drug sales, and otherwise—that deeply and adversely affect African-Americans, and especially children.

As matters stand currently, however, individual African-Americans state with deep passion that they fear the police and disrespect them. America could benefit from a new spirit of cooperation and mutual effort between police and African-American communities. Again, however, the distrust on both sides is extensive. In the absence of constructive good faith efforts, not currently in view, the two sides will not overcome the distrust.

Peaceful Protests Are Essential

Black lives matter.

That principle is a central theme of this book.

1119 "Rate of police killings in selected countries 2019" at *www.statista.com/statistics/1124039/police-killings-rate-selected-countries,* accessed Sept. 28, 2020; "American police shoot, kill and imprison more people than other developed countries. Here's the data" at *www.cnn.com/2020/06/08/us/us-police-floyd-protests-country-comparisons-intl/index.html,* accessed Sept. 2020; "Police killings by country 2020" at *worldpopulationreview.com/country-rankings/police-killings-by-country,* accessed Sept. 28, 2020.

1120 "Police killings by country 2020" at *worldpopulationreview.com/country-rankings/police-killings-by-country,* accessed Sept. 28, 2020.

The principle is not the same, however, as a blanket endorsement of a political movement.

Historically, peaceful protests calling for change have been constructive. They are a necessity in order to articulate grievances clearly when governmental abuse occurs. It is critical, however, that protests be peaceful. Violent protests are a form of self-immolation.

Unfortunately, today protestors with divergent messages forcefully attack each other. To protect rights, Americans must speak up to defend peaceful protests, regardless of whether one agrees with the protesters' message. If Americans do not do so, it will undermine important freedoms.

Violent actions seeking to harm police, individuals expressing opinions, or property are inappropriate and deserve sharp opposition. Violence and encouragement of violence is not justifiable by protesters espousing any cause. Even in the name of justice, it is fundamentally wrong to attack a person physically merely for expressing a view no matter how much one may disagree with that view.

JOHN LEWIS ON
<u>IMPORTANCE OF PROTEST</u>

"When you see something that is not right, not fair, not just, you have to speak up. You have to say something; you have to do something."

"10 John Lewis Quotes That Will Inspire You to Get Into 'Good Trouble'" at *www.globalcitizen.org/en/content/john-lewis-quotes/*, accessed Sept. 28, 2020

It also is completely unacceptable for public officials either to inflame passions or to fail to restrain overly-aggressive protestors.

Attempts to silence protests on any side will only provoke reactions. People simply will react and resist. They are entitled to articulate their points of view.

Peaceful protests have a long and successful history in America. They require restraint and patience. America's Slavery Heroes—Frederick Douglass, Sojourner Truth, William Wells Brown, Harriet Tubman, and others used a variety of persistent peaceful protests that, with support from abolitionists, Abraham Lincoln, and the Union Army, achieved the ultimate goal of slavery's end. They were highly effective.

In contrast, violence has proved to be counterproductive. It feeds directly into the historic substantial fear that whites have of African-Americans.

When slaves did not have access to a peaceful means of protest, they used violence. It was their only option to voice objections to their fates. Nat Turner in 1831, slaves in North Carolina also in 1831, and Charles Deslondes in Louisiana in 1811, all engaged in violent protests. Following each of those revolts, the slave society executed slaves, displaying their heads along public roads. The slave society then responded with ever more repressive laws and practices.

Following the Civil War and the 13th Amendment, the fear of the slave society's heirs did not disappear.

In those conditions, most freed slaves lived in poverty. Few had meaningful assets. Most owned no land. Most agricultural laborers lacked other marketable skills. They had little wealth to pass to the next generation. The slave society's adherents, re-assuming control following Reconstruction, continued to deny education to African-Americans for decades. Even when the government provided education, it was segregated and inferior. The slave society enacted tyrannical Black Codes and gave birth to the Ku Klux Klan.

Generation after generation, decade after decade, in the absence of wealth for African-Americans to pass on and without education, they have lived in persistent poverty.

Finally, a century after slavery ended, with Martin Luther King, Jr., John Lewis and other significant and effective organizers, African-Americans found charismatic and effective leadership once again giving voice through peaceful protests. The bus rides and marches across the South and the lunch counter sit-ins were aggressive, but peaceful. As in the mid-1800s a century earlier, the persistent peaceful protests gained widespread support. With that support, they brought an end to legal segregation. The 1960s were a momentous time for affirmative change.

But Dr. King was murdered. The angry violence in the aftermath of Dr. King's assassination was understandable, but counterproductive. It induced a repressive reaction and yet more decades of economic stagnation for African-Americans.

Overall, in terms of the ability to engage in routine societal daily life and access to public accommodations, together with greater white acceptance, African-Americans are in a substantially-improved position today in contrast with that of segregation before the 1960s. Assisted by the progress of the 1960s, especially creative and assertive individuals are able to escape poverty. Due to defective educations, others remain trapped.

JOHN LEWIS ON
PERSISTENT, PEACEFUL PROTEST

"You are a light. You are the light. Never let anyone — any person or any force — dampen, dim or diminish your light ... Release the need to hate, to harbor division, and the enticement of revenge. Release all bitterness. Hold only love, only peace in your heart, knowing that the battle of good to overcome evil is already won."

10 John Lewis Quotes That Will Inspire You to Get Into 'Good Trouble' at *www.globalcitizen.org/en/content/john-lewis-quotes/*, accessed Sept. 28, 2020

Since the 1960s, overall there has been little economic progress for African-Americans. In the meantime, as in the century from the mid-1800s to the mid-1900s, generation after generation, decade after decade, significant numbers of African-Americans remain in persistent poverty.

Echoing the end of slavery over the decades, overall, African-Americans still have few assets. They still are unable to obtain acceptable educations, and consequently cannot find rewarding employment, purchase decent housing or health care, create wealth, fund retirement plans, or pass wealth to their children.

There is substantial justification for African-American anger.

I am deeply saddened that there is no vehicle for moderate Americans who care very much about the plight of African-Americans to express their opinions in constructive, peaceful means without fear of radical elements from multiple political and social directions that endanger them.

Peaceful forms of protest and common sense goals matter.

Unhappily, America is trapped in a never-ending cycle of anger and repression dating directly back to the time of slavery and even further back to the Duke of York. That anger and repression also are of America's own making.

Yet do not fall into the trap of believing resolution of issues surrounding police practices would result in greater income or wealth equality for black Americans. It won't. The core issue—educational inadequacy—would remain as the most significant barrier.

Slavery's remnants continue to haunt America.

WHAT TO DO?

What is America able to do? What will it actually do?

I advocate the following steps, among others, to begin a long, difficult process of healing America's soul and making amends for slavery:

- Cease denying adequate education to disadvantaged youth—African-Americans and others; undertake fundamental reform of the education system to promote effective school choice
- Acknowledge that slavery was indeed a genuine Reign of Terror
- Apologize sincerely to African-Americans for America's treatment of their ancestors
- Educate ourselves and our children about slavery, its economic, cultural, and historical significance, and how it continues to affect us today
- Recognize and honor as role models, on a par with America's Founding Fathers and Abraham Lincoln, those brave self-reliant Heroes who fought diligently against slavery—at the risk of their freedom and their lives
- Confront statues erected in honor of Confederate generals with statues honoring the slaves to use the contrasting statues as history lessons
- Cease governmental and societal encouragement of dependence and passivity as acceptable life patterns

NATIONAL SLAVE MEMORIALS

Construct a substantial National Slave Memorial on the Washington National Mall, strategically situated between the Washington Monument and the Jefferson Memorial, and facing the Lincoln Memorial

Construct a similar substantially-sized National Slave Memorial at Georgia's beloved Stone Mountain facing directly at Jefferson Davis and Generals Robert E. Lee and Stonewall Jackson

Construct substantial slave memorials wherever monuments remain of Confederate generals or officials

Change the names of military bases, other public buildings and facilities, and cities and other governmental entities named in honor of Confederate generals or other persons instrumental in the creation or maintenance of American slavery

See, e.g., HR 196: National Slave Memorial Act, 108th Cong., 1st Sess. (2003)

In the end, however, I am highly pessimistic.

There are African-Americans who, despite the odds, through stern determination, will be able to escape the discrimination and poverty forced upon them. The persistence of America's Slavery Heroes, Adam Clayton Powell's words, and examples set by other successful African-Americans may inspire them. For initiative-taking individuals, that exercise of independence and self-sufficiency offers the primary path from poverty.

Nevertheless, while I would hope for a better result for the African-American community as a whole, in the final analysis, I do not believe that America's racial divisions will be, or even can be, overcome. There is insufficient goodwill.

Even more significantly, like the slave masters not so long ago, America's politicians are tossing out subsistence handouts hoping to keep African-Americans "in their place"—dependent and submissive in their voting habits for politicians who provide the handouts.

Just as slave masters denied slaves education in reading and writing, today's politicians of all persuasions are denying millions of young African-Americans the education and training to be able live fully-productive and self-sufficient lives. Without adequate educations, racial inequities for African-Americans in employment, income and wealth—and resulting serious housing, health, and other inequities—are inevitable.

The result is what I call "America's National Plantation."

America's slavery chickens are coming home to roost.

TREAT US LIKE PEOPLE

"I speak Americans for your good. We must and shall be free I say, in spite of you. You may do your best to keep us in wretchedness and misery..., but God will deliver us from under you. And wo, wo, will be to you if we have to obtain our freedom by fighting. Throw away your fears and prejudices then, and enlighten us ... Treat us then like people, and we will be your friends. And there is not a doubt in my mind, but that the whole of the past will be sunk into oblivion, and we yet, under God, will become a united and happy people."

D. Walker, Appeal to the Colored People of the World, But in Particular, and Very Expressly, to Those of the United States of America at 79-80 (1829), available at available at *docsouth.unc.edu*

BRINGING IT ALL TOGETHER

I have identified the Duke of York (later, King James II), his brother, King Charles II, and their colleagues as the specific individuals responsible, beginning in the 1660s, for the creation, promotion, and incentivization of American slavery for the profit of the English government. I have explained that there were less inhumane forms of slavery practiced by other cultures that the Duke and his colleagues chose not to adopt.

I have pointed out, as Dr. Peter Kolchin states, that America's slave society was one of the last surviving slave societies in the New World. I added Dr. Kolchin's observation that, by enslaving four million people, America's slave society was by far the largest remaining New World slave society—larger than all the others combined—at the time of the Civil War.

I have shown that American slavery and its aftermath were despicable. To put it bluntly: America's slave society was a Terror Society.

I have described how the slave society deliberately inflicted its terror upon millions of people. I have exposed the truth that the terror was not merely an incidental element of American history. To the contrary, the terror of slavery lasted for a majority of America's history, even as calculated today. The terror was at the core of America's development as a nation and at the center of America's economy, politics, society, culture, and history.

I have explained how the slave trade was an essential component of slavery that the Duke of York and the English government employed aggressively, again for the profit of the government and its officials. Without the slave trade, America's slave society could not have existed. I have shown that the slave trade, in which America's slave society participated actively and knowingly, constituted a racial genocide giving rise to one of the worst holocausts in World history.

I have discussed how America has buried much of that information, hiding it from open discussion. I have shown that many American schools intentionally taught falsely about slavery. I have shown that to have been, and still to be, a misguided effort to encourage a false patriotism. The politicians and schools chose, and often still choose, not to instill a genuine patriotic love for America that honestly confronts America's past and is willing to admit mistakes.

That knowledge about slavery and its terror is essential to comprehend how America has arrived at its current state of racial discord. On a personal level, large numbers of older and middle-aged white Americans formed their perspectives through that misguided education. That fraudulent education contributes directly to racial communication failures today.

Despite noteworthy progress resulting from the ratification of the 13th, 14th, and 15th Amendments and from enactment of the civil rights laws of the 1960s, poverty remains endemic in the African-American community. Significant racial inequities remain despite decades of intensive affirmative action, sensitivity training, remedial government programs, and litigation against racial discrimination. Despite support for increased funding for college education, greater access to higher education is meaningless for those who never received the necessary foundational education. Indeed, often it can be worse by cruelly setting up hopeful individuals for failure.[1121]

Just as government officials instituted American slavery as a program for the benefit of the English government and themselves, *government itself and government officials*, in the form of public school districts and public employee unions—police and teachers—comprise racial discrimination's foundation today. Capitalism, based upon freedom of labor, is not the cause.

It is intolerable that fewer than one in six African-American students in the eighth grade are proficient in reading and that fewer than one in seven are proficient in math.[1122] This is a national emergency that the government fundamentally ignores. Yet, it is a crisis far more devasting to America than the covid-19 pandemic. Government officials treat the crisis, however, with not-quite-complete, but nevertheless substantial and pervasive, silence. The silence is kept by school board members, national, state, and local government officials, and the media.

Just as America's Slavery Heroes succeeded in the past, it is possible for particularly industrious, imaginative, and fortunate African-Americans to escape poverty. Although it is difficult, there are positive examples of individuals who may be held up as role models. Without education, the larger black population does not have the same prospect for success.

Meanwhile, surrogate controversies serve as distractions from the task of crucial importance to African-Americans' quality of life.

For example, although I advocate official acknowledgement of and apology for slavery, those actions will not put food on the table. Passing out money called "reparations" to people uneducated in money management would be a waste. It would be far better to spend any such funding on encouraging competition among schools and on remedial adult education for those already harmed.

Changing place names and erecting statues to slavery heroes, which I also advocate, may be emotionally satisfying and may communicate respect for African-Americans. Those actions will not, however, enable access to better housing. They will not buy shoes for the babies.

Making constructive careful modifications in specific police practices, with which I agree, may ease a significant provocation in the African-American community. Those changes will not, however, improve access to health care or job opportunities. They will not result in increased incomes or savings for retirement or creation of wealth on which to live and which parents and grandparents may pass on to children.

Those steps, however desirable, will not give rise to equality of opportunity.

Genuine prospects for better African-American lives will occur only when there is authentic educational transformation, which the government denies. Until America radically alters its education system, large numbers of poorly-educated African-Americans will find themselves relegated to the bottom of the labor pool.

Young African-Americans will be driven to live under the same system of pitiful government subsistence handouts their parents and grandparents were forced to accept. Circumstances compel them to vote loyally for

1121 See *"Remnants of Slavery: Intolerable Discrimination in Education—Wealth Inequality Has Increased Since Enactment of the Civil Rights Laws"* above.

1122 See *"Remnants of Slavery: Intolerable Discrimination in Education—America's Educational Emergency"* above.

politicians who dispense those handouts. Yet, as was the case for slaves, subsistence is a meager living. It cannot provide independence or self-sufficiency. No wonder African-Americans express so much anger.

Without access to better-quality education in the formative years, in America there always will be substantial racial inequality in income and wealth. As a consequence, African-Americans will remain as a permanent underclass. Given the pivotal educational inequities, there always will be racial inequality in employment opportunities, housing, health care, retirement, and other key aspects of life. American blacks will continue to be unable to build wealth upon which to live comfortably.

Unfortunately, the overall quality of America's educational system for all students, including African-Americans, has declined over the past five decades in comparison to education systems of other countries.[1123] The essential fundamental reforms in education for African-Americans requires affording African-American children the same funding that benefits other students and also necessitates facilitating and encouraging genuinely effective school choice alternatives.

Choice creates competition. Competition creates innovation. Let the families and students determine how to pay for their educations from voucher funds provided by local school districts and state governments. The families are fully able to evaluate competing alternatives and to make choices that cannot be worse than the current system.

I see no evidence, however, that America's politicians and school districts will be willing to make the required changes, given unrelenting pressure from regressive teachers' unions. Reliance upon archaic funding practices and laws focused on local property taxes varying widely among school districts exacerbates the problem. America's politicians, reliant upon political contributions from teachers' unions and their members, will continue to ignore the seriousness of the problem. They will continue to overlook the havoc it creates in young lives. They will avoid acknowledging the destructiveness resulting for entire lifetimes of millions upon millions of decent people who only want to live productive lives that they have the ability to control for themselves.

Protests against police practices can constitute a distraction. As has occurred during the past five decades since the 1960s, with politicians and special interests benefiting from the educational system, despite their faithful voting patterns, until they revolt against the system African-Americans will continue to be a low priority.

As during slavery and its aftermath, denial of the foundational tools education should supply, but does not, regrettably requires them to exist on subsistence handouts throughout their entire lives.

Because the political realities and education's institutional structure are so deeply entrenched, I am not optimistic.

1123 See *"Remnants of Slavery: Intolerable Discrimination in Education—America's Educational Emergency"* above.

APPENDIX I:
AMERICAN SLAVERY TIME LINE

TIME LINE OF SELECTED EVENTS
ASSOCIATED WITH OR AFFECTING AMERICAN SLAVERY

The following Time Line[1124] lists briefly certain selected events associated with or affecting slavery in America. Even with "brief" identification of events, the Time Line is extensive.

The listing demonstrates the central significance of slavery to, and pervasive domination of slavery in, American government, society, and cultural life for hundreds of years. The Time Line reflects the imposition in the American colonies, beginning in the 1660s, of the brutal English form of slavery that contrasted with the forms of servitude practiced in Virginia and Maryland prior to that time and with the contemporaneous Dutch, Spanish, French and West African forms of slavery. Following the Declaration of Independence, virtually every significant political event in America evoked bitter disputes regarding slavery.

Contrary to the impression that American politicians and schools have created by their fraudulent sanitization of slavery, the Time Line also provides a degree of insight into how resistant slaves were to their fate. I briefly cite more prominent slave revolts. Even the revolts in the Caribbean and Guyana had an impact by pressuring Britain to emancipate slaves in its colonies, which it did in 1834. There were more revolts of varying levels of intensity and size, possibly in the hundreds, than I reflect in the Time Line.[1125]

1124 Sources: **A GUIDE TO THE HISTORY OF SLAVERY IN MARYLAND** (MD State Archives and Univ. of MD 2007); Beckles, "Slave Voyages—The Transatlantic Trade in Enslaved Africans" (United Nations Educational, Scientific and Cultural Organization); Brewer, "Slavery, Sovereignty, and 'Inheritable Blood': Reconsidering John Locke and the Origins of American Slavery" (American Historical Review Vol. 122, Issue 4, Oct. 2017); A. Baumgartner, **SOUTH TO FREEDOM: RUNAWAY SLAVES TO MEXICO AND THE ROAD TO THE CIVIL WAR** (New York: Basic Books, 2020); Grant "South to the Promised Land," (Smithsonian July-August 2022); E. McManus, **BLACK BONDAGE IN THE NORTH** (Syracuse Univ. Press 1973); E. McManus, **A HISTORY OF NEGRO SLAVERY IN NEW YORK** (Syracuse University Press 1996); L. Harris, **IN THE SHADOW OF SLAVERY—AFRICAN-AMERICANS IN NEW YORK CITY,** 1626-1863 (Univ. of Chicago Press 2003); D. Davis, **THE PROBLEM OF SLAVERY IN THE AGE OF EMANCIPATION** (Vintage Books, 2014);D. Davis, **THE PROBLEM OF SLAVERY IN THE AGE OF REVOLUTION**, 1770-1823 (Oxford Univ. Press, 1999); I. Berlin, **MANY THOUSANDS GONE: THE FIRST TWO CENTURIES OF SLAVERY IN NORTH AMERICA** (Harvard Univ. Press 1998); "Gloucester County Conspiracy (1663)" at *www.encyclopediavirginia.org/Gloucester_County_Conspiracy_1663,* accessed Nov. 12, 2020; Harper, "Slavery in the North," at *slavenorth.com; Blackpast.com; History.com; NPS.gov;* "Who Are New Afrikans" at *newafrikan77.wordpress.com,* accessed Nov. 12, 2020; Blackfacts.com.

1125 See also *Chapter Six: The Duke of York's Creation on a Rampage—Slaveholder Advertisements for Runaway Slaves."*

Year	Event(s)
1526	Spanish bring slaves to Florida; Spanish slaves have certain rights as human beings that the English later denied
1526	First slave revolt in what is now America at Spanish colony of Vasquez de Allyon (now in South Carolina); revolt stymies Spanish settlement
1528-36	Illustrating greater rights of Spanish slaves, Spanish slave, Esteban, leads Spanish expedition across North America joining Spanish explorers in Baja California 300 years before Lewis & Clark; later is appointed as de facto military commander in search of the Seven Lost Cities of Gold
1619	The English take captives from a Portuguese ship and trade them for food at Point Comfort, Virginia; the captives receive treatment with certain rights as human beings that the English later denied
1620	Pilgrims land at Plymouth with indentured servants, including my twelfth great grandfather, Edward Doten
1626	Dutch West India Company imports 11 Africans as slaves in New Netherland; slaves in New Netherland have certain rights as human beings that the English later denied
1641	Massachusetts enacts statute legalizing ownership of slaves taken captive in wars or purchased from others, which is incorporated into the Articles of the New England Confederation
1652	Rhode Island adopts similar statute
ca. 1655	Illustrating the rights of the early Virginia captives, Anthony Johnson, an early captive who became a free black slave holder and land owner through land grants, wins a dispute in court against a white property owner over ownership of a slave claimed by Mr. Johnson
1660	Restoration of the Monarchy in England; King Charles II takes the throne, then appoints his brother, James Stuart, Duke of York, as Admiral of the Navy
1660	The English government forms the Royal Adventurers, a slave trading monopoly; after reorganization, the government names the company the Royal African Company; during the Duke's control, the Royal African Company ships more than 100,000 slaves to the New World, branding many, if not all, of them with the Duke's initials, "DY"
1661	King Charles II appeals to colonial governors to enact laws supporting slavery and the Royal African Company
1661-75	England, in alliance with Portugal, fights for and ultimately gains control of Dutch forts on West African coast; the forts and associated African trading relationships, prisons, and other facilities are vital to the English slave trade
1662	King Charles II marries Catherine de Braganza, a Portuguese princess, whose dowry includes claims of West African forts controlled by the Dutch

1662	Virginia begins enacting restrictive laws formalizing brutal slavery at direction of English monarchy
1663	Slaves and indentured servants plot rebellion in Gloucester, Virginia; plot is disclosed; four plotters hanged
1663	Royal African Company officials offer land to Carolina settlers purchasing slaves (20 acres per male slave, 10 acres per female)
1664	English aggressively promote land-for-slaves policy, rewarding slave purchasers; the more slaves, the more land awarded (in Virginia, 50 acres per slave; in New Jersey, 60-75 acres per slave)
1664	Maryland begins enacting restrictive laws formalizing brutal slavery at direction of English monarchy
1664	Duke of York defeats Dutch in New Amsterdam and receives Charter from King Charles II granting the Duke control of the colony; New York is named "in honor" of the Duke
1664-88	James Stuart, as Duke of York and later as King James II, opposes representative government in New York and vetoes a Charter of Liberties petitioned by the people
1665	New York, under Duke of York, begins enacting restrictive laws, known as the "Duke's Laws," enshrining brutal slavery
1685	Duke of York takes English throne as King James II following death of King Charles II; continues slave policies and denial of representative government
1685	French King Louis XIV promulgates the *Code Noir,* granting slaves certain rights as human beings denied by the English
1686	Spanish government begins offering escaped slaves sanctuary in Florida, with rights as free citizens; over time, American slaves escape to Florida in large numbers
1688	King James II is deposed; William and Mary assume English throne
1702	Queen Anne, second daughter of the Duke of York (King James II), assumes English throne
1702 *et seq*.	English enact additional laws placing even more restrictions on slaves; still more restrictive enactments occur over many years
1708	Slaves revolt on Long Island, killing a white family; the government hangs two male slaves and burns a slave woman at the stake
1712-13	Queen Anne obtains the *Assiento,* a slave-trading monopoly contract with the Spanish, pursuant to which the English supply hundreds of thousands of slaves to the New World over several decades
1712	Slave rebellion in New York; slaves kill seven whites and set fires; dozens of slaves arrested; several slaves commit suicide to avoid capture; more than 20 slaves executed; slaves burned at the stake and broken on the wheel
1738	Spanish Florida establishes Fort Mose, a free black town

1739	Stono Rebellion in South Carolina; up to 100 slaves attempt to reach Fort Mose, Florida; kill approximately 23 whites, leaving some heads on the front steps of a store; slaves are confronted by militia, many are killed or captured, but some appear to make their escape to Florida
1741	Slave conspiracy alleged in New York based on questionable evidence; 30 slaves executed; more than a dozen slaves are burned at the stake; also four alleged white participants are executed
1760	Tacky's Rebellion in Jamaica; slaves take two plantations, but are defeated by militia; additional revolts occur across Jamaica
1764	Slave trading ship named "Hope" from Rhode Island taken over by slaves on the high seas; kill nine crew members; Spanish capture the ship
1770	Boston Massacre; Crispus Attucks, reported to have been an escaped slave, is the first to die in the American Revolution
1775	Lord Dunmore, as English Governor of Virginia, having been driven out of Virginia by revolutionaries, issues a proclamation from a ship at sea, offering freedom to slaves who escape to British
1775-83	Revolutionary War; thousands of slaves escape to British lines
1776	Declaration of Independence
1777	Vermont separates from New York; adopts State Constitution prohibiting slavery
1780	Pennsylvania statute adopts gradual abolition in which existing slaves are not freed, but their children born after the date of the statute are indentured servants to be free at age 28
1781	New York frees slaves who fought with the revolutionaries in the War
1783	Massachusetts abolishes slavery through judicial interpretation of State Constitution
1784	Rhode Island statute adopts gradual abolition in which existing slaves are not freed, but their children born after a specified date are apprentices to be free upon achieving designated ages (girls at 18, boys at 21)
1784	Connecticut statute adopts gradual abolition in which existing slaves are not freed, but their children born after a specified date are to be free upon achieving age 25
1787	Congress of the American Confederacy enacts the Northwest Ordinance; territories West of the Appalachian Mountains and North of the Ohio River are declared to be "free" territories; slaveholders from slave states have the right to capture and return fugitive slaves; the Northwest Ordinance is re-enacted in 1789 by the federal Congress after the Constitution is ratified; in 1860, Abraham Lincoln cites the Northwest Ordinance as justification for federal regulation of slavery in new territories

1788	Doctors Riot in New York occurs when blacks discover grave robbing by medical students and doctors for cadavers
1788	Constitution ratified; contemplates slavery in three provisions, including capture and return of fugitive slaves
1790	Thomas Jefferson, as Secretary of State, negotiates an end to Spain's policy of granting sanctuary to escaped slaves; slaves continue to escape into Florida interior and swamps and to Native American settlements
1791	Hattian Revolution begins
1793	First Fugitive Slave Law enacted
1794	Cotton Gin invented, creating conditions for vast expansion of internal slave trade from Upper South to Deep South and West for cotton planters; destroying families, slave traders force over a million slaves to migrate, many of them on foot, chained in slave coffles
1799	New York statute adopts gradual abolition in which existing slaves are not freed, but their children born after a specified date are indentured servants to be free at stated ages (women at 25, men at 28); slavery continues into the 1840s
1800	Gabriel Prosser, a slave, plots a rebellion in Virginia involving slaves marching on Richmond to take officials prisoner and capture arms; the plot fails after a heavy storm destroys roads and the plot is disclosed
Early 1800s	Underground Railroad begins operation to assist slaves in escaping North; activity expands over time as America acquires Florida in 1821 and abolitionism grows during 1800s
1803	In Louisiana Purchase, America gains substantial new territory giving rise to increasing disputes over potential expansion of slavery
1804	Haitian slaves finally achieve national independence; word spreads, inspiring American slaves; the slave society fears a repetition
1804	New Jersey adopts gradual abolition approach; existing slaves are not freed, but future children are freed at ages of 25 for males and 21 for females; New Jersey does not free its last slaves until the 13th Amendment is ratified
1808	International slave trade prohibited by America (Britain in 1807)
1811	German Coast Rebellion; up to 100 slaves revolt near New Orleans, Louisiana; kill some whites; defeated by U.S. Army after slaves run out of ammunition; slaves' heads are posted on spikes along roads; leader tortured, mutilated, shot, and burned to death
1812-15	War of 1812; thousands of slaves escape to British lines
1812-14	Patriot War of 1812 in Florida (yes, there was another war in 1812, a secret one); Georgia and Carolina slave holders, with support of American troops, attack Florida, lay siege to St. Augustine; Lt. Juan Bautista (Prince) Witten--an escaped slave who had received freedom in Florida--and Florida's army of black warriors defeat the slaveholders and American troops in key battle

1815	White abolitionist, George Boxley, in Spotsylvania, Virginia, plots rebellion with slaves; plan fails when disclosed; slaves executed or sent South; Mr. Boxley escapes from jail and goes North
1816	Slave revolt in Barbados led by a slave named Bussa spreads to 70 plantations and involves approximately 400 slaves; the revolt is defeated by the colonial military; Bussa is killed, but is a national hero in Barbados
1816	American Colonization Society is formed with goal of sending freed slaves to Africa; Society initially has support of slaveholders and some abolitionists; African-Americans, however, resist leaving the country of their birth for an unknown territory; over time, most abolitionists oppose colonization, and slaveholders reduce support as Society endorses immediate emancipation
1817	New York abolishes slavery as of 1827 for slaves not freed in 1799; children of many slaves remain in servitude into the 1840s
1817-18	In First Seminole War, U.S. troops led by Andrew Jackson, attack free black towns and enslave free blacks; Florida's army of black warriors aids families in escaping
1821	America acquires Florida, in part with the goal of ending the escape haven for runaway slaves
1821	Missouri Compromise admits Missouri into Union as a slave state, with agreement that, in future, slavery will not be permitted North of Missouri's Southern border; the Compromise later is undone by the Kansas-Nebraska Act
1821	Liberia is founded through funds appropriated by U.S. Congress and the American Colonization Society for freed slaves from America; few African-Americans migrate to Liberia; the rate of death from disease, climate, and wars with natives is extremely high; the cost of paying for transportation of four million slaves, even if they had been willing to go, which they most definitely were not, is prohibitive
1822	Denmark Vesey conspiracy in South Carolina fails after it is disclosed; approximately 35 persons are hanged, including Mr. Vesey
1823	Approximately 10,000 slaves revolt in what is now Guyana; hundreds of slaves are killed, and more than 25 are executed
1827	New York abolition becomes effective; children of many slaves remain in servitude into the 1840s
1829	Initial Mexican abolishion of slavery, with an exception for Texas; this action is followed by vacillation and contradictory policies over several years, creating concerns by slaveholders in Texas and by Stephen F. Austin, who was marketing a land development to slaveholders
1829	David Walker publishes his book, Appeal to the Colored Citizens of the World, passionately criticizing slavery and whites, as well as slaves for excessive passivity, and urging slaves to be prepared to revolt at the right time; the book is sent to slave states surreptitiously through traders and sailors, at times sewn into the lining of clothing, and is read to illiterate slaves by those who could read; slave states prevent blacks on ships from leaving at docks for fear of distribution of the Appeal

1830	Slave named Jerry is burned at the stake in South Carolina
1831	Nathaniel Turner's slave rebellion, with 60-70 slaves, kills 55-60 whites; for revenge, whites attack and kill hundreds of slaves randomly and post heads on roads; reportedly, whites skin Mr. Turner's body and take body parts as souvenirs; his head is missing
1831-32	Slave revolt in Jamaica results in approximately 14 white deaths and more than 500 black deaths, including in executions; the rebellion becomes an important factor in the abolition of slavery by Britain in its colonies six months later
1835-36	Texas declares independence and fights revolution against Mexico; a key factor is settlers' concern about Mexico's willingness to tolerate slavery after Mexico changes its policies repeatedly
1835-42	Second Seminole War by the U.S. army is waged against African-Americans, as well as Native Americans; Florida black warriors fight fiercely; the lengthy War is settled by allowing African-Americans to migrate West
1836	Texas adopts Constitution legalizing slavery, preventing Texas Congress from prohibiting slavery or emancipating slaves; forbids emancipation by slaveholders without approval by Texas Congress
1837	Mexico definitively abolishes slavery and offers freedom to escaping fugitives; especially fugitives from Texas and Louisiana flee to Mexico
1839	Slave ship named "Amistad" is taken over on high seas by more than 50 slaves shipped out of Cuba; after wandering for many weeks, the ship docks in New York; the slaves win their freedom after two years in court; they return to Africa
1840	Slave ship named "Creole" is taken over by 135 slaves on high seas; ship sails to Bahamas, where the slaves win their freedom
1842	In *Prigg v. Pennsylvania* , the U.S. Supreme Court rules that federal law--the Fugitive Slave Law of 1793--was supreme over Pennsylvania State law, with the result that a slaveholder was within her rights in capturing a slave woman in Pennsylvania, as well as her children, one of which was "free"
1843	Rhode Island Constitution abolishes slavery
1845	Texas, in financial ruin and diplomatic isolation, is unable to obtain international loans due to its slavery; joins the Union
1846	Within months of Texas' admission, President Polk provokes Texas border dispute, leading to Mexican-American War
1847	In *Jones v. Van Zandt* , the U.S. Supreme Court rules that, under the Fugitive Slave Act of 1793, an Ohio abolitionist who assisted a slave in escaping via the Underground Railroad was liable to a Kentucky slaveholder; abolitionist is ruined financially
1847	All slaves in Pennsylvania are freed
1848	Settlement of Mexican-American War results in significant new territory for America, opening bitter disputes over expansion of slavery

1848	Connecticut frees all slaves
1850	Fugitive Slave Law enacted; obligates officials and citizens in "free" states to assist in capturing fugitives, creates deep bitterness among abolitionists
1851	Jerry Rescue occurs in Syracuse, demonstrating after Christiana, Pennsylvania, the difficulty of enforcement of Fugitive Slave Law
1854	Kansas-Nebraska Act enacted, based on "popular sovereignty" to resolve slavery on local basis within territories; results in War in "Bleeding Kansas"
1855-56	John Brown, sons, and followers kill slavery sympathizers in Kansas with broadswords, defend Free-State settlements, fight pro-slavery "Bushwackers" and Missouri "Border Ruffians"
1856	Illustrating increasing divisions and bitterness over slavery, on the Senate floor, pro-slavery Congressman Preston Brooks brutally beats U.S. Senator Charles Sumner with a cane (which shattered) into unconsciousness in retaliation for Sumner's passionate speech against slavery in Kansas and Congressman Brooks' kinsman, U.S. Senator Andrew Butler; due to the extent of his injuries, Senator Sumner does not return to the Senate chamber for three years; Democrats in Congress wear pieces of the cane to show support for Brooks
1858	John Brown frees 11 slaves across Kansas border in Missouri, killing one slaveholder, and arranges their transport to Canada, resulting in a reward offered by President Buchanan for Brown's capture
1857	In *Dred Scott v. Sanford* , the U.S. Supreme Court rules that an African-American could not assert his "free" status in federal court because African-Americans, slave or "free," are not "citizens" under the Constitution
1859	John Brown's raid on federal armory at Harper's Ferry
1859 et seq.	Numerous slave revolts in Civil War era
1860	Lincoln elected; secession begins
1861	South Carolina attacks Fort Sumpter; Civil War begins; North fights initially to preserve Union, not to end slavery

1861-65	Civil War results in 1.5 million casualties; 200,000 African-Americans, many escaped slaves, fight on Union side; many thousands of slaves escape to Union lines
1862-63	In a change of strategy, President Lincoln makes the Civil War a war against slavery, as opposed to a war only to preserve the Union; Lincoln issues the Emancipation Proclamation on September 22, 1862, in preliminary form; it is effective on January 1, 1863; the Proclamation declares all slaves in Confederate states to be free, but does not free slaves in Union border states; it also does not free slaves in Confederate states, except where Union troops are in control; the Proclamation is a direct economic attack on Confederate wealth
1863	Upon effectiveness of the federal draft (which granted exceptions for men who could pay a substitute to take their place), the worst riots in American history erupt in New York; at first, rioters, heavily represented by Irish laborers fearing that freed slaves would come North to take their jobs, focus on government facilities; rioters turn anger on African-Americans, beating and lynching them; many are required to leave the City; the black orphanage is raided and burned; many hundreds, if not thousands, are killed
1865	On June 19, 1865, Union Major General Gordon Granger declares all slaves in Texas to be free; the date becomes an African-American holiday known as "Juneteenth"
1865	Civil War ends; slaves in Union states still are not free (except in Maryland, which abolished slavery in 1864 and the District of Columbia, which also did so in 1862 by paying slaveholders compensation for their slaves and offering money to freed slaves to leave America)
1865	13th Amendment ratified on December 6, 1865, ending slavery in America
1868	14th Amendment ratified, grants citizenship to all persons born or naturalized in America and equal protection under the law to all citizens
1870	15th Amendment ratified; grants right to vote regardless of race, color or previous condition of servitude

APPENDIX II:
KING CHARLES II's
1664 CHARTER
GRANTING TO THE DUKE OF YORK
AUTHORITY OVER NEW YORK

FIRST CHARTER GRANTED BY KING CHARLES II TO JAMES STUART, DUKE OF YORK, 1664[1126]

Charles the Second By the grace of God King of England Scotland ffrance and Ireland defender of the ffaith etc TO ALL to whom these presents shall come Greeting KNOW YEE that wee for divers good Causes and Consideracons us thereunto moveing HAVE of our especiall grace certaine knowledge and meere mocon given and Graunted And by these presents for us our heires and Successors Doe give and Graunt unto our dearest Brother James Duke of Yorke his heires and Assignes ALL that part of the Mayne land of New England beginning att a certaine Place called or knowne by the name of St. Croix next adyoyneing to New Scotland in America and from thence extending along the Sea Coast unto a certaine Place called Petuaquine or Pemaquid and (soe) upp the River thereof to the furthest head of the same as itt tendeth Northwards and extending from thence to the River of Kinebequi and soe upwards by the shortest course to the River Cannada Northward And alsoe all that Island or Islands comonly called by the severall name or names of Matowacks or Long Island scituate lyeing and being towards the west of Cape Codd and the Narro Higansetts abutting upon the Mayne land betweene the twoe Rivers there called or knowne by the severall names of Conectecutte and Hudsons River Together alsoe with the said River called Hudsons River and all the land from the west side of Connectecutte River to the East side of De la Ware Bay And alsoe all those severall Islands called or knowne by the names of Martin Vinyards and Nantukes otherwise Nantukett Together with all the lands Islands Soyles Rivers Harbours Mynes Mineralls Quarries Woods Marishes Waters Lakes ffishings hawking hunting and ffowleing and all other Royalties proffitts Comodities and hereditaments to the said severall Islands lands and premises belonging and appertaineing with their and every of their appurtennes AND all our Estate right title interest benefitt advantage Clayme and demaund of in or (to) the said lands and premisses or any part or parcell thereof AND the Revercon and Revercons Remaynder and Remaynders together with the yearely and other the Rents Revenues and proffitts of all and singuler the said premisses and of every part and parcell thereof To HAVE AND TO HOLD ALL and singuler the said lands Islands hereditaments and premisses with their and every of their appurtennes hereby given and Graunted (or hereinbefore menconed to bee given and granted) unto our said dearest Brother James Duke of Yorke his heirs and Assignes for ever To the only proper use and behoofe of the said James Duke of Yorke his heires and Assignes for ever To bee holden of us our heires and Successors as of our Manor of East Greenwich in our County of Kent in ffree and Comon Soccage and not in Capite or by Knights Service YEILDING AND RENDERING And the said James Duke of Yorke Doth for himselfe his heirs and Assignes covenant and promise to yeild and Render unto us our heires and Successors of and for the same yearely and every yeare ffortie Beaver Skynns when they shall bee demanded or within Nynety days after *AND WE DOE FURTHER of our especiall grace certaine knowledge and meere mocon for us our heires and Successors give and Graunt unto our said dearest Brother James Duke of Yorke his heires Deputyes Agents Commissioners and Assignes by these presents full and absolute power and authority to Correct punish Pardon Governe and Rule all such the Subjects of us our heires and Successors as shall from tyme to tyme Adventure themselves into any the parts or Places aforesaid or that shall or doe att any tyme thereafter Inhabite within the same according to such Lawes Orders Ordinances direccons and Instruments as by our said dearest Brother or his Assignes shall bee established And in defect thereof in Cases of necessitie according to the good discreccons of his Deputyes Commissioners Officers or Assignes respectively as well in all Causes and matters Capitall and Criminall as Civill both Marine and others SOE ALLWAYES as the said Statutes Ordinances and Proceedings bee not contrary*

1126 Colonial Laws Vol. I, at 1-6. Emphasis added.

to but as neare as conveniently may bee agreeable to the Lawes Statutes and Governement of this our Realme of England AND SAVEING and reserveing to us our heirs and Successors the receiveing heareing and determineing of the Appeale and Appeales of all or any Person or Persons of in or belonging to the Territories or Islands aforesaid in or touching any Judgment or Sentence to bee there made or given AND FURTHER that it shall and may bee lawfull to and for our said dearest Brother his heires and Assignes by these presents *from tyme to tyme to Nominate make Constitute Ordeyne and Confirme* by such Name or Names Stile or Stiles as to him or them shall seeme good and likewise to revoke discharge Change and alter as well *all and singuler Governors Officers and Ministers which hereafter shall bee by him or them thought fitt and needfull to bee made or used* within the aforesaid Parts and Islands *and alsoe to make Ordayne and Establish all manner of Orders Lawes direccons Instruccons formes and Ceremonies of Government and Magistracy fitt and necessary for and concerneing the Governement of the Territories and Islands aforesaid soe allwayes as the same bee not contrary to the Lawes and Statutes of this our Realme of England butt as neare as may bee agreeable thereunto* And the same att all tymes hereafter to putt in Execucon or abrogate revoke or change not only within the Precincts of the said Territories or Islands butt alsoe upon the Seas in goeing and comeing to and from the same as hee or they in their good discreccons shall thinke to bee fittest for the good of the Adventurers and Inhabitants there AND WE DOE FURTHER of our especiall grace certaine knowledge and meere mocon Graunt Ordeyne and Declare That such Governors Officers and Ministers as from tyme to tyme shall bee authorized and appointed in manner and forme aforesaid shall and may have full power and authority to use and exercise Marshall lawe in cases of Rebellion Insurreccon and Mutiny in as large and ample manner as our Leiftennants in our Countyes within Our Realme of England have or ought to have by force of their Comission of Leiutennancy or any lawe or Statute of this our Realme *AND WEE DOE further by these presents for us our heires and Successors Graunt unto our said dearest Brother James Duke of Yorke his heires and Assignes that itt shall and may bee lawful to and for the said James Duke of Yorke his heires and Assignes in his or their discreccons from tyme to tyme to Admitt such and soe many Person and Persons to Trade and Traffique unto and within the Territoryes and Islands aforesaid and into every or any part and parcell thereof And to have possesse and enjoye any lands or hereditaments in the parts and Places aforesaid as they shall thinke fitt according to the Lawes Orders Constitucons and Ordinances by our said Brother his heires Deputyes Comissioners and Assignes from tyme to tvme to bee made and established by virtue of and according to the true intent and meaneing of these presents and under such Condicons reservacons and Agreements as our said Brother his heires or Assignes shall sett downe Order direct and appoint and not otherwise as aforesaid* AND WEE DOE FURTHER of our especiall grace certaine knowledge and meere mocon for us our heires and Successors give and Graunt to our said deare Brother his heires and Assignes by these presents that itt shall and may bee lawfull to and for him them or any of them att all and every tyme and tymes hereafter out of any Our Realmes or Dominions whatsoever to take lead Carry and Transport in and into (their) Voyages and for and towards the Plantacon of our said Territoryes and Islands all such and soe many of our loveing Subjects or any other Strangers being not prohibited or under restraint that will become

"FULL AND ABSOLUTE POWER"

"AND WE DOE FURTHER of our especiall grace certaine knowledge and meere mocon for us our heires and Successors give and Graunt unto our said dearest Brother James Duke of Yorke his heires Deputyes Agents Commissioners and Assignes by these presents full and absolute power and authority to Correct punish Pardon Governe and Rule all such the Subjects of us our heires and Successors as shall from tyme to tyme Adventure themselves into any the parts or Places aforesaid or that shall or doe att any tyme thereafter Inhabite within the same according to such Lawes Orders Ordinances direccons and Instruments as by our said dearest Brother or his Assignes shall bee established ... ."

our loveing Subjects and live under our Allegiance as shall willingly Accompany them in the said Voyages Together with all such Cloathing Implements ffurniture and other things usually transported and not Prohibited as shall bee necessary for the Inhabitants of the said Islands and Territoryes and for their use and defence thereof and maunaging and Carrying on the Trade with the People there and in passing and returneing to and fro YEILDING AND PAYING to us our heires and Successors the Customes and Duties therefore due and payable according to the lawes and Customes of this our Realme *AND WEE DOE alsoe for us our heires and Successors Graunt to our said dearest Brother James Duke of Yorke his heires and Assignes and to all and every such Governor or Governors or other Officers or Ministers as by our said Brother his heires or Assignes shall bee appointed to have power and Authority of Governement and Commaund in or over the Inhabitants of the said Territories or Islands* that they and every of them shall and lawfully may from tyme to tyme and att all tymes hereafter for ever for their severall defence and safety encounter expulse repell and resist by force of Armes as well by Sea as by land and all wayes and meanes whatsoever all such Person and Persons as without the speciall Lycence of our said deare Brother his heires or Assignes shall attempt to inhabite within the severall Precincts and Lymitts of our said Territories and Islands AND ALSOE all and every such Person and Persons whatsoever as shall enterprize or attempt att any tyme hereafter the distruccon Invasion detriment or annoyance to the Parts Places or Islands aforesaid or any part thereof AND LASTLY OUR WILL and pleasure is and wee doe hereby declare and Graunt that these our Letters Pattents or the Inrollment thereof shall bee good and effectuall in the Law to all intents and purposes whatsoever NOTWITHSTANDING the not reciteing or menconing of the premisses or any part thereof or the Meets or Bounds thereof or of any former or other Letters Patents or Graunts heretofore made or Graunted of the premisses or of any part thereof by us or of any of our Progenitors unto any other Person or Persons whatsoever Bodyes Politique or Corporate or any Act Lawe or other Restraint incertainty or ymperfeccon whatsoever to the contrary in any wise notwithstanding ALTHOUGH EXPRESSE MENCON of the true yearely value or certainty of the premisses or of any of them or of any other Guifts or Graunts by us or by any of our Progenitors or Predecessors heretofore made to the said James Duke of Yorke in these presents is not made or any Statute Act Ordinance Provision Proclamacon or Restriccon heretofore had made Enacted Ordeyned or provided or any other matter Cause or thing whatsoever to the contrary thereof in any wise notwithstanding IN WITNES Whereof Wee have caused these our Letters to bee made Patents WITTNES our Selfe att Westminster the Twelveth day of March in the Sixteenth yeare of our Raigne.

By the King.

ACKNOWLEDGEMENTS

The subject of American slavery is extremely large. Inevitably, one feels that there is so much more to learn and to say. To quote William Wells Brown, "Slavery has never been represented; Slavery never can be represented."[1127]

It is not feasible to write such a book alone. Others became involved in varying degrees. I have deep gratitude to many people. I want to acknowledge them, but without blaming them for errors I have committed in my research and writing.

Reflecting her love, my wonderful wife encouraged me and endured and tolerated for a lengthy period piles of books and papers strewn around the house. As a talented professional writer, she provided me invaluable source information, editing comments, content suggestions, insights, and encouragement.

I acknowledge the helpful suggestions of my family members—my wife, my sister-in-law, my brother, and my children—and a long-time friend. They provided me with crucial encouragement, editorial comments, criticism, and assistance. Nevertheless, I am not providing their names. There is a very sad reason for that.

In the past few years, America has begun to assume, at what has been in the past a modest, but nevertheless real and now increasing, level of hatred, characteristics of certain other deeply-troubled countries. Extremists of the right and the left have become violent. They openly advocate the use of intimidation, threats, and actual physical and psychological attacks against those with whom they disagree. They will not tolerate even peaceful expression of views with which they disagree. Conspiracy theorists commit themselves to the most bizarre perspectives imaginable. The internet has become a haven for dissemination of abusive philosophies based upon sheer fantasy.

Some will be angry, even outraged, because I have identified in explicit terms the extreme cruelty and terror of American slavery and its central importance to America's history. They wish to believe solely in the squeaky-clean false patriotism asserted by American politicians and taught in its schools.

My opposition to defunding police may offend some. Others may be upset by my criticism of the overpowering chokehold that teachers' unions clench on the throat of America's public education system. Others may be upset that I place primary responsibility for slavery and racial inequities upon government, as opposed to capitalism.

Although I believe that America should come to terms with its past, I am unwilling to subject my family and friends to such treatment. Accordingly, they will remain unnamed. I have thanked each of them personally. They know who they are. They know that I acknowledge and appreciate what they have done.

I also have been encouraged by a number of academic historians who are unable within academia to publish a passionate book such as this. Although the book's style and manner of presentation is nonacademic, they wished me well. They did not, however, review drafts of the book or provide significant editorial comments.

1127 William Wells Brown, quoted in A. Delbanco, **THE WAR BEFORE THE WAR—FUGITIVE SLAVES AND THE STRUGGLE FOR AMERICA'S SOUL FROM THE REVOLUTION TO THE CIVIL WAR** at xviii (Penguin Books, 2019).

I benefited from the ground-breaking work of Dr. Holly Brewer of the University of Maryland. She advanced the concept that it is time to identify who did what in creating, promoting, and incentivizing slavery. I simply borrowed her idea from academia and brought it into public view, expressing it in the vivid terms it warrants. Dr. Brewer reviewed nothing in the book.

Dr. Brewer directed me to helpful resources, as did Autumn Haag, a rare book librarian at the University of Rochester, Dr. Todd Savitt and Dr. Marcus Rediker. Others wished me well.

Carl Snowden, a vigorous civil rights leader, was quite helpful in encouraging me and in educating me about matters of importance to the African-American community.

None of that assistance, however, means that any of the foregoing are responsible for anything in this book, or that they agree with my assertions, conclusions, or arguments.

I do want to acknowledge and recommend especially one person whose work on *www.DukeYork.org* has been truly outstanding. Dr. Carlton Calhoun is a website designer *par excellence.* He created the logo for the book, and made excellent recommendations for the website on which the first edition of the book is available without charge in pdf format. I appreciate his skills and his services very much!

A NOTE ON ORGANIZATION AND SOURCES

You should understand who I am and my approach.

I am not a professional academic historian. I assume that you are in the same position. Instead, I have diligently collected and present valuable information from the works of academic historians. I also have collected and present priceless information written by slaves, former slaves, black and white abolitionists, and others who lived at the time of slavery and wrote about their experiences. I have presented this information in a format and with a tone not utilized previously.

I am an everyday citizen—a retired layperson with centrist views in social and political terms. I am not writing for academic historians or history buffs who already know much, if not all, of the information I present. I have lived in the South most of my life.

I simply seek to provide the unvarnished truth for the interested average citizen able to stomach it. I caution you that there were times when I was considerably upset by information I read.

I believe strongly that America should not simply ignore slavery. America should not pretend that the terrorist slave society did not exist or, more likely, that it was and is something America should de emphasize, or even forget, today. Happily, slavery now is emerging as a topic for discussion, and justifiably so. I strongly believe in accepting responsibility for serious wrongs. That means to me that America should acknowledge and apologize for slavery in an open, sincere, and forthright manner.

In doing so, I believe that America needs to acknowledge the full magnitude of the ghastliness —the vicious cruelty, and even butchery and carnage—of slavery. Slavery entrapped millions of people. Those human beings had the legal status of chattels—animals, horses, cattle, swine—"property" to be worked, bred, sold, leased, mortgaged, inherited, punished, and in general, treated however their owners desired.

Organization and Style

I have attempted to use a conversational style of writing in the first and second person that differs from academic writing.

As much as possible, I use an anecdotal technique to describe American slavery through descriptions of specific incidents people, especially slaves and former slaves in their own words, experienced and reported. I prefer this approach because it provides to you a body of basic "raw" information in order to assist you in reaching independent conclusions.

When material is in the public domain, as with slave narratives and with abolitionist and proslavery materials, I freely copy and quote it extensively for that purpose. For other material, such as books by academic historians, I seek to summarize or to quote briefly from the author's analysis.

Sources

Although I present ideas I consider to be original, a large part of the content of this book is based upon resources already available. I conducted little research into original documentary sources. Instead, I utilized and present existing research to emphasize noteworthy ideas expressed by others, together with my own analysis.

I was able to obtain slave narratives from the Library of Congress through its arrangement with HathiTrust at *www.hathitrust.org/digital_library.* I also obtained narratives from "Documenting the American South," at the Academic Affairs Library, University of North Carolina at Chapel Hill *(docsouth.unc.edu)*. Slave narratives, being publications in the public domain, may also be readily available to you from other sources.

Much of this book is filled with first-hand, as well as some second-hand, anecdotal accounts regarding slavery and the actual conditions experienced by slaves provided by the following:

- Escaped slaves and former slaves—including with "free" blacks those people I am calling "America's Slavery Heroes"
- Members of the public who observed slavery while living in the slave society, visiting plantations, or living as members of slaveholding families and communities
- Abolitionists
- Advocates of slavery
- Laws, judicial decisions and news articles

Academic Publications

I added to those sources analyses of modern academic historians. I give very heavy weight to the work of academic historians, both books and professional articles.

The academic historians have an obligation to present fair and carefully researched publications. Their works have been extraordinarily valuable to me in interpreting and evaluating the publications from the time of slavery.

Online Resources

I have reviewed countless resources now available on the internet. I am not, however, writing an academic book, but rather one for popular consumption.

Materials Narrated by Slaves and Former Slaves

I rely especially heavily upon the slave narratives. The narratives depict the slaves' actual experiences .

There is the potential for inaccuracy, exaggeration due to anger and other emotions, and faulty recollections, but since they describe slaves' actual experiences, and since they are quite consistent with each other, I give a high degree of weight to these publications. I present much of the slaves' information as *"Stories"* designed to let you read information from a narrative spanning years. I organized that information to let you read related information in chronological order as a *"Story."*

Thus, I use an anecdotal approach from the slave narratives, allowing the former slaves to relate their own experiences directly, in their own words. The extensive anecdotes cover such matters as master/mistress-slave relations, the slave trade, slaves' daily lives, slaves' families, punishments administered to slaves, and slaves' food, clothing, housing and medical care.

I also obtained descriptions of slavery by former slaves through writings of historians or from interviews conducted as part of the Federal Writers Project during the Great Depression. Professional writers interviewed, and recorded the first-hand recollections of hundreds, if not thousands, of slaves across the nation. Archives containing various interview records are numerous. This information has its own limitations. Much depends upon the skill and biases of the writers, most, if not all, of whom were white, in asking questions and recording information.

The former slaves by this time were aged. They provided their memories from decades earlier, influenced by their own emotions. Their experiences occurred when they were young in the antebellum period immediately prior to the Civil War. As with the slave narratives, the period during which the former slaves experienced slavery was represented to be less inhumane than in earlier periods. It occurred when slaveholders argued that their "paternalism" was prevalent. Yet, slavery's extreme violence and deprivation still was evident. The interview records I read were consistent with the slave narratives.

I ascribe considerable accuracy to the former slaves' consistent recollections in the narratives and interviews, even if they may be imperfect in certain respects. The recollections are vivid, and the former slaves had lived with their memories all their lives.

Abolitionist Materials

Abolitionist publications also were an important anecdotal resource for me. Again, they are in the public domain and available through the Library of Congress' arrangement with HathiTrust at *www.hathitrust.org/digital_library* and at *docsouth.unc.edu.* I draw heavily upon them.

The abolitionists made their arguments in terms that often were highly emotional. You will be able to discern the passion and depth of feeling that abolitionists brought to the debates over slavery, especially in the antebellum period after the abolition movement came out of the shadows into the sunlight in the form of a crusade that proslavery advocates termed "fanaticism." Abolitionism evolved steadily from a weak force in the late 1700s and early 1800s into a powerful social movement by the time of the 1840s and 1850s and the Civil War, and even more so after John Brown's daring and highly-disruptive raid on the federal armory at Harper's Ferry.

Theodore Weld's book, **AMERICAN SLAVERY AS IT IS**, contains thousands of anecdotes reported by individual abolitionists and sympathizers (as well as other sources appearing in news publications at the time) regarding events and conditions they witnessed personally on a first-hand basis and also events about which they were informed by others, as second-hand information. The American Anti-Slavery Society knew and verified the second-hand sources, but kept the identities confidential.

People who provided information to Mr. Weld and the Society, which published the book, were deeply religious people—ministers and deacons among them—and some were related to slaveowners or lived in slave communities. Much information necessarily was second-hand because proslavery forces not only prohibited the distribution of abolitionist materials, but often threatened the well-being, and even the lives, of abolitionists in their midst and even reaching into free states. For that reason, people would sometimes refrain from attaching their names to information they provided.

In addition, I have included extensively ardent arguments of, and legal analyses by, abolitionists, such as George Stroud and William Goodell, and citations to the legal treatise by John Codman Hurd. Charles Dickens provided runaway slave advertisements that are quite informative about the physical conditions of escaped slaves.

Proslavery Materials

I also include materials from proslavery advocates, such as Thomas R.R. Cobb. This was a considered decision.

Since you may wonder why I did this, I want to explain my inclusion of these perspectives.

You may never have been exposed directly to unvarnished racist views. I was, especially when I was young living in the South, but also in the North. If you were exposed, the speakers may have been crude and unintelligent. I thought that you should have the opportunity to read how proslavery advocates thought at the time of slavery, as opposed to racists today. Keep in mind that, in contrast to today, when slavery advocates expressed their opinions, they were within the mainstream of acceptable thinking or behavior. Americans—North, as well as South—held those views.

I do not believe that you will be able to have an accurate portrayal of slavery without knowing the thinking of people, such as Mr. Cobb, who believed slavery to have been a perfectly acceptable, indeed desirable, and natural state of affairs. John C. Calhoun praised slavery as a "positive good." George Fitzhugh called slavery "a beautiful example of communism." Their perspectives contributed to their ability to engage in such heinous behavior.

Like the abolitionists, the proslavery advocates were highly emotional. They defended their way of life and their concept of wealth. Without slavery, the slaveowners believed they would lose an enormous amount of "asset value" and their source of income. It would disrupt relationships among social classes. Those social classes included the wealthy land-holding elite, urban business people, skilled crafts professionals, poor whites, "free" African-Americans, and at the bottom of the social order, the slaves.

For these proslavery advocates, slavery was a desirable way of life. They convinced themselves that slaves lived in conditions superior to those in Africa and to those for "free" African-Americans. They also convinced themselves that African-Americans inherently were comfortable with slavery and constitutionally were well-suited for it as inferior beings intended by God to be subordinate and submissive. One perspective was that, in Christian America, the slaves were far better off than they would have been in "pagan" Africa without a chance to go to Heaven.

The Cornerstone Speech of Alexander Stephens, the Vice President of the Confederacy should put to rest any doubt that the South fought the Civil War to preserve slavery.

The various declarations of causes by seceding states confirm that analysis. Those are readily accessible online.

Thomas R.R. Cobb[1128] was a prominent proslavery advocate and blatant racist living in the antebellum period. By the time he wrote, virtually all slaves (except for those smuggled illegally) had been born into slavery, and had lived as slaves all their lives. At that time, slavery in the South also had evolved into the classic "paternalistic" Southern slavery that had become a way of life. That is the form of slavery about which many schools taught, with omission of important substantive information regarding the extent of brutality.

Mr. Cobb expresses racist views highly offensive today. I have included those, so you should be prepared to be offended and even deeply angered. In Mr. Cobbs' day, even Northerners thought much the same way as Mr. Cobb, and often held people such as Mr. Cobb in high regard. That information is important to understand the context of America's Reign of Terror.

1128 T. Cobb, **AN INQUIRY INTO THE LAW OF NEGRO SLAVERY IN THE UNITED STATES OF AMERICA** (T. & J. W. Johnson & Co., 1858), available from the Library of Congress at *www.hathitrust.org/digital_library.*

Mr. Cobb provides useful insights regarding the slaveholders' justifications for, and laws governing, slavery. In writing his book, he received material from a Harvard Law School professor. Judicial decisions in both the North and South cited his book, regarding slavery and the rights of masters, slaves, and others under slavery.[1129]

Mr. Cobb was a former Georgia official, a successful lawyer, owner of 23 slaves, member of the Confederate Congress, influential supporter of the Confederacy, and "the leading draftsman of the Confederate Constitution."[1130] He also served as a General in the Confederate Army until killed.[1131]

I note that, as late as 1968, Supreme Court Justice William O. Douglas cited Mr. Cobb's book (together with citations to treatises written by abolitionist George Stroud and a legal treatise on slavery by Jacob Wheeler).[1132]

Emphasis on America's Slavery Heroes as Positive Role Models

Despite the undeniable horrors of slavery, it would be a serious mistake to focus excessively on the past as an excuse for failing to move forward as a nation and for African-Americans individually. It is indeed time for America to purge its soul by confession and to cease pretending that these horrible wrongs did not occur, were not actually "so bad," or occurred "too long ago" to matter.

Acknowledging and apologizing for the past does not mean, however, that African-Americans or other Americans should not strive and should not reach for the stars as did America's Slavery Heroes.

Despite all the discrimination, all the hardships, America's Slavery Heroes never gave up—and after diligent effort and many setbacks, they won!

Individual, persistent, courageous, self-reliant effort was able to triumph.

Circumstances forced America's Slavery Heroes to educate themselves. Having done so, some like Frederick Douglass and William Wells Brown, both of whom were largely self-taught, became widely read and influential authors. They and others, such as Sojourner Truth and Frances Ellen Watkins Harper, became recognized as notable lecturers. Some, like Harriet Tubman and William Wells Brown, assisted dozens of fugitive slaves in making their escapes. Others, like Harriet Jacobs and Solomon Northup, finally were able to escape after years of hope and patiently awaiting the right opportunity. Juan Bautista (Prince) Witten and the Florida army of black warriors were successful in defending their families, communities, and themselves against a slaveholders' invasion supported by American troops.

America's Slavery Heroes provide excellent models for success for African-Americans and indeed all Americans. They point African-American youth down the path to success.

Because many of America's schools simply will not provide the necessary education about these Heroes, I hope to inspire African-American youth to pull themselves up, using their own innate strength, self-reliance, determination, and willingness to confront stubborn opposition head-on. Of course, it is not fair, but it is likely the only way open.

1129 T. Cobb, **AN INQUIRY INTO THE LAW OF NEGRO SLAVERY IN THE UNITED STATES OF AMERICA** at Introduction at 17-20 (Univ. of Georgia Press, 1999, 2012) ("Cobb Reprint").

1130 Cobb Reprint, at 5.

1131 Cobb Reprint, at 6.

1132 *Jones v. Alfred H. Mayer* Co., 392 U.S. 409 (1968), concurring opinion of Justice Douglas.

Summary

There is much about slavery that is not known to members of the general public. If you fall within that description, I hope to provide you with interesting information, as well as to present an accessible and easily readable book for you to consider.

BIBLIOGRAPHY

Declaration of Independence

U.S. Constitution:

Three-fifths Compromise, counting each slave as three-fifths of a person for purposes of allocating representation in Congress, electoral votes for President, and taxes—Article I, Section II, Clause 3

Delay in prohibition of international slave trade for 20 years—Article I, Section IX, Clause 1

Fugitive slave clause—Art. IV, Sec. II, Clause 3 as in effect prior to the adoption of the 13th Amendment

Insurrection clause—Art. I, Sec. 8, Clause 15

13th Amendment

14th Amendment

15th Amendment

Constitution, Legislation and Executive Order:

The Constitution of the United States, with the acts of Congress, relating to slavery, embracing, the Constitution, the Fugitive Slave Act of 1793, the Missouri Compromise Act of 1820, the Fugitive Slave Law of 1850, and the Nebraska and Kansas Bill, carefully compiled at 11, 16-17, 19-24 (Rochester, D.M. Dewey, 1854), available from the Library of Congress at *www.hathitrust.org/digital_library*

Emancipation Proclamation

HR 196: National Slave Memorial Act, 108th Cong., 1st Sess. (2003)

Judicial Decisions:

Brown v. Board of Education, 347 U.S. 483 (1954)

Dred Scott v. Sanford, 60 U.S. 393 (1857)

Gary B., et al., v. Whitmer, Case No. 18-1855/1871 (Sixth Cir., 2020)

Jones v. Alfred H. Mayer Co., 392 U.S. 409 (1968), concurring opinion of Justice Douglas

Jones v. Van Zandt, 46 U.S. 215 (1847)

Moore v. Dempsey, 261 U.S. 86 (1923)

Plessy v. Ferguson, 163 U.S. 537 (1896)

Prigg v. Pennsylvania, 41 U.S. 539 (1842)

Somerset v Stewart (1772) 98 ER 499

Books and Chapters:

W. Allinson, **MEMOIR OF QUAMINO BUCCAU, A PIOUS METHODIST** (Henry Longstreth, 1851), Academic Affairs Library, University of North Carolina at Chapel Hill, available at *docsouth.unc.edu*

O. Anderson, **A VOICE FROM HARPER'S FERRY** (1861), available from the Library of Congress at *www.hathitrust.org/digital_library*

T. Archdeacon, **NEW YORK CITY, 1664-1710: CONQUEST AND CHANGE** (Cornell Univ. Press, 1976)

C. Ball, **SLAVERY IN THE UNITED STATES, A NARRATIVE OF THE LIFE AND ADVENTURES OF CHARLES BALL** (John S. Taylor, 1837), Davis Library, Univ. of North Carolina at Chapel Hill, available at available at docsouth.unc.edu

I. Berlin, **MANY THOUSANDS GONE: THE FIRST TWO CENTURIES OF SLAVERY IN NORTH AMERICA** (Harvard Univ. Press, 1998)

I. Berlin and L. Harris, ed., **SLAVERY IN NEW YORK** (The New Press, 2005)

H. Bibb, **NARRATIVE OF THE LIFE AND ADVENTURES OF HENRY BIBB, AN AMERICAN SLAVE WRITTEN BY HIMSELF** at 14-15 (1849), available at the Academic Affairs Library, Univ. of North Carolina at Chapel Hill, *docsouth.unc.edu*

J. Boyd, "William Still: His Life and Work to This Time" in W. Still, **STILL'S UNDERGROUND RAIL ROAD RECORDS** (Philadelphia: Wm Still, 1886), available from the Library of Congress at *www.hathitrust.org/digital_library*

S. Bradford, **HARRIETT, THE MOSES OF HER PEOPLE** (George R. Lockwood & Son, 1886), Academic Affairs Library, Univ. of North Carolina at Chapel Hill Libraries at *docsouth.unc.edu/neh/harriet/harriet.html*

S. Bradford, **SCENES IN THE LIFE OF HARRIET TUBMAN** (1869), available from the Library of Congress at *www.hathitrust.org/digital_library*

Dictated by H. Brown, written and edited by C. Stearns, **NARRATIVE OF HENRY BOX BROWN, WHO ESCAPED FROM SLAVERY** (Brown and Stearns, 1849), Academic Affairs Library, Univ. of North Carolina at Chapel Hill, available at *docsouth.unc.edu*

J. Brown, **BIOGRAPHY OF AN AMERICAN BONDMAN BY HIS DAUGHTER** (R.F. Wallcut, 1856), available from the Library of Congress at *www.hathitrust.org/digital_library*

J. Brown, **SLAVE LIFE IN GEORGIA: A NARRATIVE OF THE LIFE, SUFFERINGS, AND ESCAPE OF JOHN BROWN, A FUGITIVE SLAVE, NOW IN ENGLAND** (1855), Academic Affairs Library, Univ. of North Carolina at Chapel Hill, available at *docsouth.unc.edu/neh/jbrown/jbrown.html*

W. Brown, **CLOTEL**, or, **THE PRESIDENT'S DAUGHTER: A NARRATIVE OF SLAVE LIFE IN THE UNITED STATES, WITH A SKETCH OF THE AUTHOR'S LIFE** (London, Partridge & Oakey, 1853), Academic Affairs Library, Univ. of North Carolina at Chapel Hill, available at *docsouth.unc.edu*

W. Brown, "In A Lecture delivered before the Female Anti-Slavery Society of Salem" in E. Greenspan, ed., **WILLIAM WELLS BROWN: A READER** at 108 (Univ. of Georgia Press, Athens, 2008)

W. Brown, **NARRATIVE OF WILLIAM W. BROWN, A FUGITIVE SLAVE, WRITTEN BY HIMSELF** (Anti-Slavery Office, 2nd ed. 1848), available from the Library of Congress at *www.hathitrust.org/digital_library*

W. Brown, **THE NEGRO IN THE AMERICAN REBELLION: HIS HEROISM AND HIS FIDELITY** (Lee & Shepard, 1867) available from the Library of Congress at *www.hathitrust.org/digital_library*

A. Baumgartner, **SOUTH TO FREEDOM: RUNAWAY SLAVES TO MEXICO AND THE ROAD TO THE CIVIL WAR** (Basic Books, 2020)

R. Campbell, **AN EMPIRE FOR SLAVERY—THE PECULIAR INSTITUTION IN TEXAS**, 1821-1865 (Louisiana State University Press, 1989)

C. Chesnutt, **FREDERICK DOUGLASS** at 42-43 (Boston: Small, Maynard & Co., 1899), available from the Library of Congress at *www.hathitrust.org/digital_library*

J. Clarke, "African Resistance and Colonial Domination: The Africans in America" in Y. Ben-Jochannan and J. Clarke, **NEW DIMENSIONS IN AFRICAN HISTORY** (Brawtley Press, 1991)

T. Cobb, **AN INQUIRY INTO THE LAW OF NEGRO SLAVERY IN THE UNITED STATES OF AMERICA,** Vol I (T. & J. W. Johnson & Co., 1858), available from the Library of Congress at *www.hathitrust.org/digital_library*

T. Cobb, **AN INQUIRY INTO THE LAW OF NEGRO SLAVERY IN THE UNITED STATES OF AMERICA** (Univ. of Georgia Press, 1999, 2012)

THE COLONIAL LAWS OF NEW YORK FROM THE YEAR 1664 TO THE REVOLUTION, Vols. I-V, available from the Library of Congress at *www.hathitrust.org/digital_library*

W. Craft, **RUNNING A THOUSAND MILES FOR FREEDOM; OR, THE ESCAPE OF WILLIAM AND ELLEN CRAFT FROM SLAVERY** (London, William Tweedie, 1860), Academic Affairs Library, Univ. of North Carolina at Chapel Hill, available at *docsouth.unc.edu*

O. Cugoano, **NARRATIVE OF THE ENSLAVEMENT OF OTTOBAH CUGOANO, A NATIVE OF AFRICA; PUBLISHED BY HIMSELF** (James Bullock, 1787), Academic Affairs Library, UNC-CH, available at *docsouth.unc.edu.* The electronic edition has been transcribed from pages 120-127 of the Appendix to **"THE NEGRO'S MEMORIAL; OR, ABOLITIONIST'S CATECHISM; BY AN ABOLITIONIST."**

J. Cusick, **THE OTHER WAR OF 1812—THE PATRIOT WAR AND THE AMERICAN INVASION OF SPANISH EAST FLORIDA** (Univ. of Georgia Press, 2007)

K. Davies, **THE ROYAL AFRICAN COMPANY** (Atheneum, 1970)

D. Davis, **THE PROBLEM OF SLAVERY IN THE AGE OF EMANCIPATION** (Vintage Books, 2014)

D. Davis, **THE PROBLEM OF SLAVERY IN THE AGE OF REVOLUTION**, 1770-1823 (Oxford Univ. Press, 1999)

K. Deagan and D. MacMahon, **FORT MOSE: COLONIAL AMERICA'S BLACK FORTRESS OF FREEDOM** (Univ. Press of Florida and Florida Museum of Natural History, 1995)

A. Delbanco, **THE WAR BEFORE THE WAR—FUGITIVE SLAVES AND THE STRUGGLE FOR AMERICA'S SOUL FROM THE REVOLUTION TO THE CIVIL WAR** (Penguin Books, 2019)

C. Dickens, **AMERICAN NOTES** (Hazell, Watson & Viney, 187?), available from the Library of Congress at *www.hathitrust.org/digital_library*

F. Douglass, **JOHN BROWN** (American Classics Library, 2012)

F. Douglass, **LIFE AND TIMES OF FREDERICK DOUGLASS, WRITTEN BY HIMSELF** (Boston: De Wolfe, Fiske & Co., 1892), available from the Library of Congress at *www.hathitrust.org/digital_library*

F. Douglass, **MY BONDAGE AND MY FREEDOM** (1855), available from the Library of Congress at *www.hathitrust.org/digital_library*

F. Douglass, **THE NARRATIVE OF THE LIFE OF FREDERICK DOUGLASS** (1845), available from the Library of Congress at *www.hathitrust.org/digital_library*

W.E.B. Du Bois, **THE NEGRO** ((Henry Holt and Co., Thornton Butterworth Ltd., 1915), available from the Library of Congress at *www.hathitrust.org/digital_library*

W.E.B. Du Bois, **THE SUPPRESSION OF THE AFRICAN SLAVE TRADE TO THE UNITED STATES OF AMERICA** 1638-1870 (Longmans, Green & Co., 1896), available from the Library of Congress at *www.hathitrust.org/digital_library*

D. Eltis, **THE RISE OF AFRICAN SLAVERY IN THE AMERICAS** (Cambridge Univ. Press, 2000)

O. Equiano, **THE INTERESTING NARRATIVE OF THE LIFE OF OLAUDAH EQUIANO OR, GUSTAVUS VASSA, THE AFRICAN, WRITTEN BY HIMSELF** (T. Wilkins, 1789), available from the Library of Congress at *www.hathitrust.org/digital_library*

G. Fitzhugh, **CANNIBALS ALL! OR, SLAVES WITHOUT MASTERS** (A. Morris, 1857), available from the Library of Congress at *www.hathitrust.org/digital_library*

G. Fitzhugh, **SOCIOLOGY FOR THE SOUTH** (1854), Academic Affairs Library, Univ. of North Carolina at Chapel Hill, available at *docsouth.unc.edu*

F. Foster, ed., **A BRIGHTER COMING DAY: A FRANCES ELLEN HARPER READER** Introduction (New York: The Feminist Press at the City University of New York, 1990)

R. Freedman, **ABRAHAM LINCOLN AND FREDERICK DOUGLASS: THE STORY BEHIND AN AMERICAN FRIENDSHIP** (Houghton Mifflin Harcourt, 2012)

W. Garrison, **THE NEW "REIGN OF TERROR" IN THE SLAVEHOLDING STATES, FOR 1859-60** (American Anti-Slavery Society, 1860)

W. Goodell, **THE AMERICAN SLAVE CODE IN THEORY AND PRACTICE** (American and Foreign Anti-Slavery Society, 1853)

R. Goodwin, **CROSSING THE CONTINENT 1527-1540** (HarperCollins Publishers, 2008)

T. Gray, **THE CONFESSIONS OF NAT TURNER** (T.R. Gray, 1831), available from the Library of Congress at *www.hathitrust.org/digital_library*

Greenberg, "Name, Face, Body" in K. Greenberg, ed., **NAT TURNER: A SLAVE REBELLION IN HISTORY AND MEMORY** (Oxford Univ. Press, 2003)

R. Halpern and E. Dal Lago, ed., **SLAVERY AND EMANCIPATION** (Blackwell Publishers, Ltd., 2002)

Harding, "Symptoms of Liberty and Blackhead Signposts: David Walker and Nat Turner" in K. Greenberg, ed, **NAT TURNER: A SLAVE REBELLION IN HISTORY AND MEMORY** (Oxford Univ. Press, 2003)

L. Harris, **IN THE SHADOW OF SLAVERY—AFRICAN-AMERICANS IN NEW YORK CITY, 1626-1863** (Univ. of Chicago Press, 2003)

G. Hodges and E. Brown ed., **"PRETENDS TO BE FREE—RUNAWAY SLAVE ADVERTISEMENTS FROM COLONIAL AND REVOLUTIONARY NEW YORK AND NEW JERSEY"** (Fordham Univ. Press, 2019)

F. Holland, **FREDERICK DOUGLASS, THE COLORED ORATOR** (London and Toronto: Funk & Wagnall's Co., 1895), available at the Academic Affairs Library, Univ. of North Carolina at Chapel Hill, *docsouth.unc.edu*

T. Horowitz, **MIDNIGHT RISING** (Picador, 2011)

C. Hunter, **TO SET THE CAPTIVES FREE: REVEREND JERMAIN WESLEY LOGUEN AND THE STRUGGLE FOR FREEDOM IN CENTRAL NEW YORK, 1835-1872** (Hyrax Publishing, 2013)

J. Hurd, **THE LAW OF FREEDOM AND BONDAGE IN THE UNITED STATES,** Vol. I Little, Brown & Co., 1862)), available from the Library of Congress at *www.hathitrust.org/digital_library*

H. Jacobs, **INCIDENTS IN THE LIFE OF A SLAVE GIRL** (1861), available from the Library of Congress at *www.hathitrust.org/digital_library*

W. Jay, **AN INQUIRY INTO THE CHARACTER AND TENDENCY OF THE AMERICAN COLONIZATION, AND AMERICAN ANTI-SLAVERY SOCIETIES** (Leavitt, Lord & Co., 1835), available from the Library of Congress at *www.hathitrust.org/digital_library*

T. Jefferson, **NOTES ON THE STATE OF VIRGINIA** (J.W. Randolph, 1853), available from the Library of Congress at *www.hathitrust.org/digital_library*

J.C. Johnson, **DAMAGED HERITAGE: THE ELAINE RACE RIOT AND A STORY OF RECONCILIATION** (Pegasus Books, 2020)

H. Klein, **THE ATLANTIC SLAVE TRADE** (Cambridge Univ. Press, 2010)

J. Kleinman and E. Kurtis-Kleinman, **LIFE ON AN AFRICAN SLAVE SHIP** (Lucent Books, 2001)

P. Kolchin, **AMERICAN SLAVERY 1619-1877** (Hill and Wang, 1993, 2003)

G. Kremer, ed., **GEORGE WASHINGTON CARVER IN HIS OWN WORDS** (Univ. of Missouri Press, 2nd ed. 2017)

J. Landers, **BLACK SOCIETY IN SPANISH FLORIDA** (Univ. of Ill. Press, 1999)

K. Larson, **BOUND FOR THE PROMISED LAND—HARRIET TUBMAN, PORTRAIT OF AN AMERICAN HERO** (Ballantine Books, 2003)

J. Lepore, "Chapter 2: The Tightening Vise: Slavery and Freedom in British New York" in I. Berlin and L. Harris, ed., **SLAVERY IN NEW YORK** (The New Press, 2005)

J. Loguen, **THE REV. J. W. LOGUEN, AS A SLAVE AND AS A FREEMAN, A NARRATIVE OF REAL LIFE** (Syracuse: J.G.K. Truair & Co., 1859), Academic Affairs Library, Univ. of North Carolina at Chapel Hill, available at *docsouth.unc.edu* ("Loguen Narrative")

M. Lucas, **A HISTORY OF BLACKS IN KENTUCKY: FROM SLAVERY TO SEGREGATION, 1760-1891** (Kentucky Historical Society, 2nd ed. 2003)

E. McManus, **BLACK BONDAGE IN THE NORTH** (Syracuse University Press, 1973)

E. McManus, **A HISTORY OF NEGRO SLAVERY IN NEW YORK** (Syracuse University Press, 1996)

J. Miller, **THE STUARTS** (Hambledon Continuum, 2006)

C. Moore "Chapter 1, A World of Possibilities: Slavery and Freedom in Dutch New Amsterdam," in I. Berlin and L. Harris, ed., **SLAVERY IN NEW YORK** (The New Press, 2005)

B. Munford, **VIRGINIA'S ATTITUDE TOWARD SLAVERY AND SECESSION** (Longmans, Green, and Co., 1909; reprinted by Negro Universities Press, 1969)

S. Northup, **TWELVE YEARS A SLAVE** (1853), available from the Library of Congress at *www.hathitrust.org/digital_library*

J. Oakes, **THE CROOKED PATH TO ABOLITION: ABRAHAM LINCOLN AND THE ANTISLAVERY CONSTITUTION** (New York: W.W. Norton and Company, 2021)

Rael, "Chapter 4: The Long Death of Slavery," in I. Berlin and L. Harris, ed., **SLAVERY IN NEW YORK** (The New Press, 2005)

J. Rawley and S. Behrendt, **THE TRANSATLANTIC SLAVE TRADE** (Univ. of Nebraska Press, 2005)

M. Rediker, **THE SLAVE SHIP: A HUMAN HISTORY** (Penguin Books, 2007)

L. Rivers, **SLAVERY IN FLORIDA—TERRITORIAL DAYS TO EMANCIPATION** (Univ. Press of Florida, 2000)

E. Ruffin, **THE POLITICAL ECONOMY OF SLAVERY** (L. Towers, 1857), available from the Library of Congress at *www.hathitrust.org/digital_library*

Russell and Hodges, "Chapter 3: Liberty and Constraint: The Limits of Revolution," in **SLAVERY IN NEW YORK** (The New Press, 2005)

M. Rutherford, **A MEASURING ROD TO TEST TEXT BOOKS, AND REFERENCE BOOKS IN SCHOOLS, COLLEGES AND LIBRARIES** (1919) (reprinted by Forgotten Books, 2018), also available at *archive.org/details/measuringrodtot00ruth/page/n3/mode/2up*

A. Singer, **NEW YORK AND SLAVERY—TIME TO TEACH THE TRUTH** (Excelsior Editions, State Univ. of New York, Albany, 2008)

J. Spears, **THE AMERICAN SLAVE TRADE: AN ACCOUNT OF ITS ORIGINS, GROWTH AND SUPPRESSION** (Scribner, 1907), available from the Library of Congress at *www.hathitrust.org/digital_library*

D. Stannard, **AMERICAN HOLOCAUST** (Oxford Univ. Press, 1992)

J. Stauffer, **GIANTS: THE PARALLEL LIVES OF FREDERICK DOUGLASS AND ABRAHAM LINCOLN** (New York and Boston: Twelve, Hachette Book Group, 2008)

W. Still, **THE UNDERGROUND RAILROAD: A RECORD** at (Philadelphia: Porter & Coates, 1872), available from the Library of Congress at *www.hathitrust.org/digital_library*

G. Stroud, **A SKETCH OF THE LAWS RELATING TO SLAVERY IN THE SEVERAL STATES OF THE UNITED STATES OF AMERICA** (H. Longstreth, 1856), available from the Library of Congress at *www.hathitrust.org/digital_library*

H. Thomas, **THE SLAVE TRADE—THE STORY OF THE ATLANTIC SLAVE TRADE: 1440-1870** (Simon & Schuster, 1997)

A. Torget, **SEEDS OF EMPIRE—COTTON, SLAVERY, AND THE TRANSFORMATION OF THE TEXAS BORDERLANDS, 1800-1850** (Univ. of North Carolina Press, 2015)

Dictated by S. Truth, written and edited by O. Gilbert, **SOJOURNER TRUTH'S NARRATIVE AND BOOK OF LIFE** (1875), available from the Library of Congress at *www.hathitrust.org/digital_library*

D. Walker, **APPEAL TO THE COLORED PEOPLE OF THE WORLD, BUT IN PARTICULAR, AND VERY EXPRESSLY, TO THOSE OF THE UNITED STATES OF AMERICA, WRITTEN IN BOSTON, STATE OF MASSACHUSETTS** (1829), Academic Affairs Library, Univ. of North Carolina at Chapel Hill, available at available at docsouth.unc.edu

B.T. Washington, **UP FROM SLAVERY** (Doubleday, Page & Co., 1901), available from the Library of Congress at *www.hathitrust.org/digital_library*

H. Washington, **MEDICAL APARTHEID: THE DARK HISTORY OF MEDICAL EXPERIMENTATION ON BLACK AMERICANS FROM COLONIAL TIMES TO THE PRESENT** (Anchor Books, 2006)

A. Wasserman, **A PEOPLE'S HISTORY OF FLORIDA, 1513-1876, HOW AFRICANS, SEMINOLES, AND LOWER CLASS WHITES SHAPED THE SUNSHINE STATE** (4th ed. 2010)

T. Weld, **AMERICAN SLAVERY AS IT IS: TESTIMONY OF A THOUSAND WITNESSES** (American Anti-Slavery Society, 1839), available from the Library of Congress at *www.hathitrust.org/digital_library*

I. Wells-Barnett, **THE ARKANSAS RACE RIOT** (1920), available at *archive.org/details/TheArkansasRaceRiot/page/n1/mode/2up*

J. Wheeler, **A PRACTICAL TREATISE ON THE LAW OF SLAVERY** (A. Pollock, Jr., 1837), available from the Library of Congress at *www.hathitrust.org/digital_library*

C.G. Woodson, **THE MIS-EDUCATION OF THE NEGRO** (1933)

Articles, Reports and Papers:

Ball, "Retracing Slavery's Trail of Tears" (Smithsonian Magazine, Nov. 2015) at *www.smithsonianmag.com/history/slavery-trail-of-tears-180956968/*

Beckles, "Slave Voyages—The Transatlantic Trade in Enslaved Africans" (United Nations Educational, Scientific and Cultural Organization)

Bloomberg, "A Wake-Up Call for Public Education: Falling Enrollment in America's schools is a sign of a system in crisis" at *www.bloomberg.com/opinion/articles/2022-06-02/declining-school-enrollment-signals-challenge-for-us-public-education*

Bloomberg.com Editorial Board, "Biden Shouldn't Let Teachers Unions Hold Students Back" (July 16, 2020) at *www.bloomberg.com/opinion/articles/2020-07-16/biden-shouldn-t-let-teachers-unions-dictate-education-policy*

Brewer, "Slavery, Sovereignty, and 'Inheritable Blood': Reconsidering John Locke and the Origins of American Slavery" (American Historical Review Vol. 122, Issue 4, Oct. 2017)

Cohodes, "Charter Schools and the Achievement Gap" (The Future of Children, Princeton-Brookings, Winter 2018) at *futureofchildren.princeton.edu/news/charter-schools-and-achievement-gap#:~:text=Charter Schools and the Achievement Gap*

Dean, "'Who Controls the Past Controls the Future:' The Virginia History Textbook Controversy" (Virginia Magazine of History and Biography, vol 17, no. 4, 2009)

Egalite, "The National Charter School Landscape" (Hoover Institution, July 1, 2020) at *www.hoover.org/research/national-charter-school-landscape*

Finkelman, "John Marshall's Proslavery Jurisprudence: Racism, Property, and the 'Great' Chief Justice" at *lawreviewblog.uchicago.edu/2020/08/31/marshall-slavery-pt2/*

Finkelman, "Master John Marshall and the Problem of Slavery" at *lawreviewblog.uchicago.edu/2020/08/31/marshall-slavery-pt1/*

Grandin, "Capitalism and Slavery" (The Nation, May 1, 2015) at *www.thenation.com/article/archive/capitalism-and-slavery/*

Grant "South to the Promised Land,) at 78, 84 (Smithsonian July-August 2022)

Hamm, "Daniel Worth: Persistent Abolitionist, A Thesis Presented to the Department of History and The University Honors Committee, Butler University" (1979), republished at "Antislavery Roots: A Call to end Slavery—The Wesleyan Methodist Church 1843-1865" at *www.wesleyan.org/antislavery-roots-229*

Hannah-Jones, "Our democracy's founding ideals were false when they were written. Black Americans have fought to make them true," at *www.nytimes.com/interactive/2019/08/14/magazine/black-history-american-democracy.html/*

Harper, "Slavery in the North" at *slavenorth.com*

Harper, "Slavery in the North" at *slavenorth.com/delaware.htm*

Harper, "Slavery in the North," at *slavenorth.com/denial.htm*

Harper, "Slavery in the North," at *slavenorth.com/emancipation.htm*

Harper, "Slavery in the North" at *slavenorth.com/massachusetts.htm*

Harper, "Slavery in the North" at *slavenorth.com/northwest.htm*

Harper, "Slavery in the North" at *slavenorth.com/ohio.htm*

Harper, "Slavery in the North," at *slavenorth.com/profits.htm*

Heim, "Teaching America's Truth" (Wash. Post Online, Aug. 28, 2019) at *www.washingtonpost.com/education/2019/08/28/teaching-slavery-schools/?arc404=true*

Kaufman, "The Teacher Union's Tiny New Enemy: The behemoth National Education Association seeks to squash popular pandemic microschools" at *www.wsj.com/articles/the-teachers-unions-tiny-new-enemy-11602709305*

Kenny, "'I can do the child no good': Dr. Sims and the Enslaved Infants of Montgomery, Alabama, Social History of Medicine" at 4 (2007), at *www.researchgate.net/publication/5246334_'I_can_do_the_child_no_good'_Dr_Sims_and_the_Enslaved_Infants_of_Montgomery_Alabama*

Mintz, "Historical Context: American Slavery in Comparative Perspective" at *www.gilderlehrman.org/history resources/teaching-resource/historical-context-american-slavery-comparative-perspective*

National Assessment of Educational Progress, Institute of Education Sciences, "The Condition of Education 2020" (May 2020) at *nces.ed.gov/pubs2020/2020144.pdf*

Rhodes, "Mother of the Domestic Slave Trade, Econ Focus," Richmond Federal Reserve (2nd Quarter, 2013) at *www.richmondfed.org/-/media/richmondfedorg/publications/research/econ_focus/2013/q2/pdf/economic_history.pdf*

Rodrigue, "Slavery in French Colonial Louisiana," at *64parishes.org/entry/slavery-in-french-colonial-louisiana*

Savitt, "The Use of Blacks for Medical Experimentation and Demonstration in the Old South," Jour. Of Southern History, Vol. 48, No. 3 (Aug. 1982)

Serfilippi, "'As Odious and Immoral a Thing': Alexander Hamilton's Hidden History as an Enslaver" (Schuyler Mansion State Historic Site, 2020) at *parks.ny.gov/documents/historic-sites/SchuylerMansionAlexanderHamiltonsHiddenHistoryasanEnslaver.pdf*

Shakeel and Peterson, "Charter Schools Show Steeper Upward trend in Student Achievement than District Schools" at *www.educationnext.org/charter-schools-show-steeper-upward-trend-student-achievement-first-nationwide-study/*

Uenuma, "The Massacre of Black Sharecroppers That Led the Supreme Court to Curb the Racial Disparities of the Justice System" (Smithsonian Magazine, Aug. 2, 2018) at *www.smithsonianmag.com/history/death-hundreds-elaine-massacre-led-supreme-court-take-major-step-toward-equal-justice-african-americans-180969863/*

Ware, "The Burning of Jerry: The Last Slave Execution by Fire in South Carolina?" The South Carolina Historical Magazine, Vol. 91, 100-06 (Apr. 1990)

White, "'Massacring Whites' in Arkansas" (The Nation, Dec. 6, 1919)

Wolf and Egalite, "Pursuing Innovation: How Can Educational Choice Transform K-12 Education in the U.S.?" at 3 (Friedman Foundation for Educational Choice, 2016)

Speeches:

"Adam Clayton Powell, Jr., What's in Your Hand Speech, 1967" at *www.allreadable.com/2979EmEx*

Douglass, "Inhumanity of Slavery—Extract from a Lecture on Slavery at Rochester, December 1, 1850" contained in F. Douglass, **MY BONDAGE AND MY FREEDOM** at 435 *et seq.* (1855), available from the Library of Congress at *www.hathitrust.org/digital_library*

"(1845) Frederick Douglass, My Slave Experience in Maryland'" at *www.blackpast.org/african-american-history/1845-frederick-douglass-my-slave-experience-maryland/*

Douglass, "Reception Speech at Finnsbury Chapel, Moorsfield, England, May 12, 1846," reprinted in F. Douglass, **MY BONDAGE AND MY FREEDOM** (Miller, Orton & Mulligan, 1855), available from the Library of Congress at www.hathitrust.org/digital_library, and also republished at *worldhistoryproject.org/1846/5/12/douglass-delivers-london-reception-speech-at-finsbury-chapel*

Douglass, "What to the Slave Is the Fourth of July?" (July 5, 1852), reprinted in part in F. Douglass, **MY BONDAGE AND MY FREEDOM at 446-47** (1855), available from the Library of Congress at *www.hathitrust.org/digital_library*

Douglass, "What to the Slave Is the Fourth of July?" (July 5, 1852) at "Text of Douglass's Speech" at *www.owleyes.org/text/what-to-the-slave-is-the-fourth-of-july/read/text-of-douglasss-speech#root-162*

"John Brown's Speech to the Court at His Trial" (Nov. 2, 1859), available at John Brown's Speech to the Court at his Trial at *nationalcenter.org/JohnBrown'sSpeech.html*

"Alexander Stephens, Vice President of the Confederacy, The Cornerstone Speech (1861)" at *www.owleyes.org/search?q=cornerstone%20speech*

"Text of Douglass's Speech" at *www.owleyes.org/text/what-to-the-slave-is-the-fourth-of-july/read/text-of-douglasss-speech#root-162*

"Text of Lincoln's Speech Delivered at Washington, D. C. March 4, 1865" at *www.owleyes.org/text/second-inaugural-address/read/text-of-lincolns-speech*

Other Online Resources:

"10 John Lewis Quotes That Will Inspire You to Get Into 'Good Trouble'" at *www.globalcitizen.org/en/content/john-lewis-quotes/*

"13th Amendment to the U.S. Constitution: Abolition of Slavery (1865)" at *www.ourdocuments.gov/doc.php?flash=true&doc=40*

"(1776) The Deleted Passage of the Declaration of Independence" at *www.blackpast.org/african-american-history/declaration-independence-and-debate-over-slavery/*

"1811 German Coast Slave Uprising" at *genealogytrails.com/main/events/slavery_1811uprising.html*

"1830: The slave Jerry, the last American execution by burning?" at *www.executedtoday.com/2011/05/01/1830-the-slave-jerry-the-last-american-execution-by-burning/*

"1860 United States Census, Introduction" at viii at *www2.census.gov/library/publications/decennial/1860/population/1860a-02.pdf*

"5 Things You May Not Know About Abraham Lincoln, Slavery and Emancipation" at *www.history.com/news/5-things-you-may-not-know-about-lincoln-slavery-and-emancipation*

"Abolition in the District of Columbia" at *www.loc.gov/item/today-in-history/april-16*

"Aboard a Slave Ship: An Account by The Rev. Robert Walsh, 1829" at *www.thirteen.org/wnet/historyofus/web05/features/source/docs/C04.pdf*

"Abraham Lincoln" at *www.history.com/topics/us-presidents/abraham-lincoln*

"Abraham Lincoln, Second Annual Message" at *www.presidency.ucsb.edu/documents/second-annual-message-9*

"Abraham Lincoln's Second Inaugural Address" at *www.loc.gov/rr/program/bib/ourdocs/lincoln2nd.html*

"A declaration of the causes which impel the State of Texas to secede from the Federal Union" at *www.tsl.texas.gov/ref/abouttx/secession/2feb1861.html*

"A Declaration of the Immediate Causes which Induce and Justify the Secession of the State of Mississippi from the Federal Union" at *www.battlefields.org/learn/articles/declarations-causes#mississippi*

"African Americans Speak for Themselves: Most Want School Choice" at *www.cato.org/blog/african-americans-speak-themselves-most-want-school-choice*

"African-American support of charter schools" at *www.federationforchildren.org/african-american-support-charter-schools*

"A Historical Overview of DC Emancipation" at *emancipation.dc.gov/node/105922*

"A Look Back at the Disturbing Practice of Gibbeting" at *allthatsinteresting.com/gibbet*

"Amazing Albany Facts" at *www.albany.org/media/amazing-facts*

"American police shoot, kill and imprison more people than other developed countries. Here's the data" at *www.cnn.com/2020/06/08/us/us-police-floyd-protests-country-comparisons-intl/index.html*

Anderson, "Harvard EdCast: Replicating Effective Charter School Practice" (Feb. 20, 2019) at *www.gse.harvard.edu/news/19/02/harvard-edcast-replicating-effective-charter-school-practice*

"Anne: Queen of Great Britain and Ireland" at *www.britannica.com/biography/Anne-queen-of-Great-Britain-and-Ireland*

"Asiento de negros" at *www.britannica.com/topic/asiento-de-negros*

"Assize" at *www.britannica.com/topic/assize*

"Badge of Slavery definitions," Webster's New World Law Dictionary Copyright© 2010 by Wiley Publishing, Inc., Hoboken, New Jersey, quoted at "Badge-of-Slavery" at *www.yourdictionary.com/badge-of-slavery*

Balingit and Meckler, "Trump alleges 'left-wing indoctrination' in schools, says he will create national commission to push more 'pro-American' history" (Wash. Post, Sept. 17, 2020) at *www.washingtonpost.com/education/trump-history-education/2020/09/17/f40535ec-ee2c-11ea-ab4e-581edb849379_story.html*

"Baltimore Riot (April 19,1861)" at *civilwarhome.com/baltimoreriot.htm*

"Baltimore Riot of 1861" at *www.historynet.com/baltimore-riot-of-1861.htm*

"B. Banneker, letter dated Aug. 19, 1791, to Thomas Jefferson," available at *founders.archives.gov/documents/Jefferson/01-22-02-0049*

"Barracoon" at *www.merriam-webster.com/dictionary/barracoon*

"Benjamin Banneker Biography" at *www.biography.com/scientist/benjamin-banneker*

Berry and LeFlouria, "Five Myths—Slavery" at B3 (Wash. Post Feb. 9, 2020) and at *www.washingtonpost.com/outlook/five-myths/five-myths-about-slavery/2020/02/07/d4cb0e6a-42e0-11ea-b503-2b077c436617_story.html*

"Black Americans Want Police to Retain Local Presence" at *news.gallup.com/poll/316571/black-americans-police-retainlocal-presence.aspx*

"Black and slave population of the United States from 1790 to 1880" at *www.statista.com/statistics/1010169/black-and-slave-population-us-1790-1880/#:~:text=By 1860%2C the final census taken before the,free African Americans in all of the US.*

"Black Codes" at *www.american-historama.org/1866-1881-reconstruction-era/black-codes.htm#:~:text=The%20Black%20Codes%20were%20laws%20that%20were%20introduced,of%20ex-slaves%20was%20restricted%20in%20numerous%20ways%20including%3A*

"Black Codes of Mississippi" at *www.thirteen.org/wnet/slavery/experience/legal/docs6.html*

Blackfacts.com

"Blackhead Signpost Road needs another sign" at *www.thetidewaternews.com/2015/08/15/blackhead-signpost-road-needs-another-sign/#:~:text=In Southampton County%2C the scene of the 1831,black as a warning against any future outrage.".*

Blackpast.com

Blackthen.com

Bordewich, Review of W. Thomas, **WHEN SLAVES HAD THEIR DAY IN COURT** (Yale Univ. Press, 2020) at C7 (Wall St. J., Nov. 14, 2020) at *www.wsj.com/articles/a-question-of-freedom-review-slavery-on-trial-11605282554*

Bordewich, "'Wilmington's Lie' Review: An American Tragedy" (Wall St. J., Jan. 3, 2020) at *www.wsj.com/articles/wilmingtons-lie-review-an-american-tragedy-11578067530*

Britannica.com

Brown, "Frederick Douglass needed to see Lincoln. Would the president meet with a former slave?" (Feb. 14, 2018) at *www.washingtonpost.com/news/retropolis/wp/2018/02/14/frederick-douglass-needed-to-see-lincoln-would-the-president-meet-with-a-former-slave/*

Campbell, "Slavery" at *tshaonline.org/handbook/online/articles/yps01*

"Cat-o'-nine-tails" at *www.merriam-webster.com/dictionary/cat-o'-nine-tails*

"Chattel" at *www.merriam-webster.com/dictionary/chattel#note-1*

Chervinsky and Hopkins, "The Enslaved Household of President John Quincy Adams" at *www.whitehousehistory.org/the-enslaved-household-of-john-quincy-adams*

"Children in single-parent families by race in the United States" at datacenter. *kidscount.org/data/tables/107-children-in-single-parent-families-by#detailed/1/any/false/37,871,870,573,869,36,868,867,133,38/10,11,9,12,1,185,13/432,431*

"City of York—The First Capital of the United States" at *www.yorkcity.org/about/history*

"Civil War Casualties" at *www.battlefields.org/learn/articles/civil-war-casualties*

"Clabber" at *www.merriam-webster.com/dictionary/clabber*

"Clauber" at *www.merriam-webster.com/dictionary/clauber*

"Coffle" at *www.lexico.com/en/definition/coffle*

"Colony of New York: A Brief History" at *www.celebrateboston.com/history/new-york.htm*

"Compromise of 1850" at *www.americanhistorycentral.com/entries/compromise-of-1850/*

"Cooper Union Speech (February 27, 1860)" at *housedivided.dickinson.edu/sites/lincoln/cooper-union-speech-february-27-1860/*

Cottman, "The Ghosts of the Henrietta Marie" at *www.washingtonpost.com/wp-srv/national/daily/feb99/excerpt07.htm*

"David Walker Biography (c. 1796-c. 1830)" at *www.biography.com/writer/david-walker*

"David Walker's Appeal" at *www.pbs.org/wgbh/aia/part4/4h2931.html*

"David Walker's Appeal to the Colored Citizens of the World" at *www.davidwalkermemorial.org/appeal*

"DC Emancipation Day" at *emancipation.dc.gov/page/ending-slavery-district-columbia*

Deagan and MacMahon, at 7; "Florida History Built on Slavery" at *usslave.blogspot.com/2013/06/florida-history-built-on-slavery.html*

Dearstyne, "Syracuse Hero Jermain Loguen, Abolition and The Jerry Rescue" at *www.newyorkalmanack.com/2022/02/syracuse-hero-jermain-loguen-abolition-the-jerry-rescue/*

"Declaration of the Immediate Causes Which Induce and Justify the Secession of South Carolina from the Federal Union" (Dec. 20, 1860) at *teachingamericanhistory.org/library/document/south-carolina-declaration-of-causes-of-secession/*

"Disruptive Innovation" at *www.investopedia.com/terms/d/disruptive-innovation.asp,* accessed Sept. 14, 2020

"Draft Riot of 1863" at *www.britannica.com/event/Draft-Riot-of-1863*

Dunbar, "George Washington Slave Catcher" (NY Times, Feb. 16, 2015) at *www.nytimes.com/2015/02/16/opinion/george-washington-slave-catcher.html*

"Electoral College is 'vestige' of slavery, say some Constitutional scholars" (Nov. 6, 2016), at *www.pbs.org/newshour/politics/electoral-college-slavery-constitution*

"Elijah Lovejoy, American Abolitionist" at www.britannica.com/biography/Elijah-P-Lovejoy

"Fatal Force: 1,010 people have been shot and killed by police in the past year" (Wash. Post Online, Sept. 23, 2020) (Updated Nov. 11, 2020) at *www.washingtonpost.com/graphics/investigations/police-shootings-database/*

"February 26, 1638, First Slaves Arrive in Massachusetts" at *www.massmoments.org/moment-details/first-slaves-arrive-in-massachusetts.html*

"Florida History Built on Slavery" at *usslave.blogspot.com/2013/06/florida-history-built-on-slavery.html*

"Founders Online; Letter from Thomas Jefferson to John Holmes, 22, April 1820" at *founders.archives.gov/documents/Jefferson/03-15-02-0518*

"Frances Ellen Watkins Harper" at *www.africanamericanpoetry.org/frances-e-w-harper*

Ganeshram, "In 1795, George Washington gave thanks for liberty. The feasts chef had none." at R4 (Wash. Post, Nov. 22, 2020) at *www.washingtonpost.com/food/2020/11/19/washington-thanksgiving-hercules/*

Gates, "Did Black People Own Slaves?" (March 4, 2013) at *www.africanamerica.org/topic/did-black-people-own-slaves*

Gates, "Slavery by the Numbers" at *www.theroot.com/slavery-by-the-numbers-1790874492*

"Genocide" at *www.merriam-webster.com/dictionary/genocide*

"George Mason and Slavery" at *gmufourthestate.com/2016/10/24/george-mason-and-slavery/*

"Georgia Declaration of Causes for Secession" at *www.battlefields.org/learn/articles/declarations-causes#georgia*

"Gloucester County Conspiracy (1663)" at *www.encyclopediavirginia.org/Gloucester_County_Conspiracy_1663*

Hansen, "Here's What The Racial Wealth Gap In America Looks Like Today" at *www.forbes.com/sites/sarahhansen/2020/06/05/heres-what-the-racial-wealth-gap-in-america-looks-like-today/#3be6c333164c*

Harper, "How Slave Labor Made New York" at *www.theroot.com/how-slave-labor-made-new-york-1790895122*

Heim, "Teaching America's Truth" (Wash. Post Online, Aug.28, 2019) at *www.washingtonpost.com/education/2019/08/28/teaching-slavery-schools/?arc404=true*

"'Henrietta King'; an excerpt from Weevils in the Wheat" (1976) at *www.encyclopediavirginia.org/_Henrietta_King_an_excerpt_from_Weevils_in_the_Wheat_1976*

"Henry 'Box' Brown" at *www.biography.com/activist/henry-box-brown*

"Henry 'Box' Brown" at *www.pbs.org/black-culture/shows/list/underground-railroad/stories-freedom/henry-box-brown/*

"Henry 'Box' Brown: A Slave Signed, Sealed and Delivered" at *www.historynet.com/henry-box-brown-a-slave-signed-sealed-and-delivered.htm*

history.com

"History Is a Weapon: David Walker's Appeal" at *www.historyisaweapon.com/defcon1/walkerappeal.html*

"History of Annapolis" at *www.annapolis.gov/588/History-of-Annapolis#:~:text=The Many Names of Annapolis The capital of,of Lord Baltimore%2C who owned the proprietary colony.*

"Holocaust" at *www.merriam-webster.com/dictionary/holocaust*

"How a Movement to Send Freed Slaves to Africa Created Liberia" at *www.history.com/news/slavery-american-colonization-society-liberia*

"International Comparison of Math, Reading, and Science Skills Among 15-Year-Olds" at *www.infoplease.com/us/education/international-comparison-math-reading-and- science-skills*

"Investigators find a mass grave while searching for 1921 Tulsa race massacre victims" at *www.cnn.com/2020/10/21/us/tulsa-massacre-excavation/index.html*

"Inspiring Speeches by Frances Watkins Harper, 19th-Century Reformer & Author" at *www.literaryladiesguide.com/author-quotes/inspiring-speeches-by-frances-watkins-harper, accessed March 1, 2022*

"James Stewart" at www.commonwealthbooksllc.homestead.com/james—Duke-of-York.html

"Jermain Wesley Loguen" at *www.nationalabolitionhalloffameandmuseum.org/jermain-wesley-loguen.html*

"John Adams and Slavery" at *www.johnadamsinfo.com/john-adams-and-slavery/89/*

"John Wilkes Booth: American actor and assassin" at *www.britannica.com/biography/John-Wilkes-Booth*

"Jubilo! The Emancipation Century" at *jubiloemancipationcentury.wordpress.com/2013/02/18/list-of-slave-holding-presidents/*

"K-12 Disparity Facts and Statistics" at *uncf.org/pages/K-12-Disparity-Facts-and-stats*

Kaufman, "The Teacher Union's Tiny New Enemy: The behemoth National Education Association seeks to squash popular pandemic microschools" (Wall St. J., Oct. 14, 2020) at *www.wsj.com/articles/the-teachers-unions-tiny-new-enemy-11602709305*

"Kansas enters the Union" at *www.history.com/this-day-in-history/kansas-enters-the-union*

"Kansas-Nebraska Act" at *www.britannica.com/topic/Kansas-Nebraska-Act*

"Kansas-Nebraska Act" at *www.history.com/topics/19th-century/kansas-nebraska-act*

Kelkar, "Electoral College is 'vestige' of slavery, say some Constitutional scholars" (Nov. 6, 2016), at *www.pbs.org/newshour/politics/electoral-college-slavery-constitution*

Klein, "Alexander Hamilton's Complicated Relationship to Slavery" at *www.history.com/news/alexander-hamilton-slavery-facts*

"Last Public Address—Abe Lincoln" at *abelincolnhistory.com/speeches/last-public-address.htm#:~:text=Last%20Public%20Address%20-%20Abe%20Lincoln.%20After%20this,the%20United%20States%20after%20the%20American%20Civil%20War%2C*

"Le Code Noir" at *thelouvertureproject.org/index.php?title=Le_Code_Noir*

"Letter dated Aug. 25, 1814, from Thomas Jefferson to Edward Coles" available at *www.encyclopediavirginia.org/Letter_from_Thomas_Jefferson_to_Edward_Coles_August_25_1814*

"Life on board slave ships" at *www.liverpoolmuseums.org.uk/history-of-slavery/middle-passage#section--log-book-of-the-unity,-1769-1770*

"Lincoln Home—Fourth Debate: Charleston, Illinois" at *www.nps.gov/liho/learn/historyculture/debate4.htm*

"Lincoln's Cooper Union Address: New York City Speech Propelled Lincoln to the White House" at *www.thoughtco.com/lincolns-cooper-union-address-1773575*

"Lincoln's Peoria Speech, October 16, 1854," at *www.nps.gov/liho/learn/historyculture/peoriaspeech.htm,* accessed Oct. 13, 2021

Little, "How Woodrow Wilson Tried to Reverse Black American Progress" at *www.history.com/news/woodrow-wilson-racial-segregation-jim-crow-ku-klux-klan*

Long and Van Dam, "The black-white economic divide is as wide as it was in 1968" (Wash. Post, June 4, 2020) at *www.washingtonpost.com/business/2020/06/04/economic-divide-black-households*

"Lord Dunmore's Proclamation, 1775" at *www.gilderlehrman.org/history-resources/spotlight-primary-source/lord-dunmores-proclamation-1775*

"Lynching of Pregnant 19-Year-Old Mary Turner" at *blackthen.com/lynching-of-pregnant-19-year-old-mary-turner/*

"Lynchings by Year and Race" at *law2.umkc.edu/Faculty/projects/ftrials/shipp/lynchingyear.html*

"Manumission" at www.merriam-webster.com/dictionary/manumission

"Martha Washington as a Slaveowner" at *www.mountvernon.org/george-washington/slavery/martha-washington-as-a-slaveowner/*

Minton, "The lies our textbooks told my generation of Virginians about slavery," at B4 (Wash. Post, July 31, 2020) and at *www.washingtonpost.com/outlook/slavery-history-virginia-textbook/2020/07/31/d8571eda-d1f0-11ea-8c55-61e7fa5e82ab_story.html*

Morrar and Reese, "Inexperienced teachers are often sent to low-income schools in Sacramento. Why that Matters" (Sacramento Bee, Feb.13, 2020) at *www.sacbee.com/article239922318.html*

"Negro Head Road" at *www.ncpedia.org/negro-head-road*

"New Africans" at *Newafrikan77.wordpress.com*

"New York Draft Riots" at *www.history.com/topics/american-civil-war/draft-riots*

"New York History Blog, Historical Views and News from The Empire State—Reckoning with Our Legacy of Slavery" (Oct. 21, 2019), Comment by Alan J. Singer, at *www.newyorkalmanack.com/2019/10/reckoning-with-our-legacy-of-slavery/*

"New York State Name Origin" at *statesymbolsusa.org/symbol-official-item/new-york/state-name-origin-state-quarter/origin-new-york*

"Nine Charts about Wealth Inequality in America (Updated)" at *apps.urban.org/features/wealth-inequality-charts/*

"Northwest Ordinance" at *quaqua.org/northwest.htm#:~:text=Northwest Ordinance The Northwest Ordinancewas enacted in 1787%2C,Michigan%2C and other portions of the upper Midwest*

"Northwest Ordinance" at *www.tjheritage.org/blog/2017/8/4/northwest-ordinance-1#*

"Northwest Ordinance of 1787: Before the Constitution, an Early Federal Law Impacted Slavery" at *www.thoughtco.com/northwest-ordinance-of-1787-4177006*

"Northwest Ordinances" at *www.britannica.com/event/Northwest-Ordinances*

"Northwest Territory" at *www.encyclopedia.com/places/united-states-and-canada/miscellaneous-us-geography/northwest-territory*

NPS.gov

"Presidential Elections and the 3/5 Compromise" at *americanrevolutionblog.blogspot.com/2007/11/presidential-elections-and-35.html?m=1,* accessed Sept. 30, 2020

"Reported number of slaves owned by U.S. presidents who served from 1789 to 1877 (throughout their lifetimes)" at *www.statista.com/statistics/1121963/slaves-owned-by-us-presidents/*

"Ona Judge" at *www.mountvernon.org/library/digitalhistory/digital-encyclopedia/article/ona-judge*

"Osnaburg" at *www.merriam-webster.com/dictionary/osnaburg*

"Our Say: Everybody's wrong in Anne Arundel County teachers union dispute" (Capital Gazette, Oct. 2, 2017) at *www.capitalgazette.com/opinion/our-say/ac-ce-our-say-20171002-story.html,* accessed Sept. 17, 2020

Patricia Smith, "Speculum Oris," at *rattle.com/speculum-oris-by-patricia-smith/*

"Peck" at *www.britannica.com/science/peck*

"Pisgah" at *www.lexico.com/en/definition/pisgah*

"Police killings by country 2020" at *worldpopulationreview.com/country-rankings/police-killings-by-country*

"Poll: Support for School Choice Spiked 10 Percent among Public School Families during Covid Shutdown" at *www.nationalreview.com/news/poll-support-for-school-choice-spiked-10-percent-among-public-school-families-during-covid-shutdown*

"Presidential Elections and the 3/5 Compromise" at *americanrevolutionblog.blogspot.com/2007/11/presidential-elections-and-35.html?m=1*

"Prince Hall Freemasonry" at *freemasoninformation.com/what-is-freemasonry/family-of-freemasonry/prince-hall-freemasonry/*

"Proclamation of Earl of Dunmore" at *www.pbs.org/wgbh/aia/part2/2h42t.html*

"Project 1619" at *project1619.org*

"Q&A: Did Slaves Build the White House?" at *www.whitehousehistory.org/questions/did-slaves-build-the-white-house*

"Queen Anne" at *www.npg.org.uk/learning/digitalhistpry/abolition-of-slavery/queen-anne*

"Queen Anne's County, Maryland" at *www.ereferencedesk.com/resources/counties/maryland/queen-annes.html*

"Rate of police killings in selected countries 2019" at *www.statista.com/statistics/1124039/police-killings-rate-selected-countries*

"Reconstruction" at *www.history.com/topics/american-civil-war/reconstruction*

"Reign of Terror," American Heritage® Dictionary of the English Language, Fifth Edition (Houghton Mifflin Harcourt Publishing Company 2016), quoted at *www.thefreedictionary.com/The+Reign+Of+Terror*

"Reported number of slaves owned by U.S. presidents who served from 1789 to 1877 (throughout their lifetimes)" at *www.statista.com/statistics/1121963/slaves-owned-by-us-presidents/*

"Rescued from the Fangs of the Slave Hunter:" The Case of Shadrach Minkins at *www.nps.gov/articles/-rescued-from-the-fangs-of-the-slave-hunter-the-case-of-shadrach-minkins.htm*

Riley, "Bad Teaching Is Tearing America Apart" (Wall St. J., Sept. 11, 2020) at *www.wsj.com/articles/bad-teaching-is-tearing-america-apart-11599857351*

Riva, "Moore v. Dempsey" at *encyclopediaofarkansas.net/entries/moore-v-dempsey-5200/* (Last Updated 11/19/20)

"Roger Taney" at *housedivided.dickinson.edu/sites/slavery/people/roger%ADtaney/#:~:text=Originally%20from%20Maryland%2C%20Taney%20had%20been%20a%20slaveholder*

Rosenberg, "Mitch McConnell's ancestors owned slaves, according to a new report. He opposes reparations" (Wash. Post. July 8, 2019) at *www.washingtonpost.com/politics/2019/07/09/mitch-mcconnells-ancestors-owned-slaves-according-new-report-he-opposes-reparations/*

Rosenwald, "At least 2,000 more black people were lynched by white mobs than previously reported, new research finds" at *www.washingtonpost.com/history/2020/06/16/lynchings-report-equal-justice-initiative-reconstruction-racial-terror/*

Ruane, "It was the nation's largest auction of enslaved people. Now, a search for descendants of the 'weeping time'" at C1 (Wash. Post, Oct. 13, 2019) at *gratefulamericanfoundation.com/weeping-time/*

Schwartz, "George Mason: Forgotten Founder, He Conceived the Bill of Rights" at *www.smithsonianmag.com/history/george-mason-forgotten-founder-he-conceived-the-bill-of-rights-64408583/*

"Sept. 22, 1862: Preliminary Emancipation Proclamation Announced" at *learning.blogs.nytimes.com/2011/09/22/sept-22-1862-preliminary-emancipation-proclamation-announced/*

Shakeel and Peterson, "Charter Schools Show Steeper Upward Trend in Student Achievement than District Schools" at *www.educationnext.org/charter-schools-show-steeper-upward-trend-student-achievement-first-nationwide-study/*

"Shall Not Be Denied" at *www.loc.gov/exhibitions/women-fight-for-the-vote/about-this-exhibition/new-tactics-for-a-new-generation-1890-1915/western-states-pave-the-way/i-speak-of-wrongs-frances-ellen-watkins-harper/,* accessed March 1, 2022.

"Sharecropper" at *www.merriam-webster.com/dictionary/sharecropper*

"Sire" at *www.meriam-webster.com/dictionary/sire*

"Slavery and the Abolition Society" at *www.benjamin-franklin-history.org/slavery-abolition-society*

"Slavery a Positive Good" at *teacherpress.ocps.net/stephenhansen/files/2016/07/Calhoun-Slavery_a_Positive_Good_.pdf*

"Slavery at Whitehaven" at *www.nps.gov/articles/slavery-at-white-haven.htm*

"Slavery in Missouri" at *centerplace.org/history/misc/soc/soc14.htm*

"Slavery in South Carolina" at *www.womenhistoryblog.com/2008/07/slavery-in-south-carolina.html*

"Slavery one of the greatest crimes of history: Bush" at *www.smh.com.au/world/slavery-one-of-the-greatest-crimes-of-history-bush-20030709-gdh2ew.html*

"Slaves and Emancipation" at *civilwarmo.org/educators/resources/info sheets/slaves-and-emancipation*

"Slave Voyages" at *www.slavevoyages.org*

"Stephen A. Douglas" (Updated Aug. 21, 2108) at *www.history.com/topics/us-politics/stephen-a-douglas*

Strauss, "Michigan settles historic lawsuit after court rules students have a constitutional right to a 'basic' education, including literacy" (Wash. Post, May 14, 2020) at *www.washingtonpost.com/education/2020/05/14/michigan-settles-historic-lawsuit-after-court-rules-students-have-constitutional-right-basic-education-including-literacy/*

Sweig, "Alexandria to New Orleans: The Human Tragedy of the Interstate Slave Trade, Parts I-IV" (The Connection Newspapers, Oct. 8, 15, 23, 2014) at *connectionarchives.com/PDF/2014/Slave%20Trader/Slave%20Trader.PDF; www.alexandriagazette.com/news/2014/oct/08/alexandria-new-orleans-human-tragedy-interstate-sl/; www.alexandriagazette.com/news/2014/oct/15/alexandria-new-orleans/; www.connectionnewspapers.com/news/2014/oct/23/alexandria-new-orleans-human-tragedy-interstate-sl/*

Sweig, "At Least George Washington Let His Slaves Have Families" (Wash. Post, Sept. 25, 1983) at *www.washingtonpost.com/archive/opinions/1983/09/25/at-least-george-washington-let-his-slaves-have-families/feca420d-c4ba-4563-9b88-5ba42f9b656b*The Life of Sally Hemings at *www.monticello.org/sallyhemings*

Takahama, "Is math racist? New course outlines prompt conversations about identity, race in Seattle classrooms" at *www.seattletimes.com/education-lab/new-course-outlines-prompt-conversations-about-identity-race-in-seattle-classrooms-even-in-math/*

"Ten Facts About Martha Washington" at *www.mountvernon.org/george-washington/martha-washington/ten-facts-about-martha-washington/*

"Terrorism" at *www.merriam-webster.com/dictionary/terrorism*

"Text of the Northwest Ordinance" at *www.varsitytutors.com/earlyamerica/text-northwest-ordinance#:~:text=Text of The Northwest Ordinance. Be it ordained,in the opinion of Congress%2C make it expedient.*

"The Abolition of Slavery in Virginia" at *www.encyclopediavirginia.org/the_abolition_of_slavery_in_virginia*

"The American Colonization Society" at *www.whitehousehistory.org/the-american-colonization-society*

"The Angolan Connection and Slavery in Virginia" at *www.historyisfun.org/learn/learning-center/the-angolan-connection-and-slavery-in-virginia/*

"The Business of Enslavement" at *www.bbc.co.uk/history/british/abolition/slavery_business_gallery_06.shtml*

The Christiana Riot: Violent Resistance to Fugitive Slave Law at *www.thoughtco.com/the-christiana-riot-1773557*

"The Cooper Union Address: The Making of a Candidate" at *www.nps.gov/liho/learn/historyculture/aboutcooper.htm#:~:text=The Cooper Union Address%3A The Making of a, Our Living Representative Men%2C Prepared for Presidential Purposes.*

"The Death of David Walker" at *www.davidwalkermemorial.org/david-walker/death-of-david-walker*

"The House 'Gag Rule'" at *history.house.gov/Historical-Highlights/1800-1850/The-House-of-Representatives-instituted-the-"gag-rule"/*

"The KKK kills three civil rights workers" at *www.history.com/this-day-in-history/the-kkk-kills-three-civil-rights-activists*

"The Life of Sally Hemings" at *www.monticello.org/sallyhemings/*

"The Lincoln-Douglas Debates" at *www.ushistory.org/us/32b.asp#:~:text=The debates attracted tens of thousands of voters,was%2C he said%2C a sacred right of self-government*

"The Nation's Report Card: How Did U.S. Students Perform in the Most Recent Assessment? (Public Schools Only vs. Private Schools Only)" at *www.nation's reportcard.gov*

"The Nation's Report Card, National Results Overview," at *www.nationsreportcard.gov/reading_math_2015/#reading?grade=4*

"The Nation's Report Card: Public, Private, and Charter Schools Dashboard (Average scores in NAEP reading for Black Students by grade and type of school: 2019 (grade 4), 2019 (grade 8), and 2015 (grade 12)" at *www.nation's reportcard.gov*

"The Northwest Ordinance of 1787" at *history.house.gov/Historical-Highlights/1700s/Northwest-Ordinance-1787/*

"The Northwest Ordinance of 1787 and Its Effects" at *www.americanhistoryusa.com/northwest-ordinance-1787-effects*

"The Papers of John Jay: Jay and Slavery" at *www.columbia.edu/cu/libraries/inside/dev/jay/JaySlavery.html*

"The President's House in Philadelphia" at *www.ushistory.org/presidentshouse/plans/eisterhold/04-Systems-and-Methods-of-Slavery.php*

Theroot.com

"The Slave Ship" at *cbsnews.com/news/the-slave-ship-60-minutes/*

"The Slaves Who Built Washington DC" at *zmblackhistorymonth2012.blogspot.com/2012/02/slaves-who-built-washington-dc.html*

"The State of New York" at *www.netstate.com/states/intro/ny_intro.htm*

"The trade triangle" at *liverpoolmuseums.org.uk/history-of-slavery/transatlantic-slave-trade*

"Thomas Jefferson, letter dated Aug. 30, 1791, to Benjamin Banneker" at *www.loc.gov/exhibits/jefferson/79.html*

"Thomas Jefferson, Monticello" at *www.monticello.org*

"Transatlantic Slave Trade" at *wayback.archive-it.org/10611/20180704133101/http://www.unesco.org/new/en/social-and-human-sciences/themes/slave-route/transatlantic-slave-trade*

"Trans-Atlantic Slave Trade Database" at *slavevoyages.org*

"Tulsa Race Massacre" at *www.history.com/topics/roaring-twenties/tulsa-race-massacre*

"Tulsa race massacre of 1921" at *www.britannica.com/event/Tulsa-race-riot-of-1921*

"Value of $1,000 from 1850 to 2020" at *www.officialdata.org/us/inflation/1850?amount=1000*

"Virtual Jamestown: Laws on Slavery" at *www.virtualjamestown.org/laws1.html*

"West Virginia History" at *www.wvculture.org/history/journal_wvh/wvh21-1.html*

"What happened when Trump visited the African American History Museum" (Aug. 31, 2019), at *www.chron.com/national/article/What-happened-when-Trump-visited-the-African-14404817.php*

"What Is Genocide" at *www.theholocaustexplained.org/what-was-the-holocaust/what-was-genocide/the-cambodian-genocide/*

"What Lincoln Said in His Final Speech" at *www.history.com/news/what-lincoln-said-in-his-final-speech*

"What was the Royal African Company?" at *www.history.com/news/what-was-the-royal-african-company*

"William Lloyd Garrison and the Liberator" at *www.ushistory.org/US/28a.asp*

"William Penn and James, Duke of York" at *pennsylvaniahistory.wordpress.com/2012/08//11/William-penn-and-james-duke-of-york*

"World Population" review at *worldpopulationreview.com/states/*

State Archives:

A GUIDE TO THE HISTORY OF SLAVERY IN MARYLAND (MD State Archives and Univ. of MD, 2007)

Archives of Maryland (Biographical Series), "Josiah 'Joe' Bailey (b. 1828-d.?)" at *msa.maryland.gov/megafile/msa/speccol/sc5400/sc5496/001500/001535/html/001535bio.html*

"George Armwood, Lynched in Princess Anne, October 18, 1933," Archives of Maryland (Biographical Series) at *msa.maryland.gov/megafile/msa/speccol/sc3500/sc3520/013700/013750/html/13750bio.html*

"Henry Davis, Lynched in Annapolis, Maryland, December 21, 1906," Archives of Maryland (Biographical Series) at *msa.maryland.gov/megafile/msa/speccol/sc3500/sc3520/013600/013635/html/13635bio.html#:~:text=Lynched in Annapolis%2C Maryland%2C December 21%2C 1906. Biography%3A,store in Iglehart Station in Anne Arundel County.*

Missouri State Archives, "Missouri's Early Slave Laws: A History in Documents, Laws Concerning Slavery in Missouri Territorial to 1850s" at *www.sos.mo.gov/archives/education/aahi/earlyslavelaws/slavelaws.asp*

Images:

"Elizabeth Powell is searching for her relatives," Information Wanted Ad, *The Elevator* (San Francisco, CA), May 27, 1870, *Last Seen: Finding Family After Slavery,* accessed November 18, 2020, http://www.informationwanted.org/items/show/3704

"Isaac Moore is searching for his parents and relatives," Information Wanted Ad, The Elevator (San Francisco, CA), December 29,1871, *Last Seen: Finding Family After Slavery,* accessed November 18, 2020, http://www.informationwanted.org/items/show/3689

Images from *www.slaveryimages.org:*

"A Captive", *Slavery Images: A Visual Record of the African Slave Trade and Slave Life in the Early African Diaspora,* accessed November 14, 2020, *http://slaveryimages.org/s/slaveryimages/item/1882*

"Advertisement for Sale of Newly Arrived Africans, Charleston, July 24, 1769", *Slavery Images: A Visual Record of the African Slave Trade and Slave Life in the Early African Diaspora,* accessed November 14, 2020, http://slaveryimages.org/s/slaveryimages/item/1971

"A Planter's Mansion", *Slavery Images: A Visual Record of the African Slave Trade and Slave Life in the Early African Diaspora,* accessed November 15, 2020, *http://slaveryimages.org/s/slaveryimages/item/1373*

"A Slave Auction", *Slavery Images: A Visual Record of the African Slave Trade and Slave Life in the Early African Diaspora,* accessed November 14, 2020, *http://slaveryimages.org/s/slaveryimages/item/1878*

"A Slave Auction in Virginia", *Slavery Images: A Visual Record of the African Slave Trade and Slave Life in the Early African Diaspora,* accessed November 14, 2020, *http://slaveryimages.org/s/slaveryimages/item/2226*

"A Slave-Hunt", *Slavery Images: A Visual Record of the African Slave Trade and Slave Life in the Early African Diaspora,* accessed November 15, 2020, *http://slaveryimages.org/s/slaveryimages/item/1212*

"A Slave Raid", *Slavery Images: A Visual Record of the African Slave Trade and Slave Life in the Early African Diaspora,* accessed November 16, 2020, *http://slaveryimages.org/s/slaveryimages/item/2657*

"A Slave-Shed", *Slavery Images: A Visual Record of the African Slave Trade and Slave Life in the Early African Diaspora,* accessed November 14, 2020, *http://slaveryimages.org/s/slaveryimages/item/1980*

"Black Soldiers in the Union/Federal Army, ca. 1863-64", *Slavery Images: A Visual Record of the African Slave Trade and Slave Life in the Early African Diaspora,* accessed November 27, 2020, *http://slaveryimages.org/s/slaveryimages/item/817*

"Black Troops of the Union Army, Philadelphia, early 1864", *Slavery Images: A Visual Record of the African Slave Trade and Slave Life in the Early African Diaspora,* accessed November 15, 2020, *http://slaveryimages.org/s/slaveryimages/item/798*

"Bloodhounds Being Killed by Black Union Soldiers, 1862", Slavery Images: A Visual Record of the African Slave Trade and Slave Life in the Early African Diaspora, accessed November 15, 2020, *http://slaveryimages.org/s/slaveryimages/item/820*

"Branding a Negro Woman", *Slavery Images: A Visual Record of the African Slave Trade and Slave Life in the Early African Diaspora,* accessed November 14, 2020, *http://slaveryimages.org/s/slaveryimages/item/1976*

"Broomstick Wedding, Virginia (?), 1840s", Slavery Images: A Visual Record of the African Slave Trade and Slave Life in the Early African Diaspora, accessed November 15, 2020, *http://slaveryimages.org/s/slaveryimages/item/637*

"Captured Africans Taken to the Coast (either Nigeria, 1853 or Liberia/Sierra Leone, 1840)", *Slavery Images: A Visual Record of the African Slave Trade and Slave Life in the Early African Diaspora,* accessed November 16, 2020, *http://slaveryimages.org/s/slaveryimages/item/393*

"Coffle of Enslaved, Washington, D.C., 1840s", *Slavery Images: A Visual Record of the African Slave Trade and Slave Life in the Early African Diaspora,* accessed November 14, 2020, *http://slaveryimages.org/s/slaveryimages/item/1939*

"Cotton Machine Used for Punishing Runaways, South Carolina, 1830s", *Slavery Images: A Visual Record of the African Slave Trade and Slave Life in the Early African Diaspora,* accessed November 15, 2020, *http://slaveryimages.org/s/slaveryimages/item/1206*

"Cutting Timber, Virginia, 1850s", *Slavery Images: A Visual Record of the African Slave Trade and Slave Life in the Early African Diaspora,* accessed November 21, 2020, *http://slaveryimages.org/s/slaveryimages/item/932*

"Deck of Slave Ship, Jamaica, 19th cent.", Slavery Images: A Visual Record of the African Slave Trade and Slave Life in the Early African Diaspora, accessed November 18, 2020, *http://slaveryimages.org/s/slaveryimages/item/2031*

"Dred Scott, ca. 1857", Slavery Images: A Visual Record of the African Slave Trade and Slave Life in the Early African Diaspora, accessed November 15, 2020, *http://slaveryimages.org/s/slaveryimages/item/1508*

"English Castle at Anamabou", Slavery Images: A Visual Record of the African Slave Trade and Slave Life in the Early African Diaspora, accessed November 15, 2020, *http://slaveryimages.org/s/slaveryimages/item/2087*

"Examining a Slave for Sale, Virginia, 1830", Slavery Images: A Visual Record of the African Slave Trade and Slave Life in the Early African Diaspora, accessed November 14, 2020, *http://slaveryimages.org/s/slaveryimages/item/1941*

"Fers pour négres", Slavery Images: A Visual Record of the African Slave Trade and Slave Life in the Early African Diaspora, accessed November 13, 2020, *http://slaveryimages.org/s/slaveryimages/item/2063*

"Frederick Douglass, American abolitionist, ca. 1865", Slavery Images: A Visual Record of the African Slave Trade and Slave Life in the Early African Diaspora, accessed November 15, 2020, *http://slaveryimages.org/s/slaveryimages/item/1531*

"Freed Slaves Cheering Lincoln's Emancipation Proclamation, 1863", *Slavery Images: A Visual Record of the African Slave Trade and Slave Life in the Early African Diaspora*, accessed November 15, 2020, *http://slaveryimages.org/s/slaveryimages/item/792*

"Fugitive Slave Attacked by Dogs, 19th cent. (?)", *Slavery Images: A Visual Record of the African Slave Trade and Slave Life in the Early African Diaspora,* accessed November 15, 2020, *http://slaveryimages.org/s/slaveryimages/item/1294*

"Fugitive Slaves and Bloodhounds, U.S. South, 1850s", *Slavery Images: A Visual Record of the African Slave Trade and Slave Life in the Early African Diaspora,* accessed November 30, 2020, *http://slaveryimages.org/s/slaveryimages/item/1292*

"Fugitive Slaves Escaping to Union Lines, 1864", *Slavery Images: A Visual Record of the African Slave Trade and Slave Life in the Early African Diaspora,* accessed November 15, 2020, *http://slaveryimages.org/s/slaveryimages/item/794*

"Fugitive Slaves, U.S. South, 1861", *Slavery Images: A Visual Record of the African Slave Trade and Slave Life in the Early African Diaspora,* accessed November 15, 2020, *http://slaveryimages.org/s/slaveryimages/item/1210*

"Fugitive Slave Trapped, U.S. South, 19th cent.", *Slavery Images: A Visual Record of the African Slave Trade and Slave Life in the Early African Diaspora,* accessed November 30, 2020, *http://slaveryimages.org/s/slaveryimages/item/1293*

"Funeral, Antebellum U.S. South, 19th cent.", *Slavery Images: A Visual Record of the African Slave Trade and Slave Life in the Early African Diaspora,* accessed November 15, 2020, *http://slaveryimages.org/s/slaveryimages/item/1854*

"Gathering the Cane", *Slavery Images: A Visual Record of the African Slave Trade and Slave Life in the Early African Diaspora,* accessed November 19, 2020, *http://slaveryimages.org/s/slaveryimages/item/1082*

"George Washington with Slave Laborers ", *Slavery Images: A Visual Record of the African Slave Trade and Slave Life in the Early African Diaspora,* accessed November 16, 2020, *http://slaveryimages.org/s/slaveryimages/item/1174*

"Gordon Under Medical Inspection", *Slavery Images: A Visual Record of the African Slave Trade and Slave Life in the Early African Diaspora,* accessed November 15, 2020, *http://slaveryimages.org/s/slaveryimages/item/1236*

"'Goree,' or Slave-Stick", *Slavery Images: A Visual Record of the African Slave Trade and Slave Life in the Early African Diaspora,* accessed November 16, 2020, *http://slaveryimages.org/s/slaveryimages/item/2653*

"Ginning Cotton, U.S. South, 1850s", *Slavery Images: A Visual Record of the African Slave Trade and Slave Life in the Early African Diaspora,* accessed November 16, 2020, *http://slaveryimages.org/s/slaveryimages/item/1170*

"Hanging a Slave, South Carolina, 1850s", *Slavery Images: A Visual Record of the African Slave Trade and Slave Life in the Early African Diaspora,* accessed November 15, 2020, *http://slaveryimages.org/s/slaveryimages/item/1231*

"Hauling and Shipping Cotton, Savannah, Georgia, 1871", *Slavery Images: A Visual Record of the African Slave Trade and Slave Life in the Early African Diaspora,* accessed November 19, 2020, *http://slaveryimages.org/s/slaveryimages/item/1063*

"Hauling Cotton Bales, U.S. South, 1850s", *Slavery Images: A Visual Record of the African Slave Trade and Slave Life in the Early African Diaspora,* accessed November 19, 2020, *http://slaveryimages.org/s/slaveryimages/item/1171*

"Heading Herring", *Slavery Images: A Visual Record of the African Slave Trade and Slave Life in the Early African Diaspora,* accessed November 21, 2020, *http://slaveryimages.org/s/slaveryimages/item/953*

"Hoeing and Planting Cotton Seeds, South Carolina, 1880", *Slavery Images: A Visual Record of the African Slave Trade and Slave Life in the Early African Diaspora,* accessed November 16, 2020, *http://slaveryimages.org/s/slaveryimages/item/3108*

"Holding Pen or Cells for Slaves Awaiting Sale, Alexandria, Virginia, 1863", *Slavery Images: A Visual Record of the African Slave Trade and Slave Life in the Early African Diaspora,* accessed November 14, 2020, *http://slaveryimages.org/s/slaveryimages/item/1967*

"House Servant, Baltimore, 1861", *Slavery Images: A Visual Record of the African Slave Trade and Slave Life in the Early African Diaspora,* accessed November 16, 2020, *http://slaveryimages.org/s/slaveryimages/item/2727*

"Indigo Production, South Carolina, 1757", *Slavery Images: A Visual Record of the African Slave Trade and Slave Life in the Early African Diaspora,* accessed November 19, 2020, *http://slaveryimages.org/s/slaveryimages/item/1084*

"Inspection and Sale of a Negro", *Slavery Images: A Visual Record of the African Slave Trade and Slave Life in the Early African Diaspora,* accessed November 14, 2020, *http://slaveryimages.org/s/slaveryimages/item/1909*

"Instrument of Torture Used by Slaveholders", *Slavery Images: A Visual Record of the African Slave Trade and Slave Life in the Early African Diaspora,* accessed November 15, 2020, *http://slaveryimages.org/s/slaveryimages/item/1235*

"Interior of the Seabrook Tobacco Warehouse at Richmond, Virginia", *Slavery Images: A Visual Record of the African Slave Trade and Slave Life in the Early African Diaspora,* accessed November 21, 2020, *http://slaveryimages.org/s/slaveryimages/item/2988*

"Iron Mask, Neck Collar, Leg Shackles, and Spurs, 18th cent.", *Slavery Images: A Visual Record of the African Slave Trade and Slave Life in the Early African Diaspora,* accessed November 15, 2020, *http://slaveryimages.org/s/slaveryimages/item/1298*

"Kidnapping", *Slavery Images: A Visual Record of the African Slave Trade and Slave Life in the Early African Diaspora,* accessed November 14, 2020, *http://slaveryimages.org/s/slaveryimages/item/2479*

"Marketplace, Lynchburg, Virginia, 1870s", *Slavery Images: A Visual Record of the African Slave Trade and Slave Life in the Early African Diaspora,* accessed November 15, 2020, *http://slaveryimages.org/s/slaveryimages/item/755*

"Marks of Punishment Inflicted upon a Colored Servant in Richmond, Virginia", *Slavery Images: A Visual Record of the African Slave Trade and Slave Life in the Early African Diaspora,* accessed November 15, 2020, *http://slaveryimages.org/s/slaveryimages/item/1325*

"Marks of Punishment Inflicted upon a Colored Servant in Richmond, Virginia", *Slavery Images: A Visual Record of the African Slave Trade and Slave Life in the Early African Diaspora,* accessed June 6, 2022, *http://slaveryimages.org/s/slaveryimages/item/1325*

"Metal Branding Irons with Owners' Initials", *Slavery Images: A Visual Record of the African Slave Trade and Slave Life in the Early African Diaspora,* accessed November 14, 2020, *http://slaveryimages.org/s/slaveryimages/item/1975*

"Metal Collar to Prevent Running Away, South Carolina, 1830s", *Slavery Images: A Visual Record of the African Slave Trade and Slave Life in the Early African Diaspora,* accessed November 15, 2020, *http://slaveryimages.org/s/slaveryimages/item/1207*

"Negroes Escaping Out of Slavery", *Slavery Images: A Visual Record of the African Slave Trade and Slave Life in the Early African Diaspora,* accessed November 28, 2020, *http://slaveryimages.org/s/slaveryimages/item/1326*

"Negro Village in Georgia", *Slavery Images: A Visual Record of the African Slave Trade and Slave Life in the Early African Diaspora,* accessed November 15, 2020, *http://slaveryimages.org/s/slaveryimages/item/1362*

"On Board a Slave Ship", *Slavery Images: A Visual Record of the African Slave Trade and Slave Life in the Early African Diaspora,* accessed November 14, 2020, *http://slaveryimages.org/s/slaveryimages/item/2559*

"Paddling a Slave, U.S. South, 1845", *Slavery Images: A Visual Record of the African Slave Trade and Slave Life in the Early African Diaspora,* accessed November 15, 2020, *http://slaveryimages.org/s/slaveryimages/item/1255*

"Peter Salem at the Battle of Bunker Hill, Boston, 1775", *Slavery Images: A Visual Record of the African Slave Trade and Slave Life in the Early African Diaspora,* accessed November 15, 2020, *http://slaveryimages.org/s/slaveryimages/item/819*

"Picking Cotton, Georgia, 1858", *Slavery Images: A Visual Record of the African Slave Trade and Slave Life in the Early African Diaspora,* accessed November 16, 2020, *http://slaveryimages.org/s/slaveryimages/item/1149*

"Planting Rice, U.S. South, 1859", *Slavery Images: A Visual Record of the African Slave Trade and Slave Life in the Early African Diaspora,* accessed November 19, 2020, *http://slaveryimages.org/s/slaveryimages/item/1169*

"Prayer Meeting, Georgia, 1873-74", *Slavery Images: A Visual Record of the African Slave Trade and Slave Life in the Early African Diaspora,* accessed November 27, 2020, *http://slaveryimages.org/s/slaveryimages/item/1852*

"Punishment Aboard a Slave Ship, 1792", *Slavery Images: A Visual Record of the African Slave Trade and Slave Life in the Early African Diaspora,* accessed November 13, 2020, *http://slaveryimages.org/s/slaveryimages/item/2040*

"Represents Our next door neighbor, A little black girl spinning wool", *Slavery Images: A Visual Record of the African Slave Trade and Slave Life in the Early African Diaspora,* accessed November 21, 2020, *http://slaveryimages.org/s/slaveryimages/item/959*

"Rice Harvesting, U.S. South, 1859", *Slavery Images: A Visual Record of the African Slave Trade and Slave Life in the Early African Diaspora,* accessed November 16, 2020, *http://slaveryimages.org/s/slaveryimages/item/1168*

"Scene on a Cotton Plantation: Gathering Cotton", *Slavery Images: A Visual Record of the African Slave Trade and Slave Life in the Early African Diaspora,* accessed November 16, 2020, *http://slaveryimages.org/s/slaveryimages/item/1059*

"Separating White Cotton from Yellow (Long Staple), South Carolina, 1880", *Slavery Images: A Visual Record of the African Slave Trade and Slave Life in the Early African Diaspora,* accessed November 19, 2020, *http://slaveryimages.org/s/slaveryimages/item/3111*

"Slave Coffle, Virginia, 1839", *Slavery Images: A Visual Record of the African Slave Trade and Slave Life in the Early African Diaspora,* accessed November 14, 2020, *http://slaveryimages.org/s/slaveryimages/item/1965*

"Slave Houses on a Rice Plantation, U.S. South, 1859", *Slavery Images: A Visual Record of the African Slave Trade and Slave Life in the Early African Diaspora,* accessed November 15, 2020, *http://slaveryimages.org/s/slaveryimages/item/1426*

"Slave Quarters, Kingsley Plantation, Duval County, Florida, ca. 1870", *Slavery Images: A Visual Record of the African Slave Trade and Slave Life in the Early African Diaspora,* accessed November 15, 2020, *http://slaveryimages.org/s/slaveryimages/item/1404*

"Slavers Revenging Their Losses", *Slavery Images: A Visual Record of the African Slave Trade and Slave Life in the Early African Diaspora,* accessed November 16, 2020, *http://slaveryimages.org/s/slaveryimages/item/422*

"Slaves Abandoned", *Slavery Images: A Visual Record of the African Slave Trade and Slave Life in the Early African Diaspora,* accessed November 16, 2020, *http://slaveryimages.org/s/slaveryimages/item/2899*

"Sleeping Position of Africans on Slave Ship, 1857", *Slavery Images: A Visual Record of the African Slave Trade and Slave Life in the Early African Diaspora,* accessed November 14, 2020, *http://slaveryimages.org/s/slaveryimages/item/2764*

"Stacking Wheat, Culpeper, Virginia, 1863", *Slavery Images: A Visual Record of the African Slave Trade and Slave Life in the Early African Diaspora,* accessed November 19, 2020, *http://slaveryimages.org/s/slaveryimages/item/1145*

Stockley, "Elaine Massacre of 1919" at *encyclopediaofarkansas.net/entries/elaine-massacre-of-1919-1102/*

"Stowage of the British Slave Ship Brookes under the Regulated Slave Trade Act of 1788", *Slavery Images: A Visual Record of the African Slave Trade and Slave Life in the Early African Diaspora,* accessed November 13, 2020, *http://slaveryimages.org/s/slaveryimages/item/2553*

"Sugar Plantation, Louisiana, 1873-74", *Slavery Images: A Visual Record of the African Slave Trade and Slave Life in the Early African Diaspora,* accessed November 15, 2020, *http://slaveryimages.org/s/slaveryimages/item/2893*

"Sunday Meeting of Colored People at Chicago", *Slavery Images: A Visual Record of the African Slave Trade and Slave Life in the Early African Diaspora,* accessed November 15, 2020, *http://slaveryimages.org/s/slaveryimages/item/2272*

"The Africans of the Slave Bark 'Wildfire'", *Slavery Images: A Visual Record of the African Slave Trade and Slave Life in the Early African Diaspora,* accessed November 14, 2020, *http://slaveryimages.org/s/slaveryimages/item/2575*

"The Cook", *Slavery Images: A Visual Record of the African Slave Trade and Slave Life in the Early African Diaspora,* accessed November 16, 2020, *http://slaveryimages.org/s/slaveryimages/item/520*

"The Droves", *Slavery Images: A Visual Record of the African Slave Trade and Slave Life in the Early African Diaspora,* accessed November 21, 2020, *http://slaveryimages.org/s/slaveryimages/item/900*

"The Effects of the Proclamation: Freed Negroes Coming into Our Lines at Newbern, North Carolina", *Slavery Images: A Visual Record of the African Slave Trade and Slave Life in the Early African Diaspora,* accessed November 15, 2020, *http://slaveryimages.org/s/slaveryimages/item/534*

"The First Cotton-Gin", *Slavery Images: A Visual Record of the African Slave Trade and Slave Life in the Early African Diaspora,* accessed November 16, 2020, *http://slaveryimages.org/s/slaveryimages/item/1119*

"To be sold on board the ship Bance-Island … a choice cargo of about 250 fine healthy Negroes." *Slavery Images: A Visual Record of the African Slave Trade and Slave Life in the Early African Diaspora,* accessed November 14, 2020, *http://slaveryimages.org/s/slaveryimages/item/1913*

"Traversée: Danse de négres", *Slavery Images: A Visual Record of the African Slave Trade and Slave Life in the Early African Diaspora,* accessed November 27, 2020, *http://slaveryimages.org/s/slaveryimages/item/2554*

"Untitled Image (Iron Shackles)", *Slavery Images: A Visual Record of the African Slave Trade and Slave Life in the Early African Diaspora,* accessed November 13, 2020, *http://slaveryimages.org/s/slaveryimages/item/2619*

"Untitled Image (Portrait of John Brown)", *Slavery Images: A Visual Record of the African Slave Trade and Slave Life in the Early African Diaspora,* accessed November 15, 2020, *http://slaveryimages.org/s/slaveryimages/item/2512*

"Untitled Image (Slave Dealer, Virginia)", *Slavery Images: A Visual Record of the African Slave Trade and Slave Life in the Early African Diaspora,* accessed November 14, 2020, *http://slaveryimages.org/s/slaveryimages/item/2998*

"Untitled Image (Sleeping Positions of Captive Africans on the French Slave Ship L'Aurore)", *Slavery Images: A Visual Record of the African Slave Trade and Slave Life in the Early African Diaspora,* accessed November 13, 2020, *http://slaveryimages.org/s/slaveryimages/item/2552*

"View of Darlington Courthouse and the Sycamore Tree Where Amy Spain, the Negro Slave, Was Hung by the Citizens of Darlington, South Carolina", S*lavery Images: A Visual Record of the African Slave Trade and Slave Life in the Early African Diaspora,* accessed November 28, 2020, *http://slaveryimages.org/s/slaveryimages/item/1324*

"Weeding Rice Field, U.S. South, 19th cent.", *Slavery Images: A Visual Record of the African Slave Trade and Slave Life in the Early African Diaspora,* accessed November 16, 2020, *http://slaveryimages.org/s/slaveryimages/item/1151*

"Whipping a Slave, Brazil, 1816-1831", *Slavery Images: A Visual Record of the African Slave Trade and Slave Life in the Early African Diaspora,* accessed November 15, 2020, *http://slaveryimages.org/s/slaveryimages/item/1286*

"Whipping a Slave, Virginia, 19th cent.", *Slavery Images: A Visual Record of the African Slave Trade and Slave Life in the Early African Diaspora,* accessed November 15, 2020, *http://slaveryimages.org/s/slaveryimages/item/1237*

"Whipping of a Fugitive Slave, French West Indies, 1840s", *Slavery Images: A Visual Record of the African Slave Trade and Slave Life in the Early African Diaspora,* accessed November 15, 2020, *http://slaveryimages.org/s/slaveryimages/item/3107*

"Whipping Slaves, Missouri, 1856", *Slavery Images: A Visual Record of the African Slave Trade and Slave Life in the Early African Diaspora,* accessed November 15, 2020, *http://slaveryimages.org/s/slaveryimages/item/1284*

Index

Symbols

A

C

D

E

F

G

H

I

J

K

L

M

N

O

P

Q

R

S

T

U

V

W

Z

CPSIA information can be obtained
at www.ICGtesting.com
Printed in the USA
JSHW041110220123
36576JS00005B/7

9 781947 741744